head case

head case:
treat yourself to better mental health.

Dr Pamela Stephenson Connolly

headline

First published in 2007 by
HEADLINE PUBLISHING GROUP

1

Cataloguing in Publication Data is available from the British Library

Hardback ISBN 978 0 7553 1287 0
Trade paperback ISBN 978 0 7553 1721 9

Typeset in Minion by Avon DataSet Ltd, Bidford-on-Avon, Warwickshire

Printed and bound in Great Britain by Clays Ltd, St Ives plc

Headline's policy is to use papers that are natural, renewable and
recyclable products and made from wood grown in sustainable forests.
The logging and manufacturing processes are expected to conform
to the environmental regulations of the country of origin.

HEADLINE PUBLISHING GROUP
An Hachette Livre UK Company
338 Euston Road
London NW1 3BH

www.headline.co.uk
www.hodderheadline.com

Contents

Dedication

This book is dedicated to those who, as Thoreau observed, 'live their lives in quiet desperation' – in the hope that they may one day emerge into noisy joy.

Acknowledgements

I would like to thank my colleagues in the UK and USA who read the manuscript and provided feedback – especially Dr Leo Weisbender. As ever, I am indebted to publisher Val Hudson, as well as to Philippa Hobbs, Caitlin Raynor and all the Headline team.

introduction

"I've got the bowl, the bone, the big yard. I know I <u>should</u> be happy."

'stiff upper lip'

Millions of people are suffering needlessly. Lack of resources, mistaken beliefs, poverty and fear mean that they are not getting treatment for their mental health problems. In some countries, such simple changes as access to assessment procedures and the availability of anti-psychotic medication could mean, for example, that instead of being chained to a wall in a filthy hospital, people with schizophrenia could go home to their families and lead a productive life.

In relatively affluent societies, the situation is more complex. Very often the resources and information are available, but people do not seek treatment out of fear, ignorance, distrust or lack of family support. Sometimes the unwillingness to seek treatment is based on a sense of shame. Whereas the appearance of a physical ailment would prompt a quick call to a GP, the arrival of a psychological difficulty such as depression, anxiety, fear of going out or the onset of panic attacks heralds a protracted period of suffering in silence, misguided attempts to solve the problem alone and a worsening of symptoms. All this can lead to debilitation, lifelong misery – sometimes even suicide – and very often it is needless. There is sufficient scientific research, as well as ample clinically based knowledge, to know that modern mental-health treatments do work.

In my view, the values of 'stiff upper lip' stoicism and the misguided 'do buck up' attitude are inappropriate when it comes to mental health. British people are becoming more aware of psychological issues, largely through media coverage. While not as au fait with mental-health terminology as their American cousins (they don't watch as much *Oprah*!) they are nevertheless beginning to understand such subtleties as the difference between feeling blue in the absence of a loved one and becoming depressed. But we have a long way to go, particularly in the area of psychological education. The ongoing distaste for psychological explanations regarding human behaviour (especially crime) still abounds, while the use of the word 'psychobabble' is a defensive reaction to being confronted by a paradigm one has not yet grasped.

It has recently been estimated that 40 per cent of the British public will undergo psychological difficulties at some time in their lives, so we really need to be a bit more open about seeking help for mental anguish, depression, anxiety and a whole range of mental-health problems. Unfortunately, we do not have nearly enough psychologists to treat everyone, and there is no sign that such a deficit is being corrected. In fact their numbers are actually dwindling. This fact has been one of my prime motivations for writing *Head Case*. If psychotherapy is not immediately available, following the self-help suggestions in this book will help a person begin to heal and become proactive about the problem.

Information in this book is based on current research, professional literature and clinical experience, and international psychological research is ongoing. The fact that so many of the books listed in the reading lists are published in America (although they are also mostly available internationally) is simply a reflection of the fact that the USA seems to be 'Self Help Central'. From time to time, new information brings paradigm shifts as well as changes in diagnosis and treatment protocols. Internet searches for psychological data can turn up misinformation (some trustworthy websites are listed at the end of Chapter 13), but in each section of this book I have included suggestions for additional reading. I have provided extensive explanations for those who are curious about the way they might be diagnosed by a mental-health professional. Most importantly, besides professional treatment options I have given numerous self-help suggestions – so there is something to be getting on with while awaiting formal help. My suggestions are based on theory, science or clinical experience; however, they do not imply that there is a therapeutic relationship between author and reader, and I cannot guarantee that they will work for everybody every time. I have tried to explain how psychological problems arise, including how early psychological events, plus our biologically determined traits affect our adult lives. I have included basic information about the neurochemical aspects of each disorder, because I believe that improved understanding of the science of psychological problems will help to remove the stigma of having a mental-health problem.

I have included case studies with positive outcomes to illustrate how people with a wide range of mental disorders can be helped and healed via psychotherapeutic interventions, and go on to benefit enormously in their subsequent lives. Naturally, I have changed names and identifying features of the people I've helped in therapy. The sections and diagnostic categories in this book follow those set out in the American Psychiatric Association's *Diagnostic and Statistical Manual of Mental Disorders*, which is commonly used in the UK. The most current version of this manual is a text revision of the fourth edition (DSM-IV-TR), but from hereon in this book I shall refer to it as simply the DSM-IV. I have simplified (and in some cases, condensed) the DSM-IV diagnostic criteria (that is, the list of symptoms that suggests a particular diagnosis) and put it into easier language. The end result is that, in some cases, I have presented my own interpretations of those criteria, with which the authors of the DSM-IV may not necessarily always agree. In certain diagnostic categories, the DSM-IV makes provision for people whose symptoms are due to a medical condition, medication or substances, or whose symptoms don't quite fit the category but are still close enough to deserve a special mention. I have not bothered to include those 'special cases', but I do want to make it clear that not everybody fits neatly into a particular diagnostic category.

Why have I been the first to provide all this information for the public, straight from the 'bible' of mental-health professionals? Because I believe it is important to demystify psychology and psychotherapy and thereby provide sufferers with the background knowledge to help themselves and courage to seek treatment when necessary. I wanted to provide a springboard for both self-help and professional intervention (if it is available) and give everyone access to an understanding of how their symptoms might be viewed by people like me. Our job is not to judge, 'tut-tut' or revel in knowing more than the people we are treating, it is to try to understand humbly, compassionately and respectfully, and help each individual to the very best of our abilities. Each individual seen in therapy arrives with a unique background, style, personality and set of symptoms, so there is no such thing as a 'one size fits all' treatment approach. Just for starters, the UK is a multicultural society, and diagnostic categories created for Western people with European backgrounds may be entirely irrelevant and inappropriate for people from other cultures, especially for those who have recently arrived from non-Western countries. All good therapists try hard to be culturally sensitive and aware, but it is understandable that a person might prefer to seek therapy from a professional with a similar cultural background – in fact, I would recommend that.

If a set of symptoms does not bother a person, he or she would usually not be diagnosed as having a mental disorder, although there are a few exceptions, such as people who have lost touch with reality. If symptoms do bother a person, a diagnosis can usually be made, and there will be matching treatment options. Not all mental-health problems can be self-treated, and this book is not a substitute for face-to-face psychological treatment. However if a person lacks immediate access to professional care it can go a long way to helping someone first to have a basic understanding of his or her mental condition, and secondly to have some helpful tools for working towards resolution of painful issues and a move towards better mental health. I have clearly indicated which mental disorders require urgent professional attention, but for every problem there are many self-help strategies, and I have provided a range of those that I consider to be the most useful. At the very least, a sufferer (or person close to the sufferer) can learn about the symptoms, design a self-help treatment plan, gather support from family and friends, and evaluate professional treatment options. I hope the simple explanations, self-assessment tools and down-to-earth information within these pages will be a relief to those who may have hitherto found the concept of psychological intervention both confusing and threatening. I have tried hard to make the professional jargon accessible to all.

In many ways, this book is the true follow-up to the biography I wrote about my husband, Billy. After millions read the account of the childhood abuse and continuing struggles of my husband, there was an overwhelming outpouring from readers who had suffered similar difficulties, or were challenged by mental illness, substance abuse or past trauma. This book is designed as a one-stop launch pad to self-help for all those who seek to free themselves of psychological pain and move on to well-deserved happiness.

chapter 1
the basics

"Really, only you can tell yourself to giddyup."

When I first started studying psychology I found that the writers of much of the set literature assumed the reader understood the elementary principles. Their failure to explain basic concepts meant that I had to stop every few sentences and consult a psychological dictionary. To save you such a similar annoyance, I have set out the absolute, bottom-line basics in this chapter. In addition, there is a glossary at the end of the book to provide more definitions should you need them.

Please read this book responsibly; that is, don't start imagining you have all kinds of mental problems when there is no basis for that to be true! If you think you may qualify to be diagnosed with a particular disorder, scrutinize the criteria carefully. If they seem to fit, pay attention to the 'do not pass go' guidelines I have given concerning whether you should seek urgent help from a qualified mental-health professional, or, if you can wait a bit while trying the self-help suggestions I have set out. If you think someone close to you may qualify to be diagnosed with a mental disorder, be careful how you use that information or express your opinion. A triumphant 'See, I always knew you were crazy!' would not be kind, and it would make it less likely that he or she will either recognize the problem or seek help to fix it. I have provided many suggestions to help those close to sufferers support a move to improved mental health without putting them off.

One of the most fear-provoking questions people ask themselves about their mental health is 'Am I normal?' This is a tricky one, because what *feels* normal to some people might be, for example, a persistent low mood, a sense of euphoria that leads them to take potentially damaging risks or a tendency to protect someone who abused them in childhood. It often takes a mental-health professional to help people gently discover what it is like *not* to experience their symptoms and bring them to the realization that they were not previously as psychologically healthy as they imagined. Most of the time, however, people with mental disorders know there's something wrong, and it causes them distress and disruption to their lives.

so, what is 'normal', psychologically speaking?

Psychological normality varies according to a person's culture; so, for example, the psychological health of someone who moved to the UK from a different society and culture cannot be judged according to the standards that are in place for most Europeans. Generally, though, the broad idea of psychological normality involves being free of severe emotional conflict or distress and not having symptoms of a psychological disorder (such as severe anxiety, sadness, confusion or obsessions), as well as being able to function in the world in a reasonably effective and organized manner.

what exactly is mental health?

A person is in good mental health when (in accordance with what is considered appropriate for his or her age, stage of life and culture) he or she is functioning well emotionally, behaviourally and relationship-wise; is relatively free of disabling psychological symptoms; and can adapt reasonably well to life's ups and downs. The term is sometimes used to describe a person who is simply not suffering from a mental disorder.

what is a mental disorder?

A person might be diagnosed with a mental disorder when he or she has disabling psychological symptoms, an emotional or behavioural problem or a dysfunction in thinking, acting or feeling – all of which can cause distress and may lead to impairment in the way the person functions in the world.

what causes a mental disorder?

It may be due to a person's genetic, biochemical or psychological make-up, or a combination of these. It might be brought about by events or circumstances (past or present) in a person's social, occupational or family environment.

what is a diagnosis?

Based on symptoms, psychologists and psychiatrists have grouped people into useful categories to make it easier to study them. It also helps with their paperwork. Being given a diagnosis does not classify you, it simply describes the problem or disorder you might have. For example, a person suffering from schizophrenia should never be referred to as 'a schizophrenic' but rather as an individual who has the disorder.

Mental-health professionals in the UK follow a manual, a sort of diagnostic bible called the DSM-IV. The World Health Organization's International Statistical Classification of Diseases and Health Related Problems (ICD-10) is also used, but the diagnostic categories I've used in this book are based on the DSM-IV. Both manuals contain many categories with criteria for scores of diagnoses, but no matter how bad your mental-health problems might be, the sum total of who you are is not in there. You are an individual.

how do you know if you have a particular mental disorder or not?

Each diagnostic category is described in the DSM-IV and other manuals used by professional psychologists and psychiatrists, with a list of criteria or symptoms that would make a person's problem qualify for that particular diagnosis. In the following chapters I have tried to demystify these diagnostic categories so you can figure out how your problem might be viewed if you went to a mental-health professional. If you can self-assess from within the pages of this book, you will then be in a position to benefit from the accompanying advice and self-treatment suggestions. It is very important that you know that the DSM-IV criteria are *only guidelines*. Not everyone with, say, Bipolar Disorder (see page 25ff) fits neatly into the diagnostic category as it is written down in the manual. For most diagnostic categories in the DSM-IV, there is a slot for other, less cut-and-dried presentations of each particular disorder (that is, such-and-such a disorder: Not Otherwise Specified). There is often another slot for when symptoms are due to a medical disorder or the effects of a substance.

Aside from manuals, mental-health professionals use many other diagnostic tools, such as structured clinical interviews, standardized psychological pencil-and-paper tests, as well as clinical judgement gained through their experience and training.

what makes psychologists and other mental-health professionals think they know how to treat your mental-health problems?

Not only because they say so! They've been to university and earned a degree, plus some kind of proper and accepted accreditation, licence or certification. Never go to someone who hasn't got the proper credentials, and always ask for full information about a therapist's training (see page 397 on therapists' accreditation in the UK).

Mental-health professionals don't have all the answers, and the field is constantly evolving. There has been some research into why, when and how talking therapy works and doesn't work, but money for this type of research is not widely available. Some types of therapy have been more studied than others, but that doesn't necessarily mean they are the best types of therapy for you (see page 398 on types of therapy). The most important curative element may actually be having the right therapeutic relationship with a therapist who is right for you, no matter what style of therapy he or she practises.

what type of therapy do I practise?

There are many styles of therapy, and it is impossible to know for sure which will work best for a particular individual, so it is only fair that I disclose my own bias.

I was initially trained as a psychodynamic psychotherapist, but I also practise in an eclectic fashion, utilizing cognitive-behavioural, Gestalt and other techniques that I think will work best for certain disorders. (Explanations of these styles of therapy begin on page 399.) I also believe that Eriksonian hypnosis is a powerful healing agent and employ it in my work when appropriate. Unfortunately, hypnosis has suffered from bad PR – probably brought about by the behaviour of stage 'hypnotists'. But all hypnosis is actually *self-hypnosis* facilitated by a therapist, and no one can ever *make* you squawk like a chicken – unless you want to! Joking aside, hypnosis can be wonderfully helpful for a wide range of mental-health problems including depression, self-esteem issues, sleep problems, eating disorders and even pain.

I also work with psychiatrists from time to time, so that the people I treat may have the option to be medically evaluated and prescribed medication. Sometimes a person responds best when there is teamwork between a therapist and psychiatrist, and I have seen that pharmacological interventions can be immensely helpful – even life saving – and can help make a person capable of tolerating psychotherapy. Nevertheless, I also have sympathy and respect for people who do not wish to take prescribed medication, and will happily suggest other alternatives, such as biofeedback (see page 404) and herbal remedies.

Above all, I believe in the power of talking psychotherapy. Unfortunately, we do not have enough studies to do full, scientifically backed justice to the success rates of good psychotherapy, but millions of satisfied customers, as well as the clinical experience of myself and many colleagues, attest to it. It is a curative process that, for many problems, has a far wider range of benefits than drug therapy.

what is psychotherapy?

Psychotherapy is an interactive psychological service for individuals, couples, families or groups provided by a trained professional. It is designed to have healing effects on mental, emotional or behavioural problems or disorders, and to help people make sense of their lives.

psychologist, psychotherapist, psychoanalyst, counsellor or psychiatrist – what are the differences?

A **psychologist** is a professionally trained practitioner, researcher or teacher who may work in clinical practice as a psychotherapist, psychological counsellor or consultant, and/or provides mental-health services in settings such as educational establishments, hospitals, prisons, business organizations or clinics.

In the United States a person who calls themself a psychologist must have obtained a doctoral degree, as well as certification or formal professional licensing for the particular branch of psychology they have entered. That is not the case in the UK, so it is important to check the credentials of a mental-health professional (see guidelines on page 397).

A **psychotherapist** is someone who has been professionally trained to treat mental, behavioural and emotional problems. He or she will talk with people who seek treatment in a private situation where everything that is said must be treated as confidential.

A **psychiatrist** is a mental-health professional with a medical degree, that is, a medical doctor who specializes in mental and emotional disorders.

Unlike psychologists, he or she is qualified to prescribe medication. Some psychiatrists have been trained to perform psychotherapy.

A **psychoanalyst** (sometimes referred to simply as 'an analyst') is a therapist trained to treat mental disorders according to traditional techniques originally developed by pioneers like Sigmund Freud (1856–1939) and Carl Jung (1875–1961). The treatment involves a thorough examination of a person's 'unconscious' motivations, feelings and behaviour, so it is often an intensive long-term process.

A **counsellor** is someone who has been professionally trained to advise, evaluate and guide a person, couple or family struggling with problems such as relationship issues, substance abuse, rehabilitation or vocational conflicts. The counsellor may have another qualification or profession, such as being a nurse, social worker or pastor.

how have mental-health problems been treated in the past?

Some of the methods used in modern mental-health treatments today are rooted in the practices of ancient civilizations. Medicine men and shamans of some early African societies used drug therapy (for example, extracts of certain leaves, bark and insects), ointments and diet to soothe diseases affecting both mind and body – a close connection between the two was assumed in those days. Although no longer used in modern psychotherapy, some very early forms of psychotherapeutic practices still survive among certain peoples of the world. These include finding a 'lost soul' (employed by the pygmies of the Philippines, the Negrito people of the Malay Peninsular and the Australian Aborigines), exorcism (still used in some countries around the Mediterranean) and 'removing' objects from the sufferer's body (a practice continued today in Siberia and some Southeast Asian societies).

The first mental-health treatments were developed according to the assumed cause. For example, if a person was thought to have been a victim of sorcery, then anti-witchcraft methods were employed; if a taboo had been broken they were encouraged to make amends. The therapist's bag of tricks included ventriloquism, impersonation, dressing up, sleight of hand, ceremonial display and a strong sense of the dramatic. In fact, these techniques are still employed by shamans operating in rural areas of countries such as Indonesia, New Guinea and the Philippines. The success of all such methods relies on a person's belief that the healer can cure them, the healer's reputation and confidence and a general societal belief in the validity of the method – sound familiar? There is still a beneficial element of 'faith healing' in all medical and psychotherapeutic interventions today, and it's not just played out in the now-familiar phenomenon of the 'placebo effect'.

When it comes to healing mental problems there are even more direct connections between ancient and modern methods. Many contemporary Western mental-health treatments, for example, psychodynamic psycho-therapy, psychoanalysis and Jungian therapy (see page 399 for a brief explanation of these terms), include analyzing people's dreams in order to discover more about their unconscious desires, feelings and motivations. The power of this technique was noted by ancient Greek healers who would ask people to spend a night in a sacred cave, during which time they could have dreams that helped to cure them. One modern treatment of trauma involves a re-enactment of the initial moment of terror (psychodrama) and this principle has worked for centuries in ceremonial healing performances by groups such as the North American Pomo tribe.

Modern Western psychiatry and psychotherapy are partly derived from the earlier healing methods of magnetism (in which the healer used the power of his personality to lead someone to a curative crisis) and hypnotism. These methods were pioneered in Europe during the nineteenth and twentieth centuries by people like Franz Mesmer (1734–1815), Jean-Martin Charcot (1825–1893), Pierre Janet (1859–1947) and Sigmund Freud. These days there is an emphasis on science-based methodology, but although hundreds of new mental-health therapy treatments have emerged, few have undergone stringent research scrutiny. There have been a number of comparative studies to determine whether some types of therapy work better than some others for particular disorders, but those therapy styles that have been less studied rely on clinically gauged success rates and consumer satisfaction.

Good mental health is not elusive if our belief system is conducive to cure. That means we must awaken in ourselves the age-old human understanding that, when our minds start to create problems for us, there are ways to receive culturally sanctioned understanding, treatment and relief. And very often, we can help ourselves.

helpful books

The Discovery of the Unconscious: the History and Evolution of Dynamic Psychiatry, H. F. Ellenberger. New York: Basic Books, 1970.

The Passion of the Western Mind: Understanding the Ideas That Have Shaped Our World View, R. Tarnas. New York: Ballantine Books, 1991.

APA Dictionary of Psychology: The Language of Psychology at Your Fingertips, ed. G. R. VandenBos. Washington, DC: American Psychological Association, 2007.

chapter 2
the moody blues: mood disorders

"I have trouble keeping in touch with my silver lining."

depression

Jama had a lonely childhood. As an only child, she spent much of her time longing for attention from her busy parents. They had emigrated from Jamaica and were struggling to make a living. Jama was smart, studied hard at school and was thrilled when she received a university scholarship. But, less than a year after enrolment, she began to feel she could not continue. Far from her expectations of collegiate camaraderie, she felt separate and alone among the all-white strangers in a crowded dorm and could barely get out of bed in the morning. Even the short walk to her classes seemed very difficult. She had trouble focusing on her studies, and wondered if life was really worth living.

Jama and I talked at length about her cultural heritage and her experiences as a member of a minority group. Unfortunately, it is common to see a form of Depression in people who frequently suffer from problems such as discrimination; in fact it is a natural response to being on the receiving end of racial slurs and attacks. But Jama's Depression was so debilitating she was at risk of losing her prized scholarship, and she even contemplated committing suicide. She needed to be listened to, supported and to have some of the attention she had always craved. She also needed to learn coping strategies and receive aggressive treatment to improve her mood. Jama responded well to psycho-therapy. After a term of absence she was able to return to university and resume her studies. Eventually she was ready to focus her childhood longing onto carving out a successful career as a lawyer fighting for minority rights.

do you (or does someone close to you)

- Feel sad, blue or empty most of the time?
- No longer enjoy things that used to give you pleasure?

If one of the above has ever been true over a period of at least two con-secutive weeks, consider whether four or more of the following also apply:

- Being unusually restless or finding that it takes a lot of effort to move.
- Very low on energy most days.
- Feeling worthless and prone to self-blame.
- Sleeping quite a bit more, or quite a bit less, than usual.
- Having unexpected gains or decreases in either weight or appetite.
- Finding it hard to concentrate, be decisive or think clearly.
- Feeling a sense of hopelessness, and/or having thoughts about dying or suicide.

If most of the above is true and you are finding it hard to live life effectively, you are probably suffering from Depression. Perhaps there have previously been other low periods like that, which might imply a diagnosis of Major Depressive Disorder. Or perhaps you might have dysthymia: a chronic, but less severe, low mood. Some people with Depression have a variety of other symptoms, such as nervousness, irritability, phobias, bodily aches and pains, sleep disturbances and a feeling of numbness.

Depression can significantly interfere with a person's ability to maintain healthy relationships with partners, spouses and others. If you suspect you might be depressed, you probably are. Forget that 'stiff upper-lip' thing – it's very overrated! Depression needs to be treated right away. After some months it may eventually disappear on its own, but without treatment it will very likely return in full force at some later stage. Does it really make sense to suffer needlessly? Everyone deserves to feel happy. Take steps today to get the fun back into your life.

'do not pass go' signs

Many suicides are due to Depression. If you have thoughts about dying or suicide, and especially if you have formulated a plan for self-harm, do not delay in seeking professional help. Also, tell a trusted friend or relative how you feel so that you can be supported. Even if you feel ashamed of being so low, please do not suffer alone. Right now you are looking at the world through a dark lens – it really *can* be lifted to allow you to feel happy again. It is hard for you to imagine this right now, but after treatment you will be amazed to look back and realize that feeling better was just a few steps away.

If you know someone who seems dangerously low, especially if that person has mentioned suicide to you, make sure you do everything you can to encourage him or her to seek immediate treatment – or make that call for them (see 'A Few Words about Suicide' on page 24 for some insights into the suicidal mind).

Psychosis (for example, hearing voices or seeing things that are not there) sometimes accompanies serious Depression and can be very dangerous. If you (or someone close to you) begin to enter such a state, immediately seek help from a mental-health professional or insist on being taken to the hospital.

what causes depression?

Loss is a major factor in triggering Depression. A person may have lost a job, a loved one, or self-belief. Whereas it is normal to react to such events with sadness and low mood, such feelings can persist for some time and eventually lead to full-blown Depression. Depression can also be triggered by stress. It can follow childbirth, a change of location, or even the achievement of success. Having a parent or sibling who suffers from Depression increases your vulnerability to becoming depressed yourself. Many people with Depression also suffer from other problems such as Substance Abuse (see page 178ff), Anxiety (see page 34ff), Post-Traumatic Stress Disorder (see page 62) and Obsessive-Compulsive Disorder (see page 54ff). Depression often goes hand-in-hand with medical problems such as cancer, heart disease, hypertension and arthritis. It makes sense that having a serious physical disease might make a person depressed, but research has also shown that untreated Depression can lead, for example, to cardiovascular disease, and that Depression in people who've already had a heart attack can increase their risk of having a second one.

Depression often coexists with Substance Abuse and that can make treatment more difficult. Alcohol is a depressant. The first couple of drinks may convince you that it lifts your spirits, but the reality is the opposite.

Mood-wise, there is also a downside to the use of 'uppers', marijuana, cocaine, ecstasy and other recreational drugs. Certain prescribed medications, including some oral contraceptives, can affect a person's mood. It is always important to have a discussion with your doctor about the possible side effects of any medications you might be taking.

Trauma can lead to Depression, whether it occurred recently or in childhood. Well, it makes sense, doesn't it, that survivors of childhood abuse or children who experienced the loss of a parent via death or divorce are more likely to become depressed as adults? People who are socially isolated, in conflict with others or unhappy in their relationships, are also at risk of becoming depressed. Studies have shown that women are generally more at risk of Depression than men, although since women are the creatures they are, they're more likely to tell someone they are depressed. They are also twice as likely as men to report a family history of Mood Disorders, and tend to experience a first bout of major Depression at a younger age.

what is happening in the brain?

You know the expression 'firing on all cylinders'? It's somewhat accurate. We have cells called neurons that form pathways in the nervous system. They normally run 'feel-good' messages to keep us happy, but the pathways can become blocked if essential delivery agents called neurotransmitters (for example, serotonin and dopamine) are not doing their job properly – and that can cause Depression and other mental-health problems. Other theories suggest that certain hormones might be out of balance or the blood flow around the brain might be changing.

which treatments are likely to work?

Talking therapy can smooth those neuron pathways again, as can the right type of antidepressant medication. Research has pointed to certain types of psychotherapy as being particularly helpful in treating Depression: behavioural therapy, cognitive-behavioural therapy, brief psychodynamic psychotherapy and interpersonal therapy, but others may work just as well. Many people who seek treatment for Depression are offered antidepressant medication, which is often helpful. Nevertheless, psychotherapy can be just as effective as antidepressants and can sometimes succeed where medication fails. For chronic Depression, a combination of medication and psychotherapy might be the most appropriate. Following an exercise regimen has been known to help people recover from Depression, whereas at the other end of the scale electro-convulsive therapy is sometimes used successfully in hospitals when other treatments have failed. I know, the very mention of 'electric shock treatment' conjures up all the worst images of *One Flew over the Cuckoo's Nest*, but there are certain cases (usually for certain people in psychiatric hospitals) when it's actually a fast-working and life-saving option.

Hypnosis, too, has been advocated as a very effective treatment for Depression and some people believe acupuncture can be as effective as an antidepressant, whereas vagus nerve stimulation (VNS) is one of the new, non-medication treatments for both epilepsy and Depression. Neuro-feedback, homeopathy, relaxation training, meditation, yoga and certain over-the-counter remedies such as St John's wort can help to improve depressive symptoms, although it is worth stressing that Depression can be very serious and life-threatening – and often requires aggressive treatment.

best course of action

Make an appointment to see a mental-health professional as soon as possible. If you (or someone close to you) are having recurrent thoughts of dying or committing suicide, you must insist on immediate, urgent treatment. If you are too low on energy to be proactive, enlist a responsible and understanding friend or family member to make calls on your behalf.

in the meantime, what can you do?

1. Learn everything you can about Depression from authoritative sources (see reading list below).
2. Educate others around you about Depression.
3. Ask your physician to rule out possible medical reasons for your Depression, such as thyroid problems, hormone imbalances or disease.
4. Try to make a list of any specific concerns that may be contributing to your Depression. Is there anything on that list you could improve immediately by taking practical steps; for example, by taking charge of your finances or making adjustments to your living conditions? Try to take care of those things as best you can.
5. Is there anything on the above list you could improve through discussion or expression of feelings? For example, if it makes you sad that your spouse or partner no longer telephones you if they're going to be late, respectfully ask for a change. You will feel better when you express your needs, especially if you have some success – no matter how small.
6. Try to make a list of any positive things in your life about which you feel

hopeful. Spend some time each day focusing on those things.

7. Depressed people tend to underplay their successes and overplay their failures. Try to make an honest list of as many personal achievements and successes, no matter how small, that you can remember. Include moments of kindness such as remembering a friend's birthday.

8. Try to exercise, even if it seems incredibly difficult. First set yourself small goals each day, such as walking to the post box, supermarket or school. Gradually increase your exercise regime until it reaches a level that is appropriately challenging for you, given your age and state of physical health. It is important to check with your doctor first, to find out what level of physical activity is safe and appropriate for you.

9. Pay a little more attention to your physical appearance. People with Depression often find it hard to attend to personal grooming and hygiene. You will feel better if you maintain the same standards you did before you felt down.

10. Gather support from among your family and friends. Let them know, without making them feel responsible or guilty, that you're feeling depressed and could do with some TLC while you're waiting to be seen by a mental-health professional. Choose someone sympathetic to talk with about things that are bothering you. If that person says something like, 'Oh, do buck up!' explain to them that it's not that simple.

11. If you find yourself being irritable with people around you, discuss this with them directly, and show willingness to try not to let your mood cause conflict in your family, vocational or social life. Be quick to catch yourself and apologize.

12. Set up a system of daily reminders and affirmations; for example, place cards in places you will see them (such as inside your diary) with the positive reminders, such as 'This sad feeling will pass' and 'I have plenty to look forward to.'

13. Even if you seem to have little sense of enjoyment in your life, try to plan at least one activity every day that might give you pleasure or at least help lift your mood. An outing to a concert or the cinema, or a meal with friends can raise spirits, at least temporarily.

14. Human touch (stroking, hugs, massage), as well as satisfying sexual activity, are known to be soothing and help elevate a person's mood. Don't use sex as a mood-elevator too much, though.

15. Don't isolate yourself. Look for support among people in your community. For example, try to summon up the energy to join a club or

association that runs group events or activities you think you might enjoy, whether that be cycling, bowling, charity work or discussing books.

16. People with Depression are sometimes secretive and uncomfortable about admitting it to others. It's that old 'stiff upper-lip' thing again. Tell yourself every day that being depressed is nothing to be ashamed of and continue trying to get the professional treatment you deserve.

17. Consider the view that environmental toxins, parasite infestations, candida, food sensitivities and allergies may impact upon your mood to some extent. Seek an evaluation from reliable sources such as a certified allergist.

18. Try to eat a nutritious, healthy diet. You may be craving sugar or stodgy foods but avoid bingeing on them.

19. Do not drink alcohol or take recreational drugs, as they will almost certainly exacerbate your Depression.

20. Some over-the-counter remedies, such as SAMe, St John's wort and 5HTP (5-hydroxytryptophan) are thought by some to be helpful for Depression, so research them and consider trying them. But it is important to know that they may not mix well with some other medications (for example, St John's wort interferes with the effectiveness of some oral contraceptives).

21. Consider trying acupuncture, which is also thought to be most effective for Depression in some people.

22. Investigate homeopathic treatments for Depression and decide whether or not these may be right for you.

23. If there is a possibility that your mood may be negatively affected by seasonal changes as winter approaches, get some full-spectrum light. Do this by sitting outside for an hour or so if weather allows. If it is winter and you live in a very cold, dark place, consider investing in a specially designed light box which provides 2,500–10,000 lux of light (first check that your eyes can safely take in reflected strong light , and note that light therapy is not recommended for people with a history of Bipolar Disorder).

24. If you begin to hear voices or see strange things that others do not hear or see, get immediate help from a mental-health professional or ask someone to take you to hospital.

25. If you ever feel devoid of all hope, seek immediate help from a mental-health professional.

26. People who are suffering from Depression need structure in their day-to-day lives. Create a daily schedule of activities for yourself. Even if you

are not working, it will be helpful to stick to a plan, even one as simple
as:

8.00 a.m.	Get up and bathe
9.00 a.m.	Make tea and toast
9.30 a.m.	Tidy up
10.00 a.m.	Walk to corner shop
11.00 a.m.	Rest on the couch until noon, focusing on hopeful aspects of your life
Noon	Make and eat lunch
1.30 p.m.	Read outside if it is fine
2.30 p.m.	Write a letter or email
3.30 p.m.	Go to the post office to mail it or go for a walk
5.00 p.m.	Call a friend for a chat
6.00 p.m.	Make dinner
7.00 p.m.	Take an early evening stroll
8.00 p.m.	Watch a favourite soap opera

27. Practise the following exercises, which are designed to improve
your mood by helping you to de-stress, stop negative thoughts, reduce
your tendency to engage in distorted thinking and raise your self-
esteem:

how to reduce stress

- Identify the things that cause the most stress in your life and think
  hard about strategies that will help you to have an easier time. This
  may involve some creative or lateral thinking about the way you have
  been doing things so far, and some solutions may even 'go against the
  grain'. For example, perhaps you can persuade business associates to
  come to your neck of the woods or take care of some things online
  from your home, to avoid having to travel.
- Ask for help. Look for people who can support you, or take over some
  of your workload. Do you have a tendency to try to do everything
  yourself? Force yourself to delegate.
- Organize your time in a way that will make your week easier. This may
  involve planning ahead so you're not so rushed at your busiest times,
  or leaving home earlier to avoid rush hour.
- Prioritize your 'To Do' list. Attend to the most important things first
  and let unimportant things go.

- Learn to say 'no'. You cannot be all things to all people. Reduce your number of commitments and conserve your energy.
- Schedule breaks for yourself throughout the day.
- *Notice* the minute you start to feel overwhelmed. Immediately *stop* what you are doing and *focus on breathing slowly and deeply.*
- At least twice a day, engage in a stress-reducing activity such as meditation (see page 40), yoga, relaxation exercise (see page 41) or breathing exercise (see page 46).
- Maintain a regular physical exercise programme that is appropriate for your age and state of health.
- Get plenty of good-quality sleep. If you have problems sleeping follow the self-help suggestions for Insomnia or other Sleep Disorders (see page 361 onwards).
- Eat nutritious, well-balanced meals.
- Take steps to reduce your anxiety (see page 38).
- Be careful not to use alcohol or recreational drugs to try to reduce your stress. This will not work, and in the long-term it will cause more problems.
- Make sure you leave time in your life for fun and pleasurable activities.

exercise: thought-stopping work for depression

1. Catch yourself in the process of having negative thoughts, such as 'I'm a complete failure', or 'no-one cares about me'.
2. As you identify each negative thought, bring it into full consciousness.
3. Consider it fully and decide whether it is realistic or not, productive or counter-productive.
4. Chart that on paper.
5. Gauge how hard it is to control that particular thought or to stop it persisting (a bit difficult, quite difficult or very difficult).
6. Gauge how bad that thought makes you feel (a bit uncomfortable, quite uncomfortable, or very uncomfortable).
7. Chart that too.
8. Now, if you decide that it would be a good idea to eliminate that negative thought from your thought repertoire, dwell on that for a while (with your body as relaxed as possible).

9. Put a rubber band around your wrist. From now on snap it every time that thought returns while shouting, 'Stop!' (eventually you can just shout it inside your head).
10. Spend the next thirty seconds focusing on replacing the negative thought with a positive one, such as 'I can succeed' or 'I am loved'.
11. Work on this technique until you can regularly catch yourself and replace all your negative chatter with the positive flip-side.

exercise: distorted thinking

CATCH yourself, CONTROL those thoughts, and CHANGE them. Here are a few examples of distorted thinking:

Catastrophizing (for example, 'My husband is late home from work – that means he's probably having an affair and will end up leaving me.') The rational point of view is that there are many reasons why he may be late.

Personalizing situations (for example, 'If I don't make Christmas dinner perfect, the family will fight and it will be my fault.') The rational point of view is that families sometimes fight during holidays and other times, and a perfect meal does not have much influence one way or another.

Mistaken notions of control (for example, 'I can't take a vacation. My department at work will fall apart.') The rational point of view is that, even though work is important, a person benefits from a break at least once a year, and there are others who can hold the fort while you are away.

Black-and-white thinking (for example, 'One minute things are fabulous, the next they've gone to pot.') Work on getting in touch with the rational, realistic middle ground; for example, not, 'I'm socially brilliant' followed by 'I'm a wallflower', but instead, 'I know how to be engaging with people, but sometimes I meet people with whom I just don't click.'

Over-generalization (for example, 'My date cancelled, so I am unattractive and undesirable and I will never get married.') The rational point of view is that people sometimes cancel dates for a variety of reasons that have nothing to do with you.

Jumping to conclusions (for example, 'When I returned from lunch my boss was talking on the telephone and he seemed displeased. I think he's going to fire me.') The rational point of view is that there may be many reasons why your boss might be annoyed and talking on the telephone and seeming displeased.

Honing in on the negative (for example, 'My teeth are going to fall out. When I had my annual check-up my dentist said I need to brush more on the upper-left side. I guess I'll need a root canal before long.') The rational point of view is that having a problem area does not necessarily mean that it will deteriorate further.

how to improve your self-esteem

- Focus on your positive attributes, not on what you think are your difficulties or failures.
- Try to have faith in yourself. Say 'I can ...'
- Try new, positive things that challenge you and enjoy the sense of accomplishment afterwards.
- Learn to accept yourself, good and bad. Be kinder about the 'bad'.
- Don't have such high expectations of yourself. You're only human.
- Just do the best you can and appreciate that about yourself.
- Learn to take compliments.
- Know that in struggling with a mental disorder, you are not alone.
- Even if you do not feel self-confident, fake it for a while and see if that helps.
- Be disciplined in your attempts to feel better, but let go of things that are just too difficult to accomplish until you're 100 per cent again.
- Try to be in the 'here and now'. Savour each moment.
- Choose your battles and save your strength and energy.
- Surround yourself with people who support you, and distance yourself from those who make you feel bad about yourself.
- If you feel guilty, take steps to resolve it.
- Learn to assert yourself better (see page 38).
- Pay attention to your health.
- Pay attention to your appearance.
- Avoid overworking.
- Work on improving all your relationships – take the time to listen and be heard.

when someone close to you is suffering from depression

1. Encourage the person to seek treatment.
2. Support all healthy efforts to improve his or her mood. Do not support unhealthy efforts, such as substance abuse.
3. Being in a relationship or family with someone who is depressed can be very difficult, especially since that person will be finding it hard to be emotionally available to you. You may need to take the role of carer from

time to time and that can interfere with your relationship; for example, through causing resentment. Get some therapeutic support for yourself and the family.

4. Plan fun and enjoy regular breaks to help offset the gloom.
5. Learn everything you can about Depression.
6. Take care of yourself, physically and mentally.
7. Reduce your stress (see page 19).

depression in children and adolescents

In children and adolescents symptoms of Depression appear differently from in adults. Adolescents with Depression are particularly at risk of additional problems, such as Substance Abuse, taking part in illegal activity and suicide. Depression in children can be mistaken for other disorders such as Attention-Deficit/Hyperactivity disorder, so careful evaluation by a trained mental-health specialist is a must.

Signs of Depression in children include:

- Sadness and crying.
- Hopelessness about the future.
- Withdrawing from others.
- Self-hatred, a sense of being 'bad'.
- Not having fun.
- Taking physical risks; for example, balancing on dangerously high fences.
- Feeling responsible for all kinds of things outside his or her control.
- Feeling anxious that bad things might happen.
- Finding schoolwork too hard or failing at school.
- Tiredness.
- Sleep problems, such as insomnia, sleeping too much, nightmares or night terrors.
- Not having friends.
- Misbehaving.
- Unable to concentrate.
- Unable to make decisions.
- Irritability.
- Fighting with others.

- Feeling lonely.
- Not eating.
- Having stomach aches or other aches and pains.
- Making unfavourable comparisons with other siblings or children.
- Not feeling confident.
- Not feeling loved.
- Wanting to run away.

See also 'General Tools for Helping Children with Mental-Health Challenges' on page 255.

a few words about suicide

- Death is final. Sometimes it's hard to imagine that.
- You may have fantasies of how much people will miss you or how they will be sorry for things they might have done to you. Realistically, you will not have the opportunity to witness the effect your passing would have on others.
- You may have fantasies that no one will miss you, but that is incorrect.
- Sometimes suicide is a hostile act intended to hurt those left behind. There are other ways of expressing your anger that will allow you to survive and have a chance of future happiness.
- Most people who have been depressed enough to contemplate suicide have looked back after recovering from their Mood Disorder and been thankful they didn't do it. Those people received personal proof that they can get better and enjoy life once more – you will too.
- Sometimes suicidal thoughts are there, but barely recognized by the sufferer. Here are some covert signs in yourself that you are at risk of suicide:
  1. You start preparing others to lose you.
  2. You start giving away things you own.
  3. You start finding another home for your pet.

  Here are more overt signs:
  4. You plan exactly how you are going to take your own life.
  5. You start reading up about lethal levels of over-the-counter or prescription medications.
  6. You start sourcing and hoarding medication that might provide you with a lethal overdose.

- If you notice any of the above symptoms in yourself, take immediate steps to stop yourself spiralling down any further. Tell someone responsible and let them help you seek professional help today.
- If you have noticed any of the above signs in anyone else, take immediate steps to get some professional help for them. People who threaten suicide often carry it out. Do not let them hold you emotionally hostage by agreeing not to tell others. This is one of the rare times when confidences need to be broken. In order to save his or her life, you must pay attention and act today.

helpful books

Getting Your Life Back: A Complete Guide to Recovery from Depression, Jesse H. Wright and Monica Ramirez Basco. New York: Touchstone Books, 2003.

The Freedom from Depression Workbook, L. Carter and Frank Minirth. Nashville, Tenn.: Thomas Nelson Publishers, 1995.

The Depression Workbook: A Guide for Living with Depression and Manic Depression, Mary Ellen Copeland. Oakland, Calif.: New Harbinger Publications, 1992.

I Don't Want to Talk about It: Overcoming the Secret Legacy of Male Depression, T. Real. New York: Fireside, 1997.

Noonday Demon: An Atlas of Depression, Andrew Solomon. New York: Touchstone Books, 2002.

Exercising Your Way to Better Mental Health: Combat Stress, Fight Depression, and Improve Your Overall Mood and Self-Concept with These Simple Exercises, L. M. Leith. Morgantown, W.Va.: Fitness Information Technology, 1998.

Meditation for Busy People: 60 Seconds to Serenity, D. Croves. San Rafael, Calif.: New World Library, 1993.

bipolar disorder

case study: Hamish

Hamish was a struggling recording artist. Although he was clearly talented he lacked confidence in his own ability, except during certain seemingly unpredictable periods in his life. Then he would suddenly swing into a heady, euphoric state in which he would sleep little, write many songs and engage in risky sexual behaviour that he believed enhanced his creativity. To Hamish, these manic episodes seemed useful, exciting and even necessary; but unfortunately, each one was followed by a downside. His ensuing periods of Depression were extremely debilitating. They caused him to be confined to bed, eschewing all potentially supportive relationships and contemplating suicide. He had already made two attempts to end his life by the time I met him.

Hamish needed better mood stability. It was difficult to convince him that, with treatment, he would eventually not only be able to maintain his creativity but would sustain it better – without his lost weeks of 'black dog days'. But once he was taking medication that stabilized his mood he was able to tolerate psychotherapy, in which he learned to predict his mood swings and head them off by using various strategies such as reducing his stress. He stopped the alcohol and drug use that had been contributing to his Depression, and was finally able to have longer-term, positive relationships. His confidence and self-esteem grew, and with that came greater artistic success, reliability and a recording contract.

Bipolar Disorder used to be called Manic Depression, from the old idea that people suffering from it always swing from the high end of the emotional scale (mania) to the other extreme (deep Depression). In fact, people with Bipolar Disorder do have problematic mood swings, but not all of them experience full-blown mania (some have abnormally 'up' moods known as hypomania, meaning 'just under manic'), and not all of them swing down into deep or long-lasting Depression.

Bipolar Disorder is a complex diagnosis because it takes several forms. For example, a person might swing from normal to extremely manic and back again, or spiral down from a hypomanic episode to a depressed state. The various types of Bipolar Disorder are known by psychologists as Bipolar I, Bipolar II and Cyclothymia. Only Bipolar I involves true mania.

What exactly is mania? You would probably recognize it if you saw someone having a great time dancing dangerously on the rooftops (or the equivalent), but if you (or someone close to you) experienced periods of intense productivity that included staying up most of the night, feeling particularly brilliant, successful and sexy, would you necessarily see that as a problem? Even if you crashed afterwards? And if someone suggested you had a problem, would you tell him or her to take a hike? Right. That's one of the big issues with this disorder – recognizing it. So what does mania look like?

manic episode

have you (or has someone close to you):

- Ever experienced an excessively 'up' or irritated mood that lasted at least a week?
- During that time also experienced three or four of the following:
  1. Had an overly grand sense of your own importance.
  2. Seemed to need less sleep.
  3. Became more talkative than usual.
  4. Couldn't slow down the ideas and thoughts that were racing into your mind.
  5. Became easily distracted from one thing to another.
  6. Became unusually intent on certain goals in work, leisure or sex life (or your body became very restless).
  7. Became swept up in high-risk, fun activities that were likely to cause problems later, for example, sexual indiscretions, spending sprees or madcap business schemes.

If the above signs of mania have ever applied, even if serious Depression has never been present, you (or someone close to you) may have a Bipolar Disorder.

People in the throes of a manic episode can 'lose their grip' to a dangerous degree. They can become deluded (holding highly improbable beliefs) or experience hallucinations (seeing or hearing things that aren't there). Anyone who has ever had a manic episode that included one of those symptoms would fall into the Bipolar I category. People who have experienced hypomania only, plus Major Depression, would more likely be diagnosed with Bipolar II Disorder. Cyclothymia is another variation, where a person struggles with both hypomania plus a shorter-lasting or less serious form of Depression. The term *rapid cycling* is used when a person has four or more episodes in one year, and mental-health practitioners refer to a *mixed episode* when a person experiences both Depression and mania almost every day for at least a week.

children and adolescents with bipolar symptoms

Early symptoms of Bipolar Disorder in children and adolescents can appear as misbehaviour, or may be mistaken for other disorders such as Attention-Deficit/Hyperactivity Disorder (see page 264ff). It's all too easy to dismiss an adolescent's 'up all night' antics or deep moodiness as 'typical teenage stuff', and as a result many young people fail to be diagnosed or receive the treatment they desperately need. This is one of the reasons why any unusual behaviour, mood swings or 'acting out' in children should be investigated by a mental-health specialist.

'do not pass go' signs

Mania can become so out of control that people can lose touch with reality and become a risk to themselves or others. In such cases, hospitalization becomes necessary. At the other end of the mood swing, deep Depression can lead a person to commit suicide. In addition, the risky choices sometimes made by a person in the throes of mania (such as physical risk-taking, out-of-control spending or unprotected sex) will often lead to long-lasting problems. Bipolar Disorder is a potentially life-threatening condition. It can be managed with psychotherapeutic help, but medication is usually necessary.

Substance Abuse, particularly that involving stimulants such as cocaine and amphetamines, sometimes goes hand-in-hand with Bipolar Disorder. Many sufferers also struggle with Anxiety, Panic Attacks, Phobias, Personality Disorders, Eating Disorders, Post-Traumatic Stress Disorder and Obsessive-Compulsive Disorder. In particular, the presence of Anxiety is thought to increase the risk of suicide in people with Bipolar Disorder.

Psychosis (for example, hearing voices or seeing things that are not there) sometimes accompanies Bipolar Disorder and can be very dangerous. If you (or someone close to you) begin to enter such a state, immediately seek help from a mental-health professional or insist on being taken to hospital.

what causes bipolar disorder?

There is a strong genetic basis. People who are closely related to sufferers of Bipolar I Disorder have a higher rate than others of also having either a Bipolar Disorder or Depression. Stress is thought to be an important trigger. For example, chronic family, romantic and peer relationship stress has been linked to changes in mood among adolescents with Bipolar Disorder.

what is happening in your brain?

Some researchers believe an imbalance in the levels of certain neuro-transmitters (brain chemicals that facilitate neural connections) can cause people to become either manic or depressed. The neural signalling system may become faulty, that is, the messages either whizz along too fast and cause mania, or slow down and cause Depression. Some researchers point to dysfunction in the brain-parts known as mitochondria.

which treatments are likely to work?

Medication is usually a must. Drugs that stabilize a person's mood are the first line of attack for Bipolar Disorder. Another type of drug (known as an anti-psychotic) might be added if a sufferer is having trouble maintaining a grip on reality. A psychotherapist can help a person with Bipolar Disorder understand the condition, manage his or her moods, reduce the risk of relapse, deal with stress and other triggers of manic episodes and stay on medication. But many experts agree that people with Bipolar Disorder are at great risk if they are not also on medication.

Unfortunately, many people who have been prescribed medication to help them with Bipolar Disorder have trouble staying on it. This is partly because they enjoy the sense of euphoria they feel during manic episodes and partly because of drug side effects. But the abrupt cessation of certain medications suddenly can trigger a manic episode and put a person in a potentially damaging or life-threatening situation.

best course of action

If, in your opinion or that of someone close to you, you might have a Bipolar Disorder, especially Bipolar I, you MUST immediately seek help from a psychiatrist; that is, someone who can prescribe medication. Try to find a psychotherapist as well. It is vital that you stay on your medication. You also need support from responsible people in your life. Do not imagine you can handle it on your own; you deserve to have some proper help.

in the meantime, what can you do?

1. A manic episode can be triggered by stress, changes in sleep patterns, work-schedule changes or family conflict. Take immediate steps to put your life in order so that you are following regular sleep and work patterns, reducing your stress, limiting your contact with people who upset you and surrounding yourself with supportive friends and family.
2. Start to work on recognizing the warning signs for returning symptoms

of Depression and/or mania. You can reduce the severity of those symptoms if you act quickly.

3. Learn more about Bipolar Disorder (see the suggested reading list below).
4. Educate the people close to you about Bipolar Disorder.
5. Identify your own particular symptoms and write them down.
6. Identify your past mood patterns, being specific about dates, times and level of feeling up or down. Using 10 as the most 'up' you've ever felt and 0 as the most 'down', make a graph to illustrate your fluctuations in black and white.
7. Monitor your moods by always entering them on your graph from now on and learn to predict when they begin to change.
8. Decide which elements in your life are likely to trigger your symptoms, whether they be lack of sleep, schedule changes, crises in some areas of your life or perhaps conflicts at home or in your love relationships. Work to eliminate these stressors.
9. How do you feel about having Bipolar Disorder? (Angry? Sad? Betrayed? Confused?) Write down your feelings as a means of beginning to come to terms with them.
10. While acknowledging your feelings, try also to take a practical approach to managing your symptoms.
11. Do you sabotage yourself? Do you sometimes do things that exacerbate your mood swings? Be honest, and vow to catch yourself when you are tempted to do so.
12. Strengthen your healthy habits, such as getting enough sleep, exercising, and eating well.
13. If you have already been prescribed medication, how do you feel about it? Do you sometimes avoid taking it? If so, notice this dangerous form of self-sabotage. From now on make sure you comply with all your treatment protocols, including turning up on time to therapy sessions.
14. Do not use recreational drugs or alcohol. They will almost certainly exacerbate your Mood Disorder.
15. If you think you may also have a problem with substance or alcohol abuse, or if trusted people close to you believe that to be the case, seek immediate harm-reduction evaluation and treatment or a twelve-step programme (for example, from Alcoholics Anonymous). Harm-reduction treatment for Substance Abuse has been found to work well by helping people to reduce their substance use gradually while they are working on the underlying issues. If you choose a twelve-step programme, make sure the meetings you attend support the taking of

medication for Bipolar Disorder. There is a greater level of understanding for 'dual diagnosis' these days (that is, having a mental disorder as well as a problem with Substance Abuse) and it is important that your struggles with Bipolar Disorder are recognized.

16. When or if you feel you are falling into Depression, do not isolate yourself. You need to be in the company of healthy, supportive people.

17. Work on strengthening the positive relationships in your life.

18. What are your low moods like for you? Write down what you feel when you enter those states.

19. Follow all the relevant self-help steps for Depression (see page 16ff).

20. Join a Bipolar support group.

21. What is mania/hypomania like for you? Write down both the enjoyable features (for example, increased productivity and feeling confident) and problematic aspects (such as consequences and risks) if/when you enter that state.

22. Make plans, just in case you slip and have another manic/hypomanic episode. Ask key, supportive people around you to carry out important responsibilities (such as getting you to hospital).

23. Educate people around you about how you would like them to act if you become manic (that is, not to reinforce your manic behaviours, but not to be cold or abandoning either).

24. Identify your risk-taking tendencies and have a frank discussion with your partner or people close to you about the warning signs in you that they may notice and how to help (for example, if you have a tendency to go on spending sprees, give permission to your spouse or partner that if it should ever happen again they should cancel your credit cards and thus avoid both of you getting into serious debt).

25. Consider your libido, and how to handle it if it increases during a manic phase. Sexual risk-taking can have serious consequences. Ensure you have some preventative measures in place (for example, by asking for assistance from people you can trust).

26. Since stress is known to trigger manic and depressive episodes, it is important you take steps to reduce it. Learn some relaxation techniques (see page 41), practise meditation (see page 40) and/or listen to soothing music.

27. Establish consistent sleep patterns and work on always getting plenty of good-quality sleep. If you frequently have problems sleeping, follow the self-help suggestions for Insomnia or other Sleep Disorders (see page 361 onwards).

28. Avoid being over-stimulated. Identify and reduce noise, mess or chaos in your surroundings.

29. There are some negative side effects of some medications used to treat Bipolar Disorder. Pay attention to any that you may experience; for example, address weight gain by working on diet changes and exercise to counterbalance it. Note that a Chinese study has shown that the dizziness and fatigue sometimes brought about by the use of carbamazine (an anticonvulsant and analgesic drug) can be helped by the herbal medicine Free and Easy Wanderer Plus, which may be worth trying.

30. Try to include omega-3 fatty acids, found naturally in fish oils, flaxseed oil, soybeans and walnuts, in your diet. They have been found to help control certain types of Depression and mania successfully.

when someone close to you is suffering from bipolar disorder:

1. Encourage that person to seek immediate treatment. If she or he is in the throes of mania or Depression you may have to summon it for him or her.

2. Do not be fooled into thinking you can manage this person's problem on your own. It is simply too hard for most lay people, and since there are serious safety risks involved (many people with Bipolar Disorder commit suicide) it would be dangerous to try.

3. People with Bipolar Disorder often have trouble being compliant with their prescription drugs so, once the sufferer is in the care of a mental-health professional, one of the most useful things you can do is encourage adherence to medication and doctor's orders.

4. Support all appropriate and healthy efforts to improve symptoms and mood.

5. Do not support actions that will add to the sufferer's problems, such as substance abuse.

6. Support the sufferer's efforts to notice the triggers for mood swings and take preventative measures.

7. If the sufferer is having a manic or hypomanic episode do not reinforce the manic behaviours (for example, do not go out on the town or drink/ do drugs with him or her), but do not be cold or abandoning either.

8. Keep key telephone numbers handy (for example, for the sufferer's psychiatrist and therapist). Be prepared to call them if necessary, especially if the sufferer is at risk of harm to self or others.

9. Support the sufferer's efforts to reduce stress, to engage in appropriate regular exercise, and to eat well-balanced, nutritious meals.

10. Being in a relationship or family with someone who has Bipolar Disorder can be very challenging. You may have to act as a carer from time to time and resentment can creep in. Get some therapeutic support for yourself and the family.
11. Plan enjoyable breaks from time to time.
12. Learn everything you can about Bipolar Disorder.
13. Take care of yourself, physically and mentally.
14. Reduce your own stress (see page 19).

helpful books

The Bipolar Workbook: Tools for Controlling Your Mood Swings, Monica Ramirez Basco, Ph.D. New York: The Guilford Press, 2006.

Why Am I Up and Why Am I Down?: Understanding Bipolar Disorder, Roger Granet and Elizabeth Ferber. New York: Dell Publications, 1999.

The Bipolar Disorder Survival Guide: What You and Your Family Need to Know, D. J. Miklowitz. New York: The Guilford Press.

New Hope for People with Bipolar Disorder, Jan Fawcett, Bernard Golden and Nancy Rosenfeld. Rosevilles, Calif.: Prima Publishing, 2000.

The Depression Workbook: A Guide for Living with Depression and Manic Depression, Mary Ellen Copeland. Oakland, Calif.: New Harbinger Publications, 1992.

Healing Depression & Bipolar Disorder without Drugs: Inspiring Stories of Restoring Mental Health through Natural Therapies, G. Guyol. New York: Walker & Company 1996.

Exercising Your Way to Better Mental Health: Combat Stress, Fight Depression, and Improve Your Overall Mood and Self-Concept with These Simple Exercises, L. M. Leith. Morgantown, W.Va.: Fitness Information Technology, 1998.

Meditation for Busy People: 60 Seconds to Serenity, D. Croves. San Rafael, Calif.: New World Library, 1993.

books for close friends and family

Loving Someone with Bipolar Disorder: Understanding and Helping Your Partner, Julie A. Fast and John D. Preston. Oakland, Calif.: New Harbinger Publications, 2004.

Surviving Manic Depression: A Manual on Bipolar Disorder for Patients, Families, and Providers (1st ed.), Torrey E. Fuller. New York: Basic Books, 2002.

Acquainted with The Night: A Parent's Quest to Understand Depression and Bipolar Disorder in His Children, P. Raeburn. Broadway Books, 2004.

chapter 3
a case of the jitters: anxiety disorders

anxiety

Everyone gets a little nervous from time to time, and a touch of the butterflies before a job interview, making a speech or meeting your prospective in-laws can actually help you with motivation and performance. Anxiety, though, is a state of severe worry and apprehension that goes way beyond the usual concern a person might have about an upcoming exam or change of location. It is a pervasive, and sometimes acute, sense of agitation and distress that affects both body and mind. Physiological symptoms such as increased heartbeat, sweating, dry mouth, nausea and muscle tension combine with intense mental uneasiness that might include fear of losing control altogether – or even dying. With body and mind in such a state, it's easy to see why a person might start behaving in unusual ways that are designed to avoid or assuage the Anxiety. Thus, phobias, compulsions, obsessions or Panic Disorder can begin to develop and gradually worsen, until the sufferer's quality of life is seriously compromised. Unfortunately, some people have been suffering from Anxiety Disorders ever since they were children and have never sought treatment.

generalized anxiety disorder

case study: Dean

Dean had overcome many obstacles in order to become a judge. He lost a leg and an eye when he fell from a roof at seven years old, and in addition to his physical challenges his father had always told him he would never amount to anything. Those words continued to haunt him, even after he had achieved his goal to sit in one of the most important courtrooms in the country. He came to see me after presiding over a particularly difficult case in which the plaintiff – a vicious, bullying gangster – had reminded him of his father. This had aroused in him fear, panic and self-doubt, and he was afraid he would have to step down from his position. Dean said he had suffered from Anxiety for as long as he could remember, but had never taken steps to seek treatment until now, when his career and livelihood were threatened.

Dean needed to be helped to heal from the trauma of having such a rejecting, sneering father. In addition, I taught him how to relax his body and mind (he learned to do this in the courtroom rather than sit there full of tension), how to reduce his overall Anxiety and how to monitor the highly critical inner voice that led him to doubt himself. He learned to recognize people who pushed his buttons and to protect himself from them instantly with on-the-spot visualizations. He continues to serve as a fine judge who is now confident that neither Anxiety nor his childhood trauma can threaten his ability to maintain impartiality.

do you (or does someone close to you)
- Feel very worried and anxious most of the time? Has this been for the case for the past six months or more?
- Find it very difficult to calm yourself?

if both of the above are true, consider whether the following related problems also apply
- Are you more irritable than usual?
- Do you find it hard to relax?
- Are you feeling on edge much of the time?
- Do you become drained easily?
- Are you not sleeping well?

Ticking at least three of the last five items would suggest an Anxiety Disorder. Of course, no one manages to go through life without any worries at all, but an Anxiety Disorder goes well beyond the usual temporary nervousness about whether one will succeed in a new job or pass a driving test. The type of Anxiety that must be treated is overwhelming, pervasive and uncontrollable. If that's what you are feeling, it's time to put an end to it. You deserve to feel happier and free to enjoy your life, so take steps today to banish your jitters.

anxiety in children and adolescents

Young people suffering from Anxiety Disorders are not having any fun. Some have inherited an anxious disposition and some do not feel safe in the world, perhaps because they have experienced trauma. They avoid social situations, fail to play or express their creativity as other children do and grow up to be anxious, unhappy adults. They need to be identified and treated.

'do not pass go' signs

An Anxiety Disorder can be extremely debilitating. It can prevent a person from working or maintaining relationships. Some anxious people have a variety of bodily symptoms, such as twitching, trembling, sweating, nausea, diarrhoea and various types of aches and pains. Some also have related disorders such as Phobias, Panic Attacks, Depression, Post-Traumatic Stress Disorder or Substance Abuse. They may also have related medical conditions, such as irritable bowel syndrome, headaches and cardiovascular disease. People with significant Anxiety should seek professional mental-health treatment.

what causes anxiety?

If one of your parents suffered from Anxiety, you have around a one in three chance of inheriting it, but it is also thought to be triggered by other factors. Whereas some people seem to be born with a tendency to be anxious, irritable or tense, studies also suggest that negative childhood experiences such as trauma and abuse can lead to Anxiety. If you rarely feel relaxed or comforted as a child, you are likely to become a worried adult.

In addition, medical conditions such as hypoglycaemia (a deficiency of glucose in the bloodstream) and having an overactive thyroid can cause a person to experience persistent Anxiety.

what is happening in your brain?

Some believe Anxiety is caused by an imbalance in certain brain chemicals such as the neurotransmitter gamma aminobutyric acid (GABA). GABA is thought to be associated with the brain's calming response, so an imbalance or dysfunction in the way it works may contribute to the creation of Anxiety.

which treatments are likely to work?

Psychotherapy and hypnosis can help, and the effectiveness of cognitive-behavioural therapy has been well studied. Anti-Anxiety medications are commonly prescribed; however, some of these carry a risk of addiction and need to be managed very carefully.

best course of action

Try to be seen by a mental-health professional and work on the self-help and self-soothing methods (see page 255ff).

in the meantime, what can you do?

1. Learn everything you can about anxiety.
2. Educate your partner or spouse and family about the disorder.
3. What are the main conflicts or things that push your buttons in your current life? Write them down.
4. Explore the 'mind-chatter' that maintains and increases your anxiety. What exactly is that internal dialogue? Does it go something like: 'If I don't ... then ...'? Write it down.
5. Make a list of specific objects, people and situations that make you most anxious. Are any of these irrational fears (e.g. intense fear of suddenly being expected to, say, preach a sermon when there is no actual reason why you should be)? Identify the false logic inside your head and begin to create an inner dialogue that counters your irrationality (for example, 'I am not a vicar, therefore I am not required to preach a sermon.')
6. Do you have a stressful lifestyle? Identify and reduce the parts of your life that add unnecessary tension and stress (see page 19, 'How to reduce stress').
7. Establish a personal wellness programme that includes regular exercise (appropriate for your age, weight and level of fitness), good nutrition, regular sleep, and daily meditation and relaxation exercises (see below). Taking a yoga class can also be helpful.
8. Are you a perfectionist? Practise letting go of your need to get it right all the time. Set yourself more realistic goals, take time off, focus on your

successes rather than your failures, and learn to be less hard on yourself and others.

9. Increase the self-nurturing and pleasurable activities in your life. Have regular massages and spend more time enjoying human touch (hugs, stroking, holding and sex).

10. Establish a consistent pattern of good-quality sleep. If you have problems sleeping follow the self-help suggestions for Insomnia or other Sleep Disorders (see page 361 onwards).

11. Have more fun with family and friends.

12. Allow yourself to celebrate the positive things in your life.

special exercises to reduce anxiety

- People with Anxiety often engage in *distorted thinking*. Bust your tendency to catastrophize, personalize situations, over-generalize, hone in on the negative, jump to conclusions, make assumptions of control or engage in black-and-white thinking by following the Distorted Thinking exercise on page 21. Remember the 'three C's': CATCH yourself, CONTROL those thoughts and CHANGE them.

self-assertion

Some anxious people have trouble getting their needs met. Practise being assertive in your interactions with others in both your personal and vocational life. Self-assertion means being neither passive nor aggressive, but simply and directly expressing your needs, stating your concerns, asking for a change or being able to say 'no' in a simple, direct fashion, without manipulating, attacking or negating anyone else. It takes practice. Identify your style, and work on being more assertive:

- Write down some exchanges you may have had during the past week. Did you fail to say what you needed to say? For example, when a sales person tried to sell you something you didn't want. Did you react passively (that is, put up with being shown the goods even though it made you late) or did you react aggressively (that is, abruptly tell the salesperson to get out of your way)? An assertive response would have been to make it clear that you were not interested, in a simple, direct fashion, without putting the other person down or raising your voice. Identify your style, and work on being assertive.

- Work on saying 'no'. Some people find this very hard. If you are asked to do something that you are not keen on, there are a number of choices. You may want to take some time to get more details, and consider it. In that case you could say, 'I'd like to think about that and get back to you.' Do not be bullied into giving an answer right away, and you do not need to apologize. Avoid offering extra things to the person to make up for saying 'no'. Instead, be brief and specific. With some people you have to be very firm and repeat 'no' a couple more times before walking away. When you are genuinely concerned about a person's feelings, you might repeat their request, 'I understand you would very much like me to ... however I'm afraid that will not be possible.' You do not need to give an explanation, but some people prefer to give a brief one as a form of politeness. You may even be able to suggest someone else who might be more likely to say 'yes'.

how to ask for change assertively
In order to get your needs met, a useful formula is the Three-part Question:
1. **I feel** ... [annoyed/furious/unhappy/betrayed]
2. **because you** ... [state the person's behaviour simply in a non-judgemental fashion]
3. **and I would appreciate it if you would** ... [ask for what you need/want next time].

exercise: negative thought-stopping for anxiety

People with Anxiety worry excessively about the future and always imagine that things will go badly. Catch yourself in the process of having such negative thoughts, such as 'I will fail at my new job', or 'My husband is bound to leave me.' As you identify each negative thought, bring it into full consciousness. Consider it fully, and decide whether it is realistic or not, productive or counter-productive. Gauge how hard it is to control that particular thought (a bit difficult, quite difficult or very difficult) and how uncomfortable it makes you feel (a bit uneasy, quite uncomfortable, or very upset). Chart your answers on paper. If you decide that it would be a good idea to eliminate that negative thought from your thought repertoire, dwell on it for a while (with your body as relaxed as possible). Next, put a rubber band around your wrist and snap it every time that thought returns while shouting, 'Stop!' (Do this out loud in the beginning, then eventually inside your head.) Spend the next thirty seconds focusing on replacing the negative thought with a positive one, such as 'I can be successful in my job' or 'My husband loves me.' Work on this technique until you can regularly catch yourself and replace your negative worries with the positive flip-sides.

exercise: the 'mindfulness of breathing' meditation

The following Buddhist meditation, called 'the Mindfulness of Breathing', is a time-honoured technique that is particularly useful for Anxiety. Try to do it twice a day, but avoid meditating when you are sleepy.

1. Turn off your mobile phone/pager/landline.
2. Sit comfortably in a quiet place where you will not be interrupted for twenty minutes. There is no need to sit cross-legged unless you are comfortable doing so, but make sure your back is properly supported.
3. Take off your watch and place it in front of you where you can see it easily or use a silent clock.
4. You can close your eyes if you wish, but some people find it more useful to gaze at a space on the ground in front of them.
5. Turn your attention to your breathing. Notice the rise and fall of your breath. Allow it to become deeper and heavier as you relax more.
6. Begin to focus on counting your breaths, that is, breathe in and breathe out, then silently count 'one'; breathe in, breathe out, then count 'two'; breathe in, breathe out, then count 'three'; and so on. Do this up to five, then go back and start again at one. Repeat this sequence for around three minutes.
7. If other thoughts enter your head, gently push them away and try to get back to focusing on counting your breaths.
8. For the second stage of this meditation, reverse the first process; that is, count before you take each breath up to five then back to one again. Repeat for around three minutes.
9. In the third stage of the Mindfulness of Breathing meditation, do not count at all, but simply try to focus on the rise and fall of your breath for three minutes. This is a little more difficult, because you do not have the

counting to help anchor your focus. Remember, if extraneous thoughts enter your head simply push them away and get back to focusing on your breathing.

10. In the fourth and last stage, fine tune your focus by turning your attention to the place where you first experience the breath entering your body. This might be the edge of your nostrils or part of the way down your throat; wherever you first notice breath entering your body is the place that should have your complete focus for three minutes.

11. At the end, gradually allow yourself to become more alert. Notice how calm you have become. As you get better at focusing and better at meditating, you will be able to increase the time so that you are eventually managing five minutes for each section, that is, a total of twenty minutes.

12. It is very helpful to meditate with others. Look for a meditation class or Buddhist centre where you may receive support in your meditation.

exercise: progressive body relaxation

An important principle to be aware of is that *if you relax your body your mind will follow*. As a matter of fact, it is physiologically impossible for you to be overcome with Anxiety if you are physically calm. Therefore, it is vital that you learn the best way for you to relax your body. This isn't as simple as crashing onto a comfy sofa, you need to be more systematic about it. Here is an excellent technique for total body relaxation:

1. Take off your shoes and lie down comfortably on your back on the floor, a couch or bed. You can use a small pillow to support your head. (Note that if you need to do this exercise at work, on a bus or some other place where you cannot lie down, it can be done while sitting.)

2. Close your eyes.

3. Take two or three deep, satisfying breaths.

4. Starting at your toes, tense up each group of muscles as tight as you possibly can for ten seconds, then relax them for fifteen seconds. Work your way up your body to the tip of your head, tensing and relaxing; that is, after your toes, go to your ankles, shins, knees, thighs, buttocks, stomach, breast, fingers, forearms, upper arms, shoulders, neck and so on. Don't forget to tense up your jaw, scrunch up your eyes, frown heavily and raise your eyebrows.

5. When you have tensed up and relaxed every single muscle group, tense up your entire body as much as possible for ten seconds then relax it for thirty. Repeat three times.

when someone close to you is suffering from anxiety

1. Encourage the sufferer to seek treatment.
2. Encourage the sufferer to carry out self-help strategies.
3. Support the sufferer's healthy efforts to reduce stress, exercise and eat well-balanced, nutritious meals.
4. Do not support unhealthy attempts to reduce stress, such as drug or alcohol abuse.
5. Being in a relationship or family with someone who is anxious can be difficult. Sometimes it feels as if Anxiety is 'catching'. In particular, children of people with some Anxiety Disorders may end up anxious themselves. Get some therapeutic support for yourself and the family.
6. Play soothing music, plan calming activities and enjoyable, peaceful breaks.
7. Learn everything you can about Anxiety.
8. Take care of yourself, physically and mentally.
9. Reduce your own stress (see page 19).

helpful books

Healing Fear: New Approaches to Overcoming Anxiety, E. Bourne. Oakland, Calif.: New Harbinger Publications, Inc., 1988.

Anxiety & Depression: The Best Resources to Help You Cope, ed. R. Wemhoff. Issaquah, Wash.: Resource Pathways, 1998.

The Relaxation and Stress Reduction Workbook, M. Davis, E.R. Eshelman and M. McKay. Oakland, Calif.: New Harbinger Publications, 2000.

The Anxiety and Phobia Workbook, E. J. Bourne. Oakland, Calif.: New Harbinger Publications, 1995.

Five Weeks to Healing Stress: The Wellness Option, V. O'Hara. Oakland, Calif.: New Harbinger Publications, 1996.

Getting Old without Getting Anxious: Conquering Late Life Anxiety, Peter V. Rabins. Avery Publishing Group, 2004.

How to Meditate, L. LeShan. Boston: Back Bay Books, 1999.

Don't Say Yes When You Want to Say No, H. & B. Fensterheim. New York: David McKay, 1975.

Meditation for Busy People: 60 Seconds to Serenity, D. Croves. San Rafael, Calif.: New World Library, 1993.

If Your Adolescent Has an Anxiety Disorder: An Essential Resource for Parents,
   E. B. Foa and L.W. Andrews. New York: Oxford University Press, 2006.
The Anxiety Cure: An Eight-Step Program for Getting Well, R. L. DuPont,
   E. DuPont Spencer & C. M. DuPont. Hoboken, N. J.: John Wiley & Sons,
   Inc., 1998.

panic disorder (panic attacks)

case study: Jean

*Jean was a well-known stunt coordinator who worked in the film industry.
After a particularly challenging location shoot in which one of her co-workers
had a serious, accidental fall Jean turned up for work one day and found that
she was unable to get out of her car. She sat in the parking lot experiencing a
full-blown panic attack – something she'd never even heard of. Her heart was
racing so fast she thought she was having a stroke. Unable to move or call for
help she sat there for twenty-five minutes, convinced she was dying. Jean
subsequently had two similar attacks before she found her way to my office,
having been referred by her physician who assured her that her heart was
extremely healthy.*

*Jean needed to learn that she was suffering from Panic Disorder, probably
triggered by the stress she experienced over her co-worker's accident, and that
she could learn to overcome her Panic Attacks and reduce the likelihood of
reoccurrence. In therapy she soon began to recognize feelings of Anxiety that lead
up to an attack and to interrupt that process. She learned breathing techniques,
meditation, body relaxation and how to stop herself imagining catastrophic
happenings. For Jean, cognitive awareness was extremely important. She now
says that once she fully understood what had been happening to her – and that
Panic Attacks will always eventually pass – she immediately began to feel
relieved and in control again.*

do you (or does someone close to you)

- Experience mounting fears that can suddenly and unexpectedly take
  control and escalate to an overwhelming pitch within ten minutes? Plus at
  least four of the following symptoms:
- Heart palpitations
- Sweating
- Trembling or shaking
- Feeling short of breath, or having a sense of being smothered

- Feeling of choking
- Chest pain or discomfort
- Nausea or unsettled tummy
- Dizziness or light-headedness
- Feelings of being detached from reality, or of being detached from self
- Fear or going crazy or of losing control
- Fear of dying
- Experiencing numbness or tingling
- Chills or hot flushes

While having a panic attack, a person may have a sense of being in terrible danger – even though nothing in the environment is immediately threatening – and a tremendously powerful urge to escape. Each attack is usually over within thirty minutes, although untreated sufferers rarely know this.

panic attacks in children

Children do sometimes have Panic Attacks similar to those experienced by adults, but they also have different reactions to extreme worry, fear or stress. Sometimes their bodies express the problem in the form of severe tummy aches or other pains. They might refuse to go to school, or develop Separation Anxiety Disorder (see page 341).

'do not pass go' signs
Panic Attacks are very frightening and the disorder can be quite debilitating. Sometimes a sufferer becomes afraid of leaving the house in case a panic attack occurs away from home. The disorder generally limits a person's ability to enjoy or be successful in life because the fear of having a panic attack can prevent him or her from travelling, maintaining relationships or getting to work on time.

People who have Panic Attacks may also have Somatoform Disorders (see page 76ff), Mood Disorders (see Chapter 2), Personality Disorders (see Chapter 7) or other Anxiety Disorders (see Chapter 3). They may also have Substance Abuse Disorders, such as problems with alcohol, cocaine or cannabis. Adults who suffer from asthma have an increased risk of having Panic Attacks.

Despite the fact that Panic Disorder can cause substantial long-term disability, many people fail to seek mental-health treatment for it. It is important to know that it is treatable, that self-help strategies can work very well and that there is no need to put up with it.

what causes panic attacks?

Some researchers believe a first panic attack is triggered by an extremely stressful event, such as the loss of a partner, friend or relative through divorce, separation or death. Losing one's job, money or health can also trigger an initial panic attack and begin a cycle of recurrences. The body mounts a 'fight or flight' response, involving a huge surge of adrenaline, racing heart, and rising blood pressure, which lasts considerably longer than the usual reaction to any actual present danger. After that first event, the mind begins to monitor the body fearfully for warning signs of another panic attack such as an increase in heart rate. Thereafter, even a slight heartbeat increase, perhaps stimulated by a cup of coffee, can be sufficient to trigger another panic attack. Panic Attacks are also associated with current and future Anxiety, Depression, and Substance Abuse, and people with histories of childhood physical and sexual abuse may be at increased risk of panic during adulthood.

what is happening in your brain?

Some suspect a 'fear network' in the brain, interacting abnormally with other systems, may lead to panic responses. There may be neurotransmitter abnormalities, leading to cardiac symptoms and the enhanced vigilance that accompanies them. For example, researchers have found a marked increase in brain serotonin turnover in people with Panic Disorder.

which treatments are likely to work?

Panic Disorder responds particularly well to cognitive-behavioural therapy. A sufferer can receive education about Panic Attacks, as well as learning coping skills, breathing techniques and special styles of thinking that can help overcome the problem. There is a case for considering a deeper form of therapy, such as psychoanalysis or psychodynamic psychotherapy that can get to the root of the problem. Virtual-reality exposure therapy (in which a sufferer is given the healing opportunity to be safely exposed to an anxiety-producing situation on a TV screen) is a new and promising tool for the treatment of several Anxiety Disorders, including Panic Attacks. Sometimes, antidepressants and anti-Anxiety medications are prescribed. Many people who suffer from Panic Attacks do not seek treatment – they put up with a terrifying, debilitating problem that could so easily be treated.

best course of action

Seek cognitive-behavioural psychotherapy.

in the meantime, what can you do?

1. Learn to control your breathing, so that if you begin to have a panic attack you can stop it, calm yourself, and prevent yourself from hyperventilating.

exercise: the calming breath technique

- Let all the breath out of your body.
- Then take a long, deep, slow breath.
- Hold your breath for a count of three.
- Exhale very slowly, saying the word 'Relax' under your breath.
- Rest for fifteen seconds, quietening your thoughts and relaxing the muscles in your limbs, torso, jaw and face.
- Repeat the entire sequence twice – or more if you need to.

2. Mind over matter works well for Panic Attacks. Remind yourself that if panic begins to arise, you will not really be in danger and that the feelings will pass. This kind of awareness can make a huge difference to the severity of an attack and can even prevent them from happening at all.

3. Identify the main symptoms of your Panic Attacks (such as rapid heartbeat, choking sensation, vomiting and so on) and measure them according to severity (label them 0–10 with 10 being the longest and most intense experience of a particular symptom). Make a chart and try to plot and rate all symptoms of the Panic Attacks you've had in the past. This increased awareness will help you gain a sense of control over your symptoms.

4. Keep a record of any attacks that might occur or threaten to occur from now on.

5. Analyze the period just before an attack, so you can glean information to prevent one coming on. What exactly happens in your body? Do your muscles tense up? Do you hold your breath? Do you start to shallow-breathe? Once you know this, plan to head off your next attack by deliberately relaxing your muscles (see Progressive Body Relaxation

exercise page 41), and by controlling your breathing as outlined above.

6. Use daily affirmations to replace your fears with: 'I do not have to allow panic to overwhelm me' or 'I can get through this' or 'If I relax my body, my mind will follow'. Write these down and post them somewhere you will constantly see them.

7. Practise meditation twice a day (see page 40). Meditation techniques can help enormously in helping you to remain physically and mentally calm.

8. A yoga class can also provide you with useful de-stressing and calming skills.

9. Practise relaxation twice a day, and whenever you feel anxious or your heart rate starts to increase (see the Progressive Body Relaxation Exercise on page 41). If you do this whenever you feel your body start to tense up, you will help head off a panic attack.

10. Do not consume anything containing caffeine. This includes coffee, tea, fizzy drinks and non-prescription medications such as some headache tablets (read the label carefully). If you do consume caffeine, the ensuing heart-jolt could trigger a panic attack. There is some clinical evidence that, for some people, eliminating caffeine can prevent Panic Attacks altogether.

11. It is very important that you do not take cocaine, amphetamines ('speed'), PCP, LSD, ketamine, or any street drugs, especially stimulants. Even marijuana can trigger a panic attack.

12. Establish a consistent pattern of good-quality sleep. If you have problems sleeping follow the self-help suggestions for Insomnia or other Sleep Disorders (see page 361 onwards).

13. If you smoke, stop now. By aggravating your Anxiety, nicotine may be making you more vulnerable to Panic Attacks.

14. 'Self-talk' is the running commentary inside your mind. It is important to become aware of it, because it will give you very useful information. You will probably notice that many of your ruminations begin with the words, 'What if ... ?' and go on to describe worst-case scenarios, such as 'What if I have a panic attack while I'm out on a date?' The good news is that, if you monitor your self-talk, you can change it to positive statements. This technique is one of the many successful 'behaviour modification' strategies for reducing Anxiety and the likelihood of having Panic Attacks. This is how it works: NOTICE! INTERRUPT! CHANGE!

exercise: the 'NIC it' technique

- **Notice** First, you must learn to identify the type of self-talk that provokes your Anxiety. What exactly are you saying to yourself? Write down some of your catastrophizing statements, such as 'What if I die while I'm having a panic attack?' or 'What if I get so anxious I lose control and crash my car?'
- **Interrupt** Second, learn to interrupt the process and stop your unhelpful, negative self-talk. For obvious reasons this is called '*thought-stopping*' and involves simply telling yourself to notice and quit thinking those Anxiety-producing thoughts that only serve to increase your worry and lead to panic. It's helpful to signal the change by saying, 'Stop!' as loud as you can, or using some kind of discrete physical action such as slapping your knee. Some people wear rubber bands on their wrists and snap them to accentuate their thought stopping. Do what works for you.
- **Change** Thirdly, you can swap your negative self-talk with soothing and encouraging words, such as 'I won't die, faint or go crazy during a panic attack' or 'I am calm'.

when someone close to you suffers from panic attacks

1. Encourage him or her to seek treatment and carry out self-help strategies.
2. Remind the sufferer that a panic attack always passes after a short while and that he or she can avoid one by breathing deeply and relaxing.
3. Remind the sufferer to practise stress-reducing techniques.
4. Remind the sufferer not to ingest caffeine or any recreational drugs.
5. Support efforts to exercise, get plenty of good-quality sleep and eat well-balanced, nutritious meals.
6. Learn everything you can about Panic Attacks.
7. Being in a relationship or family with someone who has Panic Attacks can be difficult. Get some therapeutic support for yourself and the family.
8. Plan calming activities and enjoyable, peaceful breaks.
9. Take care of yourself, physically and mentally.
10. Reduce your own stress (see page 19).

helpful books

Thoughts and Feelings: Taking Control of Your Moods and Your Life, M. McKay, P. Fanning and M. Davis. Oakland, Calif.: New Harbinger Publications, 1998.

The Anxiety and Phobia Workbook, E. J. Bourne. Oakland, Calif.: New Harbinger Publications, 1995.

Don't Panic: Taking Control of Anxiety Attacks, R. Reid Wilson. New York: Harper Collins, 1996.

The Good News About Panic, Anxiety and Phobias: Cures, Treatments and Solutions in the New Age of Biopsychiatry, M. S. Gold. New York: Bantam Books, 1990.

Coping With Panic: A Drug-Free Approach to Dealing with Anxiety Attacks, G. A. Clum. Belmont, Calif.: Wadsworth, 1990.

Meditation for Busy People: 60 Seconds to Serenity by D. Croves. San Rafael, California: New World Library, 1993.

100 Questions & Answers about Panic Disorder, C. W. Berman. Sudbury, Mass.: Jones and Bartlett Publishers, 2005.

Master Your Panic and Take Back Your Life! Twelve Treatment Sessions to Conquer Panic, Anxiety and Agoraphobia, (3rd ed.), D. F. Beckfield Atascadero, Calif.: Impact Publishers, 2004.

Soothe Your Nerves: The Black Woman's Guide to Understanding and Overcoming Anxiety, Panic, and Fear, A. Neal-Barnett. New York: Fireside Books, 2003.

No More Panic Attacks: A 30-day Plan for Conquering Anxiety, J. Shoquist & D. Stafford. Franklin Lakes, N.J.: New Page Books, 2002.

Healing Fear: New Approaches to Overcoming Anxiety, E. Bourne. Oakland, Calif.: New Harbinger Publications, Inc., 1998.

phobias

The great film director Alfred Hitchcock had a whole career based on portraying people's phobias and fears of natural phenomena. Remember *The Birds* or *Vertigo*? As a society, we have come to be fascinated by phobias, and expressing unusual fears has even become a mark of individuality (or even a way to express vulnerability and thereby enlist help). People can become phobic about almost anything, and some of the most unusual I've come across are fears of fingernail clippings, subway signs and small round things. Some feared objects are impossible to avoid entirely, so having phobias can be extremely debilitating. Yet this problem is extremely common. Ask around the table next time you're at a dinner party and I bet there'll be at least one person who will mention something that is terrifying to either the guest himself or 'a close friend'! Phobias are usually easy to treat, so there is no need for anyone to avoid flying, going out (agoraphobia) or having a social life (social phobia).

Some researchers believe the susceptibility to having specific fears and their associated phobias is somewhat inherited, while others believe that conditioned responses play a role (that is, we *learn* to be afraid of certain things or situations). But, however phobias are created, the range of fears exhibited by people is remarkable – with spiders, heights, lifts, snakes, dirt, needles, blood and germs being some of the most common – and these represent the rich complexity and diversity of the human brain.

case study: Fiona

Fiona had lived all her life in Scotland, but she married an Irish man, and went to live with him in a small seaside town in England. Fiona was glad not to live in Ireland because she did not feel accepted or appreciated by her in-laws. Not long after she was married, Fiona developed a fear of flying. On the way back from her first visit to Ireland, she began to experience massive Anxiety, accompanied by sweating, nausea and a feeling of paralysis. After that, she would not entertain any thought of flying again, and would only take the train to and from Scotland whenever she wanted see her own friends and family. When she came to see me and began to tell me about the resentful way she felt she was treated by her husband's family, I concluded that the timing of her flying phobia indicated that her psyche had created a very useful way to ensure she never had to see them again. Her fear of flying would not leave her until she had learned to protect herself from them in other ways. I began to help her become more assertive, and when she began to feel more in control of the situation between her and her in-laws she was ready to address her flying phobia. Fiona responded very well to cognitive-behavioural methods. She was eventually able first to take a short plane trip to Scotland, and more recently graduated to a holiday in Barbados.

do you (or does someone close to you)

- Have an excessive fear of some thing or situation?
- Avoid the thing you fear?
- Feel extremely anxious or panic-stricken when exposed to it?
- Know this fear is unreasonable, perhaps because other people can tolerate being close to the same thing you fear?
- Find that the avoidance or distress this fear creates causes problems in your life?

If you or someone close to you has most of the above symptoms, you probably have a phobia. Don't put up with it.

phobias in children and adolescents

Most children have normal fears that gradually disappear over time, but some are extra fearful. These young people may have a genetic vulnerability or a greater likelihood than others of developing maladaptive fears. Although you can't exactly 'catch' a phobia from someone else, being in the vicinity of an adult with a phobia can make a child more likely to develop one. Once a phobia exists, it is maintained by certain thought processes.

'do not pass go' signs

Having a specific phobia can mean that even just hearing someone talk about the feared object can cause the sufferer to become utterly terrified and paralyzed with Anxiety. He or she may go to enormous lengths to avoid coming into contact with the source of that Anxiety, so leading a normal life can be very difficult. This would be especially true if the feared objects occur commonly in a person's environment; for example, water, telephones or cats. Although phobias have the potential to cause severe impairment in people's lives, they can easily be treated; so people who fail to do something about it are suffering needlessly.

A social phobia is fear of being with other people in a social situation, so having this form of phobia can prevent a person from being successful at work, from forming and maintaining friendships, or from getting married. A social phobia is a chronic disorder that is common worldwide. It typically begins early in life, and without treatment it can result in substantial impairment.

what causes phobias?

Some people seem to have a genetic predisposition to developing phobias, which may arise after an initial, traumatic encounter with some object or situation that then develops into a much greater fear and subsequent avoidance. A phobia may also be caused by witnessing something traumatic that happens to someone else. A parent with a phobia who displays fear and avoidance of something may pass that phobia onto his or her children.

what is happening in your brain?

People suffering from Anxiety Disorders such as phobias may have an imbalance in brain chemicals. The over-activation of the brain's fear centre may lead to hyperactivity in the autonomic nervous system and subsequent symptoms of Anxiety.

which treatments are likely to work?

Cognitive-behavioural therapy has been shown to be very successful in the treatment of phobias, while virtual-reality exposure therapy is a promising tool for the treatment of a number of Anxiety Disorders. Social phobia has been effectively treated by a combination of therapy plus antidepressants or an anti-Anxiety medication.

best course of action

Seek treatment from a psychotherapist.

in the meantime, what can you do?

Phobias are best overcome when the fear is faced, because if you continue to avoid the thing you fear you will maintain the phobia. However, that's not easy to achieve. For example, a person who suffers from arachnophobia (the irrational fear of spiders) would find it difficult to go into the garden, find a spider and get close to it – although that would actually help cure the phobia. There is a more palatable technique called 'imagery desensitization' that can help a person safely face and reduce his or her fear by combining relaxation with visualization. You can slowly train yourself to let go of your phobia by following these steps:

1. Create a list of ten imagined situations in which you picture yourself calmly facing your feared object or situation. These situations should be arranged in order of hierarchy; that is, the worst possible situation should be number ten, while the one that makes you least anxious should be number one. For example, for someone who has a phobia about riding in lifts, the first situation on the hierarchy might be, 'Just past a tall building in which lifts are installed'; the second might be, 'Walking into a building that has lifts'; the third might be, 'Walking pass a lift'; the fourth, 'Watching people come out of a lift'; the fifth, 'Watching people press the bell and wait for a lift'; the sixth, 'Pressing the lift bell'; seventh, 'Stepping in and out of a stationary lift'; eighth, 'Stepping into a lift and riding up one floor with other people'; ninth, 'Riding up one floor alone'; and finally, tenth, 'Taking the lift from the lobby to your office on the seventh floor.'

2. Practise relaxation and breathing techniques (pages 40, 41, 46) until you are sure you can relax your body and slow your breathing at will.

3. Lie down comfortably and fully relax your body and mind for about fifteen minutes. Wait until you are breathing with deep, slow diaphragmatic breaths.

4. For about one minute, picture yourself in a peaceful situation where you feel safe – perhaps lying on a beach or walking in a lovely garden.

5. When you are utterly calm, turn your attention to the first (least fear-producing) item on your hierarchy list, and try to visualize that situation in detail for one minute while trying to maintain full bodily relaxation. When you notice your anxiety rising, go back and attend to your relaxation and breathing until the anxiety diminishes. If necessary, return to your peaceful scene for another minute.

6. Return to your first situation and keep working at it until you can visualize it while remaining completely relaxed, with an absence of Anxiety.

7. Then move on to item number two and repeat the process until you can also visualize that second situation while fully relaxed without becoming anxious.

8. Continue to work through the list, interspersing each visualization with relaxation, breathing and your peaceful scene, until you have mastered even your most feared situation, number ten.

9. Finally, if it is feasible, face your phobia in real life for a period of at least forty minutes. If you have mastered your hierarchy you should be ready to do this. Maintain your relaxed state, breathe deeply and you will achieve the ultimate in 'mind over matter'.

helpful books

The Anxiety and Phobia Workbook, E. J. Bourne. Oakland, Calif.: New Harbinger Publications, 2005.

Overcoming Animal and Insect Phobias: How to Conquer Fear of Dogs, Snakes, Rodents, Bees, Spiders, and More, M. M. Anthony and R. E. McCabe. Oakland Calif.: New Harbinger Publications, 2005.

The Shyness and Social Anxiety Workbook: Proven Techniques for Overcoming Your Fears, M. M. Anthony and R. P. Swinson. Oakland, Calif.: New Harbinger Publications, 2000.

The Agoraphobia Workbook: A Comprehensive Program to End Your Fear of Symptom Attacks, C. A. Pollard and E. Zuercher-White. Oakland, Calif.: New Harbinger Publications, 2003.

Flying without Fear, D. Brown. Oakland, Calif.: New Harbinger Publications, 1996.

Meditation for Busy People: 60 Seconds to Serenity, D. Croves. San Rafael, Calif.: New World Library, 1993.

If Your Adolescent Has an Anxiety Disorder: An Essential Resource for Parents by E. B. Foa and L. W. Andrews. New York: Oxford University Press, 2006.

obsessive-compulsive disorder

Have you seen the actor Jack Nicholson portray a person with severe Obsessive-Compulsive Disorder (OCD) in the film *As Good As It Gets*? It was an engaging, Oscar-winning performance, but I worried that people who actually suffer from OCD might be upset by it. People with the disorder usually feel very ashamed of having obsessions and compulsions they can't control, and they don't want anyone to know about it. In any case, not everyone with OCD is as impaired as Nicholson's character was. In fact, the DSM-IV describes a 'milder form' of OCD (Obsessive-Compulsive Personality Disorder, see page 171) that applies to overly organized people or people whose need to do something perfectly interferes with their ability to finish it.

OCD is a neurobiological disorder that someone once described as a 'hiccup of the brain'. It can present itself in quite a number of different ways, including fears of contamination; doubting and checking; counting or touching compulsions; worries about imperfections or incompleteness; religious, sexual, or aggressive obsessions; and compulsive hoarding. It tends to start quite early in life and can lead to a lot of misery and an unnecessarily poor quality of life for many of the people who suffer from it. Something in the mind is always urging them either to do something, think about something or avoid something – and that can take up an awful lot of time and drastically interfere with their lives. As I said, people with OCD tend to be rather secretive about it and try to hide it from others, including mental-health professionals. But OCD is treatable, and those who suffer from it should be gently encouraged to seek help.

case study: Sheree

As a child, Sheree began to count. It was not just maths homework, however. An insistent urge in Sheree's mind drove her to count the decorative plaster darts on her bedroom ceiling, the patches on her quilt and the post boxes on her way to school. It seemed to Sheree that something terrible would happen to her or her family if she did not complete her counting rituals every morning. After a while this self-imposed requirement had escalated to the counting of all lockers outside her classroom, all windows and light switches on a particular floor of her school, all pictures hanging outside the art class and every piece of chalk in her teacher's box. Even though she lived nearby, she began to be late for school because of the length of time it took her to complete these rituals. Although she was a good student, all this affected her school success.

By the time Sheree was in her thirties, she had managed to obtain a degree in education, but was doing afternoon shift work in a local fast-food restaurant because her rituals were taking up such a large proportion of her day that she could not work in her desired profession. She lived alone in a room covered in piles of newspapers that she felt compelled to horde. She had failed to develop good social skills, and the one boyfriend she had ever had left because he was unable to cope with her compulsions and obsessions. She needed urgent treatment in order to be free of her need to count, to help her connect with people and to enable her to feel safe in the world. During psychotherapy, Sheree was helped to understand that she was suffering from a treatable complaint called Obsessive-Compulsive Disorder (OCD). Like many people with OCD, Sheree felt ashamed of her compulsions, and had been very secretive about them. But cognitive-behavioural therapy combined with anti-depressant medication immediately helped her urges to become more controllable. Her Anxiety began to be assuaged through talking therapy, and she learned to self-soothe, self-monitor and have more appropriate interactions with people round her. She eventually got a job as a valued office manager for a successful but disorganized architect – who really needed her to put his life in order. Five years later, she married him.

do you (or does someone close to you)

- Have obsessions, that is, you are troubled by the way your mind comes up with thoughts, images or impulses that you probably know go well beyond simply stressing about your real-life problems? You try to ignore or push away these obsessions, or attempt to keep them at bay with some other thought or action.

OR

- Have compulsions, that is, you feel driven to do certain things repetitively (such as counting, touching or checking certain objects; washing your hands; or putting things in order)? Even though you may know it's unrealistic, you do this to soothe yourself, because in your mind it seems that you can thus avoid something you fear or prevent something terrible from happening.

- Find that your obsessions or compulsions cause difficulties in your life, either because they take up a lot of your time, stress you out or create problems socially, at work or in your relationships?

OCD in children and adolescents

Children do sometimes show signs of obsessive behaviour and compulsive thinking. They may have inherited this or it may have been triggered either by Anxiety or trauma. Fearful imaginings, counting steps, touching every door handle in the vicinity or putting their toys in a special and exact order – these are just some of the ways a child's brain might force him or her to act in order to ward off 'disaster'.

'do not pass go' signs

A person can become paralyzed by OCD. It can prevent him or her from functioning in the world by causing avoidance of the things that other people can do quickly and easily. In addition, the stress and state of fear the disorder creates for both mind and body may lead to physical ailments, and prevent happiness. This disorder is easily treated, so there is no need to suffer.

what causes OCD?

OCD may be the result of the mind's response to Anxiety, fear or trauma, and is often a genetically determined condition that runs in families. If someone in your family has OCD, you have a greater chance of developing it. It can develop under certain circumstances; for example, some parents develop the disorder after the birth of a child. OCD may occasionally be triggered by head injury, autoimmune diseases or epilepsy.

what is happening in your brain?

Neurotransmitters, especially serotonin, have been implicated in the development of OCD. Due to new brain-imaging techniques, researchers have discovered that people with OCD have observable brain differences, especially in the sensory processing centre, the emotional memory centre and in the areas responsible for learning, motivation and voluntary movement. The part of the brain that is responsible for filtering thoughts and processing sensory stimulation is called the caudate nucleus. In people with OCD, the caudate nucleus doesn't do its job properly so, instead of sifting out undesirable and unnecessary thoughts, they are allowed to intrude unchecked. This sets off a series of problematic reactions in other parts of the brain.

which treatments are likely to work?

Cognitive-behavioural therapy (individual or group) has been shown to be very effective in treating OCD. Antidepressants can also be helpful, and the best answer for severe OCD is often a combination of therapy and medication.

best course of action

Seek cognitive-behavioural therapy.

in the meantime, what can you do?

1. People with OCD tend to be uncomfortable disclosing the extent of their obsessions, compulsions and the exact nature of their rituals, but if you think you may have OCD, appreciate that you have a condition that is shared by many other people and that it can be treated. You will not be judged on it if you see a good therapist. Instead, you will be respectfully and compassionately helped.

2. Start by being honest about the exact nature of your OCD. What are your specific rituals: Checking? Counting? Hoarding? Repeating? Washing? Cleaning? Thinking the worst? List them on paper and identify whether they are obsessions (they take place in your mind) or compulsions (you tend to act them out).

3. Be honest about how much time these rituals (either thoughts or actions) take up during your day. List the ways these rituals cause problems for you.

4. Learn everything you can about OCD (see suggested reading below).

5. Educate people around you about OCD, especially anyone who is directly affected by your symptoms. The reason for doing this would be to gain some support and understanding.

6. OCD symptoms become worse when you are under stress. Identify and take steps to reduce the stressors in your occupational, social and family life.

7. If your OCD symptoms appeared after experiencing a traumatic event, appreciate that you will need treatment for the trauma.

8. Practise Progressive Body Relaxation (see page 41).

9. Practise the Calming Breath Technique (see page 46).

10. Practise meditation (see page 40).

11. Begin a self-directed Exposure and Response Prevention programme. The concepts are outlined below, followed by specific instructions explaining how to go about it:

Exposure The idea is to expose yourself deliberately to a feared situation, thought or image; for example, if you tend to check locks or switches, to have a go at trying to make yourself do that only once. If you avoid touching certain objects or surfaces, this will involve forcing yourself to do so, without washing afterwards. If your fears concern something that cannot actually be done, exposure will involve forcing yourself to imagine it vividly instead. If you have fearful imaginings, you will force yourself to think directly about the terrifying scenarios.

Response Prevention This is about blocking your rituals, that is, not allowing yourself to carry out any of the compulsions you normally engage in to avoid Anxiety. In the case of checking rituals, for example, you will try to avoid checking for at least thirty minutes, then gradually increase that time. Even though it's hard to make yourself experience the discomfort you will be greatly helping to change your symptoms of OCD.

how to train yourself using exposure and response prevention

- Start by making a list of ten feared situations for each of your obsessions and/or compulsions, rated from bad to worst. For example, if you are a 'checker', this might begin with 'Locking the back door, checking it three times, then leaving the house for 30 minutes.' The tenth and most Anxiety-producing item on your list might be 'Locking the back door, not checking it at all, then staying elsewhere overnight.'
- Now work through this list, starting at the least threatening, until you can achieve every item without having to engage in any compulsions or obsessions to relieve your Anxiety. Practise relaxation and breathing at all times during this procedure.
- Next, go on to your second ten-item list and work though that, followed by all your other lists.
- Take courage. I know this process of exposing yourself to your fears will require great fortitude and you will have to deal with powerful feelings. Your job is to tolerate those feelings for as long as it takes to become calm. In doing so, you will be retraining your brain to deal with your specific, feared elements without triggering Anxiety. You will be well on your way to overcoming your OCD, freeing up your mind and allowing you to be happy.

when someone close to you is suffering from OCD

1. Encourage the sufferer to seek treatment, but be aware that most people with OCD feel very ashamed of it. You will have to exercise great sensitivity in your approach; useful language would be, 'I really care about you, but I've noticed that your mind seems to sabotage your ability to be relaxed and enjoy life/our ability to enjoy our life together. Would that be fair to say? I know there is a way you can be helped – how about giving it a go?'

2. Support all healthy efforts to reduce Anxiety and OCD symptoms, such as relaxation, breathing, meditation, yoga and following the self-help guidelines above.

3. Do not support unhealthy efforts to assuage Anxiety, such as substance abuse.

4. Continuing to engage in OCD behaviour and thoughts only maintains them. Until therapy is available to the sufferer, be understanding about the person's need to carry out the rituals, but encourage him or her to stop by following the Exposure and Response Prevention programme (see above).

5. Learn everything you can about OCD.

6. Being in a relationship or family with someone who has OCD can be very difficult. That person may be so busy attending to rituals that he or she will find it hard to be emotionally available to you. Get some therapeutic support for yourself and the family.

7. There is a price to pay for becoming too much of a carer in a relationship. At the end of the day, an adult is responsible for him or herself. Allow mental-health professionals to take care of the sufferer and do not take on more than you can manage.

8. Take care of yourself, physically and mentally.

9. Plan fun and enjoyable breaks to help create more fun and relaxation in your life.

10. Reduce your stress (see page 19).

helpful books

The OCD Workbook (2nd ed.) Your Guide to Breaking Free from Obsessive-Compulsive Disorder, Bruce M. Hyman, Ph.D. and Cherry Pedrick, R. N. Oakland, Calif.: New Harbinger Publications Inc., 2005.

Just Checking: Scenes from the Life of an Obsessive Compulsive, E. Colas. New York: Washington Square Press, 1999.

The Boy Who Couldn't Stop Washing: The Experience and Treatment of

Obsessive-Compulsive Disorder, J. L. Rapoport. New York: Plume/Penguin, 1989.

How to Meditate, L. LeShan. Boston: Back Bay Books, 1999.

Meditation for Busy People: 60 Seconds to Serenity, D. Croves. San Rafael, Calif.: New World Library, 1993.

Overcoming Obsessive Thoughts: How to Gain Control of Your OCD, C. Purdon and D. A. Clark,. Oakland, Calif.: New Harbinger Publications, 2005.

Overcoming Compulsive Washing: Free Your Mind from OCD, P. R. Munford. Oakland, Calif.: New Harbinger Publications, 2005.

Soothe Your Nerves: The Black Woman's Guide to Understanding and Overcoming Anxiety, Panic, and Fear, A. Neal-Barnett. New York: Fireside Books, 2003.

Obsessive Compulsive Disorder: Practical, Tried-and-Tested Strategies to Overcome OCD, (2nd ed.), F. Toates and O. Coschug-Toates. Barb Mew, London: Class Publishing, 2002.

The Imp of the Mind: Exploring the Silent Epidemic of Obsessive Bad Thoughts, L. Baer. New York: Dutton/Penguin Books, 2001.

Obsessive-Compulsive Disorders: A Complete Guide to Getting Well and Staying Well, F. Penzel. New York: Oxford University Press, 2002.

Obsessive-Compulsive Disorder: The Facts (2nd ed.), P. de Silva and S. Rachman. New York: Oxford University Press, 1999.

Stop Obsessing: How to Overcome Your Obsessions and Compulsions, E. B. Foa, B. Wilson and R. Reid. New York: Bantam Books, 2001.

help for partners, friends and family

Loving Someone with OCD: Help for You and Your Family, Karen Landsman, Kathy Ruppertus and Cherry Pedrick. Oakland, Calif.: New Harbinger Publications, 2005.

Obsessive Compulsive Disorder: A Survival Guide for Family and Friends, Roy C. New Hyde Park, New York: Obsessive Compulsive Anonymous, Inc., 1993.

Obsessive Compulsive Disorder: New Help for the Family, Herbert L. Gravitz. Santa Barbara, Calif.: Healing Visions Press, 1998.

Five Weeks to Healing Stress: The Wellness Option, V. O'Hara. Oakland, Calif.: New Harbinger Publications, 1996.

If Your Adolescent Has an Anxiety Disorder: An Essential Resource for Parents, E. B. Foa and L. W. Andrews. New York: Oxford University Press, 2006.

Freeing Your Child from Obsessive-Compulsive Disorder: A Powerful, Practical Program For Parents of Children and Adolescents, T. E. Chansky and P. Stern (illus.). Norwalk, Conn.: Crown House Publishing Limited, 2000.

chapter 4
'mind-blowing' experiences: trauma and adjusting

"Have you ever considered another line of work?"

post-traumatic stress disorder

We're hearing more and more about the disabling problem of Post-Traumatic Stress Disorder (PTSD) in the media. People are now becoming aware that soldiers who have experienced the horrors of war, and victims of terrorist attacks, often struggle to come to terms with the psychological aftermath. But PTSD can be seen in anyone who has been involved in or witnessed a terrifying traumatic event, such as an earthquake or another natural disaster, a violent crime, a car or airplane accident or a physical attack. After a while, he or she may begin to re-experience that horrible occurrence in the form of distressing recurrent memories, nightmares, flashbacks or hallucinations. PTSD can also occur after childhood trauma; as adults, the sufferers may have problems in areas related to their trauma, such as sexuality, self-esteem, trust and relationships.

Not everyone who has experienced trauma is consciously aware of it. The mind is capable of submerging dreadful memories of trauma so a person who has, say, been sexually abused might not consciously remember it. In addition, there is a tendency to protect an abuser, so many abused people will speak fondly or admiringly of their perpetrators. In fact, many survivors don't even know what constitutes abuse; since it has become so familiar to them they have nothing with which to compare it. In the course of my clinical work I have often come across people who would characteristically answer 'No' to the question 'Have you experienced childhood abuse?', then subsequently describe being tormented, tortured, starved, molested, raped, confined or brutally attacked in one way or another. In their minds they have come to think of such atrocities as something other than abuse, such as 'rightful punishment'.

Untreated symptoms of PTSD can persist for many years. Elements in the environment that remind a person of traumatic experiences (for example, bright lights, sudden noises or genital touching) activate regions of the brain that support intense emotions and cause them to 'overreact'. People with PTSD find it hard to describe their experiences in words. Their attention and memory frequently fail and they find it hard to 'be present', so traumatized people lose their way in the world. Without treatment, their lives may be negatively changed forever; with it, they can heal from the effects of the original trauma, learn to tolerate feelings and sensations, cease to be over-aroused and move on.

case study: Jerry

Jerry was a young Australian soldier during the Vietnam War. His tour of duty with the Australian forces over there left him physically in one piece – but mentally he returned a changed man. His childhood sweetheart welcomed him back, and within two months they were married and starting a family. But the trauma of his battlefield experiences remained with him. In those days few returning soldiers were helped for long-term symptoms of PTSD – in fact it was considered a sign of weakness to let memories or symptoms of war bother a man. It wasn't until his grown-up daughter came to see me, seeking treatment for Anxiety, that someone outside the family was alerted to Jerry's suffering. Jerry's PTSD had affected his ability to be emotionally available to his family. His symptoms included sleeplessness, flashbacks, and vivid and disturbing nightmares. He panicked whenever he was exposed to loud noises, such as a car backfiring, or bright flashes from lightning or fireworks.

Jerry had never talked to anyone – even his wife – about his time in Vietnam. In my office, as he began to recount the horrible experiences that had caused his mental scars, it was clear his visceral connection to them was still fresh and painful, even after all those years. Sadly, he had lived much of his post-war life in limbo – disconnected from the people round him. He had missed out on traditional family events such as watching the New Year's Eve firework display over Sydney Harbour. Nevertheless, after some months in therapy he was relatively free of his post-traumatic symptoms, and could feel confident driving his wife around the city without fear of reacting to a loud noise. He began to make up for lost years by reconnecting with his family.

is this you (or someone close to you)?

- You experienced, heard about or saw a terrifying event that made you feel helpless, horror-struck and at risk of death or serious injury to your body or sensibility.
- At some time after that event occurred, you began to re-experience it in the form of recurrent unwanted images, memories, nightmares, flashbacks and hallucinations. You may also become extremely distressed when something in your environment triggers a memory of that event.
- At least three of the following symptoms are present:
  1. You try hard to avoid thinking of that terrible event.
  2. You wish to stay away from people, activities or places that trigger memories of that event.
  3. You cannot remember significant aspects of the event.
  4. You lose interest in some of the things you once enjoyed.
  5. You feel detached from people round you.
  6. You feel somewhat emotionless.
  7. You do not feel very hopeful about the future.

- You are experiencing at least two of the following symptoms:
  1. You can't fall asleep or stay asleep easily.
  2. You are irritable and sometimes lash out in anger.
  3. You have trouble concentrating.
  4. You are easily startled.
  5. You are super-aware of things and people round you.

PTSD in children

Children with PTSD may show signs of fearfulness, Anxiety or Depression. They may fail to thrive, and have nightmares or night terrors. They may misbehave, feel alienated from other children, and their school work or attendance may suffer. They may also be at risk of committing suicide.

'do not pass go' signs

PTSD is strongly linked with less-than-optimum mental functioning, alcohol and drug abuse, poor social skills, Depression, difficulty concentrating, impaired judgement, interpersonal problems, Anxiety, relationship difficulties, suicidal tendency, health problems including an increased risk of coronary heart disease and risk of HIV infection. Without addressing the underlying problem (healing from the trauma itself), the survivor has a high likelihood of continuing the cycle of negative life experiences: Substance Abuse, family dysfunction, plus having mental and physical health deficits. PTSD in parents impacts children, so the cycle starts all over again. It is imperative to seek treatment and stop it continuing.

what causes PTSD?

PTSD arises after a person experiences (or witnesses) a terrifying, shocking, and often life-threatening, experience that made him or her feel extremely vulnerable. Examples of the types of events that may lead to PTSD are: childhood neglect, verbal, physical or sexual abuse, violent victimization, rape, war, accidents and natural disasters. Children of adults with PTSD are at risk of developing it too.

what is happening in the brain?

Researchers have found that trauma causes changes in the brain, especially in the parts responsible for emotional processing, language processing and memory. Some researchers believe that the symptoms of PTSD, such as nightmares and flashbacks occur because a person's mind cannot integrate such bad memories into his or her belief system. Or it may be that brain chemicals create changes that reinforce memories of the initial trauma in order to encourage a person to avoid a similar event in the future.

which treatments are likely to work?

Psychotherapy or psychoanalysis can be extremely helpful. Cognitive-behavioural treatments have been shown to be effective in helping survivors process their memories and feelings about traumatic events, and teaching them how to manage their fears and build coping skills. Hypnotherapy has been demonstrated to be effective, as have psychodynamic psychotherapy and group psychotherapy. EMDR (eye-movement desensitization and reprocessing) is a relatively new treatment method for PTSD and general trauma. Computer-based, virtual-reality exposure therapy is a promising new treatment that is now being offered to some returning soldiers and disaster workers. Medications are sometimes prescribed, especially anti-depressants and anti-anxiety medications.

best course of action
Seek psychotherapy.

in the meantime, what can you do?
1. Learn everything you can about PTSD. See reading list below.
2. Identify which symptoms of PTSD most bother you (understand that they constitute a common reaction to abnormal events) from the list below:
   - Flashbacks
   - Panic Attacks
   - Nightmares
   - Unwelcome memories
   - Body memories (having physical reminders, as if the abuse was reoccurring)
   - Phobias
   - Overwhelming fears
3. Identify the coping mechanisms you have developed to deal with your pain. Are they still useful? Which are less useful, or perhaps even hurting you today? Examples might be:
   - Substance Abuse
   - Promiscuity
   - Uncontrolled anger
   - Avoiding relationships

   Begin to work on eliminating those that serve only to keep you linked to shame and pain, for example seek Substance Abuse treatment, or follow an anger-management programme.
4. Join a survivors' support group.
5. Write down your feelings about what happened to you in detail and try to exonerate yourself from blame.
6. Make a personal pact to let go of your shame and view yourself with compassion and understanding.
7. Write down, frequently, any and all feelings that surface – your grief, sadness, loss, anger and fear. Allow yourself the time and space to feel them. Do not try to avoid or cover them up by making yourself busy, using harmful substances, shopping, over-exercising, over-eating or using any other avoidance mechanisms.
8. Express your feelings through some form of art, whether you choose

painting, clay-modelling or some other medium. Make sure you are not trying to produce something 'good' – and avoid judging your work. Simply allow your emotions to flow through your brush, pencil or fingers. No-one else needs to see it, so be free to let go. A helpful technique is to use your left hand if you are right-handed or your right hand if you typically write or paint with your left.

9. You are a survivor. Which of the strengths you have today have developed out of hardships you endured earlier on? Write down the answer and honour yourself for coping so well.

10. If you were expected to keep secrets that hid abuse, they have helped maintain your shame. Write them down and consider when and where might be an appropriate time to disclose them. Under therapeutic guidance is probably the answer, but sometimes sharing some with a trusted friend can help.

11. If you were abused, either in childhood or otherwise, write a lengthy letter to your abuser. Express all your feelings about what was done to you. You may choose not to send it, either because he or she has passed away, or because you feel it would be inappropriate for one reason or another (for example, the person now has advanced dementia due to Alzheimer's disease). The point of this letter is really to allow you the opportunity to enact 'confronting' him or her and letting your feelings out. (It would be inadvisable to confront your abuser in person without having professional support.)

12. Be safe. That means not taking unacceptable risks. It involves practising safe sex, leaving an uncomfortable situation before it goes bad and generally taking care of your mental and physical health. This is not always easy for survivors.

13. Allow yourself to cry. It will help.

14. PTSD and Substance Abuse are linked. If you are abusing alcohol, drugs, food or anything else, join a Harm-reduction, sobriety or twelve-step programme today (see page 181).

15. Take care of your body with healthy eating, regular medical and dental check-ups, and an exercise regime.

16. Establish a consistent pattern of good-quality sleep. If you have problems sleeping (perhaps arising from the nightmares that are often symptoms of PTSD) follow the self-help suggestions for Insomnia or other Sleep Disorders (see page 361 onwards).

17. Structure your day in a way that makes you feel productive but not over-worked.

18. Learn to relax your body (see exercise page 41).
19. Learn to meditate (see page 40).
20. Take a yoga class.
21. Practise setting boundaries with others, that is, stop others intruding on your life or personal space, stop allowing others to coerce you into doing things you don't want to do, never allow others to be verbally, mentally, physically or sexually abusive towards you and demand that they treat you with respect. Setting boundaries today will be harder to achieve if people invaded your boundaries in the past, but persevere. Your intuition will help you to know when someone is overstepping yours – trust it.
22. Practise self-assertion (see page 38)
23. There are community resources, such as survivors' or veterans' groups. Find them and use them.
24. Learn to say 'no' to people who want more from you than you feel comfortable giving.
25. Nurture yourself with healthy pleasures.
26. Ask people that you trust to support your healing.
27. Believe that you can and will get through this.
28. Celebrate your successes.

when someone close to you is suffering from PTSD

1. Encourage the person to seek treatment. This disorder will not go away by itself.
2. Support all healthy efforts to seek professional treatment and reduce symptoms of Anxiety and PTSD symptoms using self-help methods such as relaxation, breathing, meditation, yoga and the steps outlined above.
3. Do not support unhealthy efforts to deal with PTSD, such as substance abuse.
4. Learn everything you can about PTSD.
5. Being in a relationship or family with someone who has PTSD can be very difficult. That person may have extreme reactions such as 'over-reacting' to normal occurrences in your environment (for example, lightning or fireworks) or have horrible recurrent nightmares. He or she may find it hard to be emotionally available to you and may even try to push you away. Get some therapeutic support for yourself and the family.
6. If your spouse, partner or someone in your family has PTSD from a recent trauma, know that this will very likely affect your relationship (for

example, being raped can lead to not wanting to be sexual at all). You will benefit from couples or family therapy.

7. People with PTSD are sometimes suicidal. Take this seriously and follow the guidelines on page 24.

8. There is a price to pay for becoming too much of a carer in a relationship so take care of yourself, physically and mentally.

9. Reduce your stress (see page 19) and help the sufferer and your whole family to engage in soothing activities.

10. Create more relaxation and fun in your lives.

helpful books

The PTSD Workbook: Simple, Effective Techniques for Overcoming Traumatic Stress Symptoms, M. B. Williams and S. Poijula. Oakland, Calif.: New Harbinger Publications, 2002.

I Can't Get Over It: A Handbook for Trauma Survivors, A. Matsakis. Oakland, Calif.: New Harbinger Books, 1996.

Opening Up: The Healing Power of Expressing Emotions, J. W. Pennebaker. New York: The Guilford Press, 1997.

Healing the Shame that Binds You, J. Bradshaw. Deerfield Beach, Fla.: Health Communications, Inc., 1988.

Bradshaw on The Family: A Revolutionary Way of Self-Discovery, J. Bradshaw. Deerfield Beach, Fla.: Health Communications, Inc., 1988.

Home Coming: Reclaiming & Championing Your Inner Child, J. Bradshaw. London: Piatkus, 1990.

The Courage to Heal Workbook: For Men and Women Survivors of Child Sexual Abuse, L. Davis. New York: Harper & Row, 1990.

The Courage to Heal: A Guide for Women Survivors of Child Sexual Abuse, E. Bass and L. Davis. New York: Harper Perennial, 1988.

Male Survivors: 12-Step Recovery Program for Survivors of Childhood Sexual Abuse, T. L. Saunders. Freedom, Calif.: The Crossing Press, 1991.

The Inner Child Workbook: What to Do with Your Past When It Just Won't Go Away, C. L. Taylor. Los Angeles: Jeremy P. Tarcher Inc., 1991.

Allies in Healing: When the Person You Love Was Sexually Abused as a Child, L. Davis, New York: Harper Perennial, 1991.

How to Meditate, L. LeShan. Boston: Back Bay Books, 1999.

Meditation for Busy People: 60 Seconds to Serenity, D. Croves. San Rafael, Calif.: New World Library, 1993.

Survivor Guilt: A Self-Help Guide, A. Matsakis. Oakland, Calif.: New Harbinger Publications, Inc., 1999.

adjustment disorder

We can't just switch our emotions on and off, but different people have different reactions when awful things happen to them. Some people can lose a job one week and be back in the marketplace, confidently searching for another, within a few days; others might be so devastated they fall to pieces. The DSM-IV classification of Adjustment Disorder describes a longer-than-expected reaction (between three and six months) to negative events in a person's life, for example becoming divorced, facing economic hardship or succumbing to serious physical illness. The idea behind a diagnosis of Adjustment Disorder is that, although it is normal to react emotionally to difficult life events, that reaction sometimes lasts longer than is considered reasonable, and treatment is advisable in order to help a person to get back on track.

It seems strange, perhaps, to create an 'artificial' cut-off period for normal adjustment to a painful event as being three months, and many mental-health professionals would agree that recovering from some of life's difficult experiences sometimes takes more time. A person's reaction to bereavement, for example, is excluded from this classification because it's generally accepted that 'it takes as long as it takes' (although sometimes therapy is advisable if the mourning process goes on so long a person begins to be unable to recover as a matter of course). It's not always easy to decide when a person *began* to have a problematic reaction to a negative event; however, the category of Adjustment Disorder does provide a framework so that those who need treatment can enter the mental-health system, receive help, and move on.

case study: Mary

Mary had been married to Jim for nearly seven years. They never had children, partly because Jim's work required that he spend a great deal of time travelling. While he was away, Mary created a lovely home, tended their garden and cared for their dogs. Mary believed she and Jim were happy in their relationship, so it was a terrible shock when she discovered that not only had Jim been having a three-year affair, but that he wished to divorce Mary and marry his lover. He moved out within a week of making this announcement and Mary was left in a state of shock. Barely able to carry on, she became extremely sad and spent most of her days trying to come to terms with what had transpired. Her feelings oscillated between anger towards Jim and the 'other woman' to blaming herself for not being able to keep her husband happy. Two months after Jim left, Mary's sister noticed that, aside from her sister's extreme sadness, she appeared un-kempt and rarely left the house. Sensibly, she persuaded Mary to seek psychotherapy.

Mary definitely needed some professional help adjusting to the loss of her husband. She had begun to believe that she could never be happy again and that life was barely worth living. She needed a professional person to listen to her with empathy, help her heal and guide her into an optimistic single life with a view to eventually finding another partner. Her therapy was successful. Four years later Mary married again and adopted two children.

is this you (or someone close to you)?

As a reaction to an extremely stressful event (other than bereavement) some emotional or behavioural symptoms such as Depression or Anxiety developed within three months.

These symptoms are causing either: significant distress (far more than what one would normally expect as a result of that event), or major problems in the person's social, vocational or academic life.

'do not pass go' signs

Without treatment, some of the reactions people can have to a stressful event (for example, divorce, serious illness, changing locations, becoming an 'empty-nester', being made redundant or losing one's house) can develop into Depression, Anxiety, behaviour problems and emotional instability. These can have significant negative effects on a person's social, family, academic and vocational life. Related problems such as Substance Abuse or physical illness can also develop. If you are experiencing severe reactions to a stressful experience or occurrence in your life, or if this is true for someone close to you, seeking treatment is advisable.

what causes adjustment disorder?

Adjustment Disorder occurs as a result of a stressful or troublesome event that befalls a person. Some people are more resilient than others, and at certain stages in a person's life he or she is more vulnerable to having long-lasting problems in the aftermath of negative life occurrences.

which treatments are likely to work?

Supportive psychotherapy, hypnosis and many of the treatments already indicated for Depression and Anxiety (pages 15ff and 37ff) are likely to be helpful.

best course of action
Seek psychotherapy.

in the meantime, what can you do?

1. Write down your thoughts, feelings and behaviours about the stressful event that caused your Adjustment Disorder.

2. Write down the emotional or behavioural symptoms you are experiencing in the aftermath of the stressful event, for example wanting to drink more alcohol than usual, being irritable with children or not wanting to go out.

3. Try to make a list of the positive things in your life that you feel hopeful about. Spend some time each day focusing on those things.

4. People who are suffering from Adjustment Disorder need structure. Create a twenty-four-hour daily schedule for yourself and stick to it (see page 19)

5. Try to exercise. Even if it seems incredibly difficult, first set yourself small goals each day, such as walking to the post box, supermarket or school. Gradually increase your exercise regime until it reaches a level that is appropriately challenging for you, given your age and state of physical health. It is important to check with your doctor first to find out what level of physical activity is safe and appropriate for you.

6. Pay a little more attention to your physical appearance. People with Adjustment Disorder often find it's hard to care about personal grooming and hygiene. You will feel better if you try to maintain the same standards you did before you felt down.

7. You will probably be suffering from a sense of frustration and loss at not being able to control certain events in your life. This sense of powerlessness can be extremely troubling. Write down your feelings about this and, when you are ready, begin to allow yourself to let them go.

8. Identify the things in your life over which you do have some control. Try to come up with appropriate ways to gain more control over the rest.

9. Gather support from among your family and friends. Let them know, without making them feel responsible or guilty, that you're feeling sad, depressed or anxious and could do with some TLC while you're waiting to be seen by a mental-health professional.

10. Depending on the specific nature of the issue to which you are trying to adjust, research available community services and take advantage of them.

11. Choose someone sympathetic to talk to about things that are bothering you. If a person says something like 'Get over it!' educate him or her that it's not that simple.

12. If you find yourself being irritable with people around you, discuss this with them directly, and show willingness to try not to let your mood cause conflict in your family, vocational or social life. Be quick to catch yourself and apologize.

13. Have faith in your own ability to get over this. Say 'I *will* be able to move on.'

14. Your spiritual beliefs and practices may help you to be accepting of your situation. Consider searching out your spiritual leader for a chat and some guidance, especially if he or she is trained in providing therapy.

15. Try new, positive things that challenge you and enjoy the sense of accomplishment afterwards.

16. Try not to have overly high expectations of yourself. You're only human. Just do the best you can, and appreciate your own efforts.

17. Know that, in struggling with difficult life events, you are not alone.

18. If guilt is part of your adjustment difficulty, work on self-forgiveness.

19. If anger is part of your adjustment difficulty, work on letting go of that.

20. Try to be in the 'here and now'. Savour each moment.

21. If you are dealing with conflicts, choose your battles and save your strength and energy.

22. Surround yourself with people who support you, and distance yourself from those who make you feel bad about yourself.

23. Learn to assert yourself better (see page 38).

24. Pay attention to your health. Get regular medical and dental check-ups.

25. Avoid overworking.

26. Establish a regular pattern of good-quality sleep. If you have problems sleeping follow the self-help suggestions for Insomnia or other Sleep Disorders (see page 361 onwards).

27. Work on nurturing the supportive relationships in your life, take the time to listen and be heard.

28. Explore the 'chatter' in your mind that maintains and increases your worry and sadness. What exactly is that internal dialogue? Write it down.

29. Do you engage in distorted thinking (see page 21)? Work on it.

30. Practise thought-stopping (see page 20).

31. Try to eat a nutritious and healthy diet. You may be craving sugar or stodgy foods but avoid bingeing on them.

32. Do not drink alcohol or take recreational drugs, as they will almost certainly exacerbate your sadness.

33. Some over-the-counter remedies, such as SAMe, St John's wort, and 5HTP (5-hydroxytryptophan) are thought by some to be helpful for depressive feelings. Research them, and consider that they may well be worth trying. But it is important to know that they may not mix well with some other medications (for example, St John's wort interferes with the effectiveness of some oral contraceptives).

34. Consider trying acupuncture, which is thought to be most effective for people who are sad, depressed or out-of-sorts.

35. Investigate homeopathic treatments and decide whether or not these may be right for you.

36. If you feel hopeless, seek immediate help from a mental-health professional.

37. Work on reducing your stress (see exercises page 19).

38. Work on relaxation (see Progressive Body Relaxation exercise page 41).

39. Practise meditation (see page 40)

40. Remind yourself that you will get through this.

when someone close to you is suffering from adjustment disorder

1. Encourage that person to seek treatment.

2. Support all healthy efforts to improve his or her mood (for example, relaxation, meditation or physical exercise).

3. Do not support unhealthy efforts such as substance abuse.

4. It may be very helpful if you take the role of compassionate listener. Don't try to fix things – simply be there and just listen attentively and empathically. Never say, 'I know just how you feel'; no one ever knows exactly how another person is feeling. Instead, say, 'That must be so difficult for you/I can't even imagine how you must be feeling/I'm so sorry you are going through this.'

5. Learn everything you can about Adjustment Disorder and the situation or crisis that led to it.

6. Being in a relationship or family with someone who is suffering from Adjustment Disorder can be very difficult, especially since that person will be finding it hard to be emotionally available to you. He or she may be emotionally 'distanced' from you, or be irritable, angry or too sad to attend to any usual activities. Be understanding, but gently point out that it might be a good idea to get help.

7. You may need to take the role of carer from time to time and that can interfere with your relationship, perhaps causing resentment. Get some therapeutic support for yourself and the family.
8. Plan fun and enjoyable breaks to help lift spirits.
9. Take care of yourself, physically and mentally.
10. Reduce your own stress (see page 19).

helpful books

Thoughts and Feelings: Taking Control of Your Moods and Your Life, M. McKay, M. Davis, and P. Fanning. Oakland Calif.: New Harbinger Publications, 1997.

Five Weeks to Healing Stress: The Wellness Option, V. O'Hara. Oakland, Calif.: New Harbinger Publications, 1996.

Exercising Your Way to Better Mental Health: Combat Stress, Fight Depression, and Improve Your Overall Mood and Self-Concept with These Simple Exercises, L. M. Leith. Morgantown, W. Va.: Fitness Information Technology, 1998.

How to Meditate, L. LeShan. Boston: Back Bay Books, 1999.

The Healing Journey through Divorce: Your Journal of Understanding and Renewal, P. Rich and L. L. Schwartz. New York: John Wiley & Sons, Inc., 1999.

The Healing Journey through Grief: Your Journal for Reflection and Recovery, P. Rich. New York: John Wiley & Sons, Inc., 1999.

Meditation for Busy People: 60 Seconds to Serenity, D. Croves. San Rafael, Calif.: New World Library, 1993.

chapter 5
when your body talks for you

"Milt, I'm beginning to think that your illness is a disharmony of life energy."

somatoform disorders

Sometimes our bodies do the talking for us. They can take on all kinds of mysterious symptoms to try to get you and others to pay attention. It's not an ideal way to communicate, but it happens. The DSM-IV has a section for what some people refer to as 'Psychosomatic Illnesses', which are now called Somatoform Disorders. These include Somatization Disorder, Somatoform Disorder, Conversion Disorder, Pain Disorder, Health Anxiety (Hypochondriasis) and Body Dysmorphic Disorder. What they have in common is unexplained physical symptoms that are not intentionally produced. People with these disorders are not pretending to be ill; their bodies are simply making statements that need to be listened to. They may exhibit symptoms such as pain, paralysis, numbness, loss of vision or hearing, inability to speak, throat restriction, unexplained flushing reactions, profuse perspiration, psoriasis, eczema or loss of sensation in the fingers or other parts of the body.

Doctors' offices, emergency rooms and mental health clinics are rather busy with people who have medically unexplained physical symptoms. Their ailments can be baffling to doctors, especially since somatic problems often go hand in hand with physically based problems. What's more, physicians know that bodily symptoms with actual physical origins often go undiagnosed and should not be classed as psychological without specific evidence. No one wants to hear those horrid words, 'It's all in your head', but it's sometimes difficult for medical doctors to know how to go about encouraging people with suspected psychologically based problems to seek mental-health treatment. Consequently, those with somatic complaints may end up feeling ignored, stigmatized or simply mystified. Many traipse around from doctor to doctor trying, in vain, to get help.

Somatoform Disorders have been around for centuries; in fact a psychosomatic illness known as 'Hysteria' was common in nineteenth-century Europe, and such disorders were also were described in ancient Greek societies. These are complicated phenomena, but when people who have been confused by their symptoms finally feel safe and heard, and the extent of their suffering is validated, most will acknowledge that stress and emotions have an effect on their physical condition. Reaching this point will often make them feel open to seeking the psychological help they really need for these chronic and disabling, yet treatable disorders.

somatization disorder

case study: Sarah

Forty-one year-old Sarah brought was brought to my office by her younger sister. On the way into my consulting room she suddenly became weak at the knees and literally 'fainted' onto my couch. Far from being concerned, her sister simply rolled her eyes and pointedly told me, 'Just do your best with her.' Having fainting spells was just one of Sarah's many physical complaints. She also suffered from sudden sleep attacks, migraine headaches, sexual pain, 'weak stomach' and 'allergies' to a very extensive range of foods including meat, fish, eggs, milk, beans and most vegetables – so it was rather difficult for her to follow a nutritious diet. Sarah seemed to eat nothing but rice pudding. She complained of having a 'mass' in her lower abdomen that she constantly prodded and manipulated. Her abdomen seemed to be severely bloated, so it was unclear whether the pain she felt it caused her originated from problems associated with her diet, her own kneading or some other reason. Sarah also complained of having a 'weak left arm', experiencing pain on lifting it above 90 degrees from the body (she is left-handed). Sarah's sister had handed me a letter from Sarah's doctor. This letter stated that the results of tests he had given Sarah showed there was no currently understood medical reason for Sarah's complaints, with the exception of her migraine headaches. The letter contained typical doctors' code words for problems that cannot be explained medically.

Sarah was not faking illness, but her range of mysterious problems were extremely debilitating. She could not work, and relied on family to support and look after her. Her childhood had been an unhappy one, in which Sarah's severely depressed mother had expected her to care for her younger siblings. Deep in her psyche, she had somehow decided it was her turn to be looked after. After quite a few years of psychotherapy that involved healing from childhood trauma, hypnosis and treatment for Depression and personality issues, Sarah was finally able to take her place in the world as a well-functioning, responsible adult.

is this you (or someone close to you)?

- Starting before your thirtieth birthday, you have had a history of quite a few problematic physical complaints for which you have sought treatment.
- Have had pain in at least four different parts of the body.
- Have had a history of at least two gastrointestinal symptoms as well – perhaps vomiting, diarrhoea or difficulty tolerating certain foods.
- Have also had at least one sexual symptom such as erectile dysfunction or low desire.
- Have also had some kind of problem that suggested a neurological condition, such as losing balance, deafness, hallucinations or double vision.
- Are not feigning these symptoms, but nevertheless the doctors you have consulted have been unable to find adequate medical explanations or a reason for their severity.

If you have similar symptoms to the above, but you don't quite have the same number of complaints in all the specific areas outlined above, you may qualify for a similar diagnosis – Somatoform Disorder.

children with somatization or somatoform disorders

You've probably come across a child who gets a 'tummy ache' whenever he or she doesn't want to go to school. That is a very common somatic problem in children. Others include restlessness, blushing, palpitations, muscle tension, sweating and trembling or shaking.

'do not pass go' signs

Somatoform Disorders can be extremely debilitating. People with Somatization Disorder or Somatoform Disorder are sometimes so frustrated by their symptoms that they seek opinions and treatment from a variety of doctors at the same time, which can be dangerous if those treatments are incompatible. Diagnosis is made all the more complicated by the fact that a person with Somatization Disorder might also have an actual medical condition that is independent of his or her Somatization Disorder symptoms. There are high rates of overlap between Depression and Anxiety, and Somatization Disorder (if the Depression and Anxiety are treated, the somatic symptoms usually improve). People with Somatization Disorder may also have cognitive deficits, such as inattention, problems with concentration and impaired memory – all of which may contribute to relationship problems and poor psychosocial functioning in general. Some may even attempt suicide.

what causes somatization disorder?

Both factors and life experiences have been found to contribute to this disorder. It runs in families, to the extent that close female relatives of women with Somatization Disorder have an increased risk of having it too. People whose biological or adoptive parent had Somatization Disorder puts them at risk of being diagnosed with the same complaint.

Somatoform Disorders are linked to a diminished capacity to experience and recognize feelings consciously and express them in an adequate or healthy way. In certain societies, including the UK, it is still more acceptable to complain of physical problems than of mental suffering, so it is possible that here psychological problems are even more likely to manifest themselves as physical pain or a variety of other medical conditions.

what is happening in the brain?

Low brain-glucose metabolism has been identified in some people with severe Somatization Disorder.

which treatments are likely to work?

Individual and group psychotherapy is recommended, and hypnosis is believed to be particularly useful. Psychoanalysis is also recommended for all Somatoform Disorders. Antidepressants or anti-Anxiety drugs are sometimes prescribed, especially if the sufferer has a coexisting Mood or Anxiety Disorder.

When a person has symptoms that appear to be psychologically based, ideally physical causes should be ruled out before psychological support is provided. Many somatic symptoms form part of Anxiety, depressive or other recognizable psychological conditions and will improve when those problems are treated.

best course of action?
Encourage the sufferer to seek psychotherapy, psychoanalysis or psycho-analytic psychotherapy, ideally with a therapist also trained in hypnosis.

when someone close to you appears to be suffering from somatization disorder
1. Signs you may notice in the person are: all kinds of health complaints that are rarely given a definitive diagnosis, repeated visits to doctors without any subsequent improvement, a referral to a psychologist that comes from the doctor and perhaps a sense of frustration exhibited by doctors treating the sufferer.
2. Know that it is vital to seek mental-health treatment if a person has symptoms of this debilitating disorder. However, a person with suspected Somatization Disorder will not attend a mental-health consultation without sensitive and empathic motivation. Be careful how you make the approach.
3. Somatization Disorder is sometimes accompanied by Depression or Anxiety, so you might suggest treatment for either of those.
4. Another approach is that you could put forward the idea that perhaps the sufferer is right and the problem is physical, but that perhaps there is another (or contributory) explanation for all these complaints, and it might be worth seeing a mental-health specialist (as well as his or her doctor) so both perspectives could be explored.
5. People with Somatoform Disorders typically have a history of unsatisfying and unsuccessful involvement with the health-care system. Listen empathically to these complaints, then suggest that a therapist might be the best person to help with all the worry and anxiety this must be causing him or her.
6. People with Somatization Disorder find it difficult to be specific about all their symptoms. Without being challenging, encourage the sufferer to write down a detailed list – giving the exact dates they appeared and the

bodily location of each symptom (pinpoint positions on a drawing of the body) – to take to the next doctor's appointment.

7. Encourage the sufferer to reduce his or her stress. This can be done via relaxation exercise (page 41), meditation (see page 40), breathing exercise (see page 46) or by taking a yoga class.

8. There is now considerable evidence that regular physical exercise is helpful for a variety of disorders, including Somatoform Disorders. Encourage an appropriate regimen, consistent with the person's age, level of fitness and overall health.

9. It would be beneficial if the sufferer learned to be more verbally assertive. Encourage self-assertion (see page 38).

10. St John's wort has been found to relieve symptoms of Depression and Somatization Disorder. Have the sufferer consider it but be careful not to label him or her as being somatically disordered.

11. Have the sufferer consider the symptoms and self-help options for both Depression (see page 15ff) and Anxiety (see page 37ff). If he or she resonates with either, suggest the 'To Do' steps for improving their mood.

12. Provide positive reinforcement (praise or reward for improvements or success).

13. Worrying about someone else's mental or physical health takes its toll on the carer. Look after your own physical and mental health, reduce your stress, eat regular nutritious meals and get plenty of sleep.

helpful books

It's Not All in Your Head: How Worrying about Your Health Could Be Making You Sick – and What You Can Do about It, G. J. G. Asmundson and S. Taylor. New York: The Guilford Press, 2005.

Managing Pain before It Manages You, M. Caudill. New York: The Guilford Press, 2001.

Living beyond Your Pain: Using Acceptance and Commitment Therapy to Ease Chronic Pain, J. Dahl and T. Lundgren. Oakland, Calif.: New Harbinger Publications, 2006.

The Assertiveness Workbook: How to Express Your Ideas and Stand Up for Yourself in Work and Relationships. R. J. Paterson. Oakland, Calif.: New Harbinger Publications, 2000.

Full Catastrophe Living: Using the Wisdom of Your Body and Mind to Face Stress, Pain, and Illness, J. Kabat-Zinn. New York: Delta, 1990.

Meditation for Busy People: 60 Seconds to Serenity, D. Croves. San Rafael, Calif.: New World Library, 1993.

conversion disorder

Have you ever heard the term 'hysterical blindness'? It was used many years ago to describe astonishing cases where people became blind due to psychological processes. Then, when the trauma or psychological hardship that caused it was cured, the person was able to see again. The modern term, as described in the DSM-IV, is Conversion Disorder and it refers to a phenomenon where psychologically based physical problems appear after a traumatic or stressful event. Conversion Disorder is yet another example of how the body sometimes takes on a job that the voice has failed to articulate.

case study: Ellena

Ellena was an eighteen-year-old only daughter of a couple who had arrived from Sarajevo some ten years ago. Both parents had experienced severe hardship and trauma in their home country, and had suffered from symptoms of Post-Traumatic Stress Disorder (for example, nightmares and Panic Attacks) for many years. In particular, Ellena's father had started abusing alcohol soon after he arrived and became a violent alcoholic who was abusive to his wife. During her childhood, Ellena witnessed episodes in which her father beat and verbally abused her mother. After a while she began to have 'fits' in which she would become disoriented, 'black out' and fall to the ground. She could only be aroused when both parents teamed up to help her sit her up and provide her with soothing touch and a soft drink.

Electroencephalogram tests did not produce any evidence of seizure activity, and it did not escape her therapist's attention that Ellena's 'fits' began to occur during parental conflict – although they subsequently occurred in a variety of stressful situations. Family therapy was helpful for everyone and Ellena's father received treatment for alcoholism. During one period of relapse he was jailed for assault, but essentially the family moved forward into a healthier, happier existence. Ellena's 'fits' disappeared.

is this you (or someone close to you)?

■ The person suffers from the type of physical problems that are usually thought to be neurologically based, such as paralysis, weakness, coordination or balancing problems, loss of touch, loss of feeling, pain, blindness, deafness, double vision, hallucinations, seizures or convulsions.

- These symptoms are serious, but they seem to have a psychological basis because they either started or deteriorated after the appearance of some stressful situation or conflict.
- As far as you know, the sufferer is not pretending to be afflicted with these symptoms.
- The symptoms cannot be explained either medically, or as a culturally identifiable and acceptable experience. Neither have they appeared as the result of taking a harmful substance.

'do not pass go' signs

Just because a person fits the above description for having Conversion Disorder does not mean that his or her symptoms aren't real. But people whose serious physical problem (for example, blindness, paralysis, deafness, seizures) is suspected by professionals to be psychologically based are unlikely to believe that they need urgent psychological help. Hopefully, they will be correctly diagnosed and will be encouraged to find their way to the psychotherapeutic treatment they urgently need. Any treatable medical conditions that are physically based must first be properly ruled out.

what causes conversion disorder?

A stressful event or conflict seems to lead to the development of Conversion Disorder symptoms. The body may be expressing feelings that its owner cannot show via the spoken word and symptoms usually have a particular meaning (for example, of wishing to avoid something or some other unexpressed desire). Conversion symptoms may also co-occur with actual neurological or physical illness, or may even be a way to identify with illness in someone else. An inability to understand or express emotion may trigger conversion symptoms, and certain kinds of social contact may reinforce them. Conversion Disorders are a common cause of neurological disability, but the exact way in which psychological stress can 'unconsciously' result in physical symptoms is poorly understood.

what happens in the brain?

Emotional stress may mean that parts of the brain that should help with the conscious processing of sensory stimuli don't function properly.

which treatments are likely to work?

Psychotherapy and hypnotherapy may be particularly useful, while psychoanalysis is thought to be an excellent treatment for Conversion

Disorder. A special type of electrical stimulation has been successfully used to reverse paralysis when it is a symptom of Conversion Disorder.

best course of action
Seek treatment from a psychoanalyst or psychotherapist trained in hypnosis and the treatment of Conversion Disorder.

in the meantime what can you do if someone close to you seems to have conversion disorder?

1. Signs to watch out for might be: problems getting a diagnosis, repeated visits to doctors without improvement, a referral to a psychologist that comes from the doctor and perhaps a sense of frustration exhibited by doctors treating the sufferer.

2. Encourage the sufferer to seek mental-health treatment now. He or she will not go unless they receive sensitive and empathic motivation, so be careful how you make the approach.

3. Conversion Disorder is sometimes accompanied by Depression or Anxiety, so you might suggest treatment for either of those.

4. Alternatively, you could put forward the idea that perhaps there is another (or contributory) explanation for the physical symptom – and it might be worth seeing a mental-health specialist, as well as a doctor, so both perspectives could be explored.

5. People with Conversion Disorder typically have a history of unsatisfying and unsuccessful involvement with the health-care system. Listen empathically to these complaints, then suggest that a therapist might be the best person to help with all the worry and anxiety this must be causing him or her.

6. Because Conversion Disorder is associated with stressful events and conflict, encourage the reduction of his or her stress. This can be done via relaxation (page 41), meditation (see page 40), breathing exercise (see page 46) or by taking a yoga class.

7. Regular exercise is helpful for Conversion Disorder. Encourage an appropriate regimen consistent with the person's age, level of fitness and overall health.

8. It would be beneficial if the person with suspected Conversion Disorder learned to be more verbally assertive. Encourage self-assertion (see page 38).

9. Help the person to identify and label his or her feelings, even simple ones such as 'sad', 'mad', 'bad' or 'glad'.

10. Have the sufferer consider the symptoms and self-help options for both Depression (see page 15ff) and Anxiety (see page 37ff). If he or she resonates with either, suggest following the 'To Do' steps to improve their mood.
11. Provide positive reinforcement (praise or reward for improvements or success, for example, for signs of healthy decisions to seek psychological help).

helpful books

Your Body's Wisdom: A Body-Centered Approach to Transformation, R. Welfeld. Naperville, Ill.: Sourcebooks, 1997.
Five Weeks to Healing Stress: The Wellness Option, V. O'Hara. Oakland, Calif.: New Harbinger Publications, 1996.
The Assertiveness Workbook: How to Express Your Ideas and Stand Up for Yourself in Work and Relationships, R.J. Paterson. Oakland, Calif.: New Harbinger Publications, 2000.
How to Meditate, L. LeShan. Boston: Back Bay Books, 1999.

pain disorder

Pain is an interesting phenomenon. I am always fascinated by 'phantom pain' that occurs when people who have had an arm or leg amputated sometimes experience pain that seems to emanate right from the missing limb. Pain is both a sensory and an emotional experience. When you are hit, cut or burned, the nerves on the outside of your body are stimulated. Nerve fibres then transmit pain signals toward your spinal cord or brain stem at varying speeds, creating various types of sensations (for example, sharp or dull pain). So pain is always a mind *and* body experience, but when someone suffers from Pain Disorder, the mind is working overtime.

case study: Wendy

Wendy was a thirty-one-year-old creative director of a major publishing firm. Her partner of nine years was a woman called Gina. Their relationship was successful in every area except in their sex life. For the past two years, Wendy had complained of having severe back pain. A special chair made it possible for Wendy to sit comfortably at work, but she could not tolerate other positions, including those that made some of the couple's favourite sexual experiences possible. Gina had taken Wendy for a number of consultations with top-notch osteopaths and chiropractors, but neither X-rays, MRIs, nor physical examinations showed any diagnosable back problem or reason for her pain. Wendy had been brought up by her grandmother, who died six months before Wendy had her first symptoms. Her grandmother had been a highly religious woman, and Wendy had never told her that she was lesbian. On her deathbed, the grandmother had expressed a last wish that Wendy 'marry a nice man and raise a family'.

Wendy finally sought psychotherapy for her Pain Disorder. It seemed to her psychotherapist that Wendy's back pain was connected with her feelings about being lesbian. Wendy may have unconsciously felt that, through engaging in lesbian sexuality, she was betraying her grandmother. After working through these underlying issues her back pain disappeared, and she and Gina were able to re-establish the intimate relationship they had previously enjoyed.

is this you (or someone close to you)?

- You have serious pain in one or more parts of your body.
- It is likely that psychological factors played an important role in the start, continuation or severity of the pain.
- The pain is real, not faked.

'do not pass go' signs

Having chronic pain can seriously affect a person's life, causing disability, relationship and family problems and making it hard for the sufferer to work. Some people with Pain Disorder also have Depression, Anxiety and Insomnia, and are at risk of addiction to pain medication. Pain can be referred (felt elsewhere from the point of origination) so that must be considered.

what causes pain disorder?

Pain is both a sensory and an emotional experience. It is usually triggered when nerves on the outside of the body are stimulated through tissue damage.

Many people who have Pain Disorder are also being treated for severe medical conditions such as arthritis, back pain, shingles, sports injuries, carpal tunnel syndrome and cancer. Many are also suffering from Depression and Anxiety, and these coexisting disorders change a person's perception of pain so it may seem even worse than it is. Close relatives of people with chronic Pain Disorder may be more likely than others to suffer from chronic pain as well as Depression and alcohol dependence.

what happens in your brain?

Chronic somatic pain is often stress related and may also result from early traumatic and painful experiences stored in the memory. It is associated with alterations in the sensitivity of certain neurons and in the connectivity of brain structures that are engaged in the transmission and perception of pain.

which treatments are likely to work?
Psychotherapy is very often helpful to people with Pain Disorder. Hypnosis has been demonstrated to reduce both acute and chronic pain conditions. In particular, Eriksonian hypnotherapy (self-hypnosis) is an extremely useful technique for reducing or eliminating pain in a wide variety of circumstances (for example, dental surgery for people who cannot be anaesthetized). Other useful methods of pain reduction are biofeedback, acupuncture, meditation and stress-reduction.

best course of action?
Seek psychotherapy/hypnotherapy, perhaps with adjunctive biofeedback.

in the meantime what can you (or someone close to you) do?
1. Meditation has been shown to be helpful for pain (see exercise on page 40). Also, practise the meditation exercise designed to increase positive feelings towards your body; it can be found on page 103.
2. Practise relaxation and stress reduction (see exercises pages 41, 46).
3. What are your feelings towards your own body? Is it friend or foe? Write down your thoughts and do the exercise on page 102.
4. Engage in regular physical exercise, according to your age, state of health and physical ability.
5. Try to establish a regular pattern of good-quality sleep. If you have problems sleeping follow the self-help suggestions for Insomnia or other Sleep Disorders (see page 361 onwards).
6. Yoga has also been shown to be effective for pain. Find a yoga instructor or learn from a DVD.
7. T'ai chi has also been used for pain reduction. Find a class near you, or learn from a DVD.
8. Find a support group. If there is no pain sufferers' support group near you, look for one online.
9. If you think you might also be suffering from Anxiety or Depression, follow the self-help guidelines on pages 37ff and 15ff.
10. Arrange at least one or two pleasurable activities that you can look forward to each day.
11. Do not underestimate the power of human touch. If you do not have a partner to help soothe you with touch, arrange to have massage therapy.

12. Believe that you can get through this. Affirm it to yourself every day.

if you think someone close to you may have pain disorder?

1. Signs to watch out for might be: chronic pain, repeated visits to doctors without much improvement, a referral to a psychologist that comes from the doctor and perhaps a sense of frustration exhibited by physicians treating the sufferer.

2. Show empathy and consideration towards the person who is suffering. Remember that the pain is real, not faked.

3. Encourage the sufferer to seek mental-health treatment now. He or she will need sensitive and empathic motivation.

4. Pain Disorder is sometimes accompanied by Depression or Anxiety, so you might suggest treatment for either of those.

5. People with Pain Disorder typically have a history of unsatisfying and unsuccessful involvement with the health-care system. Listen empathically to these complaints, then suggest that a therapist might be the best person to help with all the worry and anxiety this must be causing him or her.

6. Because Pain Disorder is associated with stressful events and conflict, encourage the reduction of his or her stress. This can be done via relaxation exercises (page 41), meditation (see page 40), breathing exercise (see page 46) or by taking a yoga class.

7. Regular exercise is helpful for Pain Disorder. Encourage the appropriate regimen, consistent with the person's age, level of fitness and overall health.

8. It would be beneficial if the person with suspected Pain Disorder learned to be more verbally assertive. Encourage self-assertion training (see page 38).

9. Help the person to identify and label his or her feelings generally, even simple ones such as 'sad', 'mad', 'bad' or 'glad'.

10. Have the sufferer consider the symptoms and self-help options for both Depression (see page 15ff) and Anxiety (see page 37ff). If he or she resonates with either, suggest following the 'To Do' steps to improve their mood.

11. Provide positive reinforcement (praise or reward for improvements or success, for example, for signs of healthy decisions to seek psychological help).

12. It can be difficult to be around someone who is suffering from Pain Disorder, and being a carer takes its toll. Make sure you look after your

own mental and physical health and that others in the family are not also suffering.

13. If necessary, seek therapeutic help for yourself and the family.
14. Take steps to reduce your own stress.

helpful books

Fibromyalgia and Chronic Fatigue Syndrome: Seven Proven Steps to Less Pain and More Energy, F. Friedberg. Oakland, Calif.: New Harbinger Publications, 2006.

Managing Pain before It Manages You, M. Caudill. New York: The Guilford Press, 2001.

Living beyond Your Pain: Using Acceptance and Commitment Therapy to Ease Chronic Pain, J. Dahl and T. Lundgren. Oakland, Calif.: New Harbinger Publications, 2006.

Full Catastrophe Living: Using the Wisdom of Your Body and Mind to Face Stress, Pain, and Illness, J. Kabat-Zinn. New York: Delta, 1990.

Meditation for Busy People: 60 Seconds to Serenity, D. Croves. San Rafael, Calif.: New World Library, 1993.

health anxiety (hypochondriasis)

Our society takes a dim view of people who are always imagining they are ill. Most people consider those they describe as 'hypochondriacs' to be annoying, manipulative, whining and weak. The truth is rarely understood, that people who are constantly afraid they have undiagnosed serious illness are, in fact, truly suffering. Their anxiety and worry about their health is so severe it can actually *make* them sick. The trouble is, it's hard for people with Health Anxiety to accept the psychological nature of their problem, and so they rarely get the psychological help they need.

case study: Evan

For most people, the possibility of getting a life-threatening illness is a frightening thought that crosses the mind from time to time. But for Evan, such thoughts were not transient. Evan was constantly preoccupied with worries about contracting serious disease, even rare tropical diseases that he could not possibly get while living in the south of England. Every time a new health scare appeared elsewhere in the world, such as SARS and Avian flu, he would obsessively research all symptoms and check himself several times a day. He often found signs he believed proved that he had contracted this disease or that, but doctors he consulted always informed him that he was quite well. Evan even got to know the people who worked in the Tropical Diseases Institute and began to accost them on their way home from work, insisting that he had developed new symptoms and pleading with them to perform further tests. Evan's neighbour was a doctor, and tired of his frequent attempts to engage her in conversation about his health concerns, she finally said 'All this worry about your health is not good for you. I recommend you seek mental-health treatment for your Anxiety.' Evan took her advice and found a psychotherapist who was able to help him reduce his stress and Health Anxiety. He even came to understand that his mind created problems that weren't really there.

is this you (or someone close to you)?

- You are always afraid you have a serious disease.
- Medical opinion does not support your view that you are ill.

A person suffering from Health Anxiety is not faking illness, but the diagnosis involves far more than simply worrying about illness. Although a person with Health Anxiety is unfortunately sometimes labelled 'a hypochondriac' (the DSM-IV calls this diagnosis Hypochondriasis), he or she is truly suffering. Despite the lack of medical evidence, people with this disorder are enormously worried that they have real, possibly life-threatening illnesses that no-one has been able to diagnose. They may be preoccupied with their bodies, be terrified of developing a serious disease or they may be convinced that they may have something like cancer or heart disease – even though their doctors disagree. Such pervasive concerns can lead to anxiety, stress, tension and sometimes panic or Depression. The worry can be so debilitating that a person finds it hard to participate in everyday activities, maintain relationships or attend work. He or she will visit doctor after doctor in order to try to get a 'better' diagnosis or treatment, and this drains both energy and finances.

'do not pass go' signs

Health Anxiety is a debilitating disorder. Aside from all the time a person spends worrying about whether or not he or she has a serious illness, all the stress of frequent trips to the doctor and all the fear associated with it, Health Anxiety is also a condition that can produce physical effects of its own, including muscle tension, nausea and a quickened heart rate. Thus, a consultation with a mental-health practitioner is important.

what causes health anxiety?

A person who already tends to be somewhat anxious may misinterpret benign bodily sensations or variations, and this, in turn, may lead to increased anxiety, distorted thinking about his or her health, safety-seeking behaviour and physiological arousal (for example, edginess, panic, sweating and heart palpitations). Such responses account for the ensuing pattern of symptoms and day-to-day impairment that constitute Health Anxiety.

which treatments are likely to work?

Psychotherapy is essential, and hypnotherapy can be particularly useful. Psychoanalysis is thought to benefit people with any of the Somatoform Disorders. If a person is amenable, cognitive-behavioural therapy has also been shown to be an effective treatment for Health Anxiety. For mild Health Anxiety, psycho-education may be sufficient. Antidepressants are sometimes prescribed. Reducing stress, finding ways to relax and receiving treatment for Anxiety are also important.

best course of action?

Seek psychotherapy, hypnosis, or psychoanalysis plus stress-reducing treatments.

in the meantime, what can you do?

1. Create a chart of your past and present health anxieties and concerns for as long as you can remember, including symptoms, medical consultations, professional opinions and your feelings about the various opinions you have received. Rate your own concerns about each symptom from 1–10, with 10 being the most concerned you have ever been. Also rate your feelings about the medical opinions and quality of care you have received from 1–10, with 10 being the most frustrated you have ever felt.

2. How might your ideas about illness, symptoms, personal health threats and health behaviour have first arisen? Write down the answers as extensively as you can. List your past experiences, illnesses and medical treatment and include the medical treatment of your friends and family. Are there any other sources of your beliefs concerning your current state of health?

3. Are there discrepancies between your own beliefs about your state of health and those of the doctors you have consulted? List those discrepancies in detail.

4. Write down the distress and frustration you have experienced in trying to get others to understand, appreciate and act on your health concerns.

5. If there is a part of you that is open to evaluating an alternative understanding of your health problems, explore that in your journal.

6. What are your attitudes and religious beliefs about death? Write them down and include your thoughts about how these may influence your perception of your own mortality.

7. What are your feelings towards your own body? Is it friend or foe? Write down your thoughts and do the exercise on page 102.

8. Practise the meditation exercise (designed to increase positive feelings towards your body) on page 103.

9. Immediately take steps to reduce your stress. This can be done via relaxation (see page 41), meditation (see page 40), breathing exercises (see page 46) or by taking a yoga class. Also establish healthy eating patterns and a safe, regular exercise programme in keeping with your age and level of fitness. This will help with your mood, stress and overall well-being.

10. Establish a regular pattern of good-quality sleep. If you have problems sleeping follow the self-help suggestions for Insomnia or other Sleep Disorders (see page 361 onwards).

11. Take control of your health by exploring all your options:
    - If you believe you have serious health problems that are not receiving appropriate diagnosis or treatment, consider the following hypotheses: a) you may indeed have a serious illness that is so far undetected, or b) perhaps there is another explanation (or a contributory factor), that is that you are worried and concerned about illness, and regardless of whether or not your symptoms are physically based, the worry and concern is a major problem in itself.
    - Consider that the latter hypothesis can be helped by psychological approaches and, just as an experiment, seek some therapy to explore that.
    - Consider the fact that worrying about illness can make you sick. We know that Anxiety leads to all kinds of physical problems, such as irritable bowel syndrome, headaches and cardiovascular disease. So your symptoms could be *caused* by worry, not the other way around.
    - Consider getting immediate mental-health treatment for your Health Anxiety.

what can you encourage your partner, family member or friend to do?

- Tip-offs that someone close to you may be suffering from Health Anxiety would be: problems getting a diagnosis, repeated visits to doctors, a referral to a psychologist that comes from a doctor and perhaps a sense of frustration exhibited by doctors treating the sufferer.

- In our culture we have little tolerance for people we label 'hypochondriacs', believing them to be 'faking', 'weak' or 'manipulative'. It is important to remember that, despite public opinion, people with Health Anxiety are genuinely suffering (although not from the physical illness they believe they have). Be compassionate.

- It is vital to encourage the sufferer to seek mental-health treatment but he or she will not go to therapy without sensitive and empathic motivation. Be careful how you make the approach. Do not use the term 'hypochondriac', or be blaming or shaming in any way. Instead, say that perhaps the sufferer is right and is indeed suffering from a serious illness that no one has been able to diagnose – but that there may be another explanation. Ask if he or she would consider seeking therapy to explore that. Emphasize the fact that worrying about illness can make a person sick, because Anxiety leads to all kinds of physical problems, such as irritable bowel syndrome, headaches and cardiovascular disease. So the sufferer's symptoms could be caused by worry, not the other way around.

- People with Health Anxiety are unlikely to consider their problem to be psychologically based, but since Health Anxiety is sometimes accompanied by Depression or Anxiety, you might suggest treatment for either of those.

- Individuals with Health Anxiety typically have a history of unsatisfying and unsuccessful involvement with the health-care system. Listen respectfully and empathically to these complaints, then suggest that he or she might benefit from seeing a mental-health therapist to help with all the worry this must be causing.

- Have the sufferer consider the symptoms and self-help options for Depression (see page 15ff) and Anxiety (see page 37ff). If he or she resonates with either, encourage the reduction of stress via relaxation exercises (page 41), meditation (see page 40), breathing exercises (see page 46) or by taking a yoga class.

- There is now considerable evidence that regular exercise is a viable, cost-effective and underused treatment for Anxiety. Encourage an appropriate regimen, consistent with age, level of fitness and overall health.

- It would be beneficial if the sufferer learned to be more verbally assertive. Encourage self-assertion (see page 38).
- Help the sufferer to identify and label feelings, even simple ones such as 'sad', 'mad', 'bad' or 'glad'.
- Encourage the use of massage therapy, or other soothing body treatments; for example aromatherapy.
- Provide positive reinforcement (praise or reward for improvements or success).
- It's not easy to be in a relationship or family with someone suffering from Health Anxiety. Take care of yourself both mentally and physically.
- Take steps to reduce your own stress.
- Take relaxing breaks.

helpful books

It's Not All in Your Head: How Worrying about Your Health Could Be Making You Sick – and What You Can Do about It, G. J. G. Asmundson and S. Taylor. Guilford Press, 2005.

Five Weeks to Healing Stress: The Wellness Option, V. O'Hara. Oakland, Calif.: New Harbinger Publications, 1996.

Exercising Your Way to Better Mental Health: Combat Stress, Fight Depression, and Improve Your Overall Mood and Self-Concept with These Simple Exercises, L. M. Leith. Morgantown, W. Va.: Fitness Information Technology, 1998.

Meditation for Busy People: 60 Seconds to Serenity, D. Croves. San Rafael, Calif.: New World Library, 1993.

factitious disorder

It's nice to be looked after sometimes, isn't it? You're coming down with a cold and some kind soul tucks you up with a warm drink. But certain people develop a very strong need to be a 'patient' that goes well beyond the norm, and that problem is described in the DSM-IV as Factitious Disorder. It is not one of the Somatoform Disorders described previously in this chapter because, in this case, the sufferer is actually faking illness.

Factitious Disorder was previously called Munchausen's Syndrome. Did you ever see the film Terry Gilliam (of 'Monty Python' fame) made about Baron Munchausen, after whom this disorder was first named? The Baron was a seventeenth-century European character whose outrageous stories are considered to be fanciful lies, so the psychological problem of lying about being sick was named after him. There is another form of the disorder called Factitious Disorder by Proxy where, instead of developing an obsession with being a 'patient' themselves, people see others as the 'patient'. For example, a mother might be drawn to placing her perfectly healthy son in a 'patient' role, even resorting to creating the appearance of illness in him by feeding him substances that produce real symptoms of that illness.

case study: Brian

As a child, Brian suffered from rheumatic fever. This meant that he had to stay in bed and miss school for months at a time. His parents had only modest means, but they allowed Brian to have a telephone in his room so he could keep up his friendships with other boys. This telephone was a very exciting gift, of which Brian's brothers were extremely jealous. In fact, Brian found that being ill helped him get more attention than his brothers. Several adults lived in the house; apart from his parents there were two aunts and an uncle, and all of them paid him extra attention because he was ill. In a way, Brian's parents, aunts and uncle were unintentionally rewarding Brian for being ill. He grew into a man who relished being a 'patient'. In fact, Brian had begun to conceptualize the world beyond his sickbed as a threatening, unfriendly place. He had missed essential parts of his schooling and social education, including dating and learning how to get on with girls. When Brian recovered from his illness, he was forced to get back to school and try to make up all the work he'd missed. It was hard. No one made allowances for him or paid him special attention any more. He became depressed, and secretly wished his rheumatic fever would return. Even as an adult, Brian struggled with finding jobs and sustaining relationships. When I met him, he said he had a number of physical complaints for which he was seeing many different doctors. He entered therapy and enjoyed being on the couch, discussing the problems of his childhood and adult life. I noticed that it was hard to get Brian to leave when the therapy session was over. Brian would want to linger, would get upset at the idea that someone else was about to replace him on the couch and found all kinds of ways to delay his exit. Instead of improving, Brian seemed to be coming up with more and more problems to deal with in therapy, such as complaining about doctors he'd seen who refused to treat him any more, and asking to have more psychotherapy sessions per week. I began to understand how much Brian liked his 'patient' role and gently began to explore that with him. Just when we were beginning to make progress in helping Brian to understand his Factitious Disorder he walked into my office and announced triumphantly 'I've got cancer'. For the first time in his adult life he was truly seriously ill. Tragically, he passed away a year later. I often wonder if his mind helped to create his cancer. I also wonder if I or another therapist had met him earlier in his life whether he would still be alive today? Or did his Factitious Disorder make it easier for him to deal with having a terminal illness? Such mysteries torment many people in my field.

is this you (or someone close to you)?

- You are deliberately faking a physical or psychological disorder.
- Doing this because you want to play the role of a 'patient'.
- Not doing this for any other reasons, that is for financial gain or to avoid legal problems, and so on.

Are you feigning illness? If so you probably have feelings of guilt about it – yet you cannot stop. You feel drawn to act out the role of the 'patient' because it is the only way you can feel appreciated, loved, safe – or, you name it. If you are doing this, know that you can be helped. In a very real way, you truly *are* a 'patient' – just not exactly the kind you pretend to be. If you seek therapy now, and disclose what is really going on to your therapist, you can be helped to get your needs met in a healthier way. You will be free of the many problems that accompany your compulsion to engage in deception and far more likely to lead a happy life.

If there is someone in your life whom you believe fits the criteria above, I hope you will do whatever you can to help him or her receive mental-health treatment (see the guidelines opposite).

'do not pass go' signs

People with Factitious Disorder often undergo unnecessary medical treatments, including surgery. Some even take drugs that create altered mental states similar to symptoms of certain mental disorders. Cases involving Factitious Disorder enter the legal system in a number of ways and lead to incorrect judgements and financial costs if this disorder is not identified. Some people with Factitious Disorder also have a Personality Disorder and/or problems with substance abuse. Their preoccupation with seeking medical treatment makes it extremely difficult for them to hold down a job or maintain relationships. Naturally, they are extremely unlikely to seek psychological treatment specifically for Factitious Disorder, since that would involve admitting the deception. However, they might just undergo therapy to get help for Depression and Anxiety – or for some pretend reason.

what causes factitious disorder?

It might start with a chaotic childhood, perhaps childhood abuse, or the person may have had a real childhood medical or psychological condition that made him or her become comfortable and familiar with the 'patient' role at an early age.

which treatments are likely to work?

The nature of this disorder makes it difficult to treat, since the sufferer is partly a 'pretender'. However, psychotherapy can help the sufferer gain insight and move on from the desire to be a 'patient'. Psychotherapeutic treatment for true associated disorders, such as Depression or Anxiety, is also necessary.

best course of action?

Seek psychotherapy or psychoanalysis.

if someone close to you seems to have factitious disorder (or factitious disorder by proxy)

1. You might suspect Factitious Disorder after discovering that there are marked discrepancies between the doctor's findings and the distress or disability claimed by the person, or he or she may be failing to cooperate with doctors' orders. Perhaps you may even catch the person in the act of doing something to create the appearance of being ill (or even creating it in someone else). Factitious Disorder is especially difficult to pick up when it occurs in addition to a real disease or condition.

2. If you suspect a diagnosis of Factitious Disorder, try not to be judgemental of the person. Try to see his or her faking of illness as a style of adapting to earlier problems that became a pattern, and as a reaction to stress.

3. Recognize that the person is truly suffering, only not exactly in the way he or she is presenting to the world.

4. Try to get the sufferer to see a mental-health professional. It would be better not to confront the person directly about faking illness, but rather to suggest that psychological treatment may be necessary for all the worry and anxiety he or she is going though. Or, given that the person enjoys being a 'patient', emphasize any mental-health problem you think might resonate (for example, Depression and Anxiety) and suggest treatment for that. The therapist will figure out what's going on.

5. People with Factitious Disorder typically have a history of unsatisfying and unsuccessful involvement with the health-care system. Listen empathically to his or her complaints, then suggest that a therapist might be the best person to help with all the worry and anxiety this must be causing. A therapist can help the person in the most appropriate way, point out the risks involved in the behaviour and address issues of abuse.

6. Encourage the reduction of the sufferer's stress. This can be done via relaxation exercises (see page 41), meditation (see page 40), breathing exercises (see page 46) or by taking a yoga class.

7. Regular exercise is helpful for Factitious Disorder. Encourage an appropriate regimen, consistent with the person's age, level of fitness and overall health.

8. It would be beneficial if the sufferer learned to be more verbally assertive. Encourage self-assertion (see page 38).

9. Have the person consider the symptoms and self-help options for both Depression (see page 15ff) and Anxiety (see page 37ff). If he or she resonates with either, suggest that they follow the 'To Do' steps to improve their mood.

10. Encourage the use of massage therapy, or other soothing body treatments; for example aromatherapy.

11. Provide positive reinforcement (praise or reward for improvements or success) when the sufferer makes healthy choices, such as engaging in exercise or seeking psychotherapy.

12. It is difficult to be in a relationship with someone suffering from Factitious Disorder. Reduce your stress, and take care of yourself, both physically and mentally.

13. If you have reason to suspect that someone you know is deliberately faking an illness in another person, for example a child, elder or other dependent, then abuse may be taking place. You must urgently bring this to the attention of a therapist, social worker, physician, hospital authorities or police. Please do not delay in doing this.

helpful books

Patient or Pretender: Inside the Strange World of Factitious Disorders, M. Feldman and C. Ford with T. Reinhold. New York: John Wiley & Sons, 1994.

body dysmorphic disorder

Each of us has something we don't like about our body. Thighs, ankles, upper arms – we compare ourselves with the 'beautiful people' of the large and small screen, and find ourselves wanting. But sometimes a dislike for one's own body or body part takes on an unusually intense focus. People who fit the DSM-IV diagnostic criteria for Body Dysmorphic Disorder have trouble seeing themselves realistically. They imagine that they are blighted with hideous imperfections that make them unacceptable to others. This is a very painful disorder that involves extreme worry and anxiety and a preoccupation with the body that drastically interferes with a person's ability to be at peace with themselves and others, and enjoy life. In my practice I probably saw more of this disorder than therapists in other areas – perhaps because just walking down the street in Beverly Hills can feel like being in a beauty contest. Lillian is just one of the many women I met who may have responded to the 'catwalk' pressure.

Lillian

Lillian was a wealthy woman in her forties who came to see me after she divorced her husband for 'cheating' on her. Encouraged by a new, younger boyfriend she complained that she had only come to see me at his insistence. In my office, she sat very still, in an unusual position: her head was turned slightly away from me so that one side of her face was more in shadow than the other. I came to understand that Lillian was hiding what she believed to be an imperfection in one cheekbone, which she thought was lower than the other. Not long after our first appointment I received a call from her plastic surgeon. With Lillian's permission, I spoke to him and discovered that she had undergone nine operations in the past six months on various parts of her body, and she was now 'obsessed' (as he put it) with correcting an 'imbalance in the alignment of her cheekbones'. The surgeon was reluctant to perform any further surgery. He informed me that her physical health was at risk, and he had rightly surmised that Lillian needed to be helped for a psychological problem known as Body Dysmorphic Disorder.

Lillian was also suffering from Depression. At first, she attended therapy irregularly, but was gradually being motivated by her loving young partner to stick with treatment. Eventually, she began to let go of her desire for unattainable perfection and her Depression lifted. Her personal development reached a point where, even though her relationship with the young man did not last, she was able to handle his loss and negotiate the tricky dating world again with confidence and humour.

is this you (or someone close to you)?
- You focus on an imagined imperfection in your body or appearance.
- Your concern about this imaginary defect is excessive, and causes problems in your life.

Are you particularly preoccupied with some aspect of your body? Do other people tell you not to worry about things that seem enormously unsightly to you? If so, how do you hide or camouflage your 'defect'? Do you hide away and avoid parties or outings? If you have the symptoms of Body Dysmorphic Disorder and your life is less enjoyable as a result, try to accept that you need to do something about it. There's no need for you to suffer. A good therapist can help you put things in perspective and help you with your mood and other associated problems. At the very least follow the self-help guidelines at the end of this section. You deserve to be more at peace with yourself and to get more fun out of life.

'do not pass go' signs
People suffering from Body Dysmorphic Disorder are so concerned about their supposed 'defect' that they will go to extraordinary lengths to try to hide, improve or rectify it. They are constantly checking on it, looking in mirrors, picking at their skin, hiding themselves behind hats or sunglasses, and they usually lack the insight that their concern is excessive. They will undergo body modification such as multiple surgery and will even attempt self-surgery. Some are so concerned about the evaluation of others they become socially withdrawn, isolated and unable to work or maintain relationships. Many suffer from Anxiety, Mood Disorders or Substance Abuse. They may endure repeated hospitalizations and even attempt suicide. This disorder needs to be treated by a trained, experienced mental-health professional; however, most people with this disorder do not seek treatment themselves. It is usually up to the people close to them to try to get them some professional help.

what causes body dysmorphic disorder?
There are a number of theories about what causes Body Dysmorphic Disorder. It may have a biological or genetic basis, it may begin with childhood embarrassment or teasing – or it may be the result of childhood

abuse and neglect. It probably does not help that, as a society, we are very focused on physical appearance – although the problem does appear in other cultures in various forms. Body Dysmorphic Disorder is thought to be associated with Obsessive-Compulsive Disorder and sometimes goes hand in hand with Eating Disorders, Panic Attacks, and Substance Abuse.

what is happening in the brain?

Not surprisingly, researchers have found increased activity in the area of the brain that is linked to obsession and worry. There may be a serotonin dysfunction.

which treatments are likely to work?

Individual or group psychotherapy can help. Cognitive-behavioural therapy has been shown to have successful outcomes with this disorder, and hypnosis, too, can be very effective. Antidepressants are frequently used.

best course of action?

Seek psychotherapy.

in the meantime what can you do?

1. Try to accept that your problem is not how you look, but how you think you look.
2. Learn everything you can about Body Dysmorphic Disorder.
3. Do not undergo any more corrective physical treatments, especially surgery, at least until you have had some psychological help.
4. Do not drink alcohol or take recreational drugs, as they will almost certainly exacerbate your 'down' moods.
5. Some over-the-counter remedies, such as SAMe, St John's wort and 5HTP (5-hydroxytryptophan) are thought by some to be helpful for depressed feelings. If you are feeling low (as opposed to anxious), research these preparations and consider trying them. But it is import- ant to know that they may not mix well with some other medications (for example, St John's wort interferes with the effectiveness of some oral contraceptives).
6. Establish a personal-wellness programme that includes reducing your stress, regular moderate exercise (appropriate for your age, weight and level of fitness), good nutrition, regular sleep, daily meditation (see page 40) and relaxation exercises (see page 41). Taking a yoga class can also be helpful.

7. Reduce your Anxiety (follow guidelines page 37ff).

8. Utilize soothing body treatments such as massage or aromatherapy.

9. Set up a system of daily reminders and affirmations. Place cards where you will see them (for example, in your diary or on your bathroom mirror) with the positive reminders, such as 'I like the way I look'.

10. Even if you seem to have little sense of enjoyment in life, try to plan at least one activity every day that might give you pleasure or at least help lift your mood. Human touch (stroking or hugs) are known to be soothing and help elevate a person's mood. A casual outing to a concert or the cinema, or a meal with good friends can raise spirits and validate that your connection with others is not dependent on how you look.

11. Don't isolate yourself. Look for support among people in your community. For example, try to summon up the courage to join a club or group to engage in some activity you think you might enjoy, whether that be cycling, bowling, charity work or a book club.

12. People with Body Dysmorphic Disorder are usually secretive and uncomfortable about admitting it to others. Tell yourself every day that it is nothing to be ashamed of, and that you will get though it. Meanwhile, continue trying to get the professional treatment you deserve.

13. The following exercises are designed to help people with Body Dysmorphic Disorder make peace with their bodies, stop their negative or distorted thinking and raise their self-esteem:

exercise: body-image journal

1. Start by writing down in detail exactly how you feel about your body as a whole.

2. Write down exactly how you feel about each and every part of your body. Notice which bits you like, dislike or are neutral about.

3. Write the story of your body. Start with your birth and make a detailed timeline of your body's journey through life so far. Note all the changes, growing, strengthening, athletic achievements, illness and recovery, pregnancies and sexual learning. Take all the time you need to complete this.

4. Now write down what you have learned from writing the story of your body.

5. How do you think you have treated your body? Reflect on the possibility

that your body has done its best to serve you, and that you may have had unreasonable loathing of it in the past. Write down what you discover.

6. Reflect on the possibility that you may have had unreasonable expectations of your body in the past. Write down what you discover.

7. When you are alone, take off as much of your clothing as you are comfortable removing and stand in front of a mirror. Breathe and relax. Work hard to observe each part of your body without making any judgements. When you feel anxious, stop and breathe or relax (see Progressive Body Relaxation exercise (page 41) and then return to the exercise. Next, notice and focus on the good things about your body. After you are finished, write down all your observations.

exercise: positive regard for the body meditation practice

Sitting comfortably, take three deep, satisfying breaths and allow your body to become calm. Begin to be aware of your breathing and when it is deep and low in your body, turn your attention inwards and follow the stages set out below. This meditation takes place in five stages, each one lasting three to five minutes. Keep a watch handy so that you can glance at it and be reminded to move on from one stage to the next. If other thoughts enter your head during the process, push them gently aside and go back to your meditation practice. Do this meditation twice a day.

Stage 1 Try to direct feelings of well-being and happiness towards yourself generally. You can say (in your head) 'May I be happy, may I be well' over and over. Eventually you won't need to say this – you'll just be able to connect with the feelings of well-being.

Stage 2 Try to direct feelings of well-being and happiness towards the part of your body that you like the most. Picture it in your mind and engender appreciation and care for it. Reflect on how it has served you, and summon up feelings of gratitude towards it.

Stage 3 Now picture some part of your body about which you feel fairly neutral, perhaps an elbow for example or some part for which you have no particular feelings, either positive or negative. Try to direct towards it the same positive regard and sense of gratitude that you managed to engender for the part you like most in stage 2. You can say 'May it be well'.

Stage 4 Now turn your attention to those areas of your body you feel are imperfect. Try to engender the same feelings of positive regard for the part (or each of the parts in turn) you dislike. You can say 'May it be well'. This is much harder, but it's worth persevering.

Stage 5 Now encompass your entire body, inside and out. First, directing feelings of well-being and gratitude towards your heart. Now move on to your chest and begin to radiate those feelings towards every part of your body, external and internal, until you have managed to make a connection of positive regard with every inch of your body. You can say 'May all parts be well'.

When you have completed this meditation, slowly open your eyes. You should be feeling calm, glowing, happy and more generous towards your body. Practise it twice per day until those feelings come more easily.

exercise: negative thought-stopping for body dysmorphic disorder

1. People with Body Dysmorphic Disorder worry excessively about their appearance and have a distorted, negative image of how they appear to others. Catch yourself in the process of having such negative thoughts as 'I am ugly', or 'My chin is hideous'.
2. As you identify each negative thought about your body, bring it into full consciousness. Consider it fully, deciding whether it is realistic or not, productive or counter-productive. Gauge how difficult it is to control that particular thought (a bit hard, quite hard or very hard), and how uncomfortable it makes you feel (uneasy, quite uncomfortable or upset). Chart this.
3. If you decide that it would be a good idea to eliminate that negative notion from your thought-repertoire dwell on it for a while, with your body as relaxed as possible.
4. Now put a rubber band round your wrist and snap it every time that thought returns while shouting, 'Stop!' (out loud in the beginning, then eventually you can say it inside your head).
5. Spend the next thirty seconds focusing on replacing the negative thought with a positive one, such as 'I look nice' or 'My face is attractive'.
6. Work on this technique until you can regularly catch yourself having negative thoughts and replace them with the positive flip-sides.

exercise: distorted thinking work for body dysmorphic disorder

CATCH yourself, CONTROL those thoughts, and CHANGE them. Here are a few examples:

Catastrophizing (for example, 'I have a pimple, therefore I am deformed and others will be repulsed by me.') The rational point of view is that one small breakout does not constitute deformation and is unlikely even to be noticed.

Over-generalization (for example, 'My date cancelled, so that must mean I am hideous and unattractive and will never get married.') The rational point of view is that people sometimes cancel dates for a variety of reasons that have nothing to do with you.

Jumping to conclusions (for example, 'That person looked away because he couldn't bear to see my ugly face.') The rational point of view is that there are lots of reasons why a person may have looked one way or another – such as shyness or preoccupation.

Making inappropriate comparisons (for example, 'The model in that magazine is much better proportioned than me. I am deformed.') The rational point of view is that models don't look like most regular people, and photos in magazines are often doctored to improve their appearance. It's unfair and unreasonable to expect one's self to look the same way.

Honing in on the negative (for example, 'I have a few grey hairs and this really makes me look old.') The rational point of view is that having a couple of grey hairs does not alone signify aging or detract from a person's attractiveness.

exercise: self-esteem

1. Try to focus on your (non-physical) positive attributes, not on what you think are your difficulties or failures.
2. Try to have faith in yourself. Say 'I can ...'
3. Try new, positive things that challenge you and afterwards enjoy the sense of accomplishment.
4. Don't have such high expectations of yourself – you're only human.
5. Learn to take compliments.
6. Know that in struggling with a mental-health issue, you are not alone.

7. At those times when you do not feel self-confident, fake it for a while and see if that helps.
8. Try to be in the 'here and now' – savour each moment.
9. In your various conflicts (both with yourself and others) choose your battles and save your strength and energy.
10. Surround yourself with people who support you, and distance yourself from those who seem to expect too much from you or make you feel bad about yourself.
11. Learn to assert yourself better (see page 38).
12. Pay attention to your general physical health.
13. Avoid overworking.
14. Focus on improving all your relationships – take the time to listen and be heard.

when someone close to you has body dysmorphic disorder

1. Talk openly but empathically about Body Dysmorphic Disorder; for example, 'I've noticed that you don't seem to appreciate your positive physical attributes. Would you tell me more about that?' Listen to what the sufferer says, but don't get into a discussion about whether he or she has imperfections.
2. Do not give reassurances about the sufferer's looks, but maintain a supportive stance in other ways; for example, by focusing on the non-physical things you like about him or her.
3. Encourage the sufferer to seek immediate mental-health treatment. Do not focus on 'There's something mentally wrong with you', but instead gently suggest that he or she deserves proper help for all the worry and suffering.
4. Encourage activities that take the focus off physical appearance, such as hiking, sports and casual family events.
5. Try to be patient with the sufferer.
6. Provide positive reinforcement (praise or reward improvements and successes) when the sufferer makes healthy choices, such as engaging in relaxation exercises or attending psychotherapy.
7. Try to be hopeful.
8. It's not easy to be in a relationship or family with someone suffering from Body Dysmorphic Disorder. Take care of yourself. Maintain your own physical and mental health.
9. If the sufferer ever hints that he or she might be suicidal (that is, EVER mentions it) seek urgent, immediate care from a mental-health professional.

helpful books

The Broken Mirror: Understanding and Treating Body Dysmorphic Disorder, K. A. Phillips. Oxford: Oxford University Press, 2005.

The BDD Workbook: Overcome Body Dysmorphic Disorder and End Body Image Obsessions, J. Claiborne and C. Pedrick. Oakland, Calif.: New Harbinger Publications, 2002.

Cruel Reflections: Self-Help for Body Image Disturbance, S. Wilhelm. Guilford Press, 2005.

Love the Body You Were Born With: a Ten-Step Workbook for Women, Monica Dixon. New York: Perigree, 1994.

Bodylove: Learning to Like Our Looks and Ourselves, R. Freedman. New York: Harper & Row, 1988.

The Adonis Complex: How to Identify, Treat, and Prevent Body Obsession in Men and Boys, H. G. Pope, Jr, K. A. Phillips and R. Olivardia. The Free Press, 2002.

Feeling Good: The New Mood Therapy, (2nd ed), D. D. Burns. Avon Books, 2000.

The Body Image Workbook: An 8-Step Program for Learning to Like Your Looks, T. F. Cash. Oakland, Calif.: New Harbinger Publications, 1997.

Perfect Weight: The Complete Mind/Body Program for Achieving and Maintaining Your Ideal Weight, D. Chopra. Carmarthen: Crown Publications, 1996.

Ageless Body, Timeless Mind: A Companion Guide and Journal, D. Chopra. New York: Crown Arts & Letters/Harmony Books, 1993.

Women's Bodies, Women's Wisdom: Creating Physical and Emotional Health and Healing, C. Northrup. New York: Bantam Books, 1998.

'Eating Disorders, Anxiety, Depression: How Can I Tell if I'm Really in Trouble?', in A. Rubenstein and K. Zager *The Inside Story on Teen Girls*, Washington DC: American Psychological Association, 2002.

chapter 6
all or nothing: eating disorders

Eating Disorders can be extremely serious, and usually require urgent medical and mental-health treatment from qualified, experienced professionals. Anorexia Nervosa, in particular, has a high mortality rate, and is one of the most severe disorders that can afflict girls and young females. Maybe the 'size zero' emphasis on thinness, as promoted in Western society by the fashion industry and some parts of the media, has a negative psychological effect on body image. However, studies have identified many possible causes of Eating Disorders, including neurobiological and hereditary factors, sexual and physical abuse, and family conflict.

People with Eating Disorders fall into two DSM-IV categories: those with Anorexia Nervosa and those with Bulimia Nervosa. There is some overlap between the two (for example, some people with Anorexia binge-eat and purge just like many people with Bulimia); however, unlike people with Bulimia those suffering from Anorexia are unable to maintain a minimally normal weight for their age and height.

anorexia nervosa

case study: Talia

Talia was a twenty-two-year-old woman who, at 1.6m (5 ft 4 in) tall weighed only 31kg (5 st) when she was admitted to an Eating Disorders Programme in the psychiatric unit of a general hospital. She had begun to restrict her food intake and deliberately lose weight at the age of seventeen, after her older sister became estranged from her parents due to a conflict over a boyfriend with a drug problem. Over the ensuing five years she had used large quantities of diuretics and laxatives, as well as vomiting, to purge food from her body. She over-exercised to a drastic degree, and had often felt compelled to miss classes, so that she eventually left university without achieving her goal of becoming a vet. Despite her low body weight, Talia still believed she was grossly overweight. Fortunately, her life-threatening situation slowly improved under hospital care. In addition to a programme of healthy eating and weight gain she received psychotherapy to deal with the trauma of losing contact with her sister, education about her diagnosis of Anorexia Nervosa (binge eating/purging type) as well as nutritional guidance. After leaving the unit, Talia got a job at a veterinary practice and was able to enrol in a part-time degree course.

are you (or is someone close to you)

- Underweight (less than 85 per cent of the accepted norm for your age and height)?
- Nevertheless, very afraid of getting fat?
- Harsh with yourself about your weight or shape?
- Finding it hard to accept that you are in fact very underweight?
- Finding it hard to accept that it's a serious problem?
- For women: you may have missed three or more menstrual cycles.

If you have most of the above symptoms, try to be honest with yourself about it. You have a very dangerous condition, yet something in your mind is maintaining your unnatural eating patterns, making you miserable and driving you to hide, deceive and put yourself at such risk. Know that if you seek treatment, there will be someone to talk to who can really help. A good therapist will never make you feel ashamed of yourself. You deserve to be listened to and to heal from whatever deep problems are underlying your Anorexia Nervosa. Seeking therapy will also release you from some of the other problems you are currently facing (conflicts with family members and others are often part of the struggle for people with Eating Disorders). You can control your life *and* be healthy. I hope you will seek help today.

when children suffer from anorexia nervosa

This affects mainly girls, but boys do sometimes suffer from Anorexia. Symptoms are similar to those of adults. If a child or adolescent is showing the above signs, make sure he or she gets immediate psychological and medical help.

'do not pass go' signs

Anorexia Nervosa is a life-threatening disorder. People suffering from it are actually starving themselves and they often die. It can lead to serious heart problems such as mitral valve prolapse and congestive heart failure, as well as anaemia, liver damage, osteoporosis, potassium deficiency, cardiac irregularities, hypothermia and hypoglycaemia. Starvation symptoms often appear, such as fatigue, cognitive deficits, delayed visual tracking and lowered metabolism. Related complications include infection, dehydration and electrolyte imbalance. People with Anorexia Nervosa have a higher rate of suicide than the general population. The disorder often coexists with Depression, Bipolar Disorder, Anxiety, Obsessive-Compulsive Disorder, Panic Disorder, Phobias, Post-Traumatic Stress Disorder and Substance Abuse. Anorexia Nervosa requires urgent, intensive treatment, but sufferers are very often in denial about the seriousness of their condition. If you think you or anyone close to you may have this disorder, do not delay in seeking proper medical and psychological help.

what causes anorexia nervosa?

Anorexia Nervosa seems to have underlying neurobiological and hereditary factors, but other factors probably play a part. For example, sexual abuse, physical abuse, control issues (such as mother–daughter conflict), family dependence and family conflict have been associated with the development of the disorder.

what is happening in your brain?

Evidence suggests that disturbances similar to those that lead to Obsessive-Compulsive Disorder may be present in individuals with Anorexia Nervosa. In particular, dysfunction in systems that involve serotonin may make a person more likely to develop unusual feeding patterns, Anxiety, obsessions and extremes of impulse control (when combined with stressful elements in a person's life) often lead to the development of an Eating Disorder.

which treatments are likely to work?

Medical interventions plus psychotherapy best treat this life-threatening disorder, with additional help from a dietitian (who can determine fluid intake and calorie requirement). Once a person's physical safety is established, psychotherapy can address the underlying issues. Family therapy is also recommended for the treatment of adolescent Anorexia Nervosa. There are some Eating Disorder clinics that sufferers can attend on either an inpatient basis (often recommended) or as an outpatient. People with Anorexia very often need to be hospitalized, especially if their weight has dropped to 75 per cent of a body weight that would be normal for their height, structure and age. Antidepressant medications are frequently used.

best course of action?

Medical stability is a priority. A doctor should be monitoring a person with Anorexia if he or she reaches the point of being underweight by 15 per cent. Psychiatric care is crucial. Weight must urgently be restored to normal, and the underlying issues addressed.

in the meantime, what can you do?

1. If you fit the above diagnosis, try to accept that you may have Anorexia Nervosa and take control of your disorder.
2. Learn everything you can about Anorexia Nervosa.
3. Seek support from trusted family and friends – chances are they are already worried about you.
4. Try not to be defensive when people suggest medical and psychological treatment – you deserve all the help you can get.
5. Keep a food journal to establish the exact nature of your eating patterns. Write down in detail everything you eat, the rituals you engage in and your feelings about it. What did you learn from seeing this in black and white?
6. What are your feelings about your struggle to control your eating patterns? Write them down.
7. Be honest with yourself about your attempts to hide your weight loss, or

your pretence that you are eating. Write down any daily behaviour that involves secrecy, avoidance or lying. What are your thoughts and feelings about having to engage in a pattern of deception?

8. Do you find it hard to avoid manipulating people? Write down your thoughts and feelings about that. Try to come up with alternative ways to express your emotions and get your needs met.

9. What family issues trouble you from the past or in the present? Write down your feelings and thoughts.

10. How do you cope with troubling interpersonal or family issues? Is your style of coping related to eating or restricting food? Write down your ideas and feelings about that.

11. Explore all your fears by writing about them in a journal.

12. Explore your feelings of despair and guilt by writing them down too.

13. Have you experienced physical or sexual abuse? Emotional abuse or neglect? Write down your feelings.

14. Engage in relaxation training (see Progressive Body Relaxation exercise page 41).

15. Reduce your stress (see page 19).

16. Practise meditation, especially the body meditation on page 103.

17. Learn to assert yourself appropriately (see page 38).

18. Work on your self-esteem (see page 105).

19. Try to accept yourself, and let go of the idea that your self-worth depends on receiving a positive evaluation from other people about your physical appearance.

20. Identify your distorted and negative thinking and replace those thoughts with more accurate, positive ones. See NIC and 3 Cs techniques on pages 48 and 105.

21. Identify and engage in an activity that will help you with vocational development, such as taking a course or establishing a website.

22. Take better care of every part of yourself, mentally and physically. That includes regular medical, dental and eye check-ups. It also includes taking breaks and not overworking.

23. Get plenty of good-quality sleep.

24. Make peace with your body by writing a letter to it, expressing how you feel about it. Apologize if you feel you have abused it and promise to take better care of it in future.

25. Make a list of all the things you like about yourself and put it somewhere where you will frequently be reminded of your strengths.

26. Know that you can get through this, with professional help.

if someone close to you fits the diagnosis for anorexia, what can you do?

1. You must do everything you can to get the sufferer into treatment. Anorexia Nervosa is a life-threatening disorder.

2. Get as much education as possible about the disorder.

3. Support the treatment, and be sure you understand what you, as a helper should do; for example, if the sufferer's weight drops below a certain level, seek medical help. Keep important contact numbers handy (such as those of the person's treatment team).

4. If you are a parent, carer, spouse, partner or sibling of someone suffering from Anorexia Nervosa, seek therapeutic help for yourself as well.

5. Take care of yourself both mentally and physically. Seeing someone through a struggle with Anorexia Nervosa can be tough. If possible, share the burden with your partner or trusted friend.

6. Below are some special guidelines for how to relate to someone close to you with Anorexia Nervosa:

   - Be supportive and calming without being controlling.
   - Be assertive with the sufferer, and encourage self-assertion from him or her too.
   - Be openly affectionate, verbally and physically.
   - Never demand that the person gain weight.
   - Never humiliate, blame or put down the sufferer for not eating or for having an eating disorder.
   - Work to create a loving, supportive and nurturing environment for everyone in the family. Do not allow the person with Anorexia Nervosa to command all the focus, worry and attention.
   - Be emotionally available to the person with Anorexia Nervosa, that is do not avoid, withdraw or abandon him or her. But keep good boundaries between you (for example, do not allow him or her to manipulate you).
   - Do not allow the person with Anorexia Nervosa to control aspects of the family that involve eating, such as demanding a particular eating schedule.
   - Do not allow a child or adolescent with Anorexia Nervosa to cook or purchase food for the family (the child or adolescent needs to learn to self-nurture rather than nurture other people).
   - It is essential that the person with Anorexia Nervosa is receiving medical and mental-health treatment. Once the person is in a programme, do not directly address issues of weight loss with him or

her. If you see signs of deterioration or weight loss, directly contact
the responsible doctor and/or psychotherapist.

how to recognize signs of anorexia

- Chronic low body weight.
- Anaemia.
- Fainting and dizzy spells.
- Blueness of fingers and toes.
- Skin breakouts or rashes.
- Cessation of periods.
- Bad circulation.
- Fewer bathroom trips.
- Water retention.
- Dry, dull hair and skin.
- Dark circles under eyes.
- Dry eyes.
- Swollen tongue.
- Receding or bleeding gums.
- Blue and black skin colouration.
- Thinks he or she's overweight or 'fat' when the reality is the opposite.
- Preoccupied with weight.
- May over-exercise.
- Avoids relationships.
- Tries to hide low weight by wearing bulky clothing.

helpful books

The Anorexia Workbook: How to Accept Yourself, Heal Your Suffering, and
Reclaim Your Life, M. Heffner and G. H. Eifert. Oakland, Calif.: New
Harbinger Publications, 2004.

Feeding the Hungry Heart, G. Roth. New York: Plume/Penguin 1997.

Love the Body You Were Born With: A Ten-step Workbook for Women, M.
Dixon. New York: Perigree, 1994.

Hunger for Understanding: A Workbook for Helping Young People Overcome
Anorexia Nervosa, A. Eivors and S. Nesbit. Chichester, West Sussex: Wiley,
2005.

Bodylove: Learning to Like Our Looks and Ourselves, R. Freedman. New York:
Harper & Row, 1988.

Perfect Weight: The Complete Mind/Body Program for Achieving and Maintaining Your Ideal Weight, D. Chopra. New York: Harmony Books, 1994.

Reviving Ophelia, Mary Pipher. New York: Ballantine Books, 2002.

The Golden Cage: The Enigma of Anorexia Nervosa, H. Bruch. Cambridge, Mass.: Harvard University Press, 2001.

Ageless Body, Timeless Mind: A Companion Guide and Journal, D. Chopra. New York: Crown Arts & Letters/Harmony Books, 1993.

Women's Bodies, Women's Wisdom: Creating Physical and Emotional Health and Healing, C. Northrup. New York: Bantam Books, 1998.

'Eating Disorders, Anxiety, Depression: How Can I Tell If I'm Really in Trouble?', in A. Rubenstein and K. Zager *The Inside Story on Teen Girls*, Washington DC: American Psychological Association, 2002.

bulimia nervosa

People with Bulimia Nervosa often go unnoticed, mainly because they manage to maintain at least a minimally normal weight. The disorder gained particular media prominence when the late Princess Diana announced that she suffered from it. In fact, the frequency with which we hear about well-known people struggling with Eating Disorders would lead one to think it is a 'celebrity' disease – but that is not the case. Many, many people suffer the self-hatred, shame, Depression, self-esteem issues and threat to physical health that are associated with a diagnosis of Bulimia Nervosa. Being teased as a child, sexual abuse, and other types of trauma are associated with the development of the disorder, but it could be triggered simply by the shock of seeing one's image displayed in public, for example, an unflattering photo posted on a widely viewed website. A dieting attempt might follow, and when that is unsuccessful a person might resort to purging and begin the dangerous cycle that constitutes Bulimia Nervosa. Barbara is one example of someone who was happy with her weight before she saw herself on TV.

case study: Barbara

Barbara is a well-known actress who has appeared in a long-running TV soap opera for five years. Before she landed her current role she appeared mainly on the stage in classical plays. The switch to television led not only to a change in her acting style, but also to a re-evaluation of her appearance. She had always maintained a healthy, average weight; however, the television screen can make a person appear to be ten or more pounds heavier than they actually are, and Barbara noted her new self-image with horror. In an attempt to look 'normal' on TV she began to diet for the first time in her life. Finding it difficult to restrict her eating Barbara became desperate. She started vomiting after eating and begann to use diuretics. She hated the feeling of being hungry, but she managed to purge herself drastically until after each week's filming day. That evening she would binge, compulsively cramming everything she could find into her mouth to try to assuage the craving she had felt during the week. Overloaded with carbohydrates, sugar, fat and salt she would experience remorse, guilt and shame, yet her bingeing would continue for the next forty-eight hours until she forced herself to start purging again in preparation for her next week's filming day. No-one noticed that Barbara was suffering from Bulimia Nervosa and she herself was barely aware of the seriousness of her problem until she recognized her disorder in a magazine article on Eating Disorders. She sought therapeutic help and learned to arrest her binge–purge cycle. She became comfortable with her body once again, settling for a 'TV weight' that was just six pounds lower than usual, maintained through healthy eating and appropriate exercise.

do you (or does someone close to you)

- Binge-eat (that is, over any two-hour period you eat more food than other people would do)?
- Find it impossible to control your bingeing?
- Compensate by fasting, excessive exercise, making yourself vomit, or by misusing laxatives, enemas or diuretics?
- Find that on average, your bingeing, as well as your periods of restricting your food intake or purging have occurred at least twice a week for at least three months?
- Find that you are harsh with yourself about your weight or shape, but unlike people with Anorexia Nervosa you manage to maintain a weight that is within the accepted normal range for your age and height?

If most of the above is true for you, you may be suffering from Bulimia Nervosa. It would be very understandable if your symptoms seem 'normal' and 'necessary' to you, because many people find it hard to recognize that their eating patterns are problematic, even threatening to them. You probably receive plenty of encouragement when you're at the thinner end of your cycle when, for example people compliment you for having a flat stomach. That sort of thing will make you feel glad you purged the night before, forgetting how bad you felt just afterwards. All kinds of feelings go along with Bulimia, such as shame, self-loathing, a sense of having lost control, Depression and longing for stability. Take courage and recognize the problem. It didn't come from nowhere – something in your life, your psychological status or your genetic make-up got you into this position. There are serious risks attached to continuing your binge–purge cycle, so get yourself the treatment you deserve so that you can be healthier again both physically and mentally.

'do not pass go' signs

As in Anorexia Nervosa, some serious medical issues accompany Bulimia, although there is less risk of dying. But dehydration and electrolyte imbalances can lead to heart problems, and related complications are hair loss, oesophageal tearing and gastric ruptures. Regular throwing up can cause acid reflux, severe constipation, sore throat and destruction of tooth enamel. Substance abuse of amphetamines, tranquillizers and alcohol often accompanies Bulimia Nervosa.

what causes bulimia nervosa?

There are probably neurobiological and hereditary causes, as well as life-circumstance ones. Some studies have found that women with Bulimia Nervosa are more likely to report that they have been sexually and physically abused, as well as having a history of Depression, Substance Abuse, low self-esteem, perfectionism, obesity, family problems and parents who struggled with obesity.

what is happening in your brain?

The neurotransmitter serotonin has been implicated in the development of Bulimia Nervosa.

which treatments are likely to work?

Cognitive-behavioural therapy has been shown to be particularly effective (more so than antidepressant medication alone), and so have interpersonal psychotherapy, self-psychology psychotherapy and therapies that involve identifying and working on the roots of a person's conflict with food. Hypnosis can also be useful.

best course of action

Seek cognitive-behavioural, interpersonal or self-psychology therapy, which have all been shown to be successful.

in the meantime, what can you do?

1. Learn everything you can about Bulimia Nervosa (see suggested reading below).

2. Try to discover and work through the roots of your conflict with food. This will take effort, time and dedication. A good start is to answer the questions below fully:

   1. Write down your weight and eating history, including dieting, and try to identify if significant weight gains or losses, or periods of excessive bingeing or extreme purging were associated with specific events or feelings in your life so far. Make a chart giving approximate dates, weights, behaviour and associated events or feelings.

   2. As a child, were you deprived in any way? Identify how you may have experienced longing for something or someone.

   3. What family or interpersonal issues are troubling you, past or present? Write down your feelings and thoughts.

   4. Explore your fears, including those about stopping binge/purge behaviour. Write about them in a journal.

   5. In your journal, also explore your feelings of despair and guilt.

   6. Have you experienced physical or sexual abuse? Emotional abuse or neglect? Write down your feelings.

   7. How do you cope with troubling interpersonal or family issues? Is your style of coping related to eating or purging food? Write down your ideas and feelings about that.

   8. What are your feelings about your struggle to control your eating patterns? Write them down.

   9. How do your weight and your bingeing seem to help you? Does it seem that they protect you from something? Perhaps they make you feel better in a particular way, such as calmer, less vulnerable or unnoticed?

   10. Once you have identified how weight and bingeing have served you, come up with alternative ways to soothe or protect yourself, such as meditating, taking a yoga class or having a pedicure. Schedule these into your life.

   11. What would your life be like if your weight did not fluctuate, if you were not overweight, if you did not binge or purge? Identify your inner dialogue that begins 'If only I did not have Bulimia Nervosa . . .' Your answer may be the thing you fear – that which keeps your Bulimia in place.

   12. Be honest with yourself about your attempts to hide your weight gains and losses, your bingeing or your purging behaviour. Write down any behaviour that involves secrecy, avoidance or lying. What are your thoughts and feelings about having to engage in a pattern of deception?

13. Do you find it hard to avoid manipulating people, or hiding the truth about your weight or bingeing/purging patterns? Write down your thoughts and feelings about that. Try to come up with alternative ways to express your emotions and get your needs met.

14. Do the mirror exercise on page 103.

15. Practise the Positive Regard for the Body meditation (see page 103) twice per day.

16. How do you feel about your body? Identify all your thoughts and feelings, both good and bad.

17. Make peace with your body. Write a letter to it, expressing how you feel about it. Apologize for abusing it and promise to take better care of it in future.

18. If you identify that you have poor body image, follow the exercises for Body Dysmorphic Disorder (see page 102ff).

19. What do you like about yourself? Try to reinforce those things and affirm them daily.

20. Find and implement ways to nourish yourself with something other than food.

21. Establish a self-directed programme to control bingeing and purging, outlined below:
    - Start a daily eating chart. That means writing down everything you eat, every time you vomit/purge/use laxatives or diuretics/over-exercise, any rituals you engage in while eating/vomiting/purging/using laxatives or diuretics/over-exercising, and your feelings while doing so.
    - Do not diet.
    - Eat only when you are hungry.
    - Do not graze. Eat sitting down in a peaceful situation, with few distractions. Be fully aware of what and how much you are eating.
    - Do not sneak food; if possible, eat with others.
    - Eat only as much as you really need to satisfy you.
    - Enjoy your food.

22. Engage in relaxation training (see Progressive Body Relaxation exercise on page 41).

23. Reduce your stress (see page 19).

24. Learn to assert yourself appropriately (see page 38).

25. Work on your self-esteem (see page 105).

26. Try to accept yourself, and let go of the idea that your self-worth

depends on the positive evaluation of other people.

27. Identify your distorted and negative thinking and replace those thoughts with more accurate, positive ones. See NIC and 3 Cs techniques pages 48 and 105.

28. Identify and engage in an activity that will promote your vocational development, such as taking a course or establishing a website.

29. Take better care of every part of yourself, mentally and physically. That includes regular medical, dental and eye check-ups, not over-working and taking breaks.

30. Get plenty of good-quality sleep.

31. Make a list of all the things you like about yourself and put it some-where where you will frequently be reminded of your strengths.

if someone close to you fits the diagnosis for bulimia nervosa, what can you do?

1. Do everything you can to get them into treatment. Bulimia Nervosa is associated with serious psychological and physical problems.

2. Get as much education as possible about the disorder.

3. If you are a parent, carer, spouse, partner or sibling of someone suffering from Bulimia Nervosa seek therapeutic help for yourself as well.

4. Take care of yourself both mentally and physically. Seeing someone struggle with Bulimia Nervosa can be tough.

5. Below are some special guidelines for how to relate to someone close to you with Bulimia Nervosa:

   - Be supportive and calming without being controlling.
   - Be assertive with the sufferer and encourage self-assertion from him or her too.
   - Be openly affectionate, verbally and physically.
   - Never demand that the person stop bingeing, throwing up, or gain/lose weight.
   - Never humiliate, blame or put down the sufferer for having Bulimia Nervosa.
   - Work to create a loving, supportive and nurturing environment for everyone in the family. Do not allow the person with Bulimia Nervosa to command all the focus, worry and attention.
   - Be emotionally available to the person with Bulimia Nervosa, that is do not avoid, withdraw from or abandon him or her. But keep good boundaries between you (for example, do not allow him or her to manipulate you).

- Do not allow the person with Bulimia Nervosa to control aspects of the family that involve eating, such as demanding a particular eating schedule.
- It is essential that the person with Bulimia Nervosa receive mental-health treatment. Once the sufferer is in a programme, do not directly address issues of bingeing, purging or weight with him or her. Leave that to the professionals.

some indications of bulimia nervosa in someone you know

- Weight fluctuations. ■ Frequent dieting. ■ Preoccupied with weight. ■ Incorrect perception of weight. ■ Nausea. ■ Teeth marks on the backs of fingers. ■ Swollen glands. ■ Inflamed joints. ■ Acne. ■ Diarrhoea. ■ Constipation. ■ Water retention. ■ Poor sleep pattern. ■ Depression.

helpful books

Binge No More: Your Guide to Overcoming Compulsive Eating, J. D. Nash. Oakland, Calif.: New Harbinger Publications, 1999.

Why Weight? A Guide to Ending Compulsive Eating, G. Roth. New York: Plume/Penguin, 1989.

The Overcoming Bulimia Workbook: Your Comprehensive, Step-by-Step Guide to Recovery, R. E. McCabe and M. P. Olmstead. Oakland, Calif.: New Harbinger Publications, 2004.

Women's Conflicts About Eating and Sexuality: The Relationship Between Food and Sex, L. Weiss and R. Meadow. New York: Harper & Row, 1991.

Daily Affirmations for Compulsive Eaters: Beyond Feast or Famine, Susan Ward. Deerfield Beach, Fla.: Health Communications, 1990.

Breaking Free from Compulsive Eating, G. Roth. Plume/Penguin, 2002.

Fat Is a Feminist Issue: The Anti-Diet Guide to Permanent Weight Loss, S. Orbach. New York: Berkley Publishing Group, 1978.

Ageless Body, Timeless Mind: A Companion Guide and Journal, D. Chopra. New York: Crown Arts & Letters/Harmony Books, 1993.

Perfect Weight: The Complete Mind/Body Program for Achieving and Maintaining Your Ideal Weight, D. Chopra. Harmony Books, 1994.

'Eating Disorders, Anxiety, Depression: How Can I Tell if I'm Really in Trouble?', in A. Rubenstein & K. Zager, *The Inside Story on Teen Girls*, Washington DC: American Psychological Association, 2002.

Women's Bodies, Women's Wisdom: Creating Physical and Emotional Health and Healing, C. Northrup. New York: Bantam Books, 1998.

chapter 7
typecast: personality disorders

"You're only trying to migrate from yourself."

One's personality begins to develop at birth – perhaps even beforehand. There are a number of theories concerning personality development, but many people agree that there are a combination of biological and psychosocial factors at work. For a start, there is a set of genetic aspects that shape who a person is. Shyness, for example, is genetically determined – yet not all shy children grow into shy adults because sometimes shyness is shaped by early experiences, and sometimes people who are genetically programmed for shyness manage to overcome it. Biology aside, many psychologists believe that early relationships, one's style of interpersonal interaction, and certain formative experiences have an enormous influence on how someone's personality is formed. Being ignored as a child, being constantly afraid, being used for others' pleasure, being turned into a caretaker, or being abandoned are the kinds of traumatic experiences that will affect a person's personality development and later levels of functioning. He or she may develop a view of life, accompanied by certain feelings and behaviour, that will lead to chronic problems later on. In adulthood, such a person may have problems with intimacy, the regulation of emotions, the setting of boundaries, feeling safe among friends, or receiving criticism. Often, such aspects of an adult's personality have been established long ago, as defences against childhood challenges.

Psychologists have created diagnostic categories for Personality Disorders and have grouped them into clusters. Since most Personality Disorders involve chronic dysfunctional feelings and behaviour about which the sufferer may have poor insight, they are not easy for him or her to give up. People with Personality Disorders often view the difficulties they have with other people, situations or tasks as not being influenced by themselves, i.e. they may see themselves as victims, without recognizing how they contribute. They are unlikely to seek treatment for their Personality Disorders, but rather, their friends and family may be motivated by conflicts with them to try to induce them to seek help. Sometimes people with Personality Disorders are aware of the dysfunctional nature of some of their feelings and behaviour, but do not know how they became like that, or how to change. People with Personality Disorders rarely improve without psychotherapy; however, a good psychotherapist can work patiently and effectively to help them heal from the pain of their childhoods and recognize that their present behaviour styles are not serving them. In therapy they can learn to regulate their emotions, relate more effectively to others, and otherwise achieve positive change and greater happiness.

paranoid personality disorder

Some people simply have never learned to feel safe in the world. In childhood they may have been abused, humiliated or been presented with 'double binds', such as having to make the dangerous choice between pleasing a needy mother and of placating an angry father. Children just act in the best way they can for self-protection. When a sense of safety eludes them they find all kinds of creative ways to try to compensate. Sometimes they create a secret physical space, such as a cupboard where they can hide. Sometimes they disappear inside their own minds or even develop a new part of the self to act as protector. They often develop a state of hyper-vigilance, that is, they become acutely aware of the moods and actions of the threatening people around them so they can recognize danger before it arrives and follow their own manner of hiding and self-protection. Isn't it easy to see how a person who had such tortured childhood experiences would find it perfectly normal to continue to view everyone with great suspicion? In fact, wouldn't it seem highly dangerous to let go of such a conceptualization? When people suffering from Paranoid Personality Disorder are asked by a psychologist to draw a house, they often create unwelcoming towers, each with a couple of high windows and no door. In life, they seem to be imprisoned, high and dry inside their own suspicious minds, peering cautiously out at the world and ready to shoot an arrow if anyone approaches. Dennis was just such a person.

case study: Dennis

Dennis was a forty-something divorced man with a twelve-year-old son he adored. He worked in an electronics firm, and he first came to see me because he had frequent clashes with (mainly female) bosses and co-workers. When he was threatened with dismissal a friend advised him to seek therapy. As Dennis began to describe his experience in his workplace and then his social and family experiences, I began to understand that his perceived world was a painful, threatening place inhabited by few people he felt he could trust. He believed everyone was 'out to get him'. He was furious with, and suspicious of, his ex-wife, and it was easy to see why his marriage had failed.

As a child, Dennis had constantly been put in a 'no win' situation by his parents. He felt he could never please his mother, who was extremely intrusive. She and his elder sister frequently humiliated him, teased him and respected neither his privacy nor his personal property. His father was remote and judgemental, and rarely protected him from the abusive females in the family. It took Dennis several years of therapy before he felt safer in the world. His relationship with me was never smooth, but he learned to exclude me from his suspiciousness of all women – which gradually broadened to a softening of his attitude towards others. He eventually learned to tolerate female co-workers and to give them the benefit of the doubt. Best of all, he stopped passing on his paranoid ideas to his son, who benefited enormously from the change in his father. Dennis has never remarried, but he is learning to cope with relationships without sabotaging them due to unfounded suspicions.

is this you (or someone close to you)?

1. You are always extremely suspicious that others are hurting you, lying to you or ripping you off.
2. Doubt that people around you are loyal to you.
3. Don't want to take anyone into your confidence out of fear that they will use your secrets against you.
4. Always reading insidious meanings beneath what people say on the surface.
5. Do not forget all the slights and insults you feel people have given you.

6. Quick to counter-attack if others seem to be on the offensive.
7. Never trust that your spouse or partner is faithful.
8. The deviousness and disloyalty you see in the people you distrust is not usually noticed by others.

Is 'feeling safe' a state of mind that eludes you? Believing that people are always 'out to get you' is a very trying way to inhabit the world. It must be baffling to you that others do not seem to share your suspicions. You must be thinking, 'Can't they see how dangerous or untrustworthy such-and-such a person is?' Don't you sometimes wish you could just relax, let go of all your anxiety, fear and distrust and simply enjoy life?

'do not pass go' signs

Being able to trust others is an important aspect of human relationships and intimacy. Without this capacity it is difficult to be happy; friendships, social life, work and marriage will all suffer. Unfortunately, few people with Paranoid Personality Disorder seek treatment for it. They are more likely to undergo therapy for other problems, such as Anxiety or Depression. Substance Abuse, Panic Disorder, Phobias and Bipolar Disorder go hand in hand with Paranoid Personality Disorder.

what causes paranoid personality disorder?

Paranoia may be caused by both biological and environmental factors, and there may be inherited elements as well. There is a connection between childhood anxiety and the development of Paranoid Personality Disorder. Traumatized children, who experienced emotional, physical, sexual and verbal abuse often become extremely suspicious of others – with good reason. Many are unable to let go of that suspicion long after the threats have been removed.

which treatments are likely to work?

Long-term psychodynamic psychotherapy, hypnotherapy, cognitive-behavioural therapy, psychoanalysis and many other types of individual, group or psychotherapy would be useful.

best course of action?

Seek psychotherapy and hypnotherapy.

in the meantime what can you do?

1. Learn everything you can about Paranoid Personality Disorder (see reading list below).
2. What may have led to your seeing people as untrustworthy? Write down any incidents, perhaps in your childhood, where you felt hurt, betrayed, helpless or humiliated. Write down your feelings about those incidents.
3. Write more about your childhood experiences. Write down your feelings about your relationships with everyone in your family, and formative experiences you believe shaped the way you feel about the world.
4. Find a picture of yourself as a child. Write down your feelings as you look at this picture. What was it like to be you back then?
5. Increase your self-knowledge by writing down and completing the following: 'I think of myself as . . .', 'I am always afraid of . . .', 'I wish . . .'
6. Do you have any idea what has been the cost to you of being unable to trust others? Write down your thoughts and feelings about that.
7. Notice your tendency to be always on the lookout for conspiracies against you or hidden meanings in other people's words or actions. What does that thinking style cost you? How does it make you feel? Write down your thoughts and feelings.
8. Practise trying to let go of some of your mistrust and suspiciousness of others by deliberately giving some people the benefit of the doubt. Work on serenity, trust and acceptance.
9. Notice your thoughts, especially the negative ones you have about yourself, such as 'I am vulnerable to other people' or 'If I don't watch out, others will always take advantage of me.' Write them down, and ask for feedback (such as 'Do you think this is true?') from a friend or relative you feel you just might be able to (at least partially) trust.
10. If you have angry or jealous thoughts, write them down as a means of venting; then begin to allow yourself to let them go.
11. Work on increasing your self-esteem (see page 105).
12. Follow the anger-management steps (see page 213).
13. Do the thought-stopping exercise (see page 39).
14. Reduce your stress (see exercises page 19).
15. Practise Progressive Body Relaxation (see page 41).
16. Practise the following Buddhist meditation. It will help you to stop seeing everyone as a potential adversary:

exercise: positive regard meditation practice

Sitting comfortably, allow your body to calm down and take three deep breaths. Begin to be aware of your breathing, and when it is deep and low in your body, turn your attention to yourself. This meditation takes place in five stages, each one for 3–5 minutes. Keep a watch handy to remind to move from one stage to the next. If other thoughts enter your head during the process, push them gently aside and return to your meditation.

Stage 1 Try to direct feelings of well-being and happiness towards yourself. You can say (in your head) 'May I be happy, may I be well' over and over.

Stage 2 Try to direct feelings of well-being and happiness towards someone you care about. Picture that person, and try to engender pure empathy and care for him or her. You can say: 'May (he or she) be happy, may (he or she) be well.'

Stage 3 Now picture someone who has a neutral role in your life. Perhaps you barely know this person. It should be someone for whom you have no particular feelings, either positive or negative. Try to direct the same positive regard towards that person as you managed to engender for the person you care about in Stage 2. You can say: 'May (he or she) be happy, may (he or she) be well.'

Stage 4 Now choose someone you dislike, and try to engender the same feelings of positive regard for him or her. This is much harder, but it's worth persevering: 'May (he or she) be happy. May (he or she) be well'.

Stage 5 Now encompass all of humanity by first directing feelings of well-being and well wishes towards people in your immediate vicinity. Move on to people in the same building, then the same street, the same town, county, country and continent. Then move on to countries throughout the world, and even universes beyond. 'May all beings be happy, may they be well'.

When you have completed this meditation, slowly open your eyes. You should be feeling calm, glowing, happy and more generous towards others. If not, practise it until those feelings come more easily.

when someone close to you has paranoid personality disorder

■ People with Paranoid Personality Disorder will probably not be interested in having therapy unless they can be helped to see the value of being able to trust others and function better in interpersonal relationships. Perhaps motivation is something with which you can help; however your suggestion may be viewed with suspicion.

- Anxiety goes hand in hand with Paranoid Personality Disorder, so you may be able to encourage the sufferer to seek treatment for that disorder.
- Learn to be very respectful of the difficulty a person with Paranoid Personality Disorder has in trusting others. Try not to take it personally.
- It is not easy to be in a relationship with a person suffering from Paranoid Personality Disorder. Look after yourself both physically and mentally and seek therapeutic help for you and the family.

helpful books

Understanding Paranoia: A Guide for Professionals, Families and Sufferers, M. Kantor. Westport, Conn.: Praeger, 2004.

Healing Fear: New Approaches to Overcoming Anxiety, E. Bourne. Oakland, Calif.: New Harbinger Publications Inc., 1988.

The Relaxation and Stress Reduction Workbook, M. Davis, E. R. Eshelman and M. McKay. Oakland, Calif.: New Harbinger Publications, 2000.

schizoid personality disorder

Do you ever meet people who are die-hard loners? Who seem to be extremely closed-off from others? They may seem calm, even spiritual on the surface, but if you get close to them you may intuitively sense that underneath there are strong feelings. Some children who don't manage to bond well with their parents or carers, or who experience their early world as cold or threatening, learn very early on that showing feelings – such as getting angry about the way they are treated – is useless. There's no sense in fighting back, they decide, and withdraw inside their heads, repressing their rage. For them, this is a survival mechanism. They may grow up to be adults who are often in complete denial about their continuing, underlying anger and who go out of their way to avoid conflict. Some even harbour deep fantasies of releasing an explosion of violence upon innocent people. These fantasies are usually terrifying to them, but in extreme cases, as we see in the newspapers from time to time, it actually happens. 'He was a nice young man who kept to himself' is often the surprised comment of neighbours after a mass shooting incident.

Of course, most people with Schizoid Personality Disorder are not potential mass murderers. They struggle enormously when they are expected to interact with others, even just in their workplace. Devoid of emotional expression themselves, they cannot comprehend it in others, although they sometimes look to them for clues about how to react in certain circumstances. The film *Ordinary People* contains a marvellous portrayal of a young man with Schizoid Personality Disorder (played by Timothy Hutton) and the family environment that helped to create his personality. Just like Jennifer (see below), he was born to a mother who was unable to provide warmth or acceptance.

case study: Jennifer

A very beautiful, poised young woman came into my office one day, saying that she thought she might be suffering from Depression. She was bright and alert but she showed little expression on her face, and seemed unable to express emotion. Her husband had suggested she undergo therapy. The pair had married recently after a brief courtship, and he was worried about her. He was afraid she might be unhappy with him and unable to say so. Jennifer worked as a web master for an online company, and spent her days alone at her computer. Her husband travelled a great deal, so she spent the majority of her life by herself. When I asked her if she ever felt lonely, she barely seemed to understand the question. She had one friend, a woman with whom she sometimes walked their dogs. Gradually, Jennifer confessed that she drank heavily, usually when she was alone. She said that her husband had begun to expect her to arrange parties and business dinners since corporate entertaining was becoming an important part of his business. Unfortunately, being an accomplished hostess was impossible for Jennifer, although she did not openly express resentment towards him for expecting this. It seemed that her husband had impulsively married a 'trophy wife' who looked the part, but couldn't be the social star he'd hoped for. She, in turn, needed to learn to feel safe expressing emotions such as anger, and a husband who understood who she really was. They sought treatment just in time to save their marriage; after a year or so of individual and couples therapy, Jennifer and her husband had found ways to accept each other's personality differences.

is this you (or someone close to you)?
- You do not like to be close to people, including family.
- Prefer doing things alone.
- Are disinterested in having sex with a partner.
- Do not enjoy many activities.
- Have few friends.
- Barely notice either the positive or negative feedback from other people.
- Seem cold and unemotional to others.

If this seems like you, you may not see a problem with it. Well, you've developed this personality style for good reason. You need a lot of space between you and other people, in fact you are barely interested in having relationships at all. You tend to be passive and prefer to be alone most of the time. Being such a self-contained unit, why would you bother changing? To find the answer, search inside. I know that at a deep level you feel isolated and empty. You may believe you are a social misfit, and have a deep terror of rejection and failure. You don't know how to react in many situations and frequently try to look to others for clues. It's hard to imagine this, but there is a more comfortable way to be in the world.

'do not pass go' signs
Many people with Schizoid Personality Disorder suffer from Anxiety, Panic Attacks, and underlying chronic Depression. There may also be a connection between this disorder and Substance Abuse, particularly in women. Due to their lack of (and indifference to) interpersonal relationships, people with Schizoid Personality Disorder may be vulnerable to being taken advantage of by others.

what causes schizoid personality disorder?
It may have biological and life-circumstance causes, and seems to run in families. Childhood experiences are thought to influence its development. Depression in children may put them at risk for developing Schizoid Personality Disorder later in life, and childhood nutritional deficits may also be contributing factors.

which treatments are likely to work?
Psychodynamic psychotherapy, psychoanalysis, or cognitive-behavioural therapy may be the most useful types of therapy for this disorder.

best course of action?
Seek individual psychodynamic psychotherapy, cognitive behavioural therapy or psychoanalysis, and possibly group therapy as well.

in the meantime what can you do?
1. Read everything you can about Schizoid Personality Disorder.
2. What exactly is your experience when you are surrounded by other people? Write down your thoughts and feelings.
3. Your privacy is, no doubt, very important to you. Work out strategies for how you can maintain your privacy, but also open up a little to others.

Write down your thoughts, feelings and ideas about that.

4. Write about your childhood experiences. Write down your feelings about your relationships with everyone in your family and about the formative experiences that may have shaped the way you feel about the world.

5. Find a picture of yourself as a child. Write down your feelings as you look at this picture. What was it like to be you back then?

6. Notice your thoughts, especially the negative ones you have about yourself, such as 'I am socially inadequate' or 'I can't manage relationships'. Write them down, and ask for feedback (such as 'Do you think this is true about me?') from a trusted friend or relative.

7. Increase your self-knowledge by writing down and completing the following: 'I think of myself as . . .', 'I am always afraid of . . .', 'I wish . . .'

8. Try to get a little in touch with deep feelings you are afraid of, such as anger. Write down a few things you feel angry about. Know that anger can be safely expressed.

9. Practise self-assertion (see page 38). Especially practise expressing appropriate anger; for example if someone does something you don't like use the 'Three Part Question' (see page 39) to let them know and ask for a change.

10. Practise reciprocating with others. If someone close to you does something thoughtful for you, such as giving you a birthday gift, make sure you give one in return when it is his or her birthday.

11. Work on improving your social skills by practising:
   - Initiating conversation with others.
   - Giving compliments.
   - Accepting compliments.
   - Being assertive in your communication (see page 38).
   - Making sure you keep appointments.
   - Being on time for social events.
   - Being honest.
   - Self-disclosing to an appropriate degree.
   - Being able to set boundaries with others.
   - Maintaining eye contact.
   - Giving oneself and others an appropriate amount of personal space.
   - Learning to deal with criticism.
   - Learning to deal with teasing.

12. When you feel ready, try to let go of some of your need for autonomy and isolation and work on reciprocity and intimacy with others. Start by

spending more time around other people, even without interacting with them (for example, by attending a conference or sitting in a busy cafe). Work on breathing and relaxation when you feel anxious (see page 40). When you can tolerate that experience, move on to doing something more interactive and social than you would normally do, such as joining a book club.

13. Others may see you as cold or aloof, which may not be the impression you wish to give. Try to find ways to change the way you appear to others by finding someone who appears warm and learning from him or her. Reaching out to others may be hard for you, but there will eventually be untold benefits to you.

14. Work to increase your self-esteem (see page 105).

15. Reduce your stress (see exercises page 19).

16. Practise the Positive Regard meditation (see page 127).

17. Have a conversation with at least one trusted person in your family about Schizoid Personality Disorder. Explain what it is, and help him or her to understand that you do not mean to be distant – that's just how you are wired. If this conversation is helpful in any way, consider having a similar discussion with others. When people understand you, they will be more tolerant of your differences.

when someone close to you has schizoid personality disorder

- People with Schizoid Personality Disorder will probably not be interested in having therapy unless they can be helped to see the value of being able to have more of a social life and function better in interpersonal relationships. Perhaps motivation is something with which you can help.

- Alcohol and drug abuse sometimes go hand in hand with this Personality Disorder. If you think the person you are concerned about may be involved in Substance Abuse as well, do not hesitate to encourage treatment and lend support for recovery.

- Never perpetrate rage upon a person with Schizoid Personality Disorder. If you tend to explode with anger learn to express it more appropriately (see pages 213).

helpful books

Character Styles, S. J. Johnson. New York: W. W. Norton & Co, 1994.

The Addiction Workbook: A Step-By-Step Guide to Quitting Alcohol and Drugs, P. Fanning and J. T. O'Neill. Oakland, Calif.: New Harbinger Publications, 1996.

Addiction and Recovery for Dummies, B. Shaw, P. Ritvo and J. Irvine. Hoboken, New Jersey: Wiley Publishing Co., 2005.

How to Deal with Emotionally Explosive People, A. Bernstein. New York: McGraw-Hill, 2003.

Taking Charge of Anger: How to Resolve Conflict, Sustain Relationships, and Express Yourself without Losing Control, W. R. Nay. Guilford Press, 2004.

schizotypal (eccentric) personality disorder

Some people work at being eccentric, but others just are. The Schizotypal Personality Disorder described in the DSM-IV involves having styles of speech, appearance and ideas that others find odd. A sufferer may also have feelings of suspicion about others – but well, most people would be a bit wary if others were always calling them 'weird', wouldn't they? Some of your favourite show-business personalities or rock stars may have this particular personality style.

case study: Rex

As a teenager, Rex joined a rock band that became very famous. At that time, no one understood that he was a person with Schizotypal Personality Disorder. His eccentricities, strange attire and superstitions, which had previously attracted considerable negative attention as a teenager, were now considered just 'part of his act'. Rex was relieved to find that, among his fans and others in the music industry, his unusual behaviour was viewed as 'typical rock 'n' roll', and his social reticence labelled 'cool'. Even his odd speech was thought to be a function of illicit drug-taking. But as the band became even more famous, and the touring schedule escalated to a highly stressful, all-year-round lifestyle, Rex's interpersonal relationships with other band members fell apart and he began to disintegrate. His alcohol and drug abuse worsened, and it was only when friends managed to get him into a rehabilitation programme that a psychiatrist diagnosed him with Schizotypal Personality Disorder. Rex was fortunate that, in recovery, he was finally able to start understanding and appreciating his unique personality. He learned to keep his stress level moderate, and insisted that his manager establish a realistic work schedule. After several years of treatment he managed to surround himself with people who could protect and support him, and was finally in a position to balance his undeniable talent and career potential with his need to keep his mental-health issues under control. He married a supportive woman, raised a family and continues to be an international star.

is this you (or someone close to you)?

- Other people think your ideas are strange.
- You sometimes think certain events, objects, sounds, sights, songs, gestures or comments people make – or something you hear on the radio, see on TV or in a book or magazine – are directed at you personally.
- Have notions that others consider to be unusual (for example, certain superstitions or a belief that you have special powers).
- Others think your speech is unusual, perhaps jumping from topic to topic too quickly, perhaps digressing too much, or with odd phrasing.
- You may be extremely suspicious of others.
- Others may think you do not express your feelings in the best way – that you either let them out inappropriately or hold them in too much.
- Your behaviour and/or appearance are thought by others to be unusual or eccentric.
- You have few close friends, if any, and you feel you do not 'fit in'.
- Do not trust others enough to be socially comfortable; in fact you avoid social situations as much as possible.

If you fit this description you may be fully aware that other people view you as somewhat eccentric. Perhaps this will bother you, perhaps not. Some people with Schizotypal Personality Disorder experience considerable distress and hide from others, feeling that they are 'defective' in some way. Thus, they may become isolated, finding it difficult to achieve the social and vocational success they deserve. However, there can be many benefits to being unique, especially if this uniqueness is expressed in areas where it is fully appreciated. But if you are also struggling with Depression, Anxiety, or Substance Abuse, or if you sometimes have unsettling experiences such as hallucinations or delusions, it would be wise to seek therapy.

'do not pass go' signs

Having Schizotypal Personality Disorder causes a person to be marginalized in many social and vocational situations. Some are lucky enough to find themselves in careers where being 'eccentric' is considered to be a positive attribute (for example, the entertainment business), but, in many cases, people with the disorder struggle with ridicule, ostracism, relationship difficulties and economic hardship. In fact, connection has been found between Schizotypal Personality Disorder and homelessness.

Children who show early signs of the disorder may suffer from being teased by peers. Adults with the disorder rarely seek treatment because they do not view themselves as being disturbed or in need of any help. In fact, it is probably a good thing if they come to value their eccentricities, regarding themselves as interesting and creative individuals – despite the feedback they receive from others. However, Mood Disorders, Anxiety, alcohol and drug abuse, as well as antisocial behaviour sometimes go hand in hand with Schizotypal Personality Disorder, and treatment must be sought for those associated problems. Most importantly, it is absolutely necessary for people with the disorder to avoid personal or psychological stress, which can lead to transient hallucinations and delusions, and may even trigger the development of Schizophrenia.

what causes schizotypal personality disorder?
Schizotypal Personality Disorder is more common among close family relatives of people with Schizophrenia. Some people with the disorder display certain indicators found in Schizophrenia, such as eye-tracking impairment and attention deficits, so there may be neurodevelopmental causes of the disorder. Some believe the disorder may have its roots in psychosocial adversity, such as childhood trauma. Although Schizotypal Personality Disorder usually appears early in life (the twenties), there have been cases where it has had a later onset, that is, in the mid-thirties.

what happens in your brain?
Some researchers suspect that, for people with Schizotypal Personality Disorder, there may be brain abnormalities similar to those that afflict people with Schizophrenia (for example, an excess of the neurotransmitter dopamine, and various differences in the anatomy of the brain). Another theory suggests that disruption of normal brain development during a critical early stage of pregnancy, possibly due to prenatal exposure to influenza, may also be relevant to Schizotypal Personality Disorder.

which treatments are likely to work?
Psychotherapy is recommended, as well as social skills training. Some people recommend pharmacological intervention. If applicable, harm-reduction or twelve-step programmes are recommended for any accompanying Substance Abuse. If a mood disorder is present it will also require therapy, and possibly medication as well.

best course of action?

Seek psychotherapy. People with Schizotypal Personality Disorder typically do not seek treatment, so it is usually up to close friends or relatives to help them find a therapist. This is especially important if they are also suffering from Depression, Anxiety or Substance Abuse or if they engage in antisocial behaviour (for example, have trouble obeying rules and laws, which may put them at risk of being arrested).

in the meantime what can you do?

1. Learn everything you can about Schizotypal Personality Disorder (see reading list below).
2. Reduce your stress and keep it to a minimum as a matter of high priority. This is vital, because people with Schizotypal Personality Disorder may be at risk of developing Schizophrenia, thought to be triggered by social and psychological stress.
3. If you think you might have Schizotypal Personality Disorder, try to describe what that is like for you. Write down your feelings and thoughts about it in a journal.
4. What was life like for you when you were a child? Write about your childhood experiences.
5. Write down your feelings about your relationships with the people in your family, the formative experiences that may have shaped the way you now feel about the world.
6. Find a picture of yourself as a child. Write down your feelings as you gaze at this picture. What was it like to be you back then?
7. Research famous people in the past or present who may have been a little like you – considered by others to be eccentric, creative and somewhat odd. Work on trying to appreciate those things about you. For example, reframe 'odd' as 'individual'.
8. Notice the negative thoughts you have about yourself, such as 'I am defective' or 'I am an alien'. Write them down, and ask for feedback (for example, 'Do you think this is true about me?') from a trusted friend or relative.
9. Increase your self-knowledge by writing down and completing the following: 'I think of myself as ...', 'I am always afraid of ...', 'I wish ...'
10. Take a social skills class if possible. Otherwise, work on improving your social skills by practising:
    - Initiating conversation with others.
    - Giving compliments.
    - Accepting compliments.

- Being assertive in your communication (see page 38).
- Making sure you keep appointments.
- Being on time for social events.
- Being honest.
- Self-disclosing to an appropriate degree.
- Being able to set boundaries with others.
- Maintaining eye contact.
- Giving yourself and others an appropriate amount of personal space.
- Learning to deal with criticism.
- Learning to deal with teasing.

11. It may improve your quality of life if you work on your appearance. People will accept you more if you do not look atypical (unless you work in a field where individuality is rewarded, such as rock 'n' roll, the art world or show business!). Elicit feedback from someone you trust about how to improve your appearance and consider following that advice.

12. Write down the behaviours you engage in that may appear odd to others, that is, those for which you have received negative feedback in the past. Consider modifying them and try to come up with methods of achieving this.

13. If you can, work on maintaining eye contact with people when you are verbally interacting with them.

14. Work on reducing your social isolation. Take some small steps towards being around other people a little more, for example, by sitting in a busy cafe. Increase your level of tolerance for social interaction in incremental steps, with the goal of being able to join and participate in, say, a sports or book club.

15. Develop a list of life goals for yourself, and take a few easy steps towards accomplishing one or two.

16. Learn and practise self-assertion (see page 38).

17. Meditate (see exercises pages 40 and 127). It will help keep you centred and improve your stress level.

18. If you receive feedback that suggests you are more suspicious of others than necessary, practise the compassion meditation (see page 127).

19. Practise Progressive Body Relaxation (see page 41).

20. Eat regular, balanced meals.

21. Exercise. Apart from keeping your body healthy and strong this will improve your level of stress, depression and anxiety.

22. Do not abuse alcohol or drugs. If you tend to do so and cannot stop, seek treatment immediately (see page 182).

when someone close to you has schizotypal personality disorder

1. He or she is unlikely to seek therapy. If you feel it is necessary, that is, if the person is depressed, anxious, abusing substances, or struggling with interpersonal or vocational problems, try to motivate them to seek mental-health treatment for those issues. Be careful not to put the person down for being 'unusual'.

2. People with this disorder sometimes have strong feelings of paranoia. Don't take it personally, but work extra hard to establish trust in your relationship with him or her.

3. Encourage the sufferer to reduce his or her stress. This is essential, because for some people with the disorder there is a risk of developing Schizophrenia.

4. Encourage the sufferer to engage in physical exercise, to meditate (see page 40), practise relaxation (see page 41) and eat balanced, nutritious meals.

5. If it is important to the sufferer to reduce his or her oddness, perhaps in order to sustain a job or relationship, be prepared to give constructive feedback that may help with a mild make-over. Be sure to use words like 'individual' or 'unique' rather than pejorative, hurtful words such as 'weird'.

6. A number of people with Schizotypal Personality Disorder end up becoming homeless. Consider this concern in your contact with this person, and support his or her attempts to achieve lifetime stability.

7. Being in a relationship or family with someone who has the disorder can be difficult. Take care of your (and your family's) physical and mental health.

helpful books

Schizotypal Personality, eds A. Raine, T. Lencz and S. A. Mednick. Cambridge University Press, 1995.

The Freedom from Depression Workbook, Les Carter and Frank Minirth. Nashville, Tenn.: Thomas Nelson Publishers, 1995.

Five Weeks to Healing Stress: The Wellness Option, V. O'Hara. Oakland, Calif.: New Harbinger Publications, 1996.

antisocial (sociopathic) personality disorder

What makes a person become a cold-hearted criminal? Many people in the mental-health field believe the tendency begins with a tough childhood. Children need at least one person in their lives whom they can trust to care for them, who helps them to feel safe in the world. Without such a person (and especially if treated violently) a child may grow up without ever developing an ingrained sense of empathy, or remorse for wrongdoing. 'This dog-eat-dog world has treated me badly, so I'm going to hit back' is the sensibility that is carried into adulthood. Doesn't it make sense that such a person would see crime, including the white-collar variety, as natural behaviour? Dirk was just one such person:

case study: Dirk

Dirk ran a scam business that cheated people out of money they thought they were investing in a successful internet company. He was entirely remorseless about hurting others. He himself had been betrayed, harmed and abandoned many times as the child of a drug dealer. Dirk had behaviour problems as a child, getting into trouble for lying, stealing and for torturing a neighbour's dog. As a teenager he engaged in criminal activities with a carjacking gang, and was enlisted by his father to sell marijuana, ecstasy and other party drugs in dance clubs frequented by students. Dirk's career in crime was only halted when he faced criminal charges for his investment scam. In prison, he attended optional therapy sessions in an attempt to manipulate the therapist into helping him with his appeal. It failed.

is this you (or someone close to you)?
- You are disinterested in adhering to laws or societal rules.
- Repeatedly lie and con people.
- Tend to be impulsive, aggressive and irritable.
- Get into physical fights or assault others.
- Disregard the safety of self or others.
- Are irresponsible.
- Lack remorse.

If you accept that the above apply to you, and you would like to change, perhaps because that might help you to stay out of prison, you can be helped if you commit to therapy. A good therapist will not judge you for things you have done or your lack of remorse. If you can open up, he or she will be able to help you to heal from early trauma, to make better choices and to find ways to live and work in society without being drawn into making mistakes that have negative consequences for you. I know it is not easy to contemplate showing vulnerability to someone else – including a therapist – but in a bid to gain significant benefits, why not give it a go?

'do not pass go' signs

Because people with Antisocial Personality Disorder do not care to follow rules or laws, they tend to commit crimes. This in turn means they are very likely to fall foul of the justice system and end up in prison for extended periods. It is essential for a sufferer to be helped before that happens. Unfortunately, people with Antisocial Personality Disorder are rarely interested in seeking help, so it is usually up to families or friends to try to get them into treatment.

what causes antisocial personality disorder?

People with Antisocial Personality Disorder may have had severe early childhood problems regarding essential relationships with parents or carers. A child needs at least one person in their life who consistently loves and protects them, but people with Antisocial Personality Disorder may have grown up without such a figure. They develop 'survival' mechanisms such as becoming hardened, fiercely competitive and exploitative themselves. These mechanisms seem helpful to them at the time, but prove socially unacceptable and maladaptive later in life.

which treatments are likely to work?

Psychotherapy can be helpful for Antisocial Personality Disorder. If Depression or Anxiety is also present, treatment that includes antidepressant or anti-Anxiety medications is often appropriate.

best course of action?

Seek psychotherapy from a trained, qualified professional.

in the meantime what can you do?

1. Learn everything you can about Antisocial Personality Disorder.
2. Write about your childhood experiences. Write down your feelings about your relationships with everyone in your family and the formative

experiences that may have shaped the way you feel about the world.

3. Find a picture of yourself as a child. Write down your feelings as you look at this picture. What was it like to be you back then?

4. Notice your current thoughts, especially the negative ones you have about yourself, such as 'I am always vulnerable to attack (so I must strike first).' Write them down, and ask for feedback (such as 'Do you think this is true about me?') from a trusted friend or relative.

5. It would be helpful if you could try to let go of some of your combativeness, and learn to think carefully about the consequences of your choices. First, write down your thoughts and feelings about the prospect and experience of doing so.

6. When you have a problem, list your possible reactions to it, along with the advantages and disadvantages of making such a decision. Rate these possibilities in terms of how effective you think they will be. For example, if a regular customer at work makes a complaint against you for the way you spoke to him, you could:

   - Angrily protest your innocence. (Advantage: you might feel better because you've stood up for yourself. Disadvantage: someone else may have heard the exchange so you may be found out.)
   - Get revenge on the customer by selling him faulty goods next time. (Advantage: you'll feel you've paid him back. Disadvantage: your boss may find out and fire you.)
   - Leave the job. (Advantage: you won't have to put up with the customer. Disadvantage: you don't want to have to look for another job.)
   - Stay calm and keep your nose clean. (Advantage: you may benefit in the long run with promotion, pay rise and so on. Disadvantage: you will have to watch your mouth next time.)

7. Work on relaxation (page 41).

8. Practise the Calming Breath exercise (page 46) .

9. Try to become more aware of your tendency to be exploitative or predatory. When others point out instances of this, try to listen calmly instead of becoming defensive.

10. Work on developing more empathy and social sensitivity towards others. A good way to do this is by asking people who have been victims of a crime to describe how it felt. Listen carefully, and try to put yourself in their shoes. Write down your feelings and thoughts about this

11. Reduce your stress (see page 19).

12. Practise meditation, (see exercises page 40 and 127).

13. Practise Progressive Body Relaxation (see page 41).
14. Eat regular, balanced meals.
15. Exercise.
16. Do not abuse alcohol or drugs.

when someone close to you has antisocial personality disorder

- People with Antisocial Personality Disorder will probably not be interested in having therapy unless they can be helped to see the value of being able to obey rules and stop manipulating and exploiting others. Perhaps motivation is something with which you can help, but be aware that they will probably only seek help if they believe it is a way to avoid getting into trouble or benefiting them in some other concrete way.
- Learn to set limits with a person with Antisocial Personality Disorder. Do not allow him or her to manipulate, bully, exploit or otherwise hurt you or your family. Especially do not tolerate abuse, and do not remain in a relationship with an abusive partner.
- It is not easy to be in a relationship with a person suffering from Antisocial Personality Disorder. Look after yourself both physically and mentally, and seek therapeutic help for you and the family.

helpful books

Without Conscience: The Disturbing World of the Psychopaths Among Us, R. D. Hare. New York: Guilford Press, 1999.

Taking Charge of Anger: How to Resolve Conflict, Sustain Relationships, and Express Yourself without Losing Control, W.R. Nay. New York: Guilford Press, 2004.

borderline personality disorder

Some people have had a chronic lack of nurturance in childhood. Perhaps their parents or carers were depressed, alcoholic or chronically ill. Perhaps they left them, hurt them or failed to meet their dependency needs. A child who has not been adequately soothed or relieved when he or she needed it can end up, in adulthood, with chronic feelings of hunger and loneliness. These problems can start during a person's earliest days of infancy. If a mother is not there enough when needed, is there but ignores her infant, can't respond or suddenly leaves, the infant feels abandoned and hopeless, and if this happens often enough rage and despair can develop. Some people think our modern industrialized culture is responsible for our many unavailable mothers and the lack of extended family, creating childhood pain and the adult aftermath.

For many children, being constantly left or disappointed becomes too much to bear, so they decide, 'If I don't need anything, I can't be frustrated.' They are left with limited capacity to reach out and get their needs met. As adults they continue to be caught between the despair of their unfilled emptiness and the fear of exposing it, which carries a risk of being abandoned again. Some reach out for food, drink, drugs, or sex – but there is never enough to fill the 'black hole' they feel inside. Without treatment they are condemned to terrible loneliness, self-torture and a tendency to flip-flop between loving others and hating them. They can easily get lost in love, producing feelings of suffocation in their partners, and they will experience extreme panic at any slight threat of abandonment by others.

case study: Clarissa

Everyone 'walked on eggshells' around Clarissa. In her position as managing director of a well-known agency for fashion models, she wielded power, wealth and a raging temper. At thirty-eight, she was envied in her field for her talent, intuition and success – yet in her personal life she was a lonely, empty, deeply sad woman who engaged in binge-eating, Substance Abuse and risky sex in an attempt to assuage her chronic feelings of emptiness and longing. Clarissa was the third child of an alcoholic mother and a father who walked out on the family when the three children were young. No doubt the early trauma she experienced contributed to the development of Clarissa's personality style: intense, off–on relationships, mood swings, and dangerously impulsive behaviour. She began therapy after a suicide attempt when she was in her mid-thirties. She has made some progress, especially in controlling her Depression and mood swings, but she continues to struggle with the aftermath of her painful trauma, her tendency to be impulsive and full of rage, and her chronic feelings of emptiness.

is this you (or someone close to you)?

- You are very afraid of being abandoned and will go to any lengths to avoid that happening.
- Your relationships are very up and down – sometimes you love someone, the next minute you hate that same person.
- Have trouble knowing exactly who you are.
- Are impulsive in areas that carry risk of self-harm, such as sex, substance abuse, spending, binge eating.

- Threaten suicide or sometimes cut yourself.
- Have unstable moods.
- Feel horribly empty inside.
- Have emotional storms and at times you vent your rage.
- When stressed-out you sometimes feel quite paranoid, and can even lose touch with reality.

If you fit the description above, you are in great pain. That 'black hole' inside you is always driving you to try to soothe yourself by inappropriate means such as Substance Abuse, overeating, sex, shopping, sugar or caffeine. Perhaps you even cut yourself or have suicidal thoughts. Others are wary of you, especially when your rage emerges, yet you need them desperately. You probably overwork, over-mother, or take on too many responsibilities. You can be helped to get your needs met and reduce your pain and longing, but it involves long-term therapy. It's worth it, though, to avoid a life like yours.

'do not pass go' signs

Borderline Personality Disorder is excruciatingly painful for the sufferer, and also for the people around him or her. The term 'Borderline' was originally employed to describe people who straddled the line between being in touch with reality and otherwise. It is true that people with the disorder sometimes have episodes of psychosis (that is, their perceptions, understanding and other thought processes, as well as emotions and behaviour, become seriously disrupted or impaired). They may have episodes of paranoid thinking (wrongly imagining others are intent on harming them), dissociation (suffering memory loss and/or a disturbance in the way they process feelings, thinking, behaviour or personal identity), depersonalization (feeling detached from mind or body, as if in a dream) or magical thinking (for example, imbuing themselves with highly unrealistic abilities or special powers).

People with the disorder are under physical threat, due to their tendency to self-mutilate, engage in risk-taking behaviour (for example, unsafe sex and drug abuse) and to make suicide attempts. Their difficulties with controlling their impulses make these tendencies even more threatening. Many engage in other dangerous activities such as shoplifting, serious gambling, substance abuse, speeding, binge-eating and overspending. They do not have a stable sense of who they are or how to regulate their emotions, and that makes it hard for them to sustain relationships, jobs, family ties and social connections. Associated problems include Depression, Eating Disorders, Phobias,

Panic Disorder, Substance Abuse, other Personality Disorders and Post-Traumatic Stress Disorder.

If someone you know (including a child or adolescent) is engaging in self-mutilating behaviour such as cutting, or expresses suicidal ideas, seek urgent and immediate psychiatric help for the sufferer.

what causes borderline personality disorder?

Some studies have suggested that Borderline Personality Disorder is related to early abandonment of one kind or another. Failure to get needs met, childhood separation from one or both parents and early physical, sexual, emotional and verbal abuse are some of the experiences of people with the disorder. There may also be genetic, biological and psychosocial factors. Close family members of people diagnosed with the disorder are roughly five times as likely as others to be diagnosed with the same disorder.

what happens in your brain?

Impulsivity has been shown to be related to the neurotransmitter serotonin and, although several neurotransmitters may be influential, it is thought that abnormal levels of serotonin may result in both the impulsivity and aggression associated with Borderline Personality Disorder. People who have difficulty regulating their emotions have a smaller-than-usual volume in the hippocampus and amygdala. Electroencephalography (EEG) analyses of people with the disorder have shown disruptions in the limbic system (the part of the brain that regulates memory, learning and emotional states). The amygdala, which controls a person's fear response, may be hyper reactive, and it is also possible that the motivation/reward part of the brain does not function properly in people with the disorder. This may have an important influence on their sense of self-worth.

which treatments are likely to work?

Psychotherapeutic help to heal the trauma of abandonment and abuse is essential, and a psychotherapist can also help a person with Borderline Personality Disorder have a better sense of self, learn to set and accept boundaries, and to regulate his or her emotions. Besides psychodynamic psychotherapy and psychoanalysis, dialectical behaviour therapy is thought to be particularly helpful. This is a specific treatment for Borderline Personality Disorder that evolved from cognitive-behavioural therapy. It was developed by Dr Marsha Linehan especially for people who engage in self-destructive and self-injurious behaviour. Interpersonal group therapy has been found to be very effective. Family programmes are helpful (and necessary) for those close to people with Borderline Personality Disorder.

People with Borderline Personality Disorder sometimes face prejudice, even from the mental-health profession, because they are considered difficult to treat. But this disorder can be treated successfully, so be sure to find someone with expertise in this area. In some cases, symptom-focused medication treatment is helpful (for example, antidepressants that target serotonin levels to improve mood). Occasionally, inpatient clinic or hospital treatment may be the best answer, especially if a person becomes psychotic, self-destructive, severely depressed or suicidal.

best course of action?

Individual psychodynamic psychotherapy, psychoanalysis, dialectical behaviour therapy or interpersonal group therapy, and family therapy. Sometimes inpatient treatment is necessary.

in the meantime what can you do?

1. Learn everything you can about Borderline Personality Disorder.
2. Keep an emotions and behaviour log to record feelings, mood swings, actions and consequences.
3. How do you tend to express your emotions? Write this down, especially if others complain that you tend to express emotions inappropriately or exaggeratedly.
4. What are the consequences? Does that help you to get your needs met or not? Does it affect your relationships? Does it improve or lower your self-esteem?
5. Work on improving your mood by following the self-help directions for your symptoms of Depression (page 16), Anxiety (page 37) or Panic Attacks (page 46).
6. Do you become overwhelmed by anger or frustration? Write about how you deal with anger. Work on controlling your anger, and how you express it (see page 215). Search for more appropriate ways to express your anger.
7. Do you tend to have problems in life due to your behaviour? Write about this, especially if you tend to behave inappropriately towards others or manipulate them. What are the consequences? Does that help you get your needs met or not? Does it affect your relationships? Does it improve or lower your self-esteem?

8. Keep a log of any problems you have controlling your impulses, and the consequences.

9. Do you tend to have a problem maintaining boundaries with other people? Learn everything you can about boundary-keeping, and learn ways to improve your maintenance of appropriate boundaries with everyone in your life.

10. Practise self-assertion (see page 38).

11. Work on improving your self-esteem (see page 105).

12. Keep a log of any cutting or self-destructive behaviours, and try to write down why you engage in them. Are they designed to punish you? To redirect the pain from your mind to your body? Do they contain a message? Are you re-enacting something that someone else did to you? Write down your feelings.

13. Replace self-destructive behaviour with self-nurturing behaviour. Most importantly, if you are engaging in self-injury, you need to stop. Get help.

14. Write down details of your fears about being abandoned.

15. Reduce your stress (see page 19).

16. Meditate (see exercises page 40 and 127).

17. Practise Progressive Body Relaxation (see page 41).

18. Eat regular, balanced meals.

19. Exercise.

20. Do not drink alcohol or abuse any kind of drugs.

21. Join a healthy self-help group, community project or charity committee and see it through.

22. Join a team of people working towards healthy goals, such as a sports team, and stick with it.

23. Try to notice when you have unrealistic expectations of other people and work on modulating that tendency. Also work on forming more balanced opinions of people (that is, neither 'all good' nor 'all bad' but a combination of positive and negative attributes).

24. Seek the company of people who are mentally healthy and do not abuse drugs or alcohol.

25. No matter how abandoned you might feel by someone, try to stop yourself retaliating, either by pushing them away, punishing them or abusing them verbally or physically.

26. You tend to see things in black or white – try to see the grey. This also applies to relationships. Try to understand that, while your tendency may be to think of people as either good or bad (often flipping between

idealizing them and devaluing them) the majority of people and human interactions exist in the grey areas.

27. Set up a support system of trustworthy people who keep good boundaries.
28. Take responsibility for your own life, treatment compliance, general well-being and actions towards others.
29. Know you are not alone – many people suffer from Borderline Personality Disorder. Be patient and persistent with your journey to better mental health.
30. Foster your spirituality.

when someone close to you has borderline personality disorder

1. Suicide threats should always be taken seriously.
2. Remove all weapons or potentially harmful substances (including prescription medications that could be used for a lethal overdose).
3. Learn to set boundaries with the person who has Borderline Personality Disorder, and encourage the development of his or her responsibility.
4. Remind yourself that 'borderline behaviour' is not about you.
5. Remind yourself that it's OK to disagree with a person who has the Borderline Personality Disorder.
6. Work on improving your own sense of self-worth (see page 105).
7. Know that you cannot assume responsibility for a person with the Borderline Personality Disorder without undermining your own mental health. Make sure you have the telephone numbers of mental-health practitioners who are professionally responsible for this person.
8. Since people with the disorder have fears of abandonment, it is vital to express commitment to the relationship if you wish to maintain it.
9. Get extensive education about the disorder and how it impacts on partners and family.
10. Protect yourself, and do not allow the person suffering with Borderline Personality Disorder to abuse you either verbally or physically.
11. Establish your own support system.
12. Seek therapy for yourself and the family.

helpful books

Borderline Personality Disorder Demystified: An Essential Guide to Understanding and Living with BPD, R. O. Friedel. New York: Marlow & Company, 2004.

Stop Walking on Eggshells: Taking Your Life Back When Someone You Care About Has Borderline Personality Disorder, P. T. Mason and R. Kreger. Oakland, Calif.: New Harbinger Publications, 1998.

Character Styles, S. J. Johnson. New York: W.W. Norton & Co., 1994.

I Hate You – Don't Leave Me, J. Kreisman and H. Straus. New York: Avon Books, 1989.

Skin Game, C. Kettlewell. New York: St Martin's Press, 1999.

Borderline Personality Disorder: A Patient's Guide to Taking Control, G. Fusco and A. Freeman. New York: W.W. Norton & Company, 2004.

New Hope for People with Borderline Personality Disorder, N. Bocktian. New York: Prima Publishing 2002.

Sometimes I Act Crazy: Living with Borderline Personality Disorder, J. J. Kreisman and H. Straus. Hoboken, N.J.: John Wiley & Sons, Inc., 2004.

Lost in the Mirror: An Inside Look at Borderline Personality Disorder, R. Moskovitz. Lanham: MD.: Taylor Trade Publishing, 2006.

The Stop Walking on Eggshells Workbook: Practical Strategies for Living with Someone Who Has Borderline Personality Disorder, R. Kreger with J. Shirley. Oakland, Calif.: New Harbinger Publishers, 2002.

Hope for Parents: Helping Your Borderline Son or Daughter without Sacrificing Your Family or Yourself, K. Winkler and R. Kreger. Milwaukee, Wis.: Eggshell Press, 1999.

Boundaries: When to Say YES, How to Say NO, to Take Control of Your Life, H. Cloud and J. Townsend. Grand Rapids, Mich.: Zondervan Publishing House, 1995.

The Verbally Abusive Relationship: How to Recognize It and How To Respond, P. Evans. Holbrook, Mass.: Adams Media Corporation, 1996.

histrionic (overly flamboyant) personality disorder

Being flamboyant or dramatic in everyday life is not necessarily a problem. People with such attributes often attract the desired audience and give the impression of having a fun-filled life. But for some people, displays of extroversion and attention-getting ploys are desperate attempts to fill a painful gap in their lives. Without the ability to be the centre of attention they feel lost, abandoned and worthless. This disorder is based on painful trauma.

In childhood, such people never received the kind of genuine acceptance for their emerging selves that is every child's need and right, and they were usually exploited. Their parents or carers failed them in some important way, either because they sexually abused them, placed them in an inappropriate triangle of affections (for example, rivalry between mother and daughter for father's affections) or exploited their natural curiosity about sexuality. Without their needs for nurturance and affection being met appropriately, such children may grow up with an overly dramatic style of emotional expression. Many are women who played the role of 'Daddy's little girl' to a seductive father.

In adulthood the helpless and often irresponsible behaviour of those with Histrionic Personality Disorder motivates others to patronize or try to control them, but this is a no-win situation; at some point, they usually turn on their 'father figures' for treating them thus. Many feel evil, guilty, angry, needy and sad, and are prone to depression. Just like Patrick (see opposite) they need help to heal from their trauma so that they can give up trying to get their own way through flirting and manipulation, and become respected and respectful adults.

case study: Patrick

Patrick was a very entertaining person – so much so that I had to be careful not to allow his charm to interfere with our therapy work. The first day I met him he announced that he had found the 'love of his life', a man who worked in a retail store next door to Patrick's hairdressing salon. The following week he told me his heart had been broken and sobbed for five minutes before announcing that he was now dating another man, whom he also judged to be the 'love of his life'. To the world, Patrick presented a picture of glowing confidence, but beneath his tanned features and dramatic re-enactment, it was a different story. As Patrick provided extremely amusing details of the fling he'd had that past week, I realized that although his charisma and personality drew people to him, underneath he felt empty and unfulfilled.

Two years earlier, Patrick had married a woman to please his parents, but could not sustain the sham of a heterosexual marriage. He was depressed, anxious, self-destructive (having unprotected anal sex) and suffering from the negative effects of early trauma: sexual abuse by a family friend, an uncle and a member of the clergy in his home town. Patrick responded well to hypnosis, and began to heal from the events of his traumatic childhood. It was very hard for him to re-experience the pain of those early days, but over several years he did very well and even made a choice to confront one of his abusers. He was able to reconnect with his estranged family and began to maintain solid and supportive romantic relationships. At the present time he is considering adopting a child with a man he married in a civil ceremony.

is this you (or someone close to you)?

- You need to be the centre of attention.
- Are extremely flirtatious.
- Freely express rapidly switching emotions.
- Dress and groom to attract a lot of attention.
- Have a dramatic way of speaking that lacks detail.
- Are theatrical in self-expression.
- Suggestible.
- Imagine being closer to people than is accurate.

Are you like this? Or do others think you are like this? It takes an awful lot of energy to have to get your needs met this way, and I know you are doing it because of a very painful wound that has left you feeling insecure and needy. Perhaps deep down you do not believe people will accept you for who you are if you fail to be seductive with them. Feeling that you need to be the life of the party at all times is interfering with what you really need to do and achieve for yourself. Even if you are a professional performer (and many people like you find a natural 'home' in the theatre or on screen) you need time to just be. Consider seeking help to get yourself off the imaginary stage and into conscious, adult living.

'do not pass go' signs

People with Histrionic Personality Disorder give the appearance of being sexually confident through their flirtatious style and seductiveness, and they have highly romantic notions of love and marriage. They are lively, dramatic and often charming but tend to be unable to sustain emotional intimacy, so for them, long-term relationships are harder to achieve and are often dysfunctional. They alienate others by their manipulative behaviour, exaggeration and their expectation that they should always be the centre of attention. Other people tend to perceive them as shallow, lacking in genuineness, demanding and overly dependent. They crave attention, excitement, new experiences and instant gratification, which may create relational, vocational, social, legal and familial chaos. Their relationships are often impaired because they rapidly exhaust their partners with their neediness. When they are rejected they become depressed and at risk of suicide.

what causes histrionic personality disorder?

There is some overlap between Histrionic Personality Disorder and both Narcissistic and Borderline Personality Disorders, and they may have similar underlying causes. Some studies have suggested that these disorders are related to early childhood deprivation, to separation or alienation from one or both parents, and to early physical, sexual, emotional and verbal abuse. They may also have genetic, biological and psychosocial factors. All three of these Personality Disorders tend to run in families. Just like Narcissistic Personality Disorder, Histrionic Personality Disorder is associated with Depression, Anxiety, Substance Abuse, Eating Disorders, Gambling Disorder and Bipolar Disorder.

which treatments are likely to work?

Psychodynamic psychotherapy, psychoanalytic psychotherapy or psychoanalysis are recommended. If Depression or Anxiety is also present, treatment that includes antidepressant or anti-Anxiety medication is often appropriate.

best course of action?

Seek psychotherapy from a trained, qualified professional.

in the meantime what can you do?

1. Learn everything you can about Histrionic Personality Disorder (see reading list below).
2. What is it really like to be you? What is it like to crave attention so much? Write down your answers.
3. Write about your childhood experiences. Write down your feelings about your relationships with everyone in your family and the formative experiences that may have shaped the way you feel about the world.
4. Find a picture of yourself as a child. Write down your feelings as you look at this picture. Back then, what was it like to be you?
5. When you feel the need to engage in an extravagant emotional display, try to write down your feelings instead.
6. When you feel the need to be the centre of attention, try to avoid that impulse. Instead, sit quietly and notice what it feels like. Write down your feelings, then begin to practise tolerating what happens inside when you give someone else the floor. Set yourself personal goals to increase the time you can be the 'audience' rather than be 'onstage'.
7. Try to become more aware of the discrepancy between how you appear on the outside (looking good, confident, sexy) versus (feeling empty, bereft, needy) on the inside. Write down your feelings and thoughts about this.
8. Try to become aware of your seductive behaviour. How does it serve you? Does it help or hinder relationships? Does it help or hinder your ability to get your true needs met? Does it help or hinder your self-esteem? Write down your answers.
9. Watch out for your safety. You may not even be aware of how your seductive qualities may make you vulnerable to further abuse or sexual exploitation.
10. Try to let go of some of your tendencies to be exhibitionistic, overly expressive and impressionistic. Catch yourself by finding a way to record one or two of your conversations without being too aware of it (you'll probably need someone else's help with this). Then play it back and ask for feedback from someone who pays more attention to detail. For example, you may hear yourself say 'There were millions of people at the party.' Truth? There were roughly thirty.
11. Join a charity drive and allow someone else to be at the forefront or in charge without trying to put yourself in the limelight. Whenever you

find it difficult not to be the centre of attention, practise breathing and relaxation (see pages 46 and 41).

12. Practise taking responsibility for your own actions. Try to avoid always looking round for someone else to blame.

13. Try not to act helpless, or allow others to control you – even if part of you seems to want this.

14. Work on becoming more emotionally controlled. See breathing technique, page 46.

15. Work on becoming more thoughtful and reflective. Writing down your thoughts is a good way to do this.

16. Work on taking more responsibility for your own emotional reactions, that is, try to be more in tune with the feelings of others and not expect them to pick up the pieces when you are having a bad day.

17. Try to resist the urge to have a tantrum or some other type of broad emotional display as a means of controlling others. Catch yourself as you are about to cry, shout or pout and stop yourself. This is the NIC technique: Notice, Interrupt and Change (see page 48). Replace that display of emotion with a more appropriate approach. You will find you can get your needs met best by the direct expression of reasonable requests. Try to avoid being manipulative in any of your usual ways.

18. Work on becoming more organized. Write down three areas of your life that may need to be better structured and find ways to create some order.

19. Notice your thoughts, especially the negative ones you have about yourself, such as 'I am evil' or 'If I'm not the centre of attention I am nothing'. Write them down and ask for honest feedback ('Do you think this is true about me?') from a trusted friend or relative. Do not punish or criticize anyone who provides constructive criticism.

20. Increase your self-knowledge by writing down and completing the following: 'I think of myself as . . .', 'I am always afraid of . . .', 'I wish . . .'

21. Learn to be more self-assertive (see page 38).

22. Work on anger management (see page 213).

23. Reduce your stress (see page 19).

24. Meditate (see exercises page 40 and 127).

25. Practise Progressive Body Relaxation (see page 41).

26. Eat regular, balanced meals.

27. Exercise.

28. Do not abuse alcohol or drugs or engage in overeating, overspending or any other activities that you might use to cover up painful feelings. Get help for any of these that have become problematic.

when someone close to you has histrionic personality disorder

1. Encourage the sufferer to seek therapy. He or she is likely to be interested in doing so if you present it the right way, such as 'I sense that you have a unique personality style that only someone with very special qualifications could understand. Why don't you give yourself a chance to be listened to seriously and to have the special attention you deserve?'

2. Be careful not to put the sufferer down for being 'over-dramatic'.

3. If the sufferer is depressed, severely anxious, abusing alcohol or drugs, or has a shopping, gambling or eating problem it is important to try to motivate him or her to seek mental-health treatment. However, rather than say 'You have a drug problem so you need to get help', use the approach outlined above.

4. Remember that people with Histrionic Personality Disorder are very manipulative. Set limits to avoid being 'used' by the sufferer.

5. Try to be aware that what you see on the surface of people with Histrionic Personality Disorder is very different from who they are underneath. Be compassionate and respectful of their very considerable pain.

6. People with Histrionic Personality Disorder are often overly seductive with everyone. Usually, they are not really trying to go to bed with whoever they are talking to, so if you are in a relationship with a sufferer try not to take it personally. However, this need to be flirtatious will not improve until they are undergoing therapy.

7. Encourage the sufferer to reduce his or her stress.

8. Encourage the sufferer to engage in physical exercise, to meditate (see page 40), practise relaxation (see page 41) and eat balanced, nutritious meals.

9. Being in a relationship or family with someone who has Histrionic Personality Disorder can be very difficult, because they can be very cajoling and manipulative. It can also be very draining to feel that you always have to pick up the pieces when they act irresponsibly or inappropriately. Take care of your own (and your family's) physical and mental health, and seek therapy for yourself.

helpful books

Character Styles, S. J. Johnson. New York: W.W. Norton & Co., 1994.
The Drama of the Gifted Child, A. Miller. New York: Basic Books, 1997.

narcissistic personality disorder

In our culture, people who promote themselves are often despised. 'He's so in love with himself!' is the kind of judgemental comment that is often made about a person who seems to spend an inordinate amount of energy boasting about accomplishments, eliciting admiration and demanding special treatment. Just as Narcissus of Greek mythology was entranced by his own reflection in a pool of water, so people with Narcissistic Personality Disorder are frantically searching to be flatteringly reflected by others. But the need to do this is rooted in intensely acute psychological pain that originates in childhood. As children are developing, they need to be appreciated for who they truly are.

As children are developing, some parents or carers are unable to provide this kind of parenting because they are too self-involved, busy, depressed, absent or ill to support fully a child's need to develop a strong sense of self. These children learn that they cannot be themselves, but instead must try to be whatever the parent or carer needs them to be. This is a terrible burden for a child, who often develops a 'false self' in order to try to be accepted and loved. Underneath there are feelings of unworthiness, desperation and shame that lead to the development of a tragic and often lifelong search to be bolstered by others. If a person with Narcissistic Personality Disorder is lucky enough to receive help for the original trauma he or she can be released from this search and can move on into a less painful existence – just like Ross.

case study: Ross

Ross was a junior doctor at a large hospital in the centre of town. He came to me complaining that he was depressed and unhappy in his work. The long hours and lack of staff, he said, made him irritable. He had been accused of being 'impossible to work with' by some of the nursing staff, and had recently been told frankly by a supervisor that he was perceived as arrogant, uncaring and boastful.

Ross had been the only child of a single woman who was very self-involved. She expected Ross to fulfil many of her needs, even when he was a small child, so he had grown up feeling more like her partner than her child. When other children were out playing together he was running errands for her, or keeping her company while she engaged in her favourite and most frequent activity – TV shopping.

When Ross came to see me I realized that he was very interested in pleasing me. He wanted to be a 'model patient' – just as he had tried so hard to be a model child for his mother. But her lack of attention left him craving for love and seeking it elsewhere, and had resulted in a personality style where he was constantly in need of admiration and approval. Ross also suffered from an underlying Depression. He was in danger of losing his job, so urgent treatment was necessary. It was hard for him to understand why others perceived him so negatively, and I had to be very careful not to inadvertently hurt his feelings (people with Narcissistic Personality Disorder are extremely sensitive to criticism). Nevertheless, occasionally he had to learn to tolerate negative feedback from co-workers, since that was part of the culture of his workplace. After a 'quick fix' to stabilize his work situation, we worked on his childhood trauma and resultant Depression. As he began to mourn his 'lost' childhood fully, he slowly became less needy of outside bolstering and better able to connect with others in a genuine way.

is this you (or someone close to you)?

- You feel you are a very important person and would like others to recognize your superiority.
- Are always imagining yourself as famous, powerful, brilliant and irresistible.
- Believe you are very special and should only be surrounded by other unique people.
- Need to be admired.
- Expect to receive special treatment.
- Sometimes take advantage of others to get what you want.
- Don't have empathy for the feelings and needs of others.
- Are envious of others.
- Are sometimes accused of being arrogant.

If you have the above traits, you are almost certainly covering up an enormous amount of pain. You are largely misunderstood, because others will not recognize your struggle. It's a shame the word 'narcissism' is used to describe you, because that has become a pejorative term. Underneath, I know you are struggling with shame, humiliation and a terrible sense of worthlessness. All your strivings to be perfect and highly successful, to promote yourself, and get others to recognize how special you are and treat you accordingly are because you feel deep down that you need to protect your very being. You have what feels like a huge, open wound in your psyche, and, when people criticize or fail to appreciate you it feels like they are rubbing salt into that wound. This is such a difficult burden for you and you deserve to be helped. A good therapist will understand you and help release you from your 'prison' of trauma and need.

'do not pass go' signs

Narcissism is a very painful condition, and people with this disorder experience a high level of emotional torment. They spend a significant amount of time trying to nurse the acute psychological injuries they sustain when they receive even slight criticism. Their grandiose style, lack of empathy for others and feeling that they are entitled to special privileges alienates people around them, so they frequently experience difficulty maintaining relationships, family ties, social contacts and jobs. They strive for power, acclaim, wealth and prestige, and may be willing to manipulate people and events to achieve their ends. Despite appearances, they have a very fragile sense of self-esteem, with underlying feelings of humiliation and shame.

Narcissistic Personality Disorder is associated with Depression, Anxiety, Substance Abuse, Eating Disorders, Gambling Disorder and Bipolar Disorder.

what causes narcissistic personality disorder?

It is thought to arise from physical, emotional or sexual abuse. People with Narcissistic Personality Disorder have survived emotional deprivation in childhood that lowers their self-esteem. They are subsequently condemned to boosting their self-image by constantly soliciting approval from outside sources, even though this only invites further painful criticism from others. The disorder may run in families, especially since a person with an untreated Narcissistic Personality Disorder will probably parent children in a manner similar to that which created his or her disorder in the first place.

which treatments are likely to work?

Psychodynamic psychotherapy can be particularly useful to help heal narcissistic wounds and the trauma that caused them. It can also help to elevate a person's sense of worth. If Depression or Anxiety is also present, adding antidepressant or anti-Anxiety medication is sometimes appropriate.

best course of action?

Seek psychotherapy or psychoanalysis from a trained, qualified professional.

in the meantime what can you do?

1. Learn everything you can about Narcissistic Personality Disorder (see reading list below).

2. Write about your childhood experiences. Write down your feelings about your relationships with everyone in your family and the formative experiences that may have shaped the way you feel about the world.

3. Find a picture of yourself as a child. Write down your feelings as you look at this picture. What was it like to be you back then?

4. Focus on your deep pain. Try to write about your feelings, needs and thoughts about it.

5. Write about your experiences of trying hard to please your parents or carers. How did you do that? What did they need you to be, and how did that differ from who you felt yourself to be inside? What were the feelings that went along with that?

6. Notice the thoughts you have these days, especially the deep, negative ones you have about yourself, such as 'I am unlovable unless people prove I'm OK by admiring me.' Write these down and ask for feedback (such as 'Do you think this is true about me?') from a trusted friend or relative. Try to tolerate the answer.

7. Increase your self-understanding by writing down and completing the following: 'I think of myself as ...', 'I am always afraid of ...', 'I wish ...'

8. Work on letting go of some of your self-aggrandizement and competitiveness by imagining yourself in other people's shoes. Write down your attempts to do so and your feelings about this.

9. Practise listening to others talking about themselves without sharing your own views or experiences. Simply reflect back their experiences and feelings with comments like 'That must have been hard/uncomfortable/great for you.'

10. Practise being honest with others.

11. Practise giving compliments to others.

12. Practise keeping appointments and being on time.

13. Work on sharing more with others and being able to be part of a group. Join a charity drive and allow others to lead without trying to self-aggrandize. When you find it difficult not to be receiving praise, practise breathing and relaxation (see pages 46 and 41)

14. Consider the expectations and standards you set for yourself and others. Is it possible that you often set the bar too high? How do you feel when you or others fail to meet those standards? Write down your thoughts and feelings about this.

15. How do you feel when people criticize you? Write down your feelings.
16. How do you feel when people are insensitive to your needs? Write down your feelings.
17. Create a visualization to protect you from the pain of being wounded by criticism or lack of appreciation. Imagine you are surrounded by some kind of invisible, protective shell (you invent your own special type; for example, dome, plastic bubble or suit of armour). Imagine that protective shell being able to ward off emotional injuries and attacks. Use this visualization whenever you feel particularly vulnerable.
18. Read *The Drama of the Gifted Child* by Alice Miller. You will gain great insight from it.
19. Work on self-assertion (see page 38).
20. Work on anger management (see page 213).
21. Reduce your stress (see page 19).
22. Meditate (see exercises page 40 and 127).
23. Practise Progressive Body Relaxation (see page 41)
24. Eat regular, balanced, nutritious meals and get plenty of good-quality sleep.
25. Exercise in a manner that is appropriate for your age, state of health and physical ability.
26. Do not drink alcohol or take non-prescription drugs. These will exacerbate your disorder and slow down or prevent the healing process.
27. If you 'self-medicate' your pain with substances, eating, shopping, sex or by any other methods, recognize this and seek help for it.

when someone close to you has narcissistic personality disorder

1. Encourage the person to seek therapy. He or she is only likely to be interested in doing so if you present it the right way, such as 'I sense that you have some very unique issues that only someone with very special qualifications could understand. Why don't you give yourself a chance to have the special focus you deserve?'
2. Be careful not to put the person down for being 'self-involved'.
3. If the sufferer is also depressed, anxious, abusing alcohol or drugs, has a gambling problem or seems to have an Eating Disorder it is important to try to motivate him or her to seek mental-health treatment for those issues. However, using the above approach would be better than saying, 'You have a drug problem so you need to get help.'
4. Remember that people with Narcissistic Personality Disorder are very

sensitive to criticism. Their defences will rise very quickly if you do not approach them the right way.

5. Try to be aware that what you see on the surface of people with Narcissistic Personality Disorder is very different from who they are underneath. Be respectful of their very considerable pain.

6. Alice Miller's marvellous book *The Drama of the Gifted Child* will provide a fantastically helpful insight for people with Narcissistic Personality Disorder as well as for people close to them. Read it, and encourage the sufferer to do so too.

7. People with Narcissistic Personality Disorder often find it hard to show interest or empathy for others. Don't take it personally, but know that this will not improve until the person is undergoing therapy.

8. Encourage the sufferer to reduce his or her stress.

9. Encourage the sufferer to engage in physical exercise, to meditate (see page 40), practise relaxation (see page 41) and eat balanced, nutritious meals.

10. Being in a relationship or family with someone who has Narcissistic Personality Disorder can be very difficult, because they can be very manipulative and may lack any ability to be genuinely empathic and giving. It can be very draining to feel that you always have to flatter, bolster and provide positive feedback, especially for someone who does not return the favour. Take care of your own (and your family's) physical and mental health.

helpful books

The Drama of the Gifted Child, Alice Miller. New York: Basic Books, 1997.

Character Styles, S. J. Johnson. New York: W.W. Norton & Co., 1994. *Children of the Self-Absorbed: A Grown-Up's Guide to Getting over Narcissistic Parents*, N. Brown. Oakland, Calif.: New Harbinger Publications, 2001.

Loving the Self-Absorbed: How to Create a More Satisfying Relationship with a Narcissistic Partner, N. Brown. Oakland, Calif.: New Harbinger Publications, 2003.

Trapped in the Mirror: Adult Children of Narcissists in Their Struggle for Self, E. Golomb. New York: Quill, 1992.

avoidant personality disorder

Some children do not grow up being supported in their social interactions or helped to feel confident. Others are naturally shy, and, as a result, have early experiences of being made to feel embarrassed or ashamed of their social 'inadequacies'. Sometimes this happens when the parents themselves function well socially and expect their children to follow suit automatically. But everyone is different, and it is traumatic for a child to be expected to be something he or she is not. The painful memory of a 'disastrous' social experience can compound a child's problems, and if it is severe enough or it happens often enough a child may come to decide that, for his or her own protection, the best strategy is to avoid people as much as possible. That is what happened to Sam.

case study: Sam

Sam would like to be able to participate comfortably in social events like his brother Jimmy, but he feels that will never happen. He is terribly afraid that he is inadequate in many ways, and that he will be rejected by people if he tries to approach them. Consequently he stays way from having social contact with others, and even chooses jobs that allow him to work in isolation. He currently works a night shift, checking on machinery at a printing firm, which means he rarely needs to interact with anyone. In a way, this suits him very well, because talking to people produces great Anxiety. Recently, Sam was referred to a therapist by his GP who noticed that he seemed depressed. It took Sam several weeks to make an appointment, but he eventually summoned the courage and began a therapeutic relationship with a man who seemed to understand the difficulty he had relating to people. Sam was told it may take some time for him to become comfortable in social situations, but he is now hopeful about the possibility of achieving his mother's fondest wish – that he should start dating and eventually marry.

is this you (or someone close to you)?

- You dislike being in contact with others, either socially, vocationally or in close relationships, because you are afraid you will be rejected, criticized, shamed or ridiculed.
- In social situations, you are constantly worried about being rejected or criticized.

- Feel inhibited when you meet new people because you do not feel adequate.
- Feel unattractive and inferior to others.
- Rarely take social risks or try new things in case they cause embarrassment.

If you fit this description and avoid social situations even though you would like to be successful in them, know that you can be helped. It is most unfortunate that you suffered painful experiences in the past that understandably led you to this way of being, but the fact that you would like to be better at handling relationships and social situations is a good thing. I recommend that through treatment you give yourself a chance to prove that you can be more comfortable around others.

'do not pass go' signs

People with Avoidant Personality Disorder suffer distress in both wanting and fearing interpersonal relationships. Fear of intimacy and commitment prevents them from becoming close to others. They sometimes form what appear to be solid relationships, but they often tire of them, leave abruptly and end up often devastating their partners/victims. People with Avoidant Personality Disorder experience social distress and self-contempt, and have a tendency towards Depression and hypomania. The disorder can be particularly disabling in adolescence, when normal development requires social interaction. But treatment can help sufferers overcome their commitment fears and develop lasting, intimate relationships.

what causes avoidant personality disorder?

Avoidant Personality Disorder may start with childhood shyness and fear of being in new situations. There seems to be a connection with social phobia, and the two disorders have certain criteria in common. Sometimes such avoidance takes an acute form with physiological symptoms (as in social phobia) and sometimes it becomes an ingrained part of a person's personality structure. In adulthood, having a full-blown Avoidant Personality Disorder can seriously hamper a person's ability to take his or her place in the world.

which treatments are likely to work?

Psychodynamic psychotherapy, cognitive-behavioural therapy, social skills training, assertiveness training can all be helpful. If Depression or Anxiety is present, antidepressant or anti-Anxiety medications may also be appropriate.

best course of action?
Seek psychotherapy from a trained, qualified professional.

in the meantime what can you do?
1. Learn everything you can about Avoidant Personality Disorder (see reading list below).
2. What is your world like? Do you feel safe? Unsafe? Ambivalent? Write down your feelings and thoughts.
3. What are your fears? Write down all your feelings about the prospect of being rejected and other fears you have regarding being socially connected to other people.
4. What are loneliness and isolation like for you? Write down your feelings.
5. Write about your childhood experiences. Write down your feelings about your relationships with everyone in your family and the formative experiences that may have shaped the way you feel about the world.
6. Find a picture of yourself as a child. Write down your feelings as you look at this picture. What was it like to be you back then?
7. Work on letting go of some of your social vulnerability, inhibition and avoidance by attempting to tolerate a short period of time in a social situation. Notice your feelings and write them down.
8. Try to bring yourself to join some kind of regular social event, such as a book club. Choose something relatively easy to start with. When you notice your desire to back out, tolerate the feelings of discontent and stay. Write down your feelings about the experience.
9. Practise breathing and relaxation (see pages 46 and 41, to help you tolerate the Anxiety and desire to avoid getting close to others.
10. In order to help you become more gregarious, learn self-assertion (see page 38).
11. Practise tolerating constructive criticism. Invite some feedback about your interpersonal skills from someone you can trust to be honest without being cruel. Listen carefully, while breathing deeply to reduce your Anxiety. Do not respond with defensiveness. Instead, thank the person for the feedback.
12. Take a social skills class if possible. If not, work on improving your interpersonal skills by practising:
    - Initiating conversation with others.
    - Giving compliments.
    - Accepting compliments.
    - Being assertive in your communication.

- Making sure you keep appointments.
- Being on time for social events.
- Being honest.
- Self-disclosing to an appropriate degree.
- Being able to set boundaries with others.
- Maintaining eye contact.
- Giving oneself and others an appropriate amount of personal space.
- Learning to deal with criticism.
- Learning to deal with teasing.

13. Notice your thoughts, especially the negative ones you have about yourself, such as 'I will always be rejected' or 'If people knew the real me they wouldn't like me.' Write them down, and ask for feedback (such as 'Do you think this is true about me?') from a trusted friend or relative.
14. Notice the negative thoughts you have about getting close to others. Practise the thought-stopping exercise (see page 39).
15. Increase your self-knowledge by writing down and completing the following: 'I think of myself as ...', 'I am always afraid of ...', 'I wish ...'
16. Identify your wishful thinking. Complete the sentence, 'If only ... then I would be happy.'
17. Take social skills training.
18. Learn assertiveness training.
19. Reduce your stress (see page 19).
20. Meditate (see exercises on pages 40 and 127).
21. Practise Progressive Body Relaxation (see page 41).
22. Eat regular, balanced meals and get plenty of good-quality sleep.
23. Engage in appropriate physical exercise.
24. Do not attempt to assuage your discomfort about being around other people by drinking alcohol or taking drugs.

when someone close to you has avoidant personality disorder

1. He or she is unlikely to seek therapy. If you feel it is necessary, that is, if the person is depressed, anxious, abusing substances or struggling with interpersonal or vocational problems as a result of this personality disorder, try to motivate him or her to seek mental-health treatment. Be careful not to put the person down for being 'antisocial'.
2. People with Avoidant Personality Disorder are deeply worried about being put in social situations. Don't take it personally when they refuse to go to a dinner party or family event. However, if they do go, work

extra hard to create a sense of safety. For example, be very clear about what will be expected of them (hopefully nothing much), who will be attending, the format of the evening and so on.

3. Encourage the sufferer to reduce his or her stress. This is essential, because the anxiety experienced by a person with Avoidant Personality Disorder can be overwhelming.

4. Encourage the sufferer to engage in physical exercise, to meditate (see page 40), practise relaxation (see page 41) and eat balanced, nutritious meals.

5. A number of people with Avoidant Personality Disorder end up being socially marginalized and living out their lives alone. Consider this concern in your contact with this person, and support his or her attempts to achieve lifetime stability.

6. Being in a relationship or family with someone who has Avoidant Personality Disorder can be difficult and stressful. Take care of your (and your family's) physical and mental health.

helpful books

Character Styles, S. J. Johnson. New York: W.W. Norton & Co., 1994.

Don't Say Yes When You Want to Say No, H. and B. Fensterheim. New York: David McKay, 1975.

Five Weeks to Healing Stress: The Wellness Option, V. O'Hara. Oakland, Calif.: New Harbinger Publications, 1996.

Healing Fear: New Approaches to Overcoming Anxiety, E. Bourne. Oakland, Calif.: New Harbinger Publications Inc., 1988.

The Relaxation and Stress Reduction Workbook, M. Davis, E. R. Eshelman and M. McKay. Oakland, Calif.: New Harbinger Publications, 2000.

dependent personality disorder

Have you ever come across a couple where every time you ask one partner a question the other one answers? Some adults have never formed a strong sense of self and spend their lives living in the shadow of another. There is a point in children's development when they need to become individuated, or sufficiently psychologically separated from their parents in order to develop their own individual selves. This is most obvious when they start using the word 'No!'. But sometimes this natural attempt to achieve normal developmental autonomy and experience themselves as separate from their parents is not possible because the parents are too anxious or insecure to allow it. In fact, some children are punished for seeking it. Thus they grow up feeling that any kind of autonomy or independent thinking, feeling or behaviour will be extremely risky. As adults they will attach themselves to others who do all the hard work of living for them. They make all the decisions and provide clues about what they 'should' or 'should not' be thinking, feeling or doing. Their passivity will remain intact unless they receive the help they need to discover finally who they really are and what they really want in life.

case study: George

George, thirty-two-years-old, lives with his mother. He nearly married his girlfriend Cynthia two years ago, but his mother insisted he break off the engagement. Her objections to Cynthia were based on her belief that she was 'too bossy', but, in fact, it is George's mother who is the demanding one. Used to getting her own way, she rules the household by force and manipulation, and neither George nor his father can stand up to her. George's personality style has become one of compliance and fear of self-reliance. Despite his adult status he still cannot bear the thought of losing his mother's support and approval because that might mean he would have to fend for himself. He makes few decisions without her, and his life continues to revolve around her. Recently, George met another woman, Lydia, to whom he was strongly attracted. After they had been dating for a couple of months Lydia asked George to come with her to see her therapist. During that session, George began to have an inkling about his dependency issues and agreed to have individual therapy to explore them. Lydia is still hopeful that George will break free from his mother's clutches and strike out into a more independent life that may include marriage to her.

is this you (or someone close to you)?

- You need others to help you make decisions.
- Pass the responsibility for most things in your life on to other people.
- Hate to disagree with anyone in case they stop liking you.
- Don't trust yourself to undertake projects or carry out tasks on your own.
- Do anything, including things you hate, in order to get others to be nice to you.
- Dislike being alone because it makes you feel nervous and helpless.
- Spend a lot of time worrying about what would happen if you had to take care of yourself.

If the above set of symptoms rings bells for you, you may have developed a Dependent Personality Disorder. Somehow or other in your early life you did not receive the encouragement you needed to be a truly independent person with a separate, clear-cut identity, and that is why you rely so much on others. It may seem to you that it would be incredibly dangerous to step out of the shadows of dependency and move into a life of more autonomous living – but with help you could do it. You deserve the gift of being helped to find out who you truly are as a unique individual and have the chance to be the architect of your own life.

'do not pass go' signs

People with Dependent Personality Disorder lack self-confidence, and find it hard to make decisions. They believe themselves to be weak, incompetent and needing to rely on others to survive. They defer to those upon whom they depend and rarely take independent, self-initiated actions. They experience considerable difficulty in all their relationships, at work, in academic or social settings. They feel uncomfortable when they are alone and have a low sense of self-worth, so they rely on others to the extent that they are vulnerable to abuse by people who perceive them to be easy targets. They become extremely anxious when they think the people on whom they depend may reject or abandon them, and they may also experience Depression, Panic Disorder and Somatic Distress.

what causes dependent personality disorder?

Not being given the opportunity to go through a normal separation and individuation process in childhood can lead to this personality disorder. Separation Anxiety and chronic illness in childhood may also indicate a greater likelihood of developing Dependent Personality Disorder.

which treatments are likely to work?

Psychodynamic psychotherapy, psychoanalysis, and cognitive-behavioural psychotherapy are some of the most useful treatments. If Depression or Anxiety is also present, antidepressant or anti-Anxiety medications may be appropriate.

best course of action?

Seek psychotherapy or psychoanalysis from a trained, qualified professional.

in the meantime what can you do?

1. Learn everything you can about Dependent Personality Disorder (see reading list below).

2. Write about your childhood experiences. Write down your feelings about your relationships with everyone in your family and the formative experiences that may have shaped the way you feel about the world.

3. Find a picture of yourself as a child. Write down your feelings as you look at this picture. What was it like to be you back then?

4. Increase your self-knowledge by writing down and completing the following: 'I think of myself as . . .', 'I am always afraid of . . .', 'I wish . . .'

5. What would it be like to be more independent? Write down the feelings this thought creates for you.

6. Work on your self-esteem (see page 105).

7. Try to make a list of all the ways in which you are capable and skilled.

8. Do you suffer from an inner voice that criticizes you? What does it say, and how does it make you feel? Write down your response and the associated feelings.

9. What is it like for you to receive criticism from others? Write down your feelings.

10. What is it like for you to feel that you might be abandoned by someone on whom you depend? How does it affect your life to have those feelings about abandonment? Write down your feelings.

11. How does your sensitivity help or hinder you in the context of your relationships? Write down your thoughts.

12. Try to let go of your tendency always to seek help from others. Instead, work on becoming more self-sufficient. Do this by creating some small goals to work on, such as trying out a hobby you think you'd like that is not shared by your spouse, partner or person on whom you are dependent.

13. Deliberately expose yourself to a step towards independence that creates anxiety for you, such as walking through town alone. Practise tolerating that anxiety, even for five minutes. Slowly build up to a longer period of independent activity.

14. Create a list of five dependency skills to achieve, such as driving a car, going to the shops alone, or choosing to buy a small household or kitchen item without consulting anyone else.

15. Learn to tolerate being alone at times. Every time you are alone and begin to feel that you cannot cope, work on breathing and relaxation (see page 46) and try to sustain it for fifteen minutes longer than usual.

Increase this time slowly until you can manage a whole morning, afternoon or evening alone.

16. Attend an assertiveness training class.
17. Work on improving your social skills by practising:
    - Initiating conversation with others.
    - Giving compliments.
    - Accepting compliments.
    - Being assertive in your communication (see page 38).
    - Making sure you keep appointments.
    - Being on time for social events.
    - Being honest.
    - Self-disclosing to an appropriate degree.
    - Being able to set boundaries with others.
    - Maintaining eye contact.
    - Giving oneself and others an appropriate amount of personal space.
    - Learning to deal with criticism.
    - Learning to deal with teasing.

18. Reduce your stress (see page 19).
19. Meditate (see exercises on page 40 and 127).
20. Practise Progressive Body Relaxation (see page 41).
21. Eat regular, balanced meals.
22. Exercise.
23. Avoid drinking alcohol or taking recreational drugs, especially if you use them to assuage your anxiety about having to rely on yourself.

when someone close to you has dependent personality disorder

1. He or she is unlikely to seek therapy. If you feel it is necessary, that is, if the person is depressed, anxious, abusing substances or struggling with interpersonal or vocational problems, try to motivate them to seek mental-health treatment. Be careful not to put the person down for being 'too passive'.
2. People with Dependent Personality Disorder find it very hard to make decisions by themselves so try to avoid putting words into their mouths. Encourage them to come up with their own ideas and praise any small step towards independent thoughts or behaviour.
3. Encourage the sufferer to reduce his or her stress and anxiety (see page 19 and 38). This is essential, because people with Dependent Personality

Disorder become very worried at the thought of having to be alone or take independent action. They are more likely to be able to do so when they are breathing deeply and their bodies are relaxed.

4. Encourage the sufferer to engage in physical exercise, to meditate (see page 40), and eat balanced, nutritious meals.

5. People with Dependent Personality Disorder are vulnerable to abuse by others. Consider this concern in your contact with this person, and support his or her attempts to achieve lifetime safety and stability.

6. Being in a relationship or family with someone who has Dependent Personality Disorder may mean that you are probably the person on whom he or she depends. Know that it is time for you to help the person stand on his or her own two feet, and try to let go of your tendency to always be adviser, protector and carer.

helpful books

The Dependent Personality, R. F. Bornstein. New York: The Guilford Press, 1993.

Lean On Me: The Power of Positive Dependency in Intimate Relationships, M. Solomon. New York: Kensington, 1996.

Character Styles, S. J. Johnson. New York: W.W. Norton & Co., 1994.

Don't Say Yes When You Want to Say No, H. and B. Fensterheim. New York: David McKay, 1975.

obsessive-compulsive personality disorder

Do you know anyone who is so desperate to do everything perfectly he or she misses the point of why it's being done in the first place? Such a person might qualify for a diagnosis of Obsessive-Compulsive Personality Disorder (which is different from Obsessive-Compulsive Disorder – see page 54). Some children grow up in an over-controlled environment. They are aware their parents love them so they do their best to comply with the strict, rigid and exacting rules they are expected to follow. But their parents, who are far from fun to be around, do not pass on an appreciation for play, sensuality or spontaneity. Instead, their children grow up to be highly perfectionist, inflexible, obstinate, tight-fisted and controlling of others, with deep underlying hostility. Essentially, people with Obsessive-Compulsive Personality Disorder feel they must rigidly hang on to their emotions, bodies, words and feelings or they'll be punished. Others see them as cold, standoffish or distant, but it's more that they are afraid of doing the wrong thing. They have been discouraged from trusting their own feelings so they find it hard to make decisions and they hold on to anger, position and resentment. When it comes to romance, people with Obsessive Compulsive Personality Disorder seem to both love and hate the same person. The good news is that such people can excel in certain fields where precision is paramount – technology, accounting and medicine.

case study: Tim

Tim was an extremely bright thirty-two-year-old man who had attended one of the best universities in the country, and he went on to achieve great success as a lawyer, as others predicted he would. But in his personal and social life Tim functioned poorly. Others viewed him as rigid, inflexible and aloof – except when he had consumed large amounts of alcohol – so he had few friends. He was controlling of the women he dated and they rarely lasted more than a few weeks. One woman named Sally, whom he wanted to marry, felt that he was always angry with her for minor misdemeanours or misunderstandings. She complained that he hung onto his anger for many days, causing her great misery. He never expressed affection towards her, and while their sex life was satisfying for her, it lacked variety, sensuality or warmth. For Tim, the crunch came when Sally left him. He entered therapy to try to understand why. But there were problems in the therapeutic environment, because therapy was another thing Tim was intent on 'doing just right'. It was extremely hard for him to relax or to express emotion. After some time, however, he did learn to relax his body, tolerate his anxiety and risk making mistakes. Others began to give him feedback that he 'seemed more human', and he was even able to consider collaborating with others at work. He became a little more spontaneous and creative in his social life, and finally married a woman who was somewhat obsessive-compulsive herself. The two of them engaged in long-term therapy, partly to avoid the pitfalls of being rigid, authoritarian parents. Tim's career continued to flourish and he went on to make a significant contribution to his field.

is this you (or someone close to you)?

■ You are so obsessed with the details of organizing, such as schedules or rules, that it can become the point of what you are doing rather than the activity itself.

- Are so intent on doing things perfectly you sometimes cannot finish a task for fear it will fall short of your high standards.
- Are so focused on work that you have no time for friends or having fun.
- Others find you rigid and inflexible in your views.
- Find it hard to throw anything away.
- Cannot work with others unless they do it your way.
- Are thought to be quite miserly with money.
- Tend to be stubborn; at least that's how others see you.

If you are a person who qualifies for a diagnosis of Obsessive-Compulsive Personality Disorder, you may not recognize this in yourself. You have spent a lifetime always desperately trying to do the right thing, avoiding mistakes and staying out of trouble. 'Is that a bad thing?' you might well ask. The problem is really the *degree* of your attempts to achieve perfection as well as the absence of spontaneity, flexibility and fun in your life. You are paying a huge price for attending so rigidly to minor details, and as a result your life is devoid of variety, creativity, adventure and discovery. If you could magically let go of your rigidity for one day (without the anxiety that would normally create for you), you would be surprised at the difference it could make in your life. Consider finding ways to be more accepting of the humanness of those around you – and even of yourself.

'do not pass go' signs

The perfectionist ideals in people with Obsessive-Compulsive Disorder lead to many problems. In both work and day-to-day home tasks sufferers can be virtually incapacitated, since their fear of doing a task incorrectly, or falling short of their own very high standards is so intense that it prevents them from completing it. The business of constantly checking for mistakes and paying excessive attention to detail can make a process far longer than necessary. This can create problems at work, as can their preference to either work alone or insist that co-workers adhere to their way of doing things. Their difficulty dealing with situations that demand flexibility hampers them in interpersonal, vocational, academic and social settings. They are rigid and compartmentalizing in their thinking styles and find it hard to be in situations they cannot control. This leads to great anxiety for them, and their quality of life is often seriously compromised. People with Obsessive-Compulsive Personality Disorder see themselves as being highly conscientious and responsible for others as well as themselves. They see themselves as executing tasks in a disciplined and exact way and assume that others should think and behave similarly. They may be constricted in their range of experiences and expression. Romantic relationships can be strained, as individuals with Obsessive-Compulsive Personality Disorder cannot easily express emotion.

what causes obsessive-compulsive personality disorder?

Obsessive-Compulsive Personality Disorder seems to run in families. There may be a genetic component, but it certainly seems to be at least partially created when parents are obsessive-compulsive themselves or have strict, authoritarian parenting styles. The disorder may be associated with Anxiety, Phobias, and Eating Disorders (Obsessive-Compulsive Personality Disorder is frequently seen in people with Bulimia Nervosa). There is disagreement about whether or not it is related to Obsessive-Compulsive Disorder (see page 54).

which treatments are likely to work?

Psychodynamic psychotherapy and cognitive-behavioural psychotherapy, among others, will be helpful. If other disorders such as Depression or Anxiety are also present, antidepressant or anti-Anxiety medications may also be appropriate.

best course of action?

Seek psychotherapy from a trained, qualified professional.

in the meantime what can you do?

1. Learn everything you can about Obsessive-Compulsive Personality Disorder.
2. Where did you get the idea that it's terrible to make a mistake? Think about this for a while, then write down your answer. No one else needs to read what you write, so try to free yourself to just write whatever comes into your head without censoring it. One way to do this is to write with the opposite hand to that with which you normally write.
3. What is it like for you to need to maintain control, responsibility and be perfectly organized? Does it always serve you in your life? At work? In relationships? When does it specifically not serve you? Write down your thoughts and feelings (emphasis on feelings) about all of this.
4. It is important for you to learn to tolerate your anxiety. First study the relaxation and breathing techniques on page 46. Then copy down some sentences from this book, until you inadvertently make a mistake.

Instead of immediately correcting it, allow yourself to try to tolerate the anxiety this produces. Breathe, relax. What was that like for you? Write down your thoughts and feelings – with the emphasis on feelings.

5. What would it be like for you to let go of your need to do everything perfectly and always be in control? Write down the feelings that come up when you imagine this.

6. What is it like to have high expectations of other people? What kind of feedback have you had from others, including romantic partners? Write down your thoughts and feelings.

7. Write about other feelings you frequently feel, such as frustration and anxiety. When do these tend to arise? What are the triggers? How do you cope? Are your coping methods useful or not?

8. Work on self-assertion (see page 38).

9. Work on improving your social skills by practising:
   - Initiating conversation with others.
   - Giving compliments.
   - Accepting compliments.
   - Being assertive in your communication (see page 39).
   - Trying to relax more in social situations.
   - Giving people the benefit of the doubt.
   - Self-disclosing to an appropriate degree.
   - Smiling more at others.
   - Maintaining eye contact.
   - Giving oneself and others an appropriate amount of personal space.
   - Avoiding being critical or having overly high expectations of others.

10. Work on anger management (see page 213).

11. Try to allow yourself to be more playful and spontaneous, for example, go to a cinema without planning which film you are going to see. Make the decision when you get there, and if the timing is not right wander around the facility and have coffee or a snack instead. Practise breathing and relaxation techniques (see pages 46 and 41) when you find yourself becoming anxious.

12. Write about your childhood experiences. Write down your feelings about your relationships with everyone in your family and the formative experiences that may have shaped the way you feel about the world.

13. Find a picture of yourself as a child. Write down your feelings as you look at this picture. What was it like to be you back then?

14. Increase your self-knowledge by writing down and completing the

following: 'I think of myself as ...', 'I am always afraid of ...', 'I wish ...'

15. People with Obsessive-Compulsive Personality Disorder usually hold their bodies very rigidly and sometimes have problems with their joints. You need to engage in a regular physical exercise programme, being sure you stretch well before and after each session. Be sure your programme is appropriate for you given your age, and state of health.

16. Yoga would be very good for you too. Find a class.

17. Reduce your stress (see page 19).

18. Meditate (see exercises on page 40 and 127).

19. Practise Progressive Body Relaxation (see page 41).

20. Eat regular, balanced, nutritious meals.

21. Do not abuse alcohol or drugs.

when someone close to you has obsessive-compulsive personality disorder

1. Encourage the person to seek therapy. He or she is only likely to be interested in doing so if you present it the right way. Try a reasoning approach, such as 'Would you find it useful to learn how to relieve some of the frustration and anxiety you obviously feel when you or others don't meet your expectations?'

2. If the person is depressed, anxious, abusing alcohol or drugs, or has a gambling or Eating Disorder it is important to try to motivate him or her to seek mental-health treatment immediately. However, using the above approach would be better than saying, 'You have a drug problem so you need to get help.'

3. Be careful not to put the person down for being 'uptight'. He or she is that way as a means of self-protection.

4. Remember that people with Obsessive-Compulsive Personality Disorder have a strong need to be in control and be perfectly organized. If you get in the way of those needs you will trigger anxiety and anger.

5. People with Obsessive-Compulsive Personality Disorder often find it hard to let go of anger and resentment. If you are in a relationship with such a person, know that this will not improve until the person is undergoing therapy. Couple's therapy would also be a very good idea.

6. Encourage the sufferer to reduce his or her stress.

7. Encourage the sufferer to engage in physical exercise, to meditate (see page 40), practise relaxation (see page 41) and eat balanced, nutritious meals.

8. Being in a relationship or family with people who have Obsessive-

Compulsive Personality Disorder can be very difficult, because they find it hard to let go and have fun. They can also be irritatingly orderly, stubborn and needful of perfection. It can be very draining to feel that you always have to live up to these standards. Take care of your own (and your family's) physical and mental health.

helpful books

Character Styles, S. J. Johnson. New York: W.W. Norton & Co., 1994.

Meditation for Busy People: 60 Seconds to Serenity, D. Croves. San Rafael, Calif.: New World Library, 1993.

Five Weeks to Healing Stress: The Wellness Option, V. O'Hara. Oakland, Calif.: New Harbinger Publications, 1996.

Healing Fear: New Approaches to Overcoming Anxiety, E. Bourne. Oakland, Calif.: New Harbinger Publications Inc., 1988.

The Relaxation and Stress Reduction Workbook, M. Davis, E. R. Eshelman and M. McKay. Oakland, Calif.: New Harbinger Publications, 2000.

chapter 8
highs and lows: substance abuse

"Father drinks, doesn't he?"

People 'get high' for all kind of reasons: to feel more secure in social situations, to alter their mood either up or down, to make a political statement, to feel part of a group, to enhance athletic performance, to have fun or for spiritual enlightenment. A person's drug of choice very often resonates with his or her psychological state or brain chemistry. For example, a person with undiagnosed Attention-Deficit/Hyperactivity Disorder (see page 264) might gravitate towards stimulants like cocaine because it may actually help him or her to focus better. The trouble is, cocaine is far too strong a stimulant to be safely used to 'medicate' such a disorder. That's like using a chainsaw to kill a bug.

Our society is rich with social drug use. It takes place at cocktail parties, 'raves' or music concerts. At best, the use of alcohol, for example, fosters relaxation, fun, a sense of camaraderie, brief good feelings and good times. It has become a ritual to help people to become more open and communicative and talk more than they normally would, thus increasing a sense of connection and friendly intimacy with others. But finding and maintaining a useful and appropriate level of alcohol use is not possible for everyone. Many people use substances for less benign reasons, for example, to provide bravado for risky behaviour, or because they feel despondent without them.

In the DSM-IV, the category of Substance-Related Disorders covers problems with any kind of drug abuse or alcohol, with medication side effects, or being exposed to environmental toxins. The term *substance* refers to all the above, including alcohol, amphetamines, caffeine, nicotine, cannabis, cocaine, hallucinogens, inhalants, opioids, phencyclidine (PCP), sedatives, hypnotics and anxiolytics. Psychologists classify substance-related problems as: Substance Abuse, Substance Dependence and Substance Withdrawal. You 'abuse' a substance when you use it at a level that causes problems in your life. You are considered 'dependent' on it when you need it and can't stop, while 'withdrawal' refers to problems that occur when that substance is leaving your body.

case study: Greg

Greg was a bright young man from a small country town who moved to the city to become a stockbroker. His new world was an exciting one, in which he was introduced to a lavish lifestyle that included a chic apartment, an expensive car, a beautiful fiancée – and cocaine. He thought the latter helped him feel more confident at the trendy parties he attended and to focus on his demanding job for more than twelve hours a day. But his fiancée began to be concerned about his cocaine use. She complained that it made him irritable, even arrogant. She also noticed that he was becoming very thin, and that he was spending a fortune on the substance every week – money she thought they should be saving for their married life together. They frequently fought about Greg's cocaine abuse and when he refused to discontinue using it she decided to leave him. Two years later, when Greg began having problems with his nostrils, his doctor referred him to a Harm-reduction programme. Fortunately he chose to attend, and was able to get his life back on track.

substance abuse

is this you (or someone close to you)?

- Repeated use of a substance leads to problems at home, work or school.
- Use of the substance/s in situations that put self or others at risk (such as driving a car) and may cause legal problems (such as being arrested).

- Continuing to use the substance/s even though it is causing problems (for example, marital strife, getting into fights).

substance dependence

is this you (or someone close to you)?

- You need more and more of the chosen substance to achieve the same effect as a smaller amount once had. This is known as *tolerance*, implying a physiological and/or psychological need for the substance.
- Experience unpleasant withdrawal effects, which leads you to take more of the substance in order to avoid those effects.
- Make unsuccessful attempts to cut down or reduce your use of the substance.
- Spend a great deal of time trying to obtain the substance and using it.
- Relationships, work, social life or leisure suffer because of substance use.
- You continue using it, despite a realization that there are significant problems with it.

substance withdrawal

is this you or someone close to you?

- When a person stops taking a particular substance, he or she has a specific adverse reaction that can vary according to the particular substance and the length and quantity of usage.

'do not pass go' signs

People who abuse substances, including alcohol, run the risk of a huge variety of medical, legal, vocational, marital and social problems. It is vital that user, spouse or partner, and family start treatment immediately the problem is identified. There are very often one or more other psychological problems present (this is called 'dual diagnosis') so careful evaluation is necessary. Substance abuse problems often co-exist with other disorders such as Depression, Anxiety, Bipolar Disorder, Schizophrenia and Attention-Deficit/Hyperactivity Disorder. Some people drink because they mistakenly believe alcohol will help problems like Depression, but it actually makes them worse.

Substance Dependence is a stage where people have gained a tolerance for the substances they take, which can lead to even greater vocational, social and relational problems. In order to 'get clean', people who are dependent on substances often need help with detoxification. Withdrawal from many drugs involves serious mental and physical health risks if not managed properly. Inpatient rehabilitation programmes are often necessary.

People who abuse substances can also suffer from malnutrition and other medical problems, due to poor diet and hygiene. They may have problems related to toxic substances 'cut' with or ingested along with their drugs of choice. Snorting drugs like cocaine can cause serious nasal conditions, while the use of stimulants can lead to fatal cardiac problems. A significant number of people with Substance-Related Disorders commit suicide. Expectant mothers who abuse substances expose their unborn babies to toxic threats, causing serious conditions such as foetal alcohol syndrome.

what causes substance abuse, dependence and withdrawal?

A person's genetic make-up can make him or her more likely to have a problem with alcohol or drugs. Substance abuse runs in families, and researchers have identified chromosomal regions and individual genes that are likely to contribute to the development of this condition. Most of these genes are related to neurotransmitter systems and to alcohol metabolizing enzymes.

what happens in your brain?

Many substances affect brain chemistry so people only feel good when they take them. That presents a problem when a person develops Substance Abuse Disorder and wants to quit.

which treatments are likely to work?

Harm-reduction treatment for Substance Abuse has been found to work well by helping a person to reduce their substance use gradually while working on the underlying issues. Sobriety or twelve-step programmes are widely available, and they continue to help many people. It is important to be aware of the possibility of dual-diagnosis (that is, when a person abusing alcohol or drugs has other psychological problems that need to be treated). It stands to reason that, without treating Depression, Anxiety, and other disorders that help maintain a person's Substance Abuse, recovery is more likely to fail.

Inpatient treatment and rehabilitation centres are also available. These are particularly recommended for people who need detoxification and/or who have a long-term or well-entrenched abuse problem.

best course of action?

Seek a Harm-Reduction treatment twelve-step or sobriety programme, and be evaluated for other psychological issues that may require psychotherapeutic treatment.

in the meantime what can you do?

1. Write down your complete substance-use history. Leave nothing out. This will help you to see your problem with Substance Abuse/dependence for what it is and make it harder for you to be 'in denial' (telling yourself everything's fine when it's not). It might look something like this:

Date	Duration	Age	Substance	Feelings at the time	Repercussions
1999	18 months	19	cannabis	Trying to fit in. Had a boyfriend who used. Stopped me feeling anxious about leaving home.	Stopped attending classes, failed political science.
2001	5 years	21	Valium	After leaving university felt worried about my career. Got prescription. Valium to calm anxiety. Faked prescriptions after three years when doctor refused to continue prescribing.	Arrested and charged. Went into court-ordered rehab. Left after four days then got Valium on street. Still owe pusher money.

2. Join a Harm-reduction, sobriety or twelve-step programme (such as Alcoholics Anonymous, Narcotics Anonymous) and attend regular meetings.
3. Learn everything you can about alcohol or the particular drug, medication or toxin you are using.
4. Seek individual therapy and/or marital therapy with your spouse or partner.
5. Make sure you receive adequate nutrition. Eat three balanced, healthy meals a day.
6. Does your style of thinking help or hinder you? Identify your distorted thought patterns and change them for more helpful ones (see page 21).
7. Identify your negative self-talk (see page 20). Change self-talk statements such as 'I'll never beat my addiction' to 'I can manage this challenge, one day at a time.'

8. Identify all situations you identify with Substance Abuse. Work out strategies ahead of time about how either to avoid those situations or overcome the desire to 'use' in such situations.

9. Identify people you connect with Substance Abuse. Are they helpful in your life? True friends? Or people who gain from your Substance Abuse? Make decisions based on healthy choices about which (if any) of those people should remain in your life.

10. Focus on self-care. Take steps to improve your physical health, stamina and immune system.

11. Establish a regular pattern of good-quality sleep. If you have problems sleeping follow the self-help suggestions for Insomnia or other Sleep Disorders (see page 361 onwards).

12. Engage in regular exercise, as appropriate for your age, weight and state of health.

13. Learn to assert yourself appropriately (see page 38).

14. Learn relaxation skills (see page 41).

15. Work on clear, honest communication.

16. How do you typically deal with peer pressure? Write down the answer, then work out strategies about possible future challenging situations, that is, decide how you will behave in the future when offered your drug of choice, and so on.

17. Practise asking for help. What does that feel like? Write down your answer.

18. Identify the inappropriate ways you have behaved in order to maintain your Substance Abuse in the past, such as manipulation, lying and hiding. Write down your feelings and thoughts about this, then work out strategies about how to replace them with more appropriate behaviour; for example, alternative methods for dealing with stressful situations are meditation, breathing, listening to music.

19. Improve your social skills by practising:
   - Initiating conversation with others.
   - Giving compliments.
   - Accepting compliments.
   - Being assertive in your communication (see page 38).
   - Making sure you keep appointments.
   - Making sure you are on time for social events.
   - Being honest.
   - Self-disclosing to an appropriate degree.
   - Being able to set boundaries with others (see page 68).

- Maintaining eye contact.
- Giving oneself and others an appropriate amount of personal space.
- Learning to deal with criticism.
- Learning to deal with teasing.

20. Improve your self-esteem (see page 105).
21. How have your family/spouse/partner/friends been affected by your Substance Abuse? Write down your feelings and thoughts. When you are ready, try to make amends, perhaps in the context of the twelve-steps, if that is the programme you are following.
22. How have your spouse or partner, members of your family and circle of friends helped to maintain your Substance Abuse? This tendency of people to unwittingly do things that support the continuation of a person's drug or alcohol habit is known as 'enabling'. Without blaming or hurting your spouse, partner, family or friends try to understand the system that has enabled your Substance Abuse and take steps to dismantle it.
23. Learn about the signs of relapse (exhaustion, Depression, dishonesty, impatience, arguing, complacency, frustration, self-pity, over-confidence), and pay attention to those signs to avoid future problems.
24. Set appropriate goals for yourself and take small steps each day to attain them.
25. Develop a set of daily positive affirmations. Put them where you will constantly be reminded that you can be successful in recovering.

when someone close to you has a problem with drugs or alcohol

1. Join Al-Anon to receive support and education.
2. Learn everything you can about drugs and alcohol, particularly the substance being used by the person.
3. Help everyone in the family to reduce stress and anxiety.
4. Reduce your own stress (page 19) and find appropriate ways to engage in pleasurable activities.
5. Have family therapy.
6. Set a good example of abstinence.
7. Educate children about the dangers of drugs and alcohol abuse as early as possible.
8. Get help for any family member who exhibits a problem.
9. Families or family members sometimes 'enable' a person's Substance

Abuse, that is, they do or say things that help to maintain it. Identify any enabling patterns in your family, educate everyone about this tendency and put an end to it. Make it a topic of discussion and education in family meetings.

10. If your substance-abusing family member is 'in denial' and/or despite your encouragement will not stop abusing or seek treatment, consider setting up an intervention to get them into treatment. This is a meeting facilitated by a trained drugs and alcohol counsellor in which everyone close to the person would meet them and, supportively, try to get them to agree to treatment.

11. If you have done everything you can but the person is still using, you may need to lovingly detach, withdraw from the person and protect yourself and other family members.

12. Learn about relapse dangers and signs (exhaustion, Depression, dishonesty, impatience, arguing, complacency, frustration, self-pity, overconfidence), and be supportive of follow-up treatment.

13. Identify problems early on, and learn the signs of intoxication and withdrawal.

Substance	Intoxication	Withdrawal
Alcohol	Lack of coordination	Increased pulse rate
	Slurred speech	Sweating
	Unsteady gait	Hand shaking
	'Double' vision	Insomnia
	Impaired memory and focus	Nausea/vomiting
		Hallucinations
	Stupor/coma	Edginess
		Anxiety
		Seizures
Amphetamines ('uppers') and cocaine	Racing (or slowed) heart rate	Tiredness
		Vivid nightmares
	Dilated pupils	Insomnia, or sleeping too much
	Sweating or chills	
	Higher, or lower, blood pressure	Strong desire to repeat use
	Nausea or vomiting	Increased appetite
	Weight loss	Edginess, or slowness
	Edginess or slowness	Severe Depression

Substance	Intoxication	Withdrawal
	Irregular heartbeat, chest pain	Suicidal thoughts or attempts
	Muscle weakness	
	Breathing difficulty	
	Tics or spasms	
	Abnormal tensing of muscles	
	Disorientation, seizures or coma	
Caffeine	Edginess	Fatigue
	Nervousness	Headache
	Excitement	
	Insomnia	
	Flushed face	
	Increased need to urinate	
	Upset stomach	
	Muscle twitching	
	Rambling thoughts and speech	
	Faster, or slower, heart rate	
	Restlessness	
Cannabis	Red eyes	Anxiety, panic
	Increased appetite	Impairment of short-term memory
	Dry mouth	
	Fast heart rate	Disturbance in thought patterns
	Euphoria	Lapses in attention
	Passivity	Depersonalization
	Uncontrollable laughing	Mental confusion
		Flashbacks
		Paranoid thoughts
Hallucinogens	Dilated pupils	Gradual reduction of intoxication symptoms
	Racing heart	
	Blurred vision	
	Perspiring	
	Trembling	
	Lack of coordination	

Substance	Intoxication	Withdrawal
Inhalants	Dizziness	Gradual reduction of intoxication symptoms
	Involuntary, rapid eyeball movement	
	Lack of coordination	
	Slurred speech	
	Unsteady gait	
	Lethargy	
	Slowness of body and reflexes	
	Tremor	
	Weak muscles	
	Blurred vision	
	Stupor/coma	
	Euphoria	
Nicotine		Depressed mood
		Insomnia
		Irritability
		Anxiety
		Difficulty concentrating
		Restlessness
		Slowed heart rate
		Increased appetite/weight gain
Opioids	Sudden changes in behaviour	Depressed mood
	Psychological changes	Nausea/vomiting
	Impaired judgement	Muscle aches
	Impaired social or occupational functioning	Runny nose or eyes
		Dilated pupils
	Constricted pupils	Sweating
	Drowsiness or coma	Diarrhoea
	Slurred speech	Yawning
	Memory or focusing problems	Fever
		Insomnia

Substance	Intoxication	Withdrawal
Phencyclidine (PCP)	Vertical or horizontal Involuntary rapid eyeball movement	Gradual reduction of intoxication symptoms.
	Abnormally high blood pressure and heart rate	
	Numbness	
	Loss of coordination	
	Difficulty in speaking	
	Stiff muscles	
	Seizures/coma	
	Hearing sensitivity	
Sedatives/hypnotics/ anxiolytics (e.g. Valium, barbiturates, sleeping pills)	Sudden changes in behaviour	Sweating/high pulse rate
	Psychological changes	Hand trembling
	Impaired judgement	Insomnia
	Impaired social or occupational functioning	Nightmares
		Vomiting
	Slurred speech	Hallucinations
	Lack of coordination	Agitation
	Unsteady gait	Anxiety
	Involuntary rapid eye movement	Seizures
	Attention/memory problems	
	Stupor/coma	

helpful books

The Addiction Workbook: A Step-By-Step Guide to Quitting Alcohol and Drugs, P. Fanning and J. T. O'Neill. Oakland, Calif.: New Harbinger Publications, 1996.

Addiction and Recovery for Dummies, B. Shaw, P. Ritvo and J. Irvine Hoboken, New Jersey: Wiley Publishing Co., 2005.

Codependent No More: How to Stop Controlling Others and Start Caring for Yourself, M. Beattie. New York: HarperCollins, 1987.

The Language of Letting Go: Daily Meditations for Codependents, M. Beattie. New York: HarperCollins, 1990.

The Betty Ford Center Book of Answers: Help for Those Struggling with

Substance Abuse and for the People Who Love Them, J. West. New York: Pocket Books, 1997.

'It Will Never Happen to Me': Children of Alcoholics as Youngsters-Adolescents-Adults, C. Black. New York: Ballantine Books, 1981.

'It's Never Too Late to Have a Happy Childhood': Inspirations for Adult Children, C. Black. New York: Ballantine Books, 1989.

Games Alcoholics Play, C. Steiner. New York: Ballantine Books, 1971.

Drugs: Use, Misuse and Abuse (4th ed.), R. Schlaadt and P. T. Shannon. New Jersey: Prentice-Hall, Inc., 1994.

Marijuana and Madness, eds D. Castle and R. Murray. Cambridge University Press, 2004.

Controlling Your Drinking: Tools to Make Moderation Work for You, W. R. Miller and R. F. Muñoz. Guilford Press, 2005.

Cool, Hip & Sober: 88 Ways to Beat Booze & Drugs, B. Manville. Tom Doherty Associates, 2003.

Daily Affirmations for Adult Children of Alcoholics, R. Lerner. Deerfield Beach, Fla.: Health Communications, Inc., 1985.

Five Weeks to Healing Stress: The Wellness Option, V. O'Hara. Oakland, Calif.: New Harbinger Publications, 1996.

Family Intervention: Positive Action You Can Take to Help a Loved One – and Yourself – to Break the Cycle of Addiction and Dependency, F. L. Picard. Center City, Minn.: Hazelden, 1991.

chapter 9
'somebody stop me!': impulse-control disorders

"It was an impulse purchase."

'Naughty, but nice!' That's how some people describe the urge to do things that can get them into far more trouble than the consequences of an occasional chocolate binge. In fact, for most people who suffer from Impulse-Control Disorders the sense of enjoyment or relief that follows giving in to their urges is very fleeting. Then come remorse, guilt, shame, despair and even thoughts of suicide. Because impulse-control problems include such serious behaviour as starting fires, stealing or running up unpayable gambling debts (Pyromania, Kleptomania, and Pathological Gambling, respectively) – many of them have the potential to land a person in jail. Even those Impulse-Control Disorders that do not have the potential to invite arrest, such as Trichotillomania (pulling out one's hair) can be just as disabling in a person's life. There are many other disorders of impulse, such as compulsive skin-picking and uncontrolled shopping, which are not specifically classified in the DSM-IV, but the basic issues are similar. An Impulse-Control Disorder can have a substantial impact not only on the life of the sufferer but also on relationships, families, and society at large. They can be successfully treated, but unfortunately, the shame people feel and the desire to be extremely secretive about an Impulse-Control Disorder, mean that treatment may not be sought.

kleptomania

case study: Ginny

I met Ginny after she was arrested for shoplifting three pairs of pantyhose from a department store. The pantyhose were not in her size, in fact she claims she rarely wears such garments. When she was searched by the police they found she had more than enough money in her purse to pay for the items she stole. Ginny was extremely ashamed and embarrassed about her actions, although she confessed to me that over the past six months she had shoplifted around thirty pairs of pantyhose, sixteen pairs of ankle socks and a dozen 'pop socks'. These were not items Ginny needed, and in fact most of them remained unopened in their original packets. She told me she always felt excited at the time of stealing, but horribly guilty afterwards, and had surreptitiously returned several pairs. The guilt she felt had led her to drink heavily after each episode; in fact her alcohol abuse was becoming a problem in itself.

Ginny needed to be treated for Kleptomania and alcohol abuse. It was very difficult for her to face the court proceedings, but she got through it with the support of her family. She responded well to therapy and eventually managed to get both her urge to steal and her drink problem under control.

is this you (or someone close to you)?

- You cannot stop yourself stealing things you do not need.
- Just before carrying out each theft you feel mounting tension.
- Experience a sense of pleasure or relief after the theft.
- There is no element of vengeance or spite.

If you cannot control your urge to steal things you don't really need, I urge you to get some help. The problem is, that even though you are not a die-hard criminal, you might be treated like one in the very near future. I know you already feel very ashamed of having these urges to steal, especially when you act them out, and this contributes to a very low self-esteem that affects every area of your life. All the secrecy and embarrassment will be causing you great anxiety too. You deserve to have help in controlling this.

'do not pass go' signs

Kleptomania is a very disabling disorder. People with the disorder usually have high stress and sometimes Mood and Anxiety Disorders as well, and it can make their lives extremely difficult. Many people with Kleptomania report that they enter an altered state of consciousness during their acts of theft, and it is possible that some dissociate (lose touch with reality) while stealing. Even though the things they steal are not particularly of value to them the law takes a dim view of it, so people who suffer from Kleptomania are more than likely to end up in prison. Each episode of stealing may begin with a feeling of tension, followed by excitement or relief when the impulse is followed, then eventually feelings of shame, remorse and guilt. Some of the disorders that go hand in hand with Kleptomania are Substance Abuse, Depression, Anxiety, nicotine addiction, Bipolar Disorder, Phobias and personality problems. Treatment is urgently needed.

what causes kleptomania?

Genetic and psychosocial factors may cause Kleptomania, and it may be inherited (it is often seen in immediate relatives of people with Klepto-mania). Some think it has roots in early parenting behaviour, as chaotic, violent and distressing childhood experiences may be linked to its development. The disorder frequently co-occurs with Substance Abuse. People with Kleptomania often suffer from repetitive, intrusive thoughts about stealing, an inability to avoid the compulsion to steal and tension-relief following the theft. Certain types of Kleptomania may be similar to Obsessive-Compulsive Disorder, whereas others seem more like addictive disorders and Mood Disorders. There are a growing number of reports about people who developed Kleptomania after sustaining a brain injury. Kleptomania is associated with Depression, Post-Traumatic Stress Disorder, organic factors such as brain lesions and dementia, as well as psychiatric and family disturbances. It appears to be more common in women.

what happens in your brain?

Neurotransmitters such as gamma aminobutyric acid (GABA) and serotonin may play a role in the development of Kleptomania. Impulse-control seems to be associated with activity in brain circuits that control the processing of emotional information. These need to be functioning properly in order for a person to be able to stop and consider whether or not to steal and learn from the experience. It's easy to see how a person without these abilities can get into trouble with impulsive behaviour.

which treatments are likely to work?

Psychodynamic psychotherapy, hypnotherapy, cognitive-behavioural psychotherapy and family therapy can help. A broad range of medications have been found to be beneficial in the treatment of Kleptomania. Sometimes therapy combined with medication is a good combination.

best course of action?

Seek psychotherapy.

in the meantime what can you do?

1. Learn everything you can about Kleptomania.
2. What is your history of Kleptomania? Try to identify and list as many past experiences and situations that led to you wanting to steal as you can remember. Make a chart. Rate your stealing episodes from 1–10, with 10 being the most strongly you have needed to steal at one time. Keep your journal safe.
3. Now write down the feelings that accompanied each Kleptomania episode.
4. Try to express in writing any deeper feelings (for example, of hurt, sadness and helplessness) that caused tension and a desire to steal.
5. Write a list of the consequences of Kleptomania that you have experienced, either at home, work or socially.
6. Keep a daily log of any current stealing. Write down when the desire arises, the situation that led to your need to steal, the thoughts and feelings that went with it. Rate your level of needing to steal from 1–10.
7. Learn to assert yourself appropriately, either by taking a self-assertion class or follow the guidelines on page 38.
8. A great way to prevent your desire to steal from taking control is to implement the following:

Stop, Look, Listen, Think and Plan

When you feel the desire to steal arising:

Stop yourself doing it.
Look at your impulse to do it.

Listen either to positive reminders in your head or to the calm, soothing part of you.

Think about what you really want to do instead.

Plan an appropriate change of behaviour.

9. Identify the things that trigger your episodes of Kleptomania and try to avoid them. Location may be one of them; for example, if shops or shopping malls are places where you tend to steal, do not enter them under any circumstances – at least until you have gained greater control over your urge to steal.

10. There is a relationship between episodes of Kleptomania and stress. Take steps to reduce your stress and keep it low.

11. Practise relaxation (see Progressive Body Relaxation exercise page 41).

12. Practise meditation (see page 40).

13. Establish a regular pattern of good-quality sleep. If you have problems sleeping follow the self-help suggestions for Insomnia or other Sleep Disorders (see page 361 onwards).

14. Work on increasing your self-esteem (see page 105).

15. Write down a list of your strengths and accomplishments. Spend some time each day reminding yourself of these achievements.

16. Check your mood by reading the sections on Mood Disorders (see Chapter 2) and Anxiety (see page 37ff). If you think you may fit into any of those categories and have an underlying Depression, for example, seek immediate treatment and follow the 'what to do' suggestions.

17. Identify any link between your stealing and other types of problems such as Substance Abuse. Seek treatment for them.

18. Don't allow your guilt and need for secrecy to stop you from seeking treatment. You deserve to be happier, less stressed or guilty and free of this disorder.

for friends and family members

- Do not agree to cover up a family member's stealing habits. Instead, encourage him or her to seek treatment as a matter of urgency.

- Support the mental-health treatment throughout its course and watch for signs of relapse afterwards (for example, mounting stress, secrecy, lack of openness and communication, alcohol or drug abuse, solo shopping trips or irritability).

- Do not support efforts on the part of the person with Kleptomania to approach situations where they have, in the past, been likely to steal. This probably includes shops. You may have to shop for him or her until treatment is well underway.
- Support healthy efforts on the part of the person with Kleptomania to work on stress-reduction and relaxation, as well as to exercise and eat balanced, nutritious meals.
- Do not support or enable alcohol or drug abuse.
- Take care of your mental and physical health (and that of the family).
- Consider having individual or family therapy.
- Take steps to reduce your own stress (see page 19).

helpful books

Stop Me Because I Can't Stop Myself: Taking Control of Impulsive Behaviors, J. Grant and S. W. Kim. New York: McGraw-Hill, 2003.

The Habit Control Workbook: Simple, Concise, Step-by-Step Directions for Control of Overeating, Compulsive Spending, Gambling, Lying, Hair Pulling, Explosive Temper, Prescription Drug Misuse, Irresponsible Sex, TV and Video Game Addiction, Teeth Grinding and Smoking, N. Birkedahl. Oakland, Calif.: New Harbinger Publications, 1990.

Meditation for Busy People: 60 Seconds to Serenity, D. Croves. San Rafael, Calif.: New World Library, 1993.

The Habit Change Workbook: How to Break Bad Habits and Form Good Ones, J. Claiborn and C. Pedrick. Oakland, Calif.: New Harbinger Publications, 2001.

Five Weeks to Healing Stress: The Wellness Option, V. O'Hara. Oakland, Calif.: New Harbinger Publications, 1996.

pyromania

There is something about fire that is fascinating to everyone, but there are some people whose interest in fire is so profound that they have trouble controlling their impulse to start one. These are very often the people behind the latest news story about an out-of-control forest fire, and unfortunately the unfolding of those stories usually reveals significant damage to landscape, property and animals, and even human tragedy. People who start fires are not necessarily just acting out of a lack of impulse control, they may have experienced chaotic, violent and distressing childhood events that have led to the development of this startling form of self-expression.

case study: Davey

I met seventeen-year-old Davey through his older sister Annabel, who was suffering from Anxiety. She lived in fear of being burned alive in a fire started by her brother. Their single-parent father, a man given to sudden outbursts of extreme rage, was sent to prison for an incident that involved the deliberate destruction of cars and property, so the two siblings lived alone together in their small family house. By the time I came to work with Davey, he had a history of starting numerous fires – three in their home and four of them at his school (for which he had been expelled). He had started his first fire in the toilets of a local park, and he had also destroyed an area of forest reserve near a local beach. Davey loved fire. It gave him a feeling of satisfaction to watch the results of his destructive desire to ignite things.

Davey's first attempts at starting fires seemed to me to have been carried out in response to his father's explosive anger. Being the recipient of this terrifying rage made Davey feel horribly vulnerable, overwhelmed and frightened. In Davey's psyche, creating fire – a force that somehow matched his father's rage – provided him with a method of feeling powerful and better able to protect himself. Fortunately, during his father's time in prison, Davey was able to learn self-assertion skills and other methods of protecting himself without resorting to starting fires. He came to understand that his Pyromania was a symbolic gesture, but that it could potentially harm or even kill people who were as vulnerable as he once felt in the presence of his father's anger. He eventually learned to control those destructive impulses – and his sister's Anxiety was simultaneously soothed.

is this you (or someone close to you)?

- You engaged in deliberate fire-starting more than once.
- Felt tension mounting before you did this.
- Are fascinated by fire.
- Get pleasure or relief by lighting fires and watching the results.
- Don't light fires as an act of vengeance, for money, to hide a crime or to make a political statement, and are fully aware of what you are doing at the time.

If you start fires, you would be wise to seek help. Sooner or later you may experience very severe consequences that will have a profound effect on the rest of your life. There are reasons why you do it, and it would be a good idea to explore those reasons in therapy. That way you can heal, protect yourself, and focus on creating a life that is guaranteed to have more positive outcomes.

'do not pass go' signs

Starting fires causes destruction of forests, property and people, so the consequences of this Impulse-Control Disorder are extremely serious. Since society imposes severe penalties on people who are caught, those with Pyromania run the risk of being incarcerated. Some of the disorders that go hand in hand with Pyromania are Substance Abuse, Depression, nicotine addiction, Bipolar Disorder, Phobias and personality problems. Urgent treatment is required.

what causes pyromania?

Neuropsychological assessments of people with Pyromania have revealed impairments in attention, verbal and visual memory and executive functions. Some people start fires in response to conflicts such as parental or family problems, and there may sometimes be a genetic predisposition towards engaging in Pyromania. It is associated with Schizophrenia, Mood Disorders, Personality Disorders, Alcohol Abuse and Mental Retardation. People with Pyromania who also have other serious psychiatric disorders frequently suffer from significant social skills deficits, so it is believed that, for them, starting fires may be a vehicle for communication that brings results without having to work through their disabilities.

what happens in your brain?

Neurotransmitters may play a role in the development of Pyromania, especially serotonin. Impulse-control seems to be associated with activity in the brain circuits that control the processing of emotional information. They need to be functioning properly in order for a person to be able to stop to consider whether or not to start a fire and learn from the experience. Without these abilities, a person is likely to get into trouble by acting impulsively.

which treatments are likely to work?

Psychodynamic psychotherapy, hypnotherapy, cognitive-behavioural psychotherapy and family therapy are the types of therapy that may work best, although people with very serious fire-starting behaviour may need to be admitted to an inpatient facility. Medication may help improve rational thinking and social functioning, and it may help decrease aggressive behaviour and bring about a reduction in fire-starting incidents.

best course of action?

Seek psychotherapy.

in the meantime what can you do?

1. Learn everything you can about Pyromania.
2. What exactly is your history of Pyromania? Try to identify and write down as many past experiences and situations that led to you to start fires as you can remember. Make a chart. Rate your fire-starting sessions from 1–10, with 10 being the most serious episode of fire-starting you have ever carried out. Keep your journal safe.
3. Write down the feelings that accompanied each fire-starting episode.
4. Now try to express in writing any deeper feelings (for example, of hurt, sadness and helplessness) that caused tension and a desire to start fires.
5. What is your childhood history? Did you start fires as a child? If so, what was happening in your life just before you started?
6. Dig deep and ask yourself: what are you really trying to express by starting fires that you cannot say with words?
7. Write down a list of the consequences to you (legal, social, vocational or relational) of starting fires.
8. Write down a list of the consequences to others, including property or environmental destruction, and injury to people and animals.
9. Armed with the above information, now create a chart that illustrates the full cause and effect, plus actual or potential consequences of your fire-starting behaviour. Head each variable as 'Incident' (for example, lighting a fire in public park), 'Effect' (for example, trees lost, public toilets burned down) and 'Consequences' (for example, arrest and a period in prison).
10. Keep a daily log of any current fire-starting or your desire to do so. Write down when the desire arises, the situation that led to your need to start fires, plus the thoughts and feelings that went with them. Rate your levels of fire-starting desire and results from 1–10, with 10 being the strongest urge/the most serious fire.
11. Learn to assert yourself appropriately, either by taking a self-assertion class, or learning about self-assertion (see page 38).
12. A great way to prevent your desire to start fires from taking control is to implement the following:

'Stop, Look, Listen, Think and Plan'

When you feel the desire to start fires arising:

Stop yourself doing it. (This means becoming aware of the feelings that precede an incident of fire-starting.)

Look at your impulse to do it.

Listen either to positive reminders in your head or to the calm, soothing part of you.

Think about what you really want to do instead.

Plan an appropriate change of behaviour.

13. Make it difficult for you to be stimulated to start fires by reducing your connection with fire (for example, give-away books, DVDs, fire-fighting equipment or any other accoutrement that help sustain your interest in fire).

14. Do not watch TV coverage of raging forest fires, house fires or any other types of fires.

15. Identify any link between your fire-starting and other problems such as Substance Abuse

16. Check your mood by reading the sections on Mood Disorders (see Chapter 2). If you think you may fit into any of those categories follow the self-help suggestions and seek immediate treatment.

17. There is a relationship between episodes of Pyromania and stress. Take steps to reduce your stress and keep it low (see page 19).

18. Practise relaxation (see Progressive Body Relaxation exercise page 41).

19. Practise meditation (see page 40).

20. Establish a regular pattern of good-quality sleep. If you have problems sleeping follow the self-help suggestions for Insomnia or other Sleep disorders (see page 361 onwards).

21. Work on increasing your self-esteem (see page 105).

22. Write down a list of your strengths and accomplishments. Spend some time each day reminding yourself of these achievements.

for partners, friends and family members

- Do not agree to cover up a person's Pyromania. Instead, encourage him or her to seek treatment as a matter of urgency.

- Support the mental-health treatment throughout its course and watch for signs of relapse afterwards (for example, mounting stress, secrecy, lack of openness and communication, alcohol or drug abuse, irritability or the presence of any kind of fire-starting accoutrement).

- Do not support efforts on the part of the person with Pyromania to have any contact whatsoever with anything to do with fires, whether that be hanging around a fire station, watching news broadcasts covering fires or even just watching a film about fires.
- Support healthy efforts on the part of the person with Pyromania to work on stress reduction and relaxation, as well as to exercise and eat balanced, nutritious meals.
- Do not support or enable alcohol or drug abuse.
- Take care of your mental and physical health (and that of the family).
- Consider having individual or family therapy.
- Take steps to reduce your own stress (see page 19).

pyromania in children

There are three distinct types of juvenile fire-starters:

1. Those who do so out of curiosity. Such children usually face reprimands and other consequences, learn from them and never do it again.
2. Children who start fires as a reaction to something very difficult or traumatic that is going on in their life. After treatment or once they are over the problem they will rarely start fires again.
3. Children who start fires deliberately as one of the symptoms of Conduct Disorder (see page 318) and continue to do so despite warnings and consequences. These children tend to come from less stable homes and are more antisocial than the other two groups. Unfortunately, persistent fire-starting is a sign that a child is at great risk of developing an adult personality disorder that is characterized by a disregard for rules and laws.

Appropriate treatment for children include close observation, behaviour therapy, parenting training, special problem-solving training, relaxation training, fire safety and prevention education, individual and family therapy, and medication.

helpful books

The Habit Control Workbook: Simple, Concise, Step-by-Step Directions for Control of Overeating, Compulsive Spending, Gambling, Lying, Hair

Pulling, Explosive Temper, Prescription Drug Misuse, Irresponsible Sex, TV and Video Game Addiction, Teeth Grinding and Smoking, N. Birkedahl. Oakland, Calif.: New Harbinger Publications, 1990.

Meditation for Busy People: 60 Seconds to Serenity, D. Croves. San Rafael, Calif.: New World Library, 1993.

The Habit Change Workbook: How to Break Bad Habits and Form Good Ones, J. Claiborn and C. Pedrick. Oakland, Calif.: New Harbinger Publications, 2001.

Five Weeks to Healing Stress: The Wellness Option, V. O'Hara. Oakland, Calif.: New Harbinger Publications, 1996.

gambling disorder

A gambler's luck is fickle. Occasionally, there'll be the thrill of a sudden win that seduces the player with the idea that it can be done again and again. But that's when luck seems to disappear, dumping the player in a spiral of debt and remorse. There are three phases of gambling: victory, loss and despair. People who develop Gambling Disorder have become stuck in a cycle they cannot escape from, and their misguided attempts to try to win back losses often put them ever further into debt. The rapidly expanding gambling business has resulted in an increasing number of people with Gambling Disorder, and the problem is likely to get worse in the future. Chase was one of the luckier ones, in the true sense of the word:

case study: Chase

Chase was a young businessman who loved to visit Las Vegas. He lived in California, but that was only a twenty-minute plane ride from the city that constantly drew him to his favourite seat at the blackjack table. He had lost far more money than he had ever won, but the thrill of the occasional jackpot kept him hooked. He justified his losses by telling himself that he was a single man with no dependents, and he was free to spend his money however he wished; after all, if he lost everything the only person who would be hurt was himself – but that was not strictly true. Chase had another responsibility in his life: a new restaurant he had just opened with two other partners. He knew that it takes a while for restaurants to become established, and that for his partners' sake as well as his own, he needed to conserve his finances in case it failed to take off. But Chase kept telling himself that he could always win back any losses at the blackjack table. Unfortunately, the restaurant turned out to be unsuccessful, and it closed the week after Chase had managed to lose particularly heavily in Vegas. Faced with bankruptcy, Chase found his way to my office and laid his cards on my table.

As we talked, it became apparent that Chase did have a Gambling Disorder, but that he was also impulsive in other areas in his life. On four occasions so far he had met a woman in a casino, had sex with her and asked her to marry him – all in one twenty-four-hour period. Chase needed treatment for Gambling Disorder and for general impulsivity. Gamblers are often in denial about their problem and as a result they resist treatment. However, Chase was unusually compliant with his treatment programme – probably because he was facing such serious consequences. He was also extremely smart and eventually managed to get his life back on track. Aside from regular psychotherapy, he was helped by joining Gamblers Anonymous and attending regular meetings. After relapsing once and recovering, he nearly relapsed a second time by boarding a plane to Vegas, but managed to stop himself from leaving the terminal and flew straight back home. Chase continues to approach his recovery 'one day at a time'.

is this you (or someone close to you)?

Gambling causes you problems in five or more of the following ways:

- You are highly motivated to gamble. You like to think back on previous wins and plan your next gambling experience, and you are focused on raising money with which to gamble.
- You need to use more and more money for gambling to increase your excitement.
- You have tried to stop or control your gambling several times.
- You are out of sorts when you try to stop.
- You gamble as a way to feel better or escape from problems.
- When you lose, you are drawn to try to win back the money.
- You lie about the extent of your gambling.
- You may have resorted to fraud, forgery, theft or embezzlement in order to finance your gambling.
- Gambling has caused you major problems with relationships, at work or academically.
- You may have had to borrow money to finance gambling or repay gambling debts.

If the above applies to you, chances are you are already in trouble. You desperately want to stop, but you just can't. Part of the problem is the belief that you are 'lucky'. You like the buzz of gambling, and the 'high' of winning

– and those things feel like a powerful addiction. Truth? It's a mug's game. Instead, why not put your money on a recovery programme? Get treatment now before things get any worse. You can do it.

'do not pass go' signs

Compulsive gambling becomes a dangerous cycle. During the anticipation of a game or betting episode the gambler is tense and irritable. While actually gambling that tension is relieved, but losing brings the desire to win back those losses – one way or another. No wonder having Gambling Disorder leads to serious problems in a person's work, social and family life, and the divorce rate among gamblers is extremely high.

It is vital to stop the cycle but many try to do so and fail, until they are in even more trouble. Some of the disorders that go hand in hand with Gambling Disorder are Substance Abuse, Attention-Deficit/Hyperactivity Disorder, Depression (maybe half of all people suffering from Gambling Disorder), Anxiety, nicotine addiction, Social Phobia, Panic Disorder with Agoraphobia, Bipolar Disorder (maybe a quarter of all people suffering from Gambling Disorder), Phobias, personality problems and other Impulse-Control Disorders. For people struggling with Gambling Disorder treatment is urgently needed.

what causes gambling disorder?

Pathological gambling has some similarities with Substance Abuse disorders, and is also akin to Obsessive-Compulsive Disorder. Certain people are at higher risk of developing Gambling Disorder, including young men who live in cities, people belonging to some minority groups or lower socio-economic class groups and those with other psychological disorders. Gambling Disorder may also be related to a belief that one is 'lucky', as well as to the enjoyment associated with placing bets. Certain biological abnormalities may predispose individuals to pathological gambling, and repeated, heavy gambling may even lead to some physiological changes. Gambling seems to be maintained by the fact that occasional winning makes a person want to gamble more, and also by the tendency of many people to overestimate the odds of winning.

what happens in your brain?

There is a growing understanding of the role of the neurotransmitters dopamine and serotonin in gambling and other reward-related behaviour. The decision-making areas of the cortex are probably malfunctioning as well.

Impulse-control seems to be associated with brain circuits that control the processing of emotional information. They need to be functioning properly in order for a person to be able to stop to consider whether or not to gamble and learn from the experience.

which treatments are likely to work?

Twelve-step or Harm-reduction programmes are recommended, while psychodynamic psychotherapy, hypnotherapy, cognitive-behavioural psychotherapy and family therapy can address any additional or underlying mental-health problems, as well as helping to stop a person's gambling, maintain abstinence and improve his or her quality of life.

Gestalt therapy in a family setting can force gamblers to see themselves and their behaviour's effect on others, and to develop better ways to operate in the world. Medication is sometimes prescribed.

People who suffer from Gambling Disorder seem to be either similar to those suffering from Obsessive-Compulsive Disorder or more like sufferers of substance abuse. Many also suffer from a range of other psychological disorders such as Depression, Bipolar Disorder and Attention-Deficit/Hyperactivity Disorder. People who suffer from Gambling Disorder also differ with regard to where and how they gamble, their motivations to gamble and their mood states during or after gambling. Because of all this variation, there is no 'one size fits all' approach to treating this disorder.

best course of action?

Seek psychotherapy.

in the meantime what can you do?

1. Learn everything you can about Gambling Disorder.
2. Write down your complete gambling history, leaving nothing out. This will create a black-and-white record so you can have an accurate picture of your gambling behaviour and the consequences. Try to identify and list each cycle when it occurred, and as many past experiences and situations that led to you wanting to gamble as you can remember. Make a chart. Rate your gambling sessions from 1–10, with 10 being the most serious in terms of consequences or potential consequences.
3. Write down the feelings that accompanied each gambling episode.
4. Now try to express, in writing, any deeper feelings (for example, of hurt, sadness and helplessness) that helped create your desire to gamble.

5. Write a list of all the general consequences of gambling that you have experienced, either at home, work, socially or legally.
6. Keep a daily log of any current gambling or desire to gamble. Write down when the desire arises, the situation that led to your need to gamble, and the thoughts and feelings that accompany it. Rate your level of needing to gamble from 1–10 with 10 being the strongest.
7. Learn to assert yourself appropriately, either by taking a self-assertion class, or learning about self-assertion (see page 38).
8. A great way to prevent your desire to gamble from taking over is to implement the following:

'Stop, Look, Listen, Think and Plan'
When you feel the desire to gamble arising:

Stop yourself doing it. (This will mean becoming aware of the feelings that precede an incident of gambling.)
Look at your impulse to do it.
Listen either to positive reminders in your head, or to the calm, soothing part of you.
Think about what you really want to do instead.
Plan an appropriate change of behaviour.

9. Throw out your gambling accoutrements (for example, cards, dice, gambling-related books or DVDs).
10. Identify the triggers for your gambling episodes. Is location a factor? If so, do not allow yourself to go anywhere near gambling establishments, such as casinos or race tracks and restrict your online activity to non-gambling sites.
11. Check your mood by reading the sections on Mood Disorders (Chapter 2) and Anxiety (page 37ff). If you think you may fit into any of these categories seek immediate treatment and follow the self-help suggestions.
12. Identify any link between your gambling and other types of problems such as Substance Abuse. Take steps to get treatment for them too.
13. Join Gamblers Anonymous and attend regular meetings.
14. There is a relationship between Gambling Disorder and stress. Take steps to reduce your stress and keep it low.
15. Practise relaxation every day (see Progressive Body Relaxation exercise page 41).

16. Practise meditation (see page 40).
17. Establish a regular pattern of good-quality sleep. If you have problems sleeping follow the self-help suggestions for Insomnia or other Sleep Disorders (see page 361 onwards).
18. Work on increasing your self-esteem (see page 105).
19. Write down a list of your strengths and accomplishments. Spend some time each day reminding yourself of these achievements.

for partners, friends and family members

1. Do not agree to cover up a family member's Gambling Disorder. Instead, encourage him or her to seek treatment as a matter of urgency.
2. Support the mental-health treatment throughout its course and watch for any signs of relapse afterwards (for example, mounting stress, secrecy, lack of openness and communication, alcohol or drug abuse, irritability, visits to sites or cities known for gambling, borrowing money or the presence of any kind of gambling accoutrement).
3. Do not support efforts on the part of the person with Gambling Disorder to have any contact whatsoever with anything to do with gambling. That means staying away from casinos, betting shops and even watching *Casino Royale.*
4. Support healthy efforts on the part of the person with Gambling Disorder to work on stress reduction and relaxation, as well as to exercise and eat balanced, nutritious meals.
5. Do not support or enable alcohol or drug abuse.
6. Take care of your mental and physical health (and that of the family).
7. Consider having individual or family therapy.
8. Take steps to reduce your own stress (see page 19).

helpful books

The Poker Face of Wall Street, A. Brown. Hoboken, N.J.: John Wiley & Sons, Inc., 2006.

Secret Keeping: Overcoming Hidden Habits and Addictions, J. H. Prin. Novato, Calif.: New World Library, 2006.

'Problem Gambling', T. Broffman, in C. N. Dulmus and L. A. Rapp-Paglicci (eds) *Handbook of Preventive Interventions For Adults,* Hoboken, N.J.: John Wiley & Sons, 2005.

Don't Leave It to Chance: A Guide for Families of Problem Gamblers, E. Charles and C. Krebs. Oakland, Calif.: New Harbinger Publications, 2000.

The Habit Control Workbook: Simple, Concise, Step-by-Step Directions for Control of Overeating, Compulsive Spending, Gambling, Lying, Hair Pulling, Explosive Temper, Prescription Drug Misuse, Irresponsible Sex, TV and Video Game Addiction, Teeth Grinding and Smoking, N. Birkedahl. Oakland, Calif.: New Harbinger Publications, 1990.

Meditation for Busy People: 60 Seconds to Serenity, D. Croves. San Rafael, Calif.: New World Library, 1993.

The Habit Change Workbook: How to Break Bad Habits and Form Good Ones, J. Claiborn and C. Pedrick. Oakland, Calif.: New Harbinger Publications, 2001.

Five Weeks to Healing Stress: The Wellness Option, V. O'Hara. Oakland, Calif.: New Harbinger Publications, 1996.

trichotillomania (hair-pulling)

Now why couldn't they have named this disorder simply 'Hair-Pulling Disorder'? The unpronounceable Trichotillomania (Trick-oh-till-oh-mania) is a chronic impulse-control disorder that involves the repetitive pulling out of one's own hair, resulting in noticeable hair loss. Those who like to pull out their hair may go through three distinct phases (although that is not the case for everyone with Trichotillomania). First, they may experience tension and a strong desire to pull out some hair. While they are hair-pulling they may feel excitement and relief, but soon after they will probably feel shameful, guilty and remorseful. Some hair-pull very deliberately to relieve Anxiety, while some do it without even noticing, perhaps while watching TV. What all types of people who hair-pull have in common is a deep sense of shame, frustration that they cannot stop, and secrecy. They try to cover their bald patches with wigs, scarves and hats, but eventually other people usually notice the habit, which causes the sufferer to feel embarrassed, angry and humiliated.

case study: Carrie

Carrie never attended her end-of-university dance. She started compulsively pulling out her hair when she was around nineteen but managed to hide her Trichotillomania by wearing caps or berets on campus. She felt lucky that it was thought acceptable to do so because, if not, she would have felt it necessary to hide in her room or miss classes – so great was her shame about her bald patches. By her twenty-fifth birthday she had removed 40 per cent of her entire head of hair, and, although a handsome member of the football team had asked her to accompany him to the graduation dance, she knew there was no way to cover up her problem at such an event. She sat at home that night and cried, as she did many nights throughout her years at university. It wasn't until she was nearly twenty-six, lonely, isolated and ashamed that she finally found her way, in a state of suicidal despair, to a therapist's office. There she learned that she was not alone; many people are drawn to pull out their hair (or skin-pick which is a similar disorder) and that the condition is treatable. She received treatment for underlying Depression, learned to monitor herself and control her stress and Anxiety. After a couple of relapses, she managed to overcome the disorder. Today, she loves to attend formal dinner-dances.

is this you (or someone close to you)?

- You regularly pull out your own hair, and the resulting hair loss is noticeable.
- You like to do this, or perhaps it makes you feel relieved.

Trichotillomania can be such a disabling disorder, yet it can be treated. If you have this problem or a related one such as chronic skin-picking, understand that you do not have to suffer from it any longer. Certain things about you, such as your mood, genetic make-up and background have contributed to the creation of this disorder and your inability to stop pulling out your hair. I know that it is exceedingly frustrating for you to be unable to control it, but understand that it is not about willpower. You simply have a condition that needs treating.

'do not pass go' signs

Many people with Trichotillomania become depressed and extremely isolated, avoiding pleasurable activities such as swimming or dating in case their secret is discovered. Those who pull out pubic hair may avoid going to the gynae-cologist, which makes them vulnerable to undiagnosed health problems. All this shame and unhappiness can lead people with Trichotillomania to abuse alcohol or drugs. Some of the disorders that may coexist with Trichotillo-mania are Obsessive-Compulsive Disorder, Tourette's Disorder, Bipolar Disorder, Phobias and personality problems. Trichotillomania can be treated.

what causes trichotillomania?

Genetic and environmental factors may cause it. It has many similarities with Obsessive-Compulsive Disorder and may have the same triggers. Chaotic, violent and distressing childhood experiences and disturbed early relationships with parents or carers may also be linked to the development of Trichotillomania. In one study, over two-thirds of people with Trichotillomania reported a history of at least one traumatic event, and nearly a fifth were also diagnosed with Post-Traumatic Stress Disorder. Some researchers have speculated that in traumatized individuals, Trichotillomania may represent a form of coping. Strangely enough, it may be a way to self-soothe.

what happens in your brain?

Brain scans of people with Trichotillomania exhibit differences compared to people without the disorder. Neurotransmitters, possibly dopamine, serotonin or both may play a role in the development of the disorder. Impulse-control seems to be associated with activity in the brain circuits that control the processing of emotional information. They need to be functioning properly in order for a person to be able to stop to consider whether or not to pull out hair and learn from the experience. It's easy to see how people without these abilities can continue to hair-pull, even though they are fully aware of the negative effects it has on their lives.

which treatments are likely to work?

Behavioural therapy (especially habit-reversal training), psychotherapy, psychodynamic psychotherapy, hypnotherapy, cognitive-behavioural psychotherapy and antidepressant medication.

best course of action?

Seek therapy plus an evaluation for antidepressant medication.

in the meantime what can you do?

1. Learn everything you can about Trichotillomania.
2. Start a self-motivated habit-reversal programme. Begin by writing down your feelings about the fact that you hair-pull. Pour out your shame and sadness onto paper, and especially answer the question: 'How has Trichotillomania affected my life?'
3. Write a list of the consequences of hair-pulling that you have experienced, either at home, work or socially (for example, being embarrassed when people noticed, having to wear wigs, or getting infections from pulling eyelashes).
4. Allow yourself to feel the sadness that probably came from really looking at what your hair-pulling has meant in your life, then spend some time

acknowledging that you have a problem but trying to be hopeful about getting beyond it:

- Consider that you are not alone. Many other people in the world suffer from Trichotillomania or related problems such as skin-picking. They feel ashamed about it as well too – yet many of them have beaten it, and you can too.
- Now start to make a series of daily affirmations. Create your own, something like: 'I accept myself and my struggles', 'Hair-pulling is something I can beat' and 'I am a worthy person'.

5. Next you must become fully aware of the exact extent of your hair-pulling behaviour. What is your full history of hair-pulling? Write down what you remember, that is, when it started, attempts to stop and so on. Make a chart.

6. Write down a list of all the ways in which the after-effects of hair-pulling are and have been problematic for you (for example, 'Won't go swimming even though I enjoy it' or 'Can't let my boyfriend find out, so it affects our getting close').

7. Now make a chart of your current hair-pulling behaviour. Include the date, location, any other activity you were involved in (such as listening to music), plus the time each episode started and when it finished. Record how many hairs were pulled out during each episode and rate how strong your hair-pulling urge was on a scale from 1–10, with 10 being the strongest urge you've ever felt to pull out hair. Add how you felt during each episode, including physical sensations you experienced. Now try to express, in writing, any deeper feelings (for example, of hurt, sadness, frustration or helplessness) that caused tension and a desire to hair-pull.

8. After you have faithfully kept a record for a week, ask yourself: 'What did I learn from keeping this record?' Write down your thoughts and feelings. Were you surprised how much hair you pulled? Were you surprised at how much time it took up? Write down all your observations.

9. Now you have information about your hair-pulling it's time to analyze it:
- Write a list of all your high-risk situations, that is, the places where you are most likely to hair-pull (for example, in bed, on the couch, at the cinema).
- Write a list of the emotions that typically lead you to hair-pulling (for example, feeling tired or stressed, unhappy about how work went that day, or bored).
- Now make changes in your routine to break your habit of hair-

pulling. This means noticing the signs and predicting an urge to hair-pull, then stopping it happening by becoming aware of your urge, changing your location and choosing to do something else. That 'something else' should be your preferred relaxation exercises, either the Progressive Body Relaxation exercise (see page 41), breathing exercise (see page 46) or meditation (see page 40). You may need to stop yourself several times in one day, but soon it will be less than that.

10. In order to monitor and interrupt the chain of events that may lead you to hair-pull in future implement the following:

Notice, Interrupt and Choose Plan

Notice the desire to hair-pull.
Interrupt the chain of feelings and urges to do so, while listening to positive reminders in your head.
Choose to engage in your favourite relaxation activity instead, to engage the calm, soothing part of you.

11. It can be helpful to post notes to yourself in places where you previously had a tendency to hair-pull, such as in front of your mirror. Use every creative idea you can come up with to help you Notice, Interrupt and Choose whenever you have the urge to hair-pull.

12. Continue to write down and monitor your experiences (both successes and occasional failures) using the Notice, Interrupt and Choose plan.

13. Check your mood by reading the sections on Mood Disorders (see Chapter 2) and Anxiety (see page 37ff). If you think you may fit into any of these categories and have an underlying Depression for example, seek immediate treatment and follow the self-help suggestions.

14. Is there a link between your hair-pulling and other types of problems such as Substance Abuse? If so seek immediate treatment.

15. There is a relationship between episodes of hair-pulling and stress. Take steps to reduce your stress and keep it low.

16. Learn to assert yourself appropriately, either by taking a self-assertion class, or learning about self-assertion (see page 38).

17. Keep up your relaxation and stress-relieving exercises and add to them, perhaps with a yoga class once or twice a week, a martial arts class and some aerobic exercise if appropriate.

18. Do the meditation exercise (on page 40) twice a day.

19. Establish a regular pattern of good-quality sleep. If you have problems sleeping follow the self-help suggestions for Insomnia or other Sleep Disorders (see page 361 onwards).
20. Once you have your hair-pulling under control, stay vigilant. Be mindful of the potential for any relapse and continue to monitor your urges whenever they appear.
21. Work on increasing your self-esteem (see page 105).
22. Write down a list of your strengths and accomplishments. Spend some time each day reminding yourself of these achievements.

for partners, friends and family members

- Encourage the sufferer to seek treatment for Trichotillomania as a matter of urgency.
- Support the mental-health treatment throughout its course and watch for signs of relapse afterwards (for example, mounting stress, secrecy, lack of openness and communication, alcohol or drug abuse, irritability, becoming isolated, wearing something to cover a bald spot or refusing to participate in activities that might mean revealing a bald spot).
- Do not belittle the person for hair-pulling.
- Support healthy efforts on the part of the person with Trichotillomania to work on stress reduction and relaxation, as well as to exercise and eat balanced, nutritious meals.
- Do not support or enable alcohol or drug abuse.
- Take care of your mental and physical health (and that of the family).
- Consider having individual or family therapy.
- Take steps to reduce your own stress (see page 19).

helpful books

Help for Hair-Pullers: Understanding and Coping with Trichotillomania, N. J. Keuthen, D. Stein and G. A. Christenson. Oakland, Calif.: New Harbinger Publications, 2001.

The Habit Change Workbook: How to Break Bad Habits and Form Good Ones, J. M. Claiborn and C. Pedrick. Oakland, Calif.: New Harbinger Publications, 2000.

The Habit Control Workbook: Simple, Concise, Step-by-Step Directions for Control of Overeating, Compulsive Spending, Gambling, Lying, Hair Pulling, Explosive Temper, Prescription Drug Misuse, Irresponsible Sex, TV and Video Game Addiction, Teeth Grinding and Smoking, N. Birkedahl. Oakland, Calif.: New Harbinger Publications, 1990.

Five Weeks to Healing Stress: The Wellness Option, V. O'Hara. Oakland, Calif.:
    New Harbinger Publications, 1996.

intermittent explosive disorder

It's never pretty to watch a fully grown adult having a temper tantrum. Being
on the receiving end of it can be quite terrifying, and even watching from the
sidelines produces feelings of alarm coupled with a strong desire to back
away. But it is also extremely disturbing for the person having the rage attack
and unable to control it. People who have a combination of anger plus a
problem with impulse-control may frequently fly into an unchecked rage
without warning. They may even do something they afterwards deeply regret
(or for which they face consequences) such as resorting to violence or
destroying property. It's not hard to imagine how having this disorder can
very seriously affect a person's ability to maintain relationships or have a
stable family life, social life or job.

case study: Van

*Van had a serious anger-management problem. He was a successful company
floor manager in his early thirties who had the responsibility for over fifty
workers making fashion garments for a large clothing chain. Many of his
workers were newly arrived immigrants who were grateful to have been
employed, so for a while Van got away with venting his explosive anger on any
unfortunate worker who happened to be in the wrong place at the wrong time.
But one day, a brave employee decided she'd had enough of Van's verbal abuse
and started legal proceedings against him and the company. Then other workers
followed suit; and at that point Van's bosses 'hauled him over the carpet' and
fired him for his inappropriate management style, for costing them money and
for bringing the company into disrepute. When I met Van he was ready to take
an honest look at the way he expressed his anger, because not only had he lost
his job but also his long-suffering wife had finally had the courage to leave him,
taking the children with her.*

*Van also suffered from migraine headaches and high blood pressure. He
sought medical advice and was prescribed medication to help with these
conditions and his impulse-control disorder (which ran in his family). He also
benefited from anger-management treatment as well as therapy to fully understand the effect of his uncontrolled anger on himself and others. His wife agreed
to enter therapy also (to work on her dependence and passivity), and the couple*

did manage to stay married. The most important outcome was that their children no longer had to witness their father in the throes of out-of-control aggression.

is this you (or someone close to you)?

- You sometimes have so much pent-up aggression that you have to let it out by assaulting some person or destroying property.
- The level of fury you express when you are doing this is greatly out of proportion to whatever triggered it.

If you are like this, your aggression is hurting you as well as the people around you. It's not your anger that is the problem, it's the way you go about expressing it. Your brain, genetic make-up and past experiences are conspiring to make it hard for you to control your anger or modify the way to let it out. Yet it is possible to let people know you are angry about something without overdoing it, hurting anyone, destroying property or landing in jail. Do not delay in seeking treatment.

'do not pass go' signs

Aggressive driving is a leading cause of death and injury in motor-vehicle accidents. Treatment of mental-health problems in aggressive drivers, especially those with Intermittent Explosive Disorder, is a public safety priority. Domestic violence often occurs when one spouse or partner suffers from Intermittent Explosive Disorder and their children become part of a cycle of violence, copying the angry behaviour as adults and perpetrating the same treatment on their families. People with Intermittent Explosive Disorder have problems maintaining jobs, friendships and marriages.

what causes intermittent explosive disorder?

It may have both a biological and psychosocial base. Aggressive drivers usually have a family history of anger problems and conflict. Intermittent Explosive Disorder is associated with a variety of other psychological disorders including Bipolar Disorder, Mood Disorders, Anxiety Disorders, Substance Abuse, Eating Disorders, nicotine addiction, Personality Disorders, Sleep Disorders and other Impulse-Control Disorders. Sufferers also display high rates of migraine headaches and are at an increased risk of heart disease and high blood pressure. There can be other underlying medical problems.

what happens in your brain?

Impulse-control seems to be associated with brain circuits that control the processing of emotional information. Most importantly, these circuits evaluate the significance of, and assess the consequences of, a person's responses to emotionally charged information. They need to be functioning properly in order for a person to be able to stop to consider how to express feelings of anger and learn from the experience. It's easy to see how a person without these abilities can get into trouble by impulsively perpetrating rage onto others.

which treatments are likely to work?

Anger-management classes and psychotherapy can help. Cognitive-behavioural interventions may be valuable as part of the overall treatment for Intermittent Explosive Disorder, and there is evidence that explosive episodes tend to respond favourably to a number of different types of medication. People with Intermittent Explosive Disorder need a thorough medical check-up to rule out the possibility that they may have a serious underlying medical problem.

best course of action?

Have a medical check-up and seek psychotherapy.

in the meantime what can you do?

1. Learn everything you can about anger and Intermittent Explosive Disorder (see reading list below).
2. Try to identify and write down as many past experiences and situations that led to explosive anger as you can remember. Write down the details of any physical acting-out that accompanied that anger. Rate your anger level from 1–10, with 10 being the angriest you have ever been.
3. Now try to express, in writing, the deeper feelings (for example, of hurt, sadness and helplessness) that caused your anger.
4. Keep a daily log of your current angry feelings. Write down when anger arises, the situation that led to your anger, the thoughts that went with it and the way you chose to express it. Rate your anger intensity level from 1–10.
5. Learn to assert yourself appropriately, either by taking a self-assertion class, or learning about self-assertion (see page 38).
6. A great way to prevent your anger from taking control is to implement the following:

Stop, Look, Listen, Think and Plan

When you feel anger rising:

Stop yourself making any angry response.
Look at your impulse to fly off the handle.
Listen either to what others are saying, or to the calm, soothing part of you.
Think about what you really want to say.
Plan an appropriate response.

7. Venting anger tends to increase and maintain it. Three better ways to reduce angry feelings are breathing/counting (the old 'count to ten' trick really works!), taking physical exercise, and distracting oneself with something pleasurable or interesting.
8. Check your mood by reading the sections on Mood Disorders (see Chapter 2) and Anxiety (see page 37ff). If you think you may fit into any of these categories and have an underlying Depression for example, seek immediate treatment and follow the self-help suggestions for example on page 16.
9. Identify any link between your anger and other types of problems, such as Substance Abuse. Seek help for those too.
10. There is a relationship between episodes of rage and stress. Take steps to reduce your stress and keep it low.
11. Practise relaxation (see Progressive Body Relaxation exercise page 41).
12. Practise both the Mindfulness of Breathing meditation (see page 40) and the Positive Regard meditation (see pages 127).
13. Establish a regular pattern of good-quality sleep. If you have problems sleeping follow the self-help suggestions for Insomnia or other Sleep Disorders (see page 361 onwards).
14. Work on increasing your self-esteem (see page 105).
15. Write down a list of your strengths and accomplishments. Spend some time each day reminding yourself of these achievements.

for partners, friends and family members

- Encourage the person to seek treatment for Intermittent Explosive Disorder as a matter of urgency.
- If you (or anyone in the family) are a victim of verbal or physical abuse, perhaps from a person with Intermittent Explosive Disorder, you need to report this to a mental-health professional immediately. If your

physical safety is threatened, call the police. If necessary, leave and go somewhere safe. Do not cover up the person's behaviour or try to protect him or her. Instead, protect yourself and your family, and in doing so you will be making it more likely that the person will receive the appropriate consequences for his or her actions, and hopefully, treatment too.

- Remember that children are particularly vulnerable to the negative effects of Intermittent Explosive Disorder. Take steps to protect them as well as yourself and any others in the vicinity.
- Support the person's mental-health treatment throughout its course, and watch for signs of relapse afterwards (for example, rising stress or tension, irritability, moodiness, alcohol or drug abuse).
- Support healthy efforts on the part of the person with Intermittent Explosive Disorder to work on stress reduction and relaxation, as well as to exercise and eat balanced, nutritious meals.
- Do not support or enable alcohol or drug abuse.
- Take care of your mental and physical health (and that of the family).
- Consider having individual and family therapy.
- Take steps to reduce your own stress (see page 19).

helpful books

The Anger Control Workbook, M. McKay and P. D. Rogers. Oakland, Calif.: New Harbinger Publications, 2000.

When Anger Hurts: Quieting the Storm Within, M. McKay, P. D. Rogers and J. McKay. Oakland, Calif.: New Harbinger Publications, 2003.

Anger: The Misunderstood Emotion, C. Tavris. New York: Touchstone, 1982.

How to Deal with Emotionally Explosive People, A. Bernstein. New York: McGraw-Hill, 2003.

The Verbally Abusive Relationship: How to Recognize It and How to Respond, P. Evans. Holbrook, Mass.: Adams Media Corporation.

The Anger Workbook, L. Bilodeau. New York: MJF Books, 1997.

Meditation for Busy People: 60 Seconds to Serenity, D. Croves. San Rafael, Calif.: New World Library, 1993.

Responding to Anger: A Workbook, L. Bilodeau. Center City, Minn.: Hazelden, 2001.

Taking Charge of Anger: How to Resolve Conflict, Sustain Relationships, and Express Yourself without Losing Control, W. R. Nay. Guilford Press, 2004.

You Can't Say That to Me! Stopping the Pain of Verbal Abuse – an 8-Step Program, S. H. Elgin. New York: John Wiley & Sons, Inc., 1995.

Five Weeks to Healing Stress: The Wellness Option, V. O'Hara. Oakland, Calif.: New Harbinger Publications, 1996.

The Assertiveness Workbook: How to Express Your Ideas and Stand Up for Yourself in Work and Relationships, R. J. Paterson. Oakland, Calif.: New Harbinger Publications, 2000.

The Habit Control Workbook: Simple, Concise, Step-by-Step Directions for Control of Overeating, Compulsive Spending, Gambling, Lying, Hair Pulling, Explosive Temper, Prescription Drug Misuse, Irresponsible Sex, TV and Video Game Addiction, Teeth Grinding and Smoking, N. Birkedahl. Oakland, Calif.: New Harbinger Publications, 1990.

The Habit Change Workbook: How to Break Bad Habits and Form Good Ones, J. Claiborn and C. Pedrick. Oakland, Calif.: New Harbinger Publications, 2001.

chapter 10
losing touch with reality: dissociative and psychotic disorders

"I only exist online."

Some people need a reality check. I'm not talking about the 'There are a lot of people in the world who are worse off than you!' type of reality check, but rather, a treatment that brings a person who is truly 'out of his mind' back to a proper awareness of who they are, where they are and the current time and date. Psychologists call one type of lost reality 'dissociation'. This involves an acute but time-limited alteration in people's feelings, behaviour or thoughts, so that they do not process or experience information about themselves, certain events or the surrounding world in the normal way. Most people have everyday dissociative experiences, such as daydreaming, but there are times when dissociation creates serious problems. Amnesia, for example, involves significant memory loss; in 'derealization' people feel disconnected from their surroundings, and 'depersonalization' is a state in which people feel detached from themselves. Dissociation can even lead to a complex and fascinating process in the psyche whereby a person creates alternative personalities, with distinct names, preferences, styles of speech and behaviour. This constitutes a disorder once known as Multiple Personality Disorder, which is now called Dissociative Identity Disorder.

Why does the mind dissociate in the first place? Some experts believe that dissociation is a normal and useful process designed to protect the psyche from the pain of traumatic experiences, that is, if we can somehow manage to separate ourselves from the pain of having to remember, face or be associated with the terrible events that are 'too awful to even think about', then we have improved our chances of surviving them. But as time goes on, there are several ways in which immediate, normative dissociation can become problematic. A person who has experienced repeated childhood sexual abuse, for example, might use his or her imaginative abilities to create one or more alternative personalities – perhaps someone older and tougher who might, in fantasy, be the one to take the abuse. Another person might react to, say, witnessing a partner die in a car accident, by losing touch with the reality of his or her own identity and living circumstances. This person might wander off to another part of the country with no memory of the past and be reported as a missing person until either he or she is found, or regains their memory.

The DSM-IV classifies Dissociative Disorders into several types of reactions. First there is Dissociative Amnesia, in which a person experiences significant and troubling memory loss. Dissociative Fugue describes the condition mentioned above where a person wanders away from home, cannot remember the past and even becomes forgetful or confused about his or her personal identity. A person suffering from Depersonalization Disorder is one who frequently feels detached from his or her own mind or body, as if in a dream. Then there is Dissociative Identity Disorder, a not uncommon disorder that involves the creation of two or more distinct identities in the same person.

dissociative amnesia

Film makers and writers of fiction just love afflicting their leading characters with 'amnesia', don't they? It creates such an interesting twist to the usual 'boy-meets girl' or crime story. But despite its dramatic value, Dissociative Amnesia really causes enormous problems in people's lives, and it is a sign that something extremely stressful has affected their minds and that they need help. It is usually triggered by trauma. People who have been involved in wars, for example, are very likely to report that after a situation where they believed they were going to die, saw others die or killed someone they experienced amnesia (as well as out-of-body feelings, depersonalization, derealization and extreme detachment). In fact, a high percentage of returning soldiers have either partial or complete amnesia of their combat experiences, and their various dissociative symptoms often contribute to the development of Post-Traumatic Stress Disorder (see page 62).

case study: Juan

After a major earthquake disaster, I was asked to visit a young man in a local hospital. Juan had been brought into the emergency room by the police. He was suffering from a broken arm and superficial wounds. He was also disoriented and could not remember the events that had led to his injuries, but there were no signs of head injury. I suspected that his amnesia had been triggered by traumatic events caused by the earthquake, and that turned out to be true. Once Juan was medically stabilized I began to work with him. Under hypnosis he was able to recall that his home had collapsed during one of the aftershocks. Tragically, his wife, baby daughter and mother had died beneath the rubble but his two-year-old son had survived – Juan just had no idea where he was. In a later hypnotic session he remembered that his son had been taken to hospital – and indeed it turned out that young Xavier was in stable condition in the children's ward of the very same hospital.

is this you (or someone close to you)?

- You have become incapable of remembering important pieces of personal information, perhaps concerning something very upsetting or traumatic that has occurred in your life.
- This condition could not be mistaken for ordinary forgetfulness.
- This amnesia causes you significant problems in your life.

If the above applies to you, you are experiencing one of the amazing ways in which the mind copes with painful experiences. You may have recently returned from a combat zone, been involved in an accident or been the victim or witness of a crime. Whatever happened to you, having Dissociative Amnesia is usually a sign that you are have a deep-seated anguish about something.

'do not pass go' signs

Losing a bank of memory can be extremely problematic in terms of practical, everyday living. The sufferer should receive help, not only to restore memory but also to help him or her process and heal from the underlying cause.

what causes dissociative amnesia?

Dissociative Amnesia can be triggered or caused by a highly traumatic event such as being involved in a war, natural disaster, crime or accident. The condition arrives suddenly, immediately following the horrifying event. It might last only hours or days and quite often the recovery is spontaneous. A person may lose all memory of what happened during a specific time frame or just certain pieces of information and not even realize that he or she has Dissociative Amnesia. The person's knowledge of general information usually remains intact.

which treatments are likely to work?

Psychotherapy will help sufferers work through traumatic memories and reduce dissociation. Techniques such as hypnosis have proven helpful, along with selective use of anti-Anxiety and antidepressant medications for co-existing conditions such as Depression. Eriksonian hypnotherapy is recommended for this disorder. Hypnotherapy can help a person to recover the lost memories. (This technique has become somewhat controversial after some people who recovered memories of abuse took those they believed to be their abusers to court. However, it can be extremely effective.)

best course of action?

Seek psychotherapy from a qualified, experienced mental-health professional who is trained in Eriksonian hypnotherapy.

in the meantime what can you do?

1. Learn as much as you can about Dissociative Amnesia and trauma.
2. If you remember anything at all about a stressful or traumatic event in your life that may have triggered Dissociative Amnesia, try to focus on feelings that accompanied that event, either by writing them down in a journal or by recounting them to someone you trust. This may be difficult or painful, but it will help heal the trauma.
3. Work on relaxation (page 41).
4. Practise meditation (page 40).
5. Take steps to reduce your stress (see exercises on page 19).
6. If you have been in a combat zone, your Dissociative Amnesia may be an indication that you are also suffering from Post-Traumatic Stress Disorder (see page 62). Seek help immediately.
7. If applicable, seek psychological services from your particular military agency. New treatment techniques such as virtual exposure therapy (in

which a person receives healing re-exposure to traumatic experiences via computer images) are becoming available. Some of these have been designed for specific combat areas such as Iraq and Afghanistan.

when someone close to you is suffering from dissociative amnesia

1. Learn everything you can about Dissociative Amnesia and the particular trauma or stressful event that may have caused it.
2. Help the person suffering from Dissociative Amnesia, to get the best treatment possible.
3. Educate other family members and friends about Dissociative Amnesia, and prepare them for whatever is the expected progression of the disorder (the prognoses may vary, depending on the cause).
4. If the person with Dissociative Amnesia is unable to cope with certain aspects of day-to-day living, provide practical help and seek support from friends, family members, community services and professionals.
5. People with Dissociative Amnesia can be vulnerable. Take steps to protect the person from abuse, neglect or self-harm.
6. Get some help and support for yourself and other family members.
7. The 'quality-of-life' requirements of the sufferer need to be explored and implemented as far as possible. These include continuing to live in his or her own home, with as much independence as possible, having plenty of contact with spouse or partner, family and friends, as well as feeling happy and useful until full recovery is made.

helpful books
You are unlikely to find self-help books for Dissociative Amnesia itself. Instead, below are two self-help books for the underlying cause of Dissociative Amnesia, that is, trauma.

The Courage to Heal Workbook: For Women and Men Survivors of Child Sexual Abuse, L. Davis. New York: Harper & Row, 1990.
The Courage to Heal: A Guide for Women Survivors of Child Sexual Abuse, (3rd ed.), E. Bass and L. Davis. New York: Harper & Row, 1988.

dissociative fugue

Imagine wandering off from home one day with a bit of cash in your pocket and, as if in a dream, you take a train to a completely different part of the country. You forget everything about where you came from, and even assume a new identity. In rare cases, this does actually happen to some people. They are not criminals hiding out, or witnesses involved in a protection scheme, they are usually ordinary people reacting this way in response to a traumatic event.

case study: 'Maria'

'Maria' had been a waitress at a new restaurant in a small country town for only two months when local police were alerted to the fact that she was driving a borrowed car without a driving licence, and had no means of identification. The officer who questioned her was concerned about her inability to recall important pieces of personal information, such as her previous address. A police computer check revealed that she was really a woman called Gwen, who had been listed as a missing person over three months before. She was married with a teenage son and had lived most of her life in a city three hundred kilometres away. Gwen had been extremely close to her twin sister, who had been killed in a car crash shortly before Gwen's disappearance. The trauma of losing her sister had triggered an unusual kind of amnesia in which she had wandered away and lost track of her own identity. Gwen not only needed help to recover her true identity but she also needed to heal from the loss of her twin sister. I deduced that Gwen's Fugue state was an unconscious, symbolic acting out of the acutely painful loss of her 'other (twin) identity'. Gwen soon made a full recovery from her Dissociative Fugue, but dealing with her sister's death was a far longer process.

is this you (or someone close to you)?

- You suddenly travel away from where you live or work, and cannot remember your past.
- You become forgetful or confused about who you are or even assume a new identity.

'do not pass go' signs

Dissociative Fugue can be extremely distressing to the families of those who suffer from it, since their disappearance will be shocking and worrying. Whilst people in the midst of a Dissociative Fugue may look purposeful – taking public transport, going to restaurants and so on – they are usually completely unaware of their loss of memory of important personal information. They do not know who they really are and sometimes take on a new identity, yet people they come across would not necessarily notice anything unusual in their behaviour. When a missing person suffering from Dissociative Fugue finally begins to have some sense that he or she has become disconnected from home and seeks some answers, the person may then be reunited with family and friends. Then treatment can begin to help him or her recover their full memory and work on the underlying causes.

what causes dissociative fugue?
It may be caused by a traumatic event. Dissociative Fugue is a complex disorder that is frequently preceded by major Depression. There is often a history of childhood trauma.

which treatments are likely to work?
As with Dissociative Amnesia, psychotherapy and Eriksonian hypnotherapy are likely to be helpful. If Depression is present, or if trauma has triggered the disorder, treatment for those underlying issues will help with recovery of memories.

best course of action?
Seek psychotherapy and Eriksonian hypnotherapy, as well as stress-reduction and relaxing techniques such as yoga and meditation.

when someone close to you may be suffering from dissociative fugue
1. Learn everything you can about Dissociative Fugue, and the events that may have caused it.
2. Help the person suffering from Dissociative Fugue to receive the best treatment possible.
3. Educate other family members and friends about Dissociative Fugue, and prepare them for whatever is the expected course of the disorder (the prognoses for Dissociative Fugue may vary).
4. Make plans to help on occasions when the person with Dissociative Fugue may be receiving treatment and unable to take up family or work responsibilities.
5. People with Dissociative Fugue are vulnerable. Take steps to protect the sufferer from abuse, neglect or self-harm.
6. Get some help and support for yourself and other family members.

7. Encourage the person suffering from Dissociative Fugue to undertake exercise that is appropriate for his or her age and physical capabilities (first check with his or her physician).

8. The person's quality-of-life requirements need to be explored and implemented as far as possible. These include continuing to live in his or her own home, having as much independence as possible, having plenty of contact with spouse or partner, family and friends, as well as feeling happy and useful until a full recovery has been achieved.

9. Due to the nature of this disorder, it is usually down to a partner, family member or friend of the person suffering from Dissociative Fugue to help him or her find appropriate treatment. The partner, family member or friend will probably be useful in helping to supply pieces of missing information that cannot be retrieved by the sufferer.

10. Encourage relaxation (see page 41), as well as the reduction of stress (see page 19) and Anxiety (see page 37ff).

helpful books

You are unlikely to find self-help books for Dissociative Fugue itself, largely because when a person is suffering from a Dissociative Disorder he or she is unlikely to be sufficiently aware of the symptoms to recognize that help is needed. However, the following are two helpful books for the healing of trauma:

The Courage to Heal Workbook: For Women and Men Survivors of Child Sexual Abuse, L. Davis. New York: Harper & Row, 1990.
The Courage to Heal: A Guide for Women Survivors of Child Sexual Abuse, (3rd ed.), E. Bass and L. Davis. New York: Harper & Row, 1988.

dissociative identity disorder

Dissociative Identity Disorder (DID) was previously known as Multiple Personality Disorder and the condition has been somewhat sensationalized in a number of ways. The American comedian Rosanne Barr made headlines a few years ago when she announced she suffered from the disorder. Have you come across the book *Sybil*? It's about a woman who suffered extreme childhood abuse and, according to her psychiatrist Dr Cornelia Wilbur, developed sixteen alternative personalities. The book, written by journalist Flora Rheta Schreiber was hugely popular and was made into a TV film in 1976 starring Sally Field. Field won an Emmy for her performance, and the story of Sybil had a striking effect on both pop culture and the mental-health profession. More recently, in the film *Primal Fear*, Ed Norton plays a criminal who avoids going to prison by pretending that his crime was committed by an alternative personality of whom he was unaware (oops, I just told you the ending!).

case study: Greta

A woman called me for an appointment one day, saying she thought she needed to be treated for Anxiety but she did not turn up at the arranged time. When I called her to reschedule, she told me that she had been involved in a minor car accident. A week later, she missed another appointment, and this time she explained on the telephone that she had 'bumped' her car again. I wondered if she was ambivalent about seeking therapy. Greta finally did turn up, a month after she first telephoned me. She seemed overwhelmed – and I thought she was indeed suffering from Anxiety – but I wondered why her memories of childhood were so fragmented. She told me about things in her current life that confused her, such as discovering strange clothing in her closet and receipts for items she couldn't remember buying.

After a while, I met the first of Greta's alternative personalities – an extremely hostile male identity called 'Jim' who spoke in a very low, threatening voice. When 'Jim' was in charge, he let me know he thought it was a waste of time for Greta to be in therapy. Eventually, other alternative personalities ('alters') began to introduce themselves to me – there were eight in all. When I finally met the youngest one, 'June', who was only three years old, I understood why Greta seemed so accident-prone – apparently she let 'June' drive. I had to negotiate with Greta and all her alters to make a safer choice. 'Jim' was put in charge of motor vehicles (which pleased him) – as long as he promised to contain his road rage.

One of the most interesting aspects of Greta's DID was that she had medical symptoms that utterly baffled her gynaecologist. Greta herself was menopausal and having associated hormonal problems, but if she went to the clinic as 'Jim' or any other alters her symptoms were completely different. Once she had given me permission to explain things to her doctor, she was able to receive appropriate medical treatment. Greta worked hard to develop cooperation between all parts of herself, and eventually moved on to being sufficiently integrated to sustain a long-term relationship.

People who really do suffer from this disorder will not be able to self-diagnose, but the diagnostic criteria set out below may ring some bells for you – or perhaps you know someone who seems to have the following symptoms:

is this you (or someone close to you)?

- There are two or more distinct identities in one person.
- These personalities take it in turns to control the person's behaviour.
- There is an inability to remember important personal information, such as biographical details, which cannot be explained by ordinary forgetfulness.
- These symptoms are not caused by any substance or alcoholic intoxication.

These different identities may have different names, attitudes, speech styles, vocal tones, and even gender identity and medical conditions. They may or may not be aware of each other. For example, a particular identity may be aware of all the others, some of the others or none of them. There is usually one basic identity (referred to as the 'host' personality) that may be the closest to a 'real self'.

'do not pass go' signs

DID is a very complex condition. People who suffer from it often have difficulty with relationships, social life and work, and it stands to reason that those around them might find their personality 'switches' confusing (that is, when they change from one personality being dominant to another). There have been reported instances of one identity behaving in a way (for example, committing crimes) that would be abhorrent to other identities if they knew about it. Sometimes an identity takes on a task that he or she is not equipped to handle, such as a ten year-old identity operating heavy machinery – which is a life-threatening situation. The separate personalities sometimes have different medical problems, which can baffle doctors and hamper diagnosis and treatment. A person with DID will have significant problems with relationships and at work because co-workers will notice that he or she is sometimes a 'different person' and assume that indicates a lack of consistency and stability. Many people with DID attempt suicide, and the disorder is often accompanied by substance abuse and Eating Disorders. In order to make it possible for a person with DID to be at peace, he or she needs to be diagnosed and treated as soon as possible by someone who is an expert in this disorder.

what causes dissociative identity disorder?

Repeated childhood trauma can cause a person to dissociate in a manner that is normative and helpful to the psyche, but after a while, that dissociation may provide the basis for the development of other personality states. People with DID have usually experienced horrible traumatic events. In many cases this involved extreme, sustained and repetitive childhood sexual or physical abuse. In fact, sexual abuse (often incest) is the most common type of abuse suffered by people with DID. Many of them experienced extreme sadism, bizarre torture (sometimes ritualized) and being confined in small, dark spaces. Some people with DID were not directly abused themselves, but witnessed something horrifying happening to someone else, for example, one parent killing another, frequent abuse of a sibling, or a sibling dying at the hands of a parent. In order to avoid the horrors of reality a child's mind can create one or more personalities other than the self, who can experience the trauma instead, remember it, and allow the child to escape and forget.

which treatments are likely to work?

Psychotherapists who have worked with people with DID have developed treatments that usually involve mapping all the person's 'alters', healing the underlying traumas and either promoting personality integration or helping the identities to coexist comfortably and cooperate with each other. Treatment for trauma is an essential, and this often involves hypnosis. Choose an expert therapist or psychoanalyst with training in the treatment of DID. A modified form of eye-movement desensitization and reprocessing (EMDR), a relatively new treatment method for the treatment of PTSD and general trauma, is sometimes used, while art therapy is often helpful as well.

best course of action

The treatment of DID is complex and specialist work, so if you think you or a person you know might suffer from this disorder it is vital to find a psychotherapist or psychoanalyst with experience and training in this area.

in the meantime, what can you do?

If you suffer from untreated DID you may have little awareness of your different identities, but others may suspect this diagnosis and suggest you get treatment. One clue would be that you lose time, that is, you cannot remember or account for certain periods in your day, week, or life in general. Another clue might be that you are sometimes asked for personal details that you cannot remember. There might be other confusing signs in your life, such as seeing food in the refrigerator that you do not like and cannot remember buying. You might encounter unfamiliar clothing in your closet that seems to belong to someone else. Most people with DID who seek psychotherapy do so for other reasons, for example, they think they might be depressed. If you are not sure what is wrong with you, but suspect that you may have a Mood or Dissociative Disorder, have the courage to seek treatment and find out.

if someone close to you appears to be suffering from dissociative identity disorder

A close friend, partner or family member of someone with undiagnosed DID might notice that they mysteriously change in a way other people do not. One day they might seem nervous and softly spoken, while on the next day they are brash, confident and loud. From time to time there are observable differences in their behaviour, stance, facial appearance, vocal tone, mannerisms or posture. Different 'alters' might even have different medical conditions. In some cases, people with DID 'switch' personalities quite rapidly. The process of changing from one 'alter' to another might involve facial grimaces, blinking, eye-rolling or twitching.

- Learn everything you can about DID and show empathy towards the sufferer.
- Help the person suffering from DID to receive the best treatment possible.
- Educate other family members and friends about DID.
- Support the person with DID at times when he or she may be undergoing intensive treatment and unable to take up their usual responsibilities.
- 'Alters' can sometimes be violent or abusive towards self or others. Take steps to protect the person, as well as yourself and others, from abuse, neglect or self-harm.
- Teach everyone in the family about setting appropriate limits or boundaries with the person with DID.
- Do not support or enable unhealthy efforts on the part of the person with DID to self-treat with drugs or alcohol.
- Do not support risky behaviour.
- Encourage the person's healthy efforts to reduce stress through relaxation exercises (see page 41), appropriate physical exercise, meditation (see page 40) or yoga.
- Get some therapeutic help and support for yourself and other family members.

helpful books

Got Parts? An Insider's Guide to Managing Life Successfully with Dissociative
    Identity Disorder, A. T. W. Ann Arbor, Mich.: Loving Healing Press, 2005.
When Rabbit Howls, T. Chase. New York: Jove Books, 1987.
Diagnosis and Treatment of Multiple Personality Disorder, F. Putnam. New
    York: The Guilford Press, 1989.
Amongst Ourselves: A Self-Help Guide to Living with Dissociative Identity
    Disorder, Tracey Alderman and Karen Marshall. Oakland, Calif.: New
    Harbinger Publications, 1998.
First Person Plural: My Life As a Multiple, C. West. New York: Hyperion, 1999.
The Courage to Heal Workbook: For Women and Men Survivors of Child Sexual
    Abuse, L. Davis. New York: Harper & Row, 1990.
The Courage to Heal: A Guide for Women Survivors of Child Sexual Abuse
    (3rd ed.), E. Bass and L. Davis. New York: Harper & Row, 1988.

depersonalization disorder

Have you ever felt like a robot? People with Depersonalization Disorder feel
unreal, or estranged from themselves. Instead of 'Stop the world, I want to
get off!' the sufferer is inwardly wishing 'Help me get back on!' It's not a nice,
dreamy sensation but rather a frustrating feeling of being on the periphery
of life.

case study: Sylvia

A woman in her mid-forties came to see me one day, fearfully telling me that she
thought she was becoming insane. She based this notion on the fact that, once or
twice a week she was having long periods of feeling detached from her body. In
addition, the world around her seemed hazy, as though she was peering at it
through a veil. Sylvia said that during these episodes, each lasting several hours,
she could not think clearly and felt as though she was in a 'waking dream'. She
would shake her head or slap herself to try to be more in touch with herself and
her surroundings, but nothing worked. Recently, the detached feelings had
become more frequent, and were accompanied by a loss of balance. Sylvia had
begun to drop things and was afraid that she would lose her waitressing job.

As a child, Sylvia had been exploited by her mother who put her to work in
her brothel at the age of fourteen. Sylvia ran away two years later, married a
decent man and raised two children. She had held a steady job at the same
restaurant for nine years, but recently the place had changed hands. I realized

that the new owner-manager, who was an unpleasant and exploitative woman, reminded Sylvia of her mother; and that having a daily reminder of her early abuse had reawakened painful traumatic feelings and caused her symptoms. After a period of intensive trauma work, Sylvia began to heal from past abuse. Her depersonalization symptoms gradually disappeared.

is this you (or someone close to you)?

- You frequently feel like you are detached from your own mind or body, as if in a dream.
- At the same time, you are aware of reality around you.
- These experiences are distressing, or they may cause you problems in your life.

If the above applies to you, you will be aware that depersonalization is a very uncomfortable feeling. It's as if you are being somehow filtered out from being fully in the world. Most people who experience depersonalization are distressed by the strangeness of their experience. Some people also experience numbness in certain parts of their body or a strange sense that their body, or part of their body has changed in size (one of the most famous sufferers of Depersonalization Disorder was surely Alice in Wonderland!). Joking aside, this disorder can be moderately disabling, and it is as well to get help. Most importantly, the underlying causes need to be identified and treated.

'do not pass go' signs

Depersonalization Disorder can arrive very suddenly, but recovery is usually gradual. People suffering from it frequently have additional symptoms of Anxiety, Depression, Substance Abuse, a Personality Disorder, Hypochondriasis (or 'mind-chatter' that won't stop). A few also experience derealization, which is losing touch with one's surroundings, as well. They need help from a qualified mental-health professional.

what causes depersonalization disorder?

It is thought that severe stress, Depression, Panic Attacks, exhaustion, being faced with a traumatic event, or drug use (especially marijuana and hallucinogen ingestion) are causes of Depersonalization Disorder. It has also been associated with childhood interpersonal trauma, in particular emotional maltreatment.

what is happening in the brain?

Neurochemical discoveries have pointed to the involvement of several different brain messaging pathways. Brain imaging studies have revealed changes in those parts of the brain that control how we process sensory information, as well as changes in areas that respond to aversive events.

which treatments are likely to work?

Psychotherapy is recommended, including psychodynamic psychotherapy, psychoanalysis, trauma-focused therapy, hypnotherapy, and cognitive-behavioural therapy. Repetitive transcranial magnetic stimulation (a method of stimulating certain areas of the brain) has produced a reduction of depersonalization symptoms and medication is sometimes effectively used.

best course of action?

Seek therapy.

in the meantime what can you do?

1. Learn as much as you can about Depersonalization Disorder and trauma.
2. If there has been a stressful or traumatic event in your life that may have triggered Dissociative Amnesia, try to focus on feelings that may have accompanied that event, either by writing them down in a journal or by recounting them to someone you trust. This may be difficult or painful, but it will help heal the trauma.
3. Work on relaxation (page 41).
4. Practise meditation (page 40).
5. Take steps to reduce your stress (see exercise on page 19).
6. Avoid drugs or alcohol, especially if your Depersonalization Disorder symptoms may have been cause by drug taking, such as marijuana or hallucinogen ingestion.
7. If you have been in a combat zone or involved in a major accident, crime or other terrifying event you may also be suffering from Post-Traumatic Stress Disorder (see page 62). Seek treatment.
8. If applicable, seek psychological services from your particular military agency.

when someone close to you is suffering from depersonalization disorder

1. Learn everything you can about Depersonalization Disorder, and the particular condition, trauma or stressful event that may have caused it.

2. Help the person suffering from Depersonalization Disorder to receive the best treatment possible.

3. Educate other family members and friends about Depersonalization Disorder, and prepare them for whatever is the expected progression of the disorder (the prognoses may vary, depending on the cause).

4. If the person with Depersonalization Disorder is unable to cope with certain aspects of day-to-day living, provide practical help and seek support from friends, family, local services and professionals.

5. People with Depersonalization Disorder can be vulnerable. Take steps to protect the sufferer from abuse, neglect or self-harm.

6. Do not support or enable unhealthy efforts on the part of the person with Depersonalization Disorder to self-treat with drugs or alcohol.

7. Do not support risky behaviour.

8. Encourage the sufferer's healthy efforts to reduce stress through relaxation exercises (see page 41), appropriate physical exercise, meditation (see page 40) and yoga.

9. Get some help and support for yourself and other family members.

10. If the person is suffering from very severe Depersonalization Disorder, his or her quality-of-life requirements need to be explored and implemented as far as possible. These include continuing to live in his or her own home, with as much independence as possible, having plenty of contact with spouse or partner, family and friends, as well as feeling happy and useful until a full recovery is achieved.

helpful books

You are unlikely to find self-help books for Depersonalization Disorder itself, but the following will be helpful for the healing of any underlying trauma:

The Courage to Heal Workbook: For Women and Men Survivors of Child Sexual Abuse, L. Davis. New York: Harper & Row, 1990.

The Courage to Heal: A Guide for Women Survivors of Child Sexual Abuse, (3rd ed.), E. Bass and L. Davis. New York: Harper & Row, 1988.

psychotic disorders

In everyday speech, we tend to use words like 'delusional' or 'psychotic' with a pejorative twist or in ways that do not correspond with their actual meaning, for example, 'You want to borrow a fiver – are you delusional?' or 'Your psychotic dog tried to bite me!' However, psychosis is actually an abnormal state of mind in which a person's perceptions, understanding and other thought processes, as well as emotions and behaviour, are seriously disrupted or impaired. The person may have delusions (believing something highly improbable) and/or hallucinations (seeing, hearing, feeling, tasting or smelling things that aren't really there). The sufferer's speech may be extremely disorganized.

The DSM-IV provides categories with symptoms for several main Psychotic Disorders: Schizophrenia (matched in many ways by the similar, shorter-lasting Schizophreniform Disorder and Brief Psychotic Disorder), Schizo-affective Disorder (in which a Mood Disorder is also present), and Delusional Disorder (when a person holds highly improbable beliefs). There is also Shared Psychotic Disorder, in which close family members, partners or friends of someone with a Psychotic Disorder adopt a similar belief system. For example, the family of a man who has delusions that he is under surveillance by the Mafia may go along with his attempts to hide, move house, and even alter identities in a mistaken attempt to be safe.

schizophrenia

One per cent of all people in the world are affected by Schizophrenia, so it is a major mental-health problem for which, in many countries, there is no adequate treatment. People who live in Western countries who are diagnosed with Schizophrenia can usually, to a large degree, be helped to maintain jobs and relationships and lead relatively symptom-free lives. Unfortunately, there is still stigma attached to Schizophrenia and similar disorders, based largely on the incorrect generalization that sufferers are all 'crazy', dangerous, homeless, evil, drug-addicted and frightening, or have multiple personalities. These stereotypes come from ignorance.

case study: Jodie

When Jodie was twenty-four she was struggling to find employment. Living alone in a tiny flat in Birmingham, she began to hear voices. She would leave home in the morning to search for a job, but before she even reached the train station the voices would tell her to go somewhere else. She thought one of the voices sounded like her stepfather, who had gone to jail for domestic violence towards Jodie's mother. The voices told her that people in the streets were following and watching her, and that her landlady was trying to poison her. She began to feel more and more paranoid and eventually had trouble leaving her flat. Then she started believing that the TV, fridge and heater were all observation stations for devils and warlocks who were spying on her with a plan to kidnap and rape her. Her mother became alarmed at the change in her daughter and worried about what people would think. She persuaded Jodie to move with her to a country area outside Birmingham and cared for her as best she could, but Jodie needed far more than country air. She did not improve and, in fact, she began to believe her mother was involved in the plot to harm her. Eventually her mother got her to hospital.

After she was diagnosed with Schizophrenia, Jodie found herself asking, 'Why did this happen to me?' She blamed her stepfather and she blamed herself – until she finally understood the truth – it just happened. Jodie learned that Schizophrenia is a chronic but treatable disease, and that she could lead a pretty normal life if she followed her treatment plan, attended therapy sessions, took her medication regularly and kept her stress to a minimum. Not all people with Schizophrenia have successful treatment outcomes, but things worked out well for Jodie, who is now married, with a job she enjoys.

do you (or does someone close to you)

- Have delusions, hallucinations, strange speech and/or extremely odd or very 'flat', uncommunicative behaviour?
- Are less able than before to connect with others, to work or to attend to personal grooming and care?

If you suspect you may have Schizophrenia but have not yet sought treatment, you are probably very frightened. It is very upsetting to realize you are sometimes smelling, hearing, seeing or tasting things that others are unaware of. You may even be taking drugs or using alcohol in an attempt to mask your symptoms; some people believe it's better to be thought of as a 'junkie' than someone with mental problems. If so, you are only making your problem worse and delaying getting your life back on track. You are not 'crazy' – you just happen to be suffering from a treatable disorder.

People who have symptoms of Schizophrenia are frequently unaware that they appear odd to the people around them, so it often falls to family members to seek help for them. Here is a more detailed explanation of the types of symptoms you might observe in people with Schizophrenia:

- Their speech may be disorganized, that is, they jump from topic to topic in an unusual way that creates confusion for the listener or makes it hard for the listener to follow.
- Sometimes their speech is completely incomprehensible – a kind of 'word salad'.
- They may have delusions, that is, they misinterpret what is happening around them or have incorrect beliefs about other people, situations or events.
- They sometimes erroneously imagine that certain objects, sounds, sights, songs, gestures or comments people make, something they hear on radio or see on TV, or something they read in a book or magazine are directed at them personally.
- They might have delusions that they are being persecuted, spied upon, followed or tormented in some way.
- They might have truly bizarre delusions, such as believing that aliens are controlling their thoughts.
- They may have hallucinations, which can involve hearing voices or seeing/smelling/tasting/touching things that aren't really there.
- Their behaviour may be inappropriate for a given situation, ranging from angry ranting in public or masturbating in full view of others.
- A small percentage may become threatening to others around them, not out of a calculated desire to hurt them, but because of fears that they themselves may be harmed.
- Their personal hygiene may be neglected.
- They may be unable to follow through with day-to-day activities necessary for self-care, such as preparing meals.
- They may dress in an odd and disorganized manner.
- They may carry or wear items that they believe will ward off threatening entities (for example, wearing tin foil over their ears to stop aliens stealing their thoughts.)
- Sometimes their behaviour looks more as though they are completely unaware of their surroundings and have fallen into a stupor, that is, they hardly move at all and remain expressionless with little variation in tone when they speak.
- Some take on strange poses and remain motionless like that for a long time.

'do not pass go' signs

Without treatment, Schizophrenia is an extremely debilitating disorder, and it can be extremely hard on families and friends as well. With treatment, a person with Schizophrenia can function well and expect to lead a pretty normal life.

A number of other mental-health problems seem to go hand in hand with Schizophrenia, such as Obsessive-Compulsive Disorder and Substance Abuse, these also need to be treated.

what causes schizophrenia?

There have been many theories about the cause or development of Schizophrenia, including that it might be due to birth complications or triggered by viruses or an autoimmune problem. But most researchers now agree that it is caused by biochemical disruptions in the brain. It's not contagious, and it's no one's fault. Schizophrenia is a chronic illness that can deteriorate, or be triggered when a person experiences high stress. It runs in families, and you have a higher chance of having Schizophrenia if your parents (especially your mother) had it.

what is happening in the brain?

An underlying neurodevelopmental problem may be a cause of at least one form of Schizophrenia, that is, an early disruption of normal brain development possibly due to prenatal exposure to influenza. Some researchers consider that Schizophrenia may be caused by an excess of the neurotransmitter dopamine. Dopamine is supposed to transmit messages from neuron to neuron, and it needs to be properly balanced or the message gets confused. (A good analogy is a toy electric train set. If too little power is supplied to it the train stops; too much and the train flies right off the tracks.) Examination of the brain anatomy of people with Schizophrenia has revealed anatomical disturbances such as abnormal enlargements in certain areas.

which treatments are likely to work?

Those who live in affluent societies are extremely lucky that anti-psychotic drugs are available to treat people with Schizophrenia. With proper mental-health treatment, sufferers can live decent lives and families can have the support they need. Medication, psychotherapy and family therapy are recommended.

best course of action?

Schizophrenia usually begins when a person is in their twenties, although occasionally it starts later than that. Whenever symptoms begin to appear, it is vital to seek immediate treatment.

in the meantime what can you do?

1. Learn everything you can about Schizophrenia.
2. Learn everything you can about the treatments for Schizophrenia.
3. Learn everything about the medications for Schizophrenia, including the possible side effects.
4. Gather strong support among family, good friends, therapists and physicians.
5. If you need basic help, such as somewhere to live, ask someone you trust to help you find the appropriate services.
6. Understand that it is not shameful to be diagnosed with Schizophrenia. You deserve respect, understanding and the best treatment available.
7. Work on reducing your stress (see page 19).
8. Work on improving your social skills by practising:
   - Initiating appropriate conversation with others.
   - Giving compliments.
   - Accepting compliments.
   - Being assertive in your communication (see page 38).
   - Making sure you keep appointments.
   - Being on time for social events.
   - Being honest.
   - Knowing when it is appropriate to disclose the fact that you have Schizophrenia.
   - Being able to set boundaries with others.
   - Maintaining eye contact.
   - Giving oneself and others an appropriate amount of personal space.
   - Learning to deal with criticism.
   - Learning to deal with teasing.

9. Because Schizophrenia is a chronic illness, even at the point where treatment is working and symptoms are under control there is always the potential for relapse. The following are pointers for reducing the risk of relapse:
   - Stay on your prescribed medication and take it exactly the way your physician ordered.
   - Keep up your therapy sessions, group sessions and any other psychological services that have been recommended.
   - Keep all doctor appointments.
   - Reduce your stress.
   - Do not use alcohol or drugs.

- Eat regular, nutritious meals.
- Get decent sleep with a regular sleep schedule.
- Exercise appropriately, according to your age and physical capabilities.
- Find pleasurable activities to engage in– at least one or two every day.
- Build structure into your day.
- Keep your support system close – in particular, find someone who can help you reality-test (that is, will alert you or take charge of getting help if you show signs of becoming psychotic).
- Pay attention to your symptoms, especially those that might warn you of relapse.
- If you feel you are losing control, call your doctor immediately or go to the nearest hospital.

when someone close to you has schizophrenia

1. Learn everything you can about Schizophrenia.
2. Help the person suffering from Schizophrenia to get the best treatment possible.
3. Try to help the sufferer implement the above self-help suggestions.
4. It is particularly important for a person with Schizophrenia to keep up the treatment. Help monitor medication compliance as well as the quality of professional care that is being received.
5. Educate other family members and friends about Schizophrenia, and prepare them for whatever is the expected progression of the disorder (the prognoses vary, depending on the type).
6. Make plans for those times when the person with Schizophrenia may be partially or completely reliant on others.
7. Take steps to protect the person from abuse, neglect or self-harm.
8. Help the sufferer to raise his or her self-esteem by providing encouragement, support and positive feedback.
9. Help prevent the sufferer from being socially isolated.
10. Encourage improved communication.
11. Evaluate the sufferer for being at risk of harming self or others. This is more relevant to certain forms of Schizophrenia than to others (for example, a person suffering from Paranoid Schizophrenia may perceive the environment as threatening and may take apparently hostile steps to self-protect). If the person seems at risk of harming self or others, alert the sufferer's mental-health professionals, monitor closely and remove dangerous objects from the person's environment.
12. Learn about medication side effects.

13. Try to help the sufferer avoid being overly stimulated by his or her environment.
14. Provide soft music for soothing.
15. To increase trust and decrease suspicion, be open and honest in your dealings with the sufferer.
16. Try to provide consistency in the sufferer's environment.
17. Try to help the person maintain a consistent level of personal hygiene and self-care.
18. Encourage appropriate expression of feelings.
19. Be a role-model for appropriate behaviour, social skills and good communication, for example, remind the sufferer to stick to the topic in hand and encourage him or her to maintain appropriate eye contact.
20. Provide positive reinforcement for effort, achievement and improvement.
21. Help the sufferer to put their legal affairs in order at times when he or she is functioning well enough to understand the ramifications, make lucid decisions and consent to treatment.
22. Make decisions, hopefully with the sufferer, about who will become primary carers at times when he or she may have difficulty assuming responsibilities for family and/or self.
23. Get some help and support for yourself and other family members.
24. Encourage the person suffering from Schizophrenia to undertake appropriate physical exercise and reduce his or her stress (see page 19).
25. The person's 'quality-of-life' requirements need to be considered and implemented as far as possible. These include continuing to live in his or her own home, having as much independence as possible, and having plenty of contact with spouse or partner, family or friends, as well as feeling happy and useful.
26. Be aware that some people with Schizophrenia become homeless. Support the sufferer's efforts to establish a stable, sustainable living situation.

helpful books

Surviving Schizophrenia: A Manual for Families, Consumers, and Providers, E. Torey. New York: HarperCollins, 2001.

The Complete Family Guide to Schizophrenia: Helping Your Loved One Get the Most out of Life, K. T. Meuser and S. Gingerich. New York: The Guilford Press, 2006.

Diagnosis Schizophrenia: A Comprehensive Resource, R. Miller and S. E. Mason. New York: Columbia University Press, 2002.

Autobiography of a Schizophrenic Girl: The True Story of 'Renee', trans. Grace Rubin-Rabson. New York: Penguin, 1994.

The Family Face of Schizophrenia: True Stories of Mental Illness with Practical Advice from America's Leading Experts, P. Backlar. New York: G. P. Putnam's Sons, 1995.

Getting Your Life Back Together When You Have Schizophrenia, R. Temes. Oakland, Calif.: New Harbinger Publications, 2002.

delusional disorder

I am frequently struck by the extraordinary things the mind can achieve. It is capable of creating the most unusual scenarios, and presenting them to the self as though they are genuine. Having a Delusional Disorder involves holding a strong and well-entrenched belief in something that is highly improbable. The Clint Eastwood film *Play Misty for Me* provides a chilling portrait of a woman suffering from a particular type of Delusional Disorder known as Erotomania. In fact, well-known figures, especially film stars, are often the objects of desire for people with delusions about them (commonly and unkindly referred to as 'stalkers'). Shakespeare must have been aware of some of the symptoms of Delusional Disorder, because he created Othello, who seems to have been afflicted with the Jealous type. And what if Jack Bauer from the TV series *24* was only *imagining* the conspiracies against him? He might then be suffering from Delusional Disorder – Persecutory type.

case study – Carol

Carol, a forty-two-year-old single woman worked as a receptionist for a management organization that represented television and film actors and directors. One particular client of the company, a famous screen actor, frequented the office to attend business meetings and interviews. This actor was an attractive, engaging person, who smiled at Carol whenever he came in, and once asked her if her day was going well. Over a period of several months, Carol began to believe that this actor was secretly in love with her. She avidly read show-business magazines in the hope of finding photos of the actor with his wife, and was always relieved to be 'reassured' of her belief that the only reason this man did not openly declare his love towards her was that he was already married. Whenever he came to the office, she looked for special 'signs' that he was communicating lovers' messages with her. She spent her evenings replaying rented films that starred the object of her interest, and withdrew from all social activities. Friends teased her that they thought she was 'having an affair with a married man' which only fuelled her delusion. She would smile enigmatically at them and refuse to be drawn on the subject – which they took as a tacit 'yes'.

Two months before I met Carol, the actor she believed was in love with her suddenly left the management company. Carol took this extremely personally and began to seek him outside the office context. Since she had access to company files, she found out where he lived and began to stalk him. Once the actor had noticed her outside his gym and twice loitering outside his home, he became alarmed and called the police. At the point where a restraining order was placed against her to prevent her from approaching the actor, Carol began to disintegrate further, and this led to her starting treatment. A combination of therapy and antipsychotic medication helped her to move beyond being deluded that the actor was in love with her, although she still thinks of him as 'the passion of her life'.

is this you (or someone close to you)?

Holds erroneous beliefs (delusions) that may take a number of possible forms, such as:

Erotomanic type Mistakenly convinced that someone is in love with him or her, despite being a stranger or hardly knowing the person. The deluded person may try to send messages, gifts, or even stalk the object of his or her Erotomania.

Grandiose type Mistakenly convinced that he or she has some special and unrecognized gift or talent or has made some amazing discovery. The delusion could also be that he or she is a famous person or has a close and special relationship with a celebrity.

Jealous type Unreasonably convinced that his or her spouse, partner or lover is unfaithful, and carrying out extraordinary attempts to prove it, such as following, investigating, or punishing that person.

Persecutory type Erroneously believing that someone or some group of people or organization is intent on maliciously hurting, destroying or undermining him or her in some way. This fear and anger often leads them to react violently against his or her imagined conspirators.

Somatic type Erroneously believing that there is something unusual occurring in his or her body, such as emitting a foul odour or being infested with insects. This is a stranger and more intense belief than would be the case for Hypochondriasis.

'do not pass go' signs

People with Delusional Disorder can have problems working, fitting in socially, or maintaining relationships. In some cases they suffer from extreme social isolation. Their delusions may even be such that they completely alter their lives in inappropriate ways, (for example, hiding from those they feel are persecuting them). Sometimes they stalk, confront or act violently towards others they mistakenly feel are tormenting them, which means that there is a high risk of facing legal charges through causing harming or being a threat to others. They rarely seek psychological help while delusional, since their beliefs are very appropriate and real to them, and it is often up to family members to identify that there is some kind of problem and seek professional help. It is particularly advisable that mental-health treatment is provided, since relatives, friends and acquaintances are probably the most vulnerable to threats or violence by a delusional person.

what causes delusional disorder?

Family members of people with Schizophrenia are more likely to suffer from Delusional Disorder. It is also thought that extreme stress, low socio-economic status or having a hearing deficiency may make a person more likely to develop a Delusional Disorder.

what happens in your brain?

Brain malfunction, especially in the occipital or temporal areas, can cause delusions. Lesions in certain areas of the brain are also associated with delusions.

which treatments are likely to work?

Psychotherapy can be helpful, and medication is frequently prescribed. Inpatient treatment is sometimes necessary, especially if there seems to be a risk to self or others. Modified electroconvulsive therapy (a method of electrically stimulating the brain) is thought to be helpful, especially for delusions in elderly people.

best course of action?

It is usually down to family members to seek treatment on behalf of a person suffering from Delusional Disorder, and it may be quite hard to get him or her to agree to see a mental-health professional. It is, however, necessary to seek help as soon as possible, especially since there is a risk that the person with Delusional Disorder may carry out some kind of aggressive or intrusive action against those he or she feels are being hurtful or conspiratorial. This is rare, but it does happen. Sometimes an involuntary hospitalization is necessary.

in the meantime what can you do?

1. Learn everything you can about Delusional Disorder.
2. Help the person suffering from Delusional Disorder to receive the best treatment possible.
3. Help the person to comply with the treatment.
4. Do not support or enable unhealthy efforts on the part of the person with Delusional Disorder to self-treat with drugs or alcohol.
5. Do not support risky or illegal behaviour.
6. Encourage the person's healthy efforts to reduce stress through relaxation exercises (see page 41), appropriate physical exercise, meditation (see page 40) and yoga.
7. Reduce your own stress as well, and take care of your own physical and mental health.
8. Educate other family members and friends about Delusional Disorder, and prepare them for whatever is the expected progression of the disorder.
9. Make plans for those times, perhaps during treatment or hospitalization, when the person with Delusional Disorder may need to be reliant on others or unable to assume family responsibilities.
10. Take steps to protect the sufferer from abuse, neglect, or self-harm.
11. Take steps to protect yourself and others. Educate everyone close to the person with Delusional Disorder that violent or aggressive expressions, threats or actions should not be taken personally. However they need to be considered seriously and understood as genuine threats to safety.
12. Help the sufferer to put their legal affairs in order at a time when he or she is functioning well enough to understand the ramifications, make lucid decisions and consent to treatment.
13. Make decisions, hopefully with the sufferer, about who will become primary carers if the person becomes temporarily unable to care for self at any point.
14. Get some help and support for yourself and other family members.
15. The person's 'quality-of-life' requirements need to be explored and implemented as far as possible. These include continuing to live in his or her own home, having as much independence as possible, having plenty of contact with spouse, partner, family or friends, as well as feeling happy and useful.

helpful books

When Someone You Love Has a Mental Illness; A Handbook for Family, Friends, and Caregivers, R. Woolis. New York: Tarcher/Penguin, 1992.

Five Weeks to Healing Stress: The Wellness Option, V. O'Hara. Oakland, Calif.: New Harbinger Publications, 1996.

delirium

You would immediately know if a person is suffering from Delirium, by his or her appearance of being disorientated, lacking focus, speaking strangely and an inability to remember things. It wouldn't necessarily be a constant state but might fluctuate. Elderly people who are suffering from certain illnesses sometimes become afflicted with Delirium, but it can also affect younger people in the aftermath of injury, surgery or during a period of withdrawal from certain drugs, toxins or poisons. It is a sign of significant problems and must be taken very seriously.

case study: Drew

Drew was a freelance camera operator who worked on large-budget television documentaries. While filming an aerial sequence over an unrelenting desert he fell out of a helicopter as it was taking off and sustained multiple injuries. In the hospital he was placed on morphine and another painkiller, as well as a muscle relaxant and antibiotics. A day later he was feverish and agitated, and complaining of severe back pain. A week later Drew's temperature was still elevated and he seemed disoriented. He had trouble being able to answer simple questions such as 'What day is it?' He underwent surgery the next day, and following that his pain medication was changed – but he was still disoriented, had disorganized thinking, and had started rubbing food into his hair at mealtimes. A psychiatrist was summoned and Drew expressed concern that he 'couldn't concentrate', was sleeping very little and taking too many drugs. His Delirium began to disappear once his sedatives were discontinued and the level of his pain medication was reduced. Drew made a full recovery.

is this you (or someone close to you)?

- There is an alteration in the normal state of consciousness, so that one's surroundings may seem blurred and one cannot fully focus.
- There may be problems with memory or speech or the person may feel disoriented.

■ These changes in perceptions, orientation, memory and/or speech arise fairly quickly, and can fluctuate throughout the day.

'do not pass go' signs

Delirium involves an acute decline in attention and cognition. It is a common, life-threatening and potentially preventable clinical syndrome, usually seen among people who are aged sixty-five or older. Untreated delirium can lead to coma, seizures and even death, so it needs urgent attention.

what causes delirium?

Delirium can arise as a result of certain medical conditions, such as hypoglycaemia, cancer, epilepsy, meningitis, AIDS, diseases of the liver, pancreas, kidney, lung and cardiovascular system and head injury. It can be the result of electrolyte imbalance, systemic infections or vitamin deficiencies. It can be precipitated by having an operation, by head or body trauma, by intoxication or withdrawal from alcohol, other drugs or by poisons. In addition, it can accompany various types of dementia, such as Alzheimer's disease.

what happens in your brain?

Delirium may be brought about through an imbalance or malfunctioning of the neurotransmitter acetylcholine in the area of the brain known as the reticular formation (which is responsible for regulating attention and arousal). The Delirium that sometimes accompanies withdrawal from alcohol may be due to hyperactivity of certain neurons.

which treatments are likely to work?

Treatment usually involves medication combined with inpatient psychological support at a point where a person is cognitively ready to receive it.

best course of action?

If Delirium occurs outside a hospital situation or would otherwise go unnoticed, immediately alert a doctor and/or mental-health professional.

in the meantime what can you do for a person close to you who might be suffering from delirium?

1. Read everything you can about Delirium.
2. Help the person to receive the best possible hospital/psychiatric care.

3. Educate other family members and friends about Delirium, and prepare them for whatever is the expected progression of the disorder (the prognoses for Delirium vary, depending on the cause).
4. Make plans for the time when the person with Delirium may be completely reliant on others.
5. People with Delirium are vulnerable. Take steps to protect the person from abuse, neglect, or self-harm, including monitoring the quality of care they are receiving.
6. Put the person's legal affairs in order while he or she is functioning well enough to understand the ramifications, make lucid decisions and consent to treatment.
7. If the Delirium is due to alcohol or drug use, take urgent steps to get the sufferer into a treatment programme. Today would not be too soon.
8. Make decisions, hopefully together with the sufferer, about who will become primary carers if the person needs long-term care.
9. Get some help and support for yourself and other family members.

helpful books

When Someone You Love Has a Mental Illness: A Handbook for Family, Friends, and Caregivers, R. Woolis. New York: Tarcher/Penguin, 1992.

Five Weeks to Healing Stress: The Wellness Option, V. O'Hara. Oakland, Calif.: New Harbinger Publications, 1996.

dementia

case study: Maggie

Maggie was an energetic, successful estate agent in her mid sixties. She planned to retire at seventy, but four years before that she began to have problems with concentration. She found that her memory was slipping, and she was losing track of her progress with buyers and sellers, which seriously affected her ability to do her job. Two years earlier her husband had remarked that he thought Maggie had developed a slight tremor in her left hand, but she insisted that this was brought on by the financial stress the couple were under at the time. As the months wore on, Maggie's memory deteriorated even further, her speech became laboured and she began to withdraw from social activities and office group meetings. When Maggie found that she could not find her way to housing estates she had easily found in the past she consulted a neurologist, who diagnosed her with Parkinson's disease. A neuropsychological evaluation confirmed that

Maggie had also developed Dementia due to Parkinson's disease. She was treated with medication that helped some of her symptoms, but she decided to retire early and make the best of her remaining years with her husband.

This disorder is almost as troubling for the people close to those with Dementia as it is for the sufferers themselves. Given the choice, many people would rather be the one sliding away into fantasy-land. Unfortunately, Dementia of various kinds is quite common, and one can only hope that we will soon have new knowledge about the exact causes, better treatments and ways to prevent it. We now know more about the causes of Dementia due to Alzheimer's disease, and it's not all about aluminium pans (although they may have some effect). Lately, we have come to understand that it is very important to keep one's mind active and interested enough to engage in new activities that stimulate the brain, such as learning a new language or musical instrument. Loneliness seems to be one of the culprits, so perhaps we should learn from those cultures where seniors are not so isolated as they tend to be in our society. We tend to hear most about the type of Dementia that is due to Alzheimer's Disease, but there are many varieties: Vascular Dementia, Dementia due to HIV disease, Dementia due to head trauma, Dementia due to Huntington's disease, Dementia due to Parkinson's disease, Dementia due to Pick's disease, Dementia due to Creutzfeldt-Jakob disease and Substance-Induced Dementia.

is this you (or someone close to you)?

- You are having memory problems, either with learning new things or remembering things you have already learned.
- Having problems using your limbs and fingers to achieve certain tasks, even though they can move perfectly well physically.
- Having problems recognizing people or things you have previously known.
- Having problems organizing things, planning things, sequencing (for example, following a recipe in cooking) or thinking abstractly (for example, understanding metaphors).
- The above problems happen gradually, as a deterioration of how you previously managed.

what causes dementia?

Dementia is the result of a physiological problem arising from a medical condition, the effects of taking certain substances or a combination of several physiological or substance-based causes. There are also a number of genetic factors that suggest the disorder may be inheritable to some degree. The most common physiological conditions that can cause dementia are: Alzheimer's disease, vascular problems, HIV disease, head trauma, Parkinson's disease, Huntington's disease, Pick's disease, and Creutzfeldt-Jakob's disease. Substances that can cause a persisting Dementia include alcohol, hypnotic drugs, sedatives, inhalants, or anti-Anxiety drugs. Some toxins are thought to cause Dementia, such as lead, carbon monoxide, certain insecticides, mercury and industrial solvents. The Dementia can progress even after the use or ingesting of these drugs or toxins has ceased. In elderly people, those who are lonely have an increased risk of Dementia due to Alzheimer's disease than those who are not, while having more frequent social activity is associated with a reduced risk.

'do not pass go' signs

Dementia of the Alzheimer's type Those with this type of Dementia are suffering from a steadily worsening condition that will drastically change the way they live in the world. They will begin to lose their ability to recognize people they love, to remember important information and the ability to complete simple tasks that once made them independent adults. Aside from the emotional toll on families, Dementia can make a person extremely vulnerable in the world, and at risk of being lost, abused, attacked and otherwise taken advantage of. Dementia due to Alzheimer's disease is a progressive disorder, and people who suffer from it will experience gradually worsening symptoms. They may also undergo personality changes and gradually become more fussy and irritable. Eventually they may lose the ability to work their limbs and become bedridden and silent. It is vital that people with Dementia receive adequate care, support and treatment, and that their families are also given support and help in their accompanying struggle with the situation.

Vascular Dementia Sufferers who receive early treatment for hypertension and vascular disease may avoid suffering further progression of their Dementia.

Dementia due to HIV disease will typically lead to a slowing of mental agility, forgetfulness and difficulties with concentration and problem solving. Sufferers may become socially withdrawn and may eventually have difficulty balancing, and experience tremors and all kinds of motion problems.

Dementia due to head trauma may cause personality changes, movement problems, irritability, Anxiety, Depression, mood swings, problems focusing, and sufferers may become more aggressive. Dementia due to head trauma does not usually worsen, except in the case of repeated head trauma, such as is sometimes sustained in boxing.

Dementia due to Parkinson's disease involves a general slowing of mind and body functions, including problems remembering things. Depression often goes hand-in-hand with this type of dementia.

Dementia due to Huntington's disease typically begins with increased Anxiety, Depression and irritability, before the memory becomes impaired along with other brain functions.

Dementia due to Pick's disease usually starts with personality changes, sudden strange behaviour and language difficulties. Memory and movement difficulties eventually arise.

Dementia due to Creutzfeldt-Jakob disease may begin with Anxiety, tiredness, or problems with sleeping, eating or paying attention. After that, the sufferer may have problems with coordination, vision and walking, with a fast-progressing dementia.

Substance-Induced Persisting Dementia may also begin with personality changes and progress to memory, language and movement problems.

what happens in the brain?

Brain atrophy seems to occur in the case of people suffering from Dementia due to Alzheimer's disease. The neurotransmitter glutamate might be involved in the development of Dementia, since under pathologic conditions, it has been associated with excitotoxicity (neuron damage) and apoptosis (cell death). Problems in the limbic and cortical areas seem to be the main cause of Dementia. Neurochemical changes seem to be common. An inordinate number of lesions have been found in the nervous system of people who suffered from Vascular Dementia, while the dopamine transportation mechanisms in people with HIV-associated Dementia have been shown to be impaired.

which treatments are likely to work?

Both medical treatment and mental-health treatment are necessary, and specific treatment decisions for symptoms associated with Dementia are complex, involving the people with the condition, carers and physicians. Ginkgo biloba special extract EGb 761®, an anti-dementia drug, may enhance cognitive functioning and stabilize mood in cognitively impaired elderly subjects. Moreover, it has been found to alleviate symptoms of Anxiety in people with mental decline. Other drugs such as memantine are used in the treatment of Dementias caused by Alzheimer's disease and vascular problems.

Behavioural modification therapies that support the lowering of stress, the increase of pleasant events, problem-solving and environmental modification may be helpful. In addition, music therapy may be very effective in reducing behavioural, social, emotional and cognitive problems in people with Dementia. It may also help to reduce apathy in subjects with moderate to severe Dementia. The prognosis for Dementia is usually dependent on the underlying physiological condition or the substance that caused it.

best course of action?

Mental-health treatment is essential, as well as support and family therapy for family members.

in the meantime what can you do to help someone close to you who is suffering from dementia?

1. Learn everything you can about Dementia, and the disease or medical condition that has caused the particular type from which the person close to you is suffering.
2. Help the person suffering from Dementia to get the best treatment possible.
3. Educate other family members and friends about Dementia, and prepare them for whatever is the expected progression of the disorder (the prognoses for Dementia vary, depending on the cause).
4. Make plans for the time when the person with Dementia may be completely reliant on others. This will happen eventually with certain forms of Dementia.
5. People with Dementia are vulnerable. Take steps to protect the person from abuse, neglect or self-harm.
6. Help to put the person's legal affairs in order while he or she with Dementia is still functioning well enough to understand the ramifications, make lucid decisions and consent to treatment.
7. Make decisions, hopefully with the Dementia sufferer, about who will become primary carers if he or she is likely to need long-term care.
8. Get some help and support for yourself and other family members.
9. Get your loved one suffering from Alzheimer's disease to undertake exercise that is appropriate for his or her age and physical capabilities

(check with the doctor). Nursing home residents with Alzheimer's disease who participated in a moderate exercise programme for one hour twice weekly were found to have a significantly slower decline in performing activities of daily living than those who received routine medical care.

10. The 'quality-of-life' requirements of the person with Dementia need to be explored, and implemented as far as possible. These include continuing to live in his or her own home, as much independence as possible, having plenty of contact with spouse, partner, family or friends, as well as feeling happy and useful.

11. Consider trying a change in diet. For example, the Mediterranean diet has been found to be associated with a reduced risk of developing Alzheimer disease.

12. Consider folic acid supplements. A 2007 Dutch study showed that three-year folic acid supplementation improves cognitive performance on tests that measure information-processing speed and memory (skills that are known to decline with age) in certain older adults (those with raised total homocysteine concentrations).

13. It is not easy to watch a person close to you slide into Dementia. You will need to mourn their loss, as well as deal with the day-to-day and often unpredictable difficulties of being rejected or unrecognized by an afflicted parent, partner, family member or friend. Take care of your own physical and mental health, and seek supportive psychotherapy for yourself and the whole family.

helpful books

When Someone You Love Has a Mental Illness; A Handbook for Family, Friends, and Caregivers, R. Woolis. New York: Tarcher/Penguin, 1992.

Five Weeks to Healing Stress: The Wellness Option, V. O'Hara. Oakland, Calif.: New Harbinger Publications, 1996.

chapter 11
things to look out for in your child

"They're trying to figure out whether it's a chemical thing or I'm just a crybaby."

Many childhood disorders are brought about not only by genetic factors but also by problems the child might have adapting to things and people in his or her environment, by the impact of adverse or traumatic experiences or by a mismatch between the child's developmental needs and the resources available in the family and society. Attention-Deficit/ Hyperactivity Disorder, Conduct Disorder and Autistic Disorder are just some of the problems that can appear in childhood and which require urgent treatment.

When a child is struggling with emotional, behavioural or developmental problems, what can you, as a parent or carer, do? First, love, encourage and protect him or her to the very best of your ability, and second, make sure the child receives the very best treatment there is. You'll need to glean a lot of information about the disorder itself, including types of treatments, available resources and new developments. In addition to all the things a parent must do for any child, you will have to be extra-creative and resourceful about helping your child to find appropriate ways to learn, deal with frustration, have social success, maintain self-esteem and so much more. In some cases, your child who has a disorder will one day become an adult with that disorder, so your unique input and support will need to last a lifetime. Having a child with special needs makes you a special kind of parent. Over the years, I have met thousands of 'special' parents, and the vast majority truly live up to their name.

general tools for helping children with mental-health challenges

Some childhood difficulties are ubiquitous, and can occur either within or outside the context of any childhood disorder. Steps for helping a child through the most common of these are set out below:

1. **How to improve a child's self-esteem**
   - Address your child respectfully.
   - Treat your child respectfully.
   - Be accepting of your child.
   - Believe in your child.
   - That old adage 'children should be seen and not heard' does not help a child develop self-esteem. Instead, encourage him or her to express feelings and views in a respectful, appropriate manner.
   - Consult with your child about a variety of current, personally relevant issues or other, more general topics. Listen respectfully and affirm the importance of your child's views.
   - Collaborate with your child in identifying his or her strengths, and continue to reinforce your child's sense of being capable and successful in those areas.
   - Teach your child to problem-solve (see page 259) and provide positive reinforcement (praise or reward) when he or she achieves success or improvement.
   - Support your child when he or she takes appropriate risks in trying to attain desirable goals; for example, a shy child risks phoning a classmate with an invitation to a social event.
   - Identify goals towards your child's self-improvement, such as social or academic achievement, change in behaviour, better grooming or

hygiene, increasing participation in a sport or exercise regime, eating healthier food or reducing undesirable behaviour. These goals must be realistic and sensitively established. Support and encourage your child each step of the way, and provide positive reinforcement for both improvement and for trying.

■ When your child experiences setbacks or failures, help him or her to view these as learning opportunities and encourage perseverance.

■ Encourage your child to take responsibility for his or her mistakes.

■ Teach and instil values of decency and respect towards others. Role-play situations to help with this, for example, act out a scenario where another child makes a disparaging comment about a close friend – show him or her how to respond with loyalty and sensitivity.

■ With your child, create a series of daily affirmations designed to foster a positive self-image; for example, 'I am smart', 'I know how to dress myself' or 'I know how to be a good friend'. Write them on cards and place them where they will frequently be visible to the child.

■ Be responsive to curiosity. Answer questions in an age-appropriate manner, giving positive reinforcement to your child for his or her enquiring mind. If you don't know how to answer or if the situation does not lend itself to answering it's OK to say, 'That's a very good question. I wish I had an answer for you, but right now I don't. May we talk about it some more tonight?'

■ Encourage your child's (healthy) special interests, even if you do not share them. Find out what draws him or her to collect rocks, love butterflies or be fascinated by aviation. Provide karate lessons or take your child climbing if he or she shows interest, and attend your child's sports games, school concerts, shows or exhibitions.

■ Encourage creative activities and imaginative play.

■ Encourage the enjoyment of pleasurable activities that appeal to the senses, such as smelling sweet flowers, tasting delicious food, listening to appealing music or having pleasant tactile sensations (stroking animal fur, being wrapped in silky material or playing with dough). Discuss these sensations with your child and express your appreciation for his or her unique preferences and sense of enjoyment.

2. **How to improve a child's communication skills**

■ Help your child to notice, label and express his or her feelings. Encourage this process as much as possible.

■ Create a chart with pictures of people looking happy, angry, sad and so on, and label them. Continue to add to this chart so that your child builds an extensive vocabulary of 'feeling' words and learns to use them accurately to describe his or her own mood states. Validate his or her self-expression and help your child to tolerate feelings with observations, such as 'I see that you are upset right now, but the jigsaw belongs to Tommy and he had to take it home with him. Perhaps you can choose something else to play with to help you feel happier.'

- Always provide positive reinforcement (praise or reward) for improvements and success in your child's efforts to communicate better.

- Encourage eye contact during verbal communication. (Some children, though, such as those with Autism or Asperger's Disorder, may find it a lot easier to focus on listening without the distraction of face-to-face gaze – so for them, expectations of maintaining eye contact may be unreasonable.)

- Encourage appropriate expression of your child's personal views and ideas. Unless they are dangerously antisocial never dismiss these as 'wrong', but instead, gently guide the maladaptive ones towards more appropriate values by offering examples so that he or she can compare them and judge for themselves. For example, describe two scenarios where a child who has been hit retaliates with more violence, versus using words to respond.

- Teach your child to be assertive. Self-assertion involves being neither aggressive nor passive. Instead, he or she should be encouraged simply and directly to express feelings and ask for change. The Three-part Question is useful (see page 39).

- In consultation with your child, discuss possible situations and circumstances in which her or she might be expected to respond either verbally or non-verbally. Develop ideas about possible responses and role-play these to try out and practise, for example being bullied by a peer or ignored by a shopkeeper.

- For your child's safety, teach him or her that it is not always appropriate to obey adults, and that your child must respond with a loud refusal (shouting, screaming and physical counter-attack) if an adult is trying to cause harm, abduct him or her, or touch a private part of your child's body.

3. **How to improve a child's social skills**
   - In keeping with what is appropriate for his or her age and developmental stage, teach your child to cooperate with others. Set tasks and provide positive reinforcement (praise or reward) when he or she helps siblings, clears the table, or walks the dog. Discuss or role-play situations where your child might be expected to cooperate with others in the community, such as picking up his or her own rubbish in the playground. Demonstrate cooperative behaviour when you are in public together, such as giving assistance to a person with a disability when asked for help.
   - Encourage collaboration with others. With your child, create an appropriate project to share with a friend, and provide support, modelling (subtle demonstration) and assistance throughout.
   - Create games to help with the development of social skills.
   - Teach your child manners, etiquette and rules appropriate for his or her age and developmental stage. Repetition and reminders will be necessary. Provide positive reinforcement (praise or reward improvements and successes).

4. **How to teach a child to self-soothe**
   - First, be the one to soothe your child. Provide comforting experiences such as a loving touch, bedtime stories and having fun together.
   - Eventually your child will realize the fact that his or her anxiety or frustration can be calmed and that he or she can learn to self-soothe. But your continued help in providing soothing for your child will always be appreciated.
   - Encourage your child to sit or lie down and breathe slowly when he or she gets upset or frustrated, and to practise relaxation (see Progressive Body Relaxation page 41).
   - Encourage your child to engage in activities that help him or her cope with anxiety and frustration. Swimming, listening to music, taking a walk or playing with pets might be ideal. There are excellent children's meditation techniques, and yoga or martial arts might also be helpful.
   - Implement a programme of physical exercise, not just for health, but to help reduce frustration and anxiety.
   - It is soothing for children to feel that not only do they have structure imposed on them, but that they can create it for themselves. Encourage and support their efforts to become more organized and to follow a schedule.

5. **How to help a child improve his or her sense of responsibility**
   - Help your child to understand exactly what 'being responsible' means generally.
   - Help your child to understand exactly what responsibility entails for him or her specifically, in terms of self-care, school attendance, general behaviour, tidiness and so on.
   - Be sure to set realistic standards of responsibility for your child, as appropriate for your child's age, developmental stage and abilities.
   - Within the limitations of your child's age, developmental stage and abilities, give him or her specific family chores. Provide support and monitoring to see that they are carried out.
   - Rather than using punishment as a means of improving your child's behaviour, provide positive reinforcement (praise or reward) for achievement and improvement.
   - Consider allowing your child to have the responsibility of a pet. Provide support and encouragement for his or her care of the pet, as well as positive reinforcement for improvement and success.

6. **How to help a child develop better problem-solving skills**
   - Avoid solving all problems for your child. In as many situations as possible ask 'What do you think is the answer?' or 'What ideas do you have?' Follow with guidance and discussion, and provide positive reinforcement for improvement or success.
   - Provide practice for problem-solving. Identify some relevant problems that you believe your child can solve. Discuss them one by one, and brainstorm with your child some possible solutions (for example 'What do you think would be a better time for you to start your homework in order to get it finished before dinner time?'). Do this in a manner that helps him or her to feel safe to take risks in coming up with answers. Create opportunities for success.
   - Encourage your child to feel confident in his or her ability to problem-solve.
   - Provide positive reinforcement (praise or reward) when he or she achieves improvement or success in problem-solving.

7. **How to help a child be less defensive**
   - If your child acts defensively, it is a sign that he or she does not feel safe enough to receive constructive criticism. Your job is to help him or her to feel more confident and comfortable to receive feedback.

- In providing feedback, always use a calm, supportive tone and begin with something positive; for example 'You did a great job helping with the dishes today! Next time, though, please try not to leave the tea-towels on the floor.'
- Never label a child or name-call, for example 'You lazy, good-for-nothing!' Labels only serve to reinforce negative behaviour and self-image. Instead, use adjectives like 'clever', 'resourceful' and 'reliable' – and you will find your child becoming just that.
- If you need to point out negative behaviour, always focus on the behaviour itself rather than the person; that is, no child is intrinsically 'naughty', but all of them do 'naughty things' from time to time. A child who develops a self-image as 'bad', through hearing himself or herself described as that, will end up behaving badly.
- Collaborate with your child in coming up with strategies for improved behaviour, study habits and so on. He or she will respond more positively when consulted, rather than just being told what to do.
- Help your child to increase his or her self-esteem (see page 255).
- Help your child to be more self-assertive (see page 38).
- Always provide positive reinforcement (praise or reward for improvement or success).

8. **How to help a child who has developed ineffective coping skills**
   - Identify ineffective coping skills, such as cheating, manipulating, skipping school, stealing, lying (see below) or running away (see below) and gently confront your child about the specific behaviour.
   - Set limits for your child.
   - Give appropriate consequences to your child (that is, punishment that matches the misbehaviour). For example, if your child scratches their initials on a table teach him or her the skills to sand down and revarnish the entire piece of furniture.
   - Becoming more empathic is an important goal for your child. Help the child to become more aware of the consequences of his or her actions on others.
   - Help the child to see the consequences of his or her actions on himself or herself.
   - Make sure your child fully understands cause and effect. For children with some disorders, for example Attention Deficit Disorder, this is not easy. It needs to be emphasized frequently.

- Be careful not to become involved in a power struggle with your child.
- Do not argue, debate or bargain with your child who has developed ineffective coping skills, and there is no need to go overboard in explaining your rationale. Instead, set clear limits and rules with a calm, authoritative voice, leaving no room for discussion or manipulation.
- In the case of a violent child, seek immediate help from a qualified mental-health professional.
- Provide positive reinforcement (praise or reward for improvement, success, or trying).

9. How to help a child who lies

Lying is normal in very young children because they are still learning to distinguish true from false. Deliberate lying can occur only once they begin to understand the difference, although they might still be testing out the reactions of others to the things they say that are untrue. But if a child has reached a stage where lying begins to happen in a deliberate fashion, perhaps to cover up wrong-doing, follow the steps below:

- Identify the situations in which your child tends to tell lies.
- Gently confront the child about lying, and inquire about the reasons for doing so.
- Create ways to reduce the need for the child to lie, such as finding other ways to cope with stressful situations.
- Problem-solve with the child about alternative ways to get needs met.
- Emphasize the need to halt the lying, and insist on amends being made where possible.
- Monitor the child's truthfulness or otherwise, and provide positive reinforcement for improvement or success in attempts to be honest.
- Teach your child self-assertion skills (see page 38).
- Encourage direct expression of feelings (see page 262).

10. How to help a child who tries to run away

- Seek help from a qualified mental-health professional.
- Talk to the child gently and try to identify the feelings and circumstances that trigger his or her desire to run away.
- Work to improve the child's situation, environment and feelings.
- Help the child to problem-solve and come up with alternatives to running away.

- Help the child to be verbally self-assertive (see page 38).
- Help the child to reduce stress and anxiety (see pages 19 and 38).
- Depression in children presents itself differently than it does in adults. In children it may look like anger, misbehaviour, acting out and taking risks. Seek help from a mental-health professional if you suspect a child is depressed.

11. **How to help a child with poor impulse control**
- Help the child to reduce stress and anxiety (see pages 19 and 38).
- Help the child to learn to self-soothe (see page 258).
- Be a role model in how to tolerate frustration (for example remain calm when encountering a long queue at the cinema).
- Provide positive reinforcement when your child manages to tolerate and contain frustration; for example 'I see that you can stay calm, even though you really want to get in to see this film. Good job!'
- Help your child to identify situations where he or she finds it hard to accept delayed gratification, and discuss the consequences of acting too impulsively.
- Help your child to come up with alternative ways to handle the above specific situations, and provide positive feedback when he or she manages to do so.
- Help your child improve communication skills and express feelings (see page 256).

12. **How to help a child with anger problems**
Learning to modulate expression of feelings such as anger is one of the tasks of growing up, and young children will sometimes have temper tantrums as part of normal development. There is cause for concern, though, if these occur too often, or fail to develop into more controlled expression of anger.

- Help your child to understand the consequences of uncontrolled outbursts of anger.
- Help your child to identify the typical triggers for angry outbursts; for example a sibling who deliberately annoys him or her, or frustration at being unable to do certain things.
- Teach your child self-assertion (see page 38), which is the middle road between aggression and passivity.
- Children who have angry outbursts or tantrums often find it terrify-

ing to have overwhelming feelings that they cannot contain. But never suggest that the feelings themselves are wrong or bad. Talk to your child about feelings and let him or her know that feelings are not right or wrong, they just *are*. Help the child to understand that a person can either act impulsively on feelings or choose to express them in a more controlled way.

- Teach your child to notice when anger is arising, that is, the physiological signs of shallow breathing, tense muscles and clenched fists. Ask your child to describe what happens in his or her body, in order to increase awareness.
- Teach your child that, when anger is beginning to arise, he or she should focus on taking deep, slow breaths and relaxing the body.
- Physical exercise may help a child who has trouble letting go of sustained anger.
- Being distracted by something pleasurable will also help reduce lingering anger.
- Teach your child that it is always OK to express any feeling, including anger, as long as it is done in an appropriate way. The following is a good formula for the expression of anger by both children and adults: 'I feel [angry] because [reason], and I need [ask for change].' See self-assertion on page 38.
- Talk to your child about underlying anger or resentment, perhaps from the past, and try to facilitate an appropriate expression of that anger. Provide positive reinforcement (praise or reward) for appropriate expression of anger, even if it is directed at you.
- Model appropriate methods of conflict resolution and encourage your child to express current angry feelings directly and appropriately.
- Be a role model in letting go of anger once it is expressed, and provide positive reinforcement when your child manages to do the same.

family meetings

Families that are struggling with any kind of problem will benefit from having regular meetings, as long as they are held in the spirit of inclusiveness and cooperation, with the goal of problem-solving, support and optimism.

- Hold them regularly, at a time that is convenient for everyone.
- Expect everyone to attend.

- Take it in turns to chair the meeting and record minutes.
- Create a list of topics for each meeting ahead of time, and post it where everyone can make suggestions.
- Everyone should be allowed to have an equal say.
- Recognize the good things happening in the family not just the problems.
- Encourage everyone to listen.
- Encourage everyone to communicate appropriately and positively.
- Focus on the family as a whole, rather than singling out one member.
- Encourage everyone to brainstorm in order to come up with solutions to current problems.
- Summarize the meeting at the end, recap what has been agreed and get commitment from everyone to put decisions into practice.
- See that those commitments are followed through.
- Plan an enjoyable activity at the end of each family meeting.

attention-deficit/hyperactivity disorder

case study: Bobby

At nine years old, Bobby was the class clown. His classmates enjoyed his antics, but his teachers were fed up with the constant distractions and ensuing chaos he created. They failed to notice that Bobby was actually extremely bright because his concentration in class was so poor, his class work sloppy, his homework late or badly organized and he was always blurting out the answers, right or wrong. Bobby was labelled 'substandard', 'lazy' and 'a nuisance'.

At home, Bobby found it difficult to wait his turn during activities with his four siblings. He was so distractible when riding his bike that his parents thought him 'accident-prone' and feared for his safety. He frequently got hurt in the playground and was usually covered in scrapes and bruises.

It wasn't until a substitute teacher with special-needs training noticed the discrepancy between Bobby's intelligence and his school performance that Bobby was finally sent to a psychologist, who evaluated him for learning and attention issues. He was diagnosed with Attention-Deficit/Hyperactivity Disorder (ADHD). A psychiatrist prescribed a daily dose of a time-release stimulant medication, which immediately improved his focus. Bobby attended weekly psychotherapy sessions to help him understand his distractibility, learn to be more organized and ask for help when needed. After a while, he began to think of himself as the excellent student that he potentially was, and his teachers also saw him in a new light.

Bobby's parents were opposed to long-term stimulant use for Bobby, and after some trial and error they eventually found that he benefited from a combination of amino acids plus behaviour modification methods for improving his organizational skills and study habits. His treatment was a team effort between his mental-health professionals, teachers and family members. His parents learned a great deal about ADHD through various support organizations, and they kept abreast of new research and treatments. They worked hard to improve his self-esteem, encouraged him and supported the extra-curricular activities he liked best – painting and drawing. They debated whether or not to send him to a school for young people with special needs like Bobby, but opted to leave him in mainstream education. They attended family therapy to learn how best to support him while avoiding the pitfall of ignoring the needs of Bobby's less demanding siblings. It wasn't easy, but they got through it. By negotiating with the school authorities, Bobby was allowed to take untimed tests, which helped him achieve grades commensurate with his intelligence. He managed to graduate, and gained a place in a recognized design school.

People struggling with ADHD find it difficult to stay focused. Their impulses, emotions and behaviour have a tendency to get out of their control. They are often forgetful, restless, easily frustrated and have difficulty staying organized. ADHD is usually diagnosed in childhood and is seen as a disability, but before we had a school system that required everyone to learn the same way and follow a similar curriculum, distractible people seem to have flourished as the poets, dreamers and innovators in society. Albert Einstein, for example, is thought to have had what today would be diagnosed as ADHD. In the past century, many people with ADHD or learning differences have been terribly misunderstood. They have been labelled 'stupid', 'lazy', 'disruptive' or 'badly behaved', which has led to their growing up with poor self-esteem and never realizing their potential. Some have been lucky enough to find ways to compensate for their distractibility, becoming architects, actors, entrepreneurs and comedians. Some were supported by parents, partners, secretaries or bosses who helped them to be organized enough to capitalize on their strengths.

These days, when parents realize their child is impulsive, distractible or learns differently from others they face some tough decisions. If they are lucky enough to have educational choices, they might have the option of a good school that caters for children with special needs. But if mainstream school is all that's available, how can a parent be sure teachers will know how to help their particular child? Mental-health treatment for children with ADHD is available, but it comes in many forms – and some of those forms are becoming more and more controversial. The use of drug therapy, in particular, has its advocates and detractors – and it's never an easy decision to put a child on potent stimulants like Ritalin and Dexedrine. Many professionals, as well as parents and teachers, are concerned that, by putting so many children on stimulants, we may be exacerbating certain problems, for example overcrowded classrooms, overwhelmed teachers and deficiencies in parenting skills. It may be that we have acquired unreasonable expectations for our children.

Perhaps it is true that professionals and carers alike have been seduced into an over-reliance on pharmaceutical solutions to childrens' problems; yet in so many cases stimulants make the difference between a child's being able to stay focused in the classroom and succeed at school versus failing. However, medication does not cure the disorder – it simply treats some symptoms of people whose bodies respond well to those particular drugs. Parents of children with ADHD must study the disorder very carefully, review all possible treatment modalities, and seek reliable professional advice. Once a treatment protocol has been established, it should be constantly under review and the child's overall health must be carefully monitored, especially if stimulants are used, because they can affect growth, sleep and eating patterns. Parents must carefully observe the child's behaviour at home and communicate closely with teachers about his or her ability to stay on task and progress at school. Above all, the child's self-esteem must be bolstered, since it will be easy for him or her to fall into a mindset that reflects some of the negative attitudes and lack of understanding that, even today, continue to undermine people with ADHD.

is this your child?

- Has trouble paying attention to details where it matters (for example, at school) and tends to make careless mistakes.
- Finds it difficult to keep focused on tasks.
- Often doesn't seem to be listening when being addressed.
- Has trouble finishing set tasks, duties or work.
- Is disorganized.
- Is not keen on tasks that require staying focused for some time.
- Is always losing things.

- Is easily distracted by extraneous things in the environment.
- Is forgetful.

If six or more of the above are true, the child may be suffering from Attention Deficit Disorder (without hyperactivity or impulsivity, which are described below).

Hyperactivity:

- Frequently fidgeting or squirming.
- Finds it hard to stay seated, or in a position required by the situation.
- Feels restless, or moves about inappropriately.
- Finds it hard to attend to activities quietly.
- Is always 'on the go'.
- Is overly talkative.

Impulsivity:

- Blurts out answers to questions prematurely (e.g. in the classroom).
- Finds it difficult to wait his or her turn.
- Frequently interrupts others.

Some of these eighteen symptoms would be noticed by others, both at home and at school, when the person was younger than seven years old.

'do not pass go' signs

Although there is growing awareness of the disorder, there are many adults in the world whose ADHD went unnoticed as a child, and a significant number of them have problems associated with their distractibility. Distractible people sometimes get into trouble because they find it difficult to make the connection between cause and effect, for example 'If I break the speeding limit, I may have an accident/hurt someone, am likely to be caught, and may end up in jail'. Because of their lack of impulse-control, some of them have accidents and severe problems at work, school or in relationships. If your life, or that of someone close to you, is being significantly sabotaged by an inability to focus, maintain order or control impulses and frustration, it's time to get some immediate professional help. Likewise, children with ADHD need to be identified as soon as possible, since the sooner they receive treatment the better.

what causes attention-deficit/hyperactivity disorder?

Multiple genetic and environmental risk factors work together to cause ADHD. It runs in families and seems to be highly inheritable, although certain conditions in a child's environment may make a person more susceptible to developing ADHD. Boys are mainly affected – two or three times more males than females have the disorder.

Some of the symptoms of ADHD are similar to those of other conditions such as hyperthyroidism (overactivity of the thyroid causing rapid heartbeat), allergies, hypoglycaemia (glucose deficiency) and Depression, so careful evaluation is necessary.

what is happening in the brain?

Hypotheses about brain differences in people with ADHD include increased activity of the dopamine transporter, slower brain waves in the frontal regions and unusual behaviour by certain neurotransmitters. Other researchers have found that people with ADHD have differences in the part of the brain that is responsible for voluntary movement. People who suffer from ADHD describe a sense of being over-stimulated at all times. They report that they are so bombarded by sights, sounds and sensations that they have difficulty deciding what one they should to pay attention to. Sitting in a noisy restaurant, for example, can be an overwhelming experience for many. But so far, no one has been able to explain definitively what happens in the brain.

which treatments are likely to work?

Stimulant drug therapy, for example with Ritalin, is often used to treat symptoms of ADHD. But different people respond differently to medications depending on their individual metabolism, gene variants and other variables. If it works, stimulant medication helps people to focus in a way that is normally impossible for them. Unfortunately, there are very often side effects so stimulants have to be carefully managed. Some people believe drug therapy for ADHD is a bad idea, and prefer to use non-medication alternatives.

There are many other, controversial therapies for ADHD. Some people take homeopathic remedies, while some recommend the over-the-counter amino acids (a combination of L-glutamine, L-tyrosine and L-phenylalanine). Electroencephalograph (EEG) neurofeedback therapy has been used to treat people with ADHD, including children, and many of them believe it has helped. In neurofeedback therapy a person is hooked up to a machine that monitors brain waves and feeds back information about them via a computer. By playing a type of video game a person works at 'training' the brain to focus.

Advocates of osteopathic manipulation claim it improves ADHD symptoms by quietening the autonomic nervous system, while sensory integrative therapy has been designed to help a person with ADHD interpret incoming sensory information more accurately. The Feingold diet, developed in the 1960s seems to have worked for some people. One theory posits that ADHD may sometimes be caused by yeast infections, and that a special, low-sugar diet will help.

Psychotherapy is essential in helping a person manage the symptoms of ADHD, boost his or her self-esteem, learn to be more organized, and cope with social, emotional and vocational problems. Family therapy is very useful in helping all family members to understand and appreciate a child's struggles with ADHD.

best course of action

If you suspect that you, your child, or someone close to you has ADHD, first consult a doctor to rule out medical problems such as diabetes, hypoglycaemia, thyroid problems and vision or hearing problems. Next, get a thorough evaluation from a trained, certified mental-health professional who will rule out other psychological disorders (such as Anxiety or Depression) and determine if there are learning differences as well. Apart from a clinical interview and special tests that screen for ADHD, it is important to seek input from teachers, co-workers, friends and other family members in order to get a full picture of how the distractibility, impulse problems and other symptoms manifest themselves in a number of settings. A mental-health professional might suggest you ask your child's teacher to fill out a report to assist with making a diagnosis. Most importantly, learn everything you can about ADHD (see reading list below) and carefully consider all the options before deciding on a type of treatment.

in the meantime, what can you do?

For parents or carers of a child with ADHD:

1. If you suspect a diagnosis of ADHD in your child, do not delay seeking treatment. You need help in caring for this child and giving him or her the best possible future. Treatment is vital.
2. Know that there is hope. Although it may seem overwhelming to learn

that ADHD threatens a child's academic and social success, remember that there is much that can be done to help. Besides having a child with special needs, you also have a child who is loveable, and capable of loving. Your child is not a diagnosis, he or she is a unique, inspiring individual. He or she will lead you through a challenging journey, but you can do it and there will be surprising rewards along every step of the way.

3. You may be asking: 'Why did this happen? Why our family?' Try to let go of that question. There is no real answer – at the end of the day, that's just the way it is.

4. Fostering your spirituality may be very helpful for you and the whole family.

5. Read everything you can about ADHD. There is a large reading list below, which reflects the fact that there are many opinions about diagnosis and treatment. There are also political, social, historical and financial aspects of this diagnosis, and you need to be aware of all these viewpoints in order to make an informed decision about your child's treatment.

6. You will have to become an advocate for your child in the school and health system. Learn about available services, National Health or insurance coverage and your legal rights.

7. Identify the symptoms that cause the most significant problems you and your child face at home. Are there easily implemented interventions that could help, such as changing where your child sits to do homework in order to avoid noise and other environmental distractions?

8. Begin to write down your observations about the symptoms in your child that you think might be attributed to ADHD and how they cause problems at home or in other settings. Ask your spouse or partner and/or any other significant adult in your child's life to do the same. Take this to your first appointment when you have found the right therapist.

9. Ask several of your child's teachers if they have observed any signs or symptoms of ADHD in your child. Chances are they have already noticed some and brought them to your attention. Ask how these might be negatively affecting his or her chances of educational success.

10. Write down all feedback you receive, and create a file to keep all the information in one place in case you need it.

11. Find out about your child's learning style. Does he or she best learn by visualizing, hearing or having hands-on experience? Help to implement matching study techniques; for example if your child learns best by

hearing information rather than reading it, try to make it possible for your child to work with a recording device.

12. Work with your child's teacher to make classroom changes that will help reduce the chances of him or her being distracted, such as seating them in a part of the room that has the least traffic flow. The front of the class is usually best.

13. Not every teacher has been properly trained to understand attention or learning difficulties. If you feel your child's teacher is unsympathetic to his or her special needs, consider changing teachers, classes or even schools. Once you have help from a mental-health professional, he or she can help you with this decision. Children with ADHD tend to work better in classrooms with fewer students and more one-to-one teacher help.

14. Help your child to learn and implement organizational skills. This may mean working with him or her to redesign the bedroom so that there is less clutter, fewer pieces of distracting equipment and toys, and an effective storage system. Teach your child to use a calendar and a clock. Put up a 'To Do' chart as a reminder for tasks and chores. If your child has a particular problem getting ready in the morning, for example, create a list (shower, brush hair, teeth and so on, on a whiteboard with boxes to tick as each task is completed).

15. Praise your child when you see him or her following strategies that help reduce distractibility. Ignore attention-getting behaviour.

16. Consider using the 'time-out' strategy for just a few, particularly disruptive behaviours. 'Time-out' involves asking the child to sit in a quiet area with no distractions for a set amount of time that is appropriate for the child's age and matches the behaviour.

17. Help your child to develop strategies to improve problems at school such as forgetting books, losing assignments and being late to class. Laying out clothes the night before, developing a better filing system, implementing an easy homework chart and colour-coding school binders usually help.

18. Encourage your child to practise relaxation and engage in soothing activities to help cope with anxiety and frustration. Swimming, listening to music, taking a walk or playing with pets might be ideal. You can take your child through the progressive relaxation exercise found on page 41. There are excellent children's meditation techniques, and yoga or martial arts might also be helpful.

19. Consistency at home is important. Establish a set routine and stick to it.

Help siblings and everyone else in the family understand what ADHD is and how they can help. Family therapy for everyone would be advisable.

20. Hold regular family meetings (see page 263). Family meetings are imperative, especially if your child with ADHD causes disruptions to other family members.

21. Make sure you keep your spouse/partner in the loop. It is vital that you are a solid team not just in parenting your child with ADHD but also in making treatment decisions and facing problems that may arise with the school system, health system, insurance companies, social services, community resources providers and mental-health services, as well as other organizations and people in the world who may fail you in your attempts to get the help your child needs.

22. Seek support from appropriate members of your extended family.

23. You will need a professional assessment to begin to understand whether your child with ADHD will eventually achieve the ability to live fully independently (that is, live alone, hold down a job, drive a car, and so on). Sometimes the prognosis is uncertain, but take the worst-case scenario and do the following:

   - As difficult as this may be to consider right now, you need to take steps to arrange for the right person to care for your child with ADHD if, through death, disability or any other reason, you were suddenly unable to care for him or her.
   - Your child with ADHD will probably become an adult with ADHD. Start planning now for his or her long-term care.
   - Research community resources to help you, not just for now, but for the future and throughout your child's life.
   - With professional legal help, research and create appropriate legal documents, such as a trust that benefits your child with ADHD and/or a will that takes into consideration his or her long-term care and other needs.

24. Make sure your child eats a decent, healthy breakfast. Some people think there is a link between food, toxins, allergies and sugar and ADHD. Read up about these, and consider trying a special diet to see if your child might be one of the people who can be helped in this way.

25. If you don't already know what your child's preferred hobbies and special interests are, find out. Support appropriate interests by providing materials, reading matter, DVDs or trips to museums or interesting locations.

26. Implement a programme of physical exercise, not just for health, but to help with frustration and anxiety.

27. Boost your child's self-esteem (see page 255). Reward his or her talents, improvements and good behaviour.

28. Praise your child's accomplishments, but be careful not to base your approval on performance alone. Make sure your child feels loved for who he or she is.

29. Encourage your child to take pride in his or her own work.

30. Encourage appropriate friendships among your child's peers. Having one good friend will help him or her feel accepted and supported, even when facing setbacks and unkindness from others.

31. As well as love and protection, provide rules and structure for your child.

32. Teach your child to assert himself or herself and to ask for help when needed.

33. Teach your child problem-solving skills, and demonstrate those skills yourself. Don't be tempted to fix everything. When your child has a problem, instead of immediately suggesting a solution use the words, 'Hmm. What do you think you're going to do about that?' Be patient while he or she considers various strategies. Guide gently, while supporting and rewarding, and you will eventually see progress in their ability to come up with appropriate solutions.

34. Teach your child what to do in emergencies such as fire, flood, blackouts, attempted abduction or getting lost. Reinforce this frequently.

35. Some children with ADHD really benefit from taking a martial arts class. Consider karate, tae kwon do or other types for your child.

36. Try to teach your child to maintain eye contact and repeat directions back to you.

37. Treat your child with tenderness and respect, show love for him or her, and never allow anyone to label them as 'lazy', 'stupid' or any other slur.

38. Provide soothing experiences such as loving touch, bedtime stories and having fun together.

39. Take care of yourself. Parenting a child with special needs can be difficult, and you need breaks. Schedule a regular massage, manicure or other pleasurable activities and keep up your own exercise regime. Pay attention to your own needs.

40. Maintain your physical and emotional health.

41. Eat balanced, nutritious meals and get enough sleep.

42. Find good-quality childcare.

43. Make and keep good friends who will support you, as well as help you to relax and play.

44. Consider starting a home-based business to allow you to best juggle work and family.

45. Hang on to your goals, dreams or career. Don't fall into the trap of losing yourself amidst the intensive demands of raising a child with special needs.

For Adults with ADHD:

1. Utilizing feedback from people you trust at home, in social situations and at work, identify your specific symptoms. It is important to know your strengths and weaknesses.

2. Read everything you can about ADHD, and educate your family, friends and partner about relevant aspects of your struggle with the disorder.

3. Identify the problems having ADHD causes you in each area of your life, such as having difficulty completing tasks, being easily distracted in meetings or not being on time. Develop strategies about how to make things better; for example, if you find it hard to concentrate at work, try to create a workspace that has fewer distractions. Change your work style, so instead of starting lots of tasks you never finish, just start and complete one at a time. Break large projects down into smaller sections.

4. Work on your organizational skills. Ask someone who is well organized if he or she would mind helping you with this. Be sure to aid this helper in understanding what works for you and what doesn't. Perhaps you need to rearrange your desk, reorganize your files so that they are easier to access or clean up your computer desktop. If you have trouble following a sequence of tasks, make checklists that you can follow in order. 'Post-It notes', colour coding and 'To Do' lists may help. If you are in a position to have an executive assistant, be sure you hire a patient person who can understand your special needs and will be creative and patient in carrying them out.

5. Manage your time well. Structure your workday using hour-by-hour timesheets. These will help you to stay on task and help you to get your work finished.

6. Create a calendar or diary that really works for you. Utilize prompting alarm features on phones, computers or handheld devices.

7. Create deadlines for everything.

8. Capitalize on what you're good at, and try not to feel bad about the things you don't do well.

9. Don't hesitate to ask people to repeat themselves when you fail to take in their instructions first time round.

10. How does having ADHD affect how you relate to a significant other? Elicit feedback and begin to develop a strategy on how to improve your relationship.

11. Choose a partner who offers you encouragement. He or she should be able to understand your ADHD, be willing to help you through challenging situations, and maybe even balance the chequebook. However, there can be problems in relationships where one person is expected to assume the role of a carer. Couples therapy is recommended.

12. Delegate responsibility wherever you can. For example, it would be smart to hire a financial advisor who can make sure you pay attention to such important matters as tax, insurance, retirement plan, making a will, mortgages and so on.

13. Join an ADHD support group.

14. Attention disorders often go hand in hand with alcohol or drug abuse. In particular, people with ADHD often abuse street stimulants such as cocaine and 'uppers'. If you are abusing substances, join a twelve-step programme today.

15. Practise relaxation, take physical exercise and engage in pleasurable activities that will help soothe you and reduce your anxiety and frustration.

16. Try to think of the special way you function as uniquely creative. Search for ways to express it as a gift. You may be good at acting, comedy, art and entertaining at home. Enjoy your hobbies and the things you like that do not frustrate you.

17. Take care of yourself and learn how to pay attention to your own needs.

18. Maintain your physical and emotional health.

19. Eat balanced, nutritious meals and get enough sleep.

20. Nurture healthy friendships. If this is hard for you, get some specific therapeutic help to learn social skills and the fundamentals of personal interaction.

helpful books

Driven to Distraction, E. Hallowell and J. Ratey. New York: Pantheon Books, 1994.

Answers to Distraction, E. Hallowell and J. Ratey. New York: Bantam Books, 1996.

Living with ADD: A Workbook for Adults with Attention Deficit Disorder, M. S.

Roberts and G. J. Jansen. Oakland, Calif.: New Harbinger Publications, 1997.

You Mean I'm Not Lazy, Stupid, or Crazy?! A Self-Help Book for Adults with Attention Deficit Disorder, K. Kelly and P. Ramundo. New York: Fireside, 1996.

Attention Deficit Disorder in Adults: Practical Help for Sufferers and Their Spouses, L. Weiss. Dallas, Tex.: Taylor Publishing Company, 1992.

Beyond Ritalin: Facts about Medication and Other Strategies for Helping Children, Adolescents, and Adults with Attention Deficit Disorders, S. W. Garber, M. Garber and R. Spizman. New York: HarperCollins Books, 1997.

No Easy Answers: The Learning Disabled Child at Home and at School, S. L. Smith. Bantam Books, 1995.

Attention Deficit Disorder and Learning Disabilities: Realities, Myths and Controversial Treatments, B. Ingersoll and S. Goldstein. New York: Doubleday, 1993.

ADD Success Stories: A Guide to Fulfilment for Families with Attention Deficit Disorder, J. Ratey. Grass Valley, Calif.: 1995.

No More Ritalin: Treating ADHD without Drugs: A Mother's Journey, a Physician's Approach, M. Block. New York: Kensington Publishing Corp., 1996.

Total Concentration: How to Understand Attention Deficit Disorders with Treatment Guidelines for You and Your Doctor, H. Levinson. New York: Evans and Company, Inc., 1990.

The ADD Parenting Handbook: Practical Advice for Parents from Parents: Proven techniques for raising hyperactive children without losing your temper, C. Alexander-Roberts. Dallas, Tex.: Taylor Publishing Company, 1994.

ADD and Creativity: Tapping Your Inner Muse, L. Weiss. Dallas, Tex.: Taylor Publishing Company, 1997.

Parenting Your Complex Child: Become a Powerful Advocate for the Autistic, Down Syndrome, PDD, Bipolar, or Other Special-Needs Child, P. L. Morgan, AMACOM, 2006.

mental retardation

I wish we could get rid of the stigma that goes along with the idea of mental retardation. The DSM-IV uses the term Mental Retardation, but many people prefer the term 'intellectual disability' or even the more general term 'special needs'. In any case, neither term should be used as an adjective. Those who suffer from this disorder should be referred to as 'people with … intellectual disabilities, special needs, and so on'.

Just because a child does not have a high or even average IQ does not mean he or she will not be loveable and capable of loving, or have a happy, fulfilled life. Good parents have the ability to see their children as the unique individuals they are, but because good parents love and accept their children no matter what, they sometimes fail to notice that a child might have some differences that need to be addressed. It is always painful for a parent to learn that a child might have an intellectual disability or need mental-health treatment. However the sooner a full evaluation is sought, the sooner that child can be helped on his or her way to achieving the highest possible level of functioning. For a while, there will be a lot of focus on 'what's wrong', but it is important to keep sight of the fact that your child is not a diagnosis. He or she is a unique, inspiring individual. This child will lead you through a challenging journey, but you can do it and there will be surprising rewards along every step of the way.

case study: Wanda

Wanda was born prematurely, and had a birth weight of only 2 lbs (4.4 Kg). At age five she was evaluated by a neuropsychologist because she had not attained the expected skills in order to be accepted into the school her parents had chosen for her. A standardized measure of intelligence showed her to be suffering from a mild intellectual disability, with an IQ of around 60. Wanda was a charming child who more than made up for her intellectual deficits with her engaging manner, fun-loving spirit and warmth. She was placed in a special-needs school environment where she was able to receive one-on-one attention to help her learn to read and write. Over the next ten years she learned to type and use a computer, and overcame many of her difficulties in daily living skills. Most importantly, she was given the support and encouragement to maintain good self-esteem. Her special skills were horse-riding and kindness. When she became an adult, she was able to maintain a supervised job in a local riding school, helping out in the stables and providing a calm and nurturing presence towards the younger children who came along for their first lesson.

is this your child?

- Intellectual functioning is well below average, as measured on a proper, individual IQ test. A score for mild Mental Retardation would be from 50–55 to around 70; moderate would be 35–40 to 50–55; severe would be

20–25 to 35–40; and profound would be below 20 or 25. This lower-than-average IQ would be present before the age of eighteen.

- Fails to meet age-appropriate expectations in being able to attend to self-grooming, communicate, appropriately interact with others, achieve minimal academic milestones, play, do chores and self-protect.

'do not pass go' signs

People with Mental Retardation have difficulty meeting common life demands. They may also be at risk of being physically or sexually abused or otherwise exploited by others and denied rights and opportunities to progress. Some people with Mental Retardation also suffer from other mental disorders. Mental-health practitioners should be consulted immediately if there is cause to suspect that a child may be suffering from Mental Retardation. It is always painful for a parent to accept that a child might need mental-health treatment; however the sooner your child can be evaluated, the sooner he or she (and you) can be helped.

what causes mental retardation?

There are thought to be some heredity factors and many other possible causes, such as chromosomal changes, prenatal damage due to toxins (for example maternal alcohol use or infections), being deprived of nurturing and necessary stimulation, maternal problems during pregnancy and birth (for example, oxygen deficiency, infections or trauma), being born prematurely, and foetal malnutrition.

what happens in the brain?

Since there are so many possible causes of Mental Retardation, researchers have not been able to describe a common, defining feature. However, Positron Emission Tomography (PET), a technique that enables imaging of the distribution of radio-labelled tracers designed to track biochemical and molecular processes in the body, may eventually be key in identifying the physiological consequences of gene mutations associated with Mental Retardation.

which treatments are likely to work?

Whether your child suffers from mild or profound Mental Retardation, there are always treatments and support available to help with communication, speech, motor skills, social skills, daily living skills, age-appropriate independent behaviour, social responsibility, self-care and other important areas. The complexity of the behavioural problems and psychiatric disorders suffered by people with Mental Retardation calls for a multidimensional treatment approach. This usually involves the cooperation of different professionals, such as a psychiatrist, psychologist, teacher, social worker, nurse and, where possible, the person's carers. This integrative treatment should not just be directed towards the symptoms of the disorder but towards restoring a person's mental well-being. The disorder itself is best combated through treatment of the underlying processes that have led to its onset.

People with intellectual disabilities frequently have Mood Disorders, although these are not easy to diagnose due to the fact that the sufferers tend to have limitations in verbal ability, and their symptoms may be different than in other people. Behavioural symptoms such as aggression are frequently indications that a person with Mental Retardation may also have a Mood Disorder. Medication and electroconvulsive therapy have been found to be effective treatments for Mood Disorders in people with Mental Retardation, and a simplified form of cognitive-behavioural therapy is sometimes appropriate. Exercise programmes, for example walking, swimming, or jumping on a trampoline have been shown to improve levels of Depression and positive feelings about the self, as well as lower levels of automatic negative thoughts in people with Mental Retardation.

best course of action?

Get an evaluation for your child with experienced, qualified specialists (for example medical examination, neurological examination and/or evaluation by a neuropsychologist). Then, using the information gained from those investigations, you can research available resources and assemble a team of people who can provide the best possible individualized treatment that will help your child achieve his or her highest possible level of functioning.

in the meantime what can you do?

1. If you suspect a diagnosis of Mental Retardation in your child, do not delay seeking treatment. You need urgent help in caring for this child. Treatment is vital.

2. Know that there is hope. Although it may seem overwhelming to learn that Mental Retardation involves cognitive impairments as well as behavioural and self-care challenges, remember that you also have a child who is loveable, and capable of loving. Despite labels some people might give him or her, your child is a unique gift.

3. You will be asking: 'Why did this happen? Why our family?' Try to let go

of that question. There is no real answer. At the end of the day, that's just the way it is.

4. Fostering your spirituality may be very helpful for you and the whole family.

5. Learn everything you can about Mental Retardation and link up to community services, support groups and other resources.

6. Get some supportive therapy for yourself and the rest of your family.

7. Seek support from appropriate members of your extended family.

8. Openly admire your child's accomplishments, but be careful not to base your approval on progress or performance alone. Make sure your child feels loved for who he or she is.

9. In your child's treatment, collaborate with mental-health specialists to set specific, attainable goals for your child, for example the establishment of developmentally appropriate living skills, the acquisition of social skills, the development of problem-solving skills, making appropriate friends and decreasing social isolation. You can help with all of these by learning and implementing behaviour modification techniques. Here are some examples of the types of techniques you might implement, perhaps under the guidance of your child's therapist:

   - Draw up a list of daily living skills to work on, for example dressing, personal hygiene and travelling on public transport. If possible, do this in consultation with your child so he or she is involved in the creation of these goals. Making sure your expectations are realistic, develop a programme of first demonstrating those behaviours. Next, get your child to copy and repeat these skills. If necessary, break them down into small increments. Continue to remind him or her to engage consistently with these desired activities, using positive reinforcement. Give positive feedback to your child (praise or reward for improvements or successes).

   - To improve social skills, first role-play appropriate behaviour/ etiquette, rule-following, collaboration and cooperation with your child. Next, create situations where he or she can practise the learned skills. Repetition is important, so be consistent and constantly review these skills. Provide positive feedback and reinforcement.

   - To improve problem-solving skills, identify possible crises, for example fire, flood or finding a lost child. Rehearse the appropriate responses. Provide training for dialling emergency services and/or summoning help. Also role-play other situations in which problem-solving would be necessary. Provide positive feedback and reinforcement.

- To increase social connections, research appropriate community resources, such as camps for people with special needs, swimming teams or other sporting activities.

10. Encourage your child to take pride in his or her own work.
11. Encourage appropriate friendships among your child's peers. Having one good friend will help your child feel acceptable and supported, even when facing setbacks and unkindness from others.
12. The addition of massage therapy to an early intervention programme may enhance motor functioning and increase muscle tone for children with Down's syndrome.
13. As a person with Mental Retardation progresses through various stages in life, different problems may present themselves in keeping with their developmental stage – just like everyone else. For example, alcohol and drug abuse can affect the physical and mental health of people with intellectual disabilities, leading to behavioural and social difficulties, yet treatment services for people with Mental Retardation may not be easily available. Education, prevention and treatment programmes for them may have been overlooked, so it will probably fall to you to notice, intervene and try to find the appropriate services if necessary.
14. As well as love and protection, provide rules and structure for your child.
15. Teach your child self-assertion and to ask for help when needed.
16. Make sure you keep your spouse/partner in the loop. It is vital that you are a solid team, not just in parenting your child with Mental Retardation but also in making treatment decisions and facing problems that may arise with social services, community resource providers, mental-health services providers, the school system, health system and insurance companies, as well as other organizations and people in the world who may fail you in your attempts to get the help your child needs.
17. You will need a professional assessment to understand whether your child with Mental Retardation will eventually achieve the ability to live independently (for example live alone, drive a car and so on). Sometimes the prognosis is uncertain, but take the worst-case scenario and do the following:
    - As difficult as this may be to consider right now, you need to take steps to arrange for the right person to care for your child if, through death, disability or any other reason, you were suddenly unable to care for him or her.
    - Your child with Mental Retardation will one day become an adult with

Mental Retardation. Start planning now for his or her long-term care.

■ Research community resources to help you, not just for now, but for the future and throughout your child's life.

■ With professional legal help, research and create the appropriate legal documents, such as a trust that benefits your child and/or a will that takes into consideration his or her long-term care and other needs.

18. Take care of yourself, and learn how to pay attention to your own needs.

19. Maintain your physical and emotional health.

20. Eat balanced, nutritious meals and get enough sleep.

21. Find good-quality childcare.

22. Make and keep good friends who will support you, as well as help you to relax and play.

23. Consider starting a home-based business to allow you to juggle work and family the best.

24. Hang onto your goals, dreams or career. Don't fall into the trap of losing yourself amidst the intensive demands of raising a child with special needs.

helpful books

Guide to Mental Health for Families and Carers of People with Intellectual Disabilities, G. Holt, A. Gratsa, N. Bouras, T. Joyce, M. J. Spiller and S. Hardy. London: Jessica Kingsley Publishers, 2004.

Why Am I Different?, N. Simon. Morton Grove, Ill.: Albert Whitman & Company, 1976.

Don't Feed the Monster on Tuesdays: The Children's Self-Esteem Book, A. Moser. Kansas City, Miss.: Landmark Editions Inc., 1991.

Parenting Your Complex Child: Become a Powerful Advocate for the Autistic, Down Syndrome, PDD, Bipolar, or Other Special-Needs Child, P. L. Morgan. AMACOM, 2006.

'Language Interventions Using Scripts for Children with Down Syndrome', T. Nagasaki and M. Onozato, in David W. Shwalb, Jun Nakazawa, Barbara J. Shwalb (eds), *Applied Developmental Psychology: Theory, Practice, and Research from Japan, Advances in Applied Developmental Psychology*. IAP Information Age Publishing, 2005.

My Body Is Mine, My Feelings Are Mine: A Story Book about Body Safety for Young Children with an Adult Guide Book, S. Hoke. King of Prussia, Penn.: The Center for Applied Psychology Inc., 1995.

learning disorders

Before we began to understand that some children learn differently from others, many people grew up with a very poor self-image from having been told they were 'lazy' or 'stupid'. Nowadays, there is far more awareness, so children who tend to make writing or comprehension mistakes, who have problems recognizing numbers or whose written work is always full of mistakes can be identified as needing special help. Having a DSM-IV diagnosed Learning Disorder (or learning *difference* as I prefer to put it) does not necessarily prevent a person from becoming extremely successful – and there are many well-known people today (the actor Tom Cruise being perhaps the most famous) who are living proof of that.

is this your child?
- He or she scores much lower on an individually given, standardized test of reading, mathematics or expressive writing than is expected for his or her age, educational experience and level of intelligence.
- If the child also suffers from difficulties with sight, hearing or speech, these must be taken into consideration before assigning a diagnosis of Learning Disorder.

types of learning disorder

Reading Disorder is sometimes referred to as 'Dyslexia' and involves making comprehension mistakes, as well as substituting, omitting or altering words when reading aloud.

Mathematics Disorder includes problems in counting, recognizing numbers, understanding mathematical principles or operations, following steps to solve mathematical problems and learning multiplication tables.

Disorder of Written Expression is where the person finds it extremely difficult to compose written work that is free from grammar, spelling, paragraph construction and punctuation mistakes, as well as having extremely poor handwriting.

'do not pass go' signs
Having a Learning Disorder can make it very hard for a young person to achieve at school and to fit in with peers. The child's self-esteem can suffer

badly and there is a high rate of school drop-out. There are many ways to help him or her, but the exact problem needs to be identified as soon as possible. If you suspect that your child may have a learning difference, seek an evaluation for him or her from an experienced, qualified mental-health professional so that you can quickly summon appropriate support and treatment.

what causes learning disorders?

It is possible that there are underlying genetic causes, problems caused by perinatal injury, neurological problems or psychosocial influences. Learning Disorders sometimes go hand in hand with Attention-Deficit/Hyperactivity Disorder, Depression and Conduct Disorder. Some children have more than one Learning Disorder. For example, children with dyslexia and specific language impairment typically have reading problems too, while children with language problems are at risk of also having reading comprehension difficulties.

what happens in the brain?

Because there are many possible causes of the different types of Learning Disorders, no one factor has been identified to explain what happens. Many different functions of a person's brain can influence learning abilities and affect intelligence. For example, a deficit in long-term memory will have a detrimental effect on a person's ability to learn.

which treatments are likely to work?

The various treatments for Learning Disorders are as diverse as the many types of learning differences that come under the umbrella term of Learning Disorders. Individual assessment of strengths and weaknesses is not only necessary for identifying children with Learning Disorders but it is also useful so individualised programmes can be devised to meet their unique learning needs. All kinds of creative strategies are now available. They often involve one-to-one training with a special education therapist, speech therapist or special-needs tutor. For example, eye-tracking problems can be treated by an eye specialist, and psychotherapy is valuable for enhancing a child's self-esteem and helping him or her to overcome the problems associated with having a learning difference that might arise in every area of life. A therapist can often act as a case manager for all your child's interventions.

best course of action?

First, a careful evaluation from an experienced, qualified mental-health professional is necessary. After the exact nature of the learning difference has been identified it will be possible to find a range of treatments, educational help, support, psychotherapy, family therapy and other resources to create the best opportunities for your child.

in the meantime what can you do?

1. If you suspect a diagnosis of one or two of the Learning Disorders in your child, do not delay seeking treatment. You need help in order to provide the best prognosis. Treatment is vital.

2. Know that there is hope. Although having a Learning Disorder can create academic, social and family problems, remember that you also have a unique, exceptional and inspiring individual who is not just a diagnosis. This child will lead you through a challenging journey, but you can do it and there will be surprising rewards along every step of the way.

3. You will be asking: 'Why did this happen? Why our child?' Try to let go of that question. There is no real answer. At the end of the day, that's just the way it is.

4. Help to keep your child's self-esteem high.

5. Focus on your child's strengths, and support his or her hobbies and favourite activities.

6. Admire your child's accomplishments, but be careful not to base your approval on performance alone. Let them know they are loved for who they are.

7. Encourage your child to take pride in his or her own work.

8. Learn everything you can about Learning Disorders, particularly the type that afflicts your child.

9. Children with learning differences sometimes develop behaviour problems, often in response to the difficulties they are experiencing at school. Seek professional advice about how to manage any behavioural issues your child may be exhibiting, and collaborate with your child's teachers in implementing behaviour-modification strategies.

10. Always provide positive reinforcement (praising or rewarding good behaviour or improvements).

11. Help your child to develop responsible behaviour, problem-solving abilities and good social skills. Spend as much time as you can demonstrating and teaching these essentials.

12. Set limits with your child, and be consistent. Consistency is essential to facilitate behavioural change.

13. Provide safety and structure for your child.

14. Identify specific problems your child might have; for example, relating to teachers, forming and maintaining peer relationships, following directions or studying. Develop strategies with your child to find and implement solutions. In the process you will be providing vital, life-long problem-solving skills and helping your child to gain insight and understanding about the exact nature of his or her learning differences.

15. If your child has developed extreme defensiveness, impulse-control problems, anger problems or a tendency towards violence, you must seek immediate help from a mental-health professional, as these problems can lead to disastrous consequences that extend way beyond academic challenges.

16. Educate the rest of the family about Learning Disorders.

17. Seek support from appropriate members of your extended family.

18. Make sure you keep your spouse/partner in the loop. It is vital that you are a solid team, not just in parenting your child with a Learning Disorder but also in making treatment decisions and facing problems that may arise with the school system, health system, insurance companies, mental-health services providers, community resources providers and social services, as well as other organizations and people in the world who may fail you in your attempts to get the help your child needs.

19. If there is someone else in the family with a Learning Disorder encourage that person to seek treatment too, and empathize with his or her own struggles with it.

20. You will need professional assessment to begin to understand what your child with a Learning Disorder will eventually be able to achieve in terms of the ability to live fully independently (that is safely live alone, have a job, drive a car and so on). Sometimes the prognosis is uncertain, but take the worst-case scenario and do the following:

    ■ As difficult as this may be to consider right now, you need to take steps to arrange for the right person to care for your child if, through death, disability or any other reason, you were suddenly unable to care for him or her.

    ■ Your child with a Learning Disorder may one day become an adult with a Learning Disorder. Many improvements will be made, but there will still be struggles. Start planning now for his or her long-term support and care.

- Research community resources to help you, not just for now, but for the future and throughout your child's life.
- With professional legal help, research and create the appropriate legal documents, such as a trust that benefits your child with a Learning Disorder and/or a will that takes into consideration his or her long-term care and other needs.

21. Encourage appropriate friendships among your child's peers. Having one good friend will help your child feel acceptable and supported, even when he or she faces setbacks and unkindness from others.
22. Help your child to problem-solve by role-playing responses to various situations including emergency scenarios, such as fire, flood, black-outs, attempted abduction or getting lost.
23. As well as love and protection, provide rules and structure for your child.
24. Teach your child self-assertion and to ask for help when needed.
25. Take care of yourself, and learn how to pay attention to your own needs.
26. Maintain your physical and emotional health.
27. Eat balanced, nutritious meals and get enough sleep.
28. Find good-quality childcare.
29. Make and keep good friends who will support you, as well as help you to relax and play.
30. Consider starting a home-based business to allow you to juggle work and family best.
31. Hang onto your goals, dreams or career. Don't fall into the trap of losing yourself amidst the intensive demands of raising a child with special needs.

helpful books

The Winning Family: Increasing Self-Esteem in Your Children and Yourself, L. Hart. Oakland, Calif.: LifeSkills Press, 1987.

Parenting Your Complex Child: Become a Powerful Advocate for the Autistic, Down Syndrome, PDD, Bipolar, or Other Special-Needs Child, P. L. Morgan. AMACOM, 2006.

'Inquiry Learning and Special Education Students: Rejecting Instruction that Disables', B. Marlowe and M. Page, in Richard H. Audet, and Linda K. Jordan (eds.), Integrating Inquiry across the Curriculum. Corwin Press, 2005.

It's So Much Work to Be Your Friend: Helping the Child with Learning Disabilities Find Social Success, R. Lavoie. Touchstone Books/Simon & Schuster, Inc., 2005.

helpful books for children

Why Am I Different?, N. Simon. Morton Grove, Ill.: Albert Whitman & Company, 1976.

No Easy Answers: The Learning Disabled Child at Home and at School, S. L. Smith. Bantam Books, 1995.

No One to Play With: the Social Side of Learning Disabilities, B. Osman. Academic Therapy Publications, 1982.

The Don't-Give-Up Kid and Learning Differences, J. Gehret. Fairport, N.Y.: Verbal Images Press, 1990.

Trouble with School: A Family Story about Learning Disabilities, K. B. Dunn and A. B. Dunn. Woodbine House, 1993.

Don't Feed the Monster on Tuesdays: The Children's Self-Esteem Book, A. Moser. Kansas City, Miss.: Landmark Editions Inc., 1991.

developmental coordination disorder (motor-skills disorder)

case study: Danni

Danni's mother requested an evaluation for Danni, worried that there might be 'something wrong with her balance'. At eight years old, Danni was bright and seemed happy, but she seemed unable to control certain movements and was always dropping plates and cups, breaking toys and electronic equipment and bumping into furniture. She performed poorly in sports or gymnastics activities at school, and often begged her mother to let her stay at home on sports days. It turned out that Danni had been rather slow to achieve the usual developmental milestones of sitting, crawling, tying shoelaces and managing buttons. Her handwriting was poor but her reading and mathematical abilities were excellent. As a result of Danni's difficulties with coordination she was sometimes teased at school and had few friends. Fortunately, having an understanding of Danni's diagnosis of Developmental Coordination Disorder meant that she could have the help she needed, in improving her motor skills by working with an occupational therapist, and with the psychological effects by supportive therapy. She learned to understand her limitations and compensate in other ways, while her parents learned to promote her strengths. She became a high-achiever at school and later, at university.

Many parents worry needlessly when a child misses an expected developmental milestone, however those children who really do have a problem need to be diagnosed as soon as possible. Developmental coordination delays are sometimes first noticed when a child attempts to hold a knife and fork, do up buttons or run. It is normal for children to be clumsy or awkward at the first few attempts, but if they persistently fail to achieve tasks beyond an age when most children would become proficient it's worth getting a professional opinion. The best reason for getting a child evaluated is that treatment is available and should begin as soon as possible so that he or she can have the best start in life.

is this your child?
- Shows markedly below-average performance in everyday activities that involve motor coordination.
- Had significant delays in achieving expected milestones for his or her age; for example in crawling, sitting up, walking, tying shoelaces, playing ball games or doing puzzles.
- The motor coordination delays and difficulties cause problems at school or in everyday life.

'do not pass go' signs
Children with Developmental Coordination Disorder have motor difficulties that prevent or hinder them acquiring both functional and academic skills. Motor skills involve having the ability to make one's body move; for example, to use arms and legs (that is, *large* motor skills such as playing ball) or fingers and wrists (that is, *fine* motor skills such as writing). In addition, children with this disorder often develop psychological reactions (for example, irritability, anger, frustration and avoidance) to the difficulties they encounter at school with peers, and in specific situations such as being expected to participate in team sports.

If you think your child may have Developmental Coordination Disorder, seek an evaluation and treatment as soon as possible. It is vital to protect your child from the confusion, loss of self-esteem and peer rejection that might occur if nothing is done.

what causes developmental coordination disorder?
There is usually a neurological basis for sensorimotor coordination problems.

what happens in the brain?

There are usually problems in certain areas of the brain that are responsible for initiating and carrying out functions associated with coordination, such as fine and large motor skills.

which treatments are likely to work?

There is a relationship between motor difficulties and emotional and behavioural symptoms, so it is recommended that treatments for children with Developmental Coordination Disorder should target mental-health and behavioural problems as well as motor development. Motor-skills training, psychotherapy, family therapy and community support are all recommended, as are specific treatments to improve coordination. Although group therapy will not directly produce improvement in motor skills, there may be an associated increase in the self-confidence and self-esteem of children with Developmental Coordination Disorder. The technique known as 'verbal self-guidance' appears to have good potential in helping children with Developmental Coordination Disorder become competent in the occupations of their choice and enabling them to surmount their motor challenges.

best course of action?

Seek evaluation and treatment from an experienced and qualified mental-health professional.

in the meantime what can you do?

1. If you suspect a diagnosis of Developmental Coordination Disorder in your child, do not delay seeking treatment. You need urgent help in caring for this child to give him or her the best possible future.
2. Know that there is hope. Although it may be difficult to learn that your child has Developmental Coordination Disorder, remember that you also have a child who is loveable, and capable of loving. Your child is not a diagnosis, he or she is a unique, inspiring individual. Your child will lead you through a challenging journey, but you can do it and there will be surprising rewards along every step of the way.
3. Learn everything you can about Developmental Coordination Disorder.
4. Educate family members about Developmental Coordination Disorder.
5. Dietary supplementation with omega-3 fatty acids may help children with Developmental Coordination Disorder achieve better academically.
6. Pay a great deal of attention to boosting your child's self-esteem (see page 255).

7. Focus on his or her strengths and support hobbies and special interests.
8. Admire your child's accomplishments, but be careful not to base your approval on performance. Let them know they are loved for who they are.
9. Encourage your child to take pride in his or her own work.
10. Encourage appropriate friendships among your child's peers. Having one good friend will help him or her feel accepted and supported, even when facing setbacks and unkindness from others.
11. Help your child to problem-solve by role-playing responses to various situations, including emergency scenarios such as fire, flood, black-outs, attempted abduction or getting lost.
12. As well as love and protection, provide rules and structure for your child.
13. Teach your child to practise self-assertion and to ask for help when needed.
14. Educate other family members about Developmental Coordination Disorder.
15. Seek support from appropriate members of your extended family.
16. Make sure you keep your spouse/partner in the loop. It is vital that you are a solid team, not just in parenting your child with Developmental Coordination Disorder but also in making treatment decisions and facing problems that may arise with social services, the health system, mental-health services, community resource providers, the school system and insurance companies, as well as other organizations and people in the world who may fail you in your attempts to get the help your child needs.
17. You will need professional assessment to begin to understand whether your child with Developmental Coordination Disorder will eventually achieve the ability to live fully independently (that is, live alone, drive a car and so on). Sometimes the prognosis is uncertain, but take the worst-case scenario and do the following:
    - As difficult as this may be to consider right now, you need to take steps to arrange for the right person to care for your child with Developmental Coordination Disorder if, through death, disability or any other reason, you were suddenly unable to care for him or her.
    - Your child with Developmental Coordination Disorder may one day become an adult with Developmental Coordination Disorder. Start planning now for long-term eventualities.
    - With professional legal help, research and create appropriate legal documents, such as a trust that benefits your child with Develop-

mental Coordination Disorder and/or a will that takes into consideration his or her long-term care and other needs.

18. Take care of yourself, and learn how to pay attention to your own needs.
19. Maintain your physical and emotional health.
20. Eat balanced, nutritious meals and get enough sleep.
21. Find good-quality childcare.
22. Make and keep good friends who will support you, as well as help you to relax and play.
23. Consider starting a home-based business to allow you to juggle work and family best.
24. Hang onto your goals, dreams or career. Don't fall into the trap of losing yourself amidst the intensive demands of raising a child with special needs.

helpful books

Parenting Your Complex Child: Become a Powerful Advocate for the Autistic, Down Syndrome, PDD, Bipolar, or Other Special-Needs Child, P. L. Morgan. AMACOM, 2006.

The Winning Family: Increasing Self-Esteem in Your Children and Yourself, L. Hart. Oakland, Calif.: LifeSkills Press, 1987.

for children:

Why Am I Different?, N. Simon. Morton Grove, Ill.: Albert Whitman & Company, 1976.

No One to Play With: The Social Side of Learning Disabilities, B. Osman. Academic Therapy Publications, 1989.

Don't Feed the Monster on Tuesdays: The Children's Self-Esteem Book, A. Moser. Kansas City, Miss.: Landmark Editions Inc., 1991.

communication disorders

Many adults find it 'cute' when small children mispronounce words, make mistakes in sentence construction or inappropriately use expressions that have obviously been copied from adults around them. We can gently laugh at these mistakes because they are usually just part of normal language development, and we expect these children to develop into good conversationalists. Sometimes, though, a child may fail to develop optimal language or speech, or have trouble understanding adults' directions. In such a case the child can be helped to overcome his or her stuttering, or other communication issues. Just because there are significant numbers of adults in our society with untreated stuttering (ranging from mild to profound), this does not mean that the condition should be ignored in youngsters these days. All children with suspected Communication Disorders, of one sort or another, need to be evaluated and treated.

case study: Eminem

A couple sought treatment for their ten-year-old son because they were worried about his speech and comprehension. The boy was nicknamed 'Eminem' because he idolized the American rapper. He had a severe stutter and frequently failed to follow adults' instructions or directions – although he was not oppositional in his behaviour. He was able to memorize and reproduce many of the rap artist's biggest hits and, strangely enough, when he did so his Communication Disorder was not at all evident. The boy received acclaim from peers for his impressive impersonations, which was just as well as he was mercilessly teased for stuttering. He needed help for his comprehension as well as his stuttering, and after a couple of years working with a speech and language therapist there was a dramatic improvement. The young man went on to become a music performer in his own right.

is this your child?

Has a problem with communication either in expressive language or comprehension, because he or she stutters.

types of communication disorders

Expressive Language Disorder involves having limited vocabulary, making mistakes in the tenses and finding it hard to remember words or speak in developmentally appropriate sentences.

Mixed Receptive-Expressive Language Disorder involves having expressive language problems plus comprehension problems and difficulty following instructions, being unable to give appropriate responses or lacking conversational skills.

Phonological Disorder involves having difficulty with producing speech sounds.

Stuttering involves tripping or getting stuck on words or parts of words.

'do not pass go' signs

Communication Disorders are seen in significant numbers of children and adolescents. They frequently coexist with other disorders, and children with Communication Disorders are at risk of having persistent reading and spelling disorders in addition to their spoken communication difficulties. It's important that a child with suspected Communication Disorder is comprehensively assessed, because untreated problems in these important areas of a child's development are likely to affect him or her at school and in everyday life. It can create problems with peers, lower self-esteem, and prevent the child from establishing and maintaining important relationships.

what causes communication disorders?
These can be caused by neurological or medical conditions (for example, following a head injury or encephalitis – inflammation of the brain) and may be genetically inherited. Stuttering is believed to be the result of a combination of genetic and psychosocial factors. It is known to worsen under stress or when the sufferer is anxious.

which treatments are likely to work?
After a professional evaluation with a speech and language pathologist has confirmed the diagnosis, speech therapy, psychotherapy and family therapy are usually recommended.

Speech and language therapy is usually effective for children with phonological or expressive vocabulary difficulties, and integrating those treatments with working to achieve literacy goals appears to be crucial for children with Communication Disorders.

best course of action?
Seek a full evaluation from an experienced and qualified mental-health professional, then consider recommended treatments such as speech therapy and psychotherapy.

in the meantime what can you do?
1. If you suspect a diagnosis of a Communication Disorder in your child, do not delay seeking treatment.
2. Know that there is hope. Although it may seem overwhelming to learn that Communication Disorders involve significant language and communicating problems, remember that he or she is not a diagnosis, but is a unique, inspiring individual. Your child will lead you through a challenging journey, but you can do it and there will be surprising rewards along every step of the way.

3. Learn everything you can about Communication Disorders.
4. Educate other family members about Communication Disorders.
5. Seek support from appropriate members of your extended family.
6. If your child's problem is stuttering, make sure that you maintain your composure during your child's episodes of distress, and do not complete sentences for him or her.
7. Make sure you keep your spouse/partner in the loop. It is vital that you are a solid team, not just in parenting your child with a Communication Disorder but also in making treatment decisions and facing problems that may arise with the school system, health system, insurance companies, mental-health providers, social services and community resources providers, as well as other organizations and people in the world who may fail you in your attempts to get the help your child needs.
8. You will need professional assessment to begin to understand what the future may hold for your child with a Communication Disorder. For a small proportion of children diagnosed with a Communication Disorder, difficulties persist into adulthood. Sometimes the prognosis is uncertain, but take the worst-case scenario and do the following:
   - As difficult as this may be to consider right now, you need to take steps to arrange for the right person to care for your child with a Communication Disorder if, through death, disability or any other reason, you were suddenly unable to care for him or her.
   - Your child with a Communication Disorder may one day become an adult with a Communication Disorder. Start planning now for his or her long-term support.
   - Research community resources to help you, not just for now, but for the future and throughout your child's life.
   - With professional legal help, research and create appropriate legal documents, such as a trust that benefits your child with a Communication Disorder and/or a will that takes into consideration his or her long-term needs.

9. Boost your child's self-esteem.
10. Help your child to reduce his or her stress and anxiety.
11. Focus on your child's strengths and support his or her hobbies and special interests.
12. Admire your child's accomplishments, but be careful not to base your

approval on performance. Make sure your child knows they are loved for who they are.

13. Encourage your child to take pride in his or her own work.
14. Encourage appropriate friendships among your child's peers. Having one good friend will help him or her to feel acceptable and supported, even when facing setbacks and unkindness from others.
15. Help your child to problem-solve by role-playing responses to various situations, including emergency scenarios such as fire, flood, black-outs, attempted abduction or getting lost.
16. As well as love and protection, provide rules and structure for your child.
17. Teach your child to assert himself or herself and to ask for help when needed.
18. Take care of yourself, and learn how to pay attention to your own needs.
19. Maintain your physical and emotional health.
20. Eat balanced, nutritious meals and get enough sleep.
21. Find good-quality childcare.
22. Make and keep good friends who will support you, as well as help you to relax and play.
23. Consider starting a home-based business to allow you to juggle work and family best.

helpful books

The Winning Family: Increasing Self-Esteem in Your Children and Yourself, L. Hart. Oakland, Calif.: LifeSkills Press, 1987.

Parenting Your Complex Child: Become a Powerful Advocate for the Autistic, Down Syndrome, PDD, Bipolar, or Other Special-Needs Child, P. L. Morgan. AMACOM, 2006.

helpful books for children

Why Am I Different?, N. Simon. Morton Grove, Ill.: Albert Whitman & Company, 1976.

Don't Feed the Monster on Tuesdays: The Children's Self-Esteem Book, A. Moser. Kansas City, Miss.: Landmark Editions Inc., 1991.

pervasive developmental disorders (autism)

We are only just beginning to understand autism. In the past it has been defined in a number of different ways, but it is currently conceptualized as a spectrum of several disorders including Autistic Disorder, Asperger's Disorder (a milder form of Autistic Disorder with less profound communication problems, and fewer developmental delays), Rett's Disorder (developmental deterioration following a relatively brief period of normal development) and Childhood Disintegrative Disorder.

Autism is a neurodevelopmental disorder. Sufferers have problems in social interaction and/or communication, and a restricted range of interests and/or repetitive behaviour. It's no longer considered a rare disorder. In fact, some have described the escalating numbers of people with autism as constituting an epidemic – although it is possible that there is now simply better recognition of an issue that has long been with us. Another view is that the rise in autism cases identified by parents, schoolteachers and child-health professionals in recent years might have followed a broadening of the diagnostic definitions of autism, so that it includes more people; that is, anyone diagnosed within the current DSM-IV diagnostic criteria for all of the Pervasive Developmental Disorders.

Autism continues to be the focus of extensive study, controversial debate and media coverage. Research advances have been made recently and, as more is learned about autism, there has been less of a stigma associated with it and more people are now willing to be open about the condition. But the emotional strain on families of children with such pervasive disorders is profound. Evidence suggests that early intervention with autism is more effective than later treatment. Although children with neurodevelopmental disabilities have significant health, rehabilitation and special-educational challenges, getting a good start with the right treatment can make a real difference in providing them with optimal health and functioning. In fact, since more people have been identified and treated earlier, there has been an increase in the number of these individuals attending institutions of higher learning.

autistic disorder

case study: Benjamin

Benjamin did not speak until he was four years old. Prior to that he seemed disinterested in people, and could not maintain eye contact. He was endlessly fascinated by his own hands, which he constantly flapped and waved in circles. By three years old he was able to recognize letters and began to draw. He always drew the same things: lamps and light fittings and he became extremely good at accurate depictions of them from many different angles. After his sixth birthday Benjamin's speech improved, and he began to socialize better with other people. His parents put him in a school for children with special needs where his unusual behaviour was understood. By the age of twelve Benjamin was demonstrating that he had an excellent memory for facts, particularly in his own special interest area of lighting and electronics, and was able to succeed well academically. He was transferred to a regular school and left at eighteen after passing his exams. Although his vocabulary expanded significantly, his ability to connect with peers and teachers was limited. He was teased a lot, but he was fortunate to have excellent support from his parents and family. By his mid-twenties, Benjamin's Autism was in partial remission and he maintained a full-time job as inventory manager and buyer at a home-lighting firm.

A diagnosis of Autistic Disorder in a child is always devastating for parents, but in the past it also carried with it a sense of shame, and even stigma directed at families who were already struggling to care for their afflicted child. Fortunately, things are improving due to greater research-led knowledge and to public education generated by autism advocacy groups and media. Recently more people with Autism Spectrum Disorders have managed to enter higher education establishments, hold down paying jobs and achieve a quality of life that would have been difficult in the past. Moreover, much has been learned in the last decade about early warning signs that previously might have gone unnoticed by professionals and parents, as well as advances in understanding and treating autism in the first five years of life.

is this your child?

With at least two of the following:

- Problems maintaining socially appropriate eye-contact, facial expressions or body language.

- Inability to establish age-appropriate peer relationships.
- Not interested in sharing fun, interests or achievements with others.
- Inability to engage in social and emotional give-and-take.

With at least one of the following:

- Severe language problems or complete lack of speaking.
- Severe problems conversing with others.
- Repeating words or phrases, or using idiosyncratic or stereotyped language.
- Does not spontaneously engage in imaginative play.

With at least one of the following:

- Abnormal preoccupation with a particular narrow interest.
- Gets very upset about routine changes.
- Particular repetitive physical mannerisms.
- Preoccupation with or attached to inanimate objects or parts.

Some children are less socially interactive and communicative than others, but if you notice that your child is beginning to exhibit severe social and communication problems it is vital to seek immediate advice from a mental-health professional. If it turns out that your child falls somewhere under the diagnostic umbrella of Autism Spectrum Disorders, treatment should be started right away to give him or her the very best chance in life.

'do not pass go' signs

The things that can prevent people with Autistic Disorder from having the life they deserve include social and communication impairment and unusual behaviour, such as inflexible adherence to routines, rituals and stereotypical behaviour (for example, hand-wringing). However, we now know that early identification and treatment can lead to improvements in all these areas.

what causes autistic disorder?

There is debate about the exact causes of Autistic Disorder, although it is believed to be among the most genetically based of neuropsychiatric disorders, with a heritability estimated to be over 90 per cent. The constellation of co-occurring deficits that characterize Autistic Disorder may be the outcome of an underlying brain abnormality. Another perspective considers the origin of such deficits as related to problems in a child's early emerging neural system.

what is happening in the brain?

The brains of people with autism have been shown to be structurally different from others, including having size differences in certain areas, which some researchers suspect may be explained by hyperactivity in the part of the brain known as the amygdala.

The restricted range of interests and repetitive behaviours that are characteristic of autism may be influenced by mechanisms to do with the neurotransmitter serotonin.

which treatments are likely to work?

Children with Autistic Disorder have impaired social, behavioural and communication abilities. It is a good idea to provide them with very early therapeutic intervention, since this may increase the likelihood that they will become more verbally communicative, have fewer behavioural problems, and have an opportunity to learn many more daily adaptive and educational skills. Very early treatment is also preferred for improving long-term outcomes for children with Autistic Disorder, as it is provided at the best time to affect learning and development in both the child and the family. In addition, younger children may benefit more from treatment than older children because their brains may be more receptive to change. However, treatment is likely to have significant benefit to all people with Autistic Disorder, regardless of age or ability level.

The most effective mode of treatment is a very specific, intense programme of intervention administered as early as possible to improve academic performance, advance communication and language skills, foster social interactions and friendships with typically developing peers, reduce disruptive or ritualistic behaviour, and broaden the child's interests. There are many behavioural treatments that will effectively teach children skills such as compliance, increase receptive and expressive language and target motor skills in an ordered, structured environment.

Play therapy is an effective way to teach children how to develop symbolic thinking (something that is typically difficult for people with Autistic Disorder) and the dynamics of social interaction. Acceptance and commitment therapy may have promise in helping parents better adjust to the difficulties in raising children diagnosed with autism. Naturalistic behavioural treatment, attention skills training, learning from videos/DVDs and sibling-oriented interventions are four more of the many styles or strategies designed to help youngsters with Autistic Disorder. In addition, pivotal response treatment uses natural learning opportunities to improve communication, behaviour and social skills.

best course of action?
If you suspect that your child may have Autistic Disorder, seek a thorough evaluation from a trained mental-health practitioner as soon as possible. A medical examination to rule out physical problems such as hearing or vision impairment should also be carried out. Seek an experienced, qualified therapist, perhaps one who can provide intensive behaviour therapy, which has yielded good results in helping children with Autistic Disorder to acquire skills to help them function better and to reduce inappropriate behaviour. Having a child with Autistic Disorder can be very hard on everyone in the family, so it is also important to seek education and support via family therapy.

what can you do in the meantime?
1. If you suspect a diagnosis of Autistic Disorder in your child, do not delay seeking treatment. You need urgent help in caring for this child.
2. Know that there is hope. Although it may seem overwhelming to learn that Autistic Disorder involves multiple impairments in areas such as language, social skills and behaviour, remember that you also have a child who is loveable and capable of loving. Your child is not a diagnosis, he or she is a unique, exceptional, inspiring individual. Your child will lead you through a challenging journey, but you can do it and there will be surprising rewards along every step of the way.
3. You will be asking: 'Why did this happen? Why our family?' Try to let go of that question. There is no real answer. At the end of the day, that's just the way it is.
4. Fostering your spirituality may be very helpful for you and the whole family.
5. Learn everything you can about Autistic Disorder.
6. Educate everyone in your family about Autistic Disorder.
7. Help get the best possible treatment and care for your child with Autistic Disorder.
8. Get everyone in the family to attend family therapy.
9. Have supportive therapy with your spouse or partner, or individual therapy if you are a single parent or carer.

10. Seek support from appropriate members of your extended family.
11. Make sure you keep your spouse/partner in the loop. It is vital that you are a solid team, not just in parenting your child with Autistic Disorder but also in making treatment decisions and facing problems that may arise with the school system, health system, insurance companies, mental-health providers, social services, and community resources providers, as well as other organizations and people in the world who may fail you in your attempts to get the help your child needs.
12. Understand that your child with Autistic Disorder will probably not show physical affection or relate to you or other family members the way other children might. Try not to take it personally.
13. If your child with Autistic Disorder has a tendency to self-harm, you must intervene when he or she engages in self-injurious behaviour (have your child wear a safety helmet and mitts if necessary). Try to figure out what triggers this behaviour (for example, mounting anxiety) and try to soothe or comfort him or her.
14. Learn how to implement behaviour modification techniques.
15. At all times try to foster a sense of security, consistency and structure in your child's environment.
16. If possible, do not change anything in your child's physical environment, and keep it minimally stimulating.
17. Know that progress will probably be extremely slow. Be realistic about your expectations and your child's limitations. Instead of trying to impose your goals for improvement on your child, prepare yourself for the fact that he or she will move at his or her own pace.
18. Do your best to foster your child's trust in you through consistency, the provision of safety and structure, and positive reinforcement (praise or reward improvements and successes).
19. There is increasing evidence that fatty acid deficiencies or imbalances may contribute to the development of childhood neurodevelopmental disorders. Omega-3 fatty acids taken as supplements may be an effective treatment for children with autism.
20. You will need professional assessment to begin to understand whether your child with Autistic Disorder will eventually achieve the ability to live fully independently (that is live alone, hold a job, drive a car and so on). Sometimes the prognosis is uncertain, but take the worst-case scenario and do the following:
    - As difficult as this may be to consider right now, you need to take steps to arrange for someone else to care for your child if, through death,

disability or any other reason, you were suddenly unable to care for him or her.

- Your child with Autistic Disorder will one day become an adult with Autistic Disorder. Start planning now for his or her long-term care.
- Research community resources to help you, not just for now, but for the future and throughout your child's life.
- With professional legal help, research and create appropriate legal documents, such as a trust that benefits your child and/or a will that takes into consideration his or her long-term care and other needs.

21. Boost your child's self-esteem (see page 255).
22. Help your child to reduce his or her stress and anxiety (see page 19).
23. Focus on his or her strengths and support their hobbies and special interests.
24. Encourage appropriate friendships among your child's peers. Having one good friend will help him or her feel accepted and supported, even when facing setbacks and unkindness from others.
25. Recent evidence has found that high-quality sleep promotes brain plasticity, improves health and enriches quality of life. However people with developmental disorders have been found to sleep less and experience higher incidences of clinical sleep disorders than the general population. Treatments for apnoea, insomnia, restless limbs, and other Sleep Disorders are available and should be provided, for people with developmental disorders. Find out what is available for your child.
26. Try to help your child to problem-solve by role-playing responses to various situations, especially regarding emergency scenarios such as fire, flood, black-outs, attempted abduction or getting lost.
27. As well as love and protection, provide rules and structure for your child.
28. Teach your child to be assertive and to ask for help when needed.
29. Take care of yourself and learn how to pay attention to your own needs.
30. Maintain your physical and emotional health.
31. Eat balanced, nutritious meals and get enough sleep.
32. Find good-quality childcare.
33. Make and keep good friends who will support you, as well as help you to relax and play.
34. Consider starting a home-based business to allow you to juggle work and family best.
35. Hang onto your goals, dreams or career. Don't fall into the trap of losing

yourself amidst the intensive demands of raising a child with special needs.

helpful books

Nobody Nowhere: The Extraordinary Autobiography of an Autistic, Donna Williams. New York: Perennial, 2002.

Parenting Your Complex Child: Become a Powerful Advocate for the Autistic, Down Syndrome, PDD, Bipolar, or Other Special-Needs Child, P. L. Morgan. AMACOM, 2006.

Thinking in Pictures: My Life with Autism, T. Grandin. New York: Vintage Books, 2006.

Animals in Translation, T. Grandin. San Diego, Calif.: Harvest Books, 2006.

A Mind Apart: Understanding Children with Autism and Asperger Syndrome, P. Szatmari. New York: Guilford Press, 2004.

Demystifying Autism Spectrum Disorders: A Guide to Diagnosis for Parents and Professionals, C. T. Bruey. Woodbine House, 2004.

People with Autism Behaving Badly: Helping People with ASD Move on from Behavioral and Emotional Challenges, J. Clements. Jessica Kingsley Publishers, 2005.

Voices from the Spectrum: Parents, Grandparents, Siblings, People with Autism, and Professionals Share Their Wisdom, (eds) C. N. Ariel and R. A. Naseef. London: Jessica Kingsley Publishers, 2006.

Not Even Wrong: Adventures in Autism, P. Collins. Bloomsbury Publishing, 2004.

Topics in Autism: Incentives for Change: Motivating People with Autism Spectrum Disorders to Learn and Gain Independence, L. Delmolino and S. L. Harris. Woodbine House, 2004.

Healthcare for Children on the Autism Spectrum: A Guide to Medical, Nutritional, and Behavioral Issues, F. R. Volkmar and L. A. Wiesner. Woodbine House, 2004.

The Development of Autism: A Self-Regulatory Perspective, T. L. Whitman. Jessica Kingsley Publishers, 2004.

A Real Boy: A True Story of Autism, Early Intervention, and Recovery, C. Adams. The Berkley Publishing Group, 2005.

'Social Cognitive Development of Autistic Children: Attachment Relationships and Understanding the Existence of Minds of Others', S. Beppu, in D. W. Shwalb, J. Nakazawa, and B. J. Shwalb (eds), *Applied Developmental Psychology: Theory, Practice, and Research from Japan, Advances in Applied Developmental Psychology*, xiv. IAP Information Age Publishing, 2005, pp. 199–221.

Addressing the Challenging Behavior of Children with High-Functioning Autism/Asperger Syndrome in the Classroom: A Guide for Teachers and Parents, R. Moyes. London: Jessica Kingsley Publishers, 2002.

Parenting Your Complex Child: Become a Powerful Advocate for the Autistic, Down Syndrome, PDD, Bipolar, or Other Special-Needs Child, P. L. Morgan. AMACOM, 2006.

The Normal One: Life with a Difficult or Damaged Sibling, J. Safer. New York: Bantam Dell, 2003.

When Someone You Love Has a Mental Illness: A Handbook for Family, Friends, and Caregivers, R. Woolis. New York: Tarcher/Penguin, 1992.

Five Weeks to Healing Stress: The Wellness Option, V. O'Hara. Oakland, Calif.: New Harbinger Publications, 1996.

for children

Why Am I Different?, N. Simon. Morton Grove, Ill.: Albert Whitman & Company, 1976.

Don't Feed the Monster on Tuesdays: The Children's Self-Esteem Book, A. Moser. Kansas City, Miss.: Landmark Editions Inc., 1991.

Cat's Got Your Tongue/ A Story for Children Afraid to Speak, C. E. Schaefer. New York: Magination Press, 1992.

My Body Is Mine, My Feelings Are Mine: A Story Book about Body Safety for Young Children with an Adult Guide Book, S. Hoke. King of Prussia, Penn.: The Center for Applied Psychology Inc., 1995.

asperger's disorder

Asperger's Disorder is like a milder form of Autistic Disorder. The symptoms are the same except that there is no developmental delay in language, thinking processes or in the development of self-help skills. People with Asperger's Disorder can be some of the most interesting people you could ever meet, because they tend to be quite gifted and have extraordinarily detailed knowledge about their particular narrow field of interest.

case study: Garth

Garth knew everything there was to know about cricket. You could ask him the teatime score of a match that took place in another country twenty years ago and he'd know the answer. As a young child, Garth was a serious, preoccupied child who had an age-appropriate command of language but limited social skills or little interest in making friends. His parents worried about his inability to maintain eye contact, his strange mannerisms and his lack of peer relationships. But he was clearly bright and impressed everyone with his extraordinary memory. As Garth grew into an older child he began to 'stand out' as being 'unusual' in a number of ways. This attracted the wrong kind of attention at school for Garth, and when his parents discovered he was often teased they wanted to remove him from his mainstream school and place him in a special educational establishment. Unfortunately there was no appropriate placement for Garth, so his parents had to try to educate his teachers about Asperger's Disorder in the hope that they would help him with his social problems. By the time I met Garth he was nineteen years old. His self-esteem was very low, and he had just been in trouble for making sexual comments to a co-worker at his weekend job in a cafe. Among other things, Garth needed to be helped to understand what a unique, interesting and talented person he was, and given the tools to make appropriate social connections. His parents needed help in understanding their son and preparing to provide for his precise, long-term needs. Garth was eventually able to earn his living as a fact checker for a sports newspaper. He is currently trying to improve his daily living skills with the hope of one day becoming fully independent.

is this your child?

Has at least two of the following:

- Problems maintaining socially appropriate eye-contact, facial expressions or body language.
- Inability to establish age-appropriate peer relationships.
- Not interested in sharing fun, interests or achievements with others.
- Inability to engage in social and emotional give-and-take.

With at least one of the following:

- Abnormal preoccupation with a particular narrow interest.
- Gets very upset about routine changes.
- Particular repetitive physical mannerisms.
- Preoccupation with or attached to inanimate objects or parts.

'do not pass go' signs

People with Asperger's Disorder need to be given help with independence, social and behavioural skills and, just as with Autistic Disorder, they need to do this as early as possible.

what causes asperger's disorder?
It seems to run in families and may have similar causes to Autistic Disorder.

which treatments are likely to work?
Children with Asperger's Disorder have impaired social and behavioural abilities. It is a good idea to provide them with early therapeutic intervention, since this may increase the likelihood that they will have fewer behavioural problems and an opportunity to learn many more daily adaptive and educational skills. The most effective mode of treatment is a very specific, intense programme of intervention that might include behaviour therapy, play therapy, and motor-skills training administered as early as possible.

Acceptance and commitment therapy may also have value in helping parents better adjust to the difficulties in raising children diagnosed with Asperger's Disorder.

best course of action
Seek thorough evaluation and treatment from a trained mental-health practitioner.

what can you do in the meantime?
1. If you suspect a diagnosis of Asperger's Disorder in your child, do not delay seeking treatment. You need help in caring for this child. Early treatment is vital.
2. Know that there is hope. Although it may seem overwhelming to learn that Asperger's Disorder involves impairments in social and behavioural domains, remember that you also have a child who is loveable, and capable of loving. Your child is not a diagnosis, he or she is a unique, inspiring individual with some extraordinary talents. This child will lead you through a challenging journey, but you can do it and there will be surprising rewards along every step of the way.
3. You will be asking: 'Why did this happen? Why our child? Our family?' Try to let go of that question. There is no real answer. At the end of the day, that's just the way it is.
4. Fostering your spirituality may be very helpful for you and the whole family.
5. Learn everything you can about Asperger's Disorder.
6. Educate the rest of your family about Asperger's Disorder.
7. Boost your child's self-esteem.

8. Help your child to reduce his or her stress and anxiety.

9. Focus on your child's strengths and support his or her hobbies and special interests.

10. Admire your child's accomplishments, but be careful not to base your approval on performance alone. Let him or her know they are loved for who they are.

11. Encourage your child to take pride in his or her own work.

12. Encourage appropriate friendships among your child's peers. Having one good friend will help him or her feel accepted and supported, even when facing setbacks and unkindness from others.

13. Help your child to problem-solve by role-playing responses to various situations. Be sure to include emergency scenarios so that your child knows what to do in the event of fire, flood, an abduction or abuse attempt, or getting lost.

14. As well as love and protection, provide rules and structure for your child.

15. Teach your child to be assertive and to ask for help when needed.

16. There is increasing evidence that fatty acid deficiencies or imbalances may contribute to the development of childhood neurodevelopmental disorders. Omega-3 fatty acids taken as supplements may be an effective treatment for children with Asperger's Disorder.

17. Make sure your child gets the best possible treatment and care.

18. Attend family therapy.

19. Have supportive therapy with your spouse or partner, or individual therapy if you are a single parent or carer.

20. Nurture your marriage or partnership.

21. Make sure you keep your spouse/partner in the loop. It is vital that you are a solid team, not just in parenting your child with Asperger's Disorder but also in making treatment decisions and facing problems that may arise with the school system, health system, insurance companies, mental-health providers, social services and community service providers, as well as other organizations and people in the world who may fail you in your attempts to get the help your child needs.

22. Seek support from appropriate members of your extended family.

23. You will need professional assessment to begin to understand whether your child with Asperger's Disorder will eventually achieve the ability to live fully independently (that is, live alone, hold a job, drive a car and so on). Sometimes the prognosis is uncertain, but take the worst-case scenario and do the following:

   - As difficult as this may be to consider right now, you need to take steps to arrange for the right person to care for your child if, through death, disability or any other reason, you were suddenly unable to care for him or her.

- Your child with Asperger's Disorder will one day become an adult with Asperger's Disorder. Start planning now for his or her long-term care.
- Research community resources to help you, not just for now, but for the future and throughout your child's life.
- With professional legal help, research and create appropriate legal documents, such as a trust that benefits your child and/or a will that takes into consideration his or her long-term care and other needs.

24. Take care of yourself, and learn how to pay attention to your own needs.
25. Maintain your physical and emotional health.
26. Eat balanced, nutritious meals and get enough sleep.
27. Find good-quality childcare.
28. Make and keep good friends who will support you, as well as help you to relax and play.
29. Consider starting a home-based business to allow you to juggle work and family best.
30. Hang onto your goals, dreams or career. Don't fall into the trap of losing yourself amidst the intensive demands of raising a child with special needs.

helpful books

Demystifying Autism Spectrum Disorders: A Guide to Diagnosis for Parents and Professionals, C. T. Bruey. Woodbine House, 2004.

Mozart and the Whale: An Asperger's Love Story, J. Newport, M. Newport and J. Dodd. New York, N.Y.: Touchstone Books/Simon & Schuster, 2007.

A Mind Apart: Understanding Children with Autism and Asperger Syndrome, P. Szatmari. Guilford Press, 2004.

Voices from the Spectrum: Parents, Grandparents, Siblings, People with Autism, and Professionals Share Their Wisdom, eds C. N. Ariel and R. A. Naseef. London: Jessica Kingsley Publishers, 2006.

Asperger's Syndrome and Sexuality: From Adolescence through Adulthood, I. Hénault. Jessica Kingsley Publishers, 2006.

Parenting Your Complex Child: Become a Powerful Advocate for the Autistic, Down Syndrome, PDD, Bipolar, or other Special-Needs Child, P. L. Morgan. AMACOM, 2006.

Addressing the Challenging Behavior of Children with High-Functioning

Autism/Asperger Syndrome in the Classroom: A Guide for Teachers and Parents, R. Moyes. Philadelphia, Penn.: Jessica Kingsley Publishers, 2002.

Solutions for Adults with Asperger Syndrome: Maximizing the Benefits, Minimizing the Drawbacks to Achieve Success, J. P. Lovett. Gloucester, Mass.: Fair Winds Press, 2005.

Asperger's Syndrome: A Guide for Parents and Professionals, T. Attwood. London: Jessica Kingsley Publishers, 1997.

Finding out about Asperger Syndrome, High Functioning Autism and PDD, G. Gerland. London: Jessica Kingsley Publishers, 2000.

Pretending to be Normal: Living with Asperger's Syndrome, L. Holliday. London: Jessica Lindsay Publishers, 1999.

Learning and Behavior Problems in Asperger Syndrome, Margot Prior. New York: The Guilford Press, 2003.

The Normal One: Life with a Difficult or Damaged Sibling, J. Safer. New York: Bantam Dell, 2003.

The Winning Family: Increasing Self-Esteem in Your Children and Yourself, L. Hart. Oakland, Calif.: LifeSkills Press, 1987.

Why Am I Different?, N. Simon. Morton Grove, Ill.: Albert Whitman & Company, 1976.

Don't Feed the Monster on Tuesdays: The Children's Self-Esteem Book, A. Moser. Kansas City, Miss.: Landmark Editions Inc., 1991.

My Body Is Mine, My Feelings Are Mine: A Story Book about Body Safety for Young Children with an Adult Guide Book, S. Hoke. King of Prussia, Penn.: The Center for Applied Psychology Inc., 1995.

rett's disorder

Any sign of disintegration in a child is a red flag for physicians and mental health professionals, as well as a source of great worry for parents or carers. In the case of Rett's Disorder the regression occurs so early it might be difficult to pick up for a while, especially for the first child of new parents. But once disintegration is noticed, it must be investigated immediately so that treatment and support can begin.

case study: Sophie

After five months of being a healthy, developing baby, Sophie began to show signs of regression. She lost interest in engaging in play and 'baby talk' with others, and began to appear lethargic, except when flapping her hands. Her paediatrician noticed that her head growth had decelerated, and recommended psychiatric help. An intense therapy programme was started, and this was the beginning of long-term treatment and care for Sophie. Her favourite part of treatment was music therapy, and that was the only time she was really interested in moving her body. She went through different stages of increased agitation, and sleeplessness, and never developed proficient language. Luckily her parents were devoted and resourceful. With support from a number of local services they coped well with all Sophie's stages, and never swayed in their support and love for her. As a result, given her disorder, Sophie's quality of life and level of functioning were optimally high.

is this your child?

- A normal-seeming prenatal and perinatal development.
- Normal development for the first five months, then a regression occurs. Hand skills deteriorate and the child begins to exhibit strange movements such as hand-wringing. The child also stops interacting with others, although social connections may return later on.
- Normal head circumference at birth, but growth slows down at the age of between five and forty-eight months.
- Develops a badly coordinated walk and bodily movements.
- Language is poor.
- Disinclined to move his or her body.

The variety of physical and perceptual disabilities that afflict sufferers means that there is a need for constant therapy programmes to be administered on a regular basis throughout your child's life. Early treatment may delay the appearance of some symptoms and alleviate others.

'do not pass go' signs

Rett's Disorder is a progressive neurodevelopmental disorder, occurring mainly in girls. It initially appears as a deterioration from apparently normal development in infancy or early childhood. A slowdown in development occurs, involving deceleration of head growth, loss of interest in the environment, loss of adaptive skills (for example, moving around, feeding or toileting skills), stereotypic hand movements (for example, hand-wringing, washing or tapping/clapping), deterioration of motor functioning, irregular breathing, loss of expressive language, and eventually severe to profound mental retardation. Seizures occur in 70 per cent to 80 per cent of people with the disorder.

what causes rett's disorder?

Rett's Disorder is currently believed to be a neurological disorder of development resulting from an X-linked dominant mutation. Evidence indicates that Rett's Disorder is genetically carried.

what's happening in the brain?

A system in the brain known as the glutaminergic system, as well as one involving gamma-aminobutyric acid (usually abbreviated to GABA) are both thought to be disordered in Rett's Disorder.

which treatments are likely to work?

Since Rett's Disorder has severe debilitating characteristics, physical activity and physical therapy are highly recommended. Unfortunately, many people with the disorder dislike these interventions. They typically love music therapy, which is believed to be highly effective. So, in order to address the physical and medical needs of people with Rett's Disorder, and also take into consideration their emotional and communicative needs, the dual treatment programme of music and physical therapy seems to be a very good option. A multi-sensory environment may provide a soothing haven for them.

Behaviour techniques have been successful in modifying problematic behaviours. Calming techniques are necessary for those who show signs of agitation and discomfort. A sleep-wake problem of some description is a frequent feature of Rett's Disorder, so sleep treatments need to be introduced.

best course of action

If any child is not thriving and developing, or if you suspect the child may be suffering from Rett's Disorder, seek a thorough evaluation from a trained practitioner. Having a child with Rett's Disorder in the family can be very difficult for parents or carers and siblings, so everyone will need support, as well as education about Rett's Disorder. Family therapy is advisable, and it would also be wise for parents to have couples or individual therapy as well.

what can you do in the meantime?

1. If you suspect a diagnosis of Rett's Disorder in your child, do not delay seeking treatment. You need urgent help in caring for this child.
2. Know that there is hope. Although it may seem overwhelming to learn that Rett's Disorder involves regression and many other impairments, remember that you also have a child who is loveable, and capable of loving. Your child is not a diagnosis, he or she is a unique, inspiring

individual. This child will lead you through a challenging journey, but you can do it. And there will be surprising rewards along every step of the way.

3. You will be asking: 'Why did this happen? Why our child, our family?' Try to let go of that question. There is no real answer. At the end of the day, that's just the way it is.

4. Fostering your spirituality may be very helpful for you and the whole family.

5. Learn everything you can about Rett's Disorder.

6. Educate everyone in the family about Rett's Disorder.

7. Help your child receive the best possible treatment and care.

8. Try to help your child reduce his or her stress through relaxation, games, appropriate TV or DVDs, or listening to soothing music.

9. Make sure your child feels loved for who he or she is, rather than for progress or achievements.

10. Try to establish in your child a regular pattern of good-quality sleep. This may be particularly difficult with children at certain stages of Rett's Disorder, so seek professional help with this. Recent evidence has found that high-quality sleep promotes brain plasticity, improves health measures and enriches quality of life. However people with Developmental Disorders have been found to sleep less and experience higher incidences of clinical sleep disorders than the general population. Treatments for apnoea, insomnia, restless limbs and other Sleep Disorders should be provided for people with Developmental Disorders. Find out what is available for your child.

11. Attend family therapy. This is vital.

12. Have supportive therapy with your spouse, or individual therapy if you are a single parent or carer.

13. If you have a partner, make sure you keep him or her in the loop. You must be a solid team, not just in parenting your child with Rett's Disorder, but also in making treatment decisions and facing problems that may arise with local authorities, the health system, insurance companies, mental-health providers, community service providers or social services, as well as other organizations and people who may fail you in your attempts to get the help your child needs.

14. Seek support from appropriate members of your extended family.

15. Join a support organization for parents or carers of children with Rett's Disorder.

16. Protect your child with Rett's Disorder, who may be more vulnerable

than others. Do your best to teach him or her what to do in possible emergency scenarios such as fire, flood, black-outs, attempted abduction or getting lost.

17. You will need professional assessment to begin to understand whether your child will eventually achieve the ability to live independently (that is, live alone, hold a job, drive a car and so on). In the case of Rett's Disorder this is unlikely, so take the worst-case scenario and do the following:

   ■ As difficult as this may be to consider right now, you need to take steps to arrange for the right person to care for your child if, through death, disability or any other reason, you were suddenly unable to care for him or her.

   ■ Your child with Rett's Disorder will one day become an adult with Rett's Disorder. Start planning now for his or her long-term care.

   ■ Research community resources to help you, not just for now, but for the future and throughout your child's life.

   ■ With professional legal help, research and create the appropriate legal documents, such as a trust that benefits your child with Rett's Disorder and/or a will that takes into consideration his or her long-term care and other needs.

18. Take care of yourself, and learn how to pay attention to your own needs.

19. Maintain your physical and emotional health.

20. Eat balanced, nutritious meals and get enough sleep.

21. Find good-quality childcare.

22. Make and keep good friends who will support you, as well as help you relax and play.

23. Consider starting a home-based business to allow you to juggle work and family best.

24. Hang onto your goals, dreams, or career. Don't fall into the trap of losing yourself amidst the intensive demands of raising a child with special needs.

helpful books

Parenting Your Complex Child: Become a Powerful Advocate for the Autistic, Down Syndrome, PDD, Bipolar, or Other Special-Needs Child, P. L. Morgan. AMACOM, 2006.

The Normal One: Life with a Difficult or Damaged Sibling, J. Safer. New York: Bantam Dell, 2003.

childhood disintegrative disorder

In rare cases, a child who appears to have been developing normally until at least the age of two will suddenly start to lose ground, and parents will notice that he or she becomes unable to do things that were once achievable. This of course will make parents extremely worried. Hard as this may be, the trick is to take a deep breath and immediately make a call to get a professional evaluation.

case study: Bonnie

Bonnie was a happy baby. At six months she began to smile winningly at the adults around her, and she was also adored by her older brother, Ben who was four. When Ben was six he was proudly carrying Bonnie to his mother after she woke from a nap. He slipped on the kitchen floor and fell, and Bonnie's head hit the corner of a cupboard. Not long after that incident her parents became alarmed when they noticed that Bonnie was not smiling so much and seemed to have forgotten some of the words she had previously learned. They consulted a psychologist who arranged for her to be checked for head trauma. This was ruled out, but as the months went on, Bonnie's development continued to regress. A diagnosis of Childhood Disintegrative Disorder was made, and a programme of intensive remedial treatment was begun. To their parents' relief, there was probably no connection between Ben's mishap and Bonnie's condition. Ben continued to adore and help his little sister – and she now needed him more than ever.

is this your child?

- Was developing normally up to the age of two.
- Then, before the age of ten, began to lose the skills he or she had acquired and started to regress developmentally in areas of language, social skills, bowel or bladder control, play or motor skills.
- Has impaired ability in social interaction and communication.
- Has abnormally intense, narrow interests and rigid patterns of behaviour.

'do not pass go' signs

Any sign of deterioration in a child is a red flag for physicians and mental-health professionals, as well as a source of great worry for parents. Once noticed, it must be investigated immediately so that treatment and support can begin.

what causes childhood disintegrative disorder?

The cause is likely to be some kind of problem in the developing central nervous system. The disorder sometimes coexists with certain medical conditions.

which treatments are likely to work?

An intensive programme that may involve special behaviour therapy, as well as social skills training, and motor-skills training may be effective at various stages of this disorder.

best course of action

Seek a thorough evaluation and treatment from a trained practitioner, and have supportive therapy for you and the entire family.

in the meantime what can you do?

1. If you suspect a diagnosis of Childhood Disintegrative Disorder in your child, do not delay seeking treatment. You need urgent help in caring for this child. Treatment is vital.

2. Know that there is hope. Although it may seem overwhelming to learn that Childhood Disintegrative Disorder involves developmental regression and multiple impairments, remember that you also have a child who is loveable, and capable of loving. Your child is not a diagnosis, he or she is a unique, exceptional, inspiring individual. This child will lead you through a challenging journey, but you can do it. And there will be surprising rewards along every step of the way.

3. You will be asking: 'Why did this happen? Why our family?' Try to let go of that question. There is no real answer. At the end of the day, that's just the way it is.

4. Fostering your spirituality may be very helpful for you and the whole family.

5. Learn everything you can about Childhood Disintegrative Disorder.

6. Educate your whole family about Childhood Disintegrative Disorder.

7. Help your child to get the best possible treatment and care.

8. Attend family therapy.

9. Have supportive therapy with your spouse or partner, or individual therapy if you are a single parent or carer.

10. Make sure you keep your spouse/partner in the loop. It is vital that you are a solid team, not just in parenting your child with Childhood Disintegrative Disorder but also in making treatment decisions and facing problems that may arise with the health-care system, insurance companies, social services, mental-health providers and community resource providers, as well as other organizations and people in the world who may fail you in your attempts to get the help your child needs.

11. Seek support from appropriate members of your extended family.

12. Protect your child with Childhood Disintegrative Disorder, who may be more vulnerable than most. Do your best to teach your child what to do in emergency scenarios such as fire, flood, black-outs, attempted abduction or getting lost.

13. You will need professional assessment to begin to understand whether your child with Childhood Disintegrative Disorder will eventually achieve the ability to live fully independently (that is, live alone, hold a job, drive a car and so on). Sometimes the prognosis is uncertain, but take the worst-case scenario and do the following:

   - As difficult as this may be to consider right now, you need to take steps to arrange for the right person to care for your child if, through death, disability or any other reason, you were suddenly unable to care for him or her.

   - Start planning now for the long-term care of your child with Childhood Disintegrative Disorder.

   - Research community resources to help you, not just for now, but for the future and throughout your child's life.

   - With professional legal help, research and create appropriate legal documents, such as a trust that benefits your child with Childhood Disintegrative Disorder and/or a will that takes into consideration his or her long-term care and other needs.

14. Take care of yourself, and learn how to pay attention to your own needs.

15. Maintain your physical and emotional health.

16. Eat balanced, nutritious meals and get enough sleep.

17. Find good-quality childcare.

18. Make and keep good friends who will support you, as well as help you to relax and play.

19. Consider starting a home-based business to allow you to juggle work and family best.

20. Hang onto your goals, dreams or career. Don't fall into the trap of losing

yourself amidst the intensive demands of raising a child with special needs.

helpful books

The Normal One: Life with a Difficult or Damaged Sibling, J. Safer. New York: Bantam Dell, 2003.

Parenting Your Complex Child: Become a Powerful Advocate for the Autistic, Down Syndrome, PDD, Bipolar, or Other Special-Needs Child, P. L. Morgan. AMACOM, 2006.

disruptive behaviour disorders

During the 'terrible twos', most children normally display oppositional behaviour, but some never seem to emerge from this developmental stage, and continue to misbehave in a number of ways. During nursery school and early school-age years, this might take the form of defiance, temper tantrums, yelling and whining. During adolescence, more troubling behaviour may emerge, such as aggression, stealing and vandalism. When these occur in isolation, they can be effectively addressed through conventional disciplinary action from parents and teachers. But when they occur frequently it may represent a more serious psychiatric diagnosis. A child who repeatedly fights, steals and disobeys the rules at school may have Oppositional Defiant Disorder or Conduct Disorder, two Disruptive Behaviour Disorders described in the DSM-IV. They can be mild to severe, with the latter associated with significant consequences. Conduct problems include aggression, property offences, lying, bullying, fighting, cruelty to animals, violating family curfews and even serious crime. The causes are complex; there are physiological, environmental, academic, behavioural and social bases of these disorders.

conduct disorder

Conduct Disorder starts in childhood or early adolescence, when persistent, serious misbehaviour (taking into account the child's age) creates cause for concern. Immediate treatment is essential because, while this problematic behaviour is only transient in some children, others progress to engaging in even more serious delinquency. One type of behaviour to watch out for particularly is animal abuse, since there is a link between childhood animal cruelty and adult criminal behaviour.

case study: Giles

When Giles was three years old, his parents were killed in a terrorist attack in a marketplace near his home in France. He was brought to the UK and cared for by a great-aunt until a year later when she developed a terminal illness. Giles was placed in care and raised by a series of foster parents. Throughout his childhood he suffered from bullying attacks by several older boys, and repeated sexual abuse by a neighbour at one of his homes. Around the age of nine he began to exhibit significant behaviour problems. With a gang of other boys he began torturing stray animals and stealing from local shops. He attended as little school as possible, preferring to roam around the neighbourhood engaging in crime. By twelve he was stealing cars, and it was then that he attracted the attention of local authorities. He was sentenced to time in a juvenile facility, but he did not learn to improve his behaviour until a knife wound from a street brawl left him partially disabled. During his rehabilitation he came into contact with a social worker who offered him the opportunity for some community-based programmes that included psychological treatment. Instead of 'falling through the cracks' and ending up as an adult criminal in and out of prison – as many do in his situation – he was able to benefit from the available programmes. He also responded well to his group therapy, and began to heal from his abuse. Today, Giles has a steady job making motorcycle deliveries for a courier firm.

is this your child?

Repeatedly breaks rules or behaves in a manner that is threatening to the rights of others (for example bullies, fights, uses weapons, is cruel towards people and animals, mugging people, sexually coerces, destroys property, deliberately starts fires, breaks into buildings or cars, lies, cons, steals, stays out at night against parent's wishes, plays truant from school or runs away from home).

'do not pass go' signs

A child with Conduct Disorder may be at risk of developing an even more severe adult disorder. When childhood Conduct Disorder persists past the age of eighteen, the diagnosis becomes Antisocial Personality Disorder which indicates lifelong difficulties, including criminal behaviour and its consequences. Conduct Disorder often coexists with Substance Dependence, Attention-Deficit/Hyperactivity Disorder, Depression and Anxiety

Disorders. Many of the young people who engage in antisocial and aggressive behaviour may have other problems too, including difficulties with language, comprehension, controlling emotion, problem-solving and summoning school or family support. If the children and teenagers who are 'at risk' could only be identified early and given help for some of these problems, we might have healthier young people, families, schools and communities.

what causes conduct disorder?

It is thought to be caused by both genetic and psychosocial factors. Normal developmental mechanisms may be disrupted, putting a child at risk of engaging in problem behaviour, which may even begin in infancy. The factors that influence a child's behaviour include whether or not he or she bonded satisfactorily with a parent or carer, whether or not he or she has the capacity for empathy or to regulate his or her emotions, whether he or she has adequate cognitive abilities, whether or not trauma is present and whether or not his or her experience of being parented was satisfactory. Parent–child conflict can precede Conduct Disorder, which may be seen as a child's reaction to stress.

what is happening in the brain?

Dysfunctions in the impulse-control and executive function mechanisms in the brain, as well as the inability to connect behaviour and consequence, are some of the many processes that may account for disruptive behaviour problems. Cognitive structures, as well as individual differences in the responsiveness of several different brain systems, play a role in the development of this disorder.

which treatments are likely to work?

Getting support from parents, family, carers and others in the child's vicinity will really make a difference. Parent training combined with child therapy may be the most promising approach for preventing the escalation of conduct problems. Cognitive-behavioural therapeutic approaches may be very helpful to young people with Conduct Disorder, while a variety of medications have been shown to reduce aggression. Treating coexisting disorders, such as Depression, Attention-Deficit/Hyperactivity Disorder, Bipolar Disorder, or Substance Abuse may lead to a general reduction in antisocial symptoms. Incorporating classroom or teacher training as additional treatment can be useful. Throughout, the emphasis should be on the promotion of the young person's positive behaviour, rather than punishment.

best course of action
Seek a thorough evaluation from a trained practitioner, and get some mental-health treatment for your child and for the whole family from an experienced, qualified professional.

in the meantime what can you do?
1. Learn everything you can about Conduct Disorders.
2. Arrange for you (and your partner) to take supportive parent effectiveness training classes.
3. Get some assertiveness training for your young person and yourself.
4. Do not administer corporal punishment. Smacking and violence actively train children to become violent themselves. Instead, give consequences (natural outcomes that match the misbehaviour) and positive reinforcement (praise or reward good behaviour).
5. Turn off the TV and spend time engaged in healthy activities with your child or teenager with Conduct Disorder.
6. Hold a family meeting (see page 263) and brainstorm about solutions that will work for the young person with Conduct Disorder, individual family members, and the whole family. Focus on the positive and do not allow it to become a blaming session.
7. It is vital that you help your child or teenager fully understand the relationship between behaviour and consequences. Reinforce this by repeating, 'If you [state the undesirable behaviour] the [consequence will be]', then ask him or her to repeat it back. Then brainstorm together about better choices that could be made.
8. Spend some time with your young person clarifying household rules, expectations, chores and responsibilities, and the consequences that will be implemented if these are neglected (include your partner if you have one, together presenting a united front). Write all this down as a form of contract and have everyone sign it.
9. Teach your child better social skills by following the suggestions on page 258.
10. Identify your child's style of manipulation. Discuss and role-play

alternative ways to get his or her needs met. For example, instead of your child threatening another child with physical harm in order to get them to give up a desired toy, propose working towards earning a similar toy through sticking to an educational programme.

11. Help your young person to reduce his or her stress and anxiety.
12. Encourage appropriate self-soothing (see page 258).
13. Teach your child or teenager meditation (see page 40). Meditation may improve self-awareness, self-assessment and self-control as well as enhancing learning.
14. Help your young person to feel soothed and protected by you. Do this by being loving and consistent.
15. Encourage improved communication (see page 256).
16. Help to engender improved self-respect in your young person (see page 255).
17. Help to engender an improved sense of responsibility in your child or teenager (see page 259). Most importantly, in addition to these suggestions, focus on helping your young person to see how others are affected by his or her actions and vice versa.
18. Focus on your young person's strengths and support his or her hobbies and special interests.
19. Help your child or teenager to problem-solve by role-playing responses to various situations. Include emergency scenarios such as fire, flood or accident.
20. As well as love and protection, provide rules and structure for your child or teenager.
21. Educate your whole family about Conduct Disorder
22. Help your child or teenager to receive the best possible treatment and care.
23. Attend family therapy.
24. Have supportive therapy with your spouse or partner, or individual therapy if you are a single parent or carer.
25. If you have a partner, make sure you keep him or her in the loop. It is vital that you are a solid team, not just in parenting your child or teenager with a Conduct Disorder but also in making treatment decisions and facing problems that may arise with the school system, health system, insurance companies, legal system, mental-health providers, social services, and community resources providers, as well as other organizations and people in the world who may fail you in your attempts to get the help your child or teenager needs.

26. You will need professional assessment to begin to understand what the future may hold for your child or teenager with Conduct Disorder. Sometimes the prognosis is uncertain, but take the worst-case scenario and research community resources to help you, not just for now, but for the future and throughout your young person's life.
27. Join a support organization.
28. Educate other family members about Conduct Disorders.
29. Seek support from appropriate members of your extended family.
30. Maintain your own physical and emotional health.

helpful books

How to Talk So Kids Will Listen & Listen So Kids Will Talk, A. Faber and E. Mazlish. New York: Avon Books, 1980.

When Your Child Is Cutting: A Parent's Guide to Helping Children Overcome Self-Injury, M. McVey-Noble, S. Khemlani-Patel and F. Neziroglu. Oakland, Calif., New Harbinger Publications, 2006.

The Assertiveness Workbook: How to Express Your Ideas and Stand Up for Yourself in Work and Relationships, R. J. Paterson. Oakland, Calif.: New Harbinger Publications, 2000.

The Winning Family: Increasing Self-Esteem in Your Children and Yourself, L. Hart. Oakland, Calif.: LifeSkills Press, 1987.

P.E.T. Parent Effectiveness Training: The Tested New Way to Raise Responsible Children, T. Gordon. New York: Plume/Penguin, 1975.

Sign Here: A Contracting Book for Children and Their Parents, J. C. Dardig and W. L. Heward. Kalamzoo, Mich.: Behaviordelia, 1977.

Handbook of Parent Training: Parents as Co-Therapists for Children's Behavior Problems, eds J. M. Briesmeister and C. E. Schaefer. New York: John Wiley & Sons Inc., 1989.

How to be the Parent You Always Wanted to Be, A. Faber and E. Mazlish. New York: Hyperion, 1992.

The Seven Spiritual Laws for Parents: Guiding Your Children to Success and Fulfillment, D. Chopra. New York: Harmony Books, 1997.

oppositional defiant disorder

Children are never intrinsically 'bad'. When a child consistently misbehaves, we as parents, carers, teachers or other observers should first question whether that child might be depressed, anxious, or dealing with the aftermath of trauma. Once treatment is underway for such underlying problems, the behaviour will most likely improve.

case study: Malcolm

Malcolm's grandmother was his primary carer. She took her ten-year-old charge to see a psychotherapist because she was at her wit's end about his behaviour. Malcolm, she said, had been a pleasant enough boy until they moved to the city from a quiet country town eight months ago. When Malcolm was placed in his new school, he 'fell in with a bad lot' and shortly afterwards began to argue with her, refused to come home in time for dinner and 'made a nuisance of himself' in many other ways. The therapist diagnosed Malcolm with Oppositional Defiant Disorder and began to work, not only with the boy but also with his grandmother who needed help parenting him. Unfortunately, the child was hit by a taxi while playing truant and was subsequently hospitalized for six weeks. Despite that interruption in his treatment, Malcolm's behaviour eventually improved through behavioural psychotherapy and he grew into a responsible teenager. His grandmother always believed it was the accident that 'brought him to his senses'.

is this your child?
- Has behaved in a hostile and defiant manner for at least six months.
- At least four of the following have been aspects of his or her behaviour:
  1. Losing their temper.
  2. Arguing and talking back to adults.
  3. Will not obey rules.
  4. Deliberately makes himself or herself a nuisance.
  5. Blames others when he or she is in the wrong.
  6. Is irritable.
  7. Is often angry and resentful.
  8. Is frequently spiteful and vindictive.

'do not pass go' signs
Children with Oppositional Defiant Disorder are likely to have significant problems at school and in the world generally. Their academic achievement will be hampered, they may be expelled from school and their futures may be undermined. It is essential that they get help and treatment as soon as possible.

what causes oppositional defiant disorder?

The disorder runs in families but, although there is a genetic contribution to the development of Oppositional Defiant Disorder, psychosocial factors play a strong part. For example, Oppositional Defiant Disorder is more common in families where parents are fighting. Girls with conduct problems are more likely to come to the attention of authorities because of chaotic, unstable family relationships and they are more likely to express antisocial behaviour in the context of close relationships. Moreover, mothers with Depression are more likely to have children who have Oppositional Defiant Disorder.

which treatments are likely to work?

Parenting training, couples psychotherapy and assertiveness training for parents is recommended. Parent training and an increase in parent or carer involvement can lead to reductions in disruptive behaviour.

For the child, therapy to improve problem-solving, language processing, self-regulation skills and general mental health (including the treatment of commonly coexisting disorders such as Attention-Deficit/Hyperactivity Disorder and Bipolar Disorder) are recommended.

best course of action

1. Learn everything you can about Oppositional Defiant Disorders.
2. It is vital that you help your child to understand fully the relationship between behaviour and consequences. Reinforce this by repeating 'If you [undesirable behaviour] the [consequence will be]', then ask him or her to repeat it back. Then brainstorm together about better choices that could be made.
3. Spend some time with your spouse or partner clarifying household rules with your child, including expectations, chores and responsibilities plus the consequences that will be implemented if these are neglected. Write all this down as a form of contract, and have everyone sign it.
4. Turn off the TV and spend time engaged in healthy activities with your child.
5. Arrange for you and (if you have one) your partner to take Parent Effectiveness Training. You will find this enormously useful. In particular, learn to implement limit-setting, providing natural consequences (natural outcomes that match the misbehaviour) and positive reinforcement specific to your situation.

6. Provide some assertiveness training for your child (see page 39) and yourself (page 38).

7. Teach your child better social skills by following the suggestions on page 131.

8. Identify your child's style of manipulation. Discuss and role-play alternative ways to get his or her needs met. For example, instead of your child threatening another child with physical harm in order to get him or her to give up a desired toy, propose working towards earning a similar toy through sticking to an educational programme.

9. Encourage appropriate self-soothing (see page 258).

10. Teach your child meditation (see page 40). Meditation may improve self-awareness, self-assessment and self-control as well as enhance learning.

11. Help your child to feel soothed and protected by you. Do this by being loving and consistent.

12. Encourage improved communication skills (see page 256).

13. Help to engender improved self-respect in your child (see page 255).

14. Help to engender an improved sense of responsibility in your child (see page 259). Most importantly, in addition to these suggestions, focus on helping your child to see how others are affected by his or her actions and vice versa.

15. Focus on your child's strengths and support his or her hobbies and special interests.

16. Help your child to problem-solve by role-playing responses to various situations, including emergency scenarios such as fire and flood, being offered drugs, or an abduction attempt.

17. As well as love and protection, provide rules and structure for your child.

18. If you have a partner, make sure you keep him or her in the loop. It is vital that you are a solid team in parenting your child with Oppositional Defiant Disorder. Otherwise, your child will be able to manipulate his or her way out of following the rules and expectations you have set. You and your partner also need to be a cooperative unit in making treatment decisions and facing problems that may arise with the school system, health system, insurance companies, legal system, mental-health providers, social services, and community resource providers, as well as other organizations and people in the world who may fail you in your attempts to get the help your child needs.

19. Join a support group.
20. Educate other family members about Oppositional Defiant Disorders.
21. Hold a family meeting (see page 263) and explore how each member of the family is affected by the presence of Oppositional Defiant Disorder in your child. Brainstorm about solutions that will work for the child, individual family members and the whole family. Make sure the focus is positive, rather than blaming.
22. Seek support from appropriate members of your extended family.
23. As difficult as this may be to consider right now, you need to take steps to arrange for the right person to care for your child with Oppositional Defiant Disorder if, through death, disability or any other reason, you were suddenly unable to care for him or her.
24. Research community resources to help you, not just for now, but for the future and throughout your child's life.
25. Help to get your child the best possible treatment and care.
26. Attend family therapy.
27. Have supportive therapy with your spouse or partner, or individual therapy if you are a single parent or carer.
28. Take care of yourself, and maintain your own physical and emotional health.

helpful books

The Assertiveness Workbook: How to Express Your Ideas and Stand Up for Yourself in Work and Relationships, R. J. Paterson. Oakland, Calif.: New Harbinger Publications, 2000.

How to Talk So Kids Will Listen & Listen So Kids Will Talk, A. Faber and E. Mazlish. New York: Avon Books, 1980.

The Winning Family: Increasing Self-Esteem in Your Children and Yourself, L. Hart. Oakland, Calif.: LifeSkills Press, 1987.

P.E.T. Parent Effectiveness Training: The Tested New Way to Raise Responsible Children, T. Gordon. New York: Plume/Penguin, 1975.

Handbook of Parent Training: Parents as Co-Therapists for Children's Behavior Problems, eds J. M. Briesmeister and C. E. Schaefer. New York: John Wiley & Sons Inc., 1989.

How to be the Parent You Always Wanted to Be, A. Faber and E. Mazlish. New York: Hyperion, 1992.

The Seven Spiritual Laws for Parents: Guiding Your Children to Success and Fulfillment, D. Chopra. New York: Harmony Books, 1997.

helpful books for children:
Don't Feed the Monster on Tuesdays: The Children's Self-Esteem Book, A. Moser. Kansas City, Miss.: Landmark Editions Inc., 1991.

feeding and eating disorders in infancy or childhood

pica

I'm sure you've noticed that very young children just love to put things in their mouths, often horrifying their parents by their choices. This is a normal developmental phase. But some children (and adults) get into the habit of regularly eating non-food items. There are many reasons why a person might start doing this, and it's not just something that occurs in families that lack money to buy food – as is illustrated by the case of Tom.

case study: Tom

Tom was born an only child in an upper middle-class family. His parents owned a large house in a country town. Every evening, they ate a formal dinner prepared by a cook at 8.30 p.m., but Tom was sent upstairs to bed alone two hours earlier and was expected not to interrupt his parents' evening. Without having eaten a proper evening meal he often became hungry, but he was afraid to go downstairs to the kitchen. One day he was looking around for something to chew on and began to eat paper stationery. He developed a taste for it, found it somewhat satisfying and continued to eat it regularly well into adulthood. He was eventually helped to stop this unhealthy habit by a therapist who assisted him to heal from the pain of his childhood neglect.

is this your child?

Regularly eats dirt, clay, insects, animal droppings, sand, pebbles, paint, string, hair or other non-nutritive substances to an extent that goes well beyond the common toddler curiosity of tasting everything in the environment.

'do not pass go' signs

Pica is a dangerous habit that can result in choking, poisoning (from ingesting plants and so on), infections (for example, from eating faeces) and intestinal obstructions. Pica may result in the puncture or blockage of the digestive tract, infestation by gastrointestinal parasites and can interfere with an individual's daily learning, occupational performance and quality of life. Pica should be suspected in children with acute behaviour alterations that may suggest he or she has ingested something that is toxic to the brain. In less serious cases, Pica can be a minor but stigmatizing behaviour. It has occasionally been reported in elderly people with mental illness. In such cases the risk of mortality should be taken particularly seriously.

what causes pica?

Pica may be a form of Obsessive-Compulsive Disorder. Underlying issues include developmental disabilities, seizure disorders, Depression and Obsessive-Compulsive Disorder. Pica is not always associated with poverty, neglect and lack of parental supervision.

which treatments are likely to work?

People with Pica are often successfully treated using behaviour-modification therapy, and in addition there are a number of medication treatments for the condition. Pica behaviour often occurs in individuals with developmental disabilities; therefore, both education and clinical professionals may need to team up to identify, assess and treat the sufferer. Although restraining the sufferer has sometimes been thought necessary in life-threatening cases of Pica, recent studies have demonstrated how non-intrusive behavioural methods can be used to balance the protection of the sufferer's life with maintaining his or her dignity and quality of life.

best course of action?

Seek a thorough evaluation from a trained practitioner who can provide mental-health treatment and support.

in the meantime what can you do?

Provide regular, nutritious, balanced meals for your child and sit with him or her at the table in a relaxed environment while he or she eats them.

1. Monitor your child very closely to stop him or her eating non-food items.
2. Learn everything you can about Pica.

3. Educate your whole family about Pica.
4. If you have a partner, make sure you keep him or her in the loop. It is vital that you are a solid team, not just in parenting your child with Pica but also in making treatment decisions and facing problems that may arise with insurance companies, health services, mental-health providers, social services and community resource providers, as well as other organizations and people in the world who may fail you in your attempts to get the help your child needs.
5. Seek support from appropriate members of your extended family.
6. Join a support organization.
7. Research community resources to help you, not just for now, but for the future and throughout your child's life.
8. Help your child to receive the best possible treatment and care.
9. Attend family therapy.
10. Have supportive couples therapy with your spouse or partner, or individual supportive therapy if you are a single parent or carer.
11. Boost your child's self-esteem.
12. Help your child to reduce his or her stress and anxiety.
13. Focus on your child's strengths and support his or her hobbies and special interests.
14. Admire your child's accomplishments, but be careful not to base your approval on performance alone. Make sure your child feels loved for who he or she is.
15. Encourage your child to take pride in his or her own work.
16. Help your child to problem-solve by role-playing responses to various situations, including emergency scenarios.
17. As well as love and protection, provide rules and structure for your child.
18. Teach your child to be assertive and to ask for help when needed.
19. Maintain your own physical and emotional health.
20. Eat balanced, nutritious meals yourself, and get enough sleep.

helpful books

Starbright: Meditations for Children: Simple Visualizations to Help Children Sleep Peacefully, Free of Nightmares and Fears, Awaken Creativity, Develop Concentration, Learn to Quiet Themselves, M. Garth. San Francisco: HarperSanFrancisco, 1991.

Don't Feed the Monster on Tuesdays: The Children's Self-Esteem Book, A. Moser. Kansas City, Miss.: Landmark Editions Inc., 1991.

Parenting Your Complex Child: Become a Powerful Advocate for the Autistic,

Down Syndrome, PDD, Bipolar, or Other Special-Needs Child, P. L. Morgan. AMACOM, 2006.

rumination disorder

Rumination is a complex, potentially life-threatening disorder. It involves repeated regurgitation, re-chewing and re-swallowing food, causing weight loss and failure to thrive. The disorder generally appears between three and twenty-two months of age, but may start later in children with Mental Retardation. Among adolescents and adults it does happen, but it's rather rare.

case study: Baby Romelia

A seven-month-old infant was brought into a central city hospital by Jesus, a teenage sibling who was concerned about the baby's tendency to bring up her food. The children's mother was a woman struggling with drug addiction. She frequently left Romelia in the care of Jesus, and the boy noticed that the baby never kept her milk down but regurgitated it after every feeding. Jesus believed the baby was losing weight. Further investigation showed that the baby had gained weight during her first five months of life, but since being weighed by a social worker two months ago, she had lost a significant amount. Romelia was in jeopardy and needed medical attention. In fact her brother's action probably saved her life. Both children were eventually placed in care while their mother entered a detox and rehabilitation centre.

is this your child?
- Continually regurgitates and re-chews his or her food.
- This is not due to a medical condition.

'do not pass go' signs
Severe malnutrition, dangerous weight loss and death can occur in people with Rumination Disorder. This is a very serious disorder that requires swift treatment with careful monitoring.

what causes rumination disorder?
Infants with Rumination Disorder may have problems bonding with a carer, and childhood issues of neglect and feeding problems may be at the root of

rumination symptoms among adolescents and adults. The disorder can coexist with eating disorders such as Anorexia Nervosa and Bulimia Nervosa, but very often adult sufferers are secretive about their ruminating so it is difficult to know how common that might be. Adult sufferers may also have Depression.

which treatments are likely to work?

The treatment of feeding disorders usually combines therapy for child and mother together, therapy for the parents or carer(s), and/or individual therapy with the child. Typical types of treatments include psychodynamic psychotherapy and behaviour therapy. Health education, nutritional help and medication may be added. Hyperalimentation (intravenous feeding) is sometimes used to provide necessary nutrition. Changes in surroundings and enhanced mothering are often critical to the correction of Rumination Disorder in infants and allowing them to gain weight. In adults, a multidisciplinary approach involving individual insight-oriented psychotherapy, group therapy, medication and nutritional intervention has proved successful in relieving symptoms.

best course of action?

Seek a thorough medical evaluation and see a trained practitioner who can provide mental-health treatment and support.

in the meantime what can you do?

1. Learn everything you can about Rumination Disorder.
2. Help your child get the best possible treatment and care.
3. Educate your whole family about Rumination Disorder.
4. If you have a partner, make sure you keep him or her in the loop. It is vital that you are a solid team, not just in parenting your child with Rumination Disorder, but also in making treatment decisions and facing problems that may arise with the health system, insurance companies, social services, mental-health providers and community resource providers, as well as other organizations and people in the world who may fail you in your attempts to get the help your child needs.
5. You will need professional assessment to begin to understand what the future holds for your child with Rumination Disorder. Sometimes the prognosis is uncertain, but take the worst-case scenario and do the following:
   - As difficult as this may be to consider right now, you need to take steps

to arrange for the right person to care for your child if, through death, disability or any other reason, you were suddenly unable to care for him or her.

- Research community resources to help you, not just for now, but for the future and throughout your child's life.

6. Attend family therapy.
7. Join a support organization.
8. Boost your child's self-esteem.
9. Help your child to reduce his or her stress and anxiety.
10. Focus on his or her strengths and support their hobbies and special interests.
11. Maintain your own physical and emotional health.
12. Eat balanced, nutritious meals yourself and get enough sleep.

helpful books

Parenting Your Complex Child: Become a Powerful Advocate for the Autistic, Down Syndrome, PDD, Bipolar, or Other Special-Needs Child, P. L. Morgan. AMACOM, 2006.

tourette's disorder

When a young man called Pete who suffers from Tourette's Disorder became the final winner on the popular TV series Big Brother, he made many more people aware of the disorder. But in order to do that, he had to undergo severe stress and an absence of treatment that can hardly have been helpful to him. In his continued presence on the show and the massive interest he generated, wasn't he rather 'thrown to the lions' for other people's enjoyment? But at least most people in the UK will now know that a 'tic' is: a recurring, stereotypical, non-rhythmic vocalization or motor movement that occurs without warning and lasts for a short time. Tics can be 'motor' or 'vocal'. Motor tics may include grimacing, nose twitching, licking, body rocking, shudders, eye blinking, eye rolling or wide-eyed opening. Vocal tics can include sniffing, grunting, coughing, throat clearing and coprolalia (that is, a spontaneous, unprovoked interruption of speech flow with various obscenities). Tourette's Disorder often starts in middle childhood, and motor tics usually appear before vocal tics.

case study: Paul

As a very young child, Paul began to twitch his nose in a pattern of two or three lateral movements followed by an elongated up-down scrunch. This earned him the nickname 'Rabbit', but it wasn't long before other tics appeared: blinking, finger-flexing and shoulder-shrugging. By the age of thirteen he had begun to whoop and grunt, and he also made a barking sound, for which he was labelled 'Woofer'. Unfortunately he did not receive treatment until he was in his mid teens, and by then his self-esteem, peer relationships and social skills had suffered badly. He was also sleeping poorly and suffering from Depression. Once he started a programme of cognitive-behavioural therapy and medication he improved dramatically. In adulthood he still retained some mild symptoms, but the new outlook and coping styles he learned from therapy enabled him to function well and enjoy his life without suffering from the earlier problems that compounded his Tourette's Disorder.

is this your child?

- Has motor tics (rapid, random movements) in any part of the body (for example, grimacing, blinking, skipping).
- Or vocal tics (coughs, grunts, barks, whoops and so on).
- These tics occur frequently throughout the day.
- A small percentage of people with Tourette's Disorder suffer with coprolalia (uttering obscenities).

'do not pass go' signs

As a result of having tics, a person might suffer from social isolation, be ridiculed by peers, and have problems at school and work. Many people with Tourette's Disorder are anxious about the negative attention they can receive from others, and people with severe Tourette's may find that their ability to attend to academic work, read, write and communicate with others is impaired. Although the unusual behaviour of people with the disorder is usually the first symptom others notice, there can also be cognitive problems associated with the disorder that present even more challenges to the sufferer.

Other disorders coexist occurs in approximately 90 per cent of people with Tourette's Disorder, with Attention-Deficit/Hyperactivity Disorder and Obsessive-Compulsive Disorder being common. Bipolar Disorder and Tourette's Disorder may coexist in some individuals. Depression in people with Tourette's Disorder may be correlated with tic severity and duration, the presence of echophenomena (copying) and coprolalia, premonitory sensations (a kind of déjà vu), sleep disturbances, obsessive-compulsive behaviours, self-injurious behaviour, aggression, Conduct Disorder in childhood and ADHD. Depression in people with Tourette's Disorder has also been shown to result in a lower quality of life, potentially leading to hospitalization and suicide.

what causes tourette's disorder?

There appears to be a genetic reason why people might be predisposed towards having tics. There is compelling evidence to indicate that Tourette's Disorder has a strong biological component, since significant abnormalities have been picked up on brain-imaging studies, physiological measures and neurological testing. Several risk factors, including perinatal and psychosocial stressors, are believed to be associated with both the severity and timing of tics.

what happens in your brain?

The basal ganglia (parts of the brain concerned with coordination) have been implicated in the phenomenon of Tourette's Disorder.

which treatments are likely to work?

Behavioural therapy has shown particular promise in diminishing the symptoms associated with Tourette's Disorder. Medication is a widely employed and important treatment option for the management of symptoms associated with the disorder. Basal ganglia surgery is another treatment possibility. Many children grow out of Tourette's Disorder during adolescence and adulthood.

best course of action?

Seek a thorough evaluation from a trained practitioner who can provide mental-health treatment and support.

in the meantime what can you do?

1. Learn everything you can about Tourette's Disorder.
2. Educate your whole family about Tourette's Disorder.
3. Tourette's Disorder is a disabling disorder. You really need to seek mental-health treatment to help your child not only with motor and vocal tics but also with the various behavioural problems and associated disorders that can accompany it.

4. The impact of having Tourette's Disorder on your child's thought processes and behaviour needs to be carefully documented in order to provide maximum information to mental-health professionals who care for your child. Write down full details about tics including type, duration and severity; also any behaviour problems, as well as the social, academic and familial impact of his or her symptoms.

5. Help to get your child the best possible treatment and care.

6. Your child will have uncomfortable feelings about how Tourette's symptoms make him or her stand out from other children. Try to help your child self-soothe (see page 258).

7. Pay great attention to helping your child with Tourette's Disorder raise his or her self-esteem (see page 255).

8. Try to help your child with the special social challenges he or she faces. There may be community resources available. Seek them out.

9. Attend family therapy.

10. Have supportive couples therapy with your spouse or partner, or individual supportive therapy if you are a single parent or carer.

11. If you have a partner, make sure you keep him or her in the loop. It is vital that you are a solid team, not just in parenting your child with Tourette's Disorder, but also in making treatment decisions and facing problems that may arise with the mental health or school system, health services, insurance companies, social services and community resource providers, as well as other organizations and people in the world who may fail you in your attempts to get the help your child needs.

12. Seek support from appropriate members of your extended family.

13. Join a support organization.

14. You will need professional assessment to begin to understand whether your child with Tourette's Disorder will eventually achieve the ability to live fully independently (that is, live alone, hold a job, drive a car and so on). Sometimes the prognosis is uncertain, but take the worst-case scenario and do the following:

   - As difficult as this may be to consider right now, you need to take steps to arrange for the right person to care for your child with Tourette's Disorder if, through death, disability or any other reason, you were suddenly unable to care for him or her.

   - Your child with Tourette's Disorder may one day become an adult with Tourette's Disorder. Start planning now for his or her long-term care.

   - Research community resources to help you, not just for now, but for the future and throughout your child's life.

■ With professional legal help, research and create appropriate legal documents, such as a trust that benefits your child with Tourette's Disorder and/or a will that takes into consideration his or her long-term care and other needs.

15. Boost your child's self-esteem.
16. Help your child to reduce his or her stress and anxiety.
17. Focus on your child's strengths and support his or her hobbies and special interests.
18. Admire your child's accomplishments, but be careful not to base your approval on performance alone. Let him or her know they are loved for who they are.
19. Encourage your child to take pride in his or her own work.
20. Encourage appropriate friendships among your child's peers. Having one good friend will help him or her feel accepted and supported, even when facing setbacks and unkindness from others.
21. Help your child to problem-solve by role-playing responses to various situations such as fire, flood or getting lost.
22. As well as love and protection, provide rules and structure for your child.
23. Teach your child to be self-assertive and to ask for help when needed.
24. Take care of yourself, and learn how to pay attention to your own needs.
25. Maintain your physical and emotional health.
26. Eat balanced, nutritious meals and get enough sleep.
27. Find good-quality childcare.
28. Make and keep good friends who will support you, as well as help you to relax and play.
29. Consider starting a home-based business to allow you to juggle work and family best.
30. Hang onto your goals, dreams, or career. Don't fall into the trap of losing yourself amidst the intensive demands of raising a child with special needs.

helpful books

Parenting Your Complex Child: Become a Powerful Advocate for the Autistic, Down Syndrome, PDD, Bipolar, or Other Special-Needs Child, P. L. Morgan. AMACOM, 2006.

The Normal One: Life with a Difficult or Damaged Sibling, J. Safer. New York: Bantam Dell, 2003.

Five Weeks to Healing Stress: The Wellness Option, V. O'Hara. Oakland, Calif.: New Harbinger Publications, 1996.

Starbright: Meditations for Children: Simple Visualizations to Help Children Sleep Peacefully, Free of Nightmares and Fears, Awaken Creativity, Develop Concentration, Learn to Quiet Themselves, M. Garth. San Francisco: HarperSanFrancisco, 1991.

The Winning Family: Increasing Self-Esteem in Your Children and Yourself, L. Hart. Oakland, Calif.: LifeSkills Press, 1987.

The Seven Spiritual Laws for Parents: Guiding Your Children to Success and Fulfillment, D. Chopra. New York: Harmony Books, 1997.

helpful books for children:

Why Am I Different?, N. Simon. Morton Grove, Ill.: Albert Whitman & Company, 1976.

Don't Feed the Monster on Tuesdays: The Children's Self-Esteem Book, A. Moser. Kansas City, Miss.: Landmark Editions Inc., 1991.

elimination disorders

Bed-wetting and bowel incontinence are not uncommon childhood problems, and can badly affect a youngster's self-perception as well as his or her relationships with family members, peers and school personnel. The DSM-IV lists two Elimination Disorders: Enuresis (urinary voiding) and Encopresis (bowel incontinence). A child with Enuresis repeatedly voids urine inappropriately, such as wetting his or her clothes during the day or wetting the bed at night. In Encopresis, the child repeatedly passes faeces in inappropriate places, such as in clothing or on the floor. These disorders occur among early elementary-school-aged children in particular.

case study: Gerry

After Gerry was sent away to school at the age of seven, he began to wet the bed with great frequency. He had never done this at home and had experienced a normal toilet-training period earlier on. Going to boarding school was a difficult adjustment for Gerry, and he was aware that his parents were divided on the issue of whether or not it was the right educational choice for him. Gerry's father had attended the school in question from the same age, and he insisted that Gerry would be fine after a while – as he himself had been. But Gerry's mother felt bereft to 'lose him' at such a young age, and could not hide her sadness when they dropped him off to begin his first term. Apart from the physical discomfort of Gerry's Enuresis, he felt mortified that the dormitory staff had to be alerted to help change his bed. Most of all, he felt embarrassed that peers became aware of his problem, and it wasn't long before Gerry was teased and had a horrid nickname. The trauma of this meant that Gerry became even more anxious about his bed-wetting – and even less capable of controlling it. When his parents were made aware of it they arranged for him to see a psychologist, who thought it was significant that the bed-wetting only started once Gerry was in his stressful, new environment, about which both he and his mother felt highly ambiguous. After some weeks of family therapy, it was decided that Gerry should attend day school for at least another year. His Enuresis stopped as soon as he returned home.

is this your child?

- After the age of four or five, frequently urinates (Enuresis) or defecates (Encopresis) in inappropriate places.
- Enuresis (urination) might be either deliberate or involuntary.

'do not pass go' signs

Elimination Disorders are associated with high emotional distress for a child and parents, as well as with increased rates of accompanying behavioural disorders. The child's self-esteem is at risk, and there are a number of ways in which these disorders can affect his or her socialization (for example, by being unable to participate in overnight events in the case of Enuresis, or suffering ostracism by peers for Encopresis). Symptoms such as urinary tract infections often co-exist with Enuresis, especially with daytime wetting, so a detailed assessment of both somatic and psychological aspects is essential to ensure your child receives the best, specific treatment.

what causes elimination disorders?

An Elimination Disorder might start during a child's toilet training, and may sometimes be related to a child's anxiety and stress. Various physiological causes are also possible. Both disorders run in families.

which treatments are likely to work?

In nursery and school-age children treatment for Encopresis and Enuresis often involves a mixture of medical, behavioural, psychological, and/or biofeedback treatments. Both Enuresis and Encopresis have a high spontaneous cure rate, but that is not a reason to delay treatment since the child's relationships and self-esteem are at stake.

best course of action?

First, seek an evaluation from a medical practitioner to make sure the condition is not related to a medical problem, such as having an unstable bladder. Then seek a thorough evaluation from a trained practitioner who can provide mental-health treatment and support.

in the meantime what can you do?

1. Learn everything you can about Elimination Disorders.
2. Make a note of all episodes of incontinence or smearing, so that your mental-health provider will have full and accurate information as to the extent of this behaviour.
3. Your child's Elimination Disorder can have a detrimental effect on his or her social relationships. Do your best to help support his or her peer connections.
4. Trying hard to avoid embarrassing your child, educate 'need to know' members of your family about Elimination Disorders.
5. Help your child to receive the best possible treatment and care.
6. Have supportive couples therapy with your spouse or partner, or individual supportive therapy if you are a single parent or carer.
7. Join a support organization.
8. Boost your child's self-esteem.
9. Help your child to reduce his or her stress and anxiety.
10. Focus on your child's strengths and support his or her hobbies and special interests.
11. Encourage appropriate friendships among your child's peers. Having one good friend will help him or her feel accepted and supported, even when facing setbacks and unkindness from others.
12. Help your child to problem-solve by role-playing responses to various situations, including emergency scenarios.
13. As well as love and protection, provide rules and structure for your child.
14. Teach your child self-assertion and to ask for help when needed.
15. Maintain your own physical and emotional health.
16. Eat balanced, nutritious meals and get enough sleep.

helpful books

Starbright: Meditations for Children: Simple Visualizations to Help Children Sleep Peacefully, Free of Nightmares and Fears, Awaken Creativity, Develop Concentration, Learn to Quiet Themselves, M. Garth. San Francisco: HarperSanFrancisco, 1991.

The Winning Family: Increasing Self-Esteem in Your Children and Yourself, L. Hart. Oakland, Calif.: LifeSkills Press, 1987.

Parenting Your Complex Child: Become a Powerful Advocate for the Autistic, Down Syndrome, PDD, Bipolar, or Other Special-Needs Child, P. L. Morgan. AMACOM, 2006.

Don't Feed the Monster on Tuesdays: The Children's Self-Esteem Book, A. Moser. Kansas City, Miss.: Landmark Editions Inc., 1991.

separation anxiety disorder

You're trying to leave for work, the babysitter is there, but your young child is screaming and clinging to you as if her life depended on it. Most children will do this a few times, but there are some little ones who never seem to tolerate being away from their main carer comfortably. This can develop into a full-blown disorder.

case study: Juliet

Juliet's parents had a very busy social life. They were lively and engaging people whose business benefited from all the 'networking' they did at parties. The problem was that their four-year-old daughter did not enjoy being left alone most nights with a babysitter. She would beg them to stay with her and her tears eventually escalated into screaming fits. In the end, her parents decided to slip out without even saying good night to her, which only made matters worse. Juliet began to stay awake at night until she heard her parents return. When she did sleep, she frequently had nightmares, and in the morning she would be too tired to go to her nursery school. Fortunately, the family sought the help of a psychotherapist, who stressed the need for soothing, structure and consistency in Juliet's life. Juliet improved once her parents realized they needed to make her recovery from Separation Anxiety Disorder their main priority.

is this your child?
At least three of the following are causing distress, and making it hard for him or her to participate in, and be successful in, social and academic situations:

- Becomes excessively upset about leaving his or her home for any period, or about being separated from parents or carers to whom the child's attached.

- Is excessively worried about losing or being separated from his or her parents or carers, or that something terrible might happen to them.
- Refuses to go to school because of these worries.
- Is excessively afraid to be home alone, or in other settings without parents or carers to whom he or she is attached.
- Refuses to go to sleep without person he or she's attached to being there.
- Won't sleep away from home.
- Frequently has nightmares about being separated from person he or she's attached to.
- When facing separation, frequently has physical complaints such as stomach aches or nausea.

'do not pass go' signs

Separation Anxiety Disorder may be transient, but it can have long-lasting effects. Some believe it leads to adult Anxiety Disorders or to a personality disorder such as Paranoid Personality Disorder. It can certainly have a devastating effect on both the individual child and the family. Treatment is imperative.

what causes separation anxiety disorder?

It may start after some stressful event involving loss (for example, the death of a close family member or a move to another city). It may be more common among close family members of a person who has Separation Anxiety Disorder.

which treatments are likely to work?

Psychotherapy for child and parents and psycho-education for parents are recommended.

best course of action?

Seek a thorough evaluation from a trained practitioner who can provide mental-health treatment and support.

in the meantime what can you do?

1. Learn everything you can about Separation Anxiety Disorder (see reading list below).
2. Help your child to reduce his or her stress and anxiety.
3. Provide a soothing, structured environment for your child, and maintain consistency in your parenting.
4. Provide positive reinforcement and do not focus on negative behaviour.

5. Boost your child's self-esteem (see page 255).

6. Focus on your child's strengths and support his or her hobbies and special interests.

7. Admire your child's accomplishments, but be careful not to base your approval on performance alone. Let him or her know they are loved for who they are.

8. Encourage your child to take pride in his or her own work. Encourage appropriate friendships among your child's peers. Having one good friend will help him or her feel accepted and supported, even when facing setbacks and unkindness from others.

9. Help your child to problem-solve by role-playing responses to various emergency situations.

10. As well as love and protection, provide rules and structure for your child.

11. Teach your child self-assertion and to ask for help when needed.

12. Make sure your child receives the best possible treatment and care.

13. Attend family therapy.

14. Have supportive couples therapy with your spouse or partner, or individual supportive therapy if you are a single parent or carer.

15. If you have a partner, make sure you keep him or her in the loop. It is vital that you are a solid team, not just in parenting your child with Separation Anxiety Disorder, but also in making treatment decisions and facing problems that may arise with social services, health services, community resource providers, the school system, insurance companies, or mental-health providers, as well as other organizations and people in the world who may fail you in your attempts to get the help your child needs.

16. Join a support organization.

17. Educate your whole family about Separation Anxiety Disorder

18. Seek support from appropriate members of your extended family.

19. Research community resources to help you.

20. Take care of yourself, and learn how to pay attention to your own needs.

21. Maintain your own physical and emotional health.

22. Eat balanced, nutritious meals and get enough sleep.

23. Make and keep good friends who will support you, as well as help you to relax and play.

helpful books

Starbright: Meditations for Children: Simple Visualizations to Help Children Sleep Peacefully, Free of Nightmares and Fears, Awaken Creativity, Develop

Concentration, Learn to Quiet Themselves, M. Garth. San Francisco: HarperSanFrancisco, 1991.

The Winning Family: Increasing Self-Esteem in Your Children and Yourself, L. Hart. Oakland, California: LifeSkills Press, 1987.

The Seven Spiritual Laws for Parents: Guiding Your Children to Success and Fulfillment, D. Chopra. New York: Harmony Books, 1997.

helpful books for children

Don't Feed the Monster on Tuesdays: The Children's Self-Esteem Book, A. Moser. Kansas City, Miss.: Landmark Editions Inc., 1991.

My Body Is Mine, My Feelings Are Mine: A Story Book about Body Safety for Young Children with an Adult Guide Book, S. Hoke. King of Prussia, Penn.: The Center for Applied Psychology Inc., 1995.

selective mutism

Children find all kinds of ways to protect themselves. Developing a disorder known as Selective Mutism may be just one of the unintentional methods they come up with to counteract extreme anxiety. Selective Mutism is both a Communication Disorder and a severe type of shyness or social phobia. A child with this disorder may not speak in certain specific situations, despite the ability to speak in others. Children with Selective Mutism usually have a complicated set of symptoms, since they not only refuse to speak in particular social situations but are often shy, socially isolative, anxious, and may seem oppositional and negative in their behaviour.

case study: Jenny

Jenny's family moved from the UK to the United States when she was three years old. Jenny had begun to attend a nursery school before they left, and her parents were pleased to find a suitable nursery school for her in their new neighbourhood. But Jenny felt different in the new school. Not only were her surroundings unfamiliar, but the culture and manner of speaking were quite foreign to her. She knew her classmates were speaking English, but she did not always understand the words they used. Jenny was extremely quiet in her new school – in fact she did not speak at all. Her new teachers made allowances for this to begin with, expecting that she would eventually begin to participate and talk, but after six months Jenny had still not spoken one word. At home, though, Jenny was quite a chatterbox, and in her church group she interacted normally *with other children. Jenny's schoolteachers eventually asked to speak with her parents to discuss the fact that Jenny was not talking at school. In addition, the school psychologist evaluated Jenny and became concerned when Jenny would not speak to her either. They began weekly play therapy sessions, but after another month something interesting happened. One day, Jenny's teacher put on a video with which she was very familiar. It was* Winnie the Pooh, *and it immediately catapulted Jenny into speaking. 'Tut tut! Looks like rain!' she exclaimed, and excitedly told the rest of the story before it had unfolded on the screen. From that moment on, Jenny was her usual self in the classroom. All she had needed was little piece of her own familiar culture, speech and language to provide a transition from her old classroom to her new one.*

is this your child?

- Does not speak in certain situations, even though he or she may speak in other settings.
- This interferes with his or her ability to achieve required goals in social, educational or work situations.
- Has the ability to speak, but does not under specific circumstances.

'do not pass go' signs

This disorder may lead to serious problems at school and elsewhere. Children with Selective Mutism are often extremely anxious and are teased by other children.

The lack of communication involved in Selective Mutism not only affects the development of a child's speech and language, but also his or her cognitive and psychosocial development. It is typically diagnosed in childhood, and the disorder can last from just a few months to several years. The integration of children with Selective Mutism is a very important issue due to the special attention that these children require from their parents and teachers. Unfortunately, many children with Selective Mutism are not diagnosed, and are not referred to mental-health professionals in a timely fashion, even when symptoms of the condition are very apparent and parents express concern. Early diagnosis and treatment of both Selective Mutism and its associated disorders are keys to preventing the long-term effects of this condition, such as impaired self-esteem, peer rejection and academic problems.

what causes selective mutism?

Selective Mutism is probably an attempt to regulate a child's anxiety and other emotions, but there is debate concerning the origins and causes of this disorder. It may, for example, be a childhood form of an Anxiety Disorder such as Social Phobia. Both genetic and psychosocial factors are thought to be involved in causing it. Other possible factors include social isolation, the consequences of maternal social phobia, personality traits, developmental delay in speech and bladder control, family and cultural factors through learned behaviour and a bilingual environment. Rather than being seen as a pathological behaviour, Selective Mutism should perhaps be understood as serving a self-protective function for the child.

what happens in your brain?

When a child does not speak, this may be because he or she sometimes has no wish to do so (as in the case of Selective Mutism), or is the result of lesions in the brain, particularly in the posterior fossa. In Selective Mutism, the same types of brain mechanisms that contribute to anxiety may be operating. The most common organic cause of complete mutism is trauma to the cerebellum.

which treatments are likely to work?

Individualized, multiple treatment approaches may be best for children with Selective Mutism. Speech therapy, behaviour modification, cognitive-behavioural therapy, family systems therapy, psychodynamic psychotherapy, modern psychoanalytic psychotherapy, a modified version of social effectiveness therapy for children (SET-C), self-hypnosis and behavioural treatment for social anxiety are all possible treatments, some of which may be combined to create a multi-modal treatment plan.

Audio feedforward is another type of treatment for Selective Mutism. It involves having the child listen to audiotapes edited to depict him or her speaking in situations in which he or she does not usually speak. Play therapy can be very useful to help with communication, overcoming resistance, competence and positive emotion. Special games and exercises can help to reduce communication-related anxiety and positively reinforce all forms of communication initiated by the child.

Each type of therapy has its own conceptualization of Selective Mutism, as well as its own specialized treatment techniques. For example, the focus of behaviour modification treatments is often to help the child re-learn to speak in formerly problematic situations, while other styles of therapy may be seen as means to overcome the Selective Mutism by developing the ability to self-regulate a variety of emotions and behaviour. Whatever the treatment, it should probably include social skills training, be relevant to the child's daily activities and be targeted at both the child, the family and the school. In addition, concurrent parent training is a good idea to help with the management of the child's anxiety. Medication is sometimes prescribed.

Selective Mutism often resolves itself, but that is not a reason to delay treatment, since the disorder can have a damaging effect on a child's social, familial and academic progress.

best course of action?

Multi-modal treatments combining behavioural techniques in class and family, as well as individual therapy sessions may produce the best overall results.

in the meantime what can you do?

1. Learn everything you can about Selective Mutism.
2. Anything you can do that reduces your child's anxiety will be helpful. Encourage him or her to practise breathing exercises (see page 40), Progressive Body Relaxation (see page 41) and meditation for children (see page 330).
3. Be very careful to avoid dealing out any kind of punishment to your child for not speaking. That would be very counter-productive.
4. Never insist that your child speak.
5. Instead of punishment or insistence on speaking, positively reinforce (that is, praise or reward) all forms of communication initiated by your child with Selective Mutism.
6. Be aware that, even when your child is not speaking, he or she is still engaging in a powerful form of communication.
7. Try to understand that, rather than being oppositional, your child has developed an interesting way to protect himself or herself.
8. Anything you can do to assist your child socialize normally with other children will be helpful. The integration of children with Selective Mutism is a very important, due to the special attention that they require from you and their teachers.
9. Provide social skills training for your child from a teacher who has been trained to work with children with Selective Mutism.
10. Join a support organization for parents of children with Selective Mutism.
11. Educate your whole family about Selective Mutism
12. Make sure your child receives the best possible, immediate treatment and care. Do not opt to 'wait and see' (see 'do not pass go' section).

13. Attend family therapy.
14. Have supportive couples therapy with your spouse or partner, or supportive individual therapy if you are a single parent or carer.
15. If you have a partner, make sure you keep him or her in the loop. It is vital that you are a solid team, not just in parenting your child with Selective Mutism, but also in making treatment decisions and facing problems that may arise with the school system, health services, social services, mental-health providers, insurance companies, and community resources, as well as other organizations and people in the world who may fail you in your attempts to get the help your child needs.
16. Seek support from appropriate members of your extended family.
17. Research community resources to help you, not just for now, but if necessary for the future as well.
18. Boost your child's self-esteem (see page 255).
19. Help your child to reduce his or her stress (see page 19).
20. Focus on your child's strengths and support his or her hobbies and special interests.
21. Admire your child's accomplishments, but be careful not to base your approval on performance alone. Let him or her know they are loved for who they are.
22. Encourage your child to take pride in his or her own work. Encourage appropriate friendships among your child's peers. Having one good friend will help him or her feel accepted and supported, even when facing setbacks and unkindness from others.
23. Help your child to problem-solve by role-playing responses to various situations, including emergency scenarios.
24. As well as love and protection, provide rules and structure for your child.
25. Teach your child to be self-assertive and to ask for help when needed.
26. Take care of yourself, and learn how to pay attention to your own needs.
27. Maintain your own physical and emotional health.
28. Eat balanced, nutritious meals and get enough sleep.
29. Make and keep good friends who will support you, as well as help you to relax and play.

helpful books

Helping Your Child with Selective Mutism: Practical Steps to Overcome a Fear of Speaking, Angela E. McHolm, Charles E. Cunningham, Melanie K. Vanier. New Harbinger Publications, 2005.

Cat's Got Your Tongue: A Story for Children Afraid to Speak, C. E. Schaefer.
New York: Magination Press, 1992.

*Parenting Your Complex Child: Become a Powerful Advocate for the Autistic,
Down Syndrome, PDD, Bipolar, or Other Special-Needs Child*, P. L.
Morgan. AMACOM, 2006.

The Winning Family: Increasing Self-Esteem in Your Children and Yourself,
L. Hart. Oakland, Calif.: LifeSkills Press, 1987.

*The Seven Spiritual Laws for Parents: Guiding Your Children to Success and
Fulfillment*, D. Chopra. New York: Harmony Books, 1997.

for children

Don't Feed the Monster on Tuesdays: The Children's Self-Esteem Book,
A. Moser. Kansas City, Miss.: Landmark Editions Inc., 1991.

*My Body Is Mine, My Feelings Are Mine: A Story Book about Body Safety for
Young Children with an Adult Guide Book*, S. Hoke. King of Prussia, Penn.:
The Center for Applied Psychology Inc., 1995.

reactive attachment disorder of infancy or early childhood

Attachment is a concept developed to describe the way infants and children
cling to their primary carers for nurture and protection. This is a reciprocal
bonding process, a fundamental sense of commitment and responsibility on
the part of the carer, and of dependence on the part of the child. The carer's
response to the child and how well he or she cares for the child is related to
whether or not the child feels secure and cared for. Children are vulnerable
to the way they experience the roles of adults in meeting their basic physical
and emotional needs and protecting them from danger. They need to feel
safe and nurtured in order to thrive and be psychologically healthy.
Sometimes a child does not feel this, and consequential problems arise.

case study: Ruby

*Ruby was born in Romania. She was orphaned when she was six weeks old, and
local officials placed her in a state-run orphanage. In that facility she had very
poor care, and the few workers who manned it were responsible for so many
children they were really unable to meet the basic needs of any of the infants.
When Ruby was three years old she was 'saved' by a British couple who adopted*

her and brought her back home. But her adoptive mother and father soon discovered that Ruby bore the scars of her earlier neglect. She seemed very disturbed, had developmental delays and had problems bonding appropriately with her new parents. Her behaviour oscillated between being extremely withdrawn and fretful, to smiling winningly at complete strangers and wanting to hold their hands. Her concerned carers sought psychological help. Ruby was immediately placed in an intensive programme of sensory integration therapy to help her with her fine and large motor skills. She began to have some play therapy, and her adoptive parents received a great deal of psycho-education and training in parenting skills to help them know exactly how to meet her special needs. Ruby benefited greatly from the consistent, loving support she received after her very difficult start in life. Nevertheless, she continued to require intensive psychotherapeutic help for many years.

is this your child?

- Extremely disturbed and, before the age of five, is unable to relate to others in an appropriate manner for his or her age.
- May avoid contact with carers one minute, then approach them the next.
- May be watchful and suspicious of carers, and over-friendly with complete strangers.

'do not pass go' signs

Children with histories of maltreatment may show problematic attachment behaviour and are at significant risk of developing severe psychiatric problems. Symptoms of Reactive Attachment Disorder include withdrawn behaviour, Anxiety and Depression, social problems, thought problems, attention problems, rule-breaking behaviour and aggressive behaviour. Some have trouble initiating and responding to other people in an age-appropriate and non-ambivalent manner. They are usually sad and it is hard to comfort them. Children with Reactive Attachment Disorder may attach to others indiscriminately. Some may be aggressive or have problems relating to peers.

Children with Reactive Attachment Disorder need a great deal of help to overcome the early deprivations they have suffered. They require the care of mental-health professionals as well as a loving, supportive home environment.

what causes reactive attachment disorder?

The quality of early attachment relationships affects an infant's future personality and brain development. When a child has symptoms of Reactive Attachment Disorder it is usually because he or she has not been properly cared for. Such children are seen in settings such as foster homes or orphanages in countries where poverty, war, epidemics or famine has meant that there have been next to no resources to help them. They have not been able to form the human attachments they need, either because their own parents have been too psychologically or physically challenged to bond with and care for them, or perhaps because they have had too many carers. Sometimes this disorder occurs because carers have been grossly neglectful or abusive, denying children their physical needs as well as their basic emotional needs for affection, comfort and stimulation. Sometimes the child has simply been too impared to be receptive to bonding attempts.

which treatments are likely to work?

Young children who have experienced extremely disturbed care-giving may benefit from dyadic developmental therapy, a treatment based on attachment theory for children with trauma-attachment disorders. A psycho-educational treatment programme that includes special management and family counselling sessions can help to improve the child's social interactions and peer relationships, linguistic and learning abilities, cognitive functioning and motor development. Severely traumatized children and adolescents can be treated using sensory integration or eye movement desensitization and reprocessing (EMDR). Supportive educational counselling for the parents and family may also be helpful. If available, therapeutic nursery schools providing intensive psychotherapy are recommended.

best course of action?

Seek a thorough evaluation from a trained practitioner who can provide mental-health treatment and support.

in the meantime what can you do?

1. Learn everything you can about Reactive Attachment Disorder (see reading list below).
2. If you have become a carer for a child with Reactive Attachment Disorder, perhaps through adoption, appreciate that this will not be easy, so have some supportive therapy for yourself and your partner if you have one.
3. If your own child is suffering from Reactive Attachment Disorder you need a great deal of help and support for both you and your child. Seek this as soon as possible.
4. Help your child to receive the best possible treatment and care.
5. Depending on the exact nature of the child's relating style, you will need

to work with mental-health professionals to begin to lay the foundations of bonding and his or her greater psychological health.

6. Educate everyone else in the child's environment about Reactive Attachment Disorder.

7. Attend family therapy.

8. If you have one, make sure you keep your spouse or partner in the loop. It is vital that you are a solid team, not just in parenting your child with Reactive Attachment Disorder, but also in making treatment decisions and facing problems that may arise with the mental-health system, social services, health service, insurance companies, and community resource providers, as well as other organizations and people in the world who may fail you in your attempts to get the help your child needs.

9. Seek support from appropriate members of your extended family.

10. You will need professional assessment to begin to understand whether your child with Reactive Attachment Disorder will eventually achieve the ability to live fully independently (that is, live alone, hold a job, drive a car and so on). Sometimes the prognosis is uncertain, but take the worst-case scenario and do the following:

   - As difficult as this may be to consider right now, you need to take steps to arrange for the right person to care for your child if, through death, disability or any other reason, you were suddenly unable to care for him or her.

   - Start planning now for the long-term care of your child with Reactive Attachment Disorder.

   - Research community resources to help you, not just for now, but for the future and throughout your child's life.

   - If you are the parent, adoptive parent or guardian of a child with Reactive Attachment Disorder, research and create the appropriate legal documents (with appropriate professional legal help), such as a trust that benefits your child and/or a will that takes into consideration his or her long-term care and other needs.

11. Do everything you can to boost the child's self-esteem.

12. Help your child to reduce his or her stress and anxiety.

13. Focus on his or her strengths and support his hobbies and special interests.

14. Take care of yourself, and learn how to pay attention to your own needs.

15. Maintain your own physical and emotional health.

16. Eat balanced, nutritious meals and get enough sleep.

17. Join a support organization.
18. Make and keep good friends who will support you, as well as help you relax and play.

helpful books

Starbright: Meditations for Children: Simple Visualizations to Help Children Sleep Peacefully, Free of Nightmares and Fears, Awaken Creativity, Develop Concentration, Learn to Quiet Themselves, M. Garth. San Francisco: HarperSanFrancisco, 1991.

The Winning Family: Increasing Self-Esteem in Your Children and Yourself, L. Hart. Oakland, Calif.: LifeSkills Press, 1987.

The Seven Spiritual Laws for Parents: Guiding Your Children to Success and Fulfillment, D. Chopra. New York: Harmony Books, 1997.

stereotypic movement disorder

Children who repeatedly hit themselves, bang their heads or engage in some other self-injurious behaviour urgently need to be helped to stop; but in many cases it's not easy. Many of the sufferers develop this disorder in addition to other serious mental-health problems such as Autistic Disorder, Tourette's Disorder or Schizophrenia, and because of the potential serious harm, they urgently need to be protected.

case study: Toby

Toby couldn't stop hitting himself. His head was always bruised, because even when his mother put padded gloves on his hands he still managed to hit his head by banging it on a door or wall. He often used his own knees to hit his forehead, and his mother had to resort to making him wear a protective helmet. She took him to a clinic for treatment, but unfortunately the medication that helped many people suffering from Stereotypic Movement Disorder did not work for him. Behavioural therapy worked up to a point, but Toby was hearing impaired and he also had an intellectual disability. He adored his mother, who managed to teach him to sign and took him swimming every day. The only problem with going to the local swimming pool was that the tiled edges of the pool provided Toby with additional opportunities to bang his head. One day he swam full pelt towards the pool side and gave himself a bad head injury that could have led to him drowning if his mother had not been nearby. From then on, she insisted he swim wearing a padded, waterproof headgear that she had designed. Luckily, a new medication became available and it did help Toby resist the urge to hit himself. His pool experiences then became a lot more fun for him, and he began to enjoy greater independence and freedom of movement.

is this your child?

- Engages in repetitive behaviour (for example, hitting and/or picking at himself or herself, rocking his or her body) for no apparent reason.
- This hampers his or her participation in everyday activities, and may cause self-injury.

'do not pass go' signs

Children with Stereotypic Movement Disorder sometimes injure themselves, especially if they engage in banging their heads or hitting themselves. It is one of the most serious and conditions in child and adolescent psychiatry, and immediate treatment is essential.

what causes stereotypic movement disorder?

It may be triggered by a stressful environment (sometimes found in people who have been institutionalized) or possibly started when a painful medical condition causes the person to react by banging the affected part of the body. Self-injurious behaviour is not only seen in people with Stereotypic Movement Disorder, but is also commonly seen in several other disorders that are usually first diagnosed in infancy or childhood, including Mental Retardation, Pervasive Developmental Disorders and Tourette's Disorder. It is also seen in people with Schizophrenia or Borderline Personality Disorder, and has occasionally been reported after acquired brain injury.

which treatments are likely to work?

Medication treatment options for Stereotypic Movement Disorder with self-injurious behaviour are usually available. Brain surgery has been used (for example, cingulotomy and limbic leucotomy) in some cases. Rotary vestibular stimulation is another treatment option for Stereotypic Movement Disorder.

best course of action?

Seek a thorough evaluation from an experienced, qualified practitioner who can provide mental-health treatment and support.

in the meantime what can you do?

1. Learn everything you can about Stereotypic Movement Disorder (see reading list below).
2. Help to get your child the best possible treatment and care.
3. Attend family therapy
4. Have supportive couples therapy with your spouse or partner, or individual supportive therapy if you are a single parent or carer.
5. Join a support organization.
6. Educate your whole family about Stereotypic Movement Disorder.
7. If you have a partner, make sure you keep him or her in the loop. It is vital that you are a solid team, not just in parenting your child with Stereotypic Movement Disorder, but also in making treatment decisions and facing problems that may arise with the health system, mental health authorities, the school system, social services, community resources providers and insurance companies, as well as other organizations and people in the world who may fail you in your attempts to get the help your child needs.
8. Seek support from appropriate members of your extended family.
9. You will need professional assessment to begin to understand what the future holds for your child with Stereotypic Movement Disorder. Sometimes the prognosis is uncertain, but take the worst-case scenario and do the following:

   - As difficult as this may be to consider right now, you need to take steps to arrange for the right person to care for your child with Stereotypic Movement Disorder if, through death, disability or any other reason, you were suddenly unable to care for him or her.
   - Research community resources to help you, not just for now, but for the future and throughout your child's life.
   - With professional legal help, research and create appropriate legal documents, such as a trust that benefits your child with Stereotypic Movement Disorder and/or a will that takes into consideration his or her long-term care and other needs.

10. Try to boost your child's self-esteem.
11. Try to soothe your child, and help to reduce his or her stress and anxiety.
12. Focus on your child's strengths and support his or her hobbies and special interests.
13. Encourage appropriate friendships among your child's peers. Having one good friend will help him or her feel accepted and supported,

even when facing setbacks and unkindness from others.

14. Help your child to problem-solve by role-playing responses to various situations, including emergency scenarios.
15. As well as love and protection, provide rules and structure for your child.
16. Teach your child to be self-assertive and to ask for help when needed.
17. Take care of yourself, and learn how to pay attention to your own needs.
18. Maintain your own physical and emotional health.
19. Eat balanced, nutritious meals and get enough sleep.
20. Find good-quality childcare.
21. Make and keep good friends who will support you, as well as help you to relax and play.
22. Consider starting a home-based business to allow you to juggle work and family best.
23. Hang onto your goals, dreams, or career. Don't fall into the trap of losing yourself amidst the intensive demands of raising a child with special needs.

helpful books

The Winning Family: Increasing Self-Esteem in Your Children and Yourself, L. Hart. Oakland, California: LifeSkills Press, 1987.

Parenting Your Complex Child: Become a Powerful Advocate for the Autistic, Down Syndrome, PDD, Bipolar, or Other Special-Needs Child, P. L. Morgan. AMACOM, 2006.

Starbright: Meditations for Children: Simple Visualizations to Help Children Sleep Peacefully, Free of Nightmares and Fears, Awaken Creativity, Develop Concentration, Learn to Quiet Themselves, M. Garth. San Francisco: HarperSanFrancisco, 1991.

The Seven Spiritual Laws for Parents: Guiding Your Children to Success and Fulfillment, D. Chopra. New York: Harmony Books, 1997.

for children

Don't Feed the Monster on Tuesdays: The Children's Self-Esteem Book, A. Moser. Kansas City, Miss.: Landmark Editions Inc., 1991.

My Body Is Mine, My Feelings Are Mine: A Story Book about Body Safety for Young Children with an Adult Guide Book, S. Hoke. King of Prussia, Penn.: The Center For Applied Psychology Inc., 1995.

chapter 12
when the sandman gets it wrong: sleep disorders

Everybody sleeps badly some of the time, but some people sleep badly all the time. We really need our 'beauty sleep' – and it doesn't just make us look better in the morning. Being able to get a good night's sleep repairs and regulates the central nervous system and other parts of the body, and it has been proven to be a hugely important factor in predicting longevity – more influential than diet, exercise or heredity. So, isn't it surprising that people put up with all kinds of problems to do with sleep? They may have too much of it, not enough, disturbed sleep, trouble falling asleep, trouble staying asleep, trouble waking, unrefreshing sleep, dropping off during the daytime, persistent nightmares, waking up terrified, sleepwalking and trouble breathing at night. Few people know the facts about sleep and the price we pay when we are deprived of it, such as heart disease, a third of all fatigue-related traffic accidents and immeasurable mental and psychological disadvantages.

Sleep should not be considered a state of brain inertia, because our brains are actually extremely busy. In fact, sleep is a highly dynamic process involving numerous brain-stem areas and all physiological systems of the body. It normally occurs in a cyclical pattern that has three distinct states: wakefulness, rapid eye movement (REM) sleep and non-rapid eye movement (NREM) sleep that itself has four different stages. We need our proper pattern of stages in order to wake up feeling refreshed.

Disruption of a person's sleep pattern can result from environmental change, psychological disturbance, drugs or medications or physical disease. Approximately a third of all adults report experiencing insomnia at some time and half of those consider their problem serious. Add to this number all the adults who have breathing-related sleep apnoea, Narcolepsy and other neurological disorders involving excessive sleepiness, as well as the many millions with Circadian Rhythm Disorder and parasomnias (Nightmare Disorder, Sleep Terror Disorder, Sleep-Walking Disorder), and it becomes apparent that at least 40 per cent of all adults experience some type of Sleep Disorder in their lifetimes.

Sleep disturbance in infants, children and adolescents occurs as a significant and persistent difficulty in nodding off or staying asleep. The most common manifestations include resisting bedtime at least three times per week, delay in getting to sleep of at least thirty minutes to one hour, prolonging and resisting morning wake-up, daytime fatigue and night awakenings at least four times per week. In children, sleep problems are most common during the toddler period and may often persist into early childhood.

insomnia

Sleep is a habit. Some people have developed bad habits (for example, in their schedule, in their approach to bedtime or even in the way they arrange their place of rest) that lead to Insomnia. They may have acquired the habit of napping, which then makes it more difficult to fall asleep later in the evening. There are often physiological elements too. Their muscles may be unusually tense, their metabolic rate may be higher than others and their body may react more to stress. Some people also suffer from Anxiety and chronic Depression. A vicious cycle often develops, in which a person who tries to sleep but is unable to do so becomes frustrated and anxious, thereby making it even more difficult to doze off. Not knowing the facts about sleep can lead to the continuation of a Sleep Disorder, for example a person who cannot sleep might get up and start thinking about doing something stimulating, which only makes it less likely that he or she will feel like sleeping at that same time the following night.

case study: Spike

Spike worked in rock 'n' roll. He toured the world with bands at least four times a year, building stages in large amphitheatres where the concerts were held. This lifestyle involved long days and trying to snatch a few hours' sleep on a tour bus between cities. When Spike was at home, he also had an erratic schedule, with late nights partying with friends, an occasional day job driving a car and being at the beck and call of various band members and their managers who required him to run 'errands' at any time of day or night. Not surprisingly, Spike had very little time to sleep. When he did have a night off he found it was almost impossible to fall asleep, rested only fitfully and would wake many times. He became increasingly irritable and was wrongly accused by one of the managers of being addicted to cocaine. When I met Spike he had just come out of hospital after crashing into a wall in his car. It was immediately obvious that he suffered from severe Insomnia, which affected his mood, concentration and ability to stay alert. He needed to restructure his life and reacquire the habit of regular sleep – at least when he wasn't on the road. Once I had educated Spike about his Insomnia, he educated me that, in his opinion, a very large percentage of people in his profession also suffer from Sleep Disorders – 'It goes with the territory' he said.

is this you (or someone close to you)?
- You cannot get to sleep or stay asleep, or wake feeling not well-rested.
- This problem with sleeping, or with falling asleep during the daytime due to fatigue, causes problems at work, home, place of study, socially or in other situations.

'do not pass go' signs
People with Insomnia often have problems in their daily life due to the fact that they are irritable and find it hard to manage their work day, family activities and social events. Their relationships may suffer. They may find it hard to concentrate, and this can lead to work or car accidents. Insomnia is generally linked to decreased quality of life, diminished work productivity and increased long-term risk of medical and psychiatric diseases, such as diabetes and depression. Headaches and gastric problems can also occur. Once a person has a Mood Disorder, a sleep disturbance appears to make it worse. On top of that, Insomnia and other sleep disturbances may trigger a

new onset of depression. Yet if the sleep problem is treated, depressive symptoms often improve. If the Mood Disorder is treated, though, the Insomnia may remain until it too is treated. Many sleep problems are highly amenable to treatment, but they are under-diagnosed and under-treated.

what causes insomnia?

Disruption of a person's sleep pattern can result from worry, environmental change, psychological disturbance, drugs or physical disease. In many instances, Insomnia is assumed to be secondary to another primary medical, psychiatric or Sleep Disorders. People suffering from major Depression, Bipolar Disorder, and Anxiety Disorders often suffer from Insomnia that is connected to their mental disorder, or even due to prescribed medications. Sleep Disorders can also be related to medical conditions, or caused by alcohol or recreational drugs. Medications affecting neurotransmitters (for example, norepinephrine, serotonin, acetylcholine, and dopamine) can alter sleep patterns, and Insomnia is also an unwanted side effect of various other types of prescribed substances.

what happens in your brain?

Brainwave analysis has shown that, for people with Insomnia, parts of the brain are abnormally speeded up during sleep, that is, there are increased amounts of alpha and beta activity.

Hormones and other chemicals play a role, as well as the parts of the brain that are supposed to facilitate the process of going to sleep.

which treatments are likely to work?

Hypnotherapy can work well. Psychotherapy and/or medical help are appropriate, depending on the cause of the Insomnia. There is considerable evidence that cognitive-behavioural therapy is very effective for treating Insomnia, and is believed to produce longer-lasting effects than medication. It may be prudent to consult a sleep specialist and take a sleep-laboratory test to obtain information about the quality of sleep and the amount of oxygen the sufferer is getting at night, and to rule out sleep apnoea and other problems. Anxiety medication is sometimes prescribed if the reason for Insomnia is thought to be worry. Unfortunately, some medications can make a person a bit sluggish the following day; the person may also be intolerant to and/or become dependent upon these medications. Melatonin and related substances are sometimes used to treat Insomnia, while many herbal therapies have been considered for the treatment of Sleep Disorders in published medical reports. These include valerian, lavender, hops, kava, Chinese and Japanese herbal compounds, St John's wort and German chamomile. Other therapies include massage, exercise, acupuncture, music therapy, t'ai chi, magnetism and white noise. Gauging the comparative effects of each of these treatments, relative to each other or to conventional therapies, is difficult.

An integral part of treatment for Insomnia includes education about sleep, relaxation training and other techniques to restore normal sleeping patterns and manage stress and anxiety.

best course of action?

Seek psychotherapy. An initial evaluation will help you to find out if your Insomnia is secondary to another disorder, such as anxiety. A medical evaluation may also be necessary to rule out physiological problems, while investigations by a sleep-medicine specialist will be the best way to find out about the exact nature of your Insomnia and any associated sleep problems.

in the meantime what can you do?

1. Learn everything you can about sleep and Insomnia.
2. Keep a sleep diary for two weeks. This means writing down when you went to bed, roughly what time you fell asleep, how you felt if you couldn't sleep (agitated, worrying about things, annoyed and so on) and what you did do to try to get to sleep. Include your time of waking up (either in the morning or during the night), the number of times you woke, and how you felt in the morning (refreshed or otherwise). If you dropped off during the day you should record that too.
3. Check if any medications you are taking could be causing or exacerbating your Insomnia (ask your doctor, or research the possible side effects of your medications online).
4. It is important to create better sleeping habits. Redesign your schedule so that you go to bed at the same time every night, and wake at the same time every morning.
5. Limit your caffeine intake.
6. Make your bedroom a place for sleep. Remove work, computer and other mind-stimulating paraphernalia.
7. Create a regular, soothing bedtime routine. This may involve a warm shower or bath, a non-caffeinated hot drink (such as chamomile tea), relaxation or listening to gentle music.
8. If you cannot sleep, or if you wake during the night, do not get up and

start doing something 'productive'. Stay in bed with the light out and do some Progressive Body Relaxation (see page 41).

9. If snoring is a problem, consult a sleep specialist to check if you have breathing-related sleep apnoea (see page 358).

10. If your partner has a different schedule from you and needs or likes to be up while you are sleeping, negotiate with him or her to make sure your bedroom is dark and quiet.

11. Do not fall asleep in front of the TV. You need darkness and quiet when you sleep.

12. If there is light in your room from an alarm clock, computer, blinking video/DVD recorder or neon sign outside your window, do something about it. Turn off or cover the equipment and hang black-out curtains.

13. If street noise is a problem, consider double-glazing or shutters.

14. Work on lowering your general level of stress (see page 19).

15. Work on your general relaxation (see page 41).

16. You may think that alcohol or drugs help you sleep, but it would be very unwise to continue using them. Avoid them, at least until your Insomnia is under control, and never use them as a means to get to sleep.

17. If you have disturbing thoughts roaming through your mind at night, begin to write them down. What are the themes? Learning more about your anxieties will help you to begin to solve them, but solve them during the daytime – not at night.

18. If you think you may be suffering from Anxiety (see page 37ff) or Post-Traumatic Stress Disorder (see page 62), seek treatment and follow the self-help guidelines.

19. Practise meditation or yoga (during the daytime).

20. Exercise as much as you can safely manage. Do it in the morning, never in the evening.

21. If you have a spouse or partner, educate him or her about your Sleep Disorder and ask for help in your efforts to implement better sleep habits.

when your child suffers from insomnia

1. Establish a definite bedtime and wake-up time for your child, and consistently reinforce them.

2. Establish a consistent and soothing bedtime routine for your child, perhaps involving a bath, warm drink, bedtime story and comforting hugs.

3. If your child is worried about something, try to encourage him or her to

talk about it with you prior to the start of the bedtime routine. Try to help resolve the problem or concern so that physiological and psychological calming can take place as early as possible.

4. If your child wakes in the night, discourage him or her from getting up and doing something that might be stimulating and stop them getting back to sleep.

5. If your child is taking medication, check with your doctor to find out if Insomnia is one of the side effects.

6. Try increasing the amount of daily physical exercise your child gets, but make sure this occurs well before bedtime.

7. Make sure that your child's bedroom is a calm place without flashing lights from electronics or digital displays. If your child needs a night light, provide a low-level one.

8. Playing stimulating video games or watching exciting TV just before bedtime is a bad idea. These kinds of activities should be moved to earlier in the day.

9. Try to ascertain what is occurring in your child's mind when he or she is unable to sleep. Is there worry? Obsessing about something? Are they restless? Try to soothe him or her, but if you are unable to do so seek therapy for your child with an experienced, qualified mental-health professional.

helpful books

The Promise of Sleep: A Pioneer in Sleep Medicine Explores the Vital Connection between Health, Happiness, and a Good Night's Sleep, W. C. Dement and C. Vaughan. Dell Publishing Co., 1999.

Desperately Seeking Snoozin': The Insomnia Cure from Awake to Zzzzz, J. Wiedman. Towering Pines Press, 1999.

The Woman's Book of Sleep: A Complete Resource Guide, A. R. Wolfson, Oakland, Calif.: New Harbinger Publications, 2001.

Sleepless in America: Is Your Child Misbehaving or Missing Sleep, M. Kurcinka and M. Sheedy. HarperCollins Publishers, 2006.

'Establishing Bedtime', E. R. Christophersen, S. L. Mortweet, in Parenting That Works: Building Skills That Last a Lifetime. American Psychological Association, 2003, pp. 209–28.

hypersomnia (excessive sleepiness)

It's sometimes hard to distinguish between Insomnia and Hypersomnia, because one can lead to the other. If you don't manage to sleep until the wee hours, you're rather likely to fall asleep during the day – and vice versa. Despite appearances, sleep polysomnography (a procedure that can gauge how much real sleep a person is getting) usually reveals that a person with Hypersomnia is actually getting less sleep than expected. It's best not to be complacent when it comes to your sleep patterns. Don't put up with poor-quality sleep because it will affect the quality of your life, and worse.

case study: Andrea

Andrea's parents thought she was a 'typical' teenager – a fifteen-year-old who seemed to 'sleep half her life away' as her mother put it. She was extremely difficult to arouse in the morning, and was frequently in trouble at school for being late. She also had a tendency to drop off during the day, so much so that her parents suspected she sneaked out of the house at night, and so they began to monitor her very closely. They eventually came to the conclusion that she might have a psychological problem such as depression and took her to see a therapist. After her evaluation for depression proved negative, a sleep test showed that, rather than over sleeping, Andrea got far less good-quality sleep than she needed. She slept late in the morning and dropped off during the daytime because she was exhausted from sleeping poorly at night. Where sleep is concerned, it is often quality, not quantity, that counts.

is this you (or someone close to you)?

- You are excessively sleepy, that is you sleep too long at night or nap too much during the day.
- This causes you problems at work, home, place of study, socially or in other situations.

'do not pass go' signs

Hypersomnia, or excessive sleepiness, is an abnormal increase in the likelihood that the sufferer will fall asleep, take involuntary naps or have sleep attacks when sleep is not desired. It is fairly common. Social, family and work problems, as well as cognitive impairment are among the consequences of

Hypersomnia. The disorder can cause severe occupational problems, for example when a sufferer misses important meetings or does not seem alert on the job. It can lead to occupational injuries and to traffic accidents. Hypersomnia is associated with depression, and people with sleep complaints are generally more likely to have alcohol and drug problems. Sleep partners may suffer too, because quite often the daytime napping is caused by poor sleep at night. People with Hypersomnia often experience a decreased quality of life, so treatment is vital.

what causes hypersomnia?

Some of the causes are chronic sleep deprivation, sleep apnoea, movement disorders during sleep and use of drugs and medications. Hypersomnia can occur when a person is suffering from other disorders, such as Depression and Seasonal Affective Disorder (SAD). It can be brought about by the use of medications that have sedative side effects, including some antidepressants and anti-anxiety medication. The use and abuse of these drugs is a common cause of Hypersomnia.

what happens in your brain?

Excess theta waves means that, at times, the brain has slowed down more than it should.

which treatments are likely to work?

Sleep Disorders very often need to be treated by a collaboration of professionals from two or three different disciplines: psychology, psychiatry, respirology, neurology, pneumology or endocrinology. Certainly, a sleep-medicine specialist should be consulted, and once the correct diagnosis and cause has been found, cognitive-behavioural therapy or hypnotherapy may be appropriate. The treatment of excessive sleepiness includes treating the primary cause, if it can be identified. It is very important that a correct diagnosis be made, and that's not always easy since excessive daytime sleepiness could be actually due to a primary problem of Insomnia or sleep apnoea. One of the best tools for evaluating Hypersomnia is to keep a sleep log. Sleep time is self-recorded daily over a month. Better sleep habits for sleep deprivation, continuous positive airway pressure (CPAP) for sleep apnoea, medication, exercises for sleep-related movement disorders, light therapy and/or melatonin for Circadian Disorders, and use of stimulants are some of the current preferred treatments.

best course of action?

Consult a sleep-medicine specialist. Once a correct diagnosis and cause have been established for your excessive sleepiness, cognitive-behavioural therapy and hypnotherapy could be useful. If your Hypersomnia is secondary to a psychological disorder, such as Anxiety or Depression, you should seek therapy to treat the primary cause.

in the meantime what can you do?

1. Learn everything you can about sleep and Hypersomnia.
2. It is essential to get some accurate information about your sleep habits by keeping a sleep diary. For at least two weeks record exactly how much sleep you are getting, the times and amount. Also record your impression of the quality of sleep you get (that is, sound, medium or light) and how you feel when you wake up.
3. Ask your spouse, partner or someone who spends a lot of time with you to help evaluate your sleepiness. Some people with Hypersomnia are not fully cognizant of their pattern of sleepiness.
4. It is important to create better sleeping habits. Redesign your schedule so that you go to bed at the same time every night and wake at the same time every morning. Try not to allow yourself to exceed eight hours' sleep.
5. If you cannot sleep, or if you wake up during the night, do not get up and start doing something 'productive'. Stay in bed with the light out and do some Progressive Body Relaxation (see page 41).
6. If snoring is a problem, be sure to consult a sleep specialist to rule out sleep apnoea.
7. If you have a partner with a different schedule from you and he or she needs or likes to be up while you are sleeping, negotiate with them to make sure your bedroom is dark and quiet.
8. Educate your partner about your Sleep Disorder and ask for help in implementing better sleeping habits.
9. Do not fall asleep in front of the TV. You need darkness and quietude when you sleep.
10. If there is light in your room from a clock radio, computers, blinking video/DVD recorder, neon sign outside your window – do something about it. Turn off the equipment and hang black-out curtains.
11. If street noise is a problem, consider double-glazing or shutters.
12. Work on lowering your general level of stress (see page 19).

13. If you have disturbing thoughts roaming through your mind at night, begin to write them down. What is the theme? Learning more about your anxieties will help you to begin to solve them, but solve them during the daytime – not at night.

14. Plan a wake-up routine that involves rituals designed to stimulate you, such as a cool shower or bath, physical exercise and a cup of tea or coffee. But don't overdo the caffeine!

15. Work on lowering your general level of stress.

16. Avoid alcohol and drugs.

17. Practise meditation, t'ai chi or yoga (during the day).

18. Exercise as much as you can safely manage, but do it in the morning, never in the evening.

19. Be very careful not to drive or operate dangerous machinery when you are feeling sleepy.

when your child suffers from hypersomnia

1. Establish a definite bedtime and wake-up time for your child and consistently keep to these.

2. Establish a consistent and welcoming wake-up routine for your child encouraging him or her to rise at the same time every day and eat a nutritious breakfast.

3. Establish a consistent and soothing bedtime routine for your child, perhaps involving a bath, warm drink, bedtime story and comforting hugs.

4. Try to ascertain if your child's Hypersomnia occurs because he or she sleeps poorly during the night. If so, do the following:

   - If your child is worried about something, try to encourage him or her to talk about it with you prior to starting the bedtime routine. Try to help resolve the problem or concern so that physiological and psychological calming can take place as early as possible.

   - If your child wakes in the night, discourage him or her from getting up and doing something that might be stimulating and stop them getting back to sleep.

   - Make sure that your child's bedroom is a calm place without flashing lights from electronics or digital displays. If your child needs a night light, provide a low-level one.

   - Playing stimulating video games or watching exciting TV just before bedtime is a bad idea. These kinds of activities should be moved to earlier in the day.

- Try to ascertain what is occurring in your child's mind when he or she is unable to sleep. Is there worry? Obsessing about something? Are they restless? Try to soothe him or her, but if you are unable to do so seek therapy for your child with an experienced, qualified mental-health professional.

5. If your child is taking medication, check with your doctor to find out if Hypersomnia, or Insomnia that could lead to Hypersomnia, is one of the side effects.

6. Try increasing the amount of daily physical exercise your child gets, but make sure this occurs well before bedtime.

7. If your efforts to get your child out of bed in the morning fail to work, and he or she has all the signs of Hypersomnia, do not resort to punishment or allow yourself to become involved in a power struggle with your child. Seek help from a mental-health professional.

helpful books

The Promise of Sleep: A Pioneer in Sleep Medicine Explores the Vital Connection between Health, Happiness, and a Good Night's Sleep, W. C. Dement and C. Vaughan. Dell Publishing Co., 1999.

'Establishing Bedtime', E. R. Christophersen, S. L. Mortweet in Parenting That Works: Building Skills That Last a Lifetime, American Psychological Association, 2003, pp. 209–28.

The Woman's Book of Sleep: A Complete Resource Guide, A. R.Wolfson. Oakland, Calif.: New Harbinger Publications, 2001.

narcolepsy

Do you know anyone who drops off to sleep in broad daylight, often in the most inappropriate situations? Narcolepsy is a chronic Sleep Disorder that involves excessive daytime sleepiness, cataplexy (an abrupt, loss of skeletal muscle tone) and sleep paralysis. As sleep takes over, the person with Narcolepsy quickly drops into a rapid eye movement (REM) period. There can be very challenging consequences for the sufferer in terms of his or her quality of life, relationships and safety. In addition, public safety and productivity can be compromised when a person with Narcolepsy has job responsibilities that affect other people.

case study: Professor Kay

Professor Kay was responsible for many students at the university where he had been given a post as senior lecturer in psychology. As part of their training, undergraduate psychotherapists were expected to attend group therapy sessions facilitated by the professor. Unfortunately, their training was jeopardized when he developed a Sleep Disorder. Just as a student was earnestly expressing deep feelings about the loss of a friend or some painful childhood experience, Professor Kay would suddenly slump in his chair, overtaken by sleep and begin to snore. When this happened, the students reacted in various ways – with shock, titters, disgust or indignant protests. Some students even believed they were retraumatized by this seeming disregard for their feelings. Unfortunately this state of affairs continued for some time because the psychology students empathised with the professor's problem and failed to complain. Eventually, the beloved professor was made aware of the seriousness of his problem – and so were the university authorities. He sought treatment for his Narcolepsy and all students breathed a sigh of relief.

is this you (or someone close to you)?

- You cannot help suddenly falling asleep several times during the daytime.
- Your body suddenly goes limp (usually after feeling some strong emotion).
- Signs of REM sleep such as body paralysis and sleep-wake hallucinations occur between sleep and wakefulness.

'do not pass go' signs

Narcolepsy is associated with Depression, due to the decrease in cognitive and social activities that happens when a person keeps dropping off to sleep during the daytime. There is a lack of public awareness of the disorder and, as a result, sufferers are often viewed at school or work as being 'lazy' or even 'hung over'. Of particular concern is the risk of a serious car accident when a person with Narcolepsy remains untreated. People with Narcolepsy are often reluctant to seek treatment for fear of losing their driver's licence, but appropriate treatment must be provided in order to increase their safety, quality of life and chances of continuing to work.

Sometimes Narcoleptic symptoms mimic those of epileptic seizure, and misdiagnosis can lead to unnecessary investigations and inappropriate treatment. Occasionally, a person with Narcolepsy experiences a schizophrenia-like psychosis; however this is most commonly related to the effects of medication. Narcolepsy sometimes occurs in children, and again, diagnosis and treatment are vital.

what causes narcolepsy?

Narcolepsy may be a neurodegenerative or auto-immune disorder resulting in the loss of particular neurons.

what happens in your brain?

There may be an imbalance between certain neurotransmitters and, in addition, the absence of brain chemicals that promote wakefulness and inhibit REM sleep may permit inappropriate transitions between wakefulness and sleep.

which treatments are likely to work?

The treatments used for Narcolepsy, either pharmacological or behavioural, are diverse. A sleep-medicine specialist must be consulted. Once a diagnosis is confirmed, a combination of cognitive-behavioural therapy, possibly with hypnosis plus medication may work the best. Medication prescribed for Narcolepsy might be stimulants to counteract sleepiness, antidepressants for cataplexy and sedatives for the disturbed nocturnal sleep. Scheduled naps can be beneficial to combat sleepiness, while the combination of scheduled naps and regular nocturnal sleep times can significantly reduce both symptom severity and the amount of unscheduled daytime sleep.

The successful treatment of Narcolepsy requires an accurate diagnosis to exclude other Sleep Disorders (which have different treatments) and to avoid unnecessary complications of drug treatment. To evaluate the severity of Narcolepsy, polysomnography (a sleep test) might be suggested by a sleep-medicine specialist. These days, a person does not necessarily have to spend two nights in a sleep laboratory in order to undergo a polysomnography test; in some areas it is now possible to sleep at home hooked up to a portable assessment device, such as the actigraph.

Narcolepsy clearly has a negative effect on quality of life. Early diagnosis and treatment after the onset of symptoms is important in order to reduce these negative effects. A therapist can also help with social functioning and general well-being.

best course of action?

Seek an immediate evaluation with a sleep-medicine specialist, plus psychotherapy with an experienced practitioner.

in the meantime what can you do?

1. Learn everything you can about sleep and Narcolepsy.

2. Educate your family and others around you about Narcolepsy.

3. If you have a job that involves being responsible for public safety, you need to consider taking leave until you can be treated.

4. Driving could be dangerous for you and others. It would be prudent not to get behind the wheel until you have full control over your Narcolepsy.

5. It is essential to get some accurate information about your sleep habits by keeping a sleep diary. For at least two weeks record exactly how much sleep you are getting, the times and amount, and when you drop off to sleep and wake during the day. You may need help from others to record this accurately. Also record your impression of the quality of sleep you get (that is, sound, medium or light) and how you feel when you wake up from each bout of sleep.

6. Creating a regular sleep schedule is essential for sufferers of Narcolepsy. Redesign your schedule so that you go to bed at the same time every night, and wake at the same time every morning.

7. Plan a wake-up routine that involves rituals designed to stimulate you, such as a cool shower or bath, physical exercise, and a cup of tea or coffee.

8. Establish a routine designed to keep you stimulated and as physically active as possible during the day.

9. If you cannot sleep when you want to, or if you wake up during the night, do not get up and start doing something 'productive'. Stay in bed with the light out and do some Progressive Body Relaxation (see page 41).

10. If you have a partner with a different schedule from you and he or she needs or likes to be up while you are sleeping, negotiate this with them to make sure your bedroom is dark and quiet.

11. Educate your partner about your Sleep Disorder and ask for help implementing better sleep habits.

12. Avoid alcohol and drugs.

13. Do not fall asleep in front of the TV at night. You need darkness and quiet when you sleep.

14. If there is light in your room from a clock radio, computers, blinking video/DVD recorder, neon sign outside your window – do something about it. Turn off the equipment and hang black-out curtains.

15. If street noise is a problem, consider double-glazing or shutters.

16. Work on lowering your general level of stress (see page 19).
17. Is it possible that you are also suffering from Depression or Anxiety? Check the symptoms on page 13 and 35. If this resonates with you, follow the self-help suggestions.
18. Work on relaxation (see page 41).
19. If you have disturbing thoughts roaming through your mind at night that prevent you sleeping soundly, begin to write them down. What is the theme? Learning more about your anxieties will help you to begin to solve them.
20. Practise meditation, t'ai chi or yoga.

when your child suffers from narcolepsy

1. Children with Narcolepsy need a great deal of help to deal with the consequences they face from peers, family or schoolteachers.
2. Help your child to raise his or her self-esteem (see page 255).
3. Help your child with Narcolepsy to receive the best treatment available.
4. Seek an evaluation with a sleep-medicine specialist and mental-health professional.
5. Narcolepsy can be mistaken for epilepsy or other problems, so be sure your child receives good-quality assessment and treatment.
6. Make sure your child is protected from falling asleep in situations where he or she might be in physical danger.
7. Read everything you can about Narcolepsy.
8. Establish a definite bedtime and wake-up time for your child, and consistently stick to these.
9. Establish a consistent and welcoming wake-up routine for your child encouraging him or her to rise at the same time every day and eat a nutritious breakfast.
10. Establish a consistent and soothing bedtime routine for your child, perhaps involving a bath, warm drink, bedtime story and comforting hugs.
11. Establish a regular lunchtime or afternoon nap for your child to help ward off sudden sleepiness.
12. If your child sleeps poorly during the night, do the following:
    - If your child is worried about something, try to encourage him or her to talk about it with you prior to the start of the bedtime routine. Try to help resolve the problem or concern so that physiological and psychological calming can take place as early as possible.

- If your child wakes in the night, discourage him or her from getting up and doing something that might be stimulating and stop them getting back to sleep.
- Make sure that your child's bedroom is a calm place without flashing lights from electronics or digital displays. If your child needs a night light, provide a low-level one.
- Playing stimulating video games or watching exciting TV just before bedtime is a bad idea. These kinds of activities should be moved to earlier in the day.
- Try to ascertain what is occurring in your child's mind when he or she is unable to sleep. Is there worry? Obsessing about something? Are they restless? Try to soothe him or her, but if you are unable to do so seek therapy for your child with an experienced, qualified mental-health professional.

13. Try increasing the amount of daily physical exercise your child gets, but make sure this occurs well before bedtime.
14. Do not resort to punishing your child for dropping off at inappropriate times or allow yourself to become involved in a power struggle with him or her. Seek help from a mental-health professional.
15. Remember that child sufferers need a great deal of help adjusting to Narcolepsy.

helpful books

The Promise of Sleep: A Pioneer in Sleep Medicine Explores the Vital Connection between Health, Happiness, and a Good Night's Sleep, W. C. Dement and C. Vaughan. Dell Publishing Co., 1999.

Desperately Seeking Snoozin': The Insomnia Cure from Awake to Zzzzz, J. Wiedman. Towering Pines Press, 1999.

The Woman's Book of Sleep: A Complete Resource Guide, A. R. Wolfson. Oakland, Calif.: New Harbinger Publications, 2001.

breathing-related sleep disorder

Snoring isn't just annoying – it's a potential killer. If that sounds overly dramatic, consider that in men a snoring problem that is severe enough to lead to Breathing-Related Sleep Disorder due to obstructive sleep apnoea significantly increases the risk of cardiovascular problems and may also be associated with hypertension, diabetes, myocardial infarction (heart attack), metabolic syndrome and stroke – as well as with depression and anxiety. In addition there is the possibility that it can cause subtle structural brain 'damage.

Obstructive sleep apnoea is a condition where the sufferer's airway either partly or completely collapses from time to time during sleep, resulting in brief cessation of breathing. This means that he or she has poor-quality sleep and less oxygen during the night than is necessary to wake refreshed and be alert and productive during the day. Obstructive sleep apnoea can lead to Breathing-Related Sleep Disorder, which in turn is associated with very serious physiological and psychological problems. It can affect a person's executive functions, including working memory, fluency of speech, cognitive flexibility and planning. Early recognition and treatment is essential, or a sufferer could have the kind of experience Bill had.

case study: Bill

Bill was an experienced, long-haul lorry driver, working for a large frozen-foods firm. He travelled on the same, three-day routine for six years until the company opened a factory in a new city. Bill's schedule changed, and he was pleased with that because it allowed him to spend twice as much time at home with his family, sleeping in his own bed. But after a month of this, his wife expressed concern that the sudden change in schedule had made him more irritable around the house. She noticed that his sleep was disturbed and his snoring worse, which meant that she herself was often woken up. Most alarmingly, she noticed that he had a habit of stopping breathing completely for quite a few seconds before making an explosive, choking sound. Sometimes she wondered if he had died.

Two weeks later, Bill had a near-fatal accident through falling asleep at the wheel of his lorry. While he was in hospital recovering from physical injuries, his unusual snoring pattern was noticed and he was evaluated for a Sleep Disorder. Bill was diagnosed with Breathing-Related Sleep Disorder due to sleep apnoea and prescribed a CPAP breathing machine. The device forces air into the lungs via a tube attached to a face mask Bill began to wear at night. He was finally able to receive more oxygen at night and get far better quality sleep, and as a result, he was less sleepy and irritable during the daytime. His wife was relieved to know that he would be safer on the road – and that she herself would get more sleep in future.

is this you (or someone close to you)?

You have disturbed sleep that leads to either Insomnia or excessive sleepiness, due to a sleep-related breathing problem such as apnoea.

'do not pass go' signs

Breathing-Related Sleep Disorder, often characterized by heavy snoring, apnoea and daytime sleepiness suggestive of the medical diagnosis of obstructive sleep apnoea, should be confirmed by an overnight sleep study. Because the person suffering from Breathing-Related Sleep Disorder has such poor quality sleep during the night he or she is excessively sleepy during the daytime and may fall asleep frequently; also, he or she may be irritable or chronically fatigued and is at great risk of having depression, anxiety and accidents. Individuals with Breathing-Related Sleep Disorder have impairments in social, cognitive and emotional functioning and an overall reduction in quality of life. In children, the disorder can also lead to hyperactivity.

what causes breathing-related sleep disorder?

Most people with this disorder have chronic, disrupted sleep because they snore loudly and, every so often, stop breathing altogether for a few seconds. This syndrome is usually diagnosed by a doctor as obstructive sleep apnoea. A person's physical make-up may cause this disorder and obesity may contribute to it. Men are more commonly affected probably due to anatomical and functional differences in the airway wall (breathing in causes it to collapse and results in apnoea). Women may be protected by the remote effects of female sex hormones that stabilize their airway walls.

which treatments are likely to work?

An immediate evaluation by a sleep-medicine specialist is essential. You may be asked to take a polysomnography test to obtain information about the quality of sleep and the amount of oxygen you are getting at night. Portable sleep-assessment devices are available in some areas so you do not need to leave home for your sleep test. Once diagnosed, relatively simple actions may be suggested : weight loss, the changing of one's sleeping position to side or prone sleeping, as well as the avoidance of alcohol and other sedative drugs – so your physician may suggest you try one or some of these first.

Psychotherapy (cognitive-behavioural and hypnotherapy) is often appropriate. Sleep apnoea can be treated using a Continuous Positive Airway Pressure (CPAP) machine that forces air into the lungs and avoids the cessation of breathing. It is highly effective for many people, including children, and besides eliminating snoring this technique substantially improves nocturnal cardiovascular function, daytime sleepiness and quality of life. Dental appliances that keep the airways open have been shown to be effective in some people. A surgical option (to remove redundant tissue in the upper airway) is sometimes chosen, while inhaling nasal corticoids are a possible alternative in light to medium severity cases of obstructive sleep apnoea. Tonsillectomy is indicated only in serious cases. Medication is sometimes prescribed.

best course of action?
Seek a consultation with a sleep-medicine specialist for evaluation, diagnosis and possible treatment of obstructive sleep apnoea. Also seek psychotherapy for associated Breathing-Related Sleep Disorder.

in the meantime what can you do?
1. Learn everything you can about sleep and Breathing-Related Sleep Disorder.
2. If you have a partner, ask him or her for feedback. Otherwise, set up a video machine to record yourself during sleep. In which position do you snore the worst, or exhibit signs that your breathing is obstructed? Which position is the best for you to avoid such problems? Once you have this information, try to sleep in the optimum position.
3. It may be that you snore less on your side. Create a sleeping arrangement that will not allow you to turn onto your back, for example wear a T-shirt that has a pocket back to front, with a tennis ball inserted in the pocket. This will be uncomfortable when you turn onto your back and cause you to reverse your position.
4. Try various pillows to see if you can create the least possible obstruction to your airways.
5. Losing weight sometimes helps. Try this, particularly if you happen to be overweight. Choose a safe and gradual weight-loss programme.
6. Stay away from alcohol and drugs.
7. It is important to establish and maintain good sleeping habits. Ensure that you go to bed at the same time every night and wake at the same time every morning. Do not allow yourself to exceed eight hours' sleep.
8. Plan a wake-up routine that involves rituals designed to stimulate you, such as a cool shower or bath, physical stretches/exercise and a cup of tea or coffee.
9. Work on lowering your general level of stress.
10. If you have disturbing thoughts roaming through your mind at night that prevent you sleeping soundly, begin to write them down. What is the

theme? Learning more about your anxieties will help you to begin to solve them, but solve them during the daytime – not at night.

11. If you think you may be suffering from Anxiety (see page 37ff) or Depression (see page 15ff), seek treatment and follow the self-help guidelines.

12. Practise meditation, t'ai chi or yoga during the day.

13. Exercise as much as you can safely manage, but do it in the morning, never in the evening.

14. If you have a spouse or partner, educate him or her about your Sleep Disorder and ask for help. Take your partner with you when you go to see your sleep specialist for the first time. He or she will be able to provide valuable information about your breathing obstruction.

15. Sleeping in the same room as someone with Breathing-Related Sleep Disorder is very difficult and can create sleep problems for a partner. Understand and be tolerant if you are asked to sleep elsewhere until your Breathing-Related Sleep Disorder is treated (don't take it personally).

16. Be very careful not to drive a vehicle or operate dangerous machinery when you are feeling sleepy.

when your child is suffering from breathing-related sleep disorder

1. Children with Breathing-Related Sleep Disorder need to be evaluated by a sleep-medicine specialist to determine the underlying physiological cause and implement treatment.

2. Seek an evaluation with a mental-health professional too.

3. Your child may have already suffered some ridicule from peers as a result of his or her snoring and/or daytime sleepiness. Help your child to raise his or her self-esteem (see page 105).

4. Help your child with Breathing-Related Sleep Disorder to receive the best treatment available.

5. Make sure your child is protected from falling asleep in situations where he or she might be in physical danger.

6. Read everything you can about Breathing-Related Sleep Disorder.

7. Establish a definite bedtime and wake-up time for your child and consistently stick to these.

8. Establish a consistent and welcoming wake-up routine for your child encouraging him or her to rise at the same time every day and eat a nutritious breakfast.

9. Establish a consistent and soothing bedtime routine for your child,

perhaps involving a bath, warm drink, bedtime story and comforting hugs.

10. Make sure that your child's bedroom is a calm place without flashing lights from electronics or digital displays. If your child needs a night light, provide a low-level one.

11. Try increasing the amount of daily physical exercise your child gets, but make sure this occurs well before bedtime.

12. Remember that child sufferers need a great deal of help adjusting to this problem and its treatment.

helpful books

The Promise of Sleep: A Pioneer in Sleep Medicine Explores the Vital Connection between Health, Happiness, and a Good Night's Sleep, W. C. Dement and C. Vaughan. Dell Publishing Co., 1999.

Desperately Seeking Snoozin': The Insomnia Cure from Awake to Zzzzz, J. Wiedman. Towering Pines Press, 1999.

The Woman's Book of Sleep: A Complete Resource Guide, A. R. Wolfson. Oakland, Calif.: New Harbinger Publications, 2001.

circadian rhythm sleep disorder

Flying in aeroplanes across time zones isn't the only way to create a problem in a person's sleep-wake cycle. Our circadian rhythms are regulated by a master circadian clock, and are synchronized by light, melatonin and social or physical activity to the twenty-four-hour cycle of day and night. So, for example, being exposed to extremely bright light at the wrong part of the day can put a person in a near-permanent state akin to jetlag.

case study: Bert

Bert, a fifty-year-old leather-worker, was admitted to a sleep institute complaining of severe fatigue and daytime sleepiness. Previously, he had been diagnosed with Depression and chronic fatigue syndrome, and was given antidepressant drugs which failed to improve his condition. He said that over the past twenty years an irregular sleep-wake pattern had evolved, and that this had caused him great distress and severe difficulty functioning at home, at work and socially. This situation had got so bad he had even been forced to switch to a part-time position seven years ago, because he was unable to maintain a regular full-time job schedule. A sleep specialist evaluated Bert, found that he had abnormal circadian rhythm patterns and diagnosed him as suffering from irregular sleep-wake pattern. He tried treatment with melatonin, but that did not improve his condition. A further investigation of the Bert's daily habits and environmental conditions revealed that his occupation required him to work under a daylight intensity lamp, and that his exposure to bright light occurred mostly at night (he worked a night shift). To improve his circadian rhythm and stabilize his sleep-wake pattern, he was asked to take melatonin in the evening, combined with bright light therapy at 9.00 a.m. every morning. He was also advised to avoid bright light in the evening. A week later his sleep-wake pattern was stable, and he reported profound improvement in staying awake during the day.

is this you (or someone close to you)?

Your sleep is frequently disturbed, leading to excessive sleepiness, because your work/shift/travel schedule is at odds with your circadian sleep-wake pattern.

This causes you problems at work, in social and other situations.

'do not pass go' signs

Excessive sleepiness can lead to accidents. Tripping, falling asleep while driving, falling off scaffolding or making errors while operating machinery can all be life-threatening occurrences. Increased irritability can accompany a lack of regular sleep, and this can cause relationship problems, parenting issues and problems in the workplace. A disturbed sleep pattern can also make a person less productive and more likely to make errors in judgement.

what causes circadian rhythm sleep disorder?

Circadian Rhythm Sleep Disorder occurs when there is an alteration of the internal circadian timing mechanisms or a misalignment between the timing of sleep and the twenty-four-hour social and physical environments. Chronic exposure to bright light at the wrong biological time (that is, during the night-time) may also have serious effects on the circadian sleep-wake patterns.

what happens in your brain?

The master circadian clock is located in a part of the brain known as the suprachiasmatic nucleus of the hypothalamus. Dysfunction in this system will bring about symptoms of Circadian Rhythm Sleep Disorder.

which treatments are likely to work?

The obvious way to improve this problem is to change your schedule, but sometimes this is not possible and it won't necessarily cure the problem. It is essential to consult a sleep-medicine specialist. In addition to good sleeping habits, both light and melatonin, appropriately timed, have been shown to improve human circadian rhythms. Melatonin can reduce core body temperature and induce sleepiness. Because behavioural and environmental factors are often involved in the development and maintenance of these disorders, treatment combining behavioural and/or pharmacological approaches is usually required. Cognitive-behavioural therapy and hypnosis can also be helpful.

best course of action?

Have a consultation with a sleep-medicine specialist, and seek psychotherapy as well from an experienced psychotherapist.

in the meantime what can you do?

1. Learn everything you can about sleep and Circadian Rhythm Sleep Disorder (see reading list below).

2. Be your own detective. What factors in your work, family or social life might be contributing to Circadian Rhythm Sleep Disorder? Do you frequently travel across time zones? Are you exposed to bright light during the night-time? Write down your thoughts about what might be throwing your circadian rhythms off track.

3. It is essential to get some accurate information about your sleep habits by keeping a sleep diary. When you see a sleep-medicine specialist, take it with you. For at least two weeks record exactly how much sleep you are getting, the times and amount, and when you drop off and wake during the day. You may need help from others to record this accurately. Also record your impression of the quality of sleep you get (that is, sound, medium or light) and how you feel when you wake up from every bout of sleep.

4. It is important to create better sleeping habits. If you can, redesign your schedule so that you go to bed at the same time every night, and wake at the same time every morning. Do not allow yourself to exceed eight hours' sleep.

5. Plan a bedtime routine that involves soothing and calming rituals such as a warm shower or bath relaxation and a cup of chamomile tea.

6. Make your bedroom a place for sleep. Remove work, computer and other mind-stimulating paraphernalia.

7. If you cannot get to sleep, do not get up and do something 'productive'. Stay in bed with the light out and practise relaxation (see exercise page 41).

8. Plan a wake-up routine that involves rituals designed to stimulate you, such as a cool shower or bath, physical exercise and a cup of tea or coffee.

9. Work on lowering your general level of stress.

10. Alcohol and drugs will not help you with this disorder, and may cause more problems in the long run. Do not be tempted to use them to treat your Circadian Rhythm Sleep Disorder.

11. If you have disturbing thoughts roaming through your mind at night that prevent you sleeping soundly, begin to write them down. What is the theme? Learning more about your anxieties will help you to begin to solve them, but solve them during the daytime – not at night.

12. You may be suffering from Anxiety (see page 37ff) or Post-Traumatic Stress Disorder (see page 62). Seek treatment and follow the self-help guidelines.

13. Practise meditation, t'ai chi or yoga during the day.

14. Exercise as much as you can safely manage, but do it in the morning, never in the evening.

15. If you have a spouse or partner, educate him or her about your Sleep Disorder and ask for help implementing better sleep habits.

16. If you have a job that involves being responsible for public safety, you need to consider taking leave until you can be treated.

17. If your Circadian Rhythm Sleep Disorder tends to make you drowsy during the day, driving could be dangerous for you and others. It would be prudent not to get behind the wheel until you have full control over your disorder.

18. Be very careful not to operate dangerous machinery when you are feeling sleepy.

when your child is suffering from circadian rhythm sleep disorder

1. Children with Circadian Rhythm Sleep Disorder need to be evaluated by a sleep-medicine specialist to determine the reason for it and implement treatment.

2. Read everything you can about Circadian Rhythm Sleep Disorder.

3. Help your child with Circadian Rhythm Sleep Disorder to receive the best treatment available.

4. Help your child to deal with problems associated with Circadian Rhythm Disorder, such as missing school (or falling asleep at school), missing out on peer activities, being excessively fatigued or wide awake in the middle of the night. Behavioural psychotherapy can be helpful.

5. Make sure your child is protected from falling asleep in situations where he or she might be in physical danger.

6. Establish a definite bedtime and wake-up time for your child, and consistently stick to these.

7. Establish a consistent and welcoming wake-up routine for your child encouraging them to rise at the same time every day and eat a nutritious breakfast.

8. Establish a consistent and soothing bedtime routine for your child, perhaps involving a bath, warm drink, bedtime story and comforting hugs.

9. Make sure that your child's bedroom is a calm place without flashing lights from electronics or digital displays. If your child needs a night light, provide a low-level one.

10. Try increasing the amount of daily physical exercise your child gets, but make sure this occurs well before bedtime.

11. Remember that child sufferers need a great deal of help adjusting to this problem and its treatment.

helpful books

The Promise of Sleep: A Pioneer in Sleep Medicine Explores the Vital Connection between Health, Happiness, and a Good Night's Sleep, W. C. Dement and C. Vaughan. Dell Publishing Co., 1999.

Desperately Seeking Snoozin': The Insomnia Cure from Awake to Zzzzz, J. Wiedman. Towering Pines Press, 1999.

The Woman's Book of Sleep: A Complete Resource Guide, A. R. Wolfson. Oakland, Calif.: New Harbinger Publications, 2001.

nightmare disorder

You're being chased by a bad man wielding an AK-47. Funny thing is, he reminds you of your boss. You wake up in something of a panic and cannot get back to sleep for hours. The following morning, you are fatigued, irritable and snap at your partner. If this happens once it's just a nightmare; if it happens repeatedly you might have a disorder.

case study: Nancy

A woman came to see me suffering from frequent, intense, terrifying nightmares. At some point each night Nancy was waking up alert with the memory of a frightening nightmare in which she was being pursued, attacked or terrorized in some other way. Nancy was a twenty-eight-year-old mother of three young children when she was very suddenly arrested and thrown into prison for a crime she did not commit. Although the fact that she was a victim of mistaken identity was discovered and she was released within days, her ordeal affected her deeply. Her fears for her children as well as for herself, and the sense that the ordered world she once knew had disintegrated without warning, had long-lasting effects. Nancy needed to be treated for the trauma she had sustained. Once she began to heal from the horrors of her false accusation her nightmares become less frequent and eventually disappeared.

is this you (or someone close to you)?
- You repeatedly wake from deep sleep or naps with the memory of terrifying nightmares. These usually follow threatening themes of threats to safety, survival or emotional integrity.
- Once awake, you immediately become alert.

'do not pass go' signs
Nightmares may affect a person's sleep quality and quantity, but of greater concern is the fact that having nightmares is one of the symptoms of Post-Traumatic Stress Disorder (see page 62), which in itself needs to be treated. If a person is consistently having bad nightmares, it is important to investigate the underlying cause. There is also a link between Nightmare Disorder and both Depression and suicide.

what causes nightmare disorder?
Nightmares are a common response to traumatic events. In addition, alcohol or sedative use, sleep deprivation, interruption to a person's sleep-wake cycle, fatigue and physical or emotional stress can make it more likely that someone will have episodes of Nightmare Disorder.

what happens in your brain?
Nightmares occur during REM sleep.

which treatments are likely to work?

Psychotherapy from a clinician who is experienced in treating Nightmare Disorder would be useful. The correct therapy can instigate an increase in sleep quality and quantity, and also play a part in reducing Anxiety, Depression and Post-Traumatic Stress Disorder symptoms. One cognitive-behavioural method that may be particularly helpful is Lucid Dreaming Treatment, in which a person is taught to realize that he or she is dreaming and alter the storyline to a more positive one during the nightmare itself. Hypnotherapy can also be extremely effective in reducing a person's nightmares, and it provides the additional benefits of increased relaxation and improved sleep. Psychoanalytically based treatment of Post-Traumatic Stress Disorder may be useful in examining the content of the nightmares, discovering the meaning, then getting to the root of the trauma and instigating long-term relief. Medication can be of value in Nightmare Disorder, but some medications and recreational drugs can exacerbate or even cause nightmares.

best course of action?

Seek psychotherapy.

in the meantime what can you do?

1. Learn everything you can about sleep and Nightmare Disorder (see reading list below).
2. Create a nightmare diary. You will have to remind yourself to write down the content of your nightmares, as well as the date and approximate time, the minute you wake up. Keep a pen and paper by your bed.
3. If your nightmares are causing you to lose sleep and/or making you excessively sleepy during the daytime, create a sleep log as well. This means writing down exactly when you sleep and when you wake, as well as a rating of the quality of sleep you get each time. Take this log and your nightmare diary with you to your psychotherapist.
4. In many cultures, such as those of Native Americans and Australian Aborigines, great attention is placed on the content of dreams, and a nightmare would be viewed as carrying important information. Dreams are also an important part of psychodynamic or psychoanalytic theory and practice. It's worth considering taking your dreams to a therapist, enrolling in a psychologically based dream-tending course, or undergoing dream analysis to help you connect with your unconscious mind and understand the true meaning of your nightmares – especially

if they are recurring. Cognitive-behavioural methods will treat the symptoms, but there is more to discover if you are willing.

5. Educate your spouse or person you sleep with about Nightmare Disorder. Understand that your nightmares are having a detrimental effect on him or her. In some cases Nightmare Disorder can trigger a Sleep Disorder in the sufferer's partner. Don't take it personally if your partner requests that you sleep separately (if possible) until treatment is underway.

6. If your nightmares are causing you to have an interrupted sleep pattern, you are also at risk for developing another Sleep Disorder such as Insomnia or Hypersomnia. It is important to create better sleeping habits. Redesign your schedule so that you go to bed at the same time every night, and wake at the same time every morning.

7. Plan a bedtime routine that involves soothing and calming rituals such as a warm shower or bath, relaxation and a cup of chamomile tea.

8. Make your bedroom a place for calm, restorative sleep. Remove work, computer and other mind-stimulating paraphernalia.

9. If you cannot get to sleep, do not get up and do something 'productive'. Stay in bed with the light out and practise relaxation (see exercise page 41).

10. Plan a wake-up routine that involves rituals designed to stimulate you, such as a cool shower or bath, physical exercise and a cup of tea or coffee.

11. Work on lowering your general level of stress.

12. Alcohol and drugs will not help cure your Nightmare Disorder. Avoid them.

13. If you have disturbing thoughts roaming through your mind at night that prevent you sleeping soundly, begin to write them down. What is the theme? Learning more about your anxieties will help you to begin to solve them, but solve them during the daytime – not at night.

14. You may be suffering from Anxiety (see page 37ff) or Post-Traumatic Stress Disorder (see page 62). Seek treatment and follow the self-help guidelines.

15. Practise meditation, t'ai chi or yoga during the day.

16. Exercise as much as you can safely manage, but do it in the morning, never in the evening.

17. Be very careful not to drive vehicles or operate dangerous machinery when you are feeling sleepy.

when your child suffers from nightmare disorder

1. Learn everything you can about Nightmare Disorder.
2. Help your child to reduce his or her stress or anxiety (see page 38).
3. Help your child to self-soothe (see page 258).
4. Establish a soothing and consistent bedtime routine for your child, perhaps involving a bath, warm drink, bedtime story and comforting hugs.
5. If your child is worried about something, try to encourage him or her to talk about it with you prior to the start of the bedtime routine. Try to help resolve the problem or concern so that physiological and psychological calming can take place as early as possible.
6. If your child wakes with a nightmare and calls out to you, do attend and try to soothe him or her, but discourage him or her from getting up and doing something that might be stimulating and stop them getting back to sleep.
7. Make sure that your child's bedroom is a calm place without flashing lights from electronics or digital displays. If your child needs a night light, provide a low-level one.
8. Limit your child's exposure to TV or video games with violent or disturbing content.
9. Playing stimulating video games or watching exciting TV just before bedtime is a bad idea. These kinds of activities should be moved to earlier in the day.
10. If your child is taking medication, check with your doctor to find out if having nightmares is one of the side effects.
11. Try increasing the amount of daily physical exercise your child gets, but make sure this occurs well before bedtime.
12. Is your child worried about something? Obsessing? Is he or she restless? Try to soothe your child, but if you are unable to do so seek therapy for your child with an experienced, qualified mental-health professional.

helpful books

Banishing Night Terrors and Nightmares: A Breakthrough Program to Heal the Traumas That Shatter Peaceful Sleep, C. R. Carranza and J. R. Dill. Kensington Books, 2004.

'Sleep Disturbances', in M. A. Leitz, C. N. Dulmus and L. A. Rapp-Paglicci (eds.), *Handbook of Preventive Interventions for Adults*, John Wiley & Sons, 2005.

sleep terror disorder

Imagine frequently waking up screaming, but not knowing why. A person experiencing the symptoms of Sleep Terror Disorder is unable to remember his or her nightmare, yet is left in a state of extreme fear. And this disorder is almost as distressing for the sufferer's partner as it is for the sufferer.

case study: Sally

A six-year-old girl was brought to my office by her grandmother Su Lin, who was her primary carer. Su Lin had first taken Sally to see their paediatrician, insisting that her granddaughter was having 'ghost attacks' at night. Su Lin had been brought up in China where local beliefs included such possibilities. Not knowing quite what to make of this, the paediatrician referred them to me. I began to inquire about the nature of these 'ghost attacks' and realized that the symptoms Su Lin ascribed to Sally sounded very similar to those associated with Sleep Terror Disorder. Sally would wake up screaming and panicking. Her grandmother would rush to her side, but Sally would have no memory of what had just occurred. Sally was made all the more anxious by the ghost stories her grandmother was now telling her before she went to sleep. I tried to educate Su Lin about Sleep Terror Disorder, but it wasn't until I suggested she set up a video camera one night so we could both observe what happened just prior to one of Sally's awakenings that we began to make progress. We viewed the tape together, and it was clear that just prior to waking Sally was having a nightmare. Su Lin was persuaded to focus on soothing Sally and encouraging her to do exercises to reduce her anxiety. She agreed that, while the stories from her culture were important and should be passed on to Sally one day, this was not the time.

is this you (or someone close to you)?
- Repeatedly wakes from sleeping with a scream that expresses panic.
- During each episode there is heightened fear, rapid breathing and sweating.
- Despite the efforts of others, cannot be comforted during the episode.
- On waking, cannot recall details of the dream and forgets that the episode occurred.

'do not pass go' signs
People experiencing Sleep Terror Disorder experience significant distress, even though they may not remember the episode. They run the risk of self-injury (especially if it is accompanied by movements such as diving out of

bed), and there is also the threat of injury to the spouse or partner from flailing limbs. Partners may develop a Sleep Disorder themselves, or suffer from daytime sleepiness, due to being repeatedly woken by loud cries, vocalizations and violent movement, as well as being concerned about their partner's distress and threat of injury to either.

Sleep problems are very prevalent during childhood and may adversely affect a child's development. Moreover, nightmares, night terrors and sleep-walking often occur together. School problems, parental divorce, physical injury and a high degree of watching TV may all be associated with night terrors.

what causes sleep terror disorder?

Sleep Terror Disorder tends to run in families, and close relatives of sufferers have a higher chance of having Sleep Terror Disorder than others do. Sleep Terror Disorder can be caused by central nervous system activation, neurologic disorders, Post-Traumatic Stress Disorder, Depression, chronic ethanol or amphetamine abuse and withdrawal, or a mixture of various disorders.

what happens in your brain?

Sleep Terror Disorder usually occurs during slow-wave sleep.

which treatments are likely to work?

Treatment of Sleep Terror Disorder usually consists of a combination of psychotherapy and medication, relaxation techniques and behaviour modification. Hypnosis is frequently used as well. It may be prudent to consult a sleep specialist to obtain information about the quality of sleep and the amount of oxygen the sufferer is getting at night, and to rule out sleep apnoea.

best course of action?

Seek psychotherapy from an experienced therapist who can perform cognitive-behavioural therapy, hypnosis, and/or psychodynamic or psychoanalytic psychotherapy. Also consult a sleep-medicine specialist.

in the meantime what can you do?

1. Learn everything you can about sleep and Sleep Terror Disorder.
2. Educate others about Sleep Terror Disorder, especially those who live with you. They will be experiencing some negative effects of your disorder.

3. If you have a partner who sleeps with you consult with him or her about your symptoms. He or she will probably be more aware of them than you are.

4. Ask your partner to help you create a diary of sleep terror events that will record the time and duration of each episode and how you behaved during it.

5. Since you will have little recollection of your sleep terrors, it would be beneficial to have your partner accompany you to provide information when you first consult with a psychotherapist and/or sleep-medicine specialist.

6. It is important to create good sleeping habits. Design your schedule so that you go to bed at the same time every night, and wake at the same time every morning.

7. Avoid having too much stimulation in the hours that precede bedtime. Horror movies, for example may be better viewed earlier on – or not at all.

8. Plan a bedtime routine that involves soothing and calming rituals such as a warm shower or bath, relaxation and a cup of chamomile tea.

9. Make your bedroom a place for soothing, refreshing sleep. Remove work, computer and other mind-stimulating paraphernalia.

10. If you cannot get back to sleep after waking in terror, do not get up to do something. Stay in bed with the light out and practise relaxation (see exercise page 41).

11. Plan a wake-up routine that involves rituals designed to stimulate you, such as a cool shower or bath, physical exercise and a cup of tea or coffee.

12. Work on lowering your general level of stress.

13. If you have disturbing thoughts roaming through your mind at night that prevent you sleeping soundly, begin to write them down. What is the theme? Learning more about your anxieties will help you to begin to solve them, but solve them during the daytime – not at night.

14. You may be suffering from Anxiety (see page 37ff) or Post-Traumatic Stress Disorder (see page 62). Seek treatment and follow the self-help guidelines.

15. Practise meditation, t'ai chi or yoga during the day.

16. Exercise as much as you can safely manage, but do it in the morning, never in the evening.

17. If you have a spouse or partner, educate him or her about your Sleep Disorder and ask for help implementing better sleep habits.

18. Be very careful not to drive or operate heavy machinery if you are feeling sleepy.

when your child suffers from sleep terror disorder

1. Learn everything you can about Sleep Terror Disorder.
2. Help your child to reduce his or her stress or anxiety (see page 19).
3. Help your child to self-soothe (see page 258).
4. Establish a soothing and consistent bedtime routine for your child, perhaps involving a bath, warm drink, bedtime story and comforting hugs.
5. If your child is worried about something, try to encourage him or her to talk about it with you prior to the start of the bedtime routine. Try to help resolve the problem or concern so that physiological and psychological calming can take place as early as possible.
6. If your child wakes in terror and calls out to you do try to soothe him or her, but discourage him or her from getting up and doing something that might be stimulating and stop them getting back to sleep.
7. Make sure that your child's bedroom is a calm place without flashing lights from electronics or digital displays. If your child needs a night light, provide a low-level one.
8. Limit your child's exposure to TV or video games with violent or disturbing content.
9. Playing stimulating video games or watching exciting TV just before bedtime is a bad idea. These kinds of activities should be moved to earlier in the day.
10. If your child is taking medication, check with your doctor to find out if having sleep terrors is one of the side effects.
11. Try increasing the amount of daily physical exercise your child gets, but make sure this occurs well before bedtime.
12. Is your child worried about something? Obsessing? Is he or she restless? Try to soothe your child, but if you are unable to do so seek therapy for your child with an experienced, qualified mental-health professional.

helpful books

Banishing Night Terrors and Nightmares: A Breakthrough Program to Heal the Traumas That Shatter Peaceful Sleep, C. R. Carranza and J. R. Dill. Kensington Books, 2004.

'Sleep Disturbances', in M. A. Leitz, C. N. Dulmus and L. A. Rapp-Paglicci (eds), *Handbook of Preventive Interventions For Adults*, John Wiley & Sons, 2005.

sleepwalking disorder

Bellini's opera *La Sonnambula* glamourized sleepwalking, but the disorder is hardly something to sing about. Sleepwalking Disorder can produce behaviour that is disturbing, embarrassing and even dangerous.

case study: Molly

Everyone on campus knew that Molly was 'into' zombies. She had a collection of black-and-white films such as the classic I Walked With a Zombie *and she organized 'Zombie Nights' showing the films in the small cinema attached to the film school where she was enrolled. So no one thought anything of it when Molly began to be seen wandering around the halls in a 'zombie-like' state – apparently asleep, expressionless, with her eyes half closed. Her unusual long, dark clothing completed the picture observers believed she was trying to present. In fact, Molly had Sleepwalking Disorder, but because no one said anything to her about seeing her like this her problem was not discovered until a year afterwards.*

During a trip to her family home, Molly terrified her younger sister Jane by entering her room late at night 'looking weird', sitting down on her bed and staring blankly at her. Their parents came in when Jane screamed and they scolded Molly for scaring her. The following night, Jane saw Molly walking slowly in a similar state along the upstairs landing. She did not call out this time, but the next day she took an axe from her father's workshop to hide under her pillow in case she was 'attacked by the zombie'. The results of all this were very nearly tragic, because when Molly entered Jane's room again a couple of nights later, her sister took out her 'weapon' and tried to attack her, targeting her head and heart as she'd learned from Molly's films. Fortunately she was not strong enough to do any real damage, but Molly was surprised to wake up and find herself bleeding and her sister with an axe at the ready. Both sisters were sent to a family therapist, who discovered the cause of it all and treated Molly for Sleepwalking Disorder. From then on, zombies ceased to play such an important role in Molly's life.

is this you (or someone close to you)?

- Frequently gets out of bed while asleep and walks about.
- During sleepwalking, has a blank face and is not responsive when people try to wake or communicate with him or her.
- Does not remember sleepwalking after waking up.

'do not pass go' signs

People have been known to injure themselves during episodes of sleepwalking. Chronic sleepwalking is frequently associated with Sleep-Related Breathing Disorder, which needs to be ruled out. Seek treatment immediately.

what causes sleepwalking disorder?

A person suffering from Sleepwalking Disorder has no voluntary control over their actions; a dysfunction in the autonomic nervous system is controlling the sleepwalker's behaviour and mood.

which treatments are likely to work?

Therapy or medication can be of value in Sleepwalking Disorder, and hypnotherapy can also work well. It may be prudent to consult a sleep specialist to obtain information about the quality of sleep and the amount of oxygen you are getting at night, and to rule out sleep apnoea and other problems. If sleep apnoea is diagnosed and treated, the Sleepwalking Disorder may disappear as well.

best course of action?

Seek psychotherapy. An initial evaluation will help you find out if your Sleepwalking Disorder is secondary to another disorder, such as Post-Traumatic Stress Disorder, Depression or Anxiety. A medical evaluation may also be necessary to rule out physiological problems.

in the meantime what can you do?

1. Learn everything you can about sleep and Sleepwalking Disorder (see reading list below).
2. Educate people close to you about Sleepwalking Disorder, especially those who live with you. They will be experiencing some negative effects of your disorder.
3. Make sure your sleeping space is safe so that you cannot injure yourself; for example, by bumping into something sharp, walking off a balcony and so on.
4. If your partner sleeps with you, consult with him or her about your symptoms. He or she will probably be more aware of them than you are. Ask them to help you create a diary of your sleepwalking events (such as when they occur and your behaviour).
5. Since you will have little recollection of your sleepwalking, it would be

beneficial to have your partner accompany you to provide information when you first consult with a psychotherapist and/or sleep-medicine specialist.

6. It is important to create better sleeping habits. Redesign your schedule so that you go to bed at the same time every night, and wake up at the same time every morning.

7. Plan a bedtime routine that involves soothing and calming rituals such as a warm shower or bath, relaxation and a cup of chamomile tea.

8. Make your bedroom a place for sleep. Remove work, computer and other mind-stimulating paraphernalia.

9. If at any point you cannot get to sleep, do not get up and do something productive. Stay in bed with the light out and practise relaxation (see exercise page 41).

10. Plan a wake-up routine that involves rituals designed to stimulate you, such as a cool shower or bath, physical exercise and a cup of tea or coffee.

11. Work on lowering your general level of stress.

12. If you have disturbing thoughts roaming through your mind at night, begin to write them down. What is the theme? Learning more about your anxieties will help you to begin to solve them, but solve them during the daytime – not at night.

13. You may be suffering from Anxiety (see page 37ff) or Post-Traumatic Stress Disorder (see page 62). Seek treatment, and follow the self-help guidelines.

14. Practise meditation, t'ai chi or yoga during the day.

15. Exercise as much as you can safely manage, but do it in the morning, never in the evening.

16. Be very careful not to drive vehicles or operate dangerous machinery if you are feeling sleepy.

when your child suffers from sleepwalking disorder

1. Learn everything you can about Sleepwalking Disorder.

2. Make sure your child is protected in his or her sleeping environment so that there is no risk of walking into danger.

3. When your child sleepwalks, gently lead him or her back to bed. Try not to wake the child.

4. If your child is taking medication, check with your doctor to find out if sleepwalking is one of the side effects.

5. Help your child to reduce his or her stress or anxiety (see page 38).

6. Help your child to self-soothe (see page 258).

7. Establish a soothing and consistent bedtime routine for your child, perhaps involving a bath, warm drink, bedtime story and comforting hugs.

8. If your child is worried about something, try to encourage him or her to talk about it with you prior to the start of the bedtime routine. Try to help resolve the problem or concern so that physiological and psychological calming can take place as early as possible.

9. Create a diary of sleepwalking for your child, and have it available when you attend an appointment with a sleep-medicine specialist or psychotherapist.

helpful books

Banishing Night Terrors and Nightmares: A Breakthrough Program to Heal the Traumas That Shatter Peaceful Sleep, C. R. Carranza and J. R. Dill. Kensington Books, 2004.

'Sleep Disturbances', in M. A. Leitz, C. N. Dulmus and L. A. Rapp-Paglicci (eds), Handbook of Preventive Interventions for Adults, John Wiley & Sons, 2005.

The Woman's Book of Sleep: A Complete Resource Guide, A. R. Wolfson. Oakland, Calif.: New Harbinger Publications, 2001.

The Promise of Sleep: A Pioneer in Sleep Medicine Explores the Vital Connection between Health, Happiness, and a Good Night's Sleep, W. C. Dement and C. Vaughan. Dell Publishing Co., 1999.

chapter 13
now what? getting the right help

You don't have to be 'abnormal', 'sick' or even suffering from one of the disorders described in this book to seek and benefit from psychotherapy. Besides being healing, the process of sitting down and talking to someone about your life, your relationships, your fears, worries, hopes and dreams can be enriching, validating and rewarding. It can make the difference between failure and success in handling a work environment, sustaining a marriage or providing good parenting for your children. It can lead to profound improvements in the way people feel, the way they view themselves and the way they interact with others.

Therapy also saves lives. Every year, many thousands of adults, adolescents and children take their own lives in preference to feeling desperately miserable; yet there are scientifically validated psychological methods that could have helped them. If you (or someone close to you) need to talk to someone, do take steps to try to find a therapist, especially if you think you might be suffering from one of the disorders described in this book. At the very least, follow the self-help suggestions.

when should you seek therapy?

If you can find appropriate ways to help yourself, for example, if following the self-help suggestions in this book works for you there is no need to seek therapy. However, there are times when it is absolutely imperative that you seek treatment:

- If you have been thinking of killing or harming yourself.
- If you have had strong desires to be violent or have frequent angry outbursts.
- If you have severe mood swings.
- If you are seeing, hearing, tasting or smelling things that are not experienced by other people.
- If you have strange or intrusive thoughts or visions.
- If you are abusing alcohol and/or drugs, gambling, shopping, stealing, pulling out your hair, cutting yourself, engaging in non-consensual sexual acts, starting fires, destroying property or committing other impulsive acts and cannot stop despite the fact that this is causing you problems.
- If your child shows signs of having one of the disorders described in Chapter 12.

The following situations are those where it would be most advisable to seek help from a therapist:

- If you have been feeling very 'down' for at least two or three weeks.
- If something traumatic has happened to you and you are having trouble getting over it.
- If, for two or more weeks, you have had severe worries that you know are being unrealistic.
- If you are having problems keeping your job or handling your work environment.
- If you have lapses in memory.
- If you have trouble concentrating.
- If you have persistent anxiety.
- If you have problems with your weight or the way you eat.
- If you are very concerned about some aspects of your physical health even though your doctor says you are fine.
- If you have severe family or relationship problems.

how to choose a therapist

Search for someone who has good qualifications (you'll probably have to be referred via your GP), which usually means being well-trained in a respected theoretical tradition of clinical work and/or a degree from an approved institution or university. Most importantly, in choosing a therapist you should feel safe and comfortable with that person. A good therapist will never be judgemental of you, will treat everything you say in therapy as completely confidential, and will never, ever make sexual advances to you. He or she will be fair and honest in financial matters, will have no other type of relationship with you (for example, be a friend, family member, employer or babysitter) and will put the focus on you. A good therapist will always explain clearly any relevant legal aspects of therapy.

Currently there is no legislation which prevents individuals without proper training from setting up a practice and calling themselves counsellors or psychotherapists, so ideally choose a therapist who is one of the below:

1. An accredited member of the British Association for Counselling and Psychotherapy (www.bacp.co.uk). Ordinary membership is no guarantee of adequate training.
2. Registered with the United Kingdom Council for Psychotherapy (www.psychotherapy.org.uk).
3. Registered with the British Confederation of Psychotherapists (www.bcp.org.uk).
4. Chartered by the British Psychological Society (www.bps.org.uk). Membership alone does not guarantee adequate clinical experience or qualification.

There is a strong tradition of psychoanalysis and psychoanalytic psychotherapy in the UK. To find a qualified psychoanalyst, analytical psychologist, psychoanalytic psychotherapist or child psychotherapist with proper training search the list provided by the British Psychoanalytical Society at: www.psychoanalysis.org.uk/uklist.htm or the websites of the BCP or the UKCP.

what happens in therapy?

Therapy can take a number of different forms, but it is usually a talking process in which you sit or lie down in a private office. You will probably first be asked why you are seeking therapy, and then the therapist might ask you about your background and history. You should be rigorously honest with your trusted therapist. You might be given homework exercises, or your therapist might suggest that you have an additional type of treatment such as biofeedback or medication.

Therapy is a tried and trusted way to get help for psychological problems but there are no guarantees and occasionally it fails to work. But in the course of my work as a psychotherapist I have seen daily successes. It is not a passive process and therapy can be hard work for the person being treated as well as for the therapist. Treatment can be brief or long, and it's as well to ask your therapist about the expected length of treatment (although it's not always possible to gauge that exactly at the beginning). Your relationship with the therapist is meant to be one-sided – in other words you will not be hearing about the therapist's life because the therapy is about you.

types of therapy

Therapy can be carried out with an individual, a couple, a group or a family as in the following:

Individual Psychotherapy, Psychoanalysis or Counselling The therapist works with one person in one of many styles (see below).

Couples Psychotherapy or Counselling Both partners of a committed relationship are treated at the same time for the relationship issues they are currently facing. If the couple is married this may also be known as marital therapy or marital counselling.

Conjoint Therapy or Counselling Both partners in a relationship or two or more family members receive therapy together, rather than being treated separately.

Co-therapy Two therapists work with one or more clients on current issues, such as improving interpersonal relationships or changing maladaptive behaviour.

Group Psychotherapy or Counselling Two or more people interact with each other, in what is designed to be a safe and trusting environment. They share their psychological issues, interpersonal struggles and emotional difficulties while one or more psychotherapists facilitate psychological improvement, mutual respect, and the deepening of self-understanding and empathy between each participant.

Family Therapy A type of therapy where therapist and clients work on improving relationships and behaviour patterns within the family.

common therapies

There are many different styles of psychotherapy and these are based on various ideas and traditions that were developed by different pioneers, and, initially, there is no precise way to know which one will be the right one for you. Even the results of studies do not tell us very much, because certain types of therapy (for example, cognitive-behavioural) lend themselves better to being scrutinized, and have been the focus of more research studies than other forms of therapy.

The best way to choose a psychotherapist is to find out which trained and qualified mental-health professionals are available to treat you in your area (if you have the luxury of choice), then sit down with each of them and decide if you feel comfortable and safe in his or her presence. Many people believe it is the therapeutic relationship that has the most curative potential, irrespective of the therapist's orientation. Nevertheless, here are some of the most common styles of therapy, in alphabetical order:

Acceptance and Commitment Therapy This is a type of cognitive-behavioural therapy in which clients are helped to accept problematic thoughts and feelings, abandon styles of coping that don't work, and act in accordance with their own values and goals.

Active-analytic Psychotherapy encompasses the approach of German psychoanalyst Wilhelm Stekel. The analyst takes a more active role than is usual for traditional psychoanalysis, and focuses more on current problems in the patient's life rather than on early childhood issues.

Activity-play Therapy In order to encourage a child to express emotion openly, he or she is given dolls and other play materials so that the child might first explore their feelings about them, and thus communicate with the therapist in a more comfortable, less direct fashion.

Affirmative Therapy In this type of therapy, which can take place in conjunction with other types, a person's socio-cultural background becomes a focus of efforts to empower him or her. It is designed to help a person deal with problems related to his or her cultural background, sexual orientation or gender identity.

Analytical Psychotherapy uses psychoanalytic principles (see Psycho-analysis) but is of shorter duration and requires fewer sessions per week. A more active role is played by the psychotherapist.

Behaviour Therapy Instead of an exploration of the underlying causes of problematic behaviour, this type of psychotherapy focuses on modifying the behaviour itself (Pavlovian conditioning is one of the principles used) and eliminating symptoms by learning processes.

Client-centred Therapy (also Rogerian Therapy) Developed by Carl Rogers, this style of therapy is non-directive. The therapist provides respectful, empathic support of the client in his or her self-discovery and development.

Clinical Counselling is goal-oriented counselling in which the counsellor listens to a client's uppermost issues, such as relationship or low self-esteem problems and then forms a treatment plan and implements it.

Cognitive Therapy is based on the theory that a client's problems are based on faulty notions and thoughts towards oneself and others. Following a process known as cognitive restructuring, the therapist helps the client to identify distorted thinking patterns and replace them with more suitable ones.

Cognitive-Analytic Therapy is an integration of the theories and techniques of both psychodynamic psychotherapy and cognitive-behaviour therapy (see below).

Cognitive-Behaviour Therapy (CBT) is a highly structured process, developed on the premise that problematic feelings, behaviour and beliefs can be replaced with more effective ones. Therapists assign homework tasks and exercises to reinforce new attitudes, behaviour and interpersonal strategies.

Didactic Group Therapy Group therapy actively led by a professional leader who may give talks, lead discussions and provide interpretations.

Eclectic Psychotherapy refers to any psychotherapy that utilizes a combination of different approaches and techniques, based on several theories, in keeping with what the therapist judges to be appropriate for the client.

Emotion-focused Therapy is based on the idea that it is our emotions that create our personalities and can lead to development and change.

Eriksonian Hypnotherapy has a focus on hypnosis according to a style developed by Milton H. Erikson. The client's own images and mythological notions are incorporated into hypnotherapy scripts, which are used to facilitate change and healing for a wide range of psychological problems.

Existential Analysis The therapist actively challenges and guides the patient, encouraging him or her to develop conscious decision-making.

Existential Psychotherapy emphasises the 'Here and Now' of the client's life. The therapist assists with the development of a greater sense of personal responsibility, decision-making and the ability to create meaning in life.

Existential-humanistic Therapy focuses on the entire person and his or her free-will, self-determination and subjective experiences, rather than just particular aspects, such as behaviour or underlying motivations.

Family Systems Therapy Therapists assume that the best way to help someone (or a family) heal is to get the whole family involved. There are a number of different approaches, but they all focus on inter-family relationships and interactions, as well as the relating style of subgroups within the family.

Feminist Therapy is based on feminist principles and the assumption that traditional types of psychotherapy are based on underlying sexism. The therapist maintains an egalitarian relationship with the client and collaborates with her in conducting an eclectic style of therapy that emphasizes her strengths.

Functional Family Therapy focuses on patterns of relating that are established within families. The therapist works to identify the benefits family members may derive from problem behaviour and highlight those that will effect change.

Gestalt Therapy In this type of psychotherapy emphasis is placed on the totality of a person's present behaviour and relationships, rather than on past experiences. Special Gestalt techniques, sometimes involving role-playing, have been developed for this therapy style.

Hypnotherapy A trained professional uses hypnosis in the psychological treatment of a wide range of problems, such as Anxiety, Substance Abuse, Insomnia, Eating Disorders, Personality Disorders, Depression and Pain Disorder.

Integrative Psychotherapy In this type of psychotherapy the therapist uses selected techniques from a number of different therapeutic models, according to the client's particular needs.

Interpersonal Psychotherapy was developed by Harry Stack Sullivan and is based on the belief that human behaviour is motivated primarily by human relationships and interaction. The therapist helps the client to explore primary relationships, understand past and present interactive experiences, and how they impacted on the person's thoughts and behaviour.

Jungian Therapy A system of analysis proposed by Carl Jung that involves the use of images, symbols and philosophical values to interpret the psyche.

Multicultural Therapy All types of therapy should take into account the cultural background and issues of each individual. However in the treatment of psychological problems Multicultural Therapy particularly focuses on the impact of race, ethnicity, history, sexual orientation and other aspects of diversity.

Play Therapy is most often used with children, in which the therapist uses dolls, clay, sand trays, blocks and figurines to assist in understanding the child's feelings, fantasies and problems.

Psychoanalysis involves a very detailed exploration of the patient's unconscious feelings, dreams and memories with a psychoanalyst (someone who has been trained in psychoanalytic theory and practice, and applies the techniques originally developed by Sigmund Freud). Traditionally, the patient attends three or four times a week, and lies down on a couch during sessions.

Psychodrama is a method of psychotherapy in which, rather than talking with a psychotherapist, patients enact events in their lives. They dramatize encounters with people, traumatic events, hopes and fantasies – in fact many aspects of their minds. It usually involves one therapist and a group of people, and sometimes a single patient is helped by a group of trained co-therapists.

Psychodynamic Psychotherapy is a procedure in which your therapist will help you to explore underlying thoughts, motivations and feelings. Psychodynamic psychotherapists take the view that unconscious motives influence a person's emotions, attitudes and personality. The focus of the therapy, therefore, is to get to the root of the problem, rather than simply treating symptoms.

Rational Emotive Behaviour Therapy is a type of cognitive-behaviour therapy in which a client is helped to replace irrational or dysfunctional thoughts, behaviour and beliefs with more useful ones.

Supportive Psychotherapy is designed to help relieve current distress without probing deeply into underlying conflicts or personality structure. It might involve advice, education, bibliotherapy (reading specific helpful books), bereavement therapy, and pastoral counselling. A number of other types of supportive therapy are mentioned below.

specific focus therapies

Anger Control Therapy is designed to help a person manage uncontrolled anger using techniques such as exposing them to cues that provoke anger, rehearsing alternative responses and providing assertiveness training. It can take place in either individual or group settings.

Animal-Assisted Therapy Animals are used in this type of therapy to help people with the loss of a loved one by giving and receiving affection, as well as helping with their emotional problems, social and communication skills and thought processes.

Art Therapy uses painting, clay modelling or other artistic forms to help a patient to facilitate the attainment of goals such as healing, communication, rehabilitation, the resolving of problems and conflicts, and the gaining of insights.

Aversion Therapy is a type of behavioural therapy in which a person is conditioned to stop engaging in a harmful behaviour (such as drinking alcohol). The patient's undesirable symptom becomes associated with something unpleasant, such as a noxious smell or nasty taste.

Bereavement Therapy (Grief Counselling) is designed to help people through the loss of a loved one.

Career Counselling is an advice and guidance service provided by counsellors specifically to help people understand their preferences, skills, strengths and weaknesses, and then decide on or change a career depending on the desired goal.

Clay Therapy In this therapy style, children and/or individuals with Mental Retardation communicate via the clay, and use it as a symbol for feelings (for example, to express anger by pounding it).

Cognitive Processing Therapy is sometimes used for the treatment of Post-Traumatic Stress Disorder. The therapist works with the client's notions of themselves, other people, and events to try to help them deal better with negative situations through a shift in perception.

Dialectical Behaviour Therapy is a specific treatment that evolved from cognitive-behaviour therapy. It was developed by Marsha Linehan especially for people who have problems managing their emotions and engage in frequent self-destructive and self-injurious behaviour.

Disaster Counselling is designed for people who have witnessed a disaster, been victims of it or helped out as emergency workers. It involves debriefing and helping traumatized people to deal with the psychological aftermath in an effort to reduce the likelihood that they will develop Post-Traumatic Stress Disorder.

Distance Therapy (or Telepsychotherapy) In instances where clients are unable to have face-to-face therapy due to lack of mobility or some other limitation, a therapist might conduct sessions by telephone, video-conferencing, audio-conferencing or via a computer connection.

Divorce Counselling is designed to help ex-partners and families cope with loss, separation and change caused by divorce.

Educational Counselling is specifically for students, and is designed to enhance their educational experience through the provision of guidance regarding choice of courses, longer-term educational plans and management of specific difficulties (for example, achieving academically despite having a Learning Disability).

Educational Therapy People who require help to achieve academically but are hampered by emotional problems, learning disabilities or behavioural issues can receive individual therapy in the educational environment from an educational therapist.

Emergency Therapy is to help people who have just experienced a traumatic incident that has left them shocked, panicking or acutely anxious.

Medical Family Therapy is designed to help families deal with illness or disability of a loved one.

Occupational Therapy is for people who require help in improving their quality of life, overcoming disability or restoring independence for people who have a mental or physical disorder.

Sex Therapy is the treatment of sexual disorders by a trained, qualified therapist. It may include cognitive-behavioural therapy, relationship counselling, homework exercises, education, bibliotherapy, video-therapy and medical interventions.

alternative or adjunctive therapies

Biofeedback is a monitoring device used to relay information to the patient so that he or she can learn to control their physiological state. It is used for the treatment of problems such as migraine headaches, stress and hypertension. Biofeedback is sometimes used as an alternative treatment for Insomnia, Anxiety and Attention-Deficit/Hyperactivity Disorder.

Body Therapies use healing techniques such as massage, body manipulation, breathing and relaxation to relieve stress, tension and other negative symptoms that contribute to psychological distress.

Brain-wave Therapy Alpha and theta brain waves are stimulated in the expectation that memory, learning and insight will be enhanced.

Creative Arts Therapy includes art therapy, music therapy, dance therapy, manual arts therapy, drama therapy and poetry therapy. These are all designed to increase self-awareness, encourage self-expression, facilitate better communication and improve psychological and physiological functioning.

Horticultural Therapy Gardening is used to aid therapeutic healing, usually by older adults, for those with mental illness or disabilities and for those involved in rehabilitation.

Light Therapy (Phototherapy) is used to treat such problems as depressed mood or sleep disturbances.

Peer Counselling involves counselling by someone who has an equal status to the recipient, such as one student helping another.

why do psychologists use tests?

Eliciting accurate information about a person's mental state is not as easy as simply asking a direct question. None of us has the ability to be completely objective about our own thought processes, mood, ability to maintain close contact with reality, learning style or general psychological health. Therefore, to produce an accurate picture of a person's internal world we must ask questions in a psychologically sophisticated manner. For example, a person suffering from Depression may not realize it because his or her experience of Depression is one of numbness rather than sadness. In such a case it does not make sense to ask someone directly 'Are you depressed?' The word 'depressed' can mean a lot of things in general parlance, and we have to use clinical assessment to find out if a person's mood signposts a disorder that should be treated.

A person with a Learning Disability who is struggling with school work might come up with a negative coping style, such as disruptive behaviour that might lead to dropping out or expulsion from school, and pretty soon that young person could be on a negative track in life without anyone being aware of the true problem. There are underlying psychological problems beneath many of the behaviours that typically land people in trouble with the law, the community, employers, families and spouses. Whether it is Post-Traumatic Stress Disorder, Attention-Deficit Disorder, Substance Abuse, a combination of all three, or something else, such difficulties need to be identified and treated. Otherwise, the sufferer is simply likely to continue a cycle of 'acting out', often in ways that replicate the early maltreatment they have received from someone else.

Psychologists have established several successful methods of delving into a person's psychological state. For example, they use pictures and designs, as well as styles of questioning that allow a person to feel safe enough to lower their defences and answer truthfully. It's not that psychologists want to catch people out or act as interrogators, but many people have so little perspective of themselves that they are unable to recognize (or verbalize) their problems.

how do psychologists know that assessment tools work?

The commonly used assessment tools that psychologists employ are carefully developed and made available for clinical use only after a great deal of work has gone into testing the validity of the questions, and whether the test actually accurately provides the information it is designed to produce for a that particular group. In a number of countries there are ethical and legal rules about psychological testing. Usually, the test results need to be kept confidential, the testing must be done only by someone with a degree and/or licence who is trained to do so, and the results must not be given to anyone in a form they might not understand.

People being tested must give written and verbal permission that they wish to be tested and that they understand the purpose of the test, plus clear guidelines about confidentiality. The test should not be given to anyone who might not understand them for either language, cultural, comprehension or literacy reasons. In particular, results need to be guarded against use or misuse in legal proceedings. This requires great care in setting up testing procedures and in collecting and storing data.

types of psychological testing

Drawing The subject is asked to draw simple objects that will then be interpreted by a psychologist.

Inkblot (Rorschach) test A set of ten symmetrical inkblots of various shapes and colours are presented to the subject who is then requested to tell the examiner what they remind him or her of.

Bender Visual Motor Gestalt test The subject is asked to copy designs set out on nine cards.

Self-report inventories (using pencil and paper, or on a computer) These involve ticking boxes beside questions inquiring about your mood, feelings, likes and dislikes and so on.

Structured clinical interview A mental-health professional spends some time with the subject one-to-one, getting to know them by asking prepared questions.

Mental Status examination A mental-health professional asks the subject questions designed to find out about their: a) Feeling (Affect and Mood), b) Perception and c) Thinking (intellectual functioning, orientation, memory, thinking, attention and concentration, insight and judgement).

uk mental-health websites

You should be able to find accurate information about mental-health issues at the following web addresses:

Mental Health Foundation UK: www.mentalhealth.org.uk

Mental Health Care: www.mentalhealthcare.org.uk

Mind: www.mind.org.uk

Psychnet-UK: www.psychnet-uk.com

Samaritans: www.samaritans.org.uk

Sane: www.sane.org.uk

1 in 4 forum: www.1in4-forum.org

Depression Alliance: www.depressionalliance.org

British Association for Counselling and Psychotherapy: www.bacp.co.uk

British Association of Psychotherapists: www.bap-psychotherapy.org

British Psychological Society: www.bps.org.uk

National Institute of Mental Health: www.nimh.nih.gov

chapter 14
celebrating life

"Our life is sort of like a bad play, but somehow we've managed to get good reviews."

thirty ways to be mentally healthier, happier and more joyful

1. **Soothing touch**. The warmth of human contact. We all need it, especially when we are sad or in pain. Infants and children who are deprived of it do not thrive. Whereas people who have had warm, physically affectionate parents tend to have good relationships and satisfying lives, those whose carers were distant, cold and remote grow into needy, depressed adults without a sense of emotional well-being. We need to learn to get our need for human touch satisfied in appropriate ways – and to tolerate receiving it. This involves teaching others what we need from them and giving hugs and soothing caresses back to others.

2. **Kind words**. Receiving verbal kindness can relax and soothe us. If we have not had parents who said soothing things to us we will find it hard to be kind to others, and may even damage them as we have been damaged. It's not too late to learn. Make the effort to say kind things to

others, to ask others for verbal kindness and to accept it when given.

3. **Cry if you need to**. It is a marvellous, healing release. Allow yourself to sob, and teach your partner or a close friend to hold you or whatever you want to happen in such a moment. Likewise, learn what your partner wants when he or she cries and reciprocate the desired type of soothing.

4. **Learn from your pain and grief**. Betrayal, loss, humiliation – so many painful human emotions beset us during the course of our lives; but we must always learn from these experiences. This is how much of human growth, and ultimately happiness, occurs.

5. **Being relaxed**. If we relax our bodies, our minds will follow. Learn to relax your body using the progressive relaxation exercise on page 41. In doing so, you will greatly reduce your worry, anxiety and potential for panic.

6. **Feeling peaceful**. It is really worth learning to meditate. There are some exercises on page 40 and 127, but beyond those you can find meditation classes throughout the UK. For thousands of years meditation has been used to calm and soothe human beings, and provide them with the sense of perspective and control over their lives that comes when anxiety is managed.

7. **Exercise**. Find some way to exercise your body, according to what is safe and appropriate for your age, weight and level of fitness. There are many psychological benefits to be gained from exercising, including reduced feelings of depression and anxiety, and a more positive outlook. Self-esteem can be elevated through regular exercise. During and after strenuous exercise, some people even receive the good feelings one can have when endorphins (or natural painkillers) are released in the body.

8. **Engage in pleasurable pastimes**. At least twice a day do something that gives you simple, guilt-free pleasure, such as walking outside in the sunshine or enjoying the scent of a flower, listening to your favourite music or dancing in your kitchen. Even if you have a demanding life, these precious moments will uplift you.

9. **Stay busy, but not too busy**. Finding a balance between work and play is never easy. We can get stuck in a stressful rut of focusing on productivity without remembering to do what helps to sustain us. Then again, we can be so enveloped in a life of little work that we become bored and start to loathe ourselves. Know that keeping the balance right is a life-long process.

10. **Seek humour in your life**. It is very healing to laugh; studies have shown that it has some remarkable benefits. As well as enjoying funny shows,

DVDs and concerts, cultivate humour in your daily life in relationships with others at home and at work. It will help reduce stress, anxiety and sadness.

11. **Enjoy sensual delights**. Savour lovely sights, music, food, scents and/or tactile experiences. Many of us have not been taught to enjoy these and experience them as only brief, unimportant indulgences. But valuing our precious sensory gifts will help relax us, lift our mood and spirits, and give us an additional zest for life.

12. **Value and tend to your sexuality**. Sex is a powerful way to increase our happiness, health, relaxation, mood stability, self-esteem and intimacy with your partner. Use it, or lose it. Despite common mythology to the contrary, you can enjoy sexuality throughout your entire life, provided you continue to engage in it.

13. **Nurture your spirituality**. Many religions provide comfort, relaxation and relief for participants. Remember that you do not have to embrace everything in your particular religion or philosophy – just focus on whatever is helpful and works for you.

14. **Learn to do nothing**. Try not to keep busy just for the sake of it. When you occasionally do nothing, you allow something important to occur. This is how we come up with some of our greatest ideas and inspirations. It is also the time when we can have important realizations about our lives that we have been pushing away by keeping busy.

15. **Enjoy the odd game**. Whether it be backgammon, football or mah-jong, just take some time to throw yourself into the pleasure of winning or losing, and tolerating either. As long as you do not set too much store by winning, this will help you relax, exercise your mind along discrete, prescribed lines and give you a chance to interact with others.

16. **Use daily affirmations**. Once you have learned something more about yourself and your psychological make-up (perhaps from within the pages of this book) design some daily sayings to repeat to yourself to encourage your development. For example, if you tend to be a little paranoid, stick a note on your mirror that says 'Today I will remember that not everyone in the world is out to get me'; if you have poor body-image, remind yourself 'Today I will make peace with my body', and so on.

17. **Keep learning**. We thrive on mental stimulation, and it can help to protect us against dementia and mental atrophy as we age. There are new and exciting books, courses, instructional websites, blogs and educational TV programmes. Every now and again walk into a bookshop with a friend and ask them to guide you as you walk around the aisles

with your eyes closed. When you feel like it, suddenly stop, reach out and grab the nearest book. It will likely be one you would not normally be interested in, but buy it and read it. Devise other ways to keep your mind open to new ideas.

18. **Engage in artistic pursuits**. Whether you enjoy painting, playing music or dancing, these largely right-side brain activities are good for you. They are relaxing, stimulate the creative and emotional centres of the brain, provide a source of self-understanding and esteem, and can help with emotional catharsis.

19. **Write**. Writing down your thoughts, and especially your feelings, helps to soothe and organize emotions. It also helps you to develop a stronger sense of self, regulate emotions and be able to be more objective about people and events.

20. **Notice your dreams**. Dreams are powerful, the 'royal road to the unconscious' as Freud put it. Write them down as soon as you wake, which means keeping writing materials next to your bed. Take them to your therapist, or learn to analyze them by taking a dream-tending course. You will learn a great deal about yourself.

21. **Don't let anger fester**. If you have trouble with anger, that is if you cannot manage it, or if you allow it to go on so that you are furious with your spouse for a long time, learn to change. Letting go and forgiveness are powerful, vital ways to maintain intimacy and stay happy and well.

22. **Eat nutritious, well-balanced meals**. There is a relationship between mental health and a decent diet. Feed your brain.

23. **Look after your physical health**. Sometimes mental-health problems are caused or exacerbated by underlying physical conditions. They need to be ruled out. Get regular check-ups and seek medical help as soon as you think you may need it.

24. **Be aware of the potency of prescription medication**. We have many useful drugs that treat a wide range of problems, both physical and psychological; however, these can have side effects. When you experience any symptoms, always take into account the possibility that they could be caused by either prescription or non-prescription (over-the-counter) drugs, or by recreational drugs or alcohol. Always read warnings on the labels and learn about the possible side effects.

25. **Don't abuse alcohol and drugs, and keep use to a minimum**. Alcohol, for example, is a central nervous system depressant. It's easy to get stuck in a habit of a few beers a night without realizing how much that can affect your mood.

26. **Avoid toxins**. There is some evidence that environmental toxins, whether they be food additives, mercury, poor-quality air or toxic components of household furniture can negatively affect the central nervous system. Do your best to live and work in a healthy environment.

27. **Enjoy water**. Whether it's a bath, a spa, a pool or the sea, we can soothe ourselves in a primal way by floating in safe water of moderate temperature. This will relax the mind and put us in touch with our very first experiences.

28. **Contact nature**. A walk in the forest, a visit to the botanical gardens, a ride across a desert or even just peeking at the stars will provide us with a calming sense of our place on the planet. This will reduce our anxiety, soothe our stress and elevate our mood.

29. **Spend time engaged in charitable activities with others**. Working as part of a team and giving our time to help others makes us feel hopeful, raises our sense of self-worth, and inspires us.

30. **Learn to give and receive love**. People who grew up feeling unloved will have a hard time with this, but it's worth working on it. Most of all, one must first be capable of feeling good about oneself, and this can be achieved using exercises such as the Postive Regard Meditation on page 127, the body image exercise on page 103 and the self-esteem exercises on page 105.

further reading

The Art of Happiness: A Handbook for Living, His Holiness the Dalai Lama and H. C. Cutler. New York: Riverhead Books, 1998.

The Science of Happiness: How Our Brains Make Us Happy – and What We Can Do to Get Happier, S. Klein. New York: Marlowe & Company, 2002.

The Art of Sexual Ecstasy, M. Arnand. Los Angeles: Jeremy P. Tarcher Inc., 1989.

The Art of Loving, Erich Fromm. New York: Harper & Row, 1956.

365 Tao Daily Meditations, Deng Ming-Dao. San Francisco: HarperSanFrancisco, 1992.

Emotional Intelligence, D. Goleman. New York: Bantam Books, 1995.

The Pleasure Zone: Why We Resist Good Feelings & How to Let Go and Be Happy, S. Resnick. Berkeley: Conari Press, 1997.

The Way of the Wizard: Twenty Spiritual Lessons for Creating the Life You Want, D. Chopra. New York: Harmony Books, 1995.

Progressive Relaxation, E. Edmundson. Chicago: University of Chicago Press, 1942.

The Practice of Happiness: Exercises for Developing Mindfulness, Wisdom and Joy, M. Fryba. Boston and London: Shambhala, 1995.

Breathing Space: Living and Working at a Comfortable Pace in a Sped-Up Society, J. Davidson. New York: MasterMedia Limited, 1991.

Self-Massage: The Complete 15-Minutes a Day Massage System for Health and Awareness, J. Young. London: Thorsons, 1992.

When I Am an Old Woman I Shall Wear Purple, ed. S. Martz Watsonville, Calif.: Papier-Mâché Press, 1987.

The Road Less Travelled: A new Psychology of Love, Traditional Values and Spiritual Growth, M. S. Peck. New York: Touchstone, 1978.

The Marriage of Sense and Soul: Integrating Science and Religion, K. Wilber. New York: Random House, 1998.

Care of the Soul: A Guide for Cultivating Depth and Sacredness in Everyday Life, T. Moore. New York: HarperCollins, 1992.

Minding the Temple of the Soul: Balancing Body, Mind, and Spirit through Traditional Jewish Prayer, Movement, and Meditation, T. Frankiel and J. Greenfeld. Woodstock, Vt.: Jewish Lights Publishing, 1997.

Quest: A Guide for Creating Your Own Vision Quest, D. Linn. New York: Ballantine Books, 1997.

A Return to Love: Reflections on the Principles of A Course in Miracles, Marianne Williamson. New York: HarperPerennial, 1993.

glossary

"What's the next best medicine?"

Acting out: Inappropriate behaviour that serves as an uncontrolled means of expressing deep-seated feelings.

Affirmation: Statement designed to be repeated by a person to remind him or her of positive self-beliefs, thoughts or actions, for example, 'I am worthy of being treated respectfully.'

Amnesia: Temporary or permanent loss of a person's partial or complete memory.

Anti-psychotic medication: Prescribed drugs designed to treat a thought disorder and to help the person get back in touch with reality.

Antisocial behaviour: Breaking societal rules by acting aggressively, destructively, impulsively or violently in a manner that violates other people's rights or property.

Attachment: Concept developed to describe the way infants and children cling to their primary carers for nurture and protection. It can be satisfactory or otherwise.

Authoritarian parenting: Style of parenting that involves a strict expectation of unquestioning obedience and strong punishment for wrongdoing.

Authoritative parenting: Style of parenting that involves a certain amount of collaboration between carer and child. Appropriate limits and restrictions are placed on the child, but there is also an encouragement of his or her independence and autonomy.

Autonomic nervous system: Part of the nervous system that is responsible for involuntary body functions, such as breathing or digestion.

Behaviour modification: Changing human behaviour by learning techniques, such as biofeedback or aversive conditioning (that is, something unpleasant occurs, such as having a bad taste, when an undesirable behaviour is performed).

Biochemical: From the point of view of chemical changes that may be occurring in the brain or body.

Biofeedback: A monitoring device is used to relay information to a person so he or she can learn to control his or her physiological state. It is used for the treatment of problems such as migraine headaches, stress and hypertension. Biofeedback is sometimes used as an adjunctive treatment for Insomnia, Anxiety and Attention-Deficit/Hyperactivity Disorder.

Boundaries: Defined limits that are set to protect relationships or situations so that an individual or participants can maintain psychological integrity.

Catastrophize: To imagine that the very worst will happen in a given situation or as the result of a particular action.

Circadian rhythm: Behavioural or physiological occurrences that normally follow a twenty-four-hour daily cycle, such as sleeping and waking.

Cognitive: To do with knowing and awareness, including functions such as remembering, judging and problem-solving.

Compulsion: Mental or physical action a person is driven to perform in a bid to reduce anxiety (for example, hand-washing, counting or checking).

Conditioned response: The way a person behaves after a type of training known as Pavlovian conditioning.

Conditioning: When a certain behaviour or action becomes more likely to be performed due to a deliberately created learning experience.

Coping style: The way a person manages or deals with stress, problems, emergencies or situations that cause anxiety.

Counsellor: Someone who has been professionally trained to advise, evaluate and guide a person, couple or family struggling with problems such as relationship issues, Substance Abuse, rehabilitation, or vocational conflicts. That person may have another qualification or profession, such as being a nurse, social worker or pastor.

Delusion: A highly improbable belief.

Dementia: Deterioration of a person's memory, language or other cognitive functions.

Denial: An unconscious refusal to acknowledge the reality of unpleasant thoughts, feelings or a situation.

Dependency needs: Normal, universal human necessities such as love, protection, food, shelter, warmth and physical care that people at certain stages or situations in their lives (for example, infancy) rely on others to provide.

Depersonalization: A state in which people feel detached from themselves.

Derealization: A state in which people feel disconnected from their surroundings

Diagnostic category: A classification of people according to a set of symptoms or characteristics in order to understand and treat them better.

Diagnostic criteria: A list of symptoms, behaviours or characteristics that qualify a person to be considered as having a particular mental disorder.

Dissociation: An acute but time-limited alteration in people's feelings, behaviour or thoughts, so that they do not process or experience information about themselves, certain events or the surrounding world in their normal way.

Distractibility: Difficulty maintaining focus or attention.

Dopamine: A neurotransmitter that is thought to have bearing on many mental problems.

Dual diagnosis: When a person abusing alcohol or drugs has other psychological problems that also need to be treated.

EEG or electroencephalography: A method of examining a person's brain-waves by placing electrodes on the head to record and monitor them.

Emotion regulation: Ability to control or modulate feelings or emotions.

Environmental causes/factors: When used in a psychological context, this usually means how the people, events and circumstances that surrounded or cared for a person (for example, early in life) affected the development of his or her psyche.

Executive function: Organizing brain processes, including reasoning, problem-solving and planning.

Flashbacks: When traumatic experiences are reawakened and relived in the mind, often triggered by sounds, smells or other reminders of the original event.

GABA or gamma-aminobutyric acid: One of several neurotransmitters that have been implicated in the development and maintenance of many mental disorders.

Genetic predisposition: The tendency for a particular psychological or physical disorder to be inherited.

Hallucination: Hearing, seeing, smelling, feeling or tasting something that is not really there.

Harm-reduction treatment: Treatment for Substance Abuse that works by helping a person to reduce his or her substance use gradually while working on the underlying issues.

Hypomania: A heightened mood state that falls just short of full mania.

Impulse-control: The ability to resist acting on a temptation or desire.

Maladaptive: Interfering with optimal functioning.

Mental disorder: Disabling psychological symptoms, an emotional or behavioural problem or a dysfunction in thinking, acting or feeling, that cause distress and may lead to impairment in the way the person functions in the world.

Mental health: When, in accordance with what is considered appropriate for his or her age, stage of life and culture, a person is functioning well emotionally, behaviourally, and, regarding relationships, is relatively free of disabling psychological symptoms and can adapt reasonably well to life's ups and downs. The term is sometimes used to describe a person who is simply not suffering from a mental disorder.

Motor skills: Ability to make one's body move; for example, to use arms, legs (that is, large motor skills such as playing ball) or fingers and wrists (that is, fine motor skills such as writing).

Neurodevelopmental: To do with the early formation of the brain and nervous system.

Neurofeedback: A technique in which people can learn to change their own brain-wave patterns through receiving information about them on a video screen or audio signal.

Neurological: To do with the brain and nervous system.

Neurons: The cells that make up the nervous system.

Neurotransmitters: Brain chemicals that help to transmit signals between neurons. Norepinephrine, serotonin, acetylcholine, GABA and dopamine are some of the most discussed due to the fact that they are implicated in the development and maintenance of many psychological problems.

Obsession: An intrusive thought or impulse that persists and creates worry or distress.

Parasomnias: A group of Sleep Disorders that include Nightmare Disorder, Sleep Terror Disorder and Sleep-Walking Disorder.

Pharmacological intervention: The prescribing of medication.

Phobia: An irrational and persistent fear of a certain object, situation, activity or living thing.

Positive reinforcement: Method of making it more likely that a particular behaviour will be repeated. In helping children to behave in a certain way, it means praising or rewarding good behaviour rather than focusing on or punishing bad behaviour.

Prognosis: A prediction of what the treatment outcome will be, of how a person's disorder is likely to progress or improve, as well as the expected duration and severity.

Psyche: All aspects of the mind.

Psychiatrist: A mental-health professional with a medical degree, that is, a physician who specializes in mental and emotional disorders. Unlike psychologists, he or she is qualified to prescribe medication. Some psychiatrists have been trained to perform psychotherapy.

Psychoanalyst (sometimes referred to simply as 'an analyst'): A therapist trained to treat mental disorders according to traditional techniques originally developed by pioneers like Sigmund Freud and Carl Jung. The person receiving treatment usually lies on a couch instead of sitting in a chair and attends three or four sessions a week.

Psycho-education: A process of learning about relevant psychological issues.

Psychological assessment: A process, carried out by a mental-health professional, of working out what seems to be wrong, and how treatment should proceed.

Psychologist: A professionally trained practitioner, researcher or teacher who may work in clinical practice as a psychotherapist, psychological counsellor or consultant and may provide mental-health services in settings such as educational establishments, hospitals, prisons, business organizations or clinics.

Psychopharmacologist: A person with a medical degree who can prescribe medication for psychological problems.

Psychosis: An abnormal state of mind in which a person's perceptions, understanding and other thought processes, as well as emotions and behaviour, are seriously disrupted or impaired.

Psychosocial: To do with both psychological and social aspects of an issue, problem or treatment.

Psychotherapist: Someone who has been professionally trained to treat mental, behavioural and emotional problems. He or she will talk with people who seek treatment in a private, boundaried situation where everything that is said must be treated as confidential.

Psychotherapy: An interactive psychological service for individuals, couples, families or groups provided by a trained professional. It is designed to have healing effects on mental, emotional or behavioural problems or disorders, and help people to make sense of their lives.

Psychotherapeutic intervention: Any kind of action taken by a psychotherapist to treat a person with a psychological problem.

REM (rapid eye movement) sleep: The stage of sleep when dreaming occurs.

Rumination: Repetitive, obsessional thinking.

Seasonal Affective Disorder (SAD): A Mood Disorder brought about by seasonal changes.

Self-assertion: Appropriately expressing one's needs, rights or opinions in a manner that is neither aggressive nor assertive.

Self-regulation: Controlling and monitoring one's own behaviour.

Self-talk: A person's internal running commentary.

Social skills: Learned abilities, such as assertiveness, communication and the ability to make and keep friends that enable a person to cope well in social situations and contexts.

Somatization: When the body expresses a psychological problem.

Stereotypic (or stereotyped) behaviour: Unchanging and often repetitive actions, such as head banging, hitting oneself or rocking.

Stimulant medication: Prescribed drugs that speed up parts of the brain or central nervous system and the body. They are sometimes intended to work paradoxically; that is, have perceived slowing effects instead.

Therapeutic relationship: The type of connection that is established between a therapist and person seeking treatment.

Thought-stopping: Technique to notice and arrest particular thoughts that are identified as being maladaptive.

references

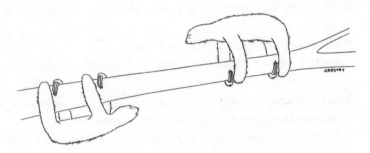

"How long have you been on antidepressants?"

depression

American Psychiatric Association (1993). *Diagnostic and statistical manual of mental disorders* (4th ed.). Washington, DC: American Psychiatric Association.

Angst, J., Angst, F., & Stassen, H. H., (1999). Suicide risk in patients with major depression disorder. *Journal of Clinical Psychiatry*, 60, 57–62.

Battino, R. (2007). Review of Hypnosis and treating depression. *American Journal of Clinical Hypnosis*, 49, 232–233.

Beck, A.T., Rush, A.J., Shaw, B.F., & Emery, G. (1979). *Cognitive Therapy of Depression*. New York: the Guilford Press.

Bodenlos, J. S., Kose, S., Borckardt, J. J.,

Nahas, Z., Shaw, D., O'Neil, P. M., & George, M. S. (2007). Vagus nerve stimulation acutely alters food craving in adults with depression. *Appetite*, 48, 145–153.

Brenes, G. A.; Williamson, J. D.; Messier, S. P.; Rejeski, W. J.; Pahor, M.; Ip, E.; Penninx, B. W. J. H. (2007). Treatment of minor depression in older adults: A pilot study comparing sertraline and exercise. *Aging & Mental Health*. Jan Vol 11(1) 61–68.

Den Boer, P. C. A. M., Wiersma, D., Ten Vaarwerk, I., Span, M. M., Stant, A. D., & Van Den Bosch, R. J. (2007). Cognitive self-therapy for chronic depression and anxiety: A multi-centre randomized controlled study. *Psychological Medicine,* 37, 329–339.

Dougherty, D. D., & Rauch, S. L. (2007). Brain Correlates of Antidepressant Treatment Outcome from Neuroimaging Studies in Depression. *Psychiatric Clinics of North America,* 30, 91–103.

Dunlop, B. W., & Nemeroff, C. B. (2007). The role of dopamine in the pathophysiology of depression. *Archives of General Psychiatry,* 64, 327–337.

Feldman, G. (2007). Cognitive and Behavioral Therapies for Depression: Overview, New Directions, and Practical Recommendations for Dissemination. *Psychiatric Clinics of North America,* 30, 39–50.

Iosifescu, D. V. (2007). Treating Depression in the Medically Ill. *Psychiatric Clinics of North America,* 30, 77–90.

Kelly, C. M., & Jorm, A. F. (2007). Stigma and mood disorders. *Current Opinion in Psychiatry,* 20, 13–16.

Kennedy, G. J. (2007). Reducing the Risk of Late-Life Suicide Through Improved Depression Care. *Primary Psychiatry,* 14, 26–28, 31–34.

Labiner, D. M., & Ahern, G. L. (2007). Vagus nerve stimulation therapy in depression and epilepsy: Therapeutic parameter settings. *Acta Neurologica Scandinavica,* 115, 23–33.

Leo, R. J., & Ligot Jr., J. S. A. (2007). A systematic review of randomized controlled trials of acupuncture in the treatment of depression. *Journal of Affective Disorders,* 97, 13–22.

Lyness, J. M., & Caine, E. D. (2000). Vascular disease and depression: Models of the interplay between psychopathology and medical comorbidity. In: *Physical Illness and Depression in Older Adults: A Handbook of Theory, Research and Practice.* G. M. Williamson, D. R. Shaffer, et al (Eds.) Dordrecht,

Netherlands: Kluwer Academic Publishers.

Mayberg, H. S. (2007). Defining the Neural Circuitry of Depression: Toward a New Nosology With Therapeutic Implications. *Biological Psychiatry,* 61, 729–730.

McCoy, D. M. (1996). Treatment considerations in patients with significant medical comorbidity. *Journal of Family Practice,* 43: S35–S44.

Morris, S. J. (2007). Attributional Biases in Subclinical Depression: A Schema-Based Account. *Clinical Psychology & Psychotherapy,* 14, 32–47.

Musselman, D. L., Evans, D. L., & Nemeroff, C. B. (1998). The relationship of depression to cardiovascular disease: Epidemiology, biology, and treatment. *Archives of General Psychiatry* 4: 1–16.

Nemeroff, C. B. (2007). The burden of severe depression: A review of diagnostic challenges and treatment alternatives. *Journal of Psychiatric Research,* 41, 189–206.

Ohayon, M. M. (2007). Epidemiology of depression and its treatment in the general population. *Journal of Psychiatric Research,* 41, 207–213.

Ostacher, M. J. (2007). Comorbid Alcohol and Substance Abuse Dependence in Depression: Impact on the Outcome of Antidepressant Treatment. *Psychiatric Clinics of North America,* 30, 69–76.

Papakostas, G. I., & Zarate Jr., C. A. (2007). Novel Augmentation Strategies for Treatment-Resistant Major Depressive Disorder. *Primary Psychiatry,* 14, 59–65.

Pruitt, I. T. P. (2007). Family Treatment Approaches for Depression in Adolescent Males. *American Journal of Family Therapy,* 35, 69–81.

Regier, D. A., Rae, D. S., Narrow, W. E., Kaelber, C. T., & Schatzberg, A. F. (1998). Prevalence of anxiety disorders and their comorbidity with mood and addictive disorders. *British Journal of Psychiatry*, 173, 24–28.

Rihmer, Z. (2007). Suicide risk in mood disorders. *Current Opinion in Psychiatry*, 20, 17–22.

Sackeim, H. A., Prudic, J., Fuller, R., Keilp, J., Lavori, P. W., & Olfson, M. (2007). The Cognitive Effects of Electroconvulsive Therapy in Community Settings. *Neuropsychopharmacology*, 32, 244–254.

Thase, M. E., & Sullivan, L. R. (1995). Relapse and recurrence of depression: A practical approach for prevention. *CNS Drugs*, 4, 261–277.

Whisman, M. (2001). The association between depression and marital dissatisfaction. In: *Marital and Family Processes in Depression: A Scientific Foundation for Clinical Practice*. S. R. H. Beach (Ed.) Washington, DC: American Psychological Association.

Williams Jr., J. W., Gerrity, M., Holsinger, T., Dobscha, S., Gaynes, B., & Dietrich, A. (2007). Systematic review of multifaceted interventions to improve depression care. *General Hospital Psychiatry*, 29, 91–116.

Yexley, M. J. (2007). Treating Postpartum Depression with Hypnosis: Addressing Specific Symptoms Presented by the Client. *American Journal of Clinical Hypnosis*, 49, 219–223.

bipolar disorder

Ackenheil, M. (2001). Neurotransmitters and signal transduction processes in bipolar affective disorders: A synopsis. *Journal of Affective Disorders*, 62, 101–111.

Altamura, A. C. (2007). Bipolar spectrum and drug addiction. Journal of Affective Disorders, 99, 285.

American Psychiatric Association (1993). *Diagnostic and statistical manual of mental disorders* (4th ed.). Washington, DC.

Antai-Otong, D. (2006). Treatment Considerations for Patients Experiencing Rapid-Cycling Bipolar Disorder. *Perspectives in Psychiatric Care*, 42, 55–57.

Benazzi, F. (2006). Mood patterns and classification in bipolar disorder. *Current Opinion in Psychiatry*, 19, 1–8.

Benazzi, F. (2007). Challenging the unipolar-bipolar division: Does mixed depression bridge the gap? *Progress in Neuro-Psychopharmacology & Biological Psychiatry*, 31, 97–103.

Benazzi, F., & Akiskal, H. (2006). The duration of hypomania in bipolar-II disorder in private practice: Methodology and validation. *Journal of Affective Disorders*, 96, 189–196.

Bernhard, B., Schaub, A., Kümmler, P., Dittmann, S., Severus, E., Seemüller, F., Born, C., Forsthoff, A., Licht, R. W., & Grunze, H. (2006). Impact of cognitive-psychoeducational interventions in bipolar patients and their relatives. *European Psychiatry*, 21, 81–86.

Bowden, C., & Singh, V. (2006). Bipolar disorders: Treatment options and patient satisfaction. *Neuropsychiatric Disease And Treatment*, 2, 149–153.

Chou, J. C. & Fazzio, L. (2006). Maintenance Treatment of Bipolar Disorder: Applying Research to Clinical Practice. *Journal of Psychiatric Practice*, 12, 283–299.

Colom, F., Vieta, E., Daban, C., Pacchiarotti, I., & Sánchez-Moreno, J. (2006). Clinical and therapeutic implications of predominant polarity in bipolar disorder. *Journal of Affective Disorders*, 93, 13–17.

Craighead, W. E., Miklowitz, D. J., Frank, E., & Vajk, F. C. (2002). Psychosocial treatments for bipolar disorder. In: P. E. Nathan & J. M. Gorman (Eds.) *A Guide to Treatments That Work*. New York: Oxford University Press.

Dager, S. R., Friedman, S. D., Parow, A.,

Demopulos, C., Stoll, A., Lyoo, L. Brain metabolic alterations in medication-free patients with bipolar disorder. In K. Demyttenaere, L. D. Renshaw, F. Perry, (Eds.) *Archives of General Psychiatry*, 61(5), May 2004, 450–458.

De Fruyt, J., Demyttenaere, K.(2007) Bipolar (Spectrum) Disorder and Mood Stabilization: Standing at the Crossroads? *Psychotherapy and Psychosomatics*. Jan Vol 76(2) 77–88.

DePaulo, J. R. Jr. (2006). Bipolar Disorder Treatment: An Evidence-Based Reality Check. *American Journal of Psychiatry*, 163, 175–176.

Di Marzo, S., Giordano, A., Pacchiarotti, I., Colom, F., Sánchez-Moreno, J., & Vieta, E. (2006). The impact of the number of episodes on the outcome of Bipolar Disorder. *European Journal of Psychiatry*, 20, 21–28.

El-Mallakh, R., Weisler, R. H., Townsend, M. H., & Ginsberg, L. D. (2006). Bipolar II Disorder: Current and future treatment options. *Annals of Clinical Psychiatry*, 18, 259–266.

Fagiolini, A., Kupfer, D. J, Rucci, P, Scott, J. A., Novick, D. M., & Frank, E. (2004). Suicide attempts and ideation in patients with bipolar I disorder. *Journal of Clinical Psychiatry*, 65, 509–514.

Fleck, D. E., Arndt, S., DelBello, M. P., & Strakowski, S. M. (2006). Concurrent tracking of alcohol use and bipolar disorder symptoms. *Bipolar Disorders*, 8, 338–344.

Frank, E., Gonzalez, J. M., & Fagiolini, A. (2006). The Importance of Routine for Preventing Recurrence in Bipolar Disorder. *American Journal of Psychiatry*, 163, 981–985.

Friedman, E., Gyulai, L., Bhargava, M., Landen, M., Wisniewski, S., Foris, J., Ostacher, M., Medina, R., & Thase, M. (2006). Seasonal changes in clinical status in bipolar disorder: A prospective study in 1000 STEP-BD patients. *Acta Psychiatrica Scandinavica*, 113, 510–517.

Gorski, E. D., & Willis, K. C. (2006). Hidden in Plain View: A Review Article on Bipolar Disorder. *Primary Psychiatry*, 13, 67–70.

Govender, S. (2006). Cognitive-Behavioural Therapy for Bipolar Disorder (Second Edition). *International Review of Psychiatry*, 18, 309.

Grant, B., Stinson, F. S., Dawson, D. A., Chou, P., Dufour, M. C., Compton, W. et al (2001). Prevalence and co-occurrence of substance use disorders and independent mood and anxiety disorders: Results from the National Epidemiology Survey on Alcohol and Related Conditions. *Archives of General Psychiatry*, 61, 807–816.

Guze, S. B., & Robins, E. (1970) Suicide and primary affective disorders. *British Journal of Psychiatry*, 117, 437–438.

Hellewell, J. S. E. (2006). A review of the evidence for the use of antipsychotics in the maintenance treatment of bipolar disorders. *Journal of Psychopharmacology*, 20, 39–45.

Hwang, J., Lyoo, I. K., Dager, S. R., Friedman, S. D., Oh, J. S., Lee, J. Y., Kim, S. J., Dunner, D. L., & Renshaw, P. F. (2006). Basal Ganglia Shape Alterations in Bipolar Disorder. *American Journal of Psychiatry*, 163, 276–285.

Kim, E. Y., Miklowitz, D. J., Biuckians, A., & Mullen, K. (2007). Life stress and the course of early-onset bipolar disorder. *Journal of Affective Disorders*, 99, 37–44.

Lingam, R., & Scott, J. (2002). Treatment non-adherence in affective disorders. *Acta Psychiatrica Scandinavica*, 105, 164–172.

MacKinnon, D. F., & Zamoiski, R. (2006). Panic comorbidity with bipolar disorder: What is the manic-panic connection? *Bipolar Disorders*, 8, 648–664.

Malkoff-Schwartz, S., Frank, E., Anderson, B., Sherill, J.T., Siegel, L., Patterson, D., et al (1998). Stressful life events and social rhythm disruption in the onset of manic and depressive bipolar episodes: A preliminary investigation. *Archives of General Psychiatry*, 62, 603–613.

McAllister-Williams, R. H. (2006). Relapse prevention in bipolar disorder: A critical review of current guidelines. *Journal of Psychopharmacology*, 20, 12–16.

McIntyre, R. S., Soczynska, J. K., Bottas, A., Bordbar, K., Konarski, J. Z., & Kennedy, S. H. (2006). Anxiety disorders and bipolar disorder: A review. *Bipolar Disorders*, 8, 665–676.

Miklowitz, D. J., & Goldstein, M. J. (1997). *Bipolar Disorder: A Family-Focused Treatment Approach*. New York: The Guilford Press.

Miklowitz, D. J., & Johnson, S. L. (2006). The Psychopathology and treatment of Bipolar Disorder. *Annual Review of Clinical Psychology*, 2, 199–235.

Mysels, D. J., Endicott, J., Nee, J., Maser, J. D., Solomon, D., Coryell, W., & Leon, A. C. (2007). The association between course of illness and subsequent morbidity in bipolar I disorder. *Journal of Psychiatric Research*, 41, 80–89.

Ozcan, M. E., Shivakumar, G., & Suppes, T. (2006). Treating Rapid Cycling Bipolar Disorder with Novel Medications. *Current Psychiatry Reviews*, 2, 361–369.

Pini, S., Maser, J. D., Dell' Osso, L., Abelli, M., Muti, M., Gesi, C., & Cassano, G. B. (2006). Social anxiety disorder comorbidity in patients with bipolar disorder: A clinical replication. *Journal of Anxiety Disorders*, 20, 1148–1157.

Post, R. M., & Leverich, G. S. (2006). The role of psychosocial stress in the onset and progression of bipolar disorder and its comorbidities: The need for earlier and alternative modes of therapeutic intervention. *Development and Psychopathology*, 18, 1181–1211.

Rihmer, Z. (2007). Suicide risk in mood disorders. *Current Opinion in Psychiatry*, 20, 17–22.

Romm, S., Avery, D. H., & Roy-Byrne, P. P. (2006). Psychological Interventions for Bipolar Disorder in Adults: Adjunctive Outpatient Treatments to Achieve and Maintain Remission. *Primary Psychiatry*, 13, 76–81.

Rosa, A. R., Marco, M., Fachel, J. M. G., Kapczinski, F., Stein, A. T., & Barros, H. M. T. (2007). Correlation between drug treatment adherence and lithium treatment attitudes and knowledge by bipolar patients. *Progress in Neuro Psychopharmacology & Biological Psychiatry*, 31, 217–224.

Scott, J. (2006). Psychotherapy for bipolar disorders – Efficacy and effectiveness. *Journal of Psychopharmacology*, 20, 46–50.

Simon, N. M., Zalta, A. K., Otto, M. W., Ostacher, M. J., Fischmann, D., Chow, C. W., Thompson, E. H., Stevens, J. C., Demopulos, C. M., Nierenberg, A. A., & Pollack, M. H. (2007). The association of comorbid anxiety disorders with suicide attempts and suicidal ideation in outpatients with bipolar disorder. *Journal of Psychiatric Research*, 41, 255–264.

Singh, J. B., & Zarate Jr., C. A. (2006). Pharmacological treatment of psychiatric comorbidity in bipolar disorder: A review of controlled trials. *Bipolar Disorders*, 8, 696–709.

Skeppar, P., & Adolfsson, R. (2006). Bipolar II and the bipolar spectrum. *Nordic Journal of Psychiatry*, 60, 7–26.

Stoll, A. L., Severus, E., Freeman, M. P., Reuter, S., Zboyan, H. A., Diamond, E., et al. (1999). Omega 3 Fatty Acids in bipolar disorder: A preliminary double-blind, placebo-controlled trial. *Archives of General Psychiatry*, 56, 407–412.

Stork, C., & Renshaw, P. F. (2005). Mitochondrial dysfunction in bipolar disorder: Evidence from magnetic resonance spectroscopy research. *Molecular Psychiatry*, 10, 900–919.

Swann, A. C. (2006). What Is Bipolar Disorder? *American Journal of Psychiatry*, 163, 177–179.

Taylor, R. (2006). Bipolar disorders: Mixed states, rapid cycling and atypical forms. *Educational Psychology in Practice*, 22, 176–177.

Tyrer, S. (2006). What does history teach us about factors associated with relapse in bipolar affective disorder? *Journal of Psychopharmacology*, 20, 4–11.

Young, A. (2006). Progress in the treatment of bipolar disorder. *Neuropsychiatric Disease And Treatment*, 2, 119–120.

Zhang, Z., Kang, W., Tan, Q., Li, Q., Gao, C., Zhang, F., Wang, H., Ma, X., Chen, C., Wang, W., Guo, L., Zhang, Y., Yang, X., & Yang, G. (2007). Adjunctive herbal medicine with carbamazepine for bipolar disorders: A double-blind, randomized, placebo-controlled study. *Journal of Psychiatric Research*, 41, 360–369.

Zutshi, A., Reddy, Y. C. J., Thennarasu, K., & Chandrashekhar, C. R. (2006). Comorbidity of anxiety disorders in patients with remitted bipolar disorder. *European Archives of Psychiatry and Clinical Neuroscience*, 256, 428–436.

anxiety

American Psychiatric Association (1993). *Diagnostic and statistical manual of mental disorders* (4th ed.). Washington, D.C. American Psychiatric Association.

Ayers, C. R., Sorrell, J. T., Thorp, S. R., & Wetherell, J. L. (2007). Evidence-Based Psychological Treatments for Late-Life Anxiety. *Psychology and Aging*, 22, 8–17.

Barlow, D.H. (1988) *Anxiety and Its Disorders: The Nature and Treatment of Anxiety and Panic.* New York: The Guilford Press.

Beck, A. T., & Emery, G. (1985). *Anxiety Disorders and Phobias.* New York: Basic Books Beidel, D. C., & Turner, S. M. (2007). Etiology of Social Anxiety Disorder. In Beidel, Deborah C.; Turner, Samuel M. *Shy children, phobic adults: Nature and treatment of social anxiety disorders* (pp. 91–119). Washington, DC, US: American Psychological Association.

Blanchard, E. B., Scharff, L., Schwarz, P., Suls, J. M., & Barlow, D. H. (1990). The role of anxiety and depression in the irritable bowel syndrome. *Behaviour Research and Therapy*, 28, 401–405.

Blanco, C., & López, O. V. (2007). Anxiety Disorders. In Grant, Jon E. (Ed.); Potenza, Marc N. (Ed.). *Textbook of men's mental health* (pp. 69-91). Washington, DC, US: American Psychiatric Publishing, Inc.

Blazer, D. G., Hughes, D., & George, L. K. (1987). Stressful life events and the onset of the generalized anxiety disorder syndrome. *American Journal of Psychiatry*, 144, 1178–1183.

Borkovec, T. D., & Inz, J. (1990). The nature of worry in generalized anxiety disorder: A predominance of thought activity. *Behaviour research and Therapy*, 28, 153–158.

Den Boer, P. C. A. M., Wiersma, D., Ten Vaarwerk, I., Span, M. M., Stant, A. D., & Van Den Bosch, R. J. (2007). Cognitive self-therapy for chronic depression and anxiety: A multi-centre randomized controlled study. *Psychological Medicine*, 37, 329–339.

Dugas, M. J., Marchand, A., & Ladouceur, R. (2005). Further validation of a cognitive-behavioral model of generalized anxiety disorder: Diagnostic and symptom specificity. *Journal of Anxiety Disorders*, 19, 329–343.

Durham, R. C., Murphy, T., Allan, T., Richard, K., Treliving, L. R, & Fenton, G. W. (1994). Cognitive therapy, analytic psychotherapy and anxiety management training for generalized anxiety disorder. *British Journal of Psychiatry*, 165, 315–323.

Kennedy, B. L., & Schwab, J. J. (1997). Utilization of medical specialists by anxiety disorder patients. *Psychosomatics*, 38, 109–112.

Lee, S. H., Ahn, S. C., Lee, Y. J., Choi, T. K., Yook, K. H., & Suh, S. Y. (2007). Effectiveness of a meditation-based stress management program as an adjunct to pharmacotherapy in patients with anxiety disorder. *Journal of Psychosomatic Research*, 62, 189–195.

Linden, M., Danker-Hopfe, H., Schulte-Herbrüggen, O., Neu, P., & Hellweg, R. (2007). Nerve growth factor serum concentrations rise after successful cognitive-behavioural therapy of generalized anxiety disorder. *Progress in Neuro-Psychopharmacology & Biological Psychiatry*, 31, 200–204.

Pull, C. B. (2007). Combined pharmacotherapy and cognitive-behavioural therapy for anxiety disorders. *Current Opinion in Psychiatry*, 20, 30–35.

Riskind, J. H., & Williams, N. L. (2005). The looming cognitive style and generalized anxiety disorder: Distinctive danger schemas and cognitive phenomenology. *Cognitive Therapy and Research*, 29, 7–27.

White, J. (1999). *Overcoming Generalized Anxiety Disorder: A Relaxation, Cognitive Restructuring, and Exposure-Based Protocol for the Treatment of GAD*. Oakland, CA: New Harbinger Publications.

panic attacks

American Psychiatric Association (1993). *Diagnostic and statistical manual of mental disorders* (4th ed.). Washington, DC: American Psychiatric Association.

Angst, J., Gamma, A., Endrass, J., Hantouche, E., Goodwin, R., Ajdacic, V., Eich, D., & Rössler, W. (2005). Obsessive-compulsive syndromes and disorders: Significance of comorbidity with bipolar and anxiety syndromes. *European Archives of Psychiatry and Clinical Neuroscience*, 255, 65–71.

Baillie, A. J., & Rapee, R. M. (2004). Predicting who benefits from psychoeducation and self help for panic attacks. *Behaviour Research and Therapy*, 42, 513–527.

Baillie, A. J., & Rapee, R. M. (2005). Panic attacks as risk markers for mental disorders. *Social Psychiatry and Psychiatric Epidemiology*, 40, 240–244.

Barnard, J. (2004). Panic disorder: The facts (2nd ed). *British Journal of Clinical Psychology*, 43, 466–467.

Bernstein, A., Zvolensky, M. J., Sachs-Ericsson, N., Schmidt, N. B., & Bonn-Miller, M. O. (2006). Associations between age of onset and lifetime history of panic attacks and alcohol use, abuse, and dependence in a representative sample. *Comprehensive Psychiatry*, 47, 342–349.

Broman-Fulks, J. J., Berman, M. E., Rabian, B. A., & Webster, M. J. (2004). Effects of aerobic exercise on anxiety sensitivity. *Behaviour Research and Therapy*, 42, 125–136.

Cabýoglu, M. T., Ergene, N., & Tan, U. (2006). The mechanism of acupuncture and clinical applications. *International Journal of Neuroscience*, 116, 115–125.

Casey, L. M., Newcombe, P. A., & Oei, T. P. S. (2005). Cognitive Mediation of Panic Severity: The Role of Catastrophic Misinterpretation of Bodily Sensations and Panic Self-Efficacy. *Cognitive Therapy and Research*, 29, 187–200.

Casey, L. M., Oei, T. P. S., & Newcombe,

P. A. (2005). Looking beyond the negatives: A time period analysis of positive cognitions, negative cognitions, and working alliance in cognitive behavior therapy for panic disorder. *Psychotherapy Research*, 15, 55–68.

Chang, S., & Chen, W. (2000). [Anxiety sensitivity and misinterpretation of ambiguous stimuli: The role of cognitive diathesis in panic pathogenesis]. *Chinese Journal of Psychology*, 42, 37–50.

Coryell, W., Dindo, L., Fyer, A., & Pine, D. S. (2006). Onset of Spontaneous Panic Attacks: A Prospective Study of Risk Factors. *Psychosomatic Medicine*, 68, 754–757.

De Masi, F. (2004). The psychodynamic of panic attacks: A useful integration of psychoanalysis and neuroscience. *International Journal of Psychoanalysis*, 85, 311–336.

Esler, M., Alvarenga, M., Pier, C., Richards, J., El-Osta, A., Barton, D., Haikerwal, D., Kaye, D., Schlaich, M., Guo, L., Jennings, G., Socratous, F., & Lambert, G. (2006). The neuronal noradrenaline transporter, anxiety and cardiovascular disease. *Journal of Psychopharmacology*, 20, 60–66.

Galassi, F., Quercioli, S., Charismas, D., Niccolai, V., & Barciulli, E. (2007). Cognitive-behavioral group treatment for panic disorder with agoraphobia. *Journal of Clinical Psychology*, 63, 409–416.

Gassner, S. M. (2004). The Role of Traumatic Experience in Panic Disorder and Agoraphobia. *Psychoanalytic Psychology*, 21, 222–243.

Goodwin, E. A., & Montgomery, D. D. (2006). A Cognitive-Behavioral, Biofeedback-Assisted Relaxation Treatment for Panic Disorder With Agoraphobia. *Clinical Case Studies*, 5, 112–125.

Goodwin, R. D., & Eaton, W. W. (2003).

Asthma and the risk of panic attacks among adults in the community. *Psychological Medicine*, 33, 879–885.

Goodwin, R. D., Fergusson, D. M., & Horwood, L. J. (2005). Childhood abuse and familial violence and the risk of panic attacks and panic disorder in young adulthood. *Psychological Medicine*, 35, 881–890.

Goodwin, R. D., Brook, J. S., & Cohen, P. (2005). Panic attacks and the risk of personality disorder. *Psychological Medicine*, 35, 227–235.

Goodwin, R. D., Lieb, R., Hoefler, M., Pfister, H., Bittner, A., Beesdo, K., & Wittchen, H. (2004). Panic Attack as a Risk Factor for Severe Psychopathology. *American Journal of Psychiatry*, 161, 2207–2214.

Goodwin, R. D., Fergusson, D. M., & Horwood, L. J. (2004). Panic attacks and the risk of depression among young adults in the community. *Psychotherapy and Psychosomatics*, 73, 158–165.

Goodwin, R. D., Pine, D. S., & Hoven, C. W. (2003). Asthma and Panic Attacks Among Youth in the Community. *Journal of Asthma*, 40, 139–145.

Goodwin, R. D., Fergusson, D. M., & Horwood, L. J. (2005). Childhood abuse and familial violence and the risk of panic attacks and panic disorder in young adulthood. *Psychological Medicine*, 35, 881–890.

Goodwin, R. D., Faravelli, C., Rosi, S., Cosci, F., Truglia, E., de Graaf, R., & Wittchen, H. U. (2005). The epidemiology of panic disorder and agoraphobia in Europe. *European Neuropsychopharmacology*, 15, 435–443.

Gorman, J. M., Kent, J. M., Sullivan, G. M., & Coplan, J. D. (2000). Neuroanatomical hypothesis of panic disorder, revised. *American Journal of Psychiatry*, 157, 493–505.

Hecker, J. E., Losee, M. C., Roberson-Nay,

R., & Maki, K. (2004). Mastery of Your Anxiety and Panic and brief therapist contact in the treatment of panic disorder. *Journal of Anxiety Disorders*, 18, 111–126.

Heninger, G. R. (1998). Catecholamines and pathogenesis in panic disorder. *Archives of General Psychiatry*, 55, 522–523.

Hinton, D. E., Pollack, M. H., Pich, V., Fama, J. M., & Barlow, D. H. (2005). Orthostatically induced panic attacks among Cambodian refugees: Flashbacks, catastrophic cognitions, and associated psychopathology. *Cognitive and Behavioral Practice*, 12, 301–311.

Jacobs, W. J., & Nadel, L. (1999). The first panic attack: A neurobiological theory. *Canadian Journal of Experimental Psychology*, 53, 92–107.

Jockers-Scherübl, M. C., Zubraegel, D., Baer, T., Goodwin, R. D., Olfson, M., Shea, S., Lantigua, R. A., Carrasquilo, O., Gameroff, M. J., & Weissman, M. M. (2003). Asthma and mental disorders in primary care. *General Hospital Psychiatry*, 25, 479–483.

Katerndahl, D. A. (2003). Predictors and outcomes in people told that they have panic attacks. *Depression and Anxiety*, 17, 98–100.

Kessler, R. C., Chiu, W. T., Jin, R., Ruscio, A. M., Shear, K., & Walters, E. E. (2006). The epidemiology of panic attacks, panic disorder, and agoraphobia in the national comorbidity survey replication. *Archives of General Psychiatry*, 63, 415–424.

Klein, B., Richards, J. C., & Austin, D. W. (2006). Efficacy of internet therapy for panic disorder. *Journal of Behavior Therapy and Experimental Psychiatry*, 37, 213–238.

O'Brien, M. S., Wu, L., & Anthony, J. C. (2005). Cocaine Use and the Occurrence of Panic Attacks in the Community: A Case-Crossover Approach. *Substance Use & Misuse*, 40, 285–297.

Pollack, M. H. (2005). The Pharmacotherapy of Panic Disorder. *Journal of Clinical Psychiatry*, 66, 23–27.

Raffa, S. D., White, K. S., & Barlow, D. H. (2004). Feared Consequences of Panic Attacks in Panic Disorder: A Qualitative and Quantitative Analysis. *Cognitive Behaviour Therapy*, 33, 199–207.

Rassovsky, Y., Abrams, K., & Kushner, M. G. (2006). Suffocation and respiratory responses to carbon dioxide and breath holding challenges in individuals with panic disorder. *Journal of Psychosomatic Research*, 60, 291–298.

Richards, J. C., Richardson, V., & Pier, C. (2002). The relative contributions of negative cognitions and self-efficacy to severity of panic attacks in panic disorder. *Behaviour Change*, 19, 102–111.

Rizq, R. (2002). Is there anybody there? A psychodynamic view of panic attack. *British Journal of Guidance & Counselling*, 30, 81–92.

Sareen, J., Cox, B. J., Clara, I., & Asmundson, G. J. G. (2005). The Relationship Between Anxiety Disorders and Physical Disorders in The US National Comorbidity Survey. *Depression and Anxiety*, 21, 193–202.

Schmidt, N. B., Lerew, D. R., & Joiner, T. E. Jr. (2000). Prospective evaluation of the etiology of anxiety sensitivity: Test of a scar model. *Behaviour Research and Therapy*, 38, 1083–1095.

Smits, J. A. J., Powers, M. B., Cho, Y., & Telch, M. J. (2004). Mechanism of Change in Cognitive-Behavioral Treatment of Panic Disorder: Evidence for the Fear of Fear Mediational Hypothesis. *Journal of Consulting and Clinical Psychology*, 72, 646–652.

Stewart, S. H., Taylor, S., Jang, K. L., Cox,

B. J., Watt, M. C., Fedoroff, I. C., & Borger, S. C. (2001). Causal modeling of relations among learning history, anxiety sensitivity, and panic attacks. *Behaviour Research and Therapy*, 39, 443–456.

Tull, M. T., Gratz, K. L., & Lacroce, D. M. (2006). The Role of Anxiety Sensitivity and Lack of Emotional Approach Coping in Depressive Symptom Severity Among a Non-Clinical Sample of Uncued Panickers. *Cognitive Behaviour Therapy*, 35, 74–87.

Uhlenhuth, E. H., Leon, A. C., & Matuzas, W. (2006). Psychopathology of panic attacks in panic disorder. *Journal of Affective Disorders*, 92, 55–62.

Valentiner, D. P., Mounts, N. S., & Deacon, B. J. (2004). Panic attacks, depression and anxiety symptoms, and substance use behaviors during late adolescence. *Journal of Anxiety Disorders*, 18, 573–585.

Watanabe, A., Nakao, K., Tokuyama, M., & Takeda, M. (2005). Prediction of first episode of panic attack among white-collar workers. *Psychiatry and Clinical Neurosciences*, 59, 119–126.

Wenzel, A., Sharp, I. R., Sokol, L., & Beck, A. T. (2006). Attentional Fixation in Panic Disorder. *Cognitive Behaviour Therapy*, 35, 65–73.

Westra, H. A., Stewart, S. H., Teehan, M., Johl, K., Dozois, D. J. A., & Hill, T. (2004). Benzodiazepine Use Associated With Decreased Memory for Psychoeducation Material in Cognitive Behavioral Therapy for Panic Disorder. *Cognitive Therapy and Research*, 28, 193–208.

Yonkers, K. A., & Howell, H. (2004). Panic and Agoraphobia. *CNS Spectrums*, 9, 6–7.

Zvolensky, M. J., Bernstein, A., Sachs-Ericsson, N., Schmidt, N. B., Buckner, J. D., & Bonn-Miller, M. O. (2006).

specific phobias

American Psychiatric Association (1993). *Diagnostic and statistical manual of mental disorders* (4th ed.). Washington, DC: American Psychiatric Association.

Antony, M. M., & Swinson, R. P. (2000). Specific phobia. In Antony, Martin M.; Swinson, Richard P. *Phobic disorders and panic in adults: A guide to assessment and treatment* (pp. 79–104). Washington, DC, US: American Psychological Association.

Barlow, D. H., Raffa, S. D., & Cohen, E. M. (2002). Psychosocial treatments for panic disorders, phobias, and generalized anxiety disorder. In Nathan, Peter E. (Ed.); Gorman, Jack M. (Ed.). *A guide to treatments that work* (2nd ed.). (pp. 301–335). New York, NY, US: Oxford University Press.

Beck, A.T., & Emery, G. (1985). *Anxiety Disorders and Phobias*. New York: Basic Books.

Beidel, D. C., & Turner, S. M. (2007). Assessment of Social Anxiety Disorder. In Beidel, Deborah C.; Turner, Samuel M. *Shy children, phobic adults: Nature and treatment of social anxiety disorders* (pp. 121–150). Washington, DC: US: American Psychological Association.

Bell, C. J., Malizia, A. L., & Nutt, D. J. (1999). The neurology of social phobia. *European Archives of Psychiatry and Clinical Neuroscience*, 249, S11–S18.

Bitran, S., & Barlow, D. H. (2004). Etiology and Treatment of Social Anxiety: A Commentary. *Journal of Clinical Psychology*, 60, 881–886.

Bor, R., Parker, J., & Papadopoulos, L. (2000). Psychological treatment of a fear of flying. *Counselling Psychology Review*, 15, 13–17.

Bracha, H. S., Bienvenu, O. J., & Eaton, W. W. (2007). Testing the Paleolithic-human-warfare hypothesis of blood-injection phobia in the Baltimore ECA Follow-up Study – Towards a more etiologically-based conceptualization for DSM-V. *Journal of Affective Disorders*, 97, 1–4.

Brosnan, M. J., & Thorpe, S. J. (2006). An evaluation of two clinically-derived treatments for technophobia. *Computers in Human Behavior*, 22, 1080–1095.

Cohn, L. G., & Hope, D. A. (2001). Treatment of social phobia: A treatments-by-dimensions review. In Hofmann, Stefan G. (Ed.); DiBartolo, Patricia Marten (Ed.). *From social anxiety to social phobia: Multiple perspectives* (pp. 354–378). Needham Heights, MA, US: Allyn & Bacon.

Davidson, J. R. T., & Connor, K. M. (2004). Treatment of Anxiety Disorders. In Schatzberg, Alan F. (Ed.); Nemeroff, Charles B. (Ed.). *The American Psychiatric Publishing Textbook of Psychopharmacology* (3rd ed.). (pp. 913–934). New York, NY, US: American Psychoanalytic Association.

Forsyth, J. P., & Chorpita, B. F. (1997). Unearthing the nonassociative origins of fears and phobias: A rejoinder. *Journal of Behavior Therapy and Experimental Psychiatry*, 28, 297–305.

Fyer, A. J. (1998). Current approaches to etiology and pathophysiology of specific phobia. *Biological Psychiatry*, 44, 1295–1304.

Gilroy, L. J., Kirkby, K. C., Daniels, B. A., Menzies, R. G., & Montgomery, I. M. (2000). Controlled comparison of computer-aided vicarious exposure versus live exposure in the treatment of spider phobia. *Behavior Therapy*, 31, 733–744.

Heading, K., Kirkby, K. C., Martin, F., Daniels, B. A., Gilroy, L. J., & Menzies, R. G. (2001). Controlled comparison of single-session treatments for spider phobia: Live graded exposure alone versus computer-aided vicarious exposure. *Behaviour Change*, 18, 103–113.

Hettema, J. M., Prescott, C. A., Myers, J. M., Neale, M. C., & Kendler, K. S. (2005). The Structure of Genetic and Environmental Risk Factors for Anxiety Disorders in Men and Women. *Archives of General Psychiatry*, 62, 182–189.

Hunt, M., Bylsma, L., Brock, J., Fenton, M., Goldberg, A., Miller, R., Tran, T., & Urgelles, J. (2006). The role of imagery in the maintenance and treatment of snake fear. *Journal of Behavior Therapy and Experimental Psychiatry*, 37, 283–298.

Jacobs, W. J., & Nadel, L. (1999). The first panic attack: A neurobiological theory. *Canadian Journal of Experimental Psychology*, 53, 92–107.

Kendler, K. S., Karkowski, L. M., & Prescott, C. A. (1999). Fears and phobias: Reliability and heritability. *Psychological Medicine*, 29, 539–553.

King, N. J., Heyne, D., & Ollendick, T. H. (2005). Cognitive-behavioral treatments for anxiety and phobic disorders in children and adolescents: A review. *Behavioral Disorders*, 30, 241–257.

King, N. J., Muris, P., & Ollendick, T. H. (2004). Specific Phobia. In Morris, Tracy L. (Ed.); March, John S. (Ed.). *Anxiety disorders in children and adolescents* (2nd ed.). (pp. 263–279). New York, NY, US: Guilford Press.

Krepps, J. M. (2002). Opening the door on claustrophobia: Utilizing client ideas and personal resources. *Journal of Systemic Therapies*, 21, 67–85.

McManus, F., Clark, D. M., & Hackmann, A. (2000). Specificity of cognitive biases in social phobia and their role in recovery. *Behavioural and Cognitive Psychotherapy*, 28, 201–209.

Muris, P., & Merckelbach, H. (2001). The etiology of childhood specific phobia: A multifactorial model. In Vasey, Michael W. (Ed.); Dadds, Mark R. (Ed.). *The developmental psychopathology of anxiety* (pp. 355–385). New York, NY, US: Oxford University Press.

Ollendick, T. H., King, N. J., & Muris, P. (2002). Fears and phobias in children: Phenomenology, epidemiology, and aetiology. *Child and Adolescent Mental Health*, 7, 98–106.

Öst, L., Ferebee, I., & Furmark, T. (1997). One-session group therapy of spider phobia: Direct versus indirect treatments. *Behaviour Research and Therapy*, 35, 721–732.

Rentz, T. O., Powers, M. B., Smits, J. A. J., Cougle, J. R., & Telch, M. J. (2003). Active-imaginal exposure: Examination of a new behavioral treatment for cynophobia (dog phobia). *Behaviour Research and Therapy*, 41, 1337–1353.

Roy-Byrne, P. P., & Cowley, D. S. (2002). Pharmacological treatments for panic disorder, generalized anxiety disorder, specific phobia, and social anxiety disorder. In Nathan, Peter E. (Ed.); Gorman, Jack M. (Ed.). *A guide to treatments that work* (2nd ed.). (pp. 337–365). New York, NY, US: Oxford University Press.

Scher, C. D., Steidtmann, D., Luxton, D., & Ingram, R. E. (2006). Specific Phobia: A Common Problem, Rarely Treated. In Plante, Thomas G. (Ed.). *Mental disorders of the new millennium: Behavioral issues* (Vol. 1). (pp. 245–264). Westport, CT, US: Praeger Publishers/Greenwood Publishing Group.

Schmidt, N. B., Koselka, M., & Woolaway-Bickel, K. (2001). Combined treatments for phobic anxiety disorders. In Sammons, Morgan T. (Ed.); Schmidt, Norman B. (Ed.). *Combined treatment for mental disorders: A guide to psychological and pharmacological interventions* (pp. 81–110). Washington, DC, US: American Psychological Association.

Schneier, F. R. (2005). Neurobiological Mechanisms of Social Anxiety Disorder. *CNS Spectrums*, 10, 8–9.

Vythilingum, B., & Stein, D. J. (2004). Specific Phobia. In Stein, Dan J. (Ed.). *Clinical manual of anxiety disorders* (pp. 43–62). Washington, DC, US: AmericanPsychiatric Publishing, Inc.

obsessive-compulsive disorder

Abramowitz, J. S., & Nelson, C. A. (2007). Treating Doubting and Checking Concerns. In Antony, Martin M. (Ed.); Purdon, Christine; Summerfeldt, Laura J. (Ed.). *Psychological treatment of obsessive compulsive disorders: Fundamentals and beyond* (pp. 169–186). Washington, DC, US: American Psychological Association.

Abramowitz, J. S., & Schwartz, S. A. (2006). Evidence-Based Treatments for Obsessive Compulsive Disorder: Deciding What Treatment Method Works for Whom? In Roberts, Albert R. (Ed.); Yeager, Kenneth R. (Ed.). *Foundations of evidence-based social work practice* (pp. 247–257). New York, NY, US: Oxford University Press.

American Psychiatric Association (1993). *Diagnostic and statistical manual of mental disorders* (4th ed.). Washington, DC.

Anderson, R. A., & Rees, C. S. (2007). Group versus individual cognitive-behavioural treatment for obsessive-compulsive disorder: A controlled trial. *Behaviour Research and Therapy*, 45, 123–137.

Anderson, K. E., & Savage, C. R. (2004). Cognitive and neurobiological findings in obsessive-compulsive disorder. *Psychiatric Clinics of North America*, 27, 37–47.

Anderson, R. A., & Rees, C. S. (2007). Group versus individual cognitive-behavioural treatment for obsessive-compulsive disorder: A controlled trial. *Behaviour Research and Therapy*, 45, 123–137.

Antony, M. M. (Ed.), Purdon, C., & Summerfeldt, L. J. (Ed.) (2007). Antony, Martin M.; Summerfeldt, Laura J. *Psychological treatment of obsessive compulsive disorders: Fundamentals and beyond.* Washington, DC, US: American Psychological Association.

Bryant, R. A., Moulds, M. L., Nixon, R. D. V., Mastrodomenico, J., Felmingham, K., & Hopwood, S. (2006). Hypnotherapy and cognitive behaviour therapy of acute stress disorder: A 3-year follow-up. *Behaviour Research and Therapy*, 44, 1331–1335.

Cherian, A. E., & Frost, R. O. (2007). Treating Compulsive Hoarding. In Antony, Martin M. (Ed.); Purdon, Christine; Summerfeldt, Laura J. (Ed.). *Psychological treatment of obsessive compulsive disorders: Fundamentals and beyond* (pp. 231–249). Washington, DC, US: American Psychological Association.

De Haan, E. (2006). Effective treatment of OCD? *Journal of the American Academy of Child & Adolescent Psychiatry*, 45, 383.

Denys, D. (2006). Pharmacotherapy of Obsessive-compulsive Disorder and Obsessive-Compulsive Spectrum Disorders. *Psychiatric Clinics of North America*, 29, 553–584.

Difede, J., Cukor, J., Patt, I., Giosan, C., & Hoffman, H. (2006). The Application of Virtual Reality to the Treatment of PTSD Following the WTC Attack. In Yehuda, Rachel (Ed.). *Psychobiology of posttraumatic stress disorders: A decade of progress* (Vol. 1071). (pp. 500–501). Malden, MA, US: Blackwell Publishing.

Evans, D. W., & Leckman, J. F. (2006). Origins of obsessive-compulsive disorder: Developmental and evolutionary perspectives. In Cicchetti, Dante (Ed.); Cohen, Donald J. (Ed.). *Developmental psychopathology*, Vol 3: Risk, disorder, and adaptation (2nd ed.). (pp. 404–435). Hoboken, NJ, US: John Wiley & Sons, Inc.

Evans, D. W., Lewis, M. D., & Iobst, E. (2004). The role of the orbitofrontal cortex in normally developing compulsive-like behaviors and obsessive-compulsive disorder. *Brain and Cognition*, 55, 220–234.

Falsetti, S. A., Resnick, H. S., & Lawyer, S. R. (2006). Combining Cognitive Processing Therapy with Panic Exposure and Management Techniques. In Schein, Leon A. (Ed.); Spitz, Henry I. (Ed.); Burlingame, Gary M. (Ed.); Muskin, Philip R. (Ed.); Vargo, Shannon (Col). *Psychological effects of catastrophic disasters: Group approaches to treatment* (pp. 629–668). New York, NY, US: Haworth Press.

House, A. S. (2006). Increasing the Usability of Cognitive Processing Therapy for Survivors of Child Sexual Abuse. *Journal of Child Sexual Abuse*, 15, 87–103.

Kraft, T., & Kraft, D. (2006). The place of hypnosis in psychiatry: Its applications in treating anxiety disorders and sleep disturbances. *Australian Journal of Clinical & Experimental Hypnosis*, 34, 187–203.

Kwan, P. S. K. (2006). The application of hypnosis in the treatment of a woman with complex trauma. *Australian Journal of Clinical & Experimental Hypnosis*, 34, 204–215.

Lee, C. W., Taylor, G., & Drummond, P D. (2006). The Active Ingredient in EMDR: Is It Traditional Exposure or Dual Focus of Attention? *Clinical Psychology & Psychotherapy*, 13, 97–107.

Maher, M. J., Rego, S. A., & Asnis, G. M. (2006). Sleep Disturbances in Patients with Post-Traumatic Stress Disorder: Epidemiology, Impact and Approaches to Management. *CNS Drugs*, 20, 567–590.

Purdon, C. (2007). Cognitive Therapy for Obsessive-Compulsive Disorder. In Antony, Martin M. (Ed.); Purdon, Christine; Summerfeldt, Laura J. (Ed.). *Psychological treatment of obsessive compulsive disorders: Fundamentals and beyond* (pp. 111–145). Washington, DC, US: American Psychological Association.

Raboni, M. R., Tufik, S., & Suchecki, D. (2006). Treatment of PTSD by Eye Movement Desensitization Reprocessing (EMDR) Improves Sleep Quality, Quality of life, and Perception of Stress. In Yehuda, Rachel (Ed.). *Psychobiology of posttraumatic stress disorders: A decade of progress* (Vol. 1071). (pp. 508–513). Malden, MA, US: Blackwell Publishing.

Riggs, D. S., & Foa, E. B. (2007). Treating Contamination Concerns and Compulsive Washing. In Antony, Martin M. (Ed.); Purdon, Christine; Summerfeldt, Laura J. (Ed.). *Psychological treatment of obsessive compulsive disorders: Fundamentals and beyond* (pp. 149–168). Washington, DC, US: American Psychological Association.

Riggs, D. S., & Foa, E. B. (2006). Obsessive-compulsive disorder. In Andrasik, Frank (Ed.). *Comprehensive handbook of personality and psychopathology*, Vol. 2: *Adult Psychopathology* (pp. 169–188). Hoboken, NJ, US: John Wiley & Sons, Inc.

Rossi, L. (2006). Obsessive-compulsive Disorder and Related Conditions. *Psychiatric Annals*, 36, 514–517.

Rowa, K., Antony, M. M., & Swinson, R. P. (2007). Exposure and Response Prevention. In Antony, Martin M. (Ed.); Purdon, Christine; Summerfeldt, Laura J. (Ed.). *Psychological treatment of obsessive*

compulsive disorders: Fundamentals and beyond (pp. 79–109). Washington, DC, US: American Psychological Association.

Stallard, P. (2006). Post-traumatic stress disorder. In Gillberg, Christopher (Ed.); Harrington, Richard (Ed.); Steinhausen, Hans-Christoph (Ed.). *A clinician's handbook of child and adolescent psychiatry.* (pp. 221–245). New York, NY, US: Cambridge University Press.

Thomsen, P. H. (2006). Obsessive-compulsive disorders. In Gillberg, Christopher (Ed.); Harrington, Richard (Ed.); Steinhausen, Hans-Christoph (Ed.). *A clinician's handbook of child and adolescent psychiatry* (pp. 188–206). New York, NY, US: Cambridge University Press.

Tolin, D. F., & Steketee, G. (2007). General Issues in Psychological Treatment for Obsessive-Compulsive Disorder. In Antony, Martin M. (Ed.); Purdon, Christine; Summerfeldt, Laura J. (Ed.). *Psychological treatment of obsessive compulsive disorders: Fundamentals and beyond* (pp. 31–59). Washington, DC, US: American Psychological Association.

Van Der Kolk, B. A. (2006). Clinical Implications of Neuroscience Research in PTSD. In Yehuda, Rachel (Ed.). *Psychobiology of posttraumatic stress disorders: A decade of progress* (Vol. 1071). (pp. 277–293). Malden, MA, US: Blackwell Publishing.

Veale, D. (2007). Treating Obsessive-Compulsive Disorder in People With Poor Insight and Overvalued Ideation. In Antony, Martin M. (Ed.); Purdon, Christine; Summerfeldt, Laura J. (Ed.). *Psychological treatment of obsessive compulsive disorders: Fundamentals and beyond* (pp. 267–280). Washington, DC, US: American Psychological Association.

Whiteside, S. P., Port, J. D., &

Abramowitz, J. S. (2004). A meta-analysis of functional neuroimaging in obsessive-compulsive disorder. *Psychiatry Research: Neuroimaging,* 132, 69–79.

post-traumatic stress disorder

American Psychiatric Association (1993). *Diagnostic and statistical manual of mental disorders* (4th ed.). Washington, DC: American Psychiatric Association.

Antai-Otong, D. (2007). Pharmacologic Management of Posttraumatic Stress Disorder. *Perspectives in Psychiatric Care,* 43, 55–59.

Briere, J., & Scott, C. (2006). Principles of trauma therapy: A guide to symptoms, evaluation, and treatment. *Thousand Oaks,* CA, US: Sage Publications, Inc.

Bryant, R. A. (2006). Post-traumatic stress disorder. In Andrasik, Frank (Ed.). *Comprehensive handbook of personality and psychopathology: Vol. 2: Adult Psychopathology.* (pp. 189–206). Hoboken, NJ, US: John Wiley & Sons, Inc.

Carolan, M. T. (2006). Handbook of stress, trauma and the family. *Journal of Marital & Family Therapy,* 32, 127–128.

Coalson, B. (1995). Nightmare help: Treatment of trauma survivors with PTSD. *Psychotherapy: Theory, Research, Practice, Training,* 32, 381–388.

De Zulueta, F. (2006). The treatment of psychological trauma from the perspective of attachment research. *Journal of Family Therapy,* 28, 334–351.

Ehlers, A., & Clark, D. M. (2006). Predictors of Chronic Posttraumatic Stress Disorder: Trauma Memories and Appraisals. In Rothbaum, Barbara Olasov (Ed.). *Pathological anxiety: Emotional processing in etiology and treatment* (pp. 39–55). New York, NY, US: Guilford Press.

Katz, C. L., & Yehuda, R. (2006). *Neurobiology of Trauma.* In Schein, Leon A. (Ed.); Spitz, Henry I. (Ed.); Burlingame, Gary M. (Ed.); Muskin, Philip R. (Ed.); Vargo, Shannon (Col). *Psychological effects of catastrophic disasters: Group approaches to treatment* (pp. 61–82). New York, NY, US: Haworth Press.

McFadden, J. (2006). Healing trauma: Attachment, mind, body and brain. *Journal of Analytical Psychology,* 51, 155–156.

Stoner, S. A. (2006). The body remembers: The psychophysiology of trauma and trauma treatment. *Journal of Sex & Marital Therapy,* 32, 275–276.

Unger, W. S., Wattenberg, M. S., Foy, D. W., & Glynn, S. M. (2006). *Trauma-Focus Group Therapy: An Evidence-Based Group Approach to Trauma with Adults.* In Schein, Leon A. (Ed.); Spitz, Henry I. (Ed.); Burlingame, Gary M. (Ed.); Muskin, Philip R. (Ed.); Vargo, Shannon (Col). *Psychological effects of catastrophic disasters: Group approaches to treatment* (pp. 731–786). New York, NY, US: Haworth Press.

Webber, J. M., Mascari, J. B., Dubi, M., & Gentry, J. E. (2006). *Moving Forward: Issues in Trauma Response and Treatment.* In Walz, Garry R. (Ed.); Bleuer, Jeanne C. (Ed.); Yep, Richard K. (Ed.). *Vistas: Compelling perspectives on counseling 2006.* (pp. 17–21). Alexandria, VA, US: American Counseling Association.

Wolfe, D. A., Rawana, J. S., & Chiodo, D. (2006). *Abuse and Trauma.* In David Wolfe, (Ed.); Mash, Eric J. (Ed.). *Behavioral and emotional disorders in adolescents: Nature, assessment, and treatment* (pp. 642–671). New York, NY, US: Guilford Publications.

Zayfert, C., & Becker, C. B. (2007). *Cognitive-behavioral therapy for PTSD: A case formulation approach.* New York, NY, US: Guilford Press.

adjustment disorder

American Psychiatric Association (1993). *Diagnostic and statistical manual of mental disorders* (4th ed.). Washington, DC: American Psychiatric Association

Greenberg, W. A., Rosenfeld, D. N., & Ortega, E. A. (1995). Adjustment disorder as an admission diagnosis. *American Journal of Psychiatry*, 152, 459–461.

Jones, R., Yates, W. R., & Zhou, M. H. (2002). Readmission rates for adjustment disorders: Comparison with other mood disorders. *Journal of Affective Disorders*, 71, 199–203.

Reeves, G., & Pruitt, D. (2006). Adjustment and Reactive Disorders. In Dulcan, Mina K.; Wiener, Jerry M. *Essentials of child and adolescent psychiatry* (pp. 505–513). Washington, DC, US: American Psychiatric Publishing, Inc.

Woelk, H., Arnoldt, K. H., Kieser, M., & Hoerr, R. (2007). Ginkgo biloba special extract EGb 761® in generalized anxiety disorder and adjustment disorder with anxious mood: A randomized, double-blind, placebo-controlled trial. *Journal of Psychiatric Research*, 41, 472–480.

somatization disorder

Abbey, S. E. (2005). Somatization and somatoform disorders. In Levenson, James L. (Ed.). *The American psychiatric publishing textbook of psychosomatic medicine.* (pp. 271–296). Washington, DC: US: American Psychiatric Publishing, Inc.

Aisenstein, M. (2006). The indissociable unity of psyche and soma: A view from the Paris Psychosomatic School. *International Journal of Psychoanalysis*, 87, 667–680.

Alexander, M., Waxman, D., & Simpson, J. (2005). Anxiety, depression and somatoform disorders. In Alexander, Matthew (Ed.); Lenahan, Patricia (Ed.); Pavlov, Anna (Ed.). *Cinemeducation: A comprehensive guide to using film in medical education* (pp. 81–87). Abingfon, United Kingdom: Radcliffe Publishing.

American Psychiatric Association (1993). *Diagnostic and statistical manual of mental disorders* (4th ed.). Washington, DC: American Psychiatric Association.

Arnold, L. M. (2005). The nature of painful and somatic complaints in depressive disorders. *CNS Spectrums*, 10, 4–6.

Barsky, A. J., Orav, E. J., & Bates, D. W. (2006). Distinctive Patterns of Medical Care Utilization in Patients Who Somatize. *Medical Care*, 44, 803–811.

Barsky, A. J., Orav, E. J., & Bates, D. W. (2005). Somatization Increases Medical Utilization and Costs Independent of Psychiatric and Medical Comorbidity. *Archives of General Psychiatry*, 62, 903–910.

Bursch, B. (2006). Somatization disorders. In Ammerman, Robert T. (Ed.). *Comprehensive handbook of personality and psychopathology*, Vol. 3. (pp. 403–421). Hoboken, NJ, US: John Wiley & Sons, Inc.

Chaves, J. E. (1996). Hypnotic Strategies for Somatoform Disorders. In Lynn, Steven Jay (Ed.); Kirsch, Irving (Ed.); Rhue, Judith W. (Ed.). *Casebook of clinical hypnosis* (pp. 131–151). Washington, DC, US: American Psychological Association.

Creed, F. (2006). Can DSM-V facilitate productive research into the somatoform disorders? *Journal of Psychosomatic Research*, 60, 331–334.

Eifert, G. H., & Zvolensky, M. J. (2005). Somatoform Disorders. In Maddux, James E. (Ed.); Winstead, Barbara A. (Ed.). *Psychopathology: Foundations for a contemporary understanding* (pp. 281–300). Mahwah, NJ, US: Lawrence Erlbaum Associates Publishers.

El-Anzi, F. O. (2006). Insomnia in Relation to Depression and Somatic Symptoms. *Psychological Reports*, 99, 171–175.

Engel, C. C. (2006). 'Mirror, mirror . . .' whose explanation is the fairest?: Evolving notions of somatization and idiopathic physical symptoms. *CNS Spectrums*, 11, 187–188.

Fall, K. A. (2005). Somatization Disorder: A Proposed Adlerian Conceptualization and Treatment. *Journal of Individual Psychology*, 61, 149–160.

Fink, P., Rosendal, M., & Olesen, F. (2005). Classification of somatization and functional somatic symptoms in primary care. *Australian and New Zealand Journal of Psychiatry*, 39, 772–781.

Fink, P., Hansen, M. S., & Sondergaard, L. (2005). Somatoform disorders among first-time referrals to a neurology service. *Psychosomatics: Journal of Consultation Liaison Psychiatry*, 46, 540–548.

Ginsburg, G. S., Riddle, M. A., & Davies, M. (2006). Somatic Symptoms in Children and Adolescents With Anxiety Disorders. *Journal of the American Academy of Child & Adolescent Psychiatry*, 45, 1179–1187.

Gipps, R. (2006). Mental Disorder and Intentional Disorder. *Philosophy, Psychiatry, & Psychology*, 13, 117–121.

Gorman, J. M. (2006). Making a diagnosis when one is not apparent: Bridging the gap between somatic patient and frustrated physician. *CNS Spectrums*, 11, 165.

Gupta, M. A. (2006). Somatization disorders in dermatology. *International Review of Psychiatry*, 18, 41–47.

Hakala, M., Vahlberg, T., Niemi, P. M., & Karlsson, H. (2006). Brain glucose metabolism and temperament in relation to severe somatization. *Psychiatry and Clinical Neurosciences*, 60, 669–675.

Hofflich, S. A., Hughes, A. A., & Kendall, P. C. (2006). Somatic complaints and childhood anxiety disorders. *International Journal of Clinical and Health Psychology*, 6, 229–242.

Jackson, J. L., & Kroenke, K. (2006). Managing Somatization: Medically Unexplained Should Not Mean Medically Ignored. *Journal of General Internal Medicine*, 21, 797–799.

Kapfhammer, H., & Rothenhäusler, H. (2006). Malingering/Münchausen: Factitious and Somatoform Disorders in Neurology and Clinical Medicine. In Hallett, Mark; Fahn, Stanley; Jankovic, Joseph; Lang, Anthony E.; Cloninger, C. Robert; et al. *Psychogenic movement disorders: Neurology and neuropsychiatry* (pp. 154–162). Philadelphia, PA, US: Lippincott Williams & Wilkins Publishers

Killgore, W. D. S., Stetz, M. C., Castro, C. A., & Hoge, C. W. (2006). The effects of prior combat experience on the expression of somatic and affective symptoms in deploying soldiers. *Journal of Psychosomatic Research*, 60, 379–385.

Kroenke, K. (2006). Physical symptom disorder: A simpler diagnostic category for somatization-spectrum conditions. *Journal of Psychosomatic Research*, 60, 335–339.

Kroenke, K., & Sharpe, M. (2006). Special mini-series on somatoform disorders. *Journal of Psychosomatic Research*, 60, 323.

Levenson, J. L. (2006). Editorial: A rose by any other name is still a rose. *Journal of Psychosomatic Research*, 60, 325–326.

Lipsitt, D. R., & Starcevic, V. (2006). Psychotherapy and Pharmacotherapy in the Treatment of Somatoform Disorders. *Psychiatric Annals*, 36, 341–348.

McDougall, J. (1989). *Theatres of the*

Body: A Psychoanalytic Approach to Psychosomatic Illness. New York: W.W. Norton & Company, Inc.

Merskey, H., & Mai, F. (2005). *Somatization and Conversion Disorders: A Review.* In Maj, Mario (Ed.); Akiskal, Hagop S. (Ed.); Mezzich, Juan E. (Ed.); Okasha, Ahmed (Ed.). *Somatoform disorders* (pp. 1–66). New York, NY, US: John Wiley & Sons Ltd.

North, C. S. (2005). *Somatoform Disorders.* In Rubin, Eugene H. (Ed.); Zorumski, Charles F. (Ed.). *Adult psychiatry* (2nd ed.). (pp. 261–274). Malden, MA, US: Blackwell Publishing.

Noyes Jr., R., Stuart, S., Watson, D. B., & Langbehn, D. R. (2006). Distinguishing between Hypochondriasis and Somatization Disorder: A Review of the Existing Literature. *Psychotherapy and Psychosomatics*, 75, 270–281.

Ovsiew, F. (2006). *An Overview of the Psychiatric Approach to Conversion Disorder.* In Hallett, Mark; Fahn, Stanley; Jankovic, Joseph; Lang, Anthony E.; Cloninger, C. Robert; et al. *Psychogenic movement disorders: Neurology and neuropsychiatry* (pp. 115–121). Philadelphia, PA, US: Lippincott Williams & Wilkins Publishrs.

Picardi, A., Porcelli, P., Pasquini, P., Fassone, G., Mazzotti, E., Lega, I., Ramieri, L., Sagoni, E., Abeni, D., Tiago, A., & Fava, G. A. (2006). Integration of multiple criteria for psychosomatic assessment of dermatological patients. *Psychosomatics: Journal of Consultation Liaison Psychiatry*, 47, 122–128.

Timmer, B., Bleichhardt, G., & Rief, W. (2006). Importance of Psychotherapy motivation in patients with somatization syndrome. *Psychotherapy Research*, 16, 348–356.

Trimble, M. (2006). *Somatization Disorder: Briquet's Hysteria.* In Hallett, Mark; Fahn, Stanley; Jankovic, Joseph; Lang, Anthony E.; Cloninger, C. Robert; et al. *Psychogenic movement disorders: Neurology and neuropsychiatry* (pp. 180–185). Philadelphia, PA, US: Lippincott Williams & Wilkins Publishers.

Trivedi, J. K., Sharma, S., Singh, A. P., Sinha, P. K., & Tandon, R. (2005). Neurocognition in Somatisation Disorder. *Hong Kong Journal of Psychiatry*, 15, 97–100.

Waller, E., & Scheidt, C. E. (2006). Somatoform disorders as disorders of affect regulation: A development perspective. *International Review of Psychiatry*, 18, 13–24.

Wenzel, A., Steer, R. A., & Beck, A. T. (2005). Are there any gender differences in frequency of self-reported somatic symptoms of depression? *Journal of Affective Disorders*, 89, 177–181.

Woolfolk, R. L., & Allen, L. A. (2007). *Treating somatization: A cognitive-behavioral approach.* New York, NY, US: Guilford Press.

Conversion Disorder

Allin, M., Streeruwitz, A., & Curtis, V. (2005). Progress in understanding conversion disorder. *Neuropsychiatric Disease And Treatment*, 1, 205–209.

American Psychiatric Association (1993). *Diagnostic and statistical manual of mental disorders* (4th ed.). Washington, DC: American Psychiatric Association.

Bhatia, M. S., & Sapra, S. (2005). Pseudo-seizures in Children: A Profile of 50 Cases. *Clinical Pediatrics*, 44, 617–621.

Bhatia, M. S., Chandra, R., & Vaid, L. (2002). Psychogenic cough: A profile of 32 cases. *International Journal of Psychiatry in Medicine*, 32, 353–360.

Campayo, J. G. (2006). Somatoform Disorders. *European Journal of Psychiatry*, 20, 55.

Cathebras, P., & Koenig, M. (2005).

Spinal Cord Astrocytoma Mistaken for Conversion Disorder. *Psychosomatics: Journal of Consultation Liaison Psychiatry*, 46, 187–188.

Chaves, J. E. (1996). *Hypnotic Strategies for Somatoform Disorders*. In Lynn, Steven Jay (Ed.); Kirsch, Irving (Ed.); Rhue, Judith W. (Ed.). *Casebook of clinical hypnosis* (pp. 131–151). Washington, DC, US: American Psychological Association.

Ciano-Federoff, L. M., & Sperry, J. A. (2005). On 'Converting' Hand Pain Into Psychological Pain: Treating Hand Pain Vicariously Through Exposure-Based Therapy for PTSD. *Clinical Case Studies*, 4, 57–71.

Couprie, W., Wijdicks, E. F. M., Rooijmans, H. G. M., & van Gijn, J. (1995). Outcome in conversion disorder: A follow-up study. *Journal of Neurology, Neurosurgery & Psychiatry*, 58, 750–752.

Crimlisk, H. L., Bhatia, K. P., Cope, H., David, A. S., Marsden, D., & Ron, M. A. (2000). Patterns of referral in patients with medically unexplained motor symptoms. *Journal of Psychosomatic Research*, 49, 217–219.

Finkenbine, R., & Miele, V. J. (2004). Globus hystericus: A brief review. *General Hospital Psychiatry*, 26, 78–82.

Fritz, G. K., Fritsch, S., & Hagino, O. (1997). Somatoform disorders in children and adolescents: A review of the past 10 years. *Journal of the American Academy of Child & Adolescent Psychiatry*, 36, 1329–1338.

Gross, M. (1983). Hypnoanalysis in conversion reaction. *Medical Hypnoanalysis*, 4, 160–165.

Harvey, S. B., Stanton, B. R., & David, A. S. (2006). Conversion disorder: Towards a neurobiological understanding. *Neuropsychiatric Disease And Treatment*, 2, 13–20.

Hurwitz, T. A. (2004). Somatization and Conversion Disorder. *Canadian Journal of Psychiatry*, 49, 172–178.

Ishikura, R., & Tashiro, N. (2002). Frustration and fulfillment of needs in dissociative and conversion disorders. *Psychiatry and Clinical Neurosciences*, 56, 381–390.

Jeste, D. V., Gierz, M., & Harris, M. J. (1990). Pseudodementia: Myths and reality. *Psychiatric Annals*, 20, 71–79.

Kozlowska, K. (2001). Good children presenting with conversion disorder. *Clinical Child Psychology and Psychiatry*, 6, 575–591.

Krem, M. M. (2004). Motor Conversion Disorders Reviewed From a Neuropsychiatric Perspective. *Journal of Clinical Psychiatry*, 65, 783–790.

Lipsitt, D. R., & Starcevic, V. (2006). Psychotherapy and Pharmacotherapy in the Treatment of Somatoform Disorders. *Psychiatric Annals*, 36, 341–348.

Looper, K. (2003). Contemporary approaches to the study of hysteria: Clinical and theoretical perspectives. *Transcultural Psychiatry*, 40, 445–448.

Lovinger, S. (2005). Conversion hysteria in a pre-adolescent girl. *Psychoanalytic Social Work*, 12, 47–61.

Lupu, V. (2005). Cognitive-behavioral therapy in the case of a teenager with conversion disorder with mixed presentation. *Journal of Cognitive and Behavioral Psychotherapies*, 5, 197–205.

Maldonado, J. R., & Spiegel, D. (2001). Conversion disorder. In Phillips, Katharine A. (Ed.). *Somatoform and factitious disorders* (pp. 95–128). Washington, DC, US: American Psychiatric Association.

Merskey, H., & Mai, F. (2005). Somatization and Conversion Disorders: A Review. In Maj, Mario (Ed.); Akiskal, Hagop S. (Ed.); Mezzich, Juan E. (Ed.); Okasha, Ahmed (Ed.). *Somatoform disorders* (pp. 1-66). New York, NY, US: John Wiley & Sons Ltd.

Milrod, B. (2002). A 9-year-old with conversion disorder, successfully treated with psychoanalysis. *International Journal of Psychoanalysis*, 83, 623–631.

Moene, F. C., Spinhoven, P., Hoogduin, K. A. L., & Dyck, R. V. (2003). A randomized controlled clinical trial of a hypnosis-based treatment for patients with conversion disorder, motor type. *International Journal of Clinical and Experimental Hypnosis*, 51, 29–50.

Moene, F. C., Landberg, E. H., Hoogduin, K. A. L., Spinhoven, P., Hertzberger, L. I., Kleyweg, R. P., & Weeda, J. (2000). Organic syndromes diagnosed as conversion disorder: Identification and frequency in a study of 85 patients. *Journal of Psychosomatic Research*, 49, 7–12.

Moene, F. C., Hoogduin, K. A. L., & Van Dyck, R. (1998). The inpatient treatment of patients suffering from (motor) conversion symptoms: A description of eight cases. *International Journal of Clinical and Experimental Hypnosis*, 46, 171–190.

Mooney, G., & Gurrister, T. (2004). Behavioral Treatment of Psychogenic Deafness: A Case Report. *Rehabilitation Psychology*, 49, 268–271.

Nakaya, M. (1995). True auditory hallucinations as a conversion symptom. *Psychopathology*, 28, 214–219.

Nash, M. R. (2005). Salient Findings: A Potentially Groundbreaking Study on the Neuroscience of Hypnotizability, A Critical Review of Hypnosis' Efficacy, and the Neurophysiology of Conversion Disorder. *International Journal of Clinical and Experimental Hypnosis*, 53, 87–93.

Oakley, D. A. (2006). Hypnosis as a tool in research: Experimental psychopathology. *Contemporary Hypnosis*, 23, 3–14.

Ovsiew, F. (2003). What is wrong in conversion disorder? *Journal of Neurology, Neurosurgery & Psychiatry*, 74, 557–557.

Peeks, B., & Levy, R. L. (1993). The girl with painful steps. In Golden, Larry B. (Ed.); Norwood, Meredith L. (Ed.). *Case studies in child counseling* (pp. 99–109). New York, NY, US: Merrill/Macmillan Publishing Co.

Razali, S. M. (1999). Conversion disorder: A case report of treatment with the Main Puteri, a Malay shamanastic healing ceremony. *European Psychiatry*, 14, 470–472.

Reisman, B., & Servis, M. (1996). Conversion disorder with pseudohallucinations. *American Journal of Psychiatry*, 153, 838.

Slaughter, J. R., & Imel, Z. E. (2004). *Conversion Disorder: A Disorder of Somatic Self-Awareness*. In Beitman, Bernard D. (Ed.); Nair, Jyotsna (Ed.). *Self-awareness deficits in psychiatric patients: Neurobiology, assessment, and treatment* (pp. 280–297). New York, NY, US: W W Norton & Co.

Schönfeldt-Lecuona, C., Connemann, B. J., Spitzer, M., & Herwig, U. (2003). Transcranial Magnetic Stimulation in the Reversal of Motor Conversion Disorder. *Psychotherapy and Psychosomatics*, 72, 286–288.

Schwartz, A. C., Calhoun, A. W., Eschbach, C. L., & Seelig, B. J. (2001). Treatment of conversion disorder in an African American Christian woman: Cultural and social considerations. *American Journal of Psychiatry*, 158, 1385–1391.

Sussman, N. (2005). Dealing With Uncertainty. *Primary Psychiatry*, 12, 12.

Rosebush, P., & Mazurek, M. F. (2006). *Treatment of Conversion Disorder*. In Hallett, Mark; Fahn, Stanley; Jankovic, Joseph; Lang, Anthony E.; Cloninger, C. Robert; et al. *Psychogenic movement disorders: Neurology and neuropsychiatry* (pp. 289–301). Philadelphia, PA, US: Lippincott Williams & Wilkins Publishers.

Slaughter, J. R., & Imel, Z. E. (2004). *Conversion Disorder: A Disorder of Somatic Self-Awareness*. In Beitman, Bernard D. (Ed.); Nair, Jyotsna (Ed.). *Self-awareness deficits in psychiatric patients: Neurobiology, assessment, and treatment* (pp. 280–297). New York, NY, US: W W Norton & Co.

Stonnington, C. M., Barry, J. J., & Fisher, R. S. (2006). Conversion Disorder. *American Journal of Psychiatry*, 163, 1510–1517.

Tkachuk, G. A., & Martin, G. L. (1999). Exercise therapy for patients with psychiatric disorders: Research and clinical implications. *Professional Psychology: Research and Practice*, 30, 275–282.

Tucher, J., & Long, M. A. (1985). A multicomponent behavioral treatment of conversion visual loss. *The Behavior Therapist*, 8, 3–4.

Viederman, M. (1995). Metaphor and meaning in conversion disorder: A brief active therapy. *Psychosomatic Medicine*, 57, 403–409.

Wald, J., Taylor, S., & Scamvougeras, A. (2004). Cognitive Behavioural and Neuropsychiatric Treatment of Post-Traumatic Conversion Disorder: A Case Study. *Cognitive Behaviour Therapy*, 33, 12–20.

pain disorder

American Psychiatric Association (1993). *Diagnostic and statistical manual of mental disorders* (4th ed.). Washington, DC: American Psychiatric Association.

Asmundson, G. J. G., & Taylor, S. (2006). PTSD and Chronic Pain: Cognitive-Behavioral Perspectives and Practical Implications. In Young, Gerald (Ed.); Kane, Andrew W. (Ed.); Nicholson, Keith (Ed.). *Psychological knowledge in court: PTSD, pain, and TBI* (pp.

225–241). New York, NY, US: Springer Science + Business Media.

Birklein, F., & Maihöfner, C. (2006). Use your imagination: Training the brain and not the body to improve chronic pain and restore function. *Neurology*, 67, 2115–2116.

Ciano-Federoff, L. M., & Sperry, J. A. (2005). On 'Converting' Hand Pain Into Psychological Pain: Treating Hand Pain Vicariously Through Exposure-Based Therapy for PTSD. *Clinical Case Studies*, 4, 57–71.

Garcia-Cebrian, A., Gandhi, P., Demyttenaere, K., & Peveler, R. (2006). The association of depression and painful physical symptoms: a review of the European literature. *European Psychiatry*, 21, 379–388.

Grazzi, L., Usai, S., & Rigamonti, A. (2005). Facial pain in children and adolescents. *Neurological Sciences*, 26, S101–S103.

Gureje, O. (2007). Psychiatric aspects of pain. *Current Opinion in Psychiatry*, 20, 42–46.

Jacobsen, L. N., Lassen, I. S., Friis, P., Videbech, P., & Licht, R. W. (2006). Bodily symptoms in moderate and severe depression. *Nordic Journal of Psychiatry*, 60, 294–298.

Keefe, F. J., Abernethy, A. P., & Campbell, L. C. (2005). Psychological Approaches to Understanding and Treating Disease-Related Pain. *Annual Review of Psychology*, 56, 601–630.

Masters, K. S. (2006). Recurrent Abdominal Pain, Medical Intervention, and Biofeedback: What Happened to the Biopsychosocial Model? *Applied Psychophysiology and Biofeedback*, 31, 155–165.

Morley, S., & Williams, A. C. d. C. (2006). RCTs of psychological treatments for chronic pain: Progress and challenges. *Pain*, 121, 171–172.

Patterson, D. R., & Jensen, M. P. (2003) Hypnosis and clinical pain.

Psychological Bulletin. 129(4), 495–521.

Saletu, B., Prause, W., Anderer, P., Mandl, M., Aigner, M., Mikova, O., & Saletu-Zyhlarz, G. M. (2005). Insomnia in Somatoform Pain Disorder: Sleep Laboratory Studies on Differences to Controls and Acute Effects of Trazodone, Evaluated by the Somnolyzer 24 x 7 and the Siesta Database. *Neuropsychobiology*, 51, 148–163.

Silberstein, S. D. (2003). Neurotoxins in the Neurobiology of Pain. *Headache: The Journal of Head and Face Pain*, 43, S2–S8.

Smith, B. H., Macfarlane, G. J., & Torrance, N. (2007). Epidemiology of chronic pain, from the laboratory to the bus stop: Time to add understanding of biological mechanisms to the study of risk factors in population-based research. *Pain*, 127, 5–10.

Tinker, R. H., & Wilson, S. A. (2005). The Phantom Limb Pain Protocol. In Shapiro, Robin (Ed.). *EMDR solutions: Pathways to healing* (pp. 147–159). New York, NY, US: W W Norton & Co.

Türkçapar, M. H., Özyurt, M. F., Örsel, S., & Türkçapar, A. F. (2005). Psychiatric morbidity in patients with pain and medically unexplained symptoms. *The Pain Clinic*, 17, 289–295.

Waldman, K. L. (2004). Psychological approaches to PAIN management: A practitioner's handbook. *Bulletin of the Menninger Clinic*, 68, 365–366.

Wise, T. N., Arnold, L. M., Malefic, V., & Ginsberg, D. L. (Ed.) (2005). Ginsberg, David L. Management of painful physical symptoms associated with depression and mood disorders. *Primary Psychiatry*, 12, 1–14.

Young, G., & Chapman, C. R. (2006). Chronic Pain and Affect as a Nonlinear Dynamical System. In Young, Gerald (Ed.); Kane, Andrew W.

(Ed.); Nicholson, Keith (Ed.). *Psychological knowledge in court: PTSD, pain, and TBI* (pp. 181–192). New York, NY, US: Springer Science + Business Media.

hypochondriasis

Abramowitz, J. S., & Braddock, A. E. (2006). Hypochondriasis: Conceptualization, Treatment, and Relationship to Obsessive-Compulsive Disorder. *Psychiatric Clinics of North America*, 29, 503–519.

Avia, M. D., & Ruiz, M. A. (2005). Recommendations for the Treatment of Hypochondriac Patients. *Journal of Contemporary Psychotherapy*, 35, 301–313.

Björgvinsson, T. (2006). Review of Treating Health Anxiety: A Cognitive-Behavioral Approach. *Bulletin of the Menninger Clinic*, 70, 341–342.

Bleichhardt, G., Timmer, B., & Rief, W. (2005). Hypochondriasis Among Patients with Multiple Somatoform Symptoms – Psychopathology and Outcome of a Cognitive-Behavioral Therapy. *Journal of Contemporary Psychotherapy*, 35, 239–249.

Furer, P., & Walker, J. R. (2005). Treatment of Hypochondriasis with Exposure. *Journal of Contemporary Psychotherapy*, 35, 251–267.

Lipsitt, D. R., & Starcevic, V. (2006). Psychotherapy and Pharmacotherapy in the Treatment of Somatoform Disorders. *Psychiatric Annals*, 36, 341–348.

McCabe, R. E. (2005). Treating Health Anxiety: A Cognitive-Behavioral Approach. *Canadian Psychology*, 46, 111–113.

Millar, K. (2004). Health anxiety: Clinical and research perspectives on hypochondriasis and related conditions. *Psycho-Oncology*, 13, 67–68.

Monopoli, J. (2005). Managing

Hypochondriasis in Elderly Clients. *Journal of Contemporary Psychotherapy*, 35, 285–300.

Neziroglu, F., & Khemlani-Patel, S. (2005). Overlap of Body Dysmorphic Disorder and Hypochondriasis with OCD. In Abramowitz, Jonathan S. (Ed.); Houts, Arthur C. (Ed.). *Concepts and controversies in obsessive-compulsive disorder* (pp. 163–175). New York, NY, US: Springer Science + Business Media.

Noyes Jr., R. (2005). Hypochondriasis: A Review. In Maj, Mario (Ed.); Akiskal, Hagop S. (Ed.); Mezzich, Juan E. (Ed.); Okasha, Ahmed (Ed.). *Somatoform disorders* (pp. 129–189). New York, NY, US: John Wiley & Sons Ltd.

Noyes, R. Jr., Woodman, C. L., Bodkin, J. A., & Yagla, S. J. (2004). Hypochondriacal Concerns in Panic Disorder and Major Depressive Disorder: A Comparison. *International Journal of Psychiatry in Medicine*, 34, 143–154.

Sisti, M. (2004). Hypochondriasis: Modern Perspectives on an Ancient Malady. *Journal of Cognitive Psychotherapy*, 18, 369–370.

Starcevic, V. (2005). Fear of Death in Hypochondriasis: Bodily Threat and Its Treatment Implications. *Journal of Contemporary Psychotherapy*, 35, 227–237.

Stuart, S., & Noyes, R. Jr. (2005). Treating Hypochondriasis with Interpersonal Psychotherapy. *Journal of Contemporary Psychotherapy*, 35, 269–283.

Taylor, S., & Asmundson, G. J. G. (2006). Hypochondriasis. In Fisher, Jane E. (Ed.); O'Donohue, William T. (Ed.). *Practitioner's guide to evidence-based psychotherapy* (pp. 313–323). New York, NY, US: Springer Science + Business Media.

Taylor, S. (2004). Understanding and treating health anxiety: A cognitive-behavioral approach. *Cognitive and Behavioral Practice*, 11, 112–123.

Taylor, S., Asmundson, G. J. G., & Coons, M. J. (2005). Current Directions in the Treatment of Hypochondriasis. *Journal of Cognitive Psychotherapy*, 19, 285–304.

Walker, J. R., & Furer, P. (2006). Treatment of Hypochondriasis and Psychogenic Movement Disorders: Focus on Cognitive-Behavior Therapy. In Hallett, Mark; Fahn, Stanley; Jankovic, Joseph; Lang, Anthony E.; Cloninger, C. Robert; et al. *Psychogenic movement disorders: Neurology and neuropsychiatry* (pp. 163–179). Philadelphia, PA, US: Lippincott Williams & Wilkins Publishers.

Wattar, U., Sorensen, P., Buemann, I., Birket-Smith, M., Salkovskis, P. M., Albertsen, M., & Strange, S. (2005). Outcome of Cognitive-Behavioural Treatment for Health Anxiety (Hypochondriasis) in a Routine Clinical Setting. *Behavioural and Cognitive Psychotherapy*, 33, 165–175.

factitious disorder

American Psychiatric Association (1993). *Diagnostic and statistical manual of mental disorders* (4th ed.). Washington, DC: American Psychiatric Association.

Eisendrath, S. J. (1996). When Munchausen becomes malingering: Factitious disorders that penetrate the legal system. *Bulletin of the American Academy of Psychiatry & the Law*, 24, 471–481.

Ford, C. V. (Ed.) (1995). Ford, Charles V. Somatoform and factitious disorders. In Gabbard, Glen O. (Ed.). *Treatments of psychiatric disorders* (2nd ed.), Vols. 1 & 2. (pp. 1711–1836). Washington, DC, US: American Psychiatric Association.

Gregory, R. J., & Jindal, S. (2006). Factitious Disorder on an Inpatient Psychiatry Ward. *American Journal of Orthopsychiatry*, 76, 31–36.

Gregory, R. J. (2003). Somatoform and

Factitious Disorders (Review of Psychiatry Series, Volume 20, Number 3). *Psychosomatics: Journal of Consultation Liaison Psychiatry*, 44, 444–445.

Huffman, J. C., & Stern, T. A. (2003). The diagnosis and treatment of Munchausen' s syndrome. *General Hospital Psychiatry*, 25, 358–363.

Krahn, L. E., Li, H., & O'Connor, M. K. (2003). Patients Who Strive to Be Ill: Factitious Disorder With Physical Symptoms. *American Journal of Psychiatry*, 160, 1163–1168.

Lau, B., & Marcoux, E. (2003). Involuntary Treatment of a Patient with Factitious Disorder: A Paradox? *Canadian Journal of Psychiatry*, 48, 284.

Peebles, R., Sabella, C., Franco, K., & Goldfarb, J. (2005). Factitious Disorder and Malingering in Adolescent Girls: Case Series and Literature Review. *Clinical Pediatrics*, 44, 237–243.

Reisner, A. D. (2006). A Case of Munchausen Syndrome by Proxy With Subsequent Stalking Behavior. *International Journal of Offender Therapy and Comparative Criminology*, 50, 245–254.

Simon, G. E. (1998). Management of somatoform and factitious disorders. In Nathan, Peter E. (Ed.); Gorman, Jack M. (Ed.). *A guide to treatments that work.* (pp. 408–422). New York, NY, US: Oxford University Press.

Smith, G. R. Jr., Ford, C. V., King, S. A., Stoudemire, A., & et al (1996). Somatoform and factitious disorders. In Gabbard, Glen O. (Ed.); Atkinson, Sarah D. (Ed.). *Synopsis of treatments of psychiatric disorders* (2nd ed.). (pp. 723–768). Washington, DC, US: American Psychiatric Association.

Sorrentino, R. (2006). Playing sick? Untangling the web of Munchausen syndrome, Munchausen by proxy, malingering, and factitious disorder. *Psychiatric Services*, 57, 149.

Swanson, D. A. (1984). Malingering and associated syndromes. *Psychiatric Medicine*, 2, 287–293.

Thompson, C. R., & Beckson, M. (2004). A Case of Factitious Homicidal Ideation. *Journal of the American Academy of Psychiatry and the Law*, 32, 277–281.

body dysmorphic disorder

Allen, A. (2006). Cognitive-Behavioral Treatment of Body Dysmorphic Disorder. *Primary Psychiatry*, 13, 70–76.

American Psychiatric Association (1993). *Diagnostic and statistical manual of mental disorders* (4th ed.). Washington, DC.

Castle, D. J., & Rossell, S. L. (2006). An update on body dysmorphic disorder. *Current Opinion in Psychiatry*, 19, 74–78.

Castle, D. J., Rossell, S., & Kyrios, M. (2006). Body Dysmorphic Disorder. *Psychiatric Clinics of North America*, 29, 521–538.

Crerand, C. E., Phillips, K. A., Menard, W., & Fay, C. (2005). Nonpsychiatric medical treatment of body dysmorphic disorder. *Psychosomatics: Journal of Consultation Liaison Psychiatry*, 46, 549–555.

da Costa, D., Nelson, T. M., Rudes, J., & Guterman, J. T. (2007). A Narrative Approach to Body Dysmorphic Disorder. *Journal of Mental Health Counseling*, 29, 67–80.

Didie, E. R., Tortolani, C. C., Pope, C. G., Menard, W., Fay, C., & Phillips, K. A. (2006). Childhood abuse and neglect in body dysmorphic disorder. *Child Abuse & Neglect*, 30, 1105–1115.

Fawcett, J. (2004). Is BDD Culturally Induced? *Psychiatric Annals*, 34, 900.

Gorbis, E. (2004). Crooked Mirrors: The Externalization of Self-Image in Body Dysmorphic Disorder. *The Behavior Therapist*, 27, 74–76.

Grant, J. E., & Phillips, K. A. (2005).

Recognizing and Treating Body Dysmorphic Disorder. *Annals of Clinical Psychiatry*, 17, 205–210.

Hadley, S. J., Kim, S., Priday, L., & Hollander, E. (2006). Pharmacologic Treatment of Body Dysmorphic Disorder. *Primary Psychiatry*, 13, 61–69.

Nardi, A. E., Lopes, F. L., & Valença, A. M. (2005). Body dysmorphic disorder treated with bupropion: Cases report. *Australian and New Zealand Journal of Psychiatry*, 39, 112.

Neziroglu, F., Roberts, M., & Yaryura-Tobias, J. A. (2004). A Behavioral Model for Body Dysmorphic Disorder. *Psychiatric Annals*, 34, 915–920.

Phillips, K.A. (2002). 'I'm as ugly as the elephant man': How to recognize and treat body dysmorphic disorder. *Current Psychiatry*, 158–65.

Phillips, K. A. (2004). Psychosis in body dysmorphic disorder. *Journal of Psychiatric Research*, 38, 63–72.

Phillips, K. A. (2004). Treating Body Dysmorphic Disorder Using Medication. *Psychiatric Annals*, 34, 945–953.

Phillips, K. A. (2005). *The broken mirror: Understanding and treating body dysmorphic disorder*. New York: Oxford University Press.

Phillips, K. A., & Castle, D. J. (2002). Body dysmorphic disorder. In Castle, David J. (Ed.); Phillips, Katharine A. (Ed.). *Disorders of body image* (pp. 101–120). Petersfield, England: Wrightson Biomedical Publishing.

Phillips, K. A., & Rasmussen, S. A. (2004). Change in psychosocial functioning and quality of life of patients with body dysmorphic disorder treated with fluoxetine: A placebo-controlled study. *Psychosomatics: Journal of Consultation Liaison Psychiatry*, 45, 438–444.

Phillips, K. A., Menard, W., Fay, C., & Pagano, M. E. (2005). Psychosocial functioning and quality of life in body dysmorphic disorder. *Comprehensive Psychiatry*, 46, 254–260.

Phillips, K. A. (2006). The Presentation of Body Dysmorphic Disorder in Medical Settings. *Primary Psychiatry*, 13, 51–59.

Phillips, K. A., Pagano, M. E., Menard, W., Fay, C., & Stout, R. L. (2005). Predictors of Remission From Body Dysmorphic Disorder: A Prospective Study. *Journal of Nervous and Mental Disease*, 193, 564–567.

Phillips, K. A., Menard, W., Pagano, M. E., Fay, C., & Stout, R. L. (2006). Delusional versus nondelusional body dysmorphic disorder: Clinical features and course of illness. *Journal of Psychiatric Research*, 40, 95–104.

Pinto, A., & Phillips, K. A. (2005). Social anxiety in body dysmorphic disorder. *Body Image*, 2, 401–405.

Ruffolo, J. S., Phillips, K. A., Menard, W., Fay, C., & Weisberg, R. B. (2006). Comorbidity of Body Dysmorphic Disorder and Eating Disorders: Severity of Psychopathology and Body Image Disturbance. *International Journal of Eating Disorders*, 39, 11–19.

Sarwer, D. B., Gibbons, L. M., & Crerand, C. E. (2004). Treating Body Dysmorphic Disorder With Cognitive-behavior Therapy. *Psychiatric Annals*, 34, 934–941.

Williams, J., Hadjistavropoulos, T., & Sharpe, D. (2006). A meta-analysis of psychological and pharmacological treatments for body dysmorphic disorder. *Behaviour Research and Therapy*, 44, 99–111.

anorexia nervosa

American Psychiatric Association (1993). *Diagnostic and statistical manual of mental disorders* (4th ed.). Washington, DC: American Psychiatric Association.

Banasiak, S. J., Paxton, S. J., & Hay, P. J. (2007). Perceptions of Cognitive Behavioural Guided Self-Help

Treatment for Bulimia Nervosa in Primary Care. *Eating Disorders: The Journal of Treatment & Prevention*, 15, 23–40.

Bryant-Waugh, R. (2006). Recent Developments in Anorexia Nervosa. *Child and Adolescent Mental Health*, 11, 76–81.

Carter, J. C., Bewell, C., Blackmore, E., & Woodside, D. B. (2006). The impact of childhood sexual abuse in anorexia nervosa. *Child Abuse & Neglect*, 30, 257–269.

Couturier, J. L., & Lock, J. (2006). Denial and minimization in adolescents with anorexia nervosa. *International Journal of Eating Disorders*, 39, 212–216.

Couturier, J., & Lock, J. (2006). What is Recovery in Adolescent Anorexia Nervosa? *International Journal of Eating Disorders*, 39, 550–555.

Derman, T., & Szabo, C. P. (2006). Why do individuals with anorexia die? A case of sudden death. *International Journal of Eating Disorders*, 39, 260–262.

Emmett, S. W., & Rabinor, J. R. (Ed.); The Sated Starver (2007). Rabinor, Judith Ruskay. The Therapist's Voice: The Sated Starver. *Eating Disorders: The Journal of Treatment & Prevention*, 15, 81–84.

Failler, A. (2006). Appetizing loss: Anorexia as an experiment in living. *Eating Disorders: The Journal of Treatment & Prevention*, 14, 99–107.

Fichter, M. M., Quadflieg, N., & Hedlund, S. (2006). Twelve-year course and outcome predictors of anorexia nervosa. *International Journal of Eating Disorders*, 39, 87–100.

Frisch, M. J., Herzog, D. B., & Franko, D. L. (2006). Residential Treatment for Eating Disorders. *International Journal of Eating Disorders*, 39, 434–442.

Gale, C., Holliday, J., Troop, N. A., Serpell, L., & Treasure, J. (2006). The Pros and Cons of Change in

Individuals with Eating Disorders: A Broader Perspective. *International Journal of Eating Disorders*, 39, 394–403.

Gillberg, I. C., Gillberg, C., Rastam, M., and Johannson, M. (1996). The cognitive profile of anorexia nervosa: A comparative study including a community-based sample. *Comprehensive Psychiatry*, 37.

Gowers, S. G. (2006). Evidence Based Research in CBT with Adolescent Eating Disorders. *Child and Adolescent Mental Health*, 11, 9–12.

Halvorsen, I., & Heyerdahl, S. (2006). Girls with Anorexia Nervosa as Young Adults: Personality, Self-Esteem, and Life Satisfaction. *International Journal of Eating Disorders*, 39, 285–293.

Herzog, D. B., Franko, D. L., Dorer, D. J., Keel, P. K., Jackson, S., & Manzo, M. P. (2006). Drug Abuse in Women with Eating Disorders. *International Journal of Eating Disorders*, 39, 364–368.

Hudson, J. I., Hiripi, E., Pope Jr., H. G., & Kessler, R. C. (2007). The Prevalence and Correlates of Eating Disorders in the National Comorbidity Survey Replication. *Biological Psychiatry*, 61, 348–358.

Kaye, W. H., Frank, G. K., Bailer, U. F., & Henry, S. E. (2005). Neurobiology of Anorexia Nervosa: Clinical Implications of Alterations of the Function of Serotonin and Other Neuronal Systems. *International Journal of Eating Disorders*, 37, S15–S19.

Key, A., O'Brien, A., Gordon, I., Christie, D., & Lask, B. (2006). Assessment of Neurobiology in Adults with Anorexia Nervosa. *European Eating Disorders Review*, 14, 308–314.

Lock, J., Couturier, J., & Agras, W. S. (2006). Comparison of Long-Term Outcomes in Adolescents With Anorexia Nervosa Treated With Family Therapy. *Journal of the American Academy of Child &*

Adolescent Psychiatry, 45, 666–672.

Lock, J., le Grange, D., Forsberg, S., & Hewell, K. (2006). Is Family Therapy Useful for Treating Children With Anorexia Nervosa? Results of a Case Series. Journal of the American Academy of Child & Adolescent Psychiatry, 45, 1323–1328.

Lynn, S. J., Kirsch, I., Crowley, M., & Campion, A. (2006). Eating Disorders and Obesity with Maryellen Crowley and Anna Campion. In Lynn, Steven Jay; Kirsch, Irving. Essentials of clinical hypnosis: An evidence-based approach. (pp. 99–120). Washington, DC, US: American Psychological Association.

Macdonald, A. J. (2006). Personality subtypes and cognitive impairment in anorexia nervosa. British Journal of Psychiatry, 188, 87–88.

McIntosh, V. V. W., Jordan, J., Luty, S. E., Carter, F. A., McKenzie, J. M., Bulik, C. M., & Joyce, P. R. (2006). Specialist Supportive Clinical Management for Anorexia Nervosa. International Journal of Eating Disorders, 39, 625–632.

Nilsson, K., & Hägglöf, B. (2006). Patient Perspectives of Recovery in Adolescent Onset Anorexia Nervosa. Eating Disorders: The Journal of Treatment & Prevention, 14, 305–311.

Nordbo, R. H. S., Espeset, E. M. S., Gulliksen, K. S., Skårderud, F., & Holte, A. (2006). The Meaning of Self-Starvation: Qualitative Study of Patients' Perception of Anorexia Nervosa. International Journal of Eating Disorders, 39, 556–564.

Pereira, T., Lock, J., & Oggins, J. (2006). Role of Therapeutic Alliance in Family Therapy for Adolescent Anorexia Nervosa. International Journal of Eating Disorders, 39, 677–684.

Roots, P., Hawker, J., & Gowers, S. (2006). The use of Target Weights in the Inpatient Treatment of Adolescent Anorexia Nervosa. European Eating Disorders Review, 14, 323–328.

Ruffolo, J. S., Phillips, K. A., Menard, W., Fay, C., & Weisberg, R. B. (2006). Comorbidity of Body Dysmorphic Disorder and Eating Disorders: Severity of Psychopathology and Body Image Disturbance. International Journal of Eating Disorders, 39, 11–19.

Shroff, H., Reba, L., Thornton, L. M., Tozzi, F., Klump, K. L., Berrettini, W. H., Brandt, H., Crawford, S., Crow, S., Fichter, M. M., Goldman, D., Halmi, K. A., Johnson, C., Kaplan, A. S., Keel, P., LaVia, M., Mitchell, J., Rotondo, A., Strober, M., Treasure, J., Woodside, D. B., Kaye, W. H., & Bulik, C. M. (2006). Features Associated With Excessive Exercise in Women with Eating Disorders. International Journal of Eating Disorders, 39, 454–461.

Silacci, J. (2007). Review of Appetite for Life: Inspiring Stories of Recovery from Anorexia, Bulimia, and Compulsive Overeating. Eating Disorders: The Journal of Treatment & Prevention, 15, 89–90.

Södersten, P., Bergh, C., & Zandian, M. (2006). Psychoneuroendocrinology of anorexia nervosa. Psychoneuroendocrinology, 31, 1149–1153.

Starzomska, M. (2006). The role of broad and narrow definitions of capacity in treating anorexic patients. Archives of Psychiatry and Psychotherapy, 8, 25–40.

Steinglass, J., & Walsh, B. T. (2006). Habit learning and anorexia nervosa: A cognitive neuroscience hypothesis. International Journal of Eating Disorders, 39, 267–275.

Stewart, M., Keel, P. K., & Schiavo, R. S. (2006). Stigmatization of Anorexia Nervosa. International Journal of Eating Disorders, 39, 320–325.

Thurfjell, B., Eliasson, M., Swenne, I., von Knorring, A. L., & Engström, I. (2006). Perceptions of Gender Ideals Predict Outcome of Eating Disorders in Adolescent Girls. *Eating Disorders: The Journal of Treatment & Prevention*, 14, 287–304.

Troisi, A., Di Lorenzo, G., Alcini, S., Nanni, R. C., Di Pasquale, C., & Siracusano, A. (2006). Body Dissatisfaction in Women With Eating Disorders: Relationship to Early Separation Anxiety and Insecure Attachment. *Psychosomatic Medicine*, 68, 449–453.

Woodside, B. D., & Staab, R. (2006). Management of Psychiatric Comorbidity in Anorexia Nervosa and Bulimia Nervosa. *CNS Drugs*, 20, 655–663.

bulimia nervosa

American Psychiatric Association (1993). *Diagnostic and statistical manual of mental disorders* (4th ed.). Washington, DC: American Psychiatric Association.

Banasiak, S. J., Paxton, S. J., & Hay, P. J. (2007). Perceptions of Cognitive Behavioural Guided Self-Help Treatment for Bulimia Nervosa in Primary Care. *Eating Disorders: The Journal of Treatment & Prevention*, 15, 23–40.

Benninghoven, D., Jürgens, E., Mohr, A., Heberlein, I., Kunzendorf, S., & Jantschek, G. (2006). Different Changes of Body-Images in Patients with Anorexia or Bulimia Nervosa During Inpatient Psychosomatic Treatment. *European Eating Disorders Review*, 14, 88–96.

Berrettini, W. H., Kaye, W. H., & Bulik, C. M. (2005). The Relation among Perfectionism, Obsessive-Compulsive Personality Disorder and Obsessive-Compulsive Disorder in Individuals with Eating Disorders. *International Journal of Eating Disorders*, 38, 371–374.

Bodenlos, J. S., Kose, S., Borckardt, J. J., Nahas, Z., Shaw, D., O'Neil, P. M., & George, M. S. (2007). Vagus nerve stimulation acutely alters food craving in adults with depression. *Appetite*, 48, 145–153.

Butryn, M. L., Lowe, M. R., Safer, D. L., & Agras, W. S. (2006). Weight Suppression Is a Robust Predictor of Outcome in the Cognitive-Behavioral Treatment of Bulimia Nervosa. *Journal of Abnormal Psychology*, 115, 62–67.

Carter, F. A., McIntosh, V. V. W., Joyce, P. R., Frampton, C. M. A., & Bulik, C. M. (2006). Cue Reactivity in Bulimia Nervosa: A Useful Self-Report Approach. *International Journal of Eating Disorders*, 39, 694–699.

Dunn, E. C., Neighbors, C., & Larimer, M. E. (2006). Motivational Enhancement Therapy and Self-Help Treatment for Binge Eaters. *Psychology of Addictive Behaviors*, 20, 44–52.

Epstein, E. M., & Sloan, D. M. (2005). Tailoring Cognitive Behavioral Therapy for Individuals Diagnosed with Bulimia Nervosa. *Journal of Contemporary Psychotherapy*, 35, 317–330.

Faris, P. L., Eckert, E. D., Kim, S., Meller, W. H., Pardo, J. V., Goodale, R. L., & Hartman, B. K. (2006). Evidence for a vagal pathophysiology for bulimia nervosa and the accompanying depressive symptoms. *Journal of Affective Disorders*, 92, 79–90.

Ferguson, C. P., & Pigott, T. A. (2000). Anorexia and bulimia nervosa: Neurobiology and pharmacotherapy. *Behavior Therapy*, 31, 237–263.

Frienderich, H., Kumari, V., Uher, R., Riga, M., Schmidt, U., Campbell, I. C., Herzog, W., & Treasure, J. (2006). Differential motivational responses to food and pleasurable cues in anorexia and bulimia nervosa: A startle reflex paradigm. *Psychological Medicine*, 36, 1327–1335.

Ghaderi, A. (2006). Attrition and outcome in self-help treatment for bulimia nervosa and binge eating disorder: A constructive replication. *Eating Behaviors*, 7, 300–308.

Gorman, S. E., & Gorman, J. M. (2004). Beyond Misconceptions: Neurobiological and Genetic Associations in Eating Disorders. *CNS Spectrums*, 9, 504.

Halmi, K. A., Tozzi, F., Thornton, L. M., Crow, S., Fichter, M. M., Kaplan, A. S., Keel, P., Klump, K. L., Lilenfeld, L. R., Mitchell, J. E., Plotnicov, K. H., Pollice, C., Rotondo, A., Strober, M., Woodside, D. B., Halmi, K. A. (2004). The Neurobiology of Eating Disorders: A Resurgence of Investigations. *CNS Spectrums*, 9, 510.

Herzog, D. B., Franko, D. L., Dorer, D. J., Keel, P. K., Jackson, S., & Manzo, M. P. (2006). Drug Abuse in Women with Eating Disorders. *International Journal of Eating Disorders*, 39, 364–368.

Hildebrandt, T., & Latner, J. (2006). Effect of Self-Monitoring on Binge Eating: Treatment Response or 'Binge Drift'? *European Eating Disorders Review*, 14, 17–22.

Kaye, W. H., Devlin, B., Barbarich, N., Bulik, C. M., Thornton, L., Bacanu, S., Fichter, M. M., Halmi, K. A., Kaplan, A. S., Strober, M., Woodside, D. B., Bergen, A. W., Crow, S., Mitchell, J., Rotondo, A., Mauri, M., Cassano, G., Keel, P., Plotnicov, K., Pollice, C., Klump, K. L., Lilenfeld, L. R., Ganjei, J. K., Quadflieg, N., & Berrettini, W. H. (2004). Genetic analysis of bulimia nervosa: Methods and sample description. *International Journal of Eating Disorders*, 35, 556–570.

Le Grange, D., & Schmidt, U. (2005). The treatment of adolescents with bulimia nervosa. *Journal of Mental Health*, 14, 587–597.

Lowe, M. R., Davis, W., Lucks, D., Annunziato, R., & Butryn, M. (2006). Weight suppression predicts weight gain during inpatient treatment of bulimia nervosa. *Physiology & Behavior*, 87, 487–492.

Mitchell, J. E., Agras, S., & Wonderlich, S.

(2007). Treatment of Bulimia Nervosa: Where Are We and Where Are We Going? *International Journal of Eating Disorders*, 40, 95–101.

Mond, J., Hay, P., Rodgers, B., & Owen, C. (2006). Self-Recognition of Disordered Eating Among Women with Bulimic-Type Eating Disorders: A Community-Based Study. *International Journal of Eating Disorders*, 39, 747–753.

Monteleone, P., Santonastaso, P., Mauri, M., Bellodi, L., Erzegovesi, S., Fuschino, A., Favaro, A., Rotondo, A., Castaldo, E., & Maj, M. (2006). Investigation of the Serotonin Transporter Regulatory Region Polymorphism in Bulimia Nervosa: Relationships to Harm Avoidance, Nutritional Parameters, and Psychiatric Comorbidity. *Psychosomatic Medicine*, 68, 99–103.

Morgan, C. D., & Marsh, C. (2006). Bulimia nervosa in an elderly male: A case report. *International Journal of Eating Disorders*, 39, 170–171.

Nevonen, L., & Broberg, A. G. (2006). A comparison of sequenced individual and group psychotherapy for patients with bulimia nervosa. *International Journal of Eating Disorders*, 39, 117–127.

Perugi, G., Toni, C., Passino, M. C. S., Akiskal, K. K., Kaprinis, S., & Akiskal, H. S. (2006). Bulimia nervosa in atypical depression: The mediating role of cyclothymic temperament. *Journal of Affective Disorders*, 92, 91–97.

Ramacciotti, C. E., Coli, E., Paoli, R., Gabriellini, G., Schulte, F., Castrogiovanni, S., Dell'Osso, L., & Garfinkel, P. E. (2005). The relationship between binge eating disorder and non-purging bulimia nervosa. *Eating and Weight Disorders*, 10, 8–12.

Ramacciotti, C. E., Coli, E., Paoli, R., Marazziti, D., & Dell'Osso, L. (2003). Serotonergic activity measured by platelet [³H] paroxetine binding in patients with eating disorders. *Psychiatry Research*, 118, 33–38.

Schapman-Williams, A. M., Lock, J., & Couturier, J. (2006). Cognitive-behavioral therapy for adolescents with binge eating syndromes: A case series. *International Journal of Eating Disorders*, 39, 252–255.

Shroff, H., Reba, L., Thornton, L. M., Tozzi, F., Klump, K. L., Berrettini, W. H., Brandt, H., Crawford, S., Crow, S., Fichter, M. M., Goldman, D., Halmi, K. A., Johnson, C., Kaplan, A. S., Keel, P., LaVia, M., Mitchell, J., Rotondo, A., Strober, M., Treasure, J., Woodside, D. B., Kaye, W. H., & Bulik, C. M. (2006). Features Associated With Excessive Exercise in Women with Eating Disorders. *International Journal of Eating Disorders*, 39, 454–461.

Troisi, A., Di Lorenzo, G., Alcini, S., Nanni, R. C., Di Pasquale, C., & Siracusano, A. (2006). Body Dissatisfaction in Women With Eating Disorders: Relationship to Early Separation Anxiety and Insecure Attachment. *Psychosomatic Medicine*, 68, 449–453.

Wilson, G. T., & Sysko, R. (2006). Cognitive-Behavioural Therapy for Adolescents with Bulimia Nervosa. *European Eating Disorders Review*, 14, 8–16.

paranoid personality disorder

American Psychiatric Association (1993). Diagnostic and statistical manual of mental disorders (4th ed.). Washington, DC: American Psychiatric Association Bender, D. S. (2005). The Therapeutic Alliance in the Treatment of Personality Disorders. *Journal of Psychiatric Practice*, 11, 73–87.

Bockian, N. R. (2006). Depression in Paranoid Personality Disorder. In Bockian, Neil R. Personality-guided therapy for depression. (pp. 41–62).

Washington, DC, US: American Psychological Association.

Ekselius, L., Tillfors, M., Furmark, T., & Fredrikson, M. (2001). Personality disorders in the general population: DSM-IV and ICD-10 defined prevalence as related to sociodemographic profile. *Personality and Individual Differences*, 30, 311–320.

Fava, M., Farabaugh, A. H., Sickinger, A. H., Wright, E., Alpert, J. E., Sonawalla, S., Nierenberg, A. A., & Worthington, J. J. III (2002). Personality disorders and depression. *Psychological Medicine*, 32, 1049–1057.

Harper, R. G. (2004). Paranoid personality. In Harper, Robert G. *Personality-guided therapy in behavioral medicine* (pp. 65–90). Washington, DC, US: American Psychological Association.

Hawkes, B. (2004). Primitive experiences of loss: Working with the paranoid-schizoid patient. *Psychodynamic Practice: Individuals, Groups and Organisations*, 10, 284–285.

Hayward, B. A. (2007). Cluster A personality disorders: Considering the 'odd-eccentric' in psychiatric nursing. *International Journal of Mental Health Nursing*, 16, 15–21.

Links, P. S., & Stockwell, M. (2004). Couples therapy with a paranoid personality-disordered client. In MacFarlane, Malcolm M. (Ed.). *Family treatment of personality disorders: Advances in clinical practice* (pp. 361–380). Binghamton, NY, US: Haworth Clinical Practice Press.

Miller, M. B., Useda, J. D., Trull, T. J., Burr, R. M., & Minks-Brown, C. (2001). Paranoid, schizoid, and schizotypal personality disorders. In Sutker, Patricia B. (Ed.); Adams, Henry E. (Ed.). *Comprehensive handbook of psychopathology* (3rd ed.). (pp. 535–559). New York, NY, US: Kluwer Academic/Plenum Publishers.

Millon, T., Grossman, S., Millon, C., Meagher, S., & Ramnath, R. (2004). *Personality disorders in modern life* (2nd ed.). Hoboken, NJ, US: John Wiley & Sons, Inc.

Oltmanns, T. F., & Okada, M. (2006). Paranoia. In Fisher, Jane E. (Ed.); O'Donohue, William T. (Ed.). *Practitioner's guide to evidence-based psychotherapy.* (pp. 503–513). New York, NY, US: Springer Science + Business Media.

Pretzer, J. (2004). Cognitive Therapy of Personality Disorders. In Magnavita, Jeffrey J. (Ed.). *Handbook of Personality Disorders: Theory and Practice* (pp. 169–193). Hoboken, NJ, US: John Wiley & Sons, Inc.

Rasmussen, P. R. (2005). The Paranoid Prototype. In Rasmussen, Paul R. *Personality-guided cognitive-behavioral therapy* (pp. 49–71). Washington, DC, US: American Psychological Association.

Sutker, P. B. (2004). Contemporary perspectives on cognitive therapy for personality disorders. *Journal of Psychopathology and Behavioral Assessment,* 26, 211–212.

Tyrer, P., Mitchard, S., Methuen, C., & Ranger, M. (2003). Treatment rejecting and treatment seeking personality disorders: Type R and Type S. *Journal of Personality Disorders,* 17, 263–267.

schizoid personality disorder

American Psychiatric Association (1993). *Diagnostic and statistical manual of mental disorders* (4th ed.). Washington, D.C. American Psychiatric Association.

Bender, D. S. (2005). The Therapeutic Alliance in the Treatment of Personality Disorders. *Journal of Psychiatric Practice,* 11, 73–87.

Bockian, N. R. (2006). Depression in Schizoid Personality Disorder. In Bockian, Neil R. *Personality-guided therapy for depression* (pp. 63–90).

Washington, DC, US: American Psychological Association.

Cornett, C. W. (1989). Schizoid adaptation in childhood: Symptomatology and treatment. *Child & Adolescent Social Work Journal,* 6, 99–113.

Costello, R. M. (1989). Schizoid personality disorder: A rare type in alcoholic populations. *Journal of Personality Disorders,* 3, 321–328.

Geiser, F., & Lieberz, K. (2000). Schizoid and narcissistic features in personality structure diagnosis. *Psychopathology,* 33, 19–24.

Harper, R. G. (2004). *Schizoid personality.* In Harper, Robert G. *Personality-guided therapy in behavioral medicine* (pp. 47–64). Washington, DC, US: American Psychological Association.

Kalus, O., Bernstein, D. P., & Siever, L. J. (1993). Schizoid personality disorder: A review of current status and implications for DSM-IV. *Journal of Personality Disorders,* 7, 43–52.

McWilliams, N. (2006). Some thoughts about schizoid dynamics. *Psychoanalytic Review,* 93, 1–24.

Rasmussen, P. R. (2005). The Schizoid Prototype. In Rasmussen, Paul R. *Personality-guided cognitive-behavioral therapy* (pp. 73–87). Washington, DC, US: American Psychological Association.

Rouff, L. (2000). Schizoid personality traits among the homeless mentally ill: A quantitative and qualitative report. *Journal of Social Distress & the Homeless,* 9, 127–141.

Slavik, S., Sperry, L., & Carlson, J. (1992). The schizoid personality disorder: A review and an Adlerian view and treatment. *Individual Psychology: Journal of Adlerian Theory, Research & Practice,* 48, 137–154.

schizotypal personality disorder

American Psychiatric Association (1993). *Diagnostic and statistical manual of mental disorders* (4th ed.). Washington, DC.

Antelman, S. M., & Chiodo, L. A. (1984). Stress: Its effect on interactions among biogenic amines and role in the induction and treatment of disease. In L. L. Iversen, S. D. Iversen, & S. H. Snyder (Eds.), *Handbook of psychopharmacology* (Vol. 18, pp. 279–341). New York: Plenum Press.

Battaglia, M., & Torgersen, S. (1996). Schizotypal disorder: At the crossroads of genetics and nosology. *Acta Psychiatrica Scandinavica*, 94, 303–310.

Bockian, N. R. (2006). Depression in Schizotypal Personality Disorder. In Bockian, Neil R. *Personality-guided therapy for depression* (pp. 91–108). Washington, DC, US: American Psychological Association.

Bornstein, R. F., Klein, D. N., Mallon, J. C., & Slater, J. F. (1988). Schizotypal personality disorder in an outpatient population: Incidence and clinical characteristics. *Journal of Clinical Psychology*, 44, 322–325.

Brunke, J. J., Pogue-Geile, M. F., Garrett, A. H., & Hall, J. K. (1991). Impaired social functioning and schizophrenia: A familial association? *Schizophrenia Research*, 4, 250–251.

Carpenter, W. T., Buchanan, R. W., Kirkpatrick, B., Tamminga, C., Thaker, G., & Breier, A. (1992). The neuroanatomy of the deficit syndrome. *Schizophrenia Research*, 6.

Chavira, D. A., Grilo, C. M., Shea, M. T., Yen, S., Gunderson, J. G., Morey, L. C., Skodol, A. E., Stout, R. L., Zanarini, M. C., & Mcglashan, T. H. (2003). Ethnicity and four personality disorders. *Comprehensive Psychiatry*, 44, 483–491.

Condray, R., & Steinhauer, S. (1992). Schizotypal personality disorder in individuals with and without schizophrenic relatives: Similarities and contrasts in neurocognitive and clinical functioning. *Schizophrenia Research*, 7, 333–41.

Coryell, W.H., & Zimmerman, M. (1988) The heritability of schizophrenia and schizoaffective disorder. A family study. *Archives of General Psychiatry*, 146, 496–502.

Coryell, W.H., & Zimmerman, M. (1989). Personality disorder in the families of depressed, schizophrenic, and never-ill probands. *American Journal of Psychiatry*, 146, 496–502.

Frangos, E., Athanassenas, G., Tsitourides, S., Katsanou, N., & Alexandrakou, P. (1985). Prevalence of DSM III schizophrenia among first-degree relatives of schizophrenia probands. *Acta Psychiatrica Scandinavica*, 72, 382–386.

Harper, R. G. (2004). Schizotypal personality. In Harper, Robert G. *Personality-guided therapy in behavioral medicine* (pp. 91–109). Washington, DC, US: American Psychological Association.

Jacobsberg, L. B., Hymowitz, P., Barasch, A., & Francis, A J. (1996). Symptoms of Schizotypal personality disorder. *American Journal of Psychiatry*, 143 (10), 1222–1227.

Kendler, K. S. (1985). Diagnostic approaches to schizotypal personality disorder: A historical perspective. *Schizophrenia Bulletin*, 11, 538–553.

Kety, S. S., Rosenthal, D.,Wender, P. H., & Schulsinger, F. (1968). The types and prevalence of mental illness in the biological and adoptive families of adopted schizophrenics. *Journal of Psychiatric Research*, 6, 345–362.

Meuser, K. T., Yarnold, P. R., Levinson, D. F., Singh, H., Bellack, A. S., Kee, K., Morrison, R.L., & Yadalam, K.G.

(1990). Prevalence of substance abuse in schizophrenia: demographic and clinical correlates. *Schizophrenia Bulletin*, 17, 555–564.

Raine, A. (2006). Schizotypal personality: Neurodevelopmental and psychosocial trajectories. *Annual Review of Clinical Psychology*, 2, 291–326.

Rasmussen, P. R. (2005). The Schizotypal Prototype. In Rasmussen, Paul R. *Personality-guided cognitive-behavioral therapy* (pp. 89–99). Washington, DC, US: American Psychological Association.

Schulz, S. C., Schulz, P. M., & Wilson, W. H. (1988). Medication treatment of schizotypal personality disorder. *Journal of Personality Disorders*, 2, 1–13.

Siever, L. J., Silverman, J. M., Horvath, T. B., Coccoro, E. F., Klar, H., Davidson, M., Pinkham, L., Apter, S. H., Mohs, R. C., & Davis, K. L. (1993). Schizophrenia-related and affective personality disorder traits in relatives of probands with schizophrenia and personality disorders. *American Journal of Psychiatry*, 150, 435–442.

Siever, L. J., Bernstein, D. P., & Silverman, J. M. (1991). Schizotypal personality disorder: A review of its current status. *Journal of Personality Disorders*, 5, 178–193.

Skodol, A. E., Pagano, M. E., Bender, D. S., Shea, M. T., Gunderson, J. G., Yen, S., Stout, R. L., Morey, L. C., Sanislow, C. A., Grilo, C. M., Zanarini, M. C., & McGlashan, T. H. (2005). Stability of functional impairment in patients with schizotypal, borderline, avoidant, or obsessive-compulsive personality disorder over two years. *Psychological Medicine*, 35, 443–451.

Squires-Wheeler, E., Skodol, A.E., Bassett, A., & Erlenmeyer-Kimling, L. (1989). DSM-III-R schizotypal personality traits in offspring of schizophrenic disorder, affective disorder, and normal control parents. *Journal of*

Psychiatric Research, 23, 229–239.

Stanley, M. A., Turner, S. M., & Borden, J. W. (1990). Schizotypal features in obsessive-compulsive disorder. *Comprehensive Psychiatry*, 31, 511–518.

Taminga, C. A., Thaker, G. K., Buchanan, R., Kirkpatrick, B., Alphs, L. D., Chase, T. N., & Carpenter, W. T. (1992) Limbic system abnormalities identified in schizophrenia using positron emission topography with fluorodeoxyglucose and neocortical alterations with deficit syndrome. *Archives of General Psychiatry*, 49, 522–530.

Thaker, G., Adami, H., Moran, M., Lahti, A., & Cassady, S. (1993). Psychiatric illnesses in families of subjects with schizophrenia-spectrum personality disorders: High morbidity risks for unspecified functional psychosis and schizophrenia. *American Journal of Psychiatry*, 150, 66–71.

Tykra, A. R., Cannon, T. D., Haslam, N., Mednick, S. A., Schulsinger, F., Schulsinger, H., & Parnas, J. (1995) The latent structure of schizotypy: Premorbid indicators of a taxon of individuals at-risk for schizophrenia spectrum disorders. *Journal of Abnormal Psychology*, 104, 173–183.

antisocial personality disorder

American Psychiatric Association (1993). *Diagnostic and statistical manual of mental disorders* (4th ed.). Washington, DC: American Psychiatric Association.

Bockian, N. R. (2006). Depression in Antisocial Personality Disorder. In Bockian, Neil R. *Personality-guided therapy for depression* (pp. 109–133). Washington, DC, US: American Psychological Association.

Cooper, S., & Tiffin, P. (2006). Psychological assessment and treatment of adolescent offenders with psychopathic personality traits. *Educational and Child Psychology*, 23, 62–74.

Kim-Cohen, J., Moffitt, T. E., Taylor, A., Pawlby, S. J., & Caspi, A. (2005). Maternal Depression and Children's Antisocial Behavior: Nature and Nurture Effects. *Archives of General Psychiatry*, 62, 173–181.

Levy, T. M., & Orlans, M. (2004). Attachment disorder, antisocial personality, and violence. *Annals of the American Psychotherapy Assn*, 7, 18–23.

Marcus, D. K., Lilienfeld, S. O., Edens, J. F., & Poythress, N. G. (2006). Is antisocial personality disorder continuous or categorical? A taxometric analysis. *Psychological Medicine*, 36, 1571–1581.

Martens, W. H. J. (2005). Multidimensional Model of Trauma and Correlated Antisocial Personality Disorder. *Journal of Loss & Trauma*, 10, 115–129.

Ogloff, J. R. P. (2006). Psychopathy/ antisocial personality disorder conundrum. *Australian and New Zealand Journal of Psychiatry*, 40, 519–528.

Pietrzak, R. H., & Petry, N. M. (2005). Antisocial personality disorder is associated with increased severity of gambling, medical, drug and psychiatric problems among treatment-seeking pathological gamblers. *Addiction*, 100, 1183–1193.

Rasmussen, P. R. (2005). The Antisocial Prototype. In Rasmussen, Paul R. *Personality-guided cognitive-behavioral therapy* (pp. 101–120). Washington, DC, US: American Psychological Association.

Reid, W. H., & Thorne, S. A. (2006). Treating Antisocial Syndromes. *Journal of Psychiatric Practice*, 12, 320–323.

Stewart, C., Mezzich, A. C., & Day, B. (2006). Parental Psychopathology and Paternal Child Neglect in Late Childhood. *Journal of Child and Family Studies*, 15, 543–554.

Vien, A., & Beech, A. R. (2006). Psychopathy: Theory, Measurement, and Treatment. *Trauma, Violence, & Abuse*, 7, 155–174.

Walsh, B. W. (2006). *Treating self-injury: A practical guide*. New York, NY, US: Guilford Press.

Westermeyer, J., & Thuras, P. (2005). Association of Antisocial Personality Disorder and Substance Disorder Morbidity in a Clinical Sample. *American Journal of Drug and Alcohol Abuse*, 31, 93–110.

borderline personality disorder

American Psychiatric Association (1993). *Diagnostic and statistical manual of mental disorders* (4th ed.). Washington, DC: American Psychiatric Association.

Aviram, R. B., Brodsky, B. S., & Stanley, B. (2006). Borderline Personality Disorder. Stigma, and Treatment Implications. *Harvard Review of Psychiatry*, 14, 249–256.

Bockian, N. R. (2006). Depression in Borderline Personality Disorder. In Bockian, Neil R. *Personality-guided therapy for depression* (pp. 135–167). Washington, DC, US: American Psychological Association.

Clarkin, J. F., Yeomans, F. E. (Ed.), & Kernberg, O. F. (2006). Yeomans, Frank E. *Psychotherapy for borderline personality: Focusing on object relations*. Washington, DC, US: American Psychiatric Publishing, Inc.

Conklin, C. Z., Bradley, R., & Westen, D. (2006). Affect regulation in borderline personality disorder. *Journal of Nervous and Mental Disease*, 194, 69–77.

Davidson, K., Norrie, J., Tyrer, P., Gumley, A., Tata, P., Murray, H., & Palmer, S. (2006). The effectiveness of cognitive behavior therapy for borderline personality disorder: Results from the borderline personality disorder study of cognitive therapy (BOSCOT) trial. *Journal of Personality Disorders*, 20, 450–465.

Fonagy, P., & Bateman, A. (2006). Progress in the treatment of borderline personality disorder. *British Journal of Psychiatry*, 188, 1–3.

Harned, M. S., Banawan, S. F., & Lynch, T. R. (2006). Dialectical Behavior Therapy: An Emotion-Focused Treatment for Borderline Personality Disorder. *Journal of Contemporary Psychotherapy*, 36, 67–75.

Hazelton, M., Rossiter, R., & Milner, J. (2006). Managing the 'unmanageable': Training staff in the use of dialectical behaviour therapy for borderline personality disorder. *Contemporary Nurse Journal*, 21, 120–130.

Horowitz, M. J. (2006). Psychotherapy for Borderline Personality: Focusing on Object Relations. *American Journal of Psychiatry*, 163, 944–945.

Kellogg, S. H., & Young, J. E. (2006). Schema therapy for borderline personality disorder. *Journal of Clinical Psychology*, 62, 445–458.

Krysinska, K., Heller, T. S., & De Leo, D. (2006). Suicide and deliberate self-harm in personality disorders. *Current Opinion in Psychiatry*, 19, 95–101.

Levy, K. N., Clarkin, J. F., Yeomans, F. E., Scott, L. N., Wasserman, R. H., & Kernberg, O. F. (2006). The mechanisms of change in the treatment of borderline personality disorder with transference focused psychotherapy. *Journal of Clinical Psychology*, 62, 481–501.

Logathas, S. (2006). Review of Understanding and Treating Borderline Personality Disorder: A Guide for Borderline Personality Disorder. *Journal of Mental Health*, 15, 503.

Lynch, T. R., Chapman, A. L., Rosenthal, M. Z., Kuo, J. R., & Linehan, M. M. (2006). Mechanisms of change in dialectical behavior therapy:

Theoretical and empirical observations. *Journal of Clinical Psychology*, 62, 459–480.

Markowitz, J. C., Skodol, A. E., & Bleiberg, K. (2006). Interpersonal psychotherapy for borderline personality disorder: Possible mechanisms of change. *Journal of Clinical Psychology*, 62, 431–444.

Oldham, J. M. (2006). Borderline Personality Disorder and Suicidality. *American Journal of Psychiatry*, 163, 20–26.

Oldham, J. M. (2006). Integrated Treatment for Borderline Personality Disorder. *Psychiatric Annals*, 36, 361–369.

Preston, J. D. (2006). *Integrative treatment for borderline personality disorders: Effective, symptom-focused techniques, simplified for private practice.* Oakland, CA, US: New Harbinger Publications.

Salsman, N. L., & Linehan, M. M. (2006). Dialectical-behavioral therapy for borderline personality disorder. *Primary Psychiatry*, 13, 51–58.

Sayrs, J., & Whiteside, U. (2006). *Borderline Personality Disorder.* In Fisher, Jane E. (Ed.); O'Donohue, William T. (Ed.). *Practitioner's guide to evidence-based psychotherapy* (pp. 151–160). New York, NY, US: Springer Science + Business/Media.

Simeon, D. (2006). Self-Injurious Behaviors. In Hollander, Eric (Ed.); Stein, Dan J. (Ed.). *Clinical manual of impulse-control disorders.* (pp. 63–86). Washington, DC, US: American Psychiatric Publishing, Inc.

Trull, T. J., Stepp, S. D., & Solhan, M. (2006). Borderline personality disorder. In Andrasik, Frank (Ed.). *Comprehensive handbook of personality and psychopathology: Vol. 2: Adult Psychopathology* (pp. 299–315). Hoboken, NJ, US: John Wiley & Sons, Inc.

histrionic personality disorder

American Psychiatric Association (1993). *Diagnostic and statistical manual of mental disorders* (4th ed.). Washington, DC: American Psychiatric Association.

Bockian, N. R. (2006). Depression in Histrionic Personality Disorder. In Bockian, Neil R. *Personality-guided therapy for depression* (pp. 169–186). Washington, DC, US: American Psychological Association.

Callaghan, G. M., Summers, C. J., & Weidman, M. (2003). The Treatment of Histrionic and Narcissistic Personality Disorder Behaviors: A Single-Subject Demonstration of Clinical Improvement Using Functional Analytic Psychotherapy. *Journal of Contemporary Psychotherapy*, 33, 321–339.

Dorfman, W. I. (2000). Histrionic personality disorder. In Hersen, Michel (Ed.); Biaggio, Maryka (Ed.). *Effective brief therapies: A clinician's guide* (pp. 355-370). San Diego, CA, US: Academic Press.

Freeman, A., Freeman, S. M., & Rosenfield, B. (2005). Histrionic personality disorder. In Gabbard, Glen O. (Ed.); Beck, Judith S. (Ed.); Holmes, Jeremy (Ed.). *Oxford textbook of psychotherapy* (pp. 305–310). New York, NY, US: Oxford University Press.

Horowitz, M. J. (1997). Psychotherapy of histrionic personality disorder. *Journal of Psychotherapy Practice & Research*, 6, 93–107.

Millon, T., Grossman, S., Millon, C., Meagher, S., & Ramnath, R. (2004). *Personality disorders in modern life* (2nd ed.). Hoboken, NJ, US: John Wiley & Sons, Inc.

Rasmussen, P. R. (2005). The Histrionic Prototype. In Rasmussen, Paul R. *Personality-guided cognitive-behavioral therapy* (pp. 147–166). Washington, DC, US: American Psychological Association.

Schwartz, R. C. (2001). Psychotherapeutic diagnosis and treatment of histrionic personality disorder. *Annals of the American Psychotherapy Assn*, 4, 12–14.

Sperry, L., & Maniacci, M. P. (1998). The histrionic-obsessive couple. In Carlson, Jon (Ed.); Sperry, Len (Ed.). *The disordered couple* (pp. 187–205). Philadelphia, PA, US: Brunner/Mazel.

narcissistic personality disorder

American Psychiatric Association (1993). *Diagnostic and statistical manual of mental disorders* (4th ed.). Washington, DC: American Psychiatric Association.

Bennett, C. S. (2006). Attachment theory and research applied to the conceptualization and treatment of pathological narcissism. *Clinical Social Work Journal*, 34, 45–60.

Brunton, J. N., Lacey, J. H., & Waller, G. (2005). Narcissism and Eating Characteristics in Young Nonclinical Women. *Journal of Nervous and Mental Disease*, 193, 140–143.

Campbell, W. K., & Baumeister, R. F. (2006). Narcissistic Personality Disorder. In Fisher, Jane E. (Ed.); O'Donohue, William T. (Ed.). *Practitioner's guide to evidence-based psychotherapy* (pp. 423–431). New York, NY, US: Springer Science + Business Media.

Dimaggio, G., Fiore, D., Salvatore, G., & Carcione, A. (2007). Dialogical Relationship Patterns in Narcissistic Personalities: Session Analysis and Treatment Implications. *Journal of Constructivist Psychology*, 20, 23–51.

Guilé, J., Mbékou, V., & Lageix, P. (2004). Child and Parent Variables Associated with Treatment Response in Narcissistic Youths: The Role of Self-Blame and Shame. *Canadian Child and Adolescent Psychiatry Review*, 13, 81–85.

Harman, M. J., & Waldo, M. (2004). Relationship enhancement family therapy with narcissistic personality disorder. In MacFarlane, Malcolm M. (Ed.). *Family treatment of personality disorders: Advances in clinical practice* (pp. 335–359). Binghamton, NY, US: Haworth Clinical Practice Press.

Imbesi, L. (2000). On the etiology of narcissistic personality disorder. *Issues in Psychoanalytic Psychology*, 22, 43–58.

Jacobowitz, J., & Newton, N. A. (1999). Dynamics and treatment of narcissism in later life. In Duffy, Michael (Ed.). *Handbook of counseling and psychotherapy with older adults* (pp. 453–469). Hoboken, NJ, US: John Wiley & Sons, Inc.

Lieberman, A. R. (2004). The Narcissistic Personality Disorder. In Masterson, James F. (Ed.); Lieberman, Anne R. (Ed.). *A therapist's guide to the personality disorders: The Masterson Approach* (pp. 73–90). Phoenix, AZ, US: Zeig, Tucker & Theisen.

Martens, W. H. J. (2005). Shame and Narcissism: Therapeutic Relevance of Conflicting Dimensions of Excessive Self Esteem, Pride, and Pathological Vulnerable Self. *Annals of the American Psychotherapy Assn*, 8, 10–17.

Rasmussen, P. R. (2005). The Narcissistic Prototype. In Rasmussen, Paul R. *Personality-guided cognitive-behavioral therapy* (pp. 167–189). Washington, DC, US: American Psychological Association.

Ronningstam, E. F. (2005). *Identifying and understand the narcissistic personality.* New York, NY, US: Oxford University Press.

Scharff, J. S., & Bagnini, C. (2003). Narcissistic disorder. In Snyder, Douglas K. (Ed.); Whisman, Mark A. (Ed.). *Treating difficult couples: Helping clients with coexisting mental and relationship disorders* (pp. 285–307). New York, NY, US: Guilford Press.

Schwartz, R. C., & Smith, S. D. (2002).

Psychotherapeutic assessment and treatment of narcissistic personality disorder. *Annals of the American Psychotherapy Assn*, 5, 20–1.

Unterberg, M. P. (2003). Personality: Personalities, personal style, and trouble getting along. In Kahn, Jeffrey P. (Ed.); Langlieb, Alan M. (Ed.). *Mental health and productivity in the workplace: A handbook for organizations and clinicians* (pp. 458–480). San Francisco, CA, US: Jossey-Bass.

Vaglum, P. (1999). The narcissistic personality disorder and addiction. In Derksen, Jan (Ed.); Maffei, Cesare (Ed.); Groen, Herman (Ed.). *Treatment of personality disorders* (pp. 241–253). Dordrecht, Netherlands: Kluwer Academic Publishers.

avoidant personality disorder

American Psychiatric Association (1993). *Diagnostic and statistical manual of mental disorders* (4th ed.). Washington, DC: American Psychiatric Association.

Baillie, A. J., & Lampe, L. A. (1998). Avoidant personality disorder: Empirical support for DSM-IV revisions. *Journal of Personality Disorders*, 12, 23–30.

Bockian, N. R. (2006). Depression in Avoidant Personality Disorder. In Bockian, Neil R. *Personality-guided therapy for depression* (pp. 209–226). Washington, DC, US: American Psychological Association.

Emmelkamp, P. M. G., Benner, A., Kuipers, A., Feiertag, G. A., Koster, H. C., & van Apeldoorn, F. J. (2006). Comparison of brief dynamic and cognitive-behavioural therapies in avoidant personality disorder. *British Journal of Psychiatry*, 189, 60–64.

Harper, R. G. (2004). Avoidant personality. In Harper, Robert G. *Personality-guided therapy in behavioral medicine* (pp. 229–249).

Washington, DC, US: American Psychological Association.

Kantor, M. (2003). *Distancing: Avoidant personality disorders* (rev. & expan.). Westport, CT, US: Praeger Publishers/Greenwood Publishing Group.

Mahgoub, N., & Hossain, A. (2007). A 60-year-old Woman with Avoidant Personality Disorder. *Psychiatric Annals*, 37, 10–12.

Porcerelli, J. H., Dauphin, V. B., Ablon, J. S., Leitman, S., & Bambery, M. (2007). Psychoanalysis With Avoidant Personality Disorder: A Systematic Case Study. *Psychotherapy: Theory, Research, Practice, Training*, 44, 1–13.

Rasmussen, P. R. (2005). The Avoidant Prototype. In Rasmussen, Paul R. *Personality-guided cognitive-behavioral therapy* (pp. 191–213). Washington, DC, US: American Psychological Association.

Schut, A. J., Castonguay, L. G., Flanagan, K. M., Yamasaki, A. S., Barber, J. P., Bedics, J. D., & Smith, T. L. (2005). Therapist Interpretation, Patient-Therapist Interpersonal Process, and Outcome in Psychodynamic Psychotherapy for Avoidant Personality Disorder. *Psychotherapy: Theory, Research, Practice, Training*, 42, 494–511.

dependent personality disorder

American Psychiatric Association (1993). *Diagnostic and statistical manual of mental disorders* (4th ed.). Washington, DC: American Psychiatric Association.

Beitz, K., & Bornstein, R. F. (2006). Dependent Personality Disorder. In Fisher, Jane E. (Ed.); O'Donohue, William T. (Ed.). *Practitioner's guide to evidence-based psychotherapy* (pp. 230–237). New York, NY, US: Springer Science + Business Media.

Bornstein, R. F. (2005). *The dependent patient: A practitioner's guide.* Washington, DC, US: American Psychological Association.

Harper, R. G. (2004). Dependent personality. In Harper, Robert G. *Personality-guided therapy in behavioral medicine* (pp. 207–228). Washington, DC, US: American Psychological Association.

Nurse, A. R. (1998). The dependent/narcissistic couple. In Carlson, Jon (Ed.); Sperry, Len (Ed.). *The disordered couple* (pp. 315–331). Philadelphia, PA, US: Brunner/Mazel.

Perry, J. C. (2005). Dependent personality disorder. In Gabbard, Glen O. (Ed.); Beck, Judith S. (Ed.); Holmes, Jeremy (Ed.). *Oxford textbook of psychotherapy* (pp. 321–328). New York, NY, US: Oxford University Press.

Rasmussen, P. R. (2005). The Dependent Prototype. In Rasmussen, Paul R. *Personality-guided cognitive-behavioral therapy* (pp. 215–234). Washington, DC, US: American Psychological Association.

Rogina, J. M., & Quilitch, H. R. (2006). Treating Dependent Personality Disorders with Logotherapy: A Case Study. *International Forum for Logotherapy*, 29, 54–61.

obsessive-compulsive personality disorder

American Psychiatric Association (1993). *Diagnostic and statistical manual of mental disorders* (4th ed.). Washington, DC: American Psychiatric Association.

Aouizerate, B., Guehl, D., Cuny, E., Rougier, A., Burbaud, P., Tignol, J., & Bioulac, B. (2005). Updated overview of the putative role of the serotoninergic system in obsessive-compulsive disorder. *Neuropsychiatric Disease And Treatment*, 1, 231–243.

Bailey, G. R. Jr. (1998). Cognitive-behavioral treatment of obsessive-compulsive personality disorder.

Journal of Psychological Practice, 4, 51–59.

Bender, D. S., Skodol, A. E., Pagano, M. E., Dyck, I. R., Grilo, C. M., Shea, M. T., Sanislow, C. A., Zanarini, M. C., Yen, S., McGlashan, T. H., & Gunderson, J. G. (2006). Prospective assessment of treatment use by patients with personality disorders. *Psychiatric Services*, 57, 254–257.

Bhar, S. S., & Kyrios, M. (2005). Obsessions and Compulsions are Associated With Different Cognitive and Mood Factors. *Behaviour Change*, 22, 81–96.

Bockian, N. R. (2006). Depression in Obsessive-Compulsive Personality Disorder. In Bockian, Neil R. *Personality-guided therapy for depression* (pp. 247–265). Washington, DC, US: American Psychological Association.

Cavedini, P., Erzegovesi, S., Ronchi, P., & Bellodi, L. (1997). Predictive value of obsessive-compulsive personality disorder in antiobsessional pharmacological treatment. *European Neuropsychopharmacology*, 7, 45–49.

Clark, D. A. (2005). Lumping Versus Splitting: A Commentary on Subtyping in OCD. *Behavior Therapy*, 36, 401–404.

Dreessen, L., Hoekstra, R., & Arntz, A. (1997). Personality disorders do not influence the results of cognitive and behavior therapy for obsessive compulsive disorder. *Journal of Anxiety Disorders*, 11, 503–521.

Fullana, M. À., Mataix-Cols, D., Trujillo, J. L., Caseras, X., Serrano, F., Alonso, P., Menchón, J. M., Vallejo, J., & Torrubia, R. (2004). Personality characteristics in obsessive-compulsive disorder and individuals with subclinical obsessive-compulsive problems. *British Journal of Clinical Psychology*, 43, 387–398.

Grant, J. E. (2005). Guest Editorial: Rethinking the Obsessive Compulsive Spectrum. *Annals of Clinical Psychiatry*, 17, 195.

Halmi, K. A. (2005). Obsessive-Compulsive Personality Disorder and Eating Disorders. *Eating Disorders: The Journal of Treatment & Prevention*, 13, 85–92.

Haslam, N., Williams, B. J., Kyrios, M., McKay, D., & Taylor, S. (2005). Subtyping Obsessive-Compulsive Disorder: A Taxometric Analysis. *Behavior Therapy*, 36, 381–391.

Mancebo, M. C., Eisen, J. L., Grant, J. E., & Rasmussen, S. A. (2005). Obsessive Compulsive Personality Disorder and Obsessive Compulsive Disorder: Clinical Characteristics, Diagnostic Difficulties, and Treatment. *Annals of Clinical Psychiatry*, 17, 197–204.

Ng, R. M. K. (2005). Cognitive Therapy for Obsessive-compulsive Personality Disorder – A Pilot Study in Hong Kong Chinese Patients. *Hong Kong Journal of Psychiatry*, 15, 50–53.

Rasmussen, P. R. (2005). The Compulsive Prototype (Obsessive-Compulsive). In Rasmussen, Paul R. *Personality-guided cognitive-behavioral therapy* (pp. 235–257). Washington, DC, US: American Psychological Association.

Rowa, K., Purdon, C., Summerfeldt, L. J., & Antony, M. M. (2005). Why are some obsessions more upsetting than others? *Behaviour Research and Therapy*, 43, 1453–1465.

Sanislow, C. A., Morey, L. C., Grilo, C. M., Gunderson, J. G., Shea, M. T., Skodol, A. E., Stout, R. L., Zanarini, M. C., & McGlashan, T. H. (2002). Confirmatory factor analysis of DSM-IV borderline, schizotypal, avoidant and obsessive-compulsive personality disorders: Findings from the Collaborative Longitudinal Personality Disorders Study. *Acta Psychiatrica Scandinavica*, 105, 28–36.

Sansone, R. A., Levitt, J. L., & Sansone, L. A. (2005). The Prevalence of

Personality Disorders Among Those with Eating Disorders. *Eating Disorders: The Journal of Treatment & Prevention*, 13, 7–21.

Seedat, S., & Stein, D. J. (2002). Hoarding in obsessive-compulsive disorder and related disorders: A preliminary report of 15 cases. *Psychiatry and Clinical Neurosciences*, 56, 17–23.

Shannahoff-Khalsa, D. S. (2003). Kundalini Yoga Meditation Techniques for the Treatment of Obsessive-Compulsive and OC Spectrum Disorders. *Brief Treatment and Crisis Intervention*, 3, 369–382.

Skodol, A. E., Pagano, M. E., Bender, D. S., Shea, M. T., Gunderson, J. G., Yen, S., Stout, R. L., Morey, L. C., Sanislow, C. A., Grilo, C. M., Zanarini, M. C., & McGlashan, T. H. (2005). Stability of functional impairment in patients with schizotypal, borderline, avoidant, or obsessive-compulsive personality disorder over two years. *Psychological Medicine*, 35, 443–451.

Strauss, J. L., Hayes, A. M., Johnson, S. L., Newman, C. F., Brown, G. K., Barber, J. P., Laurenceau, J., & Beck, A. T. (2006). Early Alliance, Alliance Ruptures, and Symptom Change in a Nonrandomized Trial of Cognitive Therapy for Avoidant and Obsessive-Compulsive Personality Disorders. *Journal of Consulting and Clinical Psychology*, 74, 337–345.

substance use, abuse and dependance

Altamura, A. C. (2007). Bipolar spectrum and drug addiction. *Journal of Affective Disorders*, 99, 285.

American Psychiatric Association (1993). *Diagnostic and statistical manual of mental disorders* (4th ed.). Washington, DC: American Psychiatric Association.

Anderson, K. G., Ramo, D. E., Schulte, M. T., Cummins, K., & Brown, S. A. (2007). Substance use treatment outcomes for youth: Integrating personal and environmental predictors. *Drug and Alcohol Dependence*, 88, 42–48.

Arendt, M., Rosenberg, R., Foldager, L., Perto, G., & Munk-Jorgensen, P. (2007). Psychopathology among cannabis-dependent treatment seekers and association with later substance abuse treatment. *Journal of Substance Abuse Treatment*, 32, 113–119.

Ball, S. A., Carroll, K. M., Canning-Ball, M., & Rounsaville, B. J. (2006). Reasons for dropout from drug abuse treatment: Symptoms, personality, and motivation. *Addictive Behaviors*, 31, 320–330.

Bellack, A. S. (2007). Issues in understanding and treating comorbidity in people with serious mental illness. *Clinical Psychology: Science and Practice*, 14, 70–76.

Brown, T. G., Dongier, M., Latimer, E., Legault, L., Seraganian, P., Kokin, M., & Ross, D. (2007). Group-Delivered Brief Intervention versus Standard Care for Mixed Alcohol/Other Drug Problems: A Preliminary Study. *Alcoholism Treatment Quarterly*, 24, 23–40.

Callaghan, R. C., Taylor, L., & Tavares, J. (2006). Addressing the needs of injection drug users in detoxification treatment. *Journal of Substance Abuse Treatment*, 30, 165–166.

Chassin, L., & Handley, E. D. (2006). Parents and Families as Contexts for the Development of Substance Use and Substance Use Disorders. *Psychology of Addictive Behaviors*, 20, 135–137.

Conason, A. H., Oquendo, M. A., & Sher, L. (2006). Psychotherapy in the treatment of alcohol and substance abusing adolescents with suicidal behavior. *International Journal of Adolescent Medicine and Health*, 18, 9–13.

Crespi, T. D., & Rueckert, Q. H. (2006).

Family Therapy and Children of Alcoholics: Implications for Continuing Education and Certification in Substance Abuse Practice. *Journal of Child & Adolescent Substance Abuse*, 15, 33–44.

Donohue, B., Romero, V., & Hill, H. H. (2006). Treatment of co-occurring child maltreatment and substance abuse. *Aggression and Violent Behavior*, 11, 626–640.

Dundas, I. (2007). The Dilemma of Confrontation: Coping with Problem Drinking in the Family. *Alcoholism Treatment Quarterly*, 24, 79–98.

Durazzo, T. C., Cardenas, V. A., Studholme, C., Weiner, M. W., & Meyerhoff, D. J. (2007). Non-treatment-seeking heavy drinkers: Effects of chronic cigarette smoking on brain structure. *Drug and Alcohol Dependence*, 87, 76–82.

Edwards, G. (2007). Review of Substance Use Among Young People in Urban Environments. *Addiction*, 102, 493–494.

Eiden, R. D., Foote, A., & Schuetze, P. (2007). Maternal cocaine use and caregiving status: Group differences in caregiver and infant risk variables. *Addictive Behaviors*, 32, 465–476.

Futterman, R., Sapadin, K., & Silverman, S. (2006). Transferring psychological technology into substance abuse treatment: Substance abuse as a psychiatric illness. *Addiction Research and Theory*, 14, 265–274.

Gallop, R. J., Crits-Christoph, P., Ten Have, T. R., Barber, J. P., Frank, A., Griffin, M. L., & Thase, M. E. (2007). Differential Transitions Between Cocaine Use and Abstinence for Men and Women. *Journal of Consulting and Clinical Psychology*, 75, 95–103.

Gifford, E., & Humphreys, K. (2007). The psychological science of addiction. *Addiction*, 102, 352–361.

Grant, B. F., Harford, T. C., Muthén, B. O., Yi, H., Hasin, D. S., & Stinson, F. S. (2007). DSM-IV alcohol dependence and abuse: Further evidence of validity in the general population. *Drug and Alcohol Dependence*, 86, 154–166.

Gruber, K. J., & Taylor, M. F. (2006). A Family Perspective for Substance Abuse: Implications from the Literature. *Journal of Social Work Practice in the Addictions*, 6, 1–29.

Hartman, C. A., Lessem, J. M., Hopfer, C. J., Crowley, T. J., & Stallings, M. C. (2006). The Family Transmission of Adolescent Alcohol Abuse and Dependence. *Journal of Studies on Alcohol*, 67, 657–664.

Hser, Y. (2007). Predicting Long-Term Stable Recovery from Heroin Addiction: Findings from a 33-year Follow-Up Study. *Journal of Addictive Diseases*, 26, 51–60.

Hser, Y., Stark, M. E., Paredes, A., Huang, D., Anglin, M. D., & Rawson, R. (2006). A 12-year follow-up of a treated cocaine-dependent sample. *Journal of Substance Abuse Treatment*, 30, 219–226.

Jones, C. G. A., Swift, W., Donnelly, N. J., & Weatherburn, D. J. (2007). Correlates of driving under the influence of cannabis. *Drug and Alcohol Dependence*, 88, 83–86.

Knudsen, H. K., Ducharme, L. J., & Roman, P. M. (2007). The adoption of medications in substance abuse treatment: Associations with organizational characteristics and technology clusters. *Drug and Alcohol Dependence*, 87, 164–174.

Leamon, M. H. (2006). When to Refer Patients for Substance Abuse Assessment and Treatment. *Primary Psychiatry*, 13, 46–51.

Leichtling, G., Gabriel, R. M., Lewis, C. K., & Vander Ley, K. J. (2006). Adolescents in Treatment: Effects of Parental Substance Abuse on Treatment Entry Characteristics and Outcomes. *Journal of Social Work*

Practice in the Addictions, 6, 155–174.

Mancinelli, R., Binetti, R., & Ceccanti, M. (2007). Woman, alcohol and environment: Emerging risks for health. *Neuroscience & Biobehavioral Reviews*, 31, 246–253.

Mark, T. L., Song, X., Vandivort, R., Duffy, S., Butler, J., Coffey, R., & Schabert, V. F. (2006). Characterizing substance abuse programs that treat adolescents. *Journal of Substance Abuse Treatment*, 31, 59–65.

Matzger, H., & Weisner, C. (2007). Nonmedical use of prescription drugs among alongitudinal sample of dependent and problem drinkers. *Drug and Alcohol Dependence*, 86, 222–229.

Miller, W. R., Sorensen, J. L., Selzer, J. A., & Brigham, G. S. (2006). Disseminating evidence-based practices in substance abuse treatment: A review with suggestions. *Journal of Substance Abuse Treatment*, 31, 25–39.

Mueser, K. T., & Drake, R. E. (2007). Comorbidity: What have we learned and where are we going? *Clinical Psychology: Science and Practice*, 14, 64–69.

Ostacher, M. J. (2007). Comorbid Alcohol and Substance Abuse Dependence in Depression: Impact on the Outcome of Antidepressant Treatment. *Psychiatric Clinics of North America*, 30, 69–76.

Piotrowski, N. A. (2007). Comorbidity and psychological science: Does one size fit all? *Clinical Psychology: Science and Practice*, 14, 6–19.

Pollack, H. A., D'Aunno, T., & Lamar, B. (2006). Outpatient substance abuse treatment and HIV prevention: An update. *Journal of Substance Abuse Treatment*, 30, 39–47.

Rassool, G. H. (Ed.) (2006). Substance abuse in black and minority ethnic communities in the United Kingdom: A neglected problem? *Journal of Addictions Nursing*, 17, 127–132.

Ross, S., & Hayden, F. (2006). *Study guide to substance abuse treatment: A companion to The American Psychiatric Publishing Textbook of Substance Abuse Treatment* (3rd ed.). Washington, DC, US: American Psychiatric Publishing, Inc.

Saatcioglu, O., Erim, R., & Cakmak, D. (2006). Role of family in alcohol and substance abuse. *Psychiatry and Clinical Neurosciences*, 60, 125–132.

Sakai, J. T., Mikulich-Gilbertson, S. K., & Crowley, T. J. (2006). Adolescent inhalant use among male patients in treatment for substance and behavior problems: Two-year outcome. *American Journal of Drug and Alcohol Abuse*, 32, 29–40.

Shearer, J. (2007). Psychosocial approaches to psychostimulant dependence: A systematic review. *Journal of Substance Abuse Treatment*, 32, 41–52.

Spadoni, A. D., McGee, C. L., Fryer, S. L., & Riley, E. P. (2007). Neuroimaging and fetal alcohol spectrum disorders. *Neuroscience & Biobehavioral Reviews*, 31, 239–245.

Stahler, G. J., Mazzella, S., Mennis, J., Chakravorty, S., Rengert, G., & Spiga, R. (2007). The effect of individual, program, and neighborhood variables on continuity of treatment among dually diagnosed individuals. *Drug and Alcohol Dependence*, 87, 54–62.

Stratyner, H. B. (2006). Multi-factorial Approaches to Substance Use Disorders and Addiction. *CNS Spectrums*, 11, 828.

Sun, A. (2007). Relapse among Substance-Abusing Women: Components and Processes. *Substance Use & Misuse*, 42, 1–21.

Tsuang, J., Fong, T. W., & Lesser, I. (2006). Psychosocial Treatment of Patients With Schizophrenia and Substance Abuse Disorders. *Addictive*

Disorders & Their Treatment, 5, 53–66.

Thompson Jr., R. G., & Auslander, W. F. (2007). Risk factors for alcohol and marijuana use among adolescents in foster care. *Journal of Substance Abuse Treatment*, 32, 61–69.

van den Bosch, L. M. C., & Verheul, R. (2007). Patients with addiction and personality disorder: Treatment outcomes and clinical implications. *Current Opinion in Psychiatry*, 20, 67–71.

Waldron, H. B., Kern-Jones, S., Turner, C. W., Peterson, T. R., & Ozechowski, T. J. (2007). Engaging resistant adolescents in drug abuse treatment. *Journal of Substance Abuse Treatment*, 32, 133–142.

Zilberman, M. L., Tavares, H., Hodgins, D. C., & el-Guebaly, N. (2007). The Impact of Gender, Depression, and Personality on Craving. Journal of Addictive Diseases, 26, 79–84.

kleptomania

Aboujaoude, E., Gamel, N., & Koran, L. M. (2004). A Case of Kleptomania Correlating With Premenstrual Dysphoria. *Journal of Clinical Psychiatry*, 65, 725–726.

Aizer, A., Lowengrub, K., & Dannon, P. N. (2004). Kleptomania after head trauma: Two case reports and combination treatment strategies. *Clinical Neuropharmacology*, 27, 211–215.

American Psychiatric Association (1993). *Diagnostic and statistical manual of mental disorders* (4th ed.). Washington, DC: American Psychiatric Association.

Dannon, P. N., Aizer, A., & Lowengrub, K. (2006). Kleptomania: Differential Diagnosis and Treatment Modalities. *Current Psychiatry Reviews*, 2, 281–283.

Dannon, P. N., & Master, R. (2006). Editorial: Impulse Control Disorders: Does the DSM-IV Classification Really Explain Everything About This Type of Disorder? *Israel Journal of Psychiatry*

and Related Sciences, 43, 71–74.

Dannon, P. N., Lowengrub, K. M., Lancu, L., & Kotler, M. (2004). Kleptomania: Comorbid Psychiatric Diagnosis in Patients and Their Families. *Psychopathology*, 37, 76–80.

Durst, R., Katz, G., & Knobler, H. Y. (1997). Buspirone augmentation of fluvoxamine in the treatment of kleptomania. *Journal of Nervous and Mental Disease*, 185, 586–588.

Feeney, D. J., & Klykylo, W. M. (1997). Treatment for kleptomania. *Journal of the American Academy of Child & Adolescent Psychiatry*, 36, 723–724.

Ginsberg, D. L. (2003). Topiramate treatment of kleptomania. *Primary Psychiatry*, 10, 17–18.

Grant, J. E. (2004). Dissociative symptoms in kleptomania. *Psychological Reports*, 94, 77–82.

Grant, J. (2005). Outcome Study of Kleptomania Patients Treated With Naltrexone: A Chart Review. *Clinical Neuropharmacology*, 28, 11–14.

Grant, J. E., Kim, S. W., & Grosz, R. L. (2003). Perceived Stress in Kleptomania. *Psychiatric Quarterly*, 74, 251–258.

Grant, J. E., & Kim, S. W. (2002). Temperament and early environmental influences in kleptomania. *Comprehensive Psychiatry*, 43, 223–228.

Grant, J. E., & Kim, S. W. (2002). Clinical characteristics and associated psychopathology of 22 patients with kleptomania. *Comprehensive Psychiatry*, 43, 378–384.

Grant, J. E. (2006). Understanding and Treating Kleptomania: New Models and New Treatments. *Israel Journal of Psychiatry and Related Sciences*, 43, 81–87.

Hocaoglu, C., & Kandemir, G. (2005). The Use of Selective Serotonin Inhibitors (SSRIs) in Kleptomania Treatment: Three Case Reports. *Arab Journal of Psychiatry*, 16, 151–160.

Hollander, E., & Rosen, J. (2000). Impulsivity. *Journal of Psychopharmacology,* 14, S39–S44.

Kindler, S., Dannon, P. N., Iancu, I., Sasson, Y., & Zohar, J. (1997). Emergence of kleptomania during treatment for depression with serotonin selective reuptake inhibitors. *Clinical Neuropharmacology,* 20, 126–129.

Kmetz, G. F., McElroy, S. L., & Collins, D. J. (1997). Response of kleptomania and mixed mania to valproate. *American Journal of Psychiatry,* 154, 580–581.

Kohn, C. S., & Antonuccio, D. O. (2002). Treatment of kleptomania using cognitive and behavioral strategies. *Clinical Case Studies,* 1, 25–38.

Kraus, J. E. (1999). Treatment of kleptomania with paroxetine. *Journal of Clinical Psychiatry,* 60, 793.

Lepkifker, E., Dannon, P. N., Ziv, R., Iancu, I., Horesh, N., & Kotler, M. (1999). The treatment of kleptomania with serotonin reuptake inhibitors. *Clinical Neuropharmacology,* 22, 40–43.

McNeilly, D. P., & Burke, W. J. (1998). Stealing lately: A case of late-onset kleptomania. *International Journal of Geriatric Psychiatry,* 13, 116–121.

Wiedemann, G. (1998). Kleptomania: Characteristics of 12 cases. *European Psychiatry,* 13, 67–77.

pyromania

American Psychiatric Association (1993). *Diagnostic and statistical manual of mental disorders* (4th ed.). Washington, DC: American Psychiatric Association.

Brett, A. (2004). 'Kindling theory' in arson: How dangerous are firesetters? *Australian and New Zealand Journal of Psychiatry,* 38, 419–425.

Bumpass, E. R., Fagelman, F. D., & Brix, R. J. (1983). Intervention with children who set fires. *American Journal of Psychotherapy,* 37, 328–345.

Cole, R., Grolnick, W., & Schwartzman, P.

(1999). Fire setting. In Ammerman, Robert T. (Ed.); Hersen, Michel (Ed.); Last, Cynthia G. (Ed.). *Handbook of prescriptive treatments for children and adolescents* (2nd ed.). (pp. 293–307). Needham Heights, MA, US: Allyn & Bacon.

Fras, I. (1997). Fire setting (pyromania) and its relationship to sexuality. In Schlesinger, Louis B. (Ed.); Revitch, Eugene (Ed.). *Sexual dynamics of anti-social behavior* (2nd ed.). (pp. 188–196). Springfield, IL, US: Charles C. Thomas Publisher

Geller, J. L. (1987). Firesetting in the adult psychiatric population. *Hospital & Community Psychiatry,* 38, 501–506.

Heath, G. A., Hardesty, V. A., Goldfine, P. E., Hinkens, A., Lind, N. A., & Stromberg, A. (1988). Childhood firesetting. In Howells, John G. (Ed.). *Modern perspectives in psychosocial pathology* (pp. 75–88). Philadelphia, PA, US: Brunner/Mazel.

Holmes, J. A., Johnson, J. L., & Roedel, A. L. (1993). Impulsivity in adult neurobehavioral disorders. In McCown, William G. (Ed.); Johnson, Judith L. (Ed.); Shure, Myrna B. (Ed.). *The impulsive client: Theory, research, and treatment* (pp. 309–321). Washington, DC, US: American Psychological Association.

Hucker, S. J. (1997). Impulsivity in DSM-IV impulse-control disorders. In Webster, Christopher D. (Ed.); Jackson, Margaret A. (Ed.). *Impulsivity: Theory, assessment, and treatment* (pp. 195–211). New York, NY, US: Guilford Press.

Kolko, D. J., & Ammerman, R. T. (1988). Firesetting. In Hersen, Michel (Ed.); Last, Cynthia G. (Ed.). *Child behavior therapy casebook* (pp. 243–262). New York, NY, US: Plenum Press.

Lion, J. R., & Scheinberg, A. W. (1996). Disorders of impulse control. In Gabbard, Glen O. (Ed.); Atkinson, Sarah D. (Ed.). *Synopsis of treatments* of psychiatric disorders (2nd ed.). (pp. 1045–1053). Washington, DC, US: American Psychiatric Association.

Lowenstein, L. F. (1989). The etiology, diagnosis and treatment of the fire-setting behaviour of children. *Child Psychiatry & Human Development*, 19, 186–194.

Monopolis, S. J., & Lion, J. R. (1986). Disorders of impulse control: Explosive disorders, pathological gambling, pyromania and kleptomania. In Curran, William J. (Ed.); McGarry, A. Louis (Ed.); Shah, Saleem A. (Ed.). *Forensic psychiatry and psychology: Perspectives and standards for interdisciplinary practice.* (pp. 409–423). Philadelphia, PA, US: F A Davis.

Opdyke, D., & Olasov Rothbaum, B. (1998). Cognitive-behavioral treatment of impulse control disorders. In Caballo, Vicente E. (Ed.). *International handbook of cognitive and behavioural treatments for psychological disorders* (pp. 417–439). Oxford, England: Pergamon/Elsevier Science Ltd.

Parks, R. W., Green, R. D. J., Girgis, S., Hunter, M. D., Woodruff, P. W. R., & Spence, S. A. (2005). Response of pyromania to biological treatment in a homeless person. *Neuropsychiatric Disease And Treatment*, 1, 277–280.

Prins, H. (1995). Adult fire-raising: Law and psychology. *Psychology, Crime & Law*, 1, 271–281.

Stewart, M. A., & Culver, K. W. (1982). Children who start fires: The clinical picture and a follow-up. *British Journal of Psychiatry*, 140, 357–363.

Stone, M. H. (1996). Psychotherapy with impulsive and compulsive patients. In Oldham, John M. (Ed.); Hollander, Eric (Ed.); Skodol, Andrew E. (Ed.). *Impulsivity and compulsivity* (pp. 231–260). Washington, DC, US: American Psychiatric Association.

Wise, M. G., & Tierney, J. G. (1996).

Impulse control disorders not elsewhere classified. In Hales, Robert E. (Ed.); Yudofsky, Stuart C. (Ed.). *The American Psychiatric Press synopsis of psychiatry* (pp. 635–652). Washington, DC, US: American Psychiatric Association.

gambling disorder

Afifi, T. O., Cox, B. J., & Sareen, J. (2006). Gambling-Related Problems Are Chronic and Persist for the Majority of Individuals With a Lifetime Diagnosis of Pathological Gambling. *American Journal of Psychiatry*, 163, 1297.

American Psychiatric Association (1993). *Diagnostic and statistical manual of mental disorders* (4th ed.). Washington, DC: American Psychiatric Association.

Angelillo, J. C. (2001). Rational-emotive behavioral therapy in the treatment of pathological gambling. In VandeCreek, Leon (Ed.); Jackson, Thomas L. (Ed.). *Innovations in clinical practice: A source book*, Vol. 19. (pp. 141–158). Sarasota, FL, US: Professional Resource Press/Professional Resource Exchange.

Blanco, C., Ibáñez, A., Sáiz-Ruiz, J., Blanco-Jerez, C., & Nunes, E. V. (2000). Epidemiology, pathophysiology and treatment of pathological gambling. *CNS Drugs*, 13, 397–407.

Blaszczynski, A., & Nower, L. (2006). Gambling and impulse disorders. In Andrasik, Frank (Ed.). *Comprehensive handbook of personality and psychopathology: Vol. 2: Adult Psychopathology.* (pp. 370–388). Hoboken, NJ, US: John Wiley & Sons, Inc.

Bondolfi, G., Osiek, C., & Ferrero, F. (2002). Pathological gambling: An increasing and underestimated disorder. *Schweizer Archiv für Neurologie und Psychiatrie*, 153, 116–122.

Dannon, P. N., Lowengrub, K., Aizer, A., & Kotler, M. (2006). Pathological

Gambling: Comorbid Psychiatric Diagnoses in Patients and their Families. *Israel Journal of Psychiatry and Related Sciences*, 43, 88–92.

Dannon, P. N., Lowengrub, K., Shalgi, B., Sasson, M., Tuson, L., Saphir, Y., & Kotler, M. (2006). Dual Psychiatric Diagnosis and Substance Abuse in Pathological Gamblers: A Preliminary Gender Comparison Study. *Journal of Addictive Diseases*, 25, 49–54.

Dannon, P. N., Lowengrub, K., Gonopolski, Y., Musin, E., & Kotler, M. (2005). Topiramate Versus Fluvoxamine in the Treatment of Pathological Gambling: A Randomized, Blind-Rater Comparison Study. *Clinical Neuropharmacology*, 28, 6–10.

Dannon, P. N., Lowengrub, K., Musin, E., Gonopolski, Y., & Kotler, M. (2005). Sustained-release bupropion versus naltrexone in the treatment of pathological gambling: A preliminary blind-rater study. *Journal of Clinical Psychopharmacology*, 25, 593–596.

Dell'Osso, B., & Hollander, E. (2005). The Impact of Comorbidity on the Management of Pathological Gambling. *CNS Spectrums*, 10, 619–621.

Goudriaan, A. E., Oosterlaan, J., de Beurs, E., & van den Brink, W. (2006). Neurocognitive functions in pathological gambling: A comparison with alcohol dependence, Tourette syndrome and normal controls. *Addiction*, 101, 534–547.

Grant, J. E., & Potenza, M. N. (2005). Pathological Gambling and Other 'Behavioral' Addictions. In Frances, Richard J. (Ed.); Miller, Sheldon I. (Ed.); Mack, Avram H. (Ed.). *Clinical textbook of addictive disorders* (3rd ed.) (pp. 303–320). New York, NY, US: Guilford Publications.

Hollander, E. (1998). Treatment of obsessive-compulsive spectrum disorders with SSRIs. *British Journal of Psychiatry*, 173, 7–12.

Hollander, E., Sood, E., Pallanti, S., Baldini-Rossi, N., & Baker, B. (2005). Pharmacological Treatments of Pathological Gambling. *Journal of Gambling Studies*, 21, 101–110.

Kim, S. W., Grant, J. E., Eckert, E. D., Faris, P. L., & Hartman, B. K. (2006). Pathological gambling and mood disorders: Clinical associations and treatment implications. *Journal of Affective Disorders*, 92, 109–116.

Korman, L. M., Toneatto, T., & Skinner, W. (2006). Pathological Gambling. In Fisher, Jane E. (Ed.); O'Donohue, William T. (Ed.). *Practitioner's guide to evidence-based psychotherapy* (pp. 291–300). New York, NY, US: Springer Science + Business Media.

Kruedelbach, N., Walker, H. I., Chapman, H. A., Haro, G., Mateu, C., & Leal, C. (2006). Comorbidity on disorders with loss of impulse-control: Pathological gambling, addictions and personality disorders. *Actas Españolas de Psiquiatría*, 34, 76–82.

Ledgerwood, D. M., & Petry, N. M. (2005). Current Trends and Future Directions in the Study of Psychosocial Treatments for Pathological Gambling. *Current Directions in Psychological Science*, 14, 89–94.

Nathan, P. E. (2005). Commentary, Special Issue, Journal of Gambling Studies. *Journal of Gambling Studies*, 21, 355–361.

Pallanti, S., Rossi, N. B., & Hollander, E. (2006). *Pathological Gambling*. In Hollander, Eric (Ed.); Stein, Dan J. (Ed.). *Clinical manual of impulse-control disorders* (pp. 251–289). Washington, DC, US: American Psychiatric Publishing, Inc.

Petry, N. M. (2005). Comorbidity of disordered gambling and other psychiatric disorders. In Petry, Nancy M. *Pathological gambling: Etiology, comorbidity, and treatment* (pp. 85–115). Washington, DC, US: American Psychological Association.

Petry, N. M. (2005). *Psychoanalytic and psychodynamic treatments.* In Petry, Nancy M. *Pathological gambling: Etiology, comorbidity, and treatment* (pp. 189–198). Washington, DC, US: American Psychological Association.

Pietrzak, R. H., & Petry, N. M. (2006). Severity of Gambling Problems and Psychosocial Functioning in Older Adults. *Journal of Geriatric Psychiatry and Neurology,* 19, 106–113.

Potenza, M. N., Xian, H., Shah, K., Scherrer, J. F., & Eisen, S. A. (2005). Shared Genetic Contributions to Pathological Gambling and Major Depression in Men. *Archives of General Psychiatry,* 62, 1015–1021.

Schmidt, S. N. (Ed.) (2006). A Simple Approach to Pathological Gambling? Don't Bet On It. *Journal of Addictions Nursing,* 17, 237–238.

Shub, N. F. (1999). A Gestalt approach to the treatment of gambling. Gestalt Review, 3, 190–204.

Slutske, W. S. (2006). Natural Recovery and Treatment-Seeking in Pathological Gambling: Results of Two U.S. National Surveys. *American Journal of Psychiatry,* 163, 297–302.

Slutske, W. S., Caspi, A., Moffitt, T. E., & Poulton, R. (2005). Personality and Problem Gambling: A Prospective Study of a Birth Cohort of Young Adults. *Archives of General Psychiatry,* 62, 769–775.

Stein, D. J., & Grant, J. E. (2005). Betting on Dopamine. *CNS Spectrums,* 10, 268–270.

Tamminga, C. A., & Nestler, E. J. (2006). Pathological Gambling: Focusing on the Addiction, Not the Activity. *American Journal of Psychiatry,* 163, 180–181.

Toneatto, T., & Millar, G. (2004). Assessing and Treating Problem Gambling: Empirical Status and Promising Trends. *Canadian Journal of Psychiatry,* 49, 517–525.

Wohl, J. A., Young, M. M., & Hart, K. E. (2007). Self-Perceptions of Dispositional Luck: Relationship to DSM Gambling Symptoms, Subjective Enjoyment of Gambling and Treatment Readiness. *Substance Use & Misuse,* 42, 43–63.

Zimmerman, M., Chelminski, I., & Young, D. (2006). Prevalence and Diagnostic Correlates of DSM-IV Pathological Gambling in Psychiatric Outpatients. *Journal of Gambling Studies,* 22, 255–262.

trichotillomania

American Psychiatric Association (1993). *Diagnostic and statistical manual of mental disorders* (4th ed.). Washington, DC: American Psychiatric Association.

Auld, J. (2006). Scripts: Tricking Trichotillomania. *Australian Journal of Clinical & Experimental Hypnosis,* 34, 216–218.

Boughn, S., & Holdom, J. A. J. (2002). Trichotillomania: Women's reports of treatment efficacy. *Research in Nursing & Health,* 25, 135–144.

Brondolo, E. (2000). Using imaginal desensitization as an adjunctive treatment for trichotillomania. *The Behavior Therapist,* 23, 169–172, 179.

Casati, J., Toner, B. B., & Yu, B. (2000). Psychosocial issues for women with trichotillomania. *Comprehensive Psychiatry,* 41, 344–351.

Diefenbach, G. J., Mouton-Odum, S., & Stanley, M. A. (2002). Affective correlates of trichotillomania. *Behaviour Research and Therapy,* 40, 1305–1315.

Diefenbach, G. J., Tolin, D. R., Hannan, S., Maltby, N., & Crocetto, J. (2006). Group Treatment for Trichotillomania: Behavior Therapy Versus Supportive Therapy. *Behavior Therapy,* 37, 353–363.

Diefenbach, G. J., Reitman, D., &

Williamson, D. A. (2000). Trichotillomania: A challenge to research and practice. *Clinical Psychology Review*, 20, 289–309.

Elliott, A. J., & Fuqua, R. W. (2000). Trichotillomania: Conceptualization, measurement, and treatment. *Behavior Therapy*, 31, 529–545.

Franklin, M. E., Tolin, D. F., & Diefenbach, G. J. (2006). Trichotillomania. In Hollander, Eric (Ed.); Keijsers, G. P. J., van Minnen, A., Hoogduin, C. A. L., Klaassen, B. N. W., Hendriks, M. J., & Tanis-Jacobs, J. (2006). Behavioural treatment of trichotillomania: Two-year follow-up results. *Behaviour Research and Therapy*, 44, 359–370.

Gershuny, B. S., Keuthen, N. J., Gentes, E. L., Russo, A. R., Emmott, E. C., Jameson, M., Dougherty, D. D., Loh, R., & Jenike, M. A. (2006). Current Posttraumatic Stress Disorder and History of Trauma in Trichotillomania. *Journal of Clinical Psychology*, 62, 1521–1529.

Inoue, N. (2000). [Treatment of Trichotillomania through Sand Play]. *Japanese Journal of Child and Adolescent Psychiatry*, 41, 38–54.

Keren, M., Ron-Miara, A., Feldman, R., & Tyano, S. (2006). Some Reflections on Infancy-Onset Trichotillomania. *The Psychoanalytic Study of the Child*, 61, 254–272.

Keuthen, N. J., Stein, D. J., & Christenson, G. A. (2001). *Help for hair pullers: Understanding and coping with trichotillomania*. Oakland, CA, US: New Harbinger Publications.

Keuthen, N. J., Aronowitz, B., Badenoch, J., & Wilhelm, S. (1999). *Behavioral treatment for trichotillomania*. In Stein, Dan J. (Ed.); Christenson, Gary A. (Ed.); Hollander, Eric (Ed.). *Trichotillomania* (pp. 147–166). Washington, DC, US: American Psychiatric Association.

Kraemer, P. A. (1999). The application of habit reversal in treating trichotillomania. *Psychotherapy: Theory, Research, Practice, Training*, 36, 289–304.

Lochner, C., Seedat, S., Niehaus, D. J. H., & Stein, D. J. (2006). Topiramate in the treatment of trichotillomania: An open-label pilot study. *International ClinicalPsychopharmacology*, 21, 255–259.

Martin, A., Scahill, L., Vitulano, L., & King, R.A. (1998). Stimulant use and trichotillomania. *Jounal of the American Academy of Child &Adolescent Psychiatry* 37, 349–350.

Michael, K. D. (2004). Behavioral Treatment of Trichotillomania: A Case Study. *Clinical Case Studies*, 3, 171–182.

Oakley, D. A. (1998). Emptying the habit: A case of trichotillomania. *Contemporary Hypnosis*, 15, 109–117.

O'Sullivan, M. J., & Redmond, H. P. (2001). Trichotillomania. *Irish Journal of Psychological Medicine*, 18, 137–139.

Pélissier, M., & O'Connor, K. (2004). Cognitive-Behavioral Treatment of Trichotillomania, Targeting Perfectionism. *Clinical Case Studies*, 3, 57–69.

Robiner, W. N., Edwards, P. E., & Christenson, G. A. (1999). *Hypnosis in the treatment of trichotillomania*. In Stein, Dan J. (Ed.); Christenson, Gary A. (Ed.); Hollander, Eric (Ed.). *Trichotillomania* (pp. 167–199). Washington, DC, US: American Psychiatric Association.

Romaniuk, C., Miltenberger, R. G., & Deaver, C. (2003). Long-term maintenance following habit reversal and adjunct treatment for trichotillomania. *Child & Family Behavior Therapy*, 25, 45–59.

Rothbaum, B. O., & Ninan, P. T. (1999). *Manual for the cognitive-behavioral treatment of trichotillomania*. In Stein, Dan J. (Ed.); Christenson, Gary A.

(Ed.); Hollander, Eric (Ed.). *Trichotillomania* (pp. 263–284). Washington, DC, US: American Psychiatric Association.

Stein, Dan J. (Ed.). Clinical manual of impulse-control disorders. (pp. 149–173). Washington, DC, US: American Psychiatric Publishing, Inc.

Stemberger, R. M. T., Stein, D. J., & Mansueto, C. S. (2003). Behavioral and Pharmacological Treatment of Trichotillomania. *Brief Treatment and Crisis Intervention*, 3, 339–352.

Wetterneck, C. T., Woods, D. W., Norberg, M. M., & Begotka, A. M. (2006). The social and economic impact of trichotillomania: Results from two nonreferred samples. *Behavioral Interventions*, 21, 97–109.

Woods, D. W., Flessner, C., Franklin, M. E., Wetterneck, C. T., Walther, M. R., Anderson, E. R., & Cardona, D. (2006). Understanding and Treating Trichotillomania: What We Know and What We Don't Know. *Psychiatric Clinics of North America*, 29, 487–501.

Zalsman, G., Hermesh, H., & Sever, J. (2001). Hypnotherapy in adolescents with trichotillomania: Three cases. *American Journal of Clinical Hypnosis*, 44, 63–68.

intermittant explosive disorder

American Psychiatric Association (1993). *Diagnostic and statistical manual of mental disorders* (4th ed.). Washington, DC: American Psychiatric Association.

Coccaro, E. F., Posternak, M. A., & Zimmerman, M. (2005). Prevalence and Features of Intermittent Explosive Disorder in a Clinical Setting. *Journal of Clinical Psychiatry*, 66, 1221–1227.

Kessler, R. C., Coccaro, E. F., Fava, M., Jaeger, S., Jin, R., & Walters, E. (2006). The Prevalence and Correlates of DSM-IV Intermittent Explosive Disorder in the National Comorbidity Survey Replication. *Archives of General Psychiatry*, 63, 669–678.

Malta, L. S., Blanchard, E. B., & Freidenberg, B. M. (2005). Psychiatric and behavioral problems in aggressive drivers. *Behaviour Research and Therapy*, 43, 1467–1484.

Olvera, R. L. (2002). Intermittent explosive disorder: Epidemiology, diagnosis and management. *CNS Drugs*, 16, 517–526.

Olvera, R. L., Pliszka, S. R., Konyecsni, W. M., Hernandez, Y., Farnum, S., & Tripp, R. F. (2001). Validation of the Interview Module for Intermittent Explosive Disorder (M-IED) in children and adolescents: A pilot study. *Psychiatry Research*, 101, 259–267.

dissociative amnesia

American Psychiatric Association (1993). *Diagnostic and statistical manual of mental disorders* (4th ed.). Washington, DC: American Psychiatric Association.

Benjamin, L. R., Benjamin, R., & Rind, B. (1998). The parenting experiences of mothers with dissociative disorders. *Journal of Marital & Family Therapy*, 24, 337–354.

Bower, G. H., & Sivers, H. (1998). Cognitive impact of traumatic events. *Development and Psychopathology*, 10, 625-653.

Brown, P., van der Hart, O., & Graafland, M. (1999). Trauma-induced dissociative amnesia in World War I combat soldiers. II. Treatment dimensions. *Australian and New Zealand Journal of Psychiatry*, 33, 392–398.

Brown, R. J. (2006). Different Types of 'Dissociation' Have Different Psychological Mechanisms. *Journal of Trauma & Dissociation*, 7, 7–28.

Cardeña, E. A., & Gleaves, D. H. (2003). *Dissociative disorders: Phantoms of the self.* In Hersen, Michel (Ed.); Turner,

Samuel M. (Ed.). *Adult psychopathology and diagnosis* (4th ed.). (pp. 476–505). Hoboken, NJ, US: John Wiley & Sons, Inc.

Classen, C., Koopman, C., & Spiegel, D. (1993). Trauma and dissociation. *Bulletin of the Menninger Clinic, 57,* 178–194.

Degun-Mather, M. (2002). Hypnosis in the treatment of a case of dissociative amnesia for a 12-year period. *Contemporary Hypnosis, 19,* 34–41.

Kihlstrom, J. R. (2005). Dissociative Disorders. *Annual Review of Clinical Psychology, 1,* 227–253.

Kluft, R. P. (2000). The psychoanalytic psychotherapy of dissociative identity disorder in the context of trauma therapy. *Psychoanalytic Inquiry, 20,* 259–286.

Loewenstein, R. J. (1996). *Dissociative amnesia and dissociative fugue.* In Michelson, Larry K. (Ed.); Ray, William J. (Ed.). *Handbook of dissociation: Theoretical, empirical, and clinical perspectives* (pp. 307–336). New York, NY, US: Plenum Press.

Loewenstein, R. J. (1991). *Psychogenic amnesia and psychogenic fugue: A comprehensive review.* In Tasman, Allan (Ed.); Goldfinger, Stephen M. (Ed.). *American Psychiatric Press review of psychiatry, Vol. 10.* (pp. 189–222). Washington, DC, US: American Psychiatric Association.

Maldonado, J. R., Butler, L. D., & Spiegel, D. (2002). *Treatments for dissociative disorders.* In Nathan, Peter E. (Ed.); Gorman, Jack M. (Ed.). *A guide to treatments that work* (2nd ed.). (pp. 463–496). New York, NY, US: Oxford University Press.

Putnam, F. W. (1995). *Traumatic stress and pathological dissociation.* In Chrousos, George P. (Ed.); McCarty, Richard (Ed.); Pacák, Karel (Ed.); Cizza, Giovanni (Ed.); Sternberg, Esther (Ed.); et al. *Stress: Basic mechanisms and clinical implications* (pp. 708–715). New York, NY, US: New York Academy of Sciences.

Vermetten, E., & Bremner, J. D. (2000). *Dissociative amnesia: Re-remembering traumatic memories.* In Berrios, German E. (Ed.); Hodges, John R. (Ed.). *Memory disorders in psychiatric practice* (pp. 400–431). New York, NY, US: Cambridge University Press.

Witztum, E., Maragalit, H., & van der Hart, O. (2002). Combat-induced dissociative amnesia: Review and case example of generalized dissociative amnesia. *Journal of Trauma & Dissociation, 3,* 35–55.

dissociative fugue

American Psychiatric Association (1993). *Diagnostic and statistical manual of mental disorders* (4th ed.). Washington, DC: American Psychiatric Association.

Degun-Mather, M. (2001). The value of hypnosis in the treatment of chronic PTSD with dissociative fugues in a war veteran. *Contemporary Hypnosis, 18,* 4–13.

Howley, J., & Ross, C. A. (2003). The Structure of Dissociative Fugue: A Case Report. *Journal of Trauma & Dissociation, 4,* 109–124.

Jasper, F. J. (2003). Working with Dissociative Fugue in a general psychotherapy practice: A cautionary tale. *American Journal of Clinical Hypnosis, 45,* 311–322.

Loewenstein, R. J. (1996). *Dissociative amnesia and dissociative fugue.* In Michelson, Larry K. (Ed.); Ray, William J. (Ed.). *Handbook of dissociation: Theoretical, empirical, and clinical perspectives* (pp. 307–336). New York, NY, US: Plenum Press.

Loewenstein, R. J. (1991). *Psychogenic amnesia and psychogenic fugue: A comprehensive review.* In Tasman, Allan (Ed.); Goldfinger, Stephen M. (Ed.). *American Psychiatric Press review of*

psychiatry, Vol. 10. (pp. 189–222).
Washington, DC, US: American
Psychiatric Association.

Macleod, A. D. (1999). Posttraumatic
stress disorder, dissociative fugue and a
locator beacon. *Australian and New
Zealand Journal of Psychiatry*, 33,
102–104.

Van der Hart, O. (1985). Metaphoric and
symbolic imagery in the hypnotic
treatment of an urge to wander: A case
report. Australian Journal of Clinical &
Experimental Hypnosis, 13, 83–95.

dissociative identity disorder

American Psychiatric Association (1993).
*Diagnostic and statistical manual of
mental disorders* (4th ed.). Washington,
DC: American Psychiatric Association.

Brand, B. L., Armstrong, J. G., &
Loewenstein, R. J. (2006).
Psychological assessment of patients
with dissociative identity disorder.
Psychiatric Clinics of North America,
29, 145–168.

Brenner, I. (2001). *Dissociation of trauma:
Theory, phenomenology, and technique.*
Madison, CT, US: International
Universities Press, Inc.

Burton, N., & Lane, R. C. (2001). The
relational treatment of dissociative
identity disorder. *Clinical Psychology
Review*, 21, 301–320.

Cox, C. T., & Cohen, B. M. (2005). The
unique role of art making in the
treatment of dissociative identity
disorder. *Psychiatric Annals*, 35, 695-
697.

Fine, C. G., & Madden, N. E. (2000).
*Group psychotherapy in the treatment of
dissociative identity disorder and allied
dissociative disorders.* In Klein, Robert
H. (Ed.); Schermer, Victor L. (Ed.).
*Group psychotherapy for psychological
trauma* (pp. 298–325). New York, NY,
US: Guilford Press.

Foote, B., Smolin, Y., Kaplan, M., Legatt,
M. E., & Lipschitz, D. (2006).
Prevalence of dissociative disorders in
psychiatric outpatients. *American
Journal of Psychiatry*, 163, 623–629.

Gold, S. N., Elhai, J. D., Rea, B. D., Weiss,
D., Masino, T., Morris, S. L., &
McIninch, J. (2001). Contextual
treatment of dissociative identity
disorder: Three case studies. *Journal of
Trauma & Dissociation*, 2, 5–36.

Greenberg, W. C. (1982). The multiple
personality. *Perspectives in Psychiatric
Care*, 20, 100–104.

Hanley, K. (2001). Case study: Narrative
of a psychotherapeutic treatment of
dissociative identity disorder in an
adolescent. *Southern African Journal of
Child and Adolescent Mental Health*, 13,
67–80.

Kellett, S. (2005). The treatment of
dissociative identity disorder with
cognitive analytic therapy:
Experimental evidence of sudden
gains. *Journal of Trauma &
Dissociation*, 6, 55–81.

Kluft, R. P. (2000). The psychoanalytic
psychotherapy of dissociative identity
disorder in the context of trauma
therapy. *Psychoanalytic Inquiry*, 20,
259–286.

Kluft, R. P. (2005). Diagnosing
dissociative identity disorder.
Psychiatric Annals, 35, 633–643.

Kluft, R. P. (2006). Dealing with alters: A
pragmatic clinical perspective.
Psychiatric Clinics of North America,
29, 281–304.

Laub, D. (2003). Trauma, early
development, and psychopathology.
*Journal of the American Psychoanalytic
Association*, 51, 669–674.

Lilienfeld, S. O., & Lynn, S. J. (2003).
*Dissociative identity disorder: Multiple
personalities, multiple controversies.* In
Lilienfeld, Scott O. (Ed.); Lynn, Steven
Jay (Ed.); Lohr, Jeffrey M. (Ed.).
*Science and pseudoscience in clinical
psychology* (pp. 109–142). New York,
NY, US: Guilford Press.

Loewenstein, R. J. (2005). Psychopharmacologic treatments for dissociative identity disorder. *Psychiatric Annals*, 35, 666–673.

Lynn, S. J., Fassler, O., Knox, J. A., & Lilienfeld, S. O. (2006). *Dissociative Identity Disorder*. In Fisher, Jane E. (Ed.); O'Donohue, William T. (Ed.). *Practitioner's guide to evidence-based psychotherapy* (pp. 248–257). New York, NY, US: Springer Science + Business Media.

Rosik, C. H. (1997). Geriatric dissociative identity disorder. *Clinical Gerontologist*, 17, 63–66.

Rosik, C. H. (2000). Some effects of world view on the theory and treatment of dissociative identity disorder. *Journal of Psychology and Christianity*, 19, 166–80.

Ross, C. A., & Gahan, P. (1988). Techniques in the treatment of multiple personality disorder. *American Journal of Psychotherapy*, 42, 40–52.

Spanos, N. P., & Burgess, C. (1994). *Hypnosis and multiple personality disorder: A sociocognitive perspective.* In Lynn, Steven Jay (Ed.); Rhue, Judith W. (Ed.). *Dissociation: Clinical and theoretical perspectives* (pp. 136–155). New York, NY, US: Guilford Press.

Twombly, J. H. (2005). *EMDR for Clients with Dissociative Identity Disorder, DDNOS, and Ego States.* In Shapiro, Robin (Ed.). *EMDR solutions: Pathways to healing* (pp. 88–120). New York, NY, US: W W Norton & Co.

Twombly, J. H. (2000). Incorporating EMDR and EMDR adaptations into the treatment of clients with dissociative identity disorder. *Journal of Trauma & Dissociation*, 1, 61–81.

Waiess, E. A. (2006). Treatment of dissociative identity disorder: 'Tortured Child Syndrome.' *Psychoanalytic Review*, 93, 477–500.

depersonalization disorder

American Psychiatric Association (1993). *Diagnostic and statistical manual of mental disorders* (4th ed.). Washington, DC: American Psychiatric Association.

Baker, D., Hunter, E., Lawrence, E., Medford, N., Patel, M., Senior, C., Sierra, M., Lambert, M. V., Khazaal, Y., Zimmermann, G., & Zullino, D. F. (2005). Dépersonnalisation – Données actuelles [Depersonalization – current data]. *Canadian Journal of Psychiatry*, 50, 101–107.

Ginsberg, D. L. (2005). Naltrexone Treatment of Depersonalization Disorder. *Primary Psychiatry*, 12, 24.

Hunter, E. C. M., Baker, D., Phillips, M. L., Sierra, M., & David, A. S. (2005). Cognitive-behaviour therapy for depersonalisation disorder: An open study. *Behaviour Research and Therapy*, 43, 1121–1130.

Jiménez-Genchi, A. M. (2004). Repetitive Transcranial Magnetic Stimulation Improves Depersonalization: A Case Report. *CNS Spectrums*, 9, 375–376.

Phillips, M. L., & David, A. S. (2003). Depersonalisation disorder: Clinical features of 204 cases. *British Journal of Psychiatry*, 182, 428–433.

Simeon, D. (2004). Depersonalisation Disorder: A Contemporary Overview. *CNS Drugs*, 18, 343–354.

Simeon, D., Guralnik, O., Schmeidler, J., & Knutelska, M. (2004). Fluoxetine therapy in depersonalisation disorder: Randomised controlled trial. *British Journal of Psychiatry*, 185, 31–36.

schizophrenia

Akbarian, S., Bunney, W. E., Jr., Potkin, S. G., Wigal, S. B., Hagman, J. O., Sandman, C. A., & Jones, E. G. (1993a). Altered distribution of nicotinamine-adenine dinucleotide phosphate-diaphorase cells in frontal lobe of schizophrenics implies disturbances of cortical development. *Archives of*

General Psychiatry, 50, 169–177.

Akbarian, S., Vinuela, A., Kim, J. J., Potkin, S. G., Bunney, W. E., Jr., & Jones, E. D. (1993b). Distorted distribution of nicotinamide-adenine dinucleotide phosphate-diaphorase neurons in temporal lobe of schizophrenics implies anomalous cortical development. Archives of General Psychiatry, 50, 178–187.

Altshuler, L.L., Conrad, A., Kovelman, J.A., & Scheibel, A. (1987). Hippocampal pyramidal cell orientation in schizophrenia. Archives of General Psychiatry, 44, 1094–1098.

American Psychiatric Association (1993). Diagnostic and statistical manual of mental disorders (4th ed.). Washington, DC.

Arnold, S. E., Hyman, B. T., Van Hoesen, G. W., & Damasio, A. R. (1991). Some cytoarchitectural abnormalities of the entorhinal cortex in schizophrenia. Archives of General Psychiatry, 48, 625–632.

Buchsbaum, M. S. (1990). The frontal lobes, basal ganglia, and temporal lobes as sites for schizophrenia. Schizophrenia Bulletin, 16, 379–389.

Buschsbaum, M. S., Haier, R. J., Potkin, S. G., Nuechterlein, K., Bracha, H. S., Katz, M., Lohr, J., Wu, J. C., Lottenberg, S., Jerabek, P. A., Trenary, M., Tafalla, R., Reynolds, C., & Bunney, W. E., Jr. (1992a). Frontostriatal disorder of cerebral metabolism in never-medicated schizophrenics. Archives of General Psychiatry, 49, 935–942.

Conley, R. R., Ascher-Svanum, H., Zhu, B., Faries, D. E., & Kinon, B. J. (2007). The burden of depressive symptoms in the long-term treatment of patients with schizophrenia. Schizophrenia Research, 90, 186–197.

Davis, K.L., Kahn, R.S., Ko, G., & Davidson, M. (1991). Dopamine in schizophrenia: A review and reconceptualization. American Journal of Psychiatry, 148, 1474–1486.

Eack, S. M., Hogarty, G. E., Greenwald, D. P., Hogarty, S. S., & Keshavan, M. S. (2007). Cognitive enhancement therapy improves emotional intelligence in early course schizophrenia: Preliminary effects. Schizophrenia Research, 89, 308–311.

Incorvaia, D., & Helmes, E. (2006). Shared Psychotic Disorder: A Psychosocial Psychosis? Current Psychiatry Reviews, 2, 353–360.

Lappin, J. M., Di Forti, M., & Murray, R. M. (2007). Foreword: Improved understanding and treatment of schizophrenia. European Neuropsychopharmacology, 17, v–vi.

Mednick, S. A., Machón, R. A., Huttunen, M. O., & Bonett, D. (1988). Adult schizophrenia following prenatal exposure to an influenza epidemic. Archives of General Psychiatry, 45, 189–192.

Mednick, S. A., Cannon, T. D., Barr, C. E., & La Fosse, J. M. (Eds.). (1991). Developmental neuropathology of schizophrenia. New York: Plenum Press.

Peralta, B., Cuesta, M. J., & deLeon, J. (1991). Premorbid personality and positive and negative symptoms in schizophrenia. Acta Psychiatrica Scandinavica, 84, 336–339.

Tamminga, C. A., Thaker, G. K., Buchanan, R., Kirkpatrick, B., Alphs, L. D., Chase, T. N., & Carpenter, W. T. (1992). Limbic system abnormalities identified in schizophrenia using positron emission topography with fluorodeoxyglucose and neocortical alterations with deficit syndrome. Archives of General Psychiatry, 49, 522–530.

Thomas, P. (2007). The stable patient with schizophrenia – From antipsychotic effectiveness to adherence. European

Neuropsychopharmacology, 17, S115–S122.

Swerdlow, N. R., & Koob, G. F. (1987). Dopamine, schizophrenia, mania, and depression: Towards a unified hypothesis of cortico-striato-pallido-thalamic function. *Behavioral and Brain Sciences*, 10, 197–245.

Waddington, J. L., Torrey, E.F., Crow, T. J., & Hirsch, S. R. (1991). Schizophrenia, neurodevelopment, and disease: The Fifth Biannual Winter Workshop on Schizophrenia. Badgastein, Austria, January 28th to February 3, 1990. *Archives of General Psychiatry*, 48, 271–273.

Weinberger, D. R. (1986). The pathogenesis of schizophrenia: A neurodevelopmental theory. In H. A. Nasrallah & D. R. Weinberger (Eds.): *The handbook of schizophrenia: The neurology of schizophrenia*. Amsterdam: Elsevier Science.

Yanos, P. T., & Moos, R. H. (2007). Determinants of functioning and well-being among individuals with schizophrenia: An integrated model. *Clinical Psychology Review*, 27, 58–77.

delusional disorder

American Psychiatric Association (1993). *Diagnostic and statistical manual of mental disorders* (4th ed.). Washington, DC: American Psychiatric Association.

Berrios, G. E., & Kennedy, N. (2002). Erotomania: A conceptual history. *History of Psychiatry*, 13, 381–400.

Dressing, H., Henn, F. A., & Gass, P. (2002). Stalking behavior – An overview of the problem and a case report of male-to-male stalking during delusional disorder. *Psychopathology*, 35, 313–318.

Eastham, J. H., & Jeste, D. V. (1997). Treatment of schizophrenia and delusional disorder in the elderly. *European Archives of Psychiatry and Clinical Neuroscience*, 247, 209–218.

Fear, C. F., & Libretto, S. E. (2002). Risperidone for the treatment of delusional disorder. *International Journal of Psychiatry in Clinical Practice*, 6, 113–116.

Felthous, A. R., Stanislaus, A., Hempel, A. G., & Gleyzer, R. (2001). Are persecutory delusions amenable to treatment? *Journal of the American Academy of Psychiatry and the Law*, 29, 461–468.

Hayashi, H., Oshino, S., Ishikawa, J., Kawakatsu, S., & Otani, K. (2004). Paroxetine treatment of delusional disorder, somatic type. *Human Psychopharmacology: Clinical and Experimental*, 19, 351–352.

Jordan, H. W., Lockert, E. W., Johnson-Warren, M., Cabell, C., Cooke, T., Greer, W., & Howe, G. (2006). Erotomania Revisited: Thirty-Four Years Later. *Journal of the National Medical Association*, 98, 787–793.

Kennedy, N., McDonough, M., Kelly, B., & Berrios, G. E. (2002). Erotomania revisited: Clinical course and treatment. *Comprehensive Psychiatry*, 43, 1–6.

Manschreck, T. C., & Khan, N. L. (2006). Recent Advances in the Treatment of Delusional Disorder. *Canadian Journal of Psychiatry*, 51, 114–119.

Morimoto, K., Miyatake, R., Nakamura, M., Watanabe, T., Hirao, T., & Suwaki, H. (2002). Delusional disorder: Molecular genetic evidence for dopamine psychosis. *Neuropsychopharmacology*, 26, 794–801.

Myers, W. C., & Ruiz, R. (2004). Aripiprazole and Psychotherapy for Delusional Disorder, Erotomanic Type. *Journal of the American Academy of Child & Adolescent Psychiatry*, 43, 1069–1070.

Ota, M., Mizukami, K., Katano, T., Sato, S., Takeda, T., & Asada, T. (2003). A case of delusional disorder, somatic type with remarkable improvement of clinical symptoms and single photon emission computed tomograpy findings following modified electroconvulsive therapy. *Progress in Neuro-Psychopharmacology & Biological Psychiatry*, 27, 881–884.

Rosch, D. S., Sajatovic, M., & Sivec, H. (2002). Behavioral characteristics in delusional pregnancy: A matched control group study. *International Journal of Psychiatry in Medicine*, 32, 295–303.

Silva, S. P., Kim, C. K., Hofmann, S. G., & Loula, E. C. (2003). To believe or not to believe: Cognitive and psychodynamic approaches to delusional disorder. *Harvard Review of Psychiatry*, 11, 20–29.

Smith, D. A., & Buckley, P. F. (2006). Pharmacotherapy of Delusional Disorders in the Context of Offending and the Potential for Compulsory Treatment. *Behavioral Sciences & the Law*, 24, 351–367.

Taylor, P. J. (2006). Delusional Disorder and Delusions: Is There a Risk of Violence in Social Interactions About the Core Symptom. *Behavioral Sciences & the Law*, 24, 313–331.

Townend, M. (2002). Individual exposure therapy for delusional disorder in the elderly: A case study of a 71-year-old-man. *Behavioural and Cognitive Psychotherapy*, 30, 103–109.

Ulzen, T. P. M., & Carpentier, R. (1997). The delusional parent: Family and multisystemic issues. *Canadian Journal of Psychiatry*, 42, 617–622.

delirium

Adamis, D., Treloar, A., Martin, F. C., & Macdonald, A. J. D. (2006). Recovery and outcome of delirium in elderly medical inpatients. *Archives of Gerontology and Geriatrics*, 43, 289–298.

Alao, A. O., & Moskowitz, L. (2006). Aripiprazole and delirium. *Annals of Clinical Psychiatry*, 18, 267–269.

American Psychiatric Association (1993). *Diagnostic and statistical manual of mental disorders* (4th ed.). Washington, DC: American Psychiatric Association.

André, C., Jaber-Filho, J. A., Bento, R. M. A., Damasceno, L. M. P., & Aquino-Neto, F. R. (2006). Delirium Following Ingestion of Marijuana Present in Chocolate Cookies. *CNS Spectrums*, 11, 262–264.

Edlund, A., Lundström, M., Karlsson, S., Brännström, B., Bucht, G., & Gustafson, Y. (2006). Delirium in Older Patients Admitted to General Internal Medicine. *Journal of Geriatric Psychiatry and Neurology*, 19, 83–90.

Inouye, S. K. (2006). Delirium in Older Persons. *New England Journal of Medicine*, 354, 1157–1165.

Kazmierski, J., Kowman, M., Banach, M., Pawelczyk, T., Okonski, P., Iwaszkiewicz, A., Zaslonka, J., Sobow, T., & Kloszewska, I. (2006). Preoperative predictors of delirium after cardiac surgery: A preliminary study. *General Hospital Psychiatry*, 28, 536–538.

Michaud, L., Büla, C., Berney, A., Camus, V., Voellinger, R., Stiefel, F., & Burnand, B.; Delirium Guidelines Development Group, Switzerland (2007). Delirium: Guidelines for general hospitals. *Journal of Psycho-somatic Research*, 62, 371–383.

Mittal, D., Majithia, D., Kennedy, R., & Rhudy, J. (2006). Differences in Char-acteristics and Outcome of Delirium as Based on Referral Patterns. *Psychosomatics: Journal of Consultation Liaison Psychiatry*, 47, 367–375.

Penttilä, J., Pasila, K., Tiisala, A., & Sipiläinen, P. (2006). Delirium in an Adolescent patient during Treatment with Cephalexin. *Journal of Adolescent Health*, 39, 782–783.

Rovasalo, A., Tohmo, H., Aantaa, R., Kettunen, E., & Palojoki, R. (2006).

Dexmedetomidine as an adjuvant in the treatment of alcohol withdrawal delirium: A case report. *General Hospital Psychiatry*, 28, 362–363.

Rudolph, J. L., Jones, R. N., Grande, L. J., Milberg, W. P., King, E. G., Lipsitz, L. A., Levkoff, S. E., & Marcantonio, E. R. (2006). Impaired Executive Function Is Associated with Delirium After Coronary Artery Bypass Graft Surgery. *Journal of the American Geriatrics Society*, 54, 937–941.

Takeuchi, T., Furuta, K., Hirasawa, T., Masaki, H., Yukizane, T., Atsuta, H., & Nishikawa, T. (2007). Perospirone in the treatment of patients with delirium. *Psychiatry and Clinical Neurosciences*, 61, 67–70.

Wright, T., Myrick, H., Henderson, S., Peters, H., & Malcolm, R. (2006). Risk Factors for Delirium Tremens: A Retrospective Chart Review. *The American Journal on Addictions*, 15, 213–219.

dementia

American Psychiatric Association (1993). *Diagnostic and statistical manual of mental disorders* (4th ed.). Washington, DC: American Psychiatric Association.

Aupperle, P. (2006). Management of aggression, agitation, and psychosis in dementia: Focus on atypical antipsychotics. *American Journal of Alzheimer's Disease and Other Dementias*, 21, 101–108.

Braaten, A. J., Parsons, T. D., McCue, R., Sellers, A., & Burns, W. J. (2006). Neurocognitive differential diagnosis of dementing diseases: Alzheimer's dementia, vascular dementia, frontotemporal dementia, and major depressive disorder. *International Journal of Neuroscience*, 116, 1271–1293.

Burns, A., & De Deyn, P. P. (2006). Risperidone for the Treatment of Neuropsychiatric Features in Dementia. *Drugs and Aging*, 23, 887–896.

Chabriat, H., & Bousser, M. G. (2006). Vascular Dementia: Potential of Antiplatelet Agents in Prevention. *European Neurology*, 55, 61–69.

Cosman, K. M., & Porsteinsson, A. P. (2006). Glutamate in the Neurobiology and Treatment of Dementias. *Primary Psychiatry*, 13, 48–55.

Dröes, R., Boelens-Van der Knoop, E. C. C., Bos, J., Meihuizen, L., Ettema, T. P., Gerritsen, D. L., Hoogeveen, F., de Lange, J., & Schölzel-Dorenbos, C. J. M. (2006). Quality of life in dementia in perspective. *Dementia: The International Journal of Social Research and Practice*, 5, 533–558.

Fulton, B. R., Edelman, P., & Kuhn, D. (2006). Streamlined models of dementia care mapping. *Aging & Mental Health*, 10, 343–351.

Golde, T. E. (2007). The Pathogenesis of Alzheimer's Disease. *Primary Psychiatry*, 14, 4–6.

Holmes, C., Knights, A., Dean, C., Hodkinson, S., & Hopkins, V. (2006). Keep music live: Music and the alleviation of apathy in dementia subjects. *International Psychogeriatrics*, 18, 623–630.

Kennedy, G. J., & Herlands, T. (2006). Missing Elements in the Treatment of Depression and Dementia. *Primary Psychiatry*, 13, 31–33.

King, B., Jones, C., & Brand, C. (2006). Relationship between dementia and length of stay of general medical patients admitted to acute care. *Australasian Journal on Ageing*, 25, 20–23.

Lavretsky, H. (2006). Diagnosis and treatment of vascular dementia. *Directions in Psychiatry*, 26, 49–67.

Lindstrom, H. A., Smyth, K. A., Sami, S. A., Dawson, N. V., Patterson, M. B., Bohinc, J. H., Post, S. G., Barber, M. J., Ollerton, S., Singer, M., & Whitehouse,

P. J. (2006). Medication use to treat memory loss in dementia: Perspectives of persons with dementia and their caregivers. *Dementia: The International Journal of Social Research and Practice*, 5, 27–50.

Lippa, C. F. (2006). An Individualized Approach to Treatment for Alzheimer's Disease, Pick's Disease, and Other Dementias. *American Journal of Alzheimer's Disease and Other Dementias*, 21, 354–359.

Logsdon, R. G., McCurry, S. M., & Teri, L. (2007). Evidence-Based Psychological Treatments for Disruptive Behaviors in Individuals With Dementia. *Psychology and Aging*, 22, 28–36.

Machado, J. C., & Caramelli, P. (2006). Treatment of dementia: Anything new? *Current Opinion in Psychiatry*, 19, 575–580.

Mazza, M., Capuano, A., Bria, P., & Mazza, S. (2006). Ginkgo biloba and donepezil: A comparison in the treatment of Alzheimer's dementia in a randomized placebo-controlled double-blind study. *European Journal of Neurology*, 13, 981–985.

Micieli, G. (2006). Vascular dementia. Neurological Sciences, 27, S37–S39.

Mountain, G. A. (2006). Self-management for people with early dementia: An exploration of concepts and supporting evidence. *Dementia: The International Journal of Social Research and Practice*, 5, 429–446.

Onor, M. L., Saina, M., Trevisiol, M., Cristante, T., & Aguglia, E. (2007). Clinical experience with risperidone in the treatment of behavioral and psychological symptoms of dementia. *Progress in Neuro-Psychopharmacology & Biological Psychiatry*, 31, 205–209.

Porsteinsson, A. P. (2006). Divalproex Sodium for the Treatment of Behavioural Problems Associated With Dementia in the Elderly. *Drugs and Aging*, 23, 877–886.

Rapaport, S. I. (1991). Positron emission topography in Alzheimer's disease in relation to disease pathogenesis: A critical review. *Cerebrovascular and brain Metabolism Reviews*, 3.

Ringman, J. M., & Cummings, J. L. (2006). Current and emerging pharmacological treatment options for dementia. *Behavioural Neurology*, 17, 5–16.

Rongve, A., & Aarsland, D. (2006). Management of Parkinson's Disease Dementia: Practical Considerations. *Drugs and Aging*, 23, 807–822.

Spector, A., & Orrell, M. (2006). Quality of Life (QoL) in Dementia: A Comparison of the Perceptions of People With Dementia and Care Staff in Residential Homes. *Alzheimer Disease & Associated Disorders*, 20, 160–165.

Stoppe, G., Haak, S., Knoblauch, A., & Maeck, L. (2007). Diagnosis of Dementia in Primary Care: A Representative Survey of Family Physicians and Neuropsychiatrists in Germany. *Dementia and Geriatric Cognitive Disorders*, 23, 207–214.

Tariot, P. N. (2007). Clinical Trials of Amyloid-Based Therapies for Alzheimer's Disease. *Primary Psychiatry*, 14, 7–10.

Wang, G., Chang, L., Volko, N. D., Telang, F., Logan, J., Ernst, T., & Fowler, J. S. (2004). Decreased brain dopaminergic transporters in HIV-associated dementia patients. *Brain: A Journal of Neurology*. 127(11), Nov 2004, 2452–2458.

Woods, B., Thorgrimsen, L., Spector, A., Royan, L., & Orrell, M. (2006). Improved quality of life and cognitive stimulation therapy in dementia. *Aging & Mental Health*, 10, 219–226.

attention-deficit/hyperactivity disorder

American Psychiatric Association (1993).

Diagnostic and statistical manual of mental disorders (4th ed.). Washington, DC: American Psychioatric Association.

Asherson, P., Chen, W., Craddock, B., & Taylor, E. (2007). Adult attention-deficit hyperactivity disorder: Recognition and tratment in general adult psychiatry. *British Journal of Psychiatry*, 190, 4–5.

Casey, B. J., & Durston, S. (2006). From Behavior to Cognition to the Brain and Back: What Have We Learned From Functional Imaging Studies of Attention Deficit Hyperactivity Disorder? *American Journal of Psychiatry*, 163, 957–960.

Daley, D. (2006). Attention deficit hyperactivity disorder: A review of the essential facts. *Child: Care, Health and Development*, 32, 193–204.

Dowson, J. H. (2006). Pharmacological Treatments for Attention-Deficit/Hyperactivity Disorder (ADHD) in Adults. *Current Psychiatry Reviews*, 2, 317–331.

DuPaul, G. J., & Weyandt, L. L. (2006). School-Based Interventions for Children and Adolescents with Attention-Deficit/Hyperactivity Disorder: Enhancing Academic and Behavioral Outcomes. *Education & Treatment of Children*, 29, 341–358.

Faraone, S.V., & Biederman, J. (1998) Neurobiology of attention deficit hyperactivity disorder. *Biological Psychiatry*, 44, 10.

Halperin, J. M., & Schulz, K. P. (2006). Revisiting the Role of the Prefrontal Cortex in the Pathophysiology of Attention-Deficit/Hyperactivity Disorder. *Psychological Bulletin*, 132, 560–581.

Hazell, P. (2007). Drug therapy for attention-deficit/hyperactivity disorder-like symptoms in autistic disorder. *Journal of Paediatrics and Child Health*, 43, 19–24.

Montague, M. (Ed.), & Dietz, S. (Ed.) (2006). Montague, Marjorie; Dietz, Samantha Attention deficit hyperactivity disorder. *Exceptionality*, 14, 1–2.

Prince, J. B. (2006). Pharmacotherapy of attention-deficit hyperactivity disorder in children and adolescents: Update on new stimulant preparations, atomoxetine, and novel treatments. *Child and Adolescent Psychiatric Clinics of North America*, 15, 13–50.

Ramsay, J. R., & Rostain, A. L. (2006). Cognitive Behavior Therapy for College Students with Attention-Deficit/Hyperactivity Disorder. *Journal of College Student Psychotherapy*, 21, 3–20.

Scahill, L., & Pachler, M. (2007). Treatment of Hyperactivity in Children with Pervasive Developmental Disorders. *Journal of Child and Adolescent Psychiatric Nursing*, 20, 59–62.

Sobanski, E. (2006). Psychiatric comorbidity in adults with attention-deficit/hyperactivity disorder (ADHD). *European Archives of Psychiatry and Clinical Neuroscience*, 256, 26–31.

Staller, J., & Faraone, S. V. (2006). Attention-Deficit Hyperactivity Disorder in Girls: Epidemiology and Management. *CNS Drugs*, 20, 107–123.

Tinius, T. (2006). Measuring the Effectiveness of Neurotherapy. *Journal of Neurotherapy*, 10, 1–3.

Trott, G. (2006). Attention-deficit/hyperactivity disorder (ADHD) in the course of life. *European Archives of Psychiatry and Clinical Neuroscience*, 256, 21–25.

Venter, A. (2006). The medical management of attention-deficit/hyperactivity disorder: Spoilt for choice? *South African Psychiatry Review*, 9, 143–151.

Wadsworth, J. S., & Harper, D. C. (2007).

Adults With Attention-Deficit/Hyperactivity Disorder: Assessment and Treatment Strategies. *Journal of Counseling & Development*, 85, 101–108.

Weisler, R. H., & Sussman, N. (2007). Treatment of Attention-Deficit/Hyperactivity Disorder. *Primary Psychiatry*, 14, 39–42.

mental retardation

American Psychiatric Association (1993). *Diagnostic and statistical manual of mental disorders* (4th ed.). Washington, DC: American Psychiatric Association.

Antshel, K. M., Phillips, M. H., Gordon, M., Barkley, R., & Faraone, S. V. (2006). Is ADHD a valid disorder in children with intellectual delays? *Clinical Psychology Review*, 26, 555–572.

Barrett, N., & Paschos, D. (2006). Alcohol-related problems in adolescents and adults with intellectual disabilities. *Current Opinion in Psychiatry*, 19, 481–485.

Bogacki, D. F., Newmark, T. S., & Gogineni, R. R. (2006). Behavioral, Psychosocial, and Pharmacologic Interventions in Adults with Developmental Disabilities. *Directions in Psychiatry*, 26, 195–206.

Dagnan, D., & Jahoda, A. (2006). Cognitive-Behavioural Intervention for People with Intellectual Disability and Anxiety Disorders. *Journal of Applied Research in Intellectual Disabilities*, 19, 91–97.

Didden, R., Korzilius, H., van Oorsouw, W., & Sturmey, P. (2006). Behavioral Treatment of Challenging Behaviors in Individuals With Mild Mental Retardation: Meta-Analysis of Single-Subject Research. *American Journal on Mental Retardation*, 111, 290–298.

Doran, S. M., Harvey, M. T., & Horner, R. H. (2006). Sleep and Developmental Disabilities: Assessment, Treatment, and Outcome Measures. *Mental Retardation*, 44, 13–27.

Dosen, A. (2007). Integrative treatment in persons with intellectual disability and mental health problems. *Journal of Intellectual Disability Research*, 51, 66–74.

Douma, J. C. H., Dekker, M. C., De Ruiter, K. P., Verhulst, F. C., & Koot, H. M. (2006). Help-Seeking Process of Parents for Psychopathology in Youth With Moderate to Borderline Intellectual Disabilities. *Journal of the American Academy of Child & Adolescent Psychiatry*, 45, 1232–1242.

Eldevik, S., Eikeseth, S., Jahr, E., & Smith, T. (2006). Effects of Low-Intensity Behavioral Treatment for Children with Autism and Mental Retardation. *Journal of Autism and Developmental Disorders*, 36, 211–224.

Esbensen, A. J., & Benson, B. A. (2006). Diathesis-stress and depressed mood among adults with mental retardation. *American Journal on Mental Retardation*, 111, 100–112.

Hackerman, F., Schmidt Jr., C. W., Dyson, C. D., Hovermale, L., & Gallucci, G. (2006). Developing a Model Psychiatric Treatment Program for Patients with Intellectual Disability in a Community Mental Health Center. *Community Mental Health Journal*, 42, 13–24.

Hall, I., Parkes, C., Samuels, S., & Hassiotis, A. (2006). Working across boundaries: Clinical outcomes for an integrated mental health service for people with intellectual disabilities. *Journal of Intellectual Disability Research*, 50, 598–607.

Hernandez-Reif, M., Field, T., Largie, S., Mora, D., Bornstein, J., & Waldman, R. (2006). Children with Down syndrome improved in motor functioning and muscle tone following massage therapy. *Early Child Development and Care*, 176, 395–410.

Hurley, A. D. (2006). Mood disorders in intellectual disability. *Current Opinion in Psychiatry*, 19, 465–469.

Hove, O. (2007). Survey on dysfunctional eating behavior in adult persons with intellectual disability living in the community. *Research in Developmental Disabilities*, 28, 1–8.

Johoda, A., Pert, C., & Trower, P. (2006). Socio-emotional understanding and frequent aggression in people with mild to moderate intellectual disabilities. *American Journal on Mental Retardation*, 111, 77–89.

Jones, M. C., Walley, R. M., Leech, A., Paterson, M., Common, S., & Metcalf, C. (2006). Using goal attainment scaling to evaluate a needs-led exercise programme for people with severe and profound intellectual disabilities. *Journal of Intellectual Disabilities*, 10, 317–335.

Kavanagh, S. (2006). Guide to Mental Health for Families and Carers of People with Intellectual Disabilities. *Journal of Applied Research in Intellectual Disabilities*, 19, 223–224.

Lew, M., Matta, C., Tripp-Tebo, C., & Watts, D. (2006). Dialectical Behavior Therapy (DBT) for individuals with intellectual disabilities: A program description. *Mental Health Aspects of Developmental Disabilities*, 9, 1–12.

McCabe, M. P., McGillivray, J. A., & Newton, D. C. (2006). Effectiveness of treatment programmes for depression among adults with mild/moderate intellectual disability. *Journal of Intellectual Disability Research*, 50, 239–247.

Owens, P. L., Kerker, B. D., Zigler, E., & Horwitz, S. M. (2006). Vision and Oral Health Needs of Individuals with Intellectual Disability. *Mental Retardation and Developmental Disabilities Research Reviews*, 12, 28–40.

Parkes, G., & Hall, I. (2006). Gender Dysphoria and Cross-Dressing in People With Intellectual Disability: A Literature Review. *Mental Retardation*, 44, 260–271.

Rojahn, J., Esbensen, A. J., & Hoch, T. A. (2006). Relationships Between Facial Discrimination and Social Adjustment in Mental Retardation. *American Journal on Mental Retardation*, 111, 366–377.

Simon, G. E., & von Korff, M. (2006). Medical co-morbidity and validity of DSM-IV depression criteria. *Psychological Medicine*, 36, 27–36.

Spevack, S., Yu, C. T., Lee, M. S., & Martin, G. L. (2006). Sensitivity of passive approach during preference and reinforcer assessments for children with severe and profound intellectual disabilities and minimal movement. *Behavioral Interventions*, 21, 165–175.

Sutor, B., Hansen, M. R., & Black, J. L. (2006). Obsessive Compulsive Disorder treatment in patients with Down syndrome: A case series. *Down Syndrome: Research & Practice*, 10, 1–3.

Tofil, N. M., Buckmaster, M. A., Winkler, M. K., Callans, B. H., Islam, M. P., & Percy, A. K. (2006). Deep Sedation with Propofol in Patients with Rett Syndrome. *Journal of Child Neurology*, 21, 210–213.

Tomasulo, D. J., & Razza, N. J. (2006). Group Psychotherapy for People With Intellectual Disabilities: The Interactive-Behavioral Model. *Journal of Group Psychotherapy, Psychodrama & Sociometry*, 59.

Vicari, S. (2006). Motor Development and Neuropsychological Patterns in Persons with Down Syndrome. *Behavior Genetics*, 36, 355–364.

Waldman, H. B., & Perlman, S. P. (2006). Mandating Education of Dental Graduates to Provide Care to Individuals With Intellectual and Developmental Disabilities. Mental Retardation, 44, 184–188.

Wallander, J. L., Dekker, M. C., & Koot,

H. M. (2006). Risk factors for psychopathology in children with intellectual disability: a prospective longitudinal population-based study. *Journal of Intellectual Disability Research*, 50, 259–268.

Weeks, L., Shane, C., MacDonald, F., Hart, C., & Smith, R. (2006). Learning from the experts: People with learning difficulties training and learning from each other. *British Journal of Learning Disabilities*, 34, 49–55.

Willner, P. (2006). Readiness for Cognitive Therapy in People with Intellectual Disabilities. *Journal of Applied Research in Intellectual Disabilities*, 19, 5–16.

learning disabilities

Ali, A., Hall, I., Taylor, C., Attard, S., & Hassiotis, A. (2006). Auditing the care programme approach for people with learning disability: A 4-year audit cycle. *Psychiatric Bulletin*, 30, 415–418.

Allen, D. (2006). Review of The Evidence Base for the Management of Imminent Violence in Learning Disability Settings. *Journal of Intellectual Disability Research*, 50, 778–779.

American Psychiatric Association (1993). *Diagnostic and statistical manual of mental disorders* (4th ed.). Washington, DC: American Psychiatric Association.

Berninger, V. W., & Hooper, S. R. (2006). Introduction to the Special Issue on Writing. *Developmental Neuropsychology*, 29, 1–4.

Burns, M. K., & VanDerHeyden, A. M. (2006). Using response to intervention to assess learning disabilities: Introduction to the Special Series. *Assessment for Effective Intervention*, 32, 3–5.

Cooney, G., Jahoda, A., Gumley, A., & Knott, F. (2006). Young people with intellectual disabilities attending mainstream and segregated schooling: perceived stigma, social comparison and future aspirations. *Journal of Intellectual Disability Research*, 50, 432–444.

Fiorello, C. A., Hale, J. B., & Snyder, L. E. (2006). Cognitive hypothesis testing and response to intervention for children with reading problems. *Psychology in the Schools*, 43, 835–853.

Fuchs, D., & Young, C. L. (2006). On the Irrelevance of Intelligence in Predicting Responsiveness to Reading Instruction. *Exceptional Children*, 73, 8–30.

Grizenko, N., Bhat, M., Schwartz, G., Ter-Stepanian, M., & Joober, R. (2006). Efficacy of methylphenidate in children with attention-deficit hyperactivity disorder and learning disabilities: A randomized crossover trial. *Journal of Psychiatry & Neuroscience*, 31, 46–51.

Hughes, T. A., & Fredrick, L. D. (2006). Teaching Vocabulary with Students with Learning Disabilities Using Classwide Peer Tutoring and Constant Time Delay. *Journal of Behavioral Education*, 15, 1–23.

Mangina, C. A., & Sokolov, E. N. (2006). Neuronal plasticity in memory and learning abilities: Theoretical position and selective review. *International Journal of Psychophysiology*, 60, 203–214.

McDermott, P. A., Goldberg, M. M., Watkins, M. W., Stanley, J. L., & Glutting, J. J. (2006). A Nationwide Epidemiologic Modeling Study of LD: Risk, Protection, and Unintended Impact. *Journal of Learning Disabilities*, 39, 230–251.

Monroe, B. W., & Troia, G. A. (2006). Teaching Writing Strategies to Middle School Students With Disabilities. *Journal of Educational Research*, 100, 21–33.

Rothenberger, A. (2006). Editorial: Learning at school and in real-life: providing an optimal setting for children. *Journal of Child Psychology and Psychiatry*, 47, 1083–1084.

Ruperto, C. R. (2006). Learning and Behavior Problems in Asperger Syndrome. *Journal of the American Academy of Child & Adolescent Psychiatry*, 45, 121–122.

Snowling, M. J., & Hayiou-Thomas, M. E. (2006). The Dyslexia Spectrum: Continuities Between Reading, Speech, and Language Impairments. *Topics in Language Disorders*, 26, 110–126.

Soo, C. A., & Bailey, J. G. (2006). A Review of Functioning of Attentional Components in Children With Attention-Deficit/Hyperactivity Disorder and Learning Disabilities. *Brain Impairment*, 7, 133–147.

Therrien, W. J., Wickstrom, K., & Jones, K. (2006). Effect of a Combined Repeated Reading and Question Generation Intervention on Reading Achievement. *Learning Disabilities Research & Practice*, 21, 89–97.

van der Aalsvoort, D. (2006). Early development risk and disability. *International Journal of Disability, Development and Education*, 53, 135–136.

Weeks, L., Shane, C., MacDonald, F., Hart, C., & Smith, R. (2006). Learning from the experts: People with learning difficulties training and learning from each other. *British Journal of Learning Disabilities*, 34, 49–55.

developmental coordination disorder

Albaret, J.-M., Zanone, P.-G., & De Castelnau, P. (2000). Une approche dynamique du trouble d'acquisition de la coordination [A dynamical approach to developmental coordination disorder]. A.N.A.E. *Approche Neuropsychologique des Apprentissages chez l'Enfant*, 12, 126–136.

American Psychiatric Association (1993). *Diagnostic and statistical manual of mental disorders* (4th ed.). Washington, DC: American Psychiatric Association.

Davidson, T., & Williams, B. (2000). Occupational therapy for children with developmental coordination disorder: A study of the effectiveness of a combined sensory integration and perceptual-motor intervention. *British Journal of Occupational Therapy*, 63, 495–499.

Elbert, J. C. (1999). *Learning and motor skills disorders*. In Netherton, Sandra D. (Ed.); Holmes, Deborah (Ed.); Walker, C. Eugene (Ed.). *Child & adolescent psychological disorders: A comprehensive textbook* (pp. 24–50). New York, NY, US: Oxford University Press.

Green, D., Baird, G., & Sugden, D. (2006). A pilot study of psychopathology in Developmental Coordination Disorder. *Child: Care, Health and Development*, 32, 741–750.

Hadders-Algra, M. (2000). The neuronal group selection theory: Promising principles for understanding and treating developmental motor disorders. *Developmental Medicine & Child Neurology*, 42, 707–715.

Macnab, J. J., Miller, L. T., & Polatajko, H. J. (2001). The search for subtypes of DCD: Is cluster analysis the answer? *Human Movement Science*, 20, 49–72.

McWilliams, S. (2005). Developmental Coordination Disorder and Self-Esteem: Do Occupational Therapy Groups have a Positive Effect? *British Journal of Occupational Therapy*, 68, 393–400.

Martin, N. C., Piek, J. P., & Hay, D. (2006). DCD and ADHD: A genetic study of their shared aetiology. *Human Movement Science*, 25, 110–124.

Martini, R., & Polatajko, H. J. (1998). Verbal self-guidance as a treatment approach for children with developmental coordination disorder: A systematic replication study.

Occupational Therapy Journal of Research, 18, 157–181.

Miller, L. T., Polatajko, H. J., Missiuna, C., Mandich, A. D., & Macnab, J. J. (2001). A pilot trial of a cognitive treatment for children with developmental coordination disorder. *Human Movement Science*, 20, 183–210.

Pless, M., & Carlsson, M. (2000). Effects of motor skill intervention on developmental coordination disorder: A meta-analysis. *Adapted Physical Activity Quarterly*, 17, 381–401.

Richardson, A. J. (2006). Omega-3 fatty acids in ADHD and related neurodevelopmental disorders. *International Review of Psychiatry*, 18, 155–172.

Stagg, V., & Burns, M. S. (1999). Specific developmental disorders. In Ammerman, Robert T. (Ed.); Hersen, Michel (Ed.); Last, Cynthia G. (Ed.). *Handbook of prescriptive treatments for children and adolescents* (2nd ed.). (pp. 48–62). Needham Heights, MA, US: Allyn & Bacon.

Wilson, P. H. (2005). Practitioner Review: Approaches to assessment and treatment of children with DCD: An evaluative review. *Journal of Child Psychology and Psychiatry*, 46, 806–82.

communication disorder

American Psychiatric Association (1993). *Diagnostic and statistical manual of mental disorders* (4th ed.). Washington, DC: American Psychiatric Association.

Crowe, B. T., Davidow, J. H., & Bothe, A. K. (2004). Quality of life measurement: Interdisciplinary implications for stuttering measurement and treatment. In Bothe, Anne K. (Ed.). *Evidence-based treatment of stuttering: Empirical bases and clinical applications* (pp. 173–198). Mahwah, NJ, US: Lawrence Erlbaum Associates Publishers.

Feinstein, C., & Phillips, J. M. (2006). Developmental Disorders of Communication, Motor Skills, and Learning. In Dulcan, Mina K.; Wiener, Jerry M. *Essentials of child and adolescent psychiatry* (pp. 203–231). Washington, DC, US: American Psychiatric Publishing, Inc.

Gillon, G. T., & Moriarty, B. C. (2007). Childhood Apraxia of Speech: Children at risk for persistent reading and spelling disorder. *Seminars in Speech & Language*, 28, 48–57.

Goldstein, B. A. (2004). Phonological Development and Disorders. In Goldstein, Brian (Ed.). *Bilingual language development and disorders in Spanish-English speakers* (pp. 259–285). Baltimore, MD, US: Paul H Brookes Publishing.

Hinshaw, S. P. (2004). Parental Mental Disorder and Children's Functioning: Silence and Communication, Stigma and Resilience. *Journal of Clinical Child and Adolescent Psychology*, 33, 400–411.

Hodge, M., & Wellman, L. (2004). Developmental Phonological Disorder. In Dewey, D. (Ed.); Tupper, D. E. (Ed.). *Developmental motor disorders: A neuropsychological perspective* (pp. 237–264). New York, NY, US: Guilford Press.

Hooper, C. R. (2004). Treatment of Voice Disorders in Children. *Language, Speech, and Hearing Services in Schools*, 35, 320–326.

Ingham, R. J., Finn, P., & Bothe, A. K. (2005). 'Roadblocks' revisited: Neural change, stuttering treatment, and recovery from stuttering. *Journal of Fluency Disorders*, 30, 91–107.

Jones, S. (2004). Augmentative and Alternative Communication: Management of Severe Communication Disorders in Children and Adults. *Journal of Applied Research in Intellectual Disabilities*, 17, 133–134.

Law, J. (2004). The Implications of Different Approaches to Evaluating Intervention: Evidence from the Study of Language Delay/Disorder. *Folia Phoniatrica et Logopaedica*, 56, 199–219.

Nippold, M. A. (2004). The child stutters and has a phonological disorder: How should treatment proceed? In Bothe, Anne K. (Ed.). *Evidence-based treatment of stuttering: Empirical bases.*

Nippold, M. A. (2004). Phonological and language disorders in children who stutter: Impact on treatment recommendations. *Clinical Linguistics & Phonetics*, 18, 145–159. *Clinical Applications.* (pp. 97–115). Mahwah, NJ, US: Lawrence Erlbaum Associates Publishers.

Packman, A., Onslow, M., & Attanasio, J. (2004). The demands and capacities model: Implications for evidence-based practice in the treatment of early stuttering. In Bothe, Anne K. (Ed.). *Evidence-based treatment of stuttering: Empirical bases and clinical applications* (pp. 65–79). Mahwah, NJ, US: Lawrence Erlbaum Associates Publishers.

Rubin, E., & Lennon, L. (2004). Challenges in Social Communication in Asperger Syndrome and High-Functioning Autism. *Topics in Language Disorders*, 24, 271–285.

Schneider, S. L., & Frens, R. A. (2005). Training four-syllable CV patterns in individuals with acquired apraxia of speech: Theoretical implications. *Aphasiology*, 19, 451–471.

Simmons-Mackie, N. (2005). Conduction Aphasia. In LaPointe, Leonard L. *Aphasia and related neurogenic language disorders* (3rd ed.). (pp. 155–168). New York, NY, US: Thieme New York.

Weiss, A. L. (2004). What child language research may contribute to the understanding and treatment of stuttering. *Language, Speech, and Hearing Services in Schools*, 35, 30–33.

autism

American Psychiatric Association (1993). *Diagnostic and statistical manual of mental disorders* (4th ed.). Washington, DC: American Psychiatric Association.

Amminger, G. P., Berger, G. E., Schäfer, M. R., Klier, C., Friedrich, M. H., & Feucht, M. (2007). Omega-3 Fatty Acids Supplementation in Children with Autism: A Double-blind Randomized, Placebo-controlled Pilot Study. *Biological Psychiatry*, 61, 551–553.

Bernier, R., Webb, S. J., & Dawson, G. (2006). Understanding Impairments in Social Engagement in Autism. In Marshall, Peter J. (Ed.); Fox, Nathan A. (Ed.). *The development of social engagement: Neurobiological perspectives* (pp. 304–330). New York, NY, US: Oxford University Press.

Bethea, T. C., & Sikich, L. (2007). Early Pharmacological Treatment of Autism: A Rationale for Developmental Treatment. *Biological Psychiatry*, 61, 521–537.

Blackledge, J. T., & Hayes, S. C. (2006). Using Acceptance and Commitment Training in the Support of Parents of Children Diagnosed with Autism. *Child & Family Behavior Therapy*, 28, 1–18.

Bonora, E., Lamb, J. A., Barnby, G., Bailey, A. J., & Monaco, A. P. (2006). Genetic Basis of Autism. In Moldin, Steven O. (Ed.); Rubenstein, John L. R. (Ed.). *Understanding autism: From basic neuroscience to treatment* (pp. 49–74). Boca Raton, FL, US: CRC Press.

Bridgemohan, C. (2007). Review of Autism Spectrum Disorders: Identification, Education and Treatment. *Journal of Developmental & Behavioral Pediatrics*, 28, 57.

Browning, S., & Miron, P. (2007).

Counseling Students With Autism and Asperger's Syndrome: A Primer for Success as a Social Being and a Student. In Lippincott, Joseph A. (Ed.); Lippincott, Ruth B. (Ed.). *Special populations in college counseling: A handbook for mental health professionals* (pp. 273–285). Alexandria, VA, US: American Counseling Association.

Carper, R. A., Wideman, G. M., & Courchesne, E. (2006). Structural Neuroimaging. In Moldin, Steven O. (Ed.); Rubenstein, John L. R. (Ed.). *Understanding autism: From basic neuroscience to treatment* (pp. 349–377). Boca Raton, FL, US: CRC Press.

Dale, E., Jahoda, A., & Knott, F. (2006). Mothers' attributions following their child's diagnosis of autistic spectrum disorder: Exploring links with maternal levels of stress, depression and expectations about their child's future. *Autism* Sep Vol 10(5) 463–479.

Faja, S., & Dawson, G. (2006). Early Intervention for Autism. In Luby, Joan L. (Ed.). *Handbook of preschool mental health: Development, disorders, and treatment.* (pp. 388–416). New York, NY, US: Guilford Press.

Ganz, M. L. (2006). The Costs of Autism. In Moldin, Steven O. (Ed.); Rubenstein, John L. R. (Ed.). *Understanding autism: From basic neuroscience to treatment* (pp. 475–502). Boca Raton, FL, US: CRC Press.

Geschwind, D. H., & Alarcón, M. (2006). Finding Genes in Spite of Heterogeneity: Endophenotypes, QTL Mapping, and Expression Profiling in Autism. In Moldin, Steven O. (Ed.); Rubenstein, John L. R. (Ed.). *Understanding autism: From basic neuroscience to treatment* (pp. 75–93). Boca Raton, FL, US: CRC Press.

Greenspan, S. I., & Wieder, S. (2006).

Engaging autism: Using the floortime approach to help children relate, communicate, and think. Cambridge, ME, US: Da Capo Press.

Ingersoll, B., & Schreibman, L. (2006). Teaching Reciprocal Imitation Skills to Young Children with Autism Using a Naturalistic Behavioral Approach: Effects on Language, Pretend Play, and Joint Attention. *Journal of Autism and Developmental Disorders*, 36, 487–505.

King, B. H., & Bostic, J. Q. (2006). An update on pharmacologic treatments for autism spectrum disorders. *Child and Adolescent Psychiatric Clinics of North America*, 15, 161–175.

Koegel, R. L., & Koegel, L. K. (2006). *Pivotal response treatments for autism: Communication, social, & academic development.* Baltimore, MD, US: Paul H Brookes Publishing.

Lockshin, S. B., Gillis, J. M., & Romanczyk, R. G. (2005). *Helping Your Child with Autism Spectrum Disorder: A Step-By-Step Workbook for Families.* Oakland, CA, US: New Harbinger Publications.

Minshew, N. J., Webb, S. J., Williams, D. L., & Dawson, G. (2006). Neuropsychology and Neurophysiology of Autism Spectrum Disorders. In Moldin, Steven O. (Ed.); Rubenstein, John L. R. (Ed.). *Understanding autism: From basic neuroscience to treatment* (pp. 379–415). Boca Raton, FL, US: CRC Press.

Mintz, M., Alessandri, M., & Curatolo, P. (2006). Treatment Approaches for the Autism Spectrum Disorders. In Tuchman, Roberto (Ed.); Rapin, Isabelle (Ed.). *Autism: A neurological disorder of early brain development* (pp. 281–307). London NW3 5RN, England: Mac Keith Press.

Moldin, S. O. (Ed.), & Rubenstein, J. L. R. (Ed.) (2006). Moldin, Steven O.; Rubenstein, John L. R. *Understanding autism: From basic neuroscience to treatment.* Boca Raton, FL, US: CRC Press.

Nacewicz, B. M., Dalton, K. M., Johnstone, T., Long, M. T., McAuliff, E. M., Oakes, T. R., Alexander, A. L., & Davidson, R. J. (2006). Amygdala Volume and Nonverbal Social Impairment in Adolescent and Adult Males With Autism. *Archives of General Psychiatry,* 63, 1417–1428.

O'Brien, M., & Daggett, J. A. (2006). *Beyond the autism diagnosis: A professional's guide to helping families.* Baltimore, MD, US: Paul H Brookes Publishing.

Reagon, K. A., Higbee, T. S., & Endicott, K. (2006). Teaching Pretend Play Skills to a Student with Autism Using Video Modeling with a Sibling as Model and Play Partner. *Education & Treatment of Children,* 29, 517–528.

Reaven, J., & Hepburn, S. (2006). The Parent's Role in the Treatment of Anxiety Symptoms. In Children With High-Functioning Autism Spectrum Disorders. *Mental Health Aspects of Developmental Disabilities,* 9, 73–80.

Rogers, S. J. (2006). Evidence-Based Interventions for Language Development in Young Children with Autism. In Charman, Tony (Ed.); Stone, Wendy (Ed.). *Social & communication development in autism spectrum disorders: Early identification, diagnosis, & intervention* (pp. 143–179). New York, NY, US: Guilford Press.

Rogers, S. J., & Ozonoff, S. (2006). Behavioral, Educational, and Developmental Treatments for Autism. In Moldin, Steven O. (Ed.); Rubenstein, John L. R. (Ed.). *Understanding autism: From basic neuroscience to treatment* (pp. 443–473). Boca Raton, FL, US: CRC Press.

Romanczyk, R. G., & Gillis, J. M. (2006). Autism and the physiology of stress and anxiety. In Baron, M. Grace (Ed.); Groden, June (Ed.); Groden, Gerald;

Lipsitt, Lewis (Ed.). *Stress and coping in autism* (pp. 183–204). New York, NY, US: Oxford University Press.

Schultz, R. T., Chawarska, K., & Volkmar, F. R. (2006). The Social Brain in Autism: Perspectives from Neuropsychology and Neuroimaging. In Moldin, Steven O. (Ed.); Rubenstein, John L. R. (Ed.). *Understanding autism: From basic neuroscience to treatment* (pp. 323–348). Boca Raton, FL, US: CRC Press.

Spector, S. G., & Volkmar, F. R. (2006). Autism Spectrum Disorders. In Wolfe, David A. (Ed.); Mash, Eric J. (Ed.). *Behavioral and emotional disorders in adolescents: Nature, assessment, and treatment* (pp. 444–460). New York, NY, US: Guilford Publications.

Vitiello, B., & Wagner, A. (2007). The Rapidly Expanding Field of Autism Research. *Biological Psychiatry,* 61, 427–428.

Whalen, C., Schreibman, L., & Ingersoll, B. (2006). The Collateral Effects of Joint Attention Training on Social Initiations, Positive Affect, Imitation, and Spontaneous Speech for Young Children with Autism. *Journal of Autism and Developmental Disorders,* 36, 655–664.

Wolfberg, P. J., & Schuler, A. L. (2006). Promoting Social Reciprocity and Symbolic Representation in Children with Autism Spectrum Disorders: Designing Quality Peer Play Interventions. In Charman, Tony (Ed.); Stone, Wendy (Ed.). *Social & communication development in autism spectrum disorders: Early identification, diagnosis, & intervention* (pp. 180–218). New York, NY, US: Guilford Press.

aspergers disorder

American Psychiatric Association (1993). *Diagnostic and statistical manual of mental disorders* (4th ed.). Washington, DC: American Psychiatric Association.

Bolton, P., Macdonald, H., Pickles, A., Rios, P., Goode, S., Crowson, M., Bailey. A., & Rutter, M. (1994). A case-control family history study of autism. *Journal of Child Psychology and Psychiatry*, 35, 5.

Browning, S., & Miron, P. (2007). Counseling Students With Autism and Asperger's Syndrome: A Primer for Success as a Social Being and a Student. In Lippincott, Joseph A. (Ed.); Lippincott, Ruth B. (Ed.). *Special populations in college counseling: A handbook for mental health professionals* (pp. 273–285). Alexandria, VA, US: American Counseling Association.

Ehlers, S., and Gillberg, C., & Wing, L. (1993). The epidemiology of Asperger syndrome. A total population study. *Journal of Child Psychology and Psychiatry*, 34, 8.

Frith, U. (1991). *Autism and Asperger Syndrome.* Cambridge; Cambridge University Press.

Gillberg, C. (1989). Asperger syndrome in 23 Swedish children. *Journal of Autism and Developmental Disorders*, 22,4.

Rickarby, G., Caruthers, A., and Mitchell, M. (1991). brief report: Biological factors associated with Asperger's syndrome. *Journal of Autism and Developmental Disorders*, 21, 3.

Shriberg, L. D., Paul, R., McSeeny, J. L., Klin, A., Cohen, D. J., & Volkmar, F. R. (2001). Speech and prosody characteristics of adolescents and adults with high-functioning autism and Asperger's syndrome. *Journal of Speech, Language, and Hearing Research*, 44.

Wing, L. (1981) Asperger's syndrome: A clinical account. *Psychological Medicine*, 11, 115–129.

rett's disorder

American Psychiatric Association (1993). *Diagnostic and statistical manual of mental disorders* (4th ed.). Washington, DC: American Psychiatric Association.

Benedek, E. P. (2006). Autism Spectrum Disorders: A Research Review for Practitioners. *American Journal of Psychiatry*, 163, 332–333.

Bishop, S. L., & Lord, C. (2006). Autism Spectrum Disorders. In Luby, Joan L. (Ed.). *Handbook of preschool mental health: Development, disorders, and treatment* (pp. 252–279). New York, NY, US: Guilford Press.

Bober, D., Robin, M., & Star, J. E. (2005). Olazapine in Rett's Disorder. *Journal of the American Academy of Child & Adolescent Psychiatry*, 44, 726–727.

Brown, R. T., McMillan, K. K., & Herschthal, A. (2005). Rett Syndrome. In Goldstein, Sam (Ed.); Reynolds, Cecil R. (Ed.). *Handbook of neurodevelopmental and genetic disorders in adults* (pp. 383–409). New York, NY, US: Guilford Press.

Brown, R. T., & Hoadley, S. L. (1999). Rett syndrome. In Goldstein, Sam (Ed.); Reynolds, Cecil R. (Ed.). *Handbook of neurodevelopmental and genetic disorders in children* (pp. 459-477). New York, NY, US: Guilford Press.

Burford, B. (2005). Perturbations in the development of infants with Rett disorder and the implications for early diagnosis. *Brain & Development*, 27, S3–S7.

Deidrick, K. M., Percy, A. K., Schanen, N. C., Mamounas, L., & Maria, B. L. (2005). Rett Syndrome: Pathogenesis, Diagnosis, Strategies, Therapies, and Future Research Directions. *Journal of Child Neurology*, 20, 708–717.

Durand, V. M., & Mapstone, E. (1999). Pervasive developmental disorders. In Silverman, Wendy K. (Ed.); Ollendick, Thomas H. (Ed.). *Developmental issues in the clinical treatment of children* (pp. 307–317). Needham Heights, MA, US: Allyn & Bacon.

Einfeld, S. (2004). Outcomes in Neurodevelopmental and Genetic Disorders. *Journal of the American Academy of Child & Adolescent Psychiatry*, 43, 1310–1311.

Elefant, C., & Lotan, M. (2004). Rett Syndrome: Dual Intervention – Music and Physical Therapy. *Nordic Journal of Music Therapy*, 13, 172–182.

Ellaway, C., Williams, K., Leonard, H., Higgins, G., Wilcken, B., & Christodoulou, J. (1999). Rett syndrome: Randomized controlled trial of {l}-carnitine. *Journal of Child Neurology*, 14, 162–167.

Goyal, M., O'Riordan, M. A., & Wiznitzer, M. (2004). Effect of Topiramate on Seizures and Respiratory Dysrhythmia in Rett Syndrome. *Journal of Child Neurology*, 19, 588–591.

Kumandas, S., Çaksen, H., Çiftçi, A., Öztürk, M., & Per, H. (2001). Lamotrigine in two cases of Rett syndrome. *Brain & Development*, 23, 240–242.

Kundert, D. K., & Trimarchi, C. L. (2006). Pervasive Developmental Disorders. In Phelps, LeAdelle (Ed.). *Chronic health-related disorders in children: Collaborative medical and psychoeducational interventions* (pp. 213–235). Washington, DC, US: American Psychological Association.

Lotan, M., & Shapiro, M. (2005). Management of young children with Rett disorder in the controlled multi-sensory (Snoezelen) environment. *Brain & Development*, 27, S88–S94.

Lotspeich, L. J. (1997). Autism, pervasive developmental disorders, and Asperger. In Steiner, Hans (Ed.). *Treating preschool children* (pp. 27–59). San Francisco, CA, US: Jossey-Bass.

Rapin, I. (2002). The autistic-spectrum disorders. *New England Journal of Medicine*, 347, 302–303.

Roane, H. S., & Piazza, C. C. (2001). Sleep disorders and Rett syndrome. In Stores, Gregory (Ed.); Wiggs, Luci (Ed.). *Sleep disturbance in children and adolescents with disorders of development: Its significance and management* (pp. 83–86). New York, NY, US: Cambridge University Press.

Roane, H. S., Piazza, C. C., Sgro, G. M., Volkert, V. M., & Anderson, C. M. (2001). Analysis of aberrant behaviour associated with Rett syndrome. *Disability and Rehabilitation: An International Multidisciplinary Journal*, 23, 139–148.

Willemsen-Swinkels, S. H. N., & Buitelaar, J. K. (2002). The autistic spectrum: Subgroups, boundaries, and treatment. *Psychiatric Clinics of North America*, 25, 811–836.

Yamashita, Y., Matsuishi, T., Murakami, Y., & Kato, H. (1999). Sleep disorder in Rett syndrome and melatonin treatment. *Brain & Development*, 21, 570.

Zwaigenbaum, L., & Szatmari, P. (1999). Psychosocial characteristics of children with pervasive developmental disorders. In Schwean, Vicki L. (Ed.); Saklofske, Donald H. (Ed.). *Handbook of psychosocial characteristics of exceptional children* (pp. 275–298). Dordrecht, Netherlands: Kluwer Academic Publishers.

childhood disintegration disorder

American Psychiatric Association (1993). *Diagnostic and statistical manual of mental disorders* (4th ed.). Washington, DC: American Psychiatric Association.

Treffert, D. A. (1999). Pervasive developmental disorders. In Netherton, Sandra D. (Ed.); Holmes, Deborah (Ed.); Walker, C. Eugene (Ed.). *Child & adolescent psychological disorders: A comprehensive textbook* (pp. 76–97). New York, NY, US: Oxford University Press.

Volkmar, F. R. (1996). The disintegrative disorders: Childhood disintegrative disorder and Rett's disorder. In Volkmar, Fred R. (Ed.). *Psychoses and pervasive developmental disorders in childhood and adolescence* (pp. 223–248). Washington, DC, US: American Psychiatric Association.

conduct disorder

American Psychiatric Association (1993). *Diagnostic and statistical manual of mental disorders* (4th ed.). Washington, DC: American Psychiatric Association.

Burt, S. A., McGue, M., Krueger, R. F., & Iacono, W. G. (2005). Sources of covariation among the child-externalizing disorders: Informant effects and the shared environment. *Psychological Medicine*, 35, 1133–1144.

Burt, S. A., Krueger, R. F., McGue, M., & Iacono, W. (2003). Parent-child conflict and the comorbidity among childhood externalizing disorders. *Archives of General Psychiatry*, 60, 505–513.

Cukrowicz, K. C., Taylor, J., Schatschneider, C., & Iacono, W. G. (2006). Personality differences in children and adolescents with attention-deficit/hyperactivity disorder, conduct disorder, and controls. *Journal of Child Psychology and Psychiatry*, 47, 151–159.

Dodge, K. A., & Pettit, G. S. (2003). A biopsychosocial model of the development of chronic conduct problems in adolescence. *Developmental Psychology*, 39, 349–371.

Drugli, M. B., & Larsson, B. (2006). Children aged 4-8 years treated with parent training and child therapy because of conduct problems: Generalisation effects to day-care and school settings. *European Child & Adolescent Psychiatry*, 15, 392–399.

Ehrensaft, M. K. (2005). Interpersonal Relationships and Sex Differences in the Development of Conduct Problems. *Clinical Child and Family Psychology Review*, 8, 39–63.

Haden, S. C., & Scarpa, A. (2005). Childhood Animal Cruelty: A Review of Research, Assessment, and Therapeutic Issues. *Forensic Examiner*, 14, 23–32.

Keenan, K., & Shaw, D. S. (2003). Starting at the beginning: Exploring the etiology of antisocial behavior in the first years of life. In Lahey, Benjamin B. (Ed.); Moffitt, Terrie E. (Ed.); Caspi, Avshalom (Ed.). *Causes of conduct disorder and juvenile delinquency* (pp. 153–181). New York, NY, US: Guilford Press.

Kotler, J. S., & McMahon, R. J. (2005). Child psychopathy: Theories, measurement, and relations with the development and persistence of conduct problems. *Clinical Child and Family Psychology Review*, 8, 291–325.

Mueser, K. T., Crocker, A. G., Frisman, L. B., Drake, R. E., Covell, N. H., & Essock, S. M. (2006). Conduct Disorder and Antisocial Personality Disorder in Persons With Severe Psychiatric and Substance Use Disorders. *Schizophrenia Bulletin*, 32, 626–636.

Nigg, J. T. (2003). Response Inhibition and Disruptive Behaviors: Toward a Multiprocess Conception of Etiological Heterogeneity for ADHD Combined Type and Conduct Disorder Early-Onset Type. In King, Jean A. (Ed.); Ferris, Craig F. (Ed.); Lederhendler, Israel I. (Ed.). *Roots of mental illness in children* (pp. 170–182). New York, NY, US: New York Academy of Sciences.

Ostrander, R. (2004). Oppositional Defiant Disorder and Conduct Disorder. In Kline, Frank M. (Ed.); Silver, Larry B. (Ed.). *The educator's guide to mental health issues in the classroom* (pp. 267–286). Baltimore, MD, US: Paul H Brookes Publishing.

Rhee, S. H., & Waldman, I. D. (2003).

Testing alternative hypotheses regarding the role of development on genetic and environmental influences underlying antisocial behavior. In Lahey, Benjamin B. (Ed.); Moffitt, Terrie E. (Ed.); Caspi, Avshalom (Ed.). *Causes of conduct disorder and juvenile delinquency* (pp. 305–318). New York, NY, US: Guilford Press.

Shaw, D. S., Dishion, T. J., Supplee, L., Gardner, F., & Arnds, K. (2006). Randomized Trial of a Family-Centered Approach to the Prevention of Early Conduct Problems: 2-Year Effects of the Family Check-Up in Early Childhood. *Journal of Consulting and Clinical Psychology*, 74, 1–9.

Smith, T. E., Sells, S. P., Rodman, J., & Reynolds, L. R. (2006). Reducing Adolescent Substance Abuse and Delinquency: Pilot Research of a Family-Oriented Psychoeducation Curriculum. *Journal of Child & Adolescent Substance Abuse*, 15, 105–115.

Sondeijker, F. E. P. L., Ferdinand, R. F., Oldehinkel, A. J., Veenstra, R., De Winter, A. F., Ormel, J., & Verhulst, F. C. (2005). Classes of adolescents with disruptive behaviors in a general population sample. *Social Psychiatry and Psychiatric Epidemiology*, 40, 931–938.

Tackett, J. L., Krueger, R. F., Iacono, W. G., & McGue, M. (2005). Symptom-Based Subfactors of DSM-Defined Conduct Disorder: Evidence for Etiologic Distinctions. *Journal of Abnormal Psychology*, 114, 483–487.

Thapar, A. (2005). Causes of conduct disorder and juvenile delinquency. *Criminal Behaviour and Mental Health*, 15, 287.

Thompson, L. L., Whitmore, E. A., Raymond, K. M., & Crowley, T. J. (2006). Measuring Impulsivity in Adolescents With Serious Substance and Conduct Problems. *Assessment*, 13, 3–15.

oppositional defiant disorder

American Psychiatric Association (1993). *Diagnostic and statistical manual of mental disorders* (4th ed.). Washington, DC: American Psychiatric Association.

Dwivedi, K. N., & Sankar, S. (2004). Promotion of Prosocial Development and Prevention of Conduct Disorders. In Dwivedi, Kedar Nath (Ed.); Harper, Peter Brinley (Ed.). *Promoting the emotional well-being of children and adolescents and preventing their mental ill health: A handbook* (pp. 198–218). London, England: Jessica Kingsley Publishers.

Essau, C. A. (Ed.) (2003). Essau, Cecilia A. *Conduct and oppositional defiant disorders: Epidemiology, risk factors, and treatment*. Mahwah, NJ, US: Lawrence Erlbaum Associates Publishers.

Farkas, B. (2004). Etiology and Pathogenesis of PTSD in Children and Adolescents. In Silva, Raul R. (Ed.). *Posttraumatic stress disorders in children and adolescents: Handbook* (pp. 123–140). New York, NY, US: W W Norton & Co.

Hicks, B. M., Krueger, R. F., Iacono, W. G., McGue, M., & Patrick, C. J. (2004). Family transmission and heritability of externalizing disorders: A twin-family study. *Archives of General Psychiatry*, 61, 922–928.

Kazdin, A. E., & Whitley, M. K. (2006). Comorbidity, Case Complexity, and Effects of Evidence-Based Treatment for Children Referred for Disruptive Behavior. *Journal of Consulting and Clinical Psychology*, 74, 455–467.

Ostrander, R. (2004). Oppositional Defiant Disorder and Conduct Disorder. In Kline, Frank M. (Ed.); Silver, Larry B. (Ed.). *The educator's guide to mental health issues in the classroom* (pp. 267–286). Baltimore, MD, US: Paul H Brookes Publishing.

Pardini, D. A., & Lochman, J. E. (2003).

Treatments for oppositional defiant disorder. In Reinecke, Mark (Ed.); Dattilio, Frank M. (Ed.); Freeman, Arthur (Ed.). *Cognitive therapy with children and adolescents: A casebook for clinical practice* (2nd ed.). (pp. 43–69). New York, NY, US: Guilford Press.

Rockhill, C. M., Collett, B. R., McClellan, J. M., & Speltz, M. L. (2006). Oppositional Defiant Disorder. In Luby, Joan L. (Ed.). *Handbook of preschool mental health: Development, disorders, and treatment* (pp. 80–114). New York, NY, US: Guilford Press.

Scott, S. (2006). Parent management training, treatment for oppositional, aggressive, and antisocial behaviour in children and adolescents. *Journal of Child Psychology and Psychiatry*, 47, 532.

Webster-Stratton, C., & Reid, M. J. (2006). Treatment and Prevention of Conduct Problems: Parent Training Interventions for Young Children (2-7 Years Old). In McCartney, Kathleen (Ed.); Phillips, Deborah (Ed.). *Blackwell handbook of early childhood development* (pp. 616–641). Malden, MA, US: Blackwell Publishing.

Whitfield, C. (2006). Childhood trauma as a cause of ADHD, aggression, violence and anti-social behaviour. In Timimi, Sami (Ed.); Maitra, Begum (Ed.). *Critical voices in child and adolescent mental health* (pp. 89–106). London, England: Free Association Books.

pica

American Psychiatric Association (1993). *Diagnostic and statistical manual of mental disorders* (4th ed.). Washington, DC: American Psychiatric Association.

Bashir, A., Loschen, E., Baluga, J., & Kirchner, L. (2002). A case of pica in a patient with mental retardation treated with venlafaxine extended release. *Mental Health Aspects of Developmental Disabilities*, 5, 87–89.

Beck, D. A., & Frohberg, N. R. (2005). Coprophagia in an elderly man: A case report and review of the literature. *International Journal of Psychiatry in Medicine*, 35, 417–427.

Burke, L., & Smith, S. L. (1999). Treatment of pica: Considering least intrusive options when working with individuals who have a developmental handicap and live in a community setting. *Developmental Disabilities Bulletin*, 27, 30–46.

Carter, S. L., Wheeler, J. J., & Mayton, M. R. (2004). Pica: A Review of Recent Assessment and Treatment Procedures. *Education and Training in Developmental Disabilities*, 39, 346–358.

Cohen, D. J., Johnson, W. T, & Caparulo, B. K. (1976). Pica and elevated blood levels in autistic and atypical children. *American Journal of Diseases of Children*, 130, 1.

Dumaguing, N. I., Singh, I., Sethi, M., & Devanand, D. P. (2003). Pica in the Geriatric Mentally Ill: Unrelenting and Potentially Fatal. *Journal of Geriatric Psychiatry and Neurology*, 16, 189–191.

Ginsberg, D. L. (2006). Bupropion SR for Nicotine-Craving Pica in a Developmentally Disabled Adult. *Primary Psychiatry*, 13, 28.

Goh, H., Iwata, B. A., & Kahng, S. W. (1999). Multicomponent assessment and treatment of cigarette pica. *Journal of Applied Behavior Analysis*, 32, 297–316.

Hagopian, L. P., & Adelinis, J. D. (2001). Response blocking with and without redirection for the treatment of pica. *Journal of Applied Behavior Analysis*, 34, 527–530.

LeBlanc, L. A., Piazza, C. C., & Krug, M. A. (1997). Comparing methods for maintaining the safety of a child with pica. *Research in Developmental Disabilities*, 18, 215–220.

McAdam, D. B., Sherman, J. A., Sheldon,

J. B., & Napolitano, D. A. (2004). Behavioral interventions to reduce the pica of persons with developmental disabilities. *Behavior Modification*, 28, 45–72.

McCord, B. E., Grosser, J. W., Iwata, B. A., & Powers, L. A. (2005). An analysis of response-blocking parameters in the prevention of pica. *Journal of Applied Behavior Analysis*, 38, 391–394.

Mihailidou, H., Galanakis, E., Paspalaki, P., Borgia, P., & Mantzouranis, E. (2002). Pica and the Elephant's Ear. *Journal of Child Neurology*, 17, 855–856.

Myles, B. S., Simpson, R. L., & Hirsch, N. C. (1997). A review of literature on interventions to reduce pica in individuals with developmental disabilities. *Autism*, 1, 77–95.

Piazza, C. C., Roane, H. S., Keeney, K. M., Boney, B. R., & Abt, K. A. (2002). Varying response effort in the treatment of pica maintained by automatic reinforcement. *Journal of Applied Behavior Analysis*, 35, 233–246.

Piazza, C. C., Fisher, W. W., Hanley, G. P., LeBlanc, L. A., Worsdell, A. S., Lindauer, S. E., & Keeney, K. M. (1998). Treatment of pica through multiple analyses of its reinforcing functions. *Journal of Applied Behavior Analysis*, 31, 165–189.

Rapp, J. T., Dozier, C. L., & Carr, J. E. (2001). Functional assessment and treatment of pica: A single-case experiment. *Behavioral Interventions*, 16, 111–125.

Ricciardi, J. N., Luiselli, J. K., Terrill, S., & Reardon, K. (2003). Alternative response training with contingent practice as intervention for pica in a school setting. *Behavioral Interventions*, 18, 219–226.

Stiegler, L. N. (2005). Understanding Pica Behavior: A Review for Clinical and Education Professionals. *Focus on Autism and Other Developmental Disabilities*, 20, 27–38.

rumination disorder

American Psychiatric Association (1993). *Diagnostic and statistical manual of mental disorders* (4th ed.). Washington, DC: American Psychiatric Association.

Anderson, C. A., & Lock, J. (1997). Feeding disorders. In Steiner, Hans (Ed.). *Treating preschool children* (pp. 187–208). San Francisco, CA, US: Jossey-Bass.

Benoit, D. (1993). Failure to thrive and feeding disorders. In Zeanah, Charles H. Jr. (Ed.). *Handbook of infant mental health* (pp. 317–331). New York, NY, US: Guilford Press.

Cohen, E., Rosen, Y., Yehuda, Y. B., & Iancu, l. (2004). Successful Multidisciplinary Treatment in an Adolescent Case of Rumination. *Israel Journal of Psychiatry and Related Sciences*, 41, 222–227.

Ellis, C. R., Parr, T. S., Singh, N. N., & Wechsler, H. A. (1997). Rumination. In Singh, Nirbhay N. (Ed.). *Prevention and treatment of severe behavior problems: Models and methods in developmental disabilities* (pp. 237–252). Belmont, CA, US: Thomson Brooks/Cole Publishing Co.

Franco, K. S., Campbell, N., Tamburrino, M. B., & Evans, C. (1993). Rumination: The eating disorder of infancy. Child Psychiatry & Human Development, 24, 91–97.

Fredericks, D. W., Carr, J. E., & Williams, W. L. (1998). Overview of the treatment of rumination disorder for adults in a residential setting. *Journal of Behavior Therapy and Experimental Psychiatry*, 29, 31–40.

Jackson, H. J., & Tierney, D. W. (1984). Rumination disorder of infancy: Some diagnostic issues in need of clarification. *Australia & New Zealand Journal of Developmental Disabilities*, 10, 243–245.

Larocca, F. E., & Della-Fera, M. A. (1986). Rumination: Its significance in adults with bulimia nervosa. *Psychosomatics: Journal of Consultation Liaison Psychiatry*, 27, 209–212.

Linscheid, T. R., & Murphy, L. B. (1999). Feeding disorders of infancy and early childhood. In Netherton, Sandra D. (Ed.); Holmes, Deborah (Ed.); Walker, C. Eugene (Ed.). *Child & adolescent psychological disorders: A comprehensive textbook.* (pp. 139–155). New York, NY, US: Oxford University Press.

Luciano Soriano, M. C., & Molina Cobos, F. J. (1992). Rumiación y vómitos: Etiología, prevención y tratamiento [Rumination and vomiting: Etiology, prevention, and treatment]. *Análisis y Modificación de Conducta*, 18, 257–277.

Mestre, J. R., Resnick, R. J., & Berman, W. F. (1983). Behavior modification in the treatment of rumination. *Clinical Pediatrics*, 22, 488–491.

Parry-Jones, B. (1994). Merycism or rumination disorder: A historical investigation and current assessment. *British Journal of Psychiatry*, 165, 303–314.

Sisson, L. A., Egan, B. S., & Van Hasselt, V. B. (1988). Rumination. In Hersen, Michel (Ed.); Last, Cynthia G. (Ed.). *Child behavior therapy casebook* (pp. 317–329). New York, NY, US: Plenum Press.

Tamburrino, M. B., Campbell, N. B., Franco, K. N., & Evans, C. L. (1995). Rumination in adults: Two case histories. *International Journal of Eating Disorders*, 17, 101–104.

Tierney, D. W., & Jackson, H. J. (1984). Psychosocial treatments of rumination disorder: A review of the literature. *Australia & New Zealand Journal of Developmental Disabilities*, 10, 81–112.

Weakley, M. M., Petti, T. A., & Karwisch, G. (1997). Case study: Chewing gum treatment of rumination in an adolescent with an eating disorder.

Journal of the American Academy of Child & Adolescent Psychiatry, 36, 1124–1127.

tourette's disorder

American Psychiatric Association (1993). *Diagnostic and statistical manual of mental disorders* (4th ed.). Washington, DC: American Psychiatric Association.

Brown, R. T., & Ivers, C. E. (1999). Gilles de la Tourette syndrome. In Goldstein, Sam (Ed.); Reynolds, Cecil R. (Ed.). *Handbook of neurodevelopmental and genetic disorders in children* (pp. 185–215). New York, NY, US: Guilford Press.

Constant, E. L., Borras, L., & Seghers, A. (2006). Aripiprazole is effective in the treatment of Tourette's disorder. *International Journal of Neuropsychopharmacology*, 9, 773–774.

Daly, R. M., & Lev, B. (2004). Tourette's syndrome: Three year follow-up of a successful treatment outcome. *Journal of Neurotherapy*, 8, 143–144.

Gilbert, D. L., & Buncher, C. R. (2005). Assessment of Scientific and Ethical Issues in Two Randomized Clinical Trial Designs for Patients With Tourette's Syndrome: A Model for Studies of Multiple Neuropsychiatric Diagnoses. *Journal of Neuropsychiatry & Clinical Neurosciences*, 17, 324–332.

Ginsberg, D. L. (2005). Aripiprazole Effective for Motor Tics in Tourette's Syndrome. *Primary Psychiatry*, 12, 21–22.

Howson, A. L., Batth, S., Ilivitsky, V., Boisjoli, A., Jaworski, M., Mahoney, C., & Knott, V. J. (2004). Clinical and attentional effects of acute nicotine treatment in Tourette's syndrome. *European Psychiatry*, 19, 102–112.

Limousin-Dowsey, P., & Tisch, S. (2005). Surgery for movement disorders: New applications? *Journal of Neurology, Neurosurgery & Psychiatry*, 76, 904.

Mansueto, C. S., & Keuler, D. J. (2005).

Tic or Compulsion?: It's Tourettic OCD. *Behavior Modification*, 29, 784–799.

Nicolson, R., Craven-Thuss, B., Smith, J., McKinlay, B. D., & Castellanos, F. X. (2005). A Randomized, Double-Blind, Placebo-Controlled Trial of Metoclopramide for the Treatment of Tourette's Disorder. *Journal of the American Academy of Child & Adolescent Psychiatry*, 44, 640–646.

Osmon, D. C., & Smerz, J. M. (2005). Neuropsychological Evaluation in the Diagnosis and Treatment of Tourette's Syndrome. *Behavior Modification*, 29, 746–783.

Phelps, L., Brown, R. T., & Power, T. J. (2002). Tics and Tourette's disorder. In Phelps, LeAdelle; Brown, Ronald T.; Power, Thomas J. *Pediatric psychopharmacology: Combining medical and psychosocial interventions* (pp. 203–229). Washington, DC, US: American Psychological Association.

Shavitt, R. G., Hounie, A. G., Campos, M. C. R., & Miguel, E. C. (2006). Tourette's Syndrome. *Psychiatric Clinics of North America*, 29, 471–486.

Stephens, R. J., Bassel, C., & Sandor, P. (2004). Olanzapine in the Treatment of Aggression and Tics in Children with Tourette's Syndrome – A Pilot Study. *Journal of Child and Adolescent Psychopharmacology*, 14, 255–266.

Verdellen, C. W. J., Keijsers, G. P. J., Cath, D. C., & Hoogduin, C. A. L. (2004). Exposure with response prevention versus habit reversal in Tourettes's syndrome: A controlled study. *Behaviour Research and Therapy*, 42, 501–511.

Woods, D. W. (2005). Introduction to the Special Issue on the Clinical Management of Tourette's Syndrome: A Behavioral Perspective. *Behavior Modification*, 29, 711–715.

elimination disorders

American Psychiatric Association (1993). *Diagnostic and statistical manual of mental disorders* (4th ed.). Washington, DC: American Psychiatric Association.

Brooks, R. C., Copen, R. M., Cox, D. J., Morris, J., Borowitz, S., & Sutphen, J. (2000). Review of the treatment literature for encopresis, functional constipation, and stool-toileting refusal. *Annals of Behavioral Medicine*, 22, 260–267.

Friman, P. C., & Jones, K. M. (1998). Elimination disorders in children. In Watson, T. Steuart (Ed.); Gresham, Frank M. (Ed.). *Handbook of child behavior therapy* (pp. 239–260). New York, NY, US: Plenum Press.

Geroski, A. M., & Rodgers, K. A. (1998). Collaborative assessment and treatment of children with enuresis and encopresis. *Professional School Counseling*, 2, 128–134.

Murphy, S., & Carney, T. (2004). The Classification of Soiling and Encopresis and a Possible Treatment Protocol. *Child and Adolescent Mental Health*, 9, 125–129.

Phelps, L., Brown, R. T., & Power, T. J. (2002). Elimination disorders. In Phelps, LeAdelle; Brown, Ronald T.; Power, Thomas J. *Pediatric psychopharmacology: Combining medical and psychosocial interventions* (pp. 87–99). Washington, DC, US: American Psychological Association.

von Gontard, A. (2006). Elimination disorders: Enuresis and encopresis. In Gillberg, Christopher (Ed.); Harrington, Richard (Ed.); Steinhausen, Hans-Christoph (Ed.). *A clinician's handbook of child and adolescent psychiatry* (pp. 625–654). New York, NY, US: Cambridge University Press.

Walker, C. E. (2003). Elimination Disorders: Enuresis and Encopresis. In Roberts, Michael C. (Ed.). *Handbook of pediatric psychology* (3rd ed.). (pp. 544–560). New York, NY, US: Guilford Press.

Walsh, T., Menvielle, E., & Khushlani, D. (2006). Disorders of Elimination. In Dulcan, Mina K.; Wiener, Jerry M. *Essentials of child and adolescent psychiatry* (pp. 581–592). Washington, DC, US: American Psychiatric Publishing, Inc.

Walsh, T., & Menvielle, E. (2004). Disorders of Elimination. In Wiener, Jerry M. (Ed.); Dulcan, Mina K. (Ed.). *The American Psychiatric Publishing Textbook of Child and Adolescent Psychiatry* (3rd ed.). (pp. 743–750). Washington, DC, US: American Psychiatric Publishing, Inc.

selective mutism

American Psychiatric Association (1993). *Diagnostic and statistical manual of mental disorders* (4th ed.). Washington, DC: American Psychiatric Association.

Anstendig, K. (1998). Selective mutism: A review of the treatment literature by modality from 1980–1996. *Psychotherapy: Theory, Research, Practice, Training*, 35, 381–391.

Baharaki, S. (1998). Selective mutism. *Psychiatriki*, 9, 177–198.

Blum, N. J., Kell, R. S., Starr, H. L., Lender, W. L., Bradley-Klug, K. L., Osborne, M. L., & Dowrick, P. W. (1998). Case study: Audio feedforward treatment of selective mutism. *Journal of the American Academy of Child & Adolescent Psychiatry*, 37, 40–43.

Cohan, S. L., Chavira, D. A., & Stein, M. B. (2006). Practitioner Review: Psychosocial interventions for children with selective mutism: a critical evaluation of the literature from 1990–2005. *Journal of Child Psychology and Psychiatry*, 47, 1085–1097.

Cook, J. A. L. (1997). Play therapy for selective mutism. In Kaduson, Heidi Gerard (Ed.); Cangelosi, Donna M. (Ed.); Schaefer, Charles E. (Ed.). *The playing cure: Individualized play therapy for specific childhood problems* (pp. 83–115). Lanham, MD, US: Jason Aronson.

Fisak, B. J. Jr., Oliveros, A., & Ehrenreich, J. T. (2006). Assessment and Behavioral Treatment of Selective Mutism. *Clinical Case Studies*, 5, 382–402.

Gordon, N. (2001). Mutism: Elective or selective, and acquired. *Brain & Development*, 23, 83-87.

Gray, R. M., Jordan, C. M., Ziegler, R. S., & Livingstone, R. B. (2002). Two sets of twins with selective mutism: Neuropsychological findings. *Child Neuropsychology*, 8, 41–51.

Güldner, M. G., & Wippo, E. (2003). Selectief mutisme. De stand van zaken [Selective mutism. The state of affairs]. *Kind en Adolescent*, 24, 200–208.

Jackson, M. F., Allen, R. S., Boothe, A. B., Nava, M. L., & Coates, A. (2005). Innovative Analyses and Interventions in the Treatment of Selective Mutism. *Clinical Case Studies*, 4, 81–112.

Kehle, T. J., Bray, M. A., & Theodore, L. A. (2006). Selective Mutism. In Bear, George G. (Ed.); Minke, Kathleen M. (Ed.). *Children's needs III: Development, prevention, and intervention* (pp. 293–302). Washington, DC, US: National Association of School Psychologists.

Kehle, T. J., Madaus, M. R., Baratta, V. S., & Bray, M. A. (1998). Augmented self-modeling as a treatment for children with selective mutism. *Journal of School Psychology*, 36, 247–260.

Kee, C. H. Y., Fung, D. S. S., & Ang, L. (2001). An electronic communication device for selective mutism. *Journal of the American Academy of Child & Adolescent Psychiatry*, 40, 389.

Kumpulainen, K. (2002). Phenomenology and treatment of selective mutism. *CNS Drugs*, 16, 175–180.

Moldan, M. B. (2005). Selective Mutism and Self-Regulation. *Clinical Social Work Journal*, 33, 291–307.

Pavlek, M. (2001). Getting ready to talk: The treatment of a mildly retarded, selectively mute adult. *Clinical Social Work Journal*, 29, 159–169.

Pionek Stone, B., Kratochwill, T. R., Sladezcek, I., & Serlin, R. C. (2002). Treatment of selective mutism: A best-evidence synthesis. *School Psychology Quarterly*, 17, 168–190.

Russell, P. S. S., Raj, S. E., & John, J. K. (1998). Multimodal intervention for selective mutism in mentally retarded children. *Journal of the American Academy of Child & Adolescent Psychiatry*, 37, 903–904.

Schwartz, R. H., Freedy, A. S., & Sheridan, M. J. (2006). Selective Mutism: Are Primary Care Physicians Missing the Silence? *Clinical Pediatrics*, 45, 43–48.

Sharkey, L., S., & Mc Nicholas, F. (2006). Female Monozygotic Twins with Selective Mutism – A Case Report. *Journal of Developmental & Behavioral Pediatrics*, 27, 129–133.

Silveira, R., Jainer, A. K., & Bates, G. (2004). Fluoxetine treatment of selective mutism in pervasive developmental disorder. *International Journal of Psychiatry in Clinical Practice*, 8, 179–180.

Standart, S., & Le Couteur, A. (2003). The quiet child: A literature review of selective mutism. *Child and Adolescent Mental Health*, 8, 154–160.

Wintgens, A. (2005). Selective mutism in children. *Child Language Teaching & Therapy*, 21, 214-216.

Zelenko, M., & Shaw, R. (2000). Case study: Selective mutism in an immigrant child. *Clinical Child Psychology and Psychiatry*, 5, 555–562.

reactive attachment disorder

American Psychiatric Association (1993). *Diagnostic and statistical manual of mental disorders* (4th ed.). Washington, DC: American Psychiatric Association.

Barth, R. P., Crea, T. M., John, K., Thoburn, J., & Quinton, D. (2005). Beyond attachment theory and therapy: Towards sensitive and evidence-based interventions with foster and adoptive families in distress. *Child & Family Social Work*, 10, 257–268.

Becker-Weidman, A. (2006). Treatment for Children with Trauma-Attachment Disorders: Dyadic Developmental Psychotherapy. *Child & Adolescent Social Work Journal*, 23, 147–171.

Becker-Weidman, A. (2006). Dyadic Developmental Psychotherapy: A Multi-Year Follow-Up. In Sturt, Stanley M. (Ed.). *New developments in child abuse research* (pp. 43–60). Hauppauge, NY, US: Nova Science Publishers.

Chaffin, M., Hanson, R., & Saunders, B. E. (2006). 'Report of the APSAC Task Force on attachment therapy, reactive attachment disorder, and attachment problems': Reply to letters. *Child Maltreatment*, 11, 381–386.

Combrink-Graham, L., & McKenna, S. B. (2006). Families with Children with Disrupted Attachments. In Combrinck-Graham, Lee (Ed.). *Children in family contexts: Perspectives on treatment* (pp. 242–264). New York, NY, US: Guilford Press.

Curtner-Smith, M. E., Middlemiss, W., Green, K., Murray, A. D., Barone, M., Stolzer, J., Parker, L., & Nicholson, B. (2006). An Elaboration on the Distinction Between Controversial Parenting and Therapeutic Practices Versus Developmentally Appropriate Attachment Parenting: A Comment on the APSAC Task Force Report. *Child Maltreatment*, 11, 373–374.

Davis, A. S., Kruczek, T., & Mcintosh, D. E. (2006). Understanding and treating psychopathology in schools: Introduction to the special issue. *Psychology in the Schools*, 43, 413–417.

Garland, K. R. (2005). The Jonathan Letters. *Journal of Prenatal & Perinatal Psychology & Health*, 19, 358–360.

Hanson, R. F., & Spratt, E. G. (2000). Reactive attachment disorder: What we know about the disorder and implications for treatment. *Child Maltreatment*, 5, 137–145.

Hardy, L. T. (2007). Attachment Theory and Reactive Attachment Disorder: Theoretical Perspectives and Treatment Implications. *Journal of Child and Adolescent Psychiatric Nursing*, 20, 27–39.

Haugaard, J. J., & Hazan, C. (2004). Recognizing and Treating Uncommon Behavioral and Emotional Disorders in Children and Adolescents Who Have Been Severely Maltreated: Reactive Attachment Disorder. *Child Maltreatment*, 9, 154–160.

Heller, S. S., Boris, N. W., Fuselier, S., Page, T., Koren-Karie, N., & Miron, D. (2006). Reactive attachment disorder in maltreated twins follow-up: From 18 months to 8 years. *Attachment & Human Development*, 8, 63–86.

Henley, D. (2005). Attachment disorders in post-institutionalized adopted children: Art therapy approaches to reactivity and detachment. *Arts in Psychotherapy*, 32, 29–46.

Hughes, D. A. (1999). Adopting children with attachment problems. *Child Welfare Journal*, 78, 541–560.

Kliman, G. (2003). International adoption: A four-year-old child with unusual behaviors adopted at six months of age: Dr. Gilbert Kliman. *Journal of Developmental & Behavioral Pediatrics*, 24, 66–67.

Mukaddes, N. M., Kaynak, F. N., Kinali, G., Bes ikci, H., & Issever, H. (2004). Psychoeducational treatment of children with autism and reactive attachment disorder. *Autism*, 8, 101–109.

Mukaddes, N. M., Bilge, S., Alyanak, B., & Kora, M. E. (2000). Clinical characteristics and treatment responses in cases diagnosed as reactive attachment disorder. *Child Psychiatry & Human Development*, 30, 273–287.

Sheperis, C. J., Renfro-Michel, E. L., & Doggett, R. A. (2003). In-home treatment of reactive attachment disorder in a therapeutic foster care system: A case example. *Journal of Mental Health Counseling*, 25, 76–88.

Stafford, B. S. (2006). Disorders of Attachment. In Fitzgerald, Hiram E. (Ed.); Lester, Barry M. (Ed.); Zuckerman, Barry (Ed.). *The crisis in youth mental health: Critical issues and effective programs, Vol 1: Childhood disorders* (pp. 55–81). Westport, CT, US: Praeger Publishers/Greenwood Publishing Group.

Taylor, R. J. (2002). Family unification with reactive attachment disorder children: A brief treatment. *Contemporary Family Therapy: An International Journal*, 24, 475–481.

Vargas, C. M., & Beatson, J. (2004). Cultural Competence in Differential Diagnosis: Post-traumatic Stress Disorder and Reactive Attachment Disorder. In Vargas, Claudia Maria (Ed.); Prelock, Patricia Ann (Ed.). *Caring for children with neurodevelop-mental disabilities and their families: An innovative approach to interdisciplinary practice* (pp. 69–112). Mahwah, NJ, US: Lawrence Erlbaum Associates Publishers.

stereotypical movement disorder

American Psychiatric Association (1993). *Diagnostic and statistical manual of mental disorders* (4th ed.). Washington, DC: American Psychiatric Association.

Anandan, S., Wigg, C. L., Thomas, C. R., & Coffey, B. (2004). Advanced Pediatric Psychopharmacology: Clinical Case Presentation. *Journal of Child and Adolescent Psychopharmacology*, 14, 531–538.

Chaleby, K., & Zawawi, A. (2006). [GABA Reuptake Inhibitor, Tiagabine in treatment of some anxiety symptoms of Pervasive Developmental Disorder]. *Arab Journal of Psychiatry*, 17, 40–51.

Lower, T. A. (2000). The effect of rotary vestibular stimulation on a stereotypic behavior: A case study. *Journal of Developmental and Physical Disabilities*, 12, 377–385.

Matthews, L. H., & Chafetz, M. D. (1999). Tic disorders and stereotypic movement disorders. In Netherton, Sandra D. (Ed.); Holmes, Deborah (Ed.); Walker, C. Eugene (Ed.). *Child & adolescent psychological disorders: A comprehensive textbook* (pp. 156–194). New York, NY, US: Oxford University Press.

McGrath, C. M., Kennedy, R. E., Hoye, W., & Yablon, S. A. (2002). Stereotypic movement disorder after acquired brain injury. *Brain Injury*, 16, 447–451.

Stein, D. J., & Niehaus, D. J. H. (2001). Stereotypic self-injurious behaviors: Neurobiology and psychopharmacology. In Simeon, Daphne (Ed.); Hollander, Eric (Ed.). *Self-injurious behaviors: Assessment and treatment* (pp. 29–48). Washington, DC, US: American Psychiatric Publishing, Inc.

Stein, D. J., & Simeon, D. (2001). Compulsive self-injurious behaviors: Neurobiology and psycho-pharmacology. In Simeon, Daphne (Ed.); Hollander, Eric (Ed.). *Self-injurious behaviors: Assessment and treatment* (pp. 71–95). Washington, DC, US: American Psychiatric Publishing, Inc.

Stein, D. J., & Simeon, D. (1998).

Pharmacotherapy of stereotypic movement disorders. *Psychiatric Annals*, 28, 327–331.

Stein, D. J., Bouwer, C., & Niehaus, D. J. (1997). Stereotypic movement disorder. *Journal of Clinical Psychiatry*, 58, 177–178.

Vogel, W., & Stein, D. J. (2000). Citalopram for head-banging. *Journal of the American Academy of Child & Adolescent Psychiatry*, 39, 544–545.

insomnia

American Psychiatric Association (1993). *Diagnostic and statistical manual of mental disorders* (4th ed.). Washington, DC: American Psychiatric Association.

Antai-Otong, D. (2006). Risks and Benefits of Non-Benzodiazepine Receptor Agonists in the Treatment of Acute Primary Insomnia in Older Adults. *Perspectives in Psychiatric Care*, 42, 196–200.

Bélanger, L., Savard, J., & Morin, C. M. (2006). Clinical Management of Insomnia Using Cognitive Therapy. *Behavioral Sleep Medicine*, 4, 179–202.

Bellon, A. (2006). Searching for New Options for Treating Insomnia: Are Melatonin and Raznelteon Beneficial? *Journal of Psychiatric Practice*, 12, 229–243.

Borja, N. L., & Daniel, K. L. (2006). Ramelteon for the Treatment of Insomnia. *Clinical Therapeutics: The International Peer-Reviewed Journal of Drug Therapy*, 28, 1540–1555.

Buysse, D. J., Germain, A., Nofzinger, E. A., & Kupfer, D. J. (2006). Mood Disorders and Sleep. In Stein, Dan J. (Ed.); Kupfer, David J. (Ed.); Schatzberg, Alan F. (Ed.). *The American Psychiatric Publishing textbook of mood disorders* (pp. 717–737). Washington, DC, US: American Psychiatric Publishing, Inc.

Carney, C. E., & Edinger, J. D. (2006). Identifying Critical Beliefs About Sleep in Primary Insomnia. *Sleep: Journal of Sleep and Sleep Disorders Research*, 29, 342–350.

Carney, C. E., Edinger, J. D., Manber, R., Garson, C., & Segal, Z. V. (2007). Beliefs about sleep in disorders characterized by sleep and mood disturbance. *Journal of Psychosomatic Research*, 62, 179–188.

Carney, C. E., & Waters, W. F. (2006). Effects of a structured problem-solving procedure on pre-sleep cognitive arousal in college students with insomnia. *Behavioral Sleep Medicine*, 4, 13–28.

Cherniack, E. P. (2006). The use of alternative medicine for the treatment of insomnia in the elderly. *Psychogeriatrics*, 6, 21–30.

Cukrowicz, K. C., Otamendi, A., Pinto, J. V., Bernert, R. A., Krakow, B., & Joiner, T. E. Jr. (2006). The Impact of Insomnia and Sleep Disturbances on Depression and Suicidality. *Dreaming*, 16, 1–10.

Currie, S. R. (2006). Sleep dysfunction. In Hersen, Michel (Ed.). *Clinician's handbook of adult behavioral assessment* (pp. 401–430). San Diego, CA, US: Elsevier Academic Press.

Graci, G., & Sexton-Radek, K. (2006). Treating Sleep Disorders Using Cognitive Behavior Therapy and Hypnosis. In Chapman, Robin A. (Ed.). *The Clinical Use of Hypnosis in Cognitive Behavior Therapy: A Practitioner's Casebook* (pp. 295–331). New York, NY, US: Springer Publishing Co.

Harvey, A. G. (2006). What about patients who can't sleep? Case formulation for insomnia. In Tarrier, Nicholas (Ed.). *Case formulation in cognitive behavior therapy: The treatment of challenging and complex cases* (pp. 293–311). New York, NY, US: Routledge/Taylor & Francis Group.

Maher, M. J., Rego, S. A., & Asnis, G. M.

(2006). Sleep Disturbances in Patients with Post-Traumatic Stress Disorder: Epidemiology, Impact and Approaches to Management. *CNS Drugs*, 20, 567–590.

McCurry, S. M., Logsdon, R. G., Teri, L., & Vitiello, M. V. (2007). Evidence-Based Psychological Treatments for Insomnia in Older Adults. *Psychology and Aging*, 22, 18–27.

McCrae, C. S., Nau, S. D., Taylor, D. J., & Lichstein, K. L. (2006). Insomnia. In Fisher, Jane E. (Ed.); O'Donohue, William T. (Ed.). *Practitioner's guide to evidence-based psychotherapy* (pp. 324–334). New York, NY, US: Springer Science + Business Media.

Neubauer, D. N., & Smith, M. T. (2006). Why Treat Insomnia? *Primary Psychiatry*, 13, 46–50.

Neubauer, D. N. (2006). New Directions in the Pharmacologic Treatment of Insomnia. *Primary Psychiatry*, 13, 51–57.

Oldham, J. (Ed.) (2006). Oldham, John From the Editor: Sleep and Exercise. *Journal of Psychiatric Practice*, 12, 201.

Rosenberg, R. P. (2006). Sleep maintenance insomnia: Strengths and weaknesses of current pharmacologic therapies. *Annals of Clinical Psychiatry*, 18, 49–56.

Rosenlicht, N. (2007). Cognitive-Behavioral Group Therapy for Insomnia. *International Journal of Group Psychotherapy*, 57, 117–121.

Roth, T., & Drak, C. (2006). Defining Insomnia: The Role of Quantitative Criteria: Comment. *Sleep: Journal of Sleep and Sleep Disorders Research*, 29, 424–425.

Schwartz, T. L., Hameed, U., & Chilton, M. (2006). The Use of Ramelteon for Secondary Insomnia Due to Mental Illness. *Primary Psychiatry*, 13, 69–73.

Sivertsen, B., Omvik, S., Pallesen, S., Bjorvatn, B., Havik, O. E., Kvale, G., Nielsen, G. H., & Nordhus, I. H.

(2006). Cognitive Behavioral Therapy vs Zopiclone for Treatment of Chronic Primary Insomnia in Older Adults: A Randomized Controlled Trial. *JAMA: Journal of the American Medical Association*, 295, 2851–2858.

Smith, M. T., & Perlis, M. L. (2006). Who Is a Candidate for Cognitive-Behavioral Therapy for Insomnia? *Health Psychology*, 25, 15–19.

Szuba, M.P., & Kloss, J. D. (2004) *Insomnia: Principles and Management.* New York: Cambridge University Press.

Tang, N. K. Y., & Harvey, A. G. (2006). Altering Misperception of Sleep in Insomnia: Behavioral Experiment Versus Verbal Feedback. *Journal of Consulting and Clinical Psychology*, 74, 767–776.

Teplin, D., Raz, B., Daiter, J., Varenbut, M., & Tyrrell, M. (2006). Screening for substance use patterns among patients referred for a variety of sleep complaints. *American Journal of Drug and Alcohol Abuse*, 32, 111–120.

Van der Heijden, K. B., Smits, M. G., Van Someren, E. J. W., Ridderinkhof, K. R., & Gunning, W. B. (2007). Effect of Melatonin on Sleep, Behavior, and Cognition in ADHD and Chronic Sleep-Onset Insomnia. *Journal of the American Academy of Child & Adolescent Psychiatry*, 46, 233–241.

Wu, R., Bao, J., Zhang, C., Deng, J., & Long, C. (2006). Comparison of Sleep Condition and Sleep-Related Psychological Activity after Cognitive-Behavior and Pharmacological Therapy for Chronic Insomnia. *Psychotherapy and Psychosomatics*, 75, 220–228.

hypersomnia

American Psychiatric Association (1993). *Diagnostic and statistical manual of mental disorders* (4th ed.). Washington, DC: American Psychiatric Association.

Bittencourt, L. R. A., Silva S., & de Bruin, P. F. C. (2006). Hypersomnolence and accidents in truck drivers: A cross-sectional study. *Chronobiology International*, 23, 963–971.

Hasler, G., Buysse, D. J., Gamma, A., Ajdacic, V., Eich, D., Rössler, W., & Angst, J. (2005). Excessive Daytime Sleepiness in Young Adults: A 20-Year Prospective Community Study. *Journal of Clinical Psychiatry*, 66, 521–529.

Leibowitz, S. M., & Black, J. E. (2005). Differential Diagnosis and Treatment of Excessive Daytime Sleepiness. *Primary Psychiatry*, 12, 57–66.

Pegram, G. V., McBurney, J., Harding, S. M., & Makris, C. M. (2004). Normal sleep and sleep disorders in adults and children. In Raczynski, James M. (Ed.); Leviton, Laura C. (Ed.). *Handbook of clinical health psychology:* Vol 2. *Disorders of behavior and health* (pp. 183–230). Washington, DC, US: American Psychological Association.

Vgontzas, A., Bixler, E. O., Kales, A., Criley, C., 7 Vela-Bueno, A (2000) Differences between nocturnal and daytime sleep between primary and psychiatric Hypersomnia: Diagnostic and treatment implications. *Psychosomatic Medicine.* 62, 220–226.

narcolepsy

American Psychiatric Association (1993). *Diagnostic and statistical manual of mental disorders* (4th ed.). Washington, DC: American Psychiatric Association.

Bailes, S., Libman, E., Baltzan, M., Amsel, R., Schondorf, R., & Fichten, C. S. (2006). Brief and distinct empirical sleepiness and fatigue scales. *Journal of Psychosomatic Research*, 60, 605–613.

Billiard, M., Bassetti, C., Dauvilliers, Y., Dolenc-Groselj, L., Lammers, G. J., Mayer, G., Pollmächer, T., Reading, P., & Sonka, K. (2006). EFNS guidelines on management of narcolepsy.

European Journal of Neurology, 13, 1035–1048.

Black, J. E., Nishino, S., & Brooks, S. N. (2005). Narcolepsy and Syndromes of Central Nervous System-Mediated Sleepiness. In Buysse, Daniel J. (Ed.). *Sleep disorders and psychiatry* (pp. 107–157). Washington, DC, US: American Psychiatric Publishing, Inc.

Bruck, D., Kennedy, G. A., Cooper, A., & Apel, S. (2005). Diurnal actigraphy and stimulant efficacy in narcolepsy. *Human Psychopharmacology: Clinical and Experimental*, 20, 105–113.

Dauvilliers, Y., Billiard, M., & Montplaisir, J. (2003). Clinical aspects and pathophysiology of narcolepsy. *Clinical Neurophysiology*, 114, 2000–2017.

Dodel, R., Peter, H., Walbert, T., Spottke, A., Noelker, C., Berger, K., Siebert, U., Oertel, W. H., Douglas, N. J. (1998). The psychosocial aspects of narcolepsy. *Neurology*, 50, S27–S30.

Ervik, S., Abdelnoor, M., Heier, M. S., Ramberg, M., & Strand, G. (2006). Health-related quality of life in narcolepsy. *Acta Neurologica Scandinavica*, 114, 198–204.

Fry, J. M. (1998). Treatment modalities for narcolepsy. *Neurology*, 50, S43–S48.

Hood, B. M., & Harbord, M. G. (2004). Narcolepsy: diagnosis and management in early childhood. *Journal of Pediatric Neurology*, 2, 65–71.

Kesper, K., Becker, H. F., & Mayer, G. (2004). The Socioeconomic Impact of Narcolepsy. *Sleep: Journal of Sleep and Sleep Disorders Research*, 27, 1123–1128.

Krahn, L. E., & Gonzalez-Arriaza, H. L. (2005). 'The Multiple Sleep Latency Test in the Diagnosis of Narcolepsy': Reply. *American Journal of Psychiatry*, 162, 2199.

Macleod, S., Ferrie, C., & Zuberi, S. M. (2005). Symptoms of narcolepsy in children misinterpreted as epilepsy. *Epileptic Disorders*, 7, 13–17.

McClellan, K. J., & Spencer, C. M. (1998). Modafinil: A review of its pharmacology and clinical efficacy in the management of narcolepsy. *CNS Drugs*, 9, 311–324.

Mamelak, M., Black, J., Montplaisir, J., & Ristanovic, R. (2004). A Pilot Study on the Effects of Sodium Oxybate on Sleep Architecture and Daytime Alertness in Narcolepsy. *Sleep: Journal of Sleep and Sleep Disorders Research*, 27, 1327–1334.

Rogers, A. E., & Mullington, J. (2003). The symptomatic management of narcolepsy. In Perlis, Michael L. (Ed.); Lichstein, Kenneth L. (Ed.). *Treating sleep disorders: Principles and practice of behavioral sleep medicine* (pp. 118–135). Hoboken, NJ, US: John Wiley & Sons, Inc.

Rogers, A. E., Aldrich, M. S., & Lin, X. (2001). A comparison of three different sleep schedules for reducing daytime sleepiness in narcolepsy. *Sleep: Journal of Sleep and Sleep Disorders Research*, 24, 385–391.

Saletu, M. T., Anderer, P., Saletu-Zyhlarz, G. M., Mandl, M., Arnold, O., Nosiska, D., Zeitlhofer, J., & Saletu, B. (2005). EEC-mapping differences between narcolepsy patients and controls and subsequent double-blind, placebo-controlled studies with modafinil. *European Archives of Psychiatry and Clinical Neuroscience*, 255, 20–32.

Scammell, T. E. (2003). The Neurobiology, Diagnosis, and Treatment of Narcolepsy. *Annals of Neurology*, 53, 154–166.

Schwartz, J. R. L., Feldman, N. T., & Bogan, R. K. (2005). Dose Effects of Modafinil in Sustaining Wakefulness in Narcolepsy Patients With Residual Evening Sleepiness. *Journal of Neuropsychiatry & Clinical Neurosciences*, 17, 405–412.

Thorpy, M. J. (2006). Cataplexy Associated with Narcolepsy: Epidemiology, Pathophysiology and

Management. *CNS Drugs*, 20, 43–50.

Walterfang, M., Upjohn, E., & Velakoulis, D. (2005). Is Schizophrenia Associated with Narcolepsy? *Cognitive and Behavioral Neurology*, 18, 113–118.

breathing-related sleep disorder

Alchanatis, M., Zias, N., Deligiorgis, N., Amfilochiou, A., Dionellis, G., & Orphanidou, D. (2005). Sleep apnea-related cognitive deficits and intelligence: An implication of cognitive reserve theory. *Journal of Sleep Research*, 14, 69–75.

American Psychiatric Association (1993). *Diagnostic and statistical manual of mental disorders* (4th ed.). Washington, DC: American Psychiatric Association.

Baran, A. S., & Richert, A. C. (2003). Obstructive sleep apnea and depression. *CNS Spectrums*, 8, 128–134.

Bardwell, W. A., Ancoli-Israel, S., & Dimsdale, J. E. (2007). Comparison of the effects of depressive symptoms and apnea severity on fatigue in patients with obstructive sleep apnea: A replication study. *Journal of Affective Disorders*, 97, 181–186.

Bittencourt, L. R. A., Silva S., & de Bruin, P. F. C. (2006). Hypersomnolence and accidents in truck drivers: A cross-sectional study. *Chronobiology International*, 23, 963–971.

Carlson, C. R., & Cordova, M. J. (1999). Sleep disorders in childhood and adolescence. In Netherton, Sandra D. (Ed.); Holmes, Deborah (Ed.); Walker, C. Eugene (Ed.). *Child & adolescent psychological disorders: A comprehensive textbook* (pp. 415–438). New York, NY, US: Oxford University Press.

El-Ad, B., & Lavie, P. (2005). Effect of sleep apnea on cognition and mood. *International Review of Psychiatry*, 17, 277–282.

Golay, A., Girard, A., Grandin, S.,

Métrailler, J., Victorion, M., Lebas, P., Ybarra, J., & Rochat, T. (2006). A new educational program for patients suffering from sleep apnea syndrome. *Patient Education and Counseling*, 60, 220–227.

Gottlieb, D. J. (2005). Can Sleep Apnea Be Treated without Modifying Anatomy? *New England Journal of Medicine*, 353, 2604–2606.

Haynes, P. L. (2005). The role of behavioral sleep medicine in the assessment and treatment of sleep disordered breathing. *Clinical Psychology Review*, 25, 673–705.

Höllinger, P., Khatami, R., Gugger, M., Hess, C. W., & Bassetti, C. L. (2006). Epilepsy and Obstructive Sleep Apnea. *European Neurology*, 55, 74–79.

Holten, K. B. (2004). How should we diagnose and treat obstructive sleep apnea?. *Journal of Family Practice*, 53, 902–903.

Hukins, C. A. (2006). Obstructive sleep apnea – management update. *Neuropsychiatric Disease And Treatment*, 2, 309–326.

Ireland, J. L., & Culpin, V. (2006). The relationship between sleeping problems and aggression, anger, and impulsivity in a population of juvenile and young offenders. *Journal of Adolescent Health*, 38, 649–655.

Marin, J. M., Carrizo, S. J., Vicente, E., & Agusti, A. G. N. (2005). Long-term cardiovascular outcomes in men with obstructive sleep apnoea-hypopnoea with or without treatment with continuous positive airway pressure: An observational study. *Lancet*, 365, 1046–1053.

McNicholas, W. T. (2006). Optimizing Continuous Positive Airway Pressure Therapy for Obstructive Sleep Apnea Syndrome: Comment. *Sleep: Journal of Sleep and Sleep Disorders Research*, 29, 421–423.

Paditz, E. (2006). Schlafstörungen im

Kleinkindesalter - Diagnostik, Differenzialdiagnostik und somatische Hintergründe [Sleep disorders in infancy - Aspects of diagnosis and somatic background]. *Praxis der Kinderpsychologie und Kinderpsychiatrie*, 55, 103–117.

Parrino, L., Thomas, R. J., Smerieri, A., Spaggiari, M. C., Felice, A. D., & Terzano, M. G. (2005). Reorganization of sleep patterns in severe OSAS under prolonged CPAP treatment. *Clinical Neurophysiology*, 116, 2228–2239.

Pierucci, P., Lacedonia, D., & Resta, O. (2005). Management of obstructive sleep apnea. *Minerva Psichiatrica*, 46, 147–157.

Saunamäki, T., & Jehkonen, M. (2007). A review of executive functions in obstructive sleep apnea syndrome. *Acta Neurologica Scandinavica*, 115, 1–11.

Strollo, P. J. Jr., & Davé, N. B. (2005). Sleep Apnea. In Buysse, Daniel J. (Ed.). *Sleep disorders and psychiatry* (pp. 77–105). Washington, DC, US: American Psychiatric Publishing, Inc.

Yang, Q., Phillips, C. L., Melehan, K. L., Rogers, N. L., Seale, J. P., & Grunstein, R. R. (2006). Effects of Short-Term CPAP Withdrawal on Neurobehavioral Performance in Patients With Obstructive Sleep Apnea. *Sleep: Journal of Sleep and Sleep Disorders Research*, 29, 545–552.

circadian rhythm sleep disorder

American Psychiatric Association (1993). *Diagnostic and statistical manual of mental disorders* (4th ed.). Washington, DC: American Psychiatric Association.

Doljansky, J. T., Kannety, H., & Dagan, Y. (2005). Working under daylight intensity lamp: An occupational risk for developing circadian rhythm sleep disorder? *Chronobiology International*, 22, 597–605.

Jan, J. E., & Freeman, R. D. (2004). Melatonin therapy for circadian rhythm sleep disorders in children with multiple disabilities: What have we learned in the last decade? *Developmental Medicine & Child Neurology*, 46, 776–782.

Kamei, Y., Hayakawa, T., Urata, J., Uchiyama, M., Shibui, K., Kim, K., Kudo, Y., & Okawa, M. (2000). Melatonin treatment for circadian rhythm sleep disorders. *Psychiatry and Clinical Neurosciences*, 54, 381–382.

Pandi-Perumal, S. R., Smits, M., Spence, W., Srinivasan, V., Cardinali, D. P., Lowe, A. D., & Kayumov, L. (2007). Dim light melatonin onset (DLMO): A tool for the analysis of circadian phase in human sleep and chronobiological disorders. *Progress in Neuro-Psychopharmacology & Biological Psychiatry*, 31, 1–11.

Skene, D. J. (2003). Optimization of Light and Melatonin to Phase-Shift Human Circadian Rhythms. *Journal of Neuroendocrinology*, 15, 438–441.

Zee, P. C. (2006). Circadian Rhythm Sleep Disorders. *Primary Psychiatry*, 13, 58–66.

nightmare disorder

American Psychiatric Association (1993). *Diagnostic and statistical manual of mental disorders* (4th ed.). Washington, DC: American Psychiatric Association.

Davis, J. L., & Wright, D. C. (2005). Case Series Utilizing Exposure, Relaxation, and Rescripting Therapy: Impact on Nightmares, Sleep Quality, and Psychological Distress. *Behavioral Sleep Medicine*, 3, 151–157.

Davis, J. L., De Arellano, M., Falsetti, S. A., & Resnick, H. S. (2003). Treatment of nightmares related to post-traumatic stress disorder in an adolescent rape victim. *Clinical Case Studies*, 2, 283–294.

Forbes, D., Phelps, A., & McHugh, T.

(2001). Treatment of combat-related nightmares using imagery rehearsal: A pilot study. *Journal of Traumatic Stress*, 14, 433–442.

Forbes, D., Phelps, A. J., McHugh, A. F., Debenham, P., Hopwood, M., & Creamer, M. (2003). Imagery Rehearsal in the Treatment of Posttraumatic Nightmares in Australian Veterans With Chronic Combat-Related PTSD: 12-Month Follow-Up Data. *Journal of Traumatic Stress*, 16, 509–513.

Germain, A., Krakow, B., Faucher, B., Zadra, A., Nielsen, T., Hollifield, M., Warner, T. D., & Koss, M. (2004). Increased Mastery Elements Associated With Imagery Rehearsal Treatment for Nightmares in Sexual Assault Survivors With PTSD. *Dreaming*, 14, 195–206.

Grandi, S., Fabbri, S., Panattoni, N., Gonnella, E., & Marks, I. (2006). Self-Exposure Treatment of Recurrent Nightmares: Waiting-List-Controlled Trial and 4-Year Follow-Up. *Psychotherapy and Psychosomatics*, 75, 384–388.

Kennedy, G. A. (2002). A review of hypnosis in the treatment of parasomnias: Nightmare, sleepwalking, and sleep terror disorders. *Australian Journal of Clinical & Experimental Hypnosis*, 30, 99–155.

Krakow, B., Hollifield, M., Johnston, L., Koss, M., Schrader, R., Warner, T. D., Tandberg, D., Lauriello, J., McBride, L., Cutchen, L., Cheng, D., Emmons, S., Germain, A., Melendrez, D., Sandoval, D., & Prince, H. (2001). Imagery rehearsal therapy for chronic nightmares in sexual assault survivors with post-traumatic stress disorder: A randomized controlled trial. *JAMA: Journal of the American Medical Association*, 286, 537–545.

Krakow, B., Hollifield, M., Schrader, R., Koss, M., Tandberg, D., Lauriello, J., McBride, L., Warner, T. D., Cheng, D., Edmond, T., & Kellner, R. (2000). A controlled study of imagery rehearsal for chronic nightmares in sexual assault survivors with PTSD: A preliminary report. *Journal of Traumatic Stress*, 13, 589–609.

Krakow, B., Lowry, C., Germain, A., Gaddy, L., Hollifield, M., Koss, M., Tandberg, D., Johnston, L., & Melendrez, D. (2000). A retrospective study on improvements in nightmares and post-traumatic stress disorder following treatment for co-morbid sleep-disordered breathing. *Journal of Psychosomatic Research*, 49, 291–298.

Krakow, B., Johnston, L., Melendrez, D., Hollifield, M., Warner, T. D., Chavez-Kennedy, D., & Herlan, M. J. (2001). An open-label trial of evidence-based cognitive behavior therapy for nightmares and insomnia in crime victims with PTSD. *American Journal of Psychiatry*, 158, 2043–2047.

Lansky, M. R. (1997). Post-traumatic nightmares: A psychoanalytic reconsideration. *Psychoanalysis & Contemporary Thought*, 20, 501–521.

Spoormaker, V. I., & van den Bout, J. (2006). Lucid Dreaming Treatment for Nightmares: A Pilot Study. *Psychotherapy and Psychosomatics*, 75, 389–394.

sleep terror disorder

American Psychiatric Association (1993). *Diagnostic and statistical manual of mental disorders* (4th ed.). Washington, DC: American Psychiatric Association.

Buysse, D. J. (Ed.) (2005). Buysse, Daniel J. *Sleep disorders and psychiatry.* Washington, DC, US: American Psychiatric Publishing, Inc.

Carlson, C. R., & Cordova, M. J. (1999). Sleep disorders in childhood and adolescence. In Netherton, Sandra D. (Ed.); Holmes, Deborah (Ed.); Walker, C. Eugene (Ed.). *Child & adolescent psychological disorders: A comprehensive textbook* (pp. 415–438).

New York, NY, US: Oxford University Press.

Dahl, R. E. (1999). Parasomnias. In Ammerman, Robert T. (Ed.); Hersen, Michel (Ed.); Last, Cynthia G. (Ed.). *Handbook of prescriptive treatments for children and adolescents* (2nd ed.). (pp. 244–260). Needham Heights, MA, US: Allyn & Bacon.

Frölich, J., Wiater, A., & Lehmkuhl, G. (2001). Successful treatment of severe parasomnias with paroxetine in a 12-year-old boy. *International Journal of Psychiatry in Clinical Practice*, 5, 215–218.

Kennedy, G. A. (2002). A review of hypnosis in the treatment of parasomnias: Nightmare, sleepwalking, and sleep terror disorders. *Australian Journal of Clinical & Experimental Hypnosis*, 30, 99–155.

Schredl, M. (2001). Night terrors in children: Prevalence and influencing factors. *Sleep and Hypnosis*, 3, 68–72.

Singh, A. N. (1997). Parasomnias and management. *International Medical Journal*, 4, 191–192.

Soldatos, C. R., & Paparrigopoulos, T. J. (2005). Sleep physiology and pathology: Pertinence to psychiatry. *International Review of Psychiatry*, 17, 213–228.

Winkelman, J. W. (2005). Parasomnias. In Buysse, Daniel J. (Ed.). *Sleep disorders and psychiatry* (pp. 163–183). Washington, DC, US: American Psychiatric Publishing, Inc.

sleepwalking disorder

American Psychiatric Association (1993). *Diagnostic and statistical manual of mental disorders* (4th ed.). Washington, DC: American Psychiatric Association.

Buysse, D. J. (Ed.) (2005). Buysse, Daniel J. *Sleep disorders and psychiatry.*

Washington, DC, US: American Psychiatric Publishing, Inc.

Cartwright, R. (2004). Sleepwalking violence: A sleep disorder, a legal dilemma, and a psychological challenge. *American Journal of Psychiatry*, 161, 1149–1158.

Guilleminault, C., Kirisoglu, C., Bao, G., Arias, V., Chan, A., & Li, K. K. (2005). Adult chronic sleepwalking and its treatment based on polysomnography. *Brain: A Journal of Neurology*, 128, 1062–1069.

Howard, B. J. (2004). A Clinical Guide to Sleep Disorders in Children and Adolescents. *Journal of Developmental & Behavioral Pediatrics*, 25, 365.

Kennedy, G. A. (2002). A review of hypnosis in the treatment of parasomnias: Nightmare, sleepwalking, and sleep terror disorders. *Australian Journal of Clinical & Experimental Hypnosis*, 30, 99–155.

Kennedy, G. A. (2002). A review of hypnosis in the treatment of parasomnias: Nightmare, sleepwalking, and sleep terror disorders. *Australian Journal of Clinical & Experimental Hypnosis*, 30, 99–155.

Sadeh, A. (2005). Cognitive-behavioral treatment for childhood sleep disorders. *Clinical Psychology Review*, 25, 612–628.

Schenck, C. H., Boyd, J. L., & Mahowald, M. W. (1997). A parasomnia overlap disorder involving sleepwalking, sleep terrors, and REM sleep behavior disorder in 33 polysomnographically confirmed cases. *Sleep: Journal of Sleep Research & Sleep Medicine*, 20, 972–981.

Winkelman, J. W. (Ed.) (2005). Winkelman, John W. Sleep Disorders Comes of Age. *Primary Psychiatry*, 12, 35–36.

index